The New Book of

POPULAR SCIENCE

The New Book of POPULAR SCIENCE

4

An imprint of

Library of Congress Cataloging-in-Publication Data

The new book of popular science.
    p. cm.
  Includes bibliographical references and index.
  ISBN 978-0-7172-1226-2 (set)
    1. Science—Encyclopedias, Juvenile. 2. Technology—
Encyclopedias, Juvenile. 3. Medicine—Encyclopedias, Juvenile.
4. Science—Popular works. 5. Technology—Popular works.
6. Medicine, Popular. I. Scholastic Library Publishing.

Q163.N55 2008
503—dc22

                                  2007041858

VOLUME 4

Contents

PLANT LIFE

Many plants seem to flourish easily. The common North American water lily (left), for example, thrives on ponds and small lakes, its colorful flowers attached to underwater stems and its leathery leaves, or lily pads, floating on the surface. Sometimes, when the number of plants of a desired variety is difficult to achieve via seeds, botanists turn to grafting, a process in which the stem of one plant is inserted into the stem, root, or branch of another (above). When successful, the two grafted parts unite and grow as one plant.

BOTANISTS
AND THEIR SCIENCE

by Peter A. Flax

Few adventurers can match the stories that British botanist Tom Hart Dyke has to tell. In his 2004 book, *The Cloud Garden*, Dyke weaves the gripping tale of an expedition through the Darien Gap, a lawless jungle on the border of Colombia and Panama. Dyke, along with his companion, battled the rough terrain in search of rare orchids until, in a dramatic turn of events, they were captured by guerrilla fighters, held for ransom, and—finally—released.

Though not all work in botany includes such harrowing—and potentially life-threatening—experiences, there is still plenty of opportunity for excitement. In the late 1990s, an IMAX film captured the exploits of Steve Perlman and Ken Wood, botanists with the National Tropical Botanical Garden, in Kauai, Hawaii, as they backpacked through dense rain forests, kayaked across rough ocean waters, and climbed sheer cliffs in search of their elusive quarry—new and endangered plant species. Along with the risks of their work, there were also rewards: the pair discovered the first new plant genus in Hawaii in more than 80 years.

Meanwhile, the academic side of the field holds its own intrigue. Paleobotanists, such as Jennifer McElwain of the Field Museum of Natural History, in Chicago, study fossilized remains in hopes of unlocking secrets from millions of years ago.

All of these modern scientists have followed in the footsteps of early botanists, researchers who also sought to find, name, categorize, and understand plants in their midst. Today, though, botanists are able to make use of modern technology to conduct their studies—

In specially equipped laboratories, botanists can control light, temperature, soil, and other factors to create the ideal conditions for growing just about any type of plant.

using electron microscopes to view tiny plant cells, modifying plant compounds to fight disease, and even launching satellites to image the world's forests.

WHAT IS BOTANY?

Simply stated, botany is the study of plants. Botany deals with facts that are of critical importance to humanity, since plants are indispensable to life on Earth. All that we eat—whether vegetable, meat, or even ice cream—owes its existence, either directly or indirectly, to plants. In addition, green plants constitute the single most important source of oxygen in the atmosphere.

The short definition just stated, however, is not entirely complete, because scientists often classify the study of other forms of life—including bacteria, fungi, and algae—within the confines of botany. As a result, the subjects studied by botanists range from the smallest bacteria to the largest living things on Earth: the mighty sequoia trees.

As a general rule, modern botanists are specialists. Some botanists study plant anatomy, while others investigate plant diseases, the medicinal properties of plant products, the nature of plants millions of years ago, or any one of the myriad other aspects of the science.

During the Renaissance, encyclopedia-like "herbals" focused on plants and their medicinal properties.

THE ROOTS OF BOTANY

Humans have harbored a great interest in and dependence on plants since ancient times. Prehistoric peoples recognized that plants could provide food, shelter, clothing, and material for tools. The origins of agriculture, for example, likely emerged from the discovery that discarded seeds sprouted into new plants. Similarly, early humans were able to identify the healing properties of certain plants, and began collecting and later growing plants for medicinal purposes. Over time, as early civilizations evolved, humans assembled information that would become the basis of a science millennia later. The ancients also recognized the beauty of plant life; in fact, the Assyrians cultivated ornamental gardens in western Asia nearly 4,000 years ago.

The ancient Greeks were the first to approach the study of plants as a science. Theophrastus, a philosopher who studied under Plato and Aristotle, is widely considered to be the "father of botany." He systematically outlined the classification, structure, and natural history of plants with unprecedented precision. Today many plants still bear the 2,300-year-old names that this pioneering botanist gave them.

Despite their flaws, the works of Theophrastus and other early Greeks remained the core of botany for many centuries.

Little new inquiry into the science occurred until the Renaissance, when scholars began to reexamine and expand upon the works of the Greeks. This intellectual reawakening heralded a new age of botanical study. With the invention of the printing press, numerous large works were compiled and published that contained illustrations of many known plants and descriptions of their medicinal properties. These books, known as "herbals," helped spur further botanical research.

The development of the microscope late in the 16th century allowed scientists to delve into the previously mysterious internal structure and life processes of plants. In 1655, England's Robert Hooke published a landmark study on the unseen cellular structure of plants. Knowledge of plant physiology was further advanced by Stephen Hales, who accurately traced the movement of water in plants and provided the foundation for explaining photosynthesis. The work of Hooke, Hales, and others marked the emergence of botany as a laboratory science.

Taxonomy took center stage in the 18th century, thanks to the groundbreaking research of Swedish naturalist Carolus Linnaeus. In a tome titled *Species plantarum*, Linnaeus faithfully described and systematically organized

Some areas of botany are highly specialized. At the California Institute of Technology (above), a research team is working to discover how flowers evolved.

6,000 different plant species from all over the world. He also introduced the use of the two-word name, or *binomial nomenclature*, as the standard way of expressing a plant's scientific name. This system is still in use today with relatively few changes. A century later, Charles Darwin's *On the Origin of Species* encouraged taxonomists to consider evolutionary characteristics when classifying plants.

During the 19th century, a number of new botanical disciplines developed into sciences in their own right. Plant pathology, for example, gained new importance when a mysterious potato blight ravaged Ireland in the 1840s, leading to widespread starvation. In the 1860s, Austrian monk Gregor Johann Mendel conducted breeding experiments with pea plants—work that initiated the study of plant heredity and laid the foundation for modern genetics.

BOTANY TODAY

During the past century, botany was again reshaped, this time by the fast-paced development of new techniques and technologies. The invention of the electron microscope, for example, enabled botanists to study the three-dimensional structure of living plant cells. Likewise, the perfection of radioactive-dating techniques allowed scientists to flesh out the long history of plant life on Earth.

Major Disciplines

As with most sciences, botany has grown in modern times to include a number of distinct fields, many of which overlap with one another.

Taxonomy. Botanical taxonomists can trace their specialty back to early botanists who diligently collected and identified plant specimens. While such research still goes on today, modern taxonomists are more often concerned with clarifying the relationships among different plants. The most widely used classification system organizes plants to reflect evolutionary relationships in a manner that resembles a family tree, based on the assumption that all plants in a given genus share a common ancestor.

In recent years, however, taxonomists have begun to develop other systems. Some new classification schemes organize plants by their chemical or genetic characteristics; others focus on ecological attributes. To aid such work, taxonomists regularly engage in sophisticated biochemistry experiments and utilize some of the world's most powerful computer systems.

Morphology. Morphology deals with the structure and form of plants. One major component of this field is plant anatomy. Many anatomists focus on the arrangement and function of a plant's structural features—its roots, stems, leaves, and flowers, for example. An important specialty within morphology is *plant cytology*, the study of plant cells. Research on cell membranes, where much of a plant's activities take place, has become a busy area of botanical study in recent years. Morphologists also study how plants grow. Consequently, they are interested in the genetic, biochemical, and physiological factors that affect a plant's growth, as well as in environmental factors (temperature, for example) that can alter plant development.

Physiology. Plant physiology concentrates on the internal functions and activities of plants: how plants germinate, grow, reproduce, and die. The most vital physiological phenomena of plants include: *photosynthesis*, the process by which plants convert energy from the Sun into

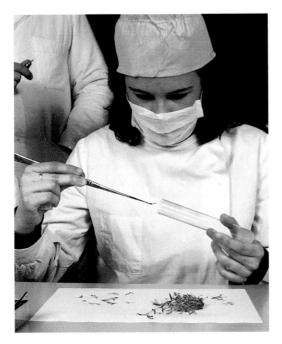

Many botanists spend hours in the lab performing painstaking experiments to advance their research. The scientist above is conducting microbotanical studies.

food; *respiration*, the way that plants obtain and use oxygen and carbon dioxide; and *transpiration*, the movement of water in plants. Some plant physiologists study hormones and their effect on such botanical processes as flowering.

Plant physiology is now a sophisticated laboratory science with close links to biochemistry and molecular genetics. Many basic biological processes—such as digestion and protein synthesis—are very similar in plants and animals. As a result, physiologists can often translate findings from their research on plants, which are relatively easy to grow and manipulate, to other living things.

Pathology. Plant disease is the focus of botanists who specialize in pathology. This specialty is concerned with the fungi, bacteria, viruses, and other living entities that cause plant disease, as well as the environmental conditions that coincide with these diseases. (Interestingly, damage caused by insects, humans, and other animals is ordinarily not included within the field.) Much of the research in this field concentrates on methods of preventing or controlling plant diseases or alleviating the damage that they can cause. Given humanity's dependence on plants for food, such work can be instrumental in protecting crops and harvests, and in improving the world's food supply.

Pathologists have a wide range of tools to help them fight plant disease. Some botanists, for example, are engaged in a fight to save the stately American chestnut, a tree that once prospered throughout the eastern United States. In recent decades, the species has been ravaged by a disease-producing fungus that causes chestnut blight. In response, plant pathologists have modified the species in the laboratory using a technique called plant tissue culture. If efforts to produce a disease-resistant strain succeed, then the American chestnut might be able to propagate as it did in the past, and these elegant trees will once again grace the landscape.

Ecology. Plant ecology is the subdiscipline of botany that studies the interactions between plants and their surrounding environments. Many ecologists research the pressures that a plant species or community faces from competing plants, other organisms, and the environment—trying to understand, for example, how plants withstand and prosper through destructive periods of fire or flooding. Plant ecologists also study the amazing ways that plant communities live together—examining, for instance, how mosses benefit from the shade of tall trees.

Botanists have played a prominent role in the development of insecticides to eradicate the Mediterranean fruit flies that periodically threaten California's fruit industry.

In recent decades, many ecologists have turned their attention to the interactions between plants and humanity. Some are researching the effects of population growth and human activities on the survival of plant species, while others are investigating how plants can help limit the effects of pollution.

Other Subspecialties

Bacteriology. Single-celled organisms called bacteria are the subject of this field. Some bacteriologists examine the life processes of bacteria, while others study bacterial diseases, such as tuberculosis and tetanus, as well as "newer" conditions like Lyme disease. Still other scientists examine the beneficial uses of bacteria, whether these be their role in decomposing organic material or their applications in the food, energy, and pharmaceutical industries. In recent years, bacteriologists have been able to harness bacteria to safely and quickly clean up hazardous waste. Through genetic engineering, bacteria have been finding numerous other medical and industrial roles.

Careers in Botany

Aspiring botanists must undergo intensive scientific education before they can enter the workforce. At the undergraduate level, most students pursue a degree in botany, biology, or a related discipline. Related course work includes chemistry, physics, and mathematics.

Most career botanists also hold advanced graduate degrees in botany. For the majority of research and teaching positions, a doctorate degree is necessary; the course of study can take more than six years to complete. During this time, many botanists receive extensive training in disciplines closely tied to their areas of specialization. Those pursuing a career in paleobotany, for example, would likely obtain a rigorous grounding in geology, while plant physiologists would seek advanced study in biochemistry.

Many aspiring botanists obtain internships at private companies or in government agricultural-research labs.

Once their formal education is complete, botanists can find work in either a basic or an applied field. Those pursuing a career in a basic science concern themselves with research purely for the sake of gaining knowledge; by contrast, applied scientists are focused more on conducting research that serves specific practical needs of society at large.

Colleges and universities are the most common employers of botanists. The academic setting allows botanists to conduct their research and to teach at the same time. Given the interdisciplinary nature of contemporary botanical specialties, many academics find that their research is aided by working in a community of scientists of every stripe.

Applied botanists may find work in a number of other settings. Academic institutions and government agencies, for example, often employ botanists to conduct research relating to ecology, agriculture, and plant diseases. Highly trained botanists are also needed at museums and botanical gardens. In the private sector, botanists pursue careers in the petroleum, biotechnology, agribusiness, chemical, and pharmaceutical industries.

Current thinking holds that the opportunities for botanists will grow rapidly in the future. As the world's population continues to grow, for example, the resulting demand for more food will likely create opportunities for those botanists expert in such areas as plant diseases and biotechnology.

Some botanists specialize in the study of kelp (above) and other forms of marine flora. Others apply techniques of biotechnology to artificially select, or in some cases to design, desirable features in certain crops (right).

Paleobotany. Using the fossilized remains of leaves, seeds, spores, and other materials, paleobotanists reconstruct whole plants as they grew in the distant past, and then use such fossil records to map out the historical and evolutionary succession of plants on Earth. Some researchers also have analyzed fossils to learn more about the climate and other environmental conditions in long-ago geologic ages.

Economic botany. Plants that have useful economic value or those that pose a threat to society are the focus of economic botany. In general, economic botanists study plants that are important sources of food, medicine, wood, and fiber. Many efforts to increase crop yields or curtail plant blights require input from economic botanists.

Ethnobotany. Ethnobotanists study the use of plants by preliterate societies, both in the present and the distant past. In many cases, such research has yielded valuable insight into the history of how plants have been used by our ancestors. Many ethnobotanists also strive to discover (or rediscover) plants whose powerful medicinal properties or other valuable traits have been forgotten over the ages.

BOTANY IN THE FUTURE

Although humans have been studying plants for thousands of years, major new areas of research are still emerging. Advancing technology—especially the field of biotechnology—is expected to drive many of the developments that will transform botany in the future. Using genetic-engineering techniques, scientists have already increased the resistance of many agricultural plants to disease, drought, frost, and herbicides. In 1994, for the first time, the U.S. government extended approval to a genetically altered food—a tomato that ripens far more slowly than do ordinary tomatoes. In 1996, U.S. farmers grew herbicide-tolerant soybeans for the first time. By 2006, 89 percent of soybean acreage was planted with this bioengineered crop, while 83 percent of cotton acreage and 61 percent of corn acreage was planted with biotech varieties.

Another area expected to grow rapidly is medical botany. Numerous plant compounds found in tropical rain forests and elsewhere have shown promise as drugs to fight cancer, AIDS, and a variety of other diseases. In some cases, biochemists may be able to synthesize these substances in laboratories to guarantee their plentiful supply without endangering the plants from which they come.

And while much growth in botany will be driven by innovative technology, many scientists will undoubtedly remain hard at work to answer elemental questions that are still unanswered. For example, botanists still do not understand the process by which tall trees carry water to their uppermost branches, or how individual plant cells develop into complex organisms with billions of cells.

What Is a Plant?

by Jessica Snyder Sachs

A young boy lies on his back in a meadow of tall grass, closing his eyes as the wind rustles through the leaves. A backpacker walks in awe through a forest of towering redwood trees. Two lovers stroll through a tropical garden. One pauses to smell a delicate orchid; the other plucks a mango from a lush shade tree.

Whatever your idea of "paradise," chances are, it involves plants. Indeed, life as we know it could not be possible without them. Directly or indirectly, all our food comes from plants, as does the oxygen we breathe and the wood we use to build our shelters.

PLANT OR PLANTLIKE?

But what exactly is a plant? Like most questions, the answer depends on whom you ask. A young child might say: "Something green that stays in one place." An older child or adult might add that a plant "makes its own food from sunlight." Taken together, these commonsense statements well describe most plants.

Virtually all food chains (including the human one) begin with plants—especially green plants and the nutrients stored within their leaves, stems, roots, and seeds.

But the scientific notion of what is and is not a plant is no longer so simple. Using powerful microscopes and sophisticated chemical tests, botanists have discovered a number of essential differences between "plantlike" organisms such as seaweeds and green algae, and true plants such as mosses, ferns, and seed plants. The result is a much more complex definition of the thing we call "plant."

According to current scientific thinking, a true plant is a multicellular (many-celled) organism whose cells are enclosed by a rigid wall made of cellulose. These cells contain the photosynthetic pigments chlorophyll a and b, which capture and harness the radiant energy of the Sun. (A few plants have lost these pigments through the course of evolution, becoming parasites on other organisms.)

But there is more to the modern-day definition of "plant." A plant's cells must be able to organize themselves into different structures such as roots for anchoring and stems for support. True plants also possess a unique way of reproducing themselves: they pass through two distinct life phases, or alternating generations. During one of these generations, a plant produces sex cells—namely, eggs and sperm. In the other, it produces spores. Many plants can also reproduce vegetatively—generating new plants from a piece of stem or root from the parent. However they begin life, many plants can continue to grow for an indefinite period of time.

They do so primarily by expanding from special growth regions called *meristems* at the tips of roots, buds, and certain parts of the stem.

A typical plant spends its life anchored in one spot. But it is a myth that plants do not move. The flowers of many species open and close each morning and evening. Some also turn their leaves throughout the day, tracking the Sun as it travels across the sky. Such movements are generally too slow for a person to discern, except with time-lapse photography. But a few unusual plants, such as the Venus's-flytrap and the sensitive plant, can move quite quickly. The flytrap snaps shut its special, toothed leaves to capture an insect within a sort of botanical prison. The sensitive plant responds to touch by suddenly closing its leaves and drooping.

THE DIVERSITY OF GREEN PLANTS

Botanists estimate that there are between 320,000 and 430,000 plant species, with more

Through the ages, humans have underscored the importance of plants by depicting them in art. Whether it be in ancient Egypt (right) or medieval Europe (below), plant cultivation has always been an essential occupation.

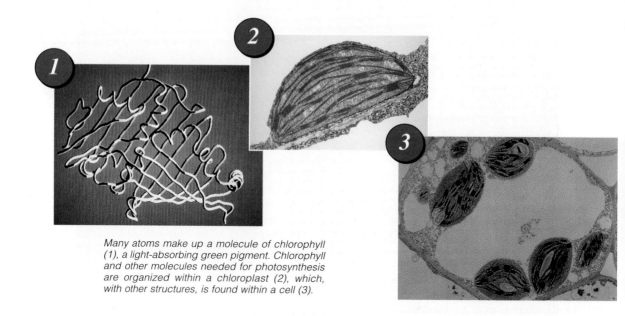

Many atoms make up a molecule of chlorophyll (1), a light-absorbing green pigment. Chlorophyll and other molecules needed for photosynthesis are organized within a chloroplast (2), which, with other structures, is found within a cell (3).

species being discovered every year. They range in size from tiny duckweeds less than 0.1 inch (2.5 millimeters) long to giant sequoias and eucalyptus trees that can soar to heights of 300 feet (90 meters) or more.

Together, the world's plants throw a distinctive green mantle over much of the planet's land surface. No land region on Earth is entirely devoid of plant life. Evolution has produced plants specially adapted to survive in most every environment, from the bitter cold of the frozen tundra to the broiling heat of the parched desert. Such adaptations have produced a tremendous diversity of plant forms—from creeping herbs and dangling vines to upright shrubs and trees of many sizes and shapes. Their stems can branch into complex patterns. Leaves likewise vary between species, assuming many patterns and shapes—broad, narrow, smooth-edged, or indented. Most astounding of all may be the array of complex structures and stunning colors seen in the blossoms of angiosperms, the "flowering plants."

There are also startling contrasts in life span. Some plants, called annuals, live for just one growing season. Others, called perennials, can live for many years. Cone-bearing trees such as pines, firs, and redwoods are among the longest-lived of all living things. Indeed, some surviving California redwoods have been determined to be more than 3,000 years old.

Over the past 10,000 years, humans have expanded nature's variety by turning desirable wild plants into domesticated crops. Selective-breeding techniques have helped produce faster-growing plants with larger fruit, tastier leaves, more-colorful blossoms, more-abundant fibers, and many other desirable traits.

IMPORTANCE OF PLANTS

Be they wild or domesticated, plants are the world's primary producers. Through the complex process of photosynthesis, they capture the radiant energy of the Sun and use it to transform carbon dioxide from the atmosphere into sugars and starch. Virtually all food chains start with plants, with their nutrients stored in the leaves, stems, roots, and seeds of green plants. Photosynthesis also produces the atmospheric oxygen animals need for respiration. (See "Photosynthesis," page 16.)

Plants play an essential role in protecting land from erosion. They anchor soil in place with their roots and rhizomes (hairlike roots on creeping stems). They blunt the force of rain and runoff, which would otherwise pit and erode the soil. Finally, plants catch and hold rain, releasing the moisture slowly to reduce runoff. Plants also cleanse our water and air by absorbing pollutants into their tissues during the respiration process.

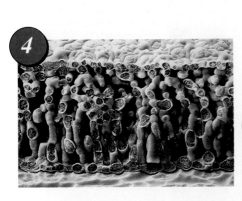

Each cell is essentially an individual functioning unit. Similar cells are grouped together within a plant to form tissues (4) that perform specific functions. Many different types of tissues are organized together to form plant structures, such as leaves (5) and other parts of a tree (6).

Over the course of history, we as humans have found even more ways to use plants to our benefit. We mine the Plant Kingdom for wood, resins, oils, and rubber—all products that became the raw materials for our first industries. We weave plant fibers into clothes, canvas, and rope. Many of the world's most-important medicines have come from plants, as do chemicals we use for everything from cleaning our homes to repelling insect pests.

PLANT EVOLUTION

How did the first plants come to be? Many people mistakenly assume that Earth's first living things must have been plants, or some type of plantlike organism. It is an understandable assumption, given that virtually all food chains start with plants—and the nutrients they create through photosynthesis.

But scientists believe that the first forms of life were too simple to perform the complex process of photosynthesis. There is no proof of this, as the first living things on Earth were probably one-celled organisms too tiny to leave fossils. Still, scientists have reconstructed a probable scenario based on the conditions that must have existed when Earth's crust was still forming. During this period, the seas were filled with organic molecules produced by the raging storms and volcanic activity that shook the early

Earth. Most likely the first living organisms on Earth were *heterotrophic*, or "outside-feeding"—organisms that consumed these organic molecules for food.

As Earth stabilized and these primitive organisms increased in number, they would have begun to use up the organic molecules on which their existence depended. As a result, there was increased competition for food. This set the stage for the evolution of the first *autotrophic*, or "self-feeding," organisms.

One or more groups of these first autotrophs evolved a system for capturing solar energy, or sunlight. These were the first photosynthetic organisms. They were very simple compared to true plants, but much more complex than the first heterotrophs.

The first photosynthetic organisms probably captured solar energy using the same pigments—or similar ones—that modern plants use today. And like modern plants, these autotrophs used solar energy to transform simple molecules of carbon dioxide into complex food molecules such as sugar.

The earliest evidence of photosynthetic organisms appears in rocks some 3.5 billion years old. This is about 100 million years after the first signs of life on Earth. With the arrival of these early plantlike organisms, the flow of life energy on Earth assumed its modern form: photosynthetic organisms used the energy of the Sun

Fruit constitutes one of the tastiest food products derived from plants. The agronomist above is checking the ripeness of jackfruit, which grows in tropical areas.

KINGDOM PLANTAE

The first true plants were "amphibians." Like the amphibians of the animal world, these early plants could survive on land, but depended on outside moisture for fertilization, or sexual reproduction. They also reproduced asexually by means of spores.

Today the surviving representatives of this ancient group are an abundance of tiny plants known as the *bryophytes*. This group includes the familiar mosses, as well as the lesser-known liverworts and hornworts. These plants lack true roots, stems, and leaves, and have little in the way of waxy covering (*cuticle*) to prevent their tissues from drying out. Only a small number of bryophytes grow more than a few inches in height, and most creep along the ground in moist or wet places.

The first vascular plants appear in the fossil record approximately 405 million to 410 million years ago. Their vascular tissue consists of a stiff, central column that conducts water and essential nutrients through the plant while supporting it. Specifically, water passes through a stiff, supportive network of dead cells called *xylem*, while food passes through a sieve of living cells called *phloem*.

Vascular plants have true roots to anchor themselves in the soil and collect from it both moisture and inorganic nutrients. One or more stems support the main photosynthetic organs—the leaves. A waxy cuticle covers the aboveground portions of the plant to help protect it from drying.

The cuticle was a great evolutionary advance because it enabled vascular plants to survive farther from water than the more-primitive bryophytes. However, this thick covering prevented the necessary exchange of gases between the plant and surrounding air. The solution was the development of *stomata*, small openings in

to create their own food; the photosynthesizers, in turn, become food for other organisms.

As photosynthetic organisms became abundant, they also transformed the planet. The process of photosynthesis created more and more oxygen, which was released into the atmosphere. Slowly but steadily, the amount of oxygen in Earth's atmosphere increased to its present level of about 21 percent. This sparked the evolution of *aerobic*, or oxygen-dependent, forms of life. It also produced a protective "shield" of ozone that wrapped around the planet in the upper reaches of the atmosphere.

The first true plants appear in the fossil record in rock some 450 million to 500 million years old. Botanists believe that these first plants evolved from green algae that floated below the surface of sunlit waters. As this aquatic green algae became abundant, it may have depleted minerals in the water, making survival more difficult. Such nutrients would have been more abundant in shallow water along the shoreline. As a result, there arose multicellular algae with special tissues for anchoring themselves to shoreline rocks and sand. From these highly developed algae—similar perhaps to the green algae known as sea lettuce (*Ulva* species)—evolved the first primitive plants.

the cuticle bordered by pairs of special *guard cells* that act as movable "doors." Stomata open and close to help a plant balance its need to conserve water with its need for oxygen and carbon dioxide from the atmosphere.

Like bryophytes, these first vascular plants were seedless and relied on water for fertilization. The modern-day representatives of this group include such "living fossils" as horsetails, club mosses, and ferns.

It was such a world—a world of giant mosses, horsetails, and ferns—that greeted the first vertebrate animals to emerge onto dry land approximately 350 million years ago. Some 100 million years later, dinosaurs roamed through forests of cycads and primitive conifers—the world's first seed plants.

Scientists believe that the first flowering plants, or *angiosperms*, did not appear until sometime during the Cretaceous period, about 127 million years ago. The early angiosperms included beech trees, figs, and magnolias, as

Many plants are cultivated for ornamental reasons. The horticulturist below specializes in growing and improving plants, and in developing hardier varieties.

well as many species that have long since vanished. A great burgeoning of angiosperms occurred approximately 100 million years ago. Not surprisingly, a great many new species of insects appeared about the same time. Then, as now, most of the flowering plants depended on insects to pollinate, or fertilize, their flowers. In return, the angiosperms developed blossoms with a dazzling array of colors, scents, and nectars to lure and reward their insect "cupids."

LIFE PROCESSES

Like all living things, plants must obtain food and respire, or breathe, in order to survive, grow, and reproduce. Unlike animals, plants are capable of producing their own food through the process of photosynthesis, which is discussed in detail in the following article. The food created during photosynthesis is then consumed in respiration. Respiration is the process by which oxygen and sugar react to produce chemical energy and carbon dioxide.

So plants, like animals, must have oxygen to survive. Plant cells produce most of their own oxygen as a by-product of photosynthesis. Indeed, plant cells give off an abundance of extra oxygen during periods of active photosynthesis. But this production of oxygen ceases when photosynthesis stops—at night, for example. Then plant cells must absorb oxygen from the atmosphere to continue respiration.

Plants "breathe" through their stomata, the tiny pores in the waxy cuticle that covers their leaves and stems. In addition to "inhaling" oxygen, plants must also "exhale" carbon dioxide—just as animals do. When plants are forced to close their stomata in times of drought, their respiration slows substantially and may eventually grind to a halt.

Plants also require a variety of inorganic nutrients, or minerals, which they absorb from their surroundings, typically through their roots. These nutrients include rather large amounts of nitrogen, sulfur, phosphorus, potassium, calcium, and magnesium, as well as small amounts of iron, copper, manganese, zinc, molybdenum, boron, cobalt, and chlorine. These 14 soil nutrients, together with carbon, hydrogen, and oxygen from the atmosphere, constitute the essential elements of plant nutrition. The lack of any one nutrient can halt plant growth.

The Plant Cell

All life on Earth is composed of cells, the fundamental units of life. The smallest organisms consist of a single cell. The largest consist of trillions of interconnected cells. A single multicellular organism may also have many different kinds of cells—each type designed to perform a particular function. Yet cells are more remarkable for their similarity than their differences. Every cell, be it plant or animal, is a self-contained unit bounded by a living envelope called the plasma membrane. This membrane controls the passage of materials in and out of the cell. Enclosed inside the membrane is the *cytoplasm*, a "cellular soup" containing the microscopic machinery of life. This "machinery" includes a variety of distinct structures and many dissolved substances.

The *nucleus* is a vital structure found in both plant and animal cells. This membrane-bound body contains the cell's chromosomes (genetic structures), and through them controls the cell's activities. All cells also contain mitochondria, where food molecules are converted to usable energy (the molecule adenosine triphosphate, or ATP). Another universal cell structure is the *endoplasmic reticulum*, a membrane network that divides the cytoplasm into a series of compartments and channels. The many folds of the endoplasmic reticulum form a large work surface, or "assembly line," for the assembly of proteins and other important compounds. Most cells also contain structures called *Golgi bodies*—flattened sacs that function as packaging centers for proteins and other products being sent to other cells.

Plant cells have four important characteristics that distinguish them from animal cells. The first is the *cell wall*. When viewed through a microscope, this may be the plant cell's most-obvious feature—a rigid wall made of cellulose that gives structure and support to the living cell within.

Also unique to plant cells are a variety of *plastids*—membrane-enclosed structures that are the site of food manufacture and storage. The most important of these are the disk-shaped *chloroplasts*, the sites of photosynthesis. A typical plant cell contains 40 to 50 chloroplasts. Each chloroplast, in turn, contains an abundance of green chlorophyll pigments and smaller amounts of yellow, orange, or red carotenoid pigments.

Other cell plastids include *chromoplasts*, which contain masses of carotenoid pigments, and *leucoplasts*, which store food in the form of starch, oil, or protein. *Vacuoles* are the third cell structure unique to plants. In essence, vacuoles are liquid-filled bubbles. An immature plant cell has several small vacuoles. They expand to enlarge the cell as it matures. Eventually the vacuoles fuse to form a large, central vacuole that occupies up to 90 percent of the cell.

Finally, plant cells are interconnected by unique structures called *plasmodesmata*. These narrow canals function as pathways between cells for the transport of substances such as sugars and amino acids.

Plant cells and animal cells have many structures in common, but also a few structures that make them unique. A cell wall, chloroplasts, and a vacuole distinguish plant cells from their animal counterparts, while centrioles are one of the unique features of animal cells.

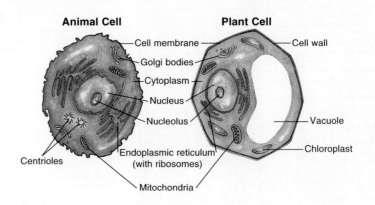

Animal Cell

- Cell membrane
- Golgi bodies
- Cytoplasm
- Nucleus
- Nucleolus
- Centrioles
- Endoplasmic reticulum (with ribosomes)
- Mitochondria

Plant Cell

- Cell wall
- Vacuole
- Chloroplast

Growth

Much of the energy produced through respiration is consumed in maintaining a plant's existing tissues. When conditions are right, additional energy is channeled into growth. Botanists generally recognize two types of plant growth: primary and secondary.

Primary growth is the process by which plants lengthen their stems and roots and produce special tissues such as leaves. They do so by adding new cells in special areas called *apical meristems*, located at the tips of roots, shoots, and buds. (By contrast, an animal adds new cells throughout its body as it grows.) In an important way, primary growth is the plant equivalent of mobility in animals. Rather than picking themselves up and walking, plants lengthen their bodies to reach new areas with fresh supplies of water, sunlight, and nutrients.

Secondary growth is the process by which woody plants increase the thickness of their roots, branches, and stems or trunks. Secondary growth arises from the production of new cells in a cylinder of tissue called the *lateral meristem*, or *cambium*. The cambium produces new cells during each year's growing season. This annual cycle of growth can be seen as a distinctive ring on the cross section of a woody stem of certain plants or the trunk of a tree. Each ring corresponds to a year of growth.

Reproduction

All species of plant pass through two distinct life phases. In the *diploid phase*, the cells of the plant contain two complete sets of chromosomes (the genetic structures containing DNA). In this phase, the plant is called a *sporophyte*, or "spore-producing plant." It produces small male spores (*microspores*) and larger female spores (*megaspores*) whose cells contain just one set of chromosomes each. These spores germinate without sexual reproduction to produce a distinct generation of male and female plants. In this phase, the plants are called *gametophytes*, or "gamete-producing plants." Like the spores from which they grew, gametophytes are haploid—that is, they contain just one set of chromosomes each. The female gametophytes produce eggs, and the male gametophytes produce sperm. The sperm and eggs unite (sexual reproduction) to form a new sporophyte, which again has two sets of chromosomes.

The enormous amount of botanical research conducted by government and university scientists bears definitive testimony to the essential role of plants in our lives.

This comparatively complex life cycle, in which plants produce different-looking generations, is clearly visible only in primitive plants such as moss and other bryophytes. Every species of moss, for example, produces distinct male and female gametophytes that can be seen growing side by side. When fertilization occurs, the female gametophyte produces a stemlike sporophyte with a spore capsule.

This is not so in most plants. Through the course of evolution, the gametophyte generation of higher plants has become quite small, while the sporophyte generation has become large. What we see as a flowering plant, for example, is the sporophyte generation. Inside each flower, one or more tiny female gametophytes grows into an embryo sac made of just seven cells. The same flower contains an abundance of even tinier male gametophytes. Each grows into a pollen grain just three cells in size. This generation of tiny male and female "individuals" produce the eggs and sperm, which unite to create an embryo, or fertile seed.

PHOTOSYNTHESIS

by Jessica Snyder Sachs

Spring arrives in a New England forest, and, almost overnight, bare branches and barren ground sprout bright green. On the Great Plains, the brown prairie becomes an emerald patchwork of wheat, corn, and hay. Even the southwestern desert shimmers with green life after a drenching spring rain.

This lush growth is fueled by a phenomenon called *photosynthesis*, the process by which plants use the energy of sunlight to create the foods on which we all depend. The word itself means "putting together" (synthesis) with "light" (photo). Specifically, photosynthesis assembles carbohydrates (sugars and starches) out of carbon dioxide (a gas) and water. The power

fueling this reaction is the energy of the Sun. The by-product, or "waste" material, of photosynthesis is pure oxygen.

Sound like a useful reaction? Indeed, it would be difficult to overestimate the tremendous importance of photosynthesis. Without it, there would be no plants, and so no plant-eating animals, nor any animals that eat plant-eating animals. Without photosynthesis, oxygen would all but disappear from our atmosphere. The only living things able to survive in such a world

Plants, green algae, and some bacteria absorb the energy of sunlight and use it to power the formation of carbohydrates—a process known as photosynthesis.

would be a few types of bacteria that could take energy from inorganic chemicals.

Although few people stop to think about it, even much of modern industry is powered by photosynthesis. Our technological society all but runs on "fossil fuels"—coal, oil, and natural gas—which come from the piled-up remains of plants that flourished, died, and were buried many millions of years ago.

In one way or another, most everyone today has at least a basic appreciation of photosynthesis and the wondrous "green machines" that we call plants. Even young schoolchildren, who may not yet know the term photosynthesis, understand that plants grow, thanks to sunlight.

So it may seem especially odd that, in the long history of science, photosynthesis was discovered less than 200 years ago. Not even in the mid-1700s, a time of great scientific renaissance and discovery, did botanists have the slightest idea that plants drew their energy from sunlight. Indeed, they still believed that plants took all the nourishment they needed from soil and water.

THE STUDY OF PHOTOSYNTHESIS

The first glimmering of understanding came in 1771, when the English chemist Joseph Priestley noticed that a candle in an airtight container burned longer if the container also included a plant. Likewise, he found that a small animal had less difficulty breathing when its airtight container also housed a living plant. Priestley concluded that plants produced some substance (which we now know to be oxygen) that "restored," or refreshed, air that had been "injured," or depleted, by a burning candle or a breathing animal. Soon after, Priestley received a medal for his discovery. It read, in part: "For

these discoveries we are assured that no vegetable grows in vain . . . but cleanses and purifies our atmosphere."

What Priestley did not realize was that sunlight was the energy fueling the plant's production of oxygen. In fact, he was baffled when his experiments failed in a shaded corner of his lab.

It was the Dutch physician Jan Ingenhousz who, in 1779, recognized that plants "purify air" only in sunlight and only with their green parts. In 1796, Ingenhousz further suggested that plants are not just exchanging "good air" for "bad," but are also absorbing carbon from the air (in the form of carbon dioxide) and using it for nourishment. Ingenhousz had the basic idea.

In 1804, the Swiss botanist Nicholas Theodore de Saussure confirmed Ingenhousz's ideas with experiments showing that a growing plant gains weight equal to the amount of carbon it draws from the air plus the amount of water taken up by its roots.

But it would be nearly half a century later (1845) before scientists finally put all the pieces together and realized that light energy from the Sun is stored as chemical energy in the carbon products, or carbohydrates, created as an outcome of photosynthesis.

The result was the formula that summarizes this important process:

$$6CO_2 + 6H_2O + \text{light energy} \rightarrow C_6H_{12}O_6 + 6O_2.$$

In this equation, the letters C, H, and O stand for the

The chlorophyll molecule is noted for its central core of magnesium (Mg) held in place by a complex of rings. The attached carbon-hydrogen chain anchors the molecule to proteins in the chloroplast. Chlorophyll b is distinguished from chlorophyll a by the chemical group attached at the site indicated by the box in the illustration.

elements carbon, hydrogen, and oxygen. In other words, carbon dioxide plus water plus light energy yields carbohydrate (such as a sugar) plus oxygen. The sugar is then available as fuel for growth and other life processes. Extra sugars are stored in plant tissues as starch.

In recent years, scientists have discovered that carbohydrate is not the only type of plant "food" that results from the process of photosynthesis. In smaller amounts, photosynthesis also produces amino acids, proteins, fats, and other organic (carbon-based) products. The creation of these and other "building materials" requires a number of additional elements such as nitrogen, phosphorus, and sulfur. Yet the photosynthetic process that produces them remains essentially the same. Indeed, it can be said, quite literally, that a plant *builds itself* through the process of photosynthesis.

PHOTOSYNTHETIC PIGMENTS

Before a plant (or other photosynthetic organism) can use the energy of the Sun, it must "catch" it. The plant does so with a pigment, a substance that absorbs visible light. Some pigments absorb all wavelengths of visible light and so appear black. But most absorb only certain wavelengths, or colors.

Chlorophylls, the most important photosynthetic pigments, absorb light primarily in the

The green of summer leaves comes from chlorophyll. As autumn progresses, the chlorophyll breaks down and the red and yellow pigments reveal themselves.

violet, blue, and red range of the spectrum. They reflect green wavelengths—and so give plants their characteristic color.

We now know that there is not just one form of chlorophyll, but at least five. All photosynthetic organisms appear to use chlorophyll a. True plants and green algae also use chlorophyll b. Other photosynthetic algae and cyanobacteria employ chlorophylls c, d, and e. Purple bacteria and sulfur bacteria use still other types.

Chlorophylls are by far the most abundant and important photosynthetic pigments. But they do not work alone. They are "assisted" by other pigments, which funnel additional energy into the process of photosynthesis. In true plants, these "helper pigments" include carotene (yellow), xanthophyll (pale yellow), betacyanin (red), and anthocyanin (reddish to purple). Typically, their colors are hidden by the green mask of chlorophyll. They become most visible in autumn, when chlorophyll breaks down. Some red algae and cyanobacteria (blue-green algae) also contain accessory pigments, called *phycobilins*.

Energy Traps

What enables these pigments to function as little energy traps? All are complex molecules made, in part, of a ring of carbon atoms. It is this ring that is able to absorb light energy—and hold onto it, if only for a moment.

Chlorophyll consists of a large circular molecule with a single metallic atom—magnesium—embedded in its heart. Around this magnesium atom is a ring made of nitrogen and carbon atoms. A long chain of carbon atoms serves as an anchor, securing the pigment in its proper place in a photosynthetic cell.

When a pigment molecule absorbs light, the electrons in its carbon ring temporarily rise to a higher, or more excited, level. When they drop back to a lower level, the extra energy channels into one of three forms:

• It may be lost as heat;
• It may produce an energetic glow, called *fluorescence;* or
• It may be captured and used in the formation of a chemical bond.

This third action is what takes place in the process of photosynthesis. But a pigment alone cannot accomplish this feat.

Indeed, when chlorophyll pigments are separated from plant tissue and placed in a test

By chance, some of these organic molecules may have formed carbon rings similar to those seen in photosynthetic pigments. Then some of these primitive pigments may have found their way inside simple one-celled organisms. At first, these simple pigments may have acted as "spark plugs," emitting flashes of energy that drove a useful reaction or two. Then, through evolution, a chemical pathway for storing this energy may have developed.

The earliest known photosynthetic organisms were the cyanobacteria, or "blue-green algae," which appeared some 3 billion years ago. Then, as today, they produced their own energy using the pigment chlorophyll. Their photosynthetic activities filled the atmosphere with

In the controlled atmosphere of the lab (above), or in the field (right), scientists have devised a number of methods and instruments for measuring the rate of photosynthesis in plants.

tube, light will cause them to fluoresce, or glow. In other words, an isolated pigment quickly reemits the energy it captures. None of the light it absorbs is converted into a form useful to living things. For the latter to happen, a photosynthetic pigment must be associated with special proteins and embedded in a living cell.

THE EVOLUTION OF PHOTOSYNTHETIC ORGANISMS

The first living things on Earth surely lacked the ability to photosynthesize. Most likely, these simple one-celled creatures merely absorbed the nutrients they needed from the "organic soup" in which they lived. As best as scientists can reconstruct it, early Earth was buffeted by powerful electric storms and solar radiation. This intense energy would have produced an abundance of complex, carbon-based (organic) molecules in the atmosphere. These would then rain down into the seas to supply early life with simple nutrients, or food.

oxygen (O_2) and threw a protective blanket of ozone (O_3) around the planet. The oxygen made possible the appearance of aerobic (oxygen-breathing) organisms. The ozone blunted the onslaught of intense solar radiation.

These first photosynthetic organisms were simple, one-celled organisms—more complex than the first living cells, but far simpler than any true plant. Like other early life, they were *prokaryotic*. That is, their single-celled bodies were not divided into membrane-bound structures such as a nucleus and chloroplasts.

By contrast, all multicellular (many celled) organisms consist of *eukaryotic* cells—cells whose contents are organized into membrane-bound structures such as a nucleus, chloroplasts, and mitochondria. All plants, animals, algae, and fungi are eukaryotic organisms.

There is a theory that the first photosynthetic eukaryotic organism was created when a simple (prokaryotic) photosynthetic bacterium infected a larger, nonphotosynthetic, eukaryotic organism. Or perhaps the bacterium was engulfed by the larger organism. No doubt, such things occurred frequently. But at least once—the theory goes—the union of the two cells proved symbiotic: the larger organism gave the smaller, photosynthetic bacterium a safe haven; in return, the bacterium supplied its host with energy.

Within their host cells, these photosynthetic bacteria are believed to have evolved into chloroplasts. A chloroplast is a kind of *plastid*, a membrane-bound cell structure unique to plants.

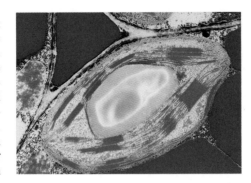

The chloroplast (above, greatly magnified) is the site of photosynthesis. The diagram below uses a series of blowups to zoom in on a chloroplast.

Specifically, it is the plastid, or cell structure, in which all plant photosynthesis takes place.

THE CHLOROPLAST

The development of the chloroplast was one of life's great evolutionary breakthroughs. It is, in essence, a highly efficient combination power plant and factory. In it, the pigments are arranged to maximize their capture of sunlight and production of energy. By contrast, in photosynthetic organisms that lack chloroplasts, photosynthesis is far less efficient. In these organisms, the photosynthetic pigments simply float freely through the cell.

In shape, a chloroplast more or less resembles a football. In size, it is about 2,500 nanome-

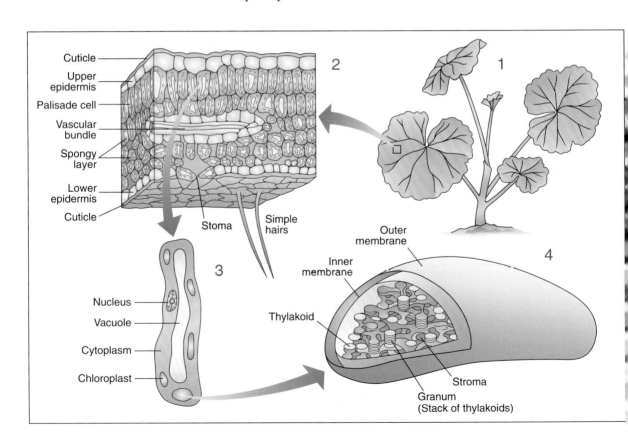

Life as we know it depends on a grand recycling effort. Not glass or aluminum or newspapers, but the element carbon is the vital material in nature's recycling plant.

To begin with, a vast reservoir of carbon fills our atmosphere in the form of carbon dioxide. Through photosynthesis, this carbon is assembled into organic (carbon-containing) compounds, such as sugars and starches. The most important photosynthesizers on our planet are plants and photosynthetic plankton. They consume some of the carbon compounds they create in respiration (breathing). This "burned" carbon returns to the atmosphere as carbon dioxide. The rest is stored in the tissues of these organisms. In this way, plants incorporate an estimated 20 billion to 30 billion tons of carbon into organic material each year. In the oceans, photosynthetic plankton incorporate about 40 billion tons more.

These plant and plankton tissues, in turn, become food for animals. Herbivorous animals feed on plants directly. Predators consume plants indirectly, through the bodies of the animals on which they prey. Like plants, all animals respire, or breathe, and so return some carbon dioxide directly into the atmosphere. The rest they store in their own body tissues.

Next in line in the carbon cycle are the decomposers. The world's most important decomposers are fungi and bacteria, which break down dead plant and animal matter as they feed upon it. Their respiration returns still more carbon to the atmosphere.

As you can see, a single atom of carbon may cycle through many life-forms before it returns again to the atmosphere as carbon dioxide. Yet, on the whole, the natural processes of photosynthesis and respiration essentially balance one another. So carbon dioxide concentrations in our atmosphere have remained fairly constant—until the past two centuries.

With the Industrial Revolution, in the mid–1800s, human activities began tipping the balance of the carbon cycle. The burning of fossil fuels (coal, oil, and natural gas) has

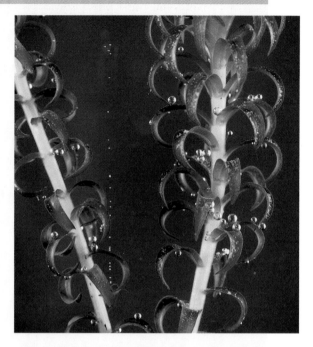

Photosynthesis provides pure oxygen to Earth's atmosphere. In water plants (above), the oxygen is visible as bubbles that float to the surface.

been releasing tremendous amounts of carbon into the atmosphere. (These fuels come from underground deposits of buried plant and animal matter millions of years old.) The same can be said about the widespread clearing of forests and other areas of natural vegetation. This destruction also releases tremendous amounts of carbon into the atmosphere (and removes an important source of atmospheric oxygen).

As a result, the amount of carbon dioxide in our atmosphere has been steadily increasing over the past century. Scientists are not yet sure what the result of this great change will be. Some predict that the extra carbon in our atmosphere will act like a greenhouse cover to warm our planet (a phenomenon called the greenhouse effect). The solution, according to some experts, is a great reduction in the burning of fossil fuels and an increase in photosynthesis—namely, the replanting and preservation of forests.

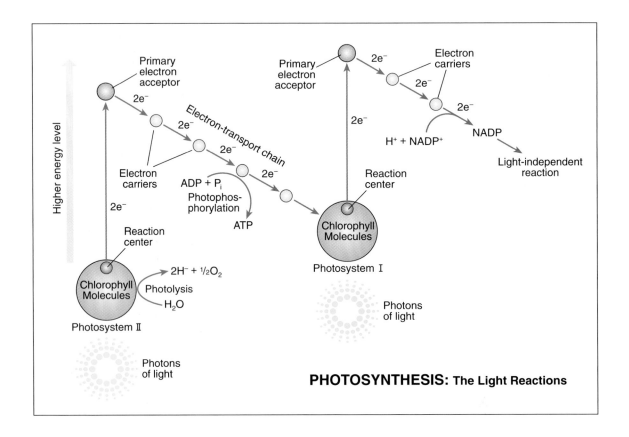

PHOTOSYNTHESIS: The Light Reactions

ters thick and 5,000 nanometers long (1 nanometer equals 0.00000004 inch). This is large enough to fill over half the "body" of a certain single-celled alga. By comparison, a typical leaf cell contains up to 200 chloroplasts.

Separating the chloroplast from the rest of the cell is its double-layered outer membrane. Several striking features can be seen within the chloroplast (as viewed with an electron microscope). Lacing throughout the chloroplast is a folded network of internal membranes called *lamellae*. Under very high magnification, one can see that the lamellae are organized into flattened disks called *thylakoids*.

The thylakoids, in turn, are stacked throughout the chloroplast like so many piles of poker chips. These stacks of chlorophyll-packed "chips" were visible as green specks to early scientists using ordinary light microscopes. They called them *grana*, meaning "grains," a term still used today. The grana are interconnected by bridgelike extensions that stretch between some of their thylakoid disks.

The light-capturing reactions of photosynthesis (described below) take place in the grana, where chlorophylls and other pigments lie embedded in the lamellae. These pigments are arranged in special units called *photosystems*. Each photosystem contains a cluster of 250 to 400 pigments linked together and held in place to maximize the efficient capture of light.

All of the pigments in the photosystem can absorb light energy. But only one pair of chlorophyll molecules can actually use this energy to fuel a photosynthetic reaction. This special pair sits at the core of the photosystem—the *reaction center*. The other pigments are called *antenna pigments*. Arranged like spokes around the reaction center, they pass their captured light energy along to the reaction center. The two chlorophyll molecules sitting in the center bundle this energy in the form of an electron. Then they pass it to a carrier molecule, which carries the electron away from the grana.

Surrounding the grana is a dense solution called the *stroma*. It is packed with the enzymes

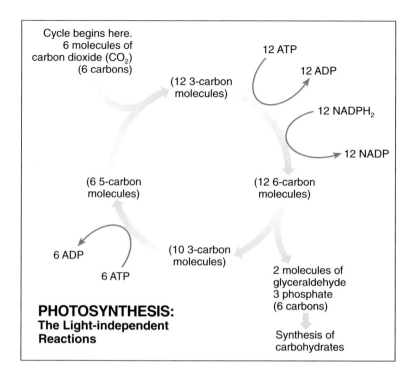

Cycle begins here.
6 molecules of
carbon dioxide (CO$_2$)
(6 carbons)

12 ATP

12 ADP

(12 3-carbon
molecules)

12 NADPH$_2$

12 NADP

(6 5-carbon
molecules)

(12 6-carbon
molecules)

6 ADP

(10 3-carbon
molecules)

6 ATP

2 molecules of
glyceraldehyde
3 phosphate
(6 carbons)

PHOTOSYNTHESIS:
The Light-independent
Reactions

Synthesis of
carbohydrates

that the dark reactions do not require the absence of light. Indeed, the term "light-independent" more accurately describes the second-stage reactions than does the term "dark reactions." In fact, these reactions typically occur during the daytime in living plants.

Light Reactions

Recall from the previous sections how the grana contain light-capturing pigments carefully arranged into "photosystems" that maximize their efficiency. We now know there are two kinds of photosystems, linked to each other and operating side by side like twin power plants. The chlorophyll pigments at the core of Photosystem I best absorb light at a slightly different wavelength than those at the core of Photosystem II. They work together as follows:

Light excites the electrons in the chlorophyll of Photosystem II—so much so that two electrons leave the chlorophyll molecule. They are immediately replaced by two electrons from a water molecule. This reaction splits the water

and small molecules needed for the "dark reactions" of photosynthesis. In these reactions, energy produced in the grana are used to convert carbon dioxide into sugar and other organic (carbon-containing) compounds. The double membrane that surrounds the chloroplast keeps the stroma from leaking out into the cell's thinner cytoplasm. If the membrane breaks, the stroma enzymes leak out and photosynthesis comes to a halt.

STAGES OF PHOTOSYNTHESIS

The grana and the stroma, described above, are the separate sites of the two stages of photosynthesis. Stage one, in the grana, involves the steps in which light energy gets captured. These steps are therefore called the *light reactions*. Stage two, in the stroma, uses the energy produced in stage one (the light reactions) to build carbon products. The reactions in this second stage do not require light, so they are often called the *dark reactions*. It should be noted, however,

Current research is exploring ways of enhancing photosynthesis so as to maximize the growth efficiency of wheat (below) and other plant species, and thereby produce a greater crop yield from a fixed amount of land.

molecules into two protons (2H+) and an atom of oxygen (O). This process is called *photolysis*, meaning "light splitting"; it yields the first important by-product of photosynthesis—oxygen.

Meanwhile, the two superenergized electrons (just boosted out of the chlorophyll) get snatched up by a carrier molecule. It passes the electrons to another carrier molecule, which does the same. As the electrons get passed through this *electron-transport chain*, some of their extra energy is used to produce two molecules of *adenosine triphosphate* (*ATP*) from *adenosine diphosphate* (*ADP*). ATP is the major source of usable energy in all living cells. So here we have the second important by-product of photosynthesis—chemical energy. It will be used later, in the "light-independent" reactions described below.

But the two liberated electrons have not yet finished their work. The electron-transport chain delivers them to the chlorophyll reaction center in Photosystem I. Light energy absorbed by the chlorophyll there boosts the electrons back into a high-energy state and out of the chlorophyll. Snatched up by a second, shorter electron-transport chain, they end up in the *electron acceptor molecule* (*NADP*). The NADP temporarily "holds" the electrons in place by picking up one of the protons (H+) left over from the previous splitting of water (H_2O), becoming NADPH. NADPH then ferries the electrons' energy out of the grana to the surrounding stroma. There the energy will be used to fuel the production of carbohydrates and other organic molecules in the "light-independent" reactions.

In summary, the light reactions of photosynthesis convert light energy into electrical energy (free electrons), which is then converted into chemical energy (in the molecular bonds of ATP and NADPH). In the words of the biochemist and author Albert Szent-Györgyi: "What drives life is … a little electric current, kept up by the sunshine."

Light-independent Reactions

At this stage of photosynthesis, the energy generated by the "power plants" in the grana flows to carbon assembly lines, or "factories," in the stroma. The raw materials used in this factory are carbon dioxide (CO_2) and hydrogen atoms from water (H_2O). Most plants absorb carbon dioxide from the air through special openings, called *stomata*, in their leaves and stems. They draw water primarily through their roots. The process of assembling simple carbon into more-complex carbon compounds is called *carbon fixation*. It takes place in a series of reactions called the *Calvin cycle* (named after biochemist Melvin Calvin). In essence, every turn of the Calvin cycle splices one molecule of carbon dioxide onto a carrier molecule, along with the hydrogen from one molecule of water. So six turns of the Calvin cycle will incorporate six carbon atoms. This produces one molecule of the sugar glucose ($C_6H_{12}O$).

Fueling this process is the ATP and NADPH produced in the light reactions. In total, six revolutions of the Calvin cycle consume, or "burn," the energy in 18 molecules of ATP and 12 molecules of NADPH.

The sugar produced by these reactions can then be "burned" by the plant as fuel, stored as starch, or used as a skeleton to build more-complicated carbon molecules such as amino acids.

Summary of Photosynthesis

Here, in summary, is what basically happens during photosynthesis:

1. Light reaches the chlorophyll and other pigments.

2. The chlorophyll absorbs the light energy and releases electrical energy (free electrons), which in turn is converted to chemical energy (ATP and NADPH).

3. Water molecules (H_2O) split to resupply the chlorophyll with electrons and the NADP with protons (H+). The by-product of this reaction is oxygen.

4. The energy produced by the above steps fuels a series of reactions (the Calvin cycle), which assemble molecules of carbon dioxide into complex carbon compounds such as the sugar glucose.

5. The resulting sugar can be consumed by the plant as fuel, stored by the plant as starch, or assembled into other building materials such as amino acids.

Steps 1 through 3 require the presence of light. Steps 4 and 5 do not.

Through this process, virtually all life on Earth receives its nourishment—either directly, as is the case with plants, algae, and photosynthetic bacteria—or indirectly, as with plant-eating animals and the animals that eat them.

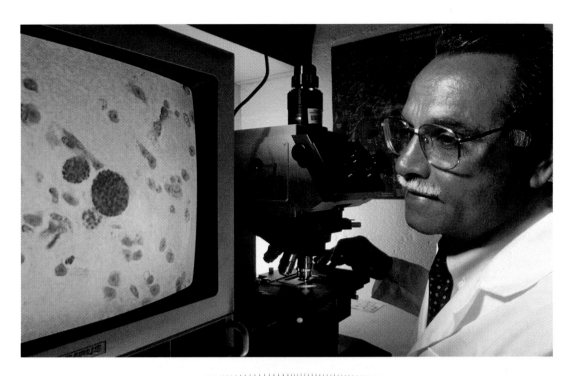

KINGDOM MONERA

by Elaine Pascoe

Science-fiction films portray alien life-forms as almond-eyed humanoids or nightmarish insect-lizard hybrids. But if (or when) life is found on other planets, it is likely to be far simpler—as simple as bacteria and other members of the kingdom Monera. Monerans are the most-numerous and the oldest living things on Earth. They are virtually everywhere. Yet they are so small that they can be seen only when they are put under a microscope or form huge colonies. We are rarely directly aware of them.

It has been more than 300 years since the Dutch lensmaker Anton van Leeuwenhoek peered through his primitive microscope and observed the existence of microbes. But it was another 200 years before scientists such as Louis Pasteur and Robert Koch demonstrated the links between bacteria and disease, and it is only in the past 50 years or so that biologists have begun to unlock the secrets of these tiniest living things. However, with recent advances in microbiology, knowledge of the monerans is expanding quite rapidly. These primitive organisms are now the focus of one of the most-exciting fields of study in biology, and they are bringing us ever closer to an understanding of how life on Earth may have originated.

WHAT ARE MONERANS?

Not long after bacteria were first observed, scientists sought to place them in one of the two existing kingdoms of living things, plant or animal. At first, bacteria were considered tiny animals, similar to one-celled protozoans, and were therefore relegated to the Animal Kingdom. Later they were placed in the Plant Kingdom, along with blue-green algae. Unfortunately, neither kingdom was a comfortable fit. Finally, in the late 1800s, the German biologist Ernst Haeckel suggested that living things be divided into three kingdoms—plants, animals, and *pro-*

Kingdom Monera has as its members the simplest forms of life on Earth. In order to view an individual moneran, scientists must use a powerful microscope.

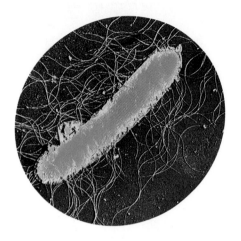

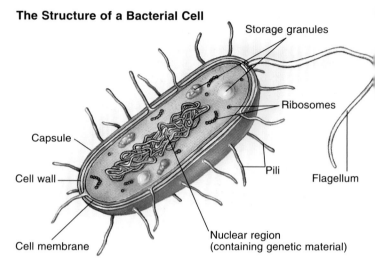

The Structure of a Bacterial Cell

Storage granules

Ribosomes

Capsule

Cell wall

Pili

Flagellum

Cell membrane

Nuclear region
(containing genetic material)

All bacteria are classified as monerans. Special structures, such as capsules, pili, or the flagella seen in the micrograph of Proteus mirabilis *(above), appear on many types of bacteria.*

tists, a group that would include one-celled creatures such as yeasts and protozoans as well as bacteria. Haeckel also holds the distinction of being the first to use the term *monera*, although not exactly in the same sense as it is used today. He attempted to draw a genealogical tree of living things, and he designated the hypothetical first ancestors of life as Monera.

By the 1950s, advances in molecular biology and improved research tools, such as the electron microscope, caused scientists to think again. Bacteria and blue-green algae not only did not fit neatly into either the plant or animal category, but there were marked differences between these organisms and others that Haeckel had termed protists. Under a new five-kingdom classification system proposed by R.H. Whittaker, they were grouped separately, as Monera.

The Whittaker system is the one in general use today. Three of the five kingdoms distinguish between living things primarily on the basis of how they obtain nutrition—through photosynthesis (green plants), by ingesting food (animals), or by absorbing nutrients (fungi). Monerans and protists, which form the remaining kingdoms in this system, are for the most part unicellular (one-celled) organisms. They are classified according to differences in cell structure, rather than by their methods of obtaining nutrients. In this scheme, the blue-green algae—previously considered plants, because they are capable of photosynthesis—are ranked with the bacteria, as cyanobacteria.

Prokaryotes

The monerans are the simplest of all living things, so simple that they are thought to resemble the earliest forms of life. The members of this kingdom are set apart chiefly by the fact that they have no clearly organized cell nuclei. Their genetic material, or DNA, is in a long double strand, coiled into one circular chromosome called a *nucleoid*, rather than arranged in multiple chromosomes like the genetic material of more-complex organisms. If the strand were uncoiled, in many cases it would be 1,000 times longer than the microscopic cell that holds it. There is no nuclear envelope around it.

Because they lack a nucleus, these simple organisms are termed *prokaryotes*, from Greek words meaning "prior to" and "nucleus." Organisms that have cell nuclei, whether they are unicellular or multicellular, are termed *eukaryotes*, from Greek words meaning "true nucleus."

Prokaryotes are set apart by a number of other structural differences. In nearly all, the cell is enclosed in a rigid wall, which in most cases is made up primarily of *peptidoglycan* (a polymer of amino acids and sugars). This material is similar, but not identical, to *chitin*, which forms the shells of crustaceans. Just inside the cell wall is a membrane made up of lipids and proteins. This structure acts as a barrier, preventing cell contents from leaking out. It also helps carry out metabolic functions that, in higher organisms, are generally handled by specialized structures within the cell, such as mitochondria and chloroplasts. These structures, or organelles, are absent in prokaryotes.

While some types of prokaryotes link together to form colonies or (in the case of some cyanobacteria) filaments, each cell remains a fully functioning individual. There is usually no cell differentiation within the colonies, as is found in multicellular organisms. Prokaryotes reproduce asexually, mainly by cell division.

The discovery of new types of bacteria and sophisticated methods of tracing relationships through cellular chemistry are causing scientists to constantly reassess the classification of prokaryotes. Traditionally, Kingdom Monera was divided into two phyla, or main groups—bacteria and cyanobacteria. Based on analysis of nucleic acids in the cells and on other differences, many scientists now recognize a separate subkingdom, Archaea. Its members, sometimes called *archaebacteria*, are simple organisms that exist in extreme conditions—without oxygen, and in hot and acidic environments. It is probable that they closely resemble the first forms of life that appeared on Earth.

RELATIONSHIP TO EARLY LIFE

Fossils of ancient microbes have been found in rocks roughly 3.5 billion years old. They represent the earliest evidence of living organisms—cells capable of metabolism and self-replication. How the first such cells arose is a matter of debate. A widely held view supposes that ultraviolet radiation and lightning discharges prompted chemical reactions on Earth's surface and in the atmosphere. The reactions formed organic compounds, and clusters of organic molecules eventually organized into functioning cells.

When the first living cells appeared, there was no oxygen in the atmosphere, and the planet was much hotter than it is today. Early microbes were thus *anaerobic* (functioning without oxygen) and *thermophilic* (heat-loving). They probably obtained energy through fermentation, breaking down chemicals in their environment. These traits can still be found in some monerans, most notably in the archaebacteria.

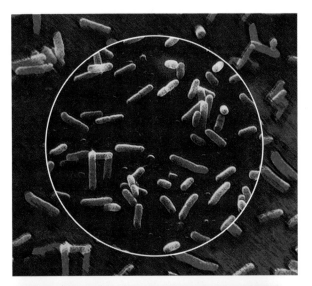

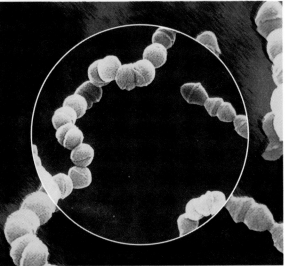

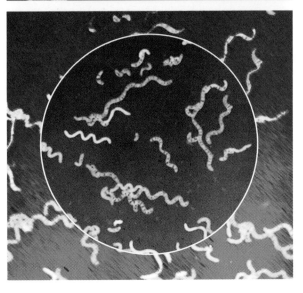

Bacteria are typically classified according to whether they are rod-shaped (Salmonella, *top), spherical* (Streptococcus, *center), or spiral* (Rhodospirillum, *right).*

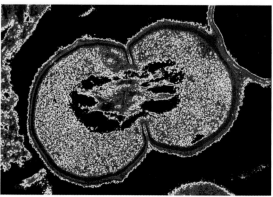

Each daughter cell that results from the dividing bacterium above is capable of living independently. Using a machine called a fermentor (left), scientists can "mass-produce" certain bacteria for laboratory research.

The development of chlorophylls marked the start of a profound change on Earth. Chlorophylls are pigments that enable cells to convert the energy of sunlight into sugars, which the cells then use for food. There are two forms of photosynthesis—*oxygenic*, which produces oxygen as a by-product, and *anoxygenic*, which does not. Oxygenic photosynthesis filled the atmosphere with oxygen and led to the formation of the atmospheric ozone layer, which shields Earth's surface from excessive ultraviolet radiation. In this protected, oxygen-rich environment, life as we know it emerged.

Microbes—eukaryotes and prokaryotes—ruled Earth for billions of years. Then, even as life diversified into ever more complex, varied, and sophisticated forms, these primitive organisms remained enormously successful.

BACTERIA

Bacteria have been found in just about every place imaginable, from steaming hot springs to rocks in Antarctica. They exist independently in soil and water, in the air, and on the ocean floor. Bacteria live on, and in, living and nonliving things. They have even been discovered in rocks thousands of feet below the surface, living off minerals there. People often think of bacteria as harmful, and understandably so. Bacterial diseases—including cholera, diphtheria, and tuberculosis—have claimed millions of lives. But bacteria play an essential role in the cycle of life, and they do more good than harm.

Characteristics

Bacteria are the smallest living things (if viruses are not considered truly living), so it will be easiest to discuss their size in terms of millimeters (1 millimeter equals 0.039 inch) and micrometers, or microns (1 micron equals 0.00039 inch). Since bacteria are seldom more than 0.005 millimeter at the longest measurement, as many as 100 million could reside in a drop of spoiled milk. Most common types take one of three shapes: spherical or ovoid (*coccus*); rod-shaped (*bacillus*); and spiral (*spirillum*). Bacteria with other shapes have been observed, including some with many branching filaments and a square type, discovered along the shore of the Red Sea in 1981.

Nearly all bacteria have cell walls, often coated with a layer of slime that the organism secretes. One exception is a group of bacteria called *mycoplasmas*, which are enclosed only by a highly stable cell membrane. (Mycoplasmas are also among the smallest bacteria, some only 0.2 micron in diameter.) Cell walls are sev-

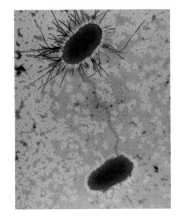

The E. coli *bacterium* at right is transferring a copy of its resistance gene to a second *bacterium—a process that will ultimately help the species resist attack by antibiotics.*

eral layers thick, and their composition varies somewhat among species. Differences in the ways that the walls absorb a stain (applied to make them visible under a microscope) led to the division of bacteria into *gram-positive* and *gram-negative* types (after the 19th-century scientist Hans Christian Gram).

Many bacteria that live in water or other liquids have *flagella*, threadlike external structures that move the organism about. Flagella, which are formed of a protein similar to that in muscle tissue, vary greatly in number and location from one species to the next. Many bacteria are *chemotactic*; that is, they move toward or away from certain chemicals. Bacterial flagella rotate constantly, and the direction of rotation determines how the bacterium moves. Counterclockwise rotation causes the bacterium to swim in a straight line, or run. Clockwise rotation causes the organism to stop and tumble around, until it sets off in a new direction. A few bacteria are able to move without flagella, gliding slowly along any solid surface with snakelike, twisting motions.

Some bacteria have protein appendages called *fimbriae* and *pili*, which resemble flagella, but do not play a role in movement. Fimbriae and pili help the organism adhere to surfaces, and they play a role in the transmission of DNA among bacteria during certain reproductive processes.

The interior of a bacterial cell is filled with cytoplasm that is about 70 percent water. Besides DNA, the cell contains RNA in ribosomes that regulate the synthesis of proteins—mainly the hundreds of different enzymes that are involved in cell functions and metabolism. Bacterial ribosomes are shorter than those found in eukaryotic cells. Many bacteria also contain

Moneran Classification

KINGDOM Monera

SUBKINGDOM Archaea: *"Ancient bacteria" found in extreme conditions (geysers, deep sea vents, etc.).*

PHYLUM Euryarcheota: *Methanogens.*

PHYLUM Crenarchaeota: *Thermoacidophiles.*

SUBKINGDOM Eubacteria: *"True bacteria."*

PHYLUM Proteobacteria: *Gram negative; includes purple bacteria, ntirogen-fixing bacteria, and pseudomonads.*

PHYLUM Spirochaetae: *Gram negative; includes spirochetes and flagellated bacteria.*

PHYLUM Cyanobacteria: *Gram negative; formerly called blue-green algae.*

PHYLUM Saprospirae: *Gram-negative fermenters.*

PHYLUM Chloroflexa: *Gram-negative green nonsulfur phototrophs.*

PHYLUM Chlorobia: *Gram negative; anoxygenic green sulfur phototrophs.*

PHYLUM Endospora: *Gram-positive, protein-walled, endospore-forming bacteria.*

PHYLUM Pirellae: *Gram-positive, stalked, protein-walled bacteria.*

PHYLUM Actinobacteria: *Gram-positive, protein-walled actinomycetes.*

PHYLUM Deinococci: *Gram-positive, protein-walled, aerobic, radioresistant bacteria.*

PHYLUM Thermotogae: *Gram-positive, protein-walled, thermophilic fermenters.*

PHYLUM Aphragmabacteria: *Bacteria without walls; mycoplasmas and spiroplasmas.*

structures called *inclusion bodies*, granules that hold stored nutrients.

When bacteria run out of nutrients or encounter unfavorable conditions, some types survive by altering their physical makeup and forming *spores*. While in this inert, resting stage, the water content of the cell drops; a thick coat forms to protect the spore while the remainder of the cell disintegrates; and cell functions are minimal or halt completely. The organism stays in this state until conditions are favorable again. Then the cell sprouts from the spore coat, fully active once again. Spores are highly resistant to heat, and thus they often survive sterilization—some can even withstand being boiled for several hours. Fortunately, most of the bacteria that cause serious diseases in people do not form resistant spores.

Nutrition and Metabolism

Like all living things, bacteria break down nutrients to obtain energy and raw materials used in growth, reproduction, and other vital activities. Aerobic bacteria draw free oxygen from air or water to facilitate this process, which is called *respiration*. Anaerobic bacteria survive without oxygen—within other organisms, in sealed cans of food, and at depths of soil and water where little or no free oxygen is present—and break down nutrients chiefly through fermentation. So-called *obligate* anaerobes grow only in these conditions, while *facultative* anaerobes are able to live with or without oxygen. *Salmonella*, which can cause severe food poisoning, is among the best known of the facultative anaerobes.

Aerobic and anaerobic bacteria alike may obtain food in any of several ways. Most bacteria feed on organic compounds produced by other living things—in wastes and dead plant or animal tissues, or in the tissues of living plants or animals. They are called *organotrophs* or *heterotrophs* (from Greek words meaning "other" and "nourishment"). Some of these bacteria have wide-ranging tastes and can consume a variety of materials; others are quite selective and require specific materials to flourish. *Rickettsia* and *chlamydia* are unusual in that they are intra-

Cyanobacteria (formerly called blue-green algae) have no distinct nuclei; unlike other bacteria, they can photosynthesize. Representative genera include Chroococcus *(mainly unicellular);* Oscillatoria *(filamentous);* Rivularia, *which grows in colonies on rocks;* Anabaena, *common in ponds; and* Dermocarpa, *which grows in colonies on algae.*

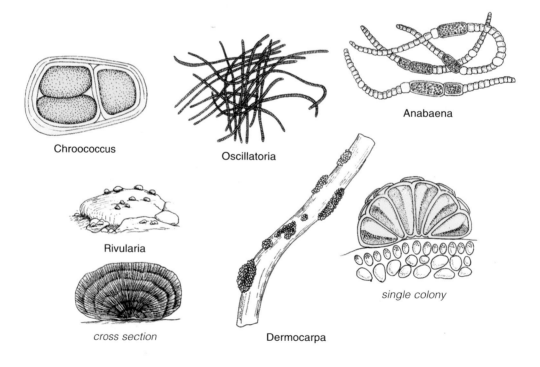

Anabaena

Chroococcus

Oscillatoria

Rivularia

cross section

Dermocarpa

single colony

Exobacteria?

No planet in the solar system has conditions that would support life as we know it on Earth. But scientists have discovered bacteria living in hot springs, deep-sea thermal vents, oil sediments, and frozen rocks. If life exists in such hostile conditions on Earth, might similar forms have evolved on other planets as well?

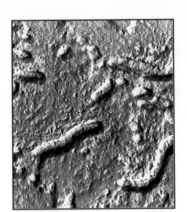

Speculation about this question intensified in 1996, when National Aeronautics and Space Administration (NASA) scientists claimed to have found evidence of life in a Martian meteorite. The Allan Hills meteorite, which was probably blasted loose from the surface of Mars 4 billion years ago, was discovered in Antarctica. In it, the scientists found traces of chemicals associated with microbes. They also observed microscopic ovoid-shaped formations (see photo above) that, they said, might be fossil evidence of so-called nanobacteria—bacteria substantially smaller than the smallest bacteria ever found on Earth.

In 2001, new evidence of extraterrestrial life came to light when British and Indian scientists detected bacteria high in Earth's atmosphere. The cells, similar to those found on the ground, were so numerous that it was unlikely that they had originated on Earth.

There are serious scientific doubts about each of these findings. Still, it's likely that Mars, and perhaps other planets, once had conditions suitable for life. Although it is cold and barren now, the Martian surface shows traces of ancient lakes, rivers, and hot springs where simple microbes might have flourished. There may still be underground reservoirs of water—and if so, microbes may currently thrive there.

If life exists on Mars or other planets, it likely developed independently from life on Earth. The idea that ancient Martian microbes might arrive on Earth in a meteorite leads to another theory: perhaps life originated on Mars and traveled to Earth the same way.

---

cellular parasites, unable to live outside an animal cell. They rely on the host cell for certain metabolic functions, and cause many diseases.

Bacteria that can manufacture their own food through photosynthesis, using energy from the Sun, are called *photoautotrophs*, from Greek words meaning "light" and "self-nourishing." Besides cyanobacteria, described below, most of these belong to a group of water dwellers known collectively as purple and green bacteria. Their method of photosynthesis differs from that of plants and cyanobacteria, and it does not produce oxygen as a by-product. Purple bacteria and green bacteria also contain different types of pigments (*bacteriochlorophyll*). In green bacteria, structures called *chlorosomes* are attached to the cell membrane and carry out the photosynthesis. Purple bacteria have internal membrane systems that accomplish the task.

A third type of bacteria, the *chemolithotrophs*, are able to use simple inorganic compounds as a source of energy. Some rely entirely on this method; others can also draw nutrition from organic sources. Chemolithotrophs, which are generally grouped according to the inorganic compounds they rely on, play important roles in the scheme of nature. For example, nitrifying bacteria in soils and water help ensure that plants have an adequate nitrogen supply for new growth by converting ammonia to nitrites, and nitrites into nitrates. Among other chemolithotrophs are bacteria that rely on sulfur compounds, iron compounds, or hydrogen compounds.

Reproduction and Genetics

Most bacteria reproduce asexually by *binary fission*, a simple process in which one cell di-

Researchers often study the course of a bacterial disease in pigs (above) or other animals in order to develop ways to treat the same disease in humans.

vides to form two. When a bacterium grows to a certain size, which varies according to the species, fission automatically takes place. The double strand of genetic material replicates and then splits, and the cell pinches off in the middle, forming two daughter cells that are identical to the first.

When temperature, moisture levels, food supply, and other conditions are optimal for growth, fission can take place with incredible frequency—as often as every 20 minutes in some types of bacteria. The population of bacteria increases exponentially until moisture or food supply begins to run out or conditions otherwise become less favorable. Then reproduction slows or stops.

In nature, optimal conditions for bacterial growth rarely exist, at least not for long. Still, the frequency with which bacteria reproduce provides plenty of opportunities for mistakes in copying genetic material. Such mistakes result in mutations. While most mutations are unsuc-

cessful, occasionally a change helps the bacteria thrive. In that case, a new strain of bacteria may arise, as the altered individuals rapidly multiply.

The genetic makeup, or *genotype*, of bacteria also changes through *recombination*, the process by which genetic material from two individuals can be combined. This happens in several ways. In *transformation*, a bacterium takes up bits of free DNA that have been released by a donor. In *transduction*, bits of DNA are carried from one bacterium to another by a *phage*, a virus that attaches to the wall of the bacterium and inserts its genetic material into the host. The virus then replicates itself inside the bacterium. Sometimes, however, bits of the host DNA are incorporated into the viral DNA during replication. These are carried along when the new virus particles are released, and infect other bacteria.

Among some bacteria, genetic recombination occurs through a process known as *conjugation*. These bacteria contain *plasmids*, tightly coiled molecules of DNA that reproduce separately from the chromosomal DNA. A plasmid-containing bacterium becomes a donor after it forms a pilus that attaches to a second bacterium, or recipient. A bridge forms between the two bacteria, and the donor transfers a copy of a plasmid to the recipient.

The DNA in many plasmids grants new attributes to bacteria, such as resistance to antibiotics, the ability to produce toxins, or the ability to break down certain materials. Some bacteria, including *E. coli*, can also transfer chromosomal genes by conjugation. These bacteria contain so-called *F factor plasmids* that integrate with the donor's chromosome, and pass along copies of specific genes, which then become part of the recipient's genome.

The altered genetic makeup is replicated as both donor and recipient undergo fission. As bacteria multiply rapidly, new strains evolve quickly. There are already bacteria that can break down synthetic chemicals that did not exist 50 years ago.

CYANOBACTERIA

Although the cyanobacteria are commonly known as blue-green algae, they have little in common with other organisms called algae—and they're not even always blue-green! Cyanobacteria have the basic prokaryote struc-

ture—simple cells with no definite nuclei—and are grouped in the same subkingdom of Monera as the bacteria. All are photoautotrophs, producing food through photosynthesis. Their photosynthetic pigments include not only green chlorophyll, but also red phycoerythrin and blue phycocyanin. While most are dark blue, members of the family range in color from near black to orange.

Some of the oldest known fossils are cyanobacteria. About 1,700 species are found worldwide today, living in water and wherever there is ample moisture—on damp stones and walls, even in the snows of Arctic regions. They are responsible for the color of the water in Yellowstone National Park's hot springs and the reddish color of the Red Sea. They sometimes contaminate drinking water, producing unpleasant odors and tastes. A few types form symbiotic partnerships with other organisms.

Like bacteria, cyanobacteria reproduce asexually. Besides the usual prokaryote structures and their photosynthetic pigments, many water-dwelling cyanobacteria contain *gas vesicles*—rigid sacs filled with air—that keep the

organism afloat. The vesicles are formed of a watertight protein that admits gas but is impermeable to liquids.

Many cyanobacteria spend their lives as single cells. Others link up to form sheets, balls, or filaments that are held together by sticky slime that the organisms secrete. *Gloeocapsa*, for example, sometimes forms little colonies of three or four cells, enclosed in a gelatinous sheet. Eventually the colony breaks up into individual cells. *Gloeocapsa* is often found as a slimy coating on damp rocks.

Anabaena forms fine, threadlike filaments known as *trichomes*. Under a microscope, the filaments look like strings of tiny green beads. *Anabaena* is one of the most-common cyanobacteria in North America, living in freshwater ponds and lakes. *Anabaena* is a source of food for fish, making it an important part of the freshwater food chain.

Oscillatoria, another common filament-forming cyanobacteria, is often seen in "blooms" of greenish pond scum in summer. It also grows in damp soil and on flowerpots. Each filament is made up of rectangular cells, lined up in single file and enclosed in a sheath. The colony grows only at each end, as the cells there undergo fission. Sometimes a filament breaks up into sections, and the sections then grow individually. *Oscillatoria* is one of the few cyanobacteria that can move, although how it does so is not fully understood. It has no flagella, but can travel along surfaces with a twisting, gliding motion.

Several recently discovered marine organisms closely resemble cyanobacteria, but are grouped separately. They include a one-celled

Pathogenic, or disease-causing, bacteria are responsible for a long list of deadly diseases, among them bacterial pneumonia, cholera, diphtheria, leprosy, meningitis, tetanus, tuberculosis, typhoid fever, and various types of dysentery. They also cause a host of less-serious illnesses, as well as localized infections in wounds. Bacterial diseases also affect animals, and they are responsible for various diseases of crop plants.

Many bacterial diseases have become less common and less serious with the development of vaccines and antibiotics. Vaccines against diseases such as cholera, diphtheria, and typhoid fever are made from killed or weakened bacteria or from products produced by the bacteria that cause the disease. They prompt the body to mount an immune response against the disease, producing antibodies against it. The antibodies circulate in the blood, ready to attack living bacteria of the same type should they appear.

Antibiotics are based on compounds produced mainly by molds and certain types of bacteria, especially those that live in soil. In nature, the compounds serve to kill or retard the growth of competing bacteria, giving the type that produces the compound an edge in the contest for space and nutrients. Harnessed by medicine, antibiotics kill pathogenic bacteria in various ways.

Increasingly, however, new strains of pathogenic bacteria are appearing—strains that are resistant to known antibiotics. Resistant forms of *Staphylococcus*, which causes a wide range of infections, and *Mycobacterium*, which causes tuberculosis, are especially worrisome. Medical researchers seem to be locked in a race with these microscopic organisms, trying to find ways to control them before they can spread.

Besides causing disease, bacteria also ruin great quantities of food—especially milk, butter, meats, and fresh fruits and vegetables. Some of the bacteria that spoil food produce deadly toxins. Refrigeration does not kill bacteria, but it does slow their actions for as long as the food is refrigerated. Drying also makes it impossible for bacteria to grow, since they require moisture. Heat kills many bacteria, a strong argument for thoroughly cooking foods such as meat. Many packaged and processed foods contain chemical preservatives that prevent or delay bacterial growth. Aerobic bacteria cannot grow in canned foods, but if cans are not processed at temperatures high enough to kill all the bacteria inside, anaerobic types can thrive. Cans that contain highly spoiled food typically appear swollen, the result of gas produced by bacterial fermentation.

Although some bacteria spoil food or cause disease, people have found ways to make use of many others. Some types of bacteria, such as *Lactobacillus*, ferment milk into products such as yogurt, buttermilk, and

organism, *prochloron*, that lives on sea squirts. The discovery of prochloron in 1975 bolstered the theory that chloroplasts, the organelles that carry out photosynthesis in plant cells, may have originated as prokaryotes that lived in symbiosis inside cells. Over time, they lost the ability to function independently.

ARCHAEA

Hydrothermal vents on the ocean floor release mineral-rich water heated by Earth's interior to temperatures as high as 716° F (380° C). Sunlight does not penetrate to these depths, and there is little, if any, available oxygen. These conditions, scientists think, mirror those on Earth billions of years ago, when life first appeared. Around the vents—and in other extreme environments—primitive organisms have been discovered, living in waters as hot as 302° F (150° C). These organisms—the *archaebacteria* (sometimes called *extremophiles*)—probably resemble the earliest forms of life.

Archaebacteria share the basic cell structure and asexual reproduction of other prokaryotes. They differ from other monerans in the chemical composition of their cell membranes and cell walls, and in the sequence of the RNA

cheese. Bacteria are responsible for the holes and the flavor of Swiss cheese. In industry, fermentation is used in leather tanning, in softening and separating some natural fibers for textiles, and in producing materials needed for products that range from plastics to cosmetics. Septic systems and other methods of sewage disposal depend on the action of organotrophic bacteria to decompose wastes. Certain chemolithotrophic bacteria are used in metal and petroleum refining.

Bacteria have become even more important in medicine and industry through genetic engineering. Using techniques of gene splicing, scientists have learned to manipulate the hereditary characteristics of these organisms, so that the bacteria produce substances that are useful as medicine or in manufacturing processes. One of the first products produced through this technique was human insulin, a substance that regulates the body's use of sugar and other nutrients. It is needed by diabetics—people who do not produce enough insulin on their own. Scientists removed a section of bacterial DNA and replaced it with a section of human DNA that would instruct the bacterial cell to produce insulin. As the bacteria multiplied, each generation carried the new genes. In this way, bacteria became an important source of insulin. This same technique is used to produce human growth hormone, which is needed to treat dwarfism.

in their ribosomes. These differences have led some scientists to classify archaebacteria separately from bacteria and cyanobacteria, in the subkingdom Archaea.

Cold-loving forms of Archaea have been found in ice cores drilled from deep within the Antarctic plateau. These organisms, called *psychrophiles*, may show how life could survive in the soil of the planet Mars.

MONERANS IN THE WEB OF LIFE

Most scientists believe that members of Kingdom Monera may have been among the earliest living things, and monerans remain essential to life on Earth. Large numbers of bacteria are at home in nonliving organic material, such as decaying plants, the bodies of dead animals, and animal wastes. These bacteria are important agents of decay, breaking down proteins and other complex organic molecules into simpler compounds such as carbon dioxide and ammonia. They are essentially recyclers, helping to clear away organic debris. In the process, they take many of the nutrients needed by plants and restore these nutrients to the soil, air, and water. Bacteria also produce organic acids that help dissolve the minerals in rock, a process that contributes to the formation of soil.

Beneficial bacteria in the intestines of many mammals, including humans, assist digestion by producing enzymes that help break down food and facilitate the absorption of nutrients. These so-called "gut flora" also help maintain the correct levels of acidity, and even manufacture vitamins, particularly the B vitamins and vitamin K. The bacteria thrive on the wealth of food that passes through, and the host benefits as well. Ruminants, such as cows, giraffes, and antelopes, are especially dependent on bacteria. These animals have in the gastrointestinal tract a chamber called the rumen, where bacteria break down the cellulose contained in grass and other plant material. The bacteria obtain nutrients through the process, but they also convert the cellulose into materials that the animal can absorb and use—something the animals cannot do on their own.

Throughout nature, there are many examples of symbiotic relationships between bacteria and other living things. One of the most important is the partnership between nitrogen-fixing bacteria and plants. These bacteria include several types that live in the roots of legumes. The roots provide carbohydrates and other nutrients for the bacteria, and the bacteria convert nitrogen gas into compounds that the plants can use. The nodules also release nitrogen compounds into the soil, increasing its fertility. Planting legumes as part of a crop-rotation plan is one way in which farmers can maintain soil fertility. Some types of cyanobacteria, including a variety sometimes found in rice paddies, can also fix nitrogen. They do this by forming specialized cells, called *heterocysts*, that function in much the same way as soil bacteria.

KINGDOM FUNGI

by Jessica Snyder Sachs

Mushrooms peeking from a damp forest floor. Molds growing on old fruit. Yeast bubbling in a baker's bowl. These are the fungi with which we are most familiar. But they are neither the most common nor the most important members of the vast Kingdom Fungi. Fungi and their spores pervade the soil, the air we breathe, even the water we drink. Some are harmful, spoiling food or causing diseases in crops, trees, domestic and wild animals, as well as humans. A few are outright deadly if eaten.

But many, if not most, fungi are beneficial. In fact, few of our crops would grow if not for their symbiotic relationship with root fungi called mycorrhizae. Other fungi help produce important foods and beverages such as bread, beer, wine, aged cheeses, and many soybean products. Some of our most important medicines come from fungi—from antibiotics such as penicillin, to cyclosporine, the drug that prevents the rejection of transplanted organs.

Indeed, whether we realize it or not, seldom does a day go by when we are not helped or harmed by fungi in some way. Most impor-

tant of all is the role fungi play as decomposers. Together with certain bacteria, fungi have the primary responsibility for recycling organic material on our planet. As they absorb nutrition from dead plants and animals, fungi release carbon dioxide into the atmosphere and return nitrogen and other vital materials to the soil. Without their efforts, the circle of life would soon grind to a screeching halt.

For these and other reasons, fungi have long been of interest to science. The study of fungi is called *mycology*, from the Greek word *mykes*, meaning "mushroom." Specialists in this field are known as mycologists.

WHAT IS A FUNGUS?

In many ways, fungi are like no other group of organisms on Earth. Unlike the simple monerans, fungi have complex cells with dis-

Scientists have identified more than 150,000 species of fungi. All fungi get their food and energy from the living organisms, such as trees (above), on which they live.

tinct nuclei. Unlike the aquatic protists, fungi are best suited for life on land. Unlike plants, they lack chlorophyll and cannot make their own food. Unlike animals, they do not move about nor do they digest food inside their bodies. For these and other reasons, scientists place fungi in a kingdom apart from all others.

A large and varied group, most fungi share two common and unique characteristics. First, they all feed by absorbing molecules from the plant or animal matter on which they grow. Second, all but the one-celled fungi grow by producing masses of filaments. These filaments, called *hyphae*, are in essence long, open-ended cells. Their rigid cell walls are made of *chitin*—the same material found in the hard shells of insects and crustaceans. Filled with cytoplasm, each hypha can contain many nuclei.

Fungi grow by producing tangled masses of threadlike hyphae called *mycelium*. Visible structures such as mushrooms consist of tightly packed mycelium made of billions of interwoven hyphae. Some kinds of fungi also produce rootlike hyphae, called *rhizoids*, and use them to anchor themselves in place. Many parasitic fungi use another type of specialized hyphae to penetrate the cells of their hosts. These are called *haustoria*.

Many fungi grow amazingly fast. The fastest may be the soil fungi, some of which can produce up to 0.5 mile (0.8 kilometer) of new mycelium in just 24 hours. Yet little of this growth is visible to the casual observer. Indeed, most of a fungus' body—or thallus—lies hidden in the soil, log, or other material from which the fungus draws nutrition. When the mycelium grows near or on the surface, it appears as a mass of loose, cottony threads.

Fungi can reach astounding size. In 1992, scientists discovered two vast underground mats of fungus. The first, in northern Michigan, was a specimen of *Armillaria gallica*, which covered more than 37 acres (15 hectares). The second, in southwestern Washington State, was a specimen of *A. ostoyae*, which stretched for more than 1,500 acres (600 hectares). In 2000, in eastern Oregon, another *A. ostoyae* was found, which covered 2,200 acres (900 hectares), and is the largest living organism known to exist.

Most visible fungal structures—be they mushrooms or the fuzzy growth seen atop spoiled fruit and vegetables—are the organism's fruiting bodies, or *sporangia*. These structures sprout from the fungus' thallus, or main body, during specific periods in its life cycle.

FUNGI BIOLOGY

As mentioned, fungi neither produce their own food (as plants do), nor actively consume food (digesting it internally as animals do). Instead, they passively absorb nutrients from organic material in their environment. All fungi are therefore either parasites (feeding on live organisms) or saprophytes (feeding on dead matter), or they live in a symbiotic (mutually beneficial) relationship with another organism. A few fungi, mainly yeasts, can generate energy by converting glucose (sugar) to ethyl alcohol.

Parasitic and saprophytic fungi secrete chemicals (digestive enzymes) that break down organic matter into relatively small, simple mol-

The study of fungi is called mycology. The mycologist below is examining a particularly large fungal specimen that comprises part of the National Fungus Collection.

Spores are formed by the reproductive mycelium in a variety of structures, such as the end of stalklike hyphae (above). Despite its name, the bread-mold fungus grows on overripe fruits (right) as well as on bread.

ecules that they can absorb. Fungi take in these nutrients through the growing tips of their open-ended hyphae. Some species of fungi can break down a broad variety of dead or decaying plant and animal matter. Others have digestive enzymes tailored to a specific material. One small fungus group, for example, grows only on dead animal hooves and horns.

Fungi also secrete a variety of toxic chemicals to use as weapons against their main competitors—bacteria. (Some bacteria, in turn, produce antifungal chemicals.) Penicillin, produced by the blue-green mold *Penicillium notatum*, was the first of a series of antibiotic drugs derived from fungi. Some of the more recently developed bacteria fighters include the powerful cephalosporin antibiotics, produced by the mold *Cephalosporium acremonium*.

In general, fungi thrive best under warm, moist conditions. But some molds can actively grow at temperatures near freezing (an ability frequently demonstrated in refrigerators). Most fungi can survive even harsher conditions as dormant (resting) spores, which germinate when warmth and moisture return.

Reproduction

When fungi reach maturity, they begin to produce reproductive cells called spores. Some fungi can produce spores in only one way; most species produce spores both sexually and asexually, at different points in their life cycle.

The spores that result from asexual reproduction tend to be dustlike. They are called *conidia* (singular: *conidium*), a term derived from the Greek word *konis*, meaning "dust." When these spores germinate, they give rise to individuals genetically identical to their parent (clones). Conidia can be scattered for hundreds, even thousands, of miles by wind, rain, insects, and other agents.

Fungi show a great deal of variation in sexual reproduction. But in all cases, the essential feature is the bringing together and fusing of two cell nuclei. In the most-primitive types of fungi, this event occurs inside a thick-walled sexual structure called a *zygosporangium*. A sexually produced spore can remain dormant for months before germinating into a new fungus.

The most-advanced fungi produce fruiting bodies after sexual reproduction. These *sporophores*, ranging in size from microscopic to gigantic, are filled with spore-producing filaments. Among the largest are mushrooms, which can grow to be more than 10 inches (25 centimeters) high and nearly as wide. Shelf fungi, which grow from the side of trees and logs, produce "shelves" nearly 20 inches (50 centimeters) wide. The largest puffball on record had a diameter of nearly 5 feet (1.5 meters)! Such giants produce trillions of spores—each able to germinate into a new individual.

EVOLUTION AND CLASSIFICATION

No one can say for sure how or from what organism the first fungi came. Some mycologists have proposed that fungi evolved from a group of algae that lost their chlorophyll. Others have proposed that fungi descended from protozoans that lost their ability to move. Most present-day mycologists agree that fungi evolved from some unique type of flagellated (swimming) one-celled organism, be it algal or protozoan. Whatever the ancestral organism, scientists have yet to discover any living counterpart.

In general, mycologists place modern-day fungi into three groups, each more evolved, or "advanced," than the next. The most primitive are the zygomycetes (phylum Zygomycota), which produce their sex cells internally. The most advanced are the basidiomycetes (phylum Basidiomycota), many of which produce fruiting bodies such as mushrooms and puffballs. Intermediate between the two are the ascomycetes (phylum Ascomycota), which share traits of both the zygomycetes and the basidiomycetes.

Zygomycota—the Primitive Fungi

This phylum of fungi is named for its distinctive zygosporangia (sexual structures). Zygosporangia are a type of thick-walled spore that can survive in a resting state (dormancy) for many years. They germinate in conditions of ample moisture, warmth, and organic matter.

Most zygomycetes are decomposers found in soil. Among the best-known species are the so-called "shotgun fungi" *(Pilobolus),* which grow on animal dung. Their sporangia, or spore capsules, grow on short, threadlike stalks. When ripe, they blast their tiny spores distances of up to 6 feet (1.8 meters).

Another familiar zygomycete is the bread-mold fungus, *Rhizopus stolonifer*. It often finds its way into kitchens, appearing as black fuzz on overripe fruit and vegetables as well as on bread; it is also used to ferment wine. Still other zygomycetes parasitize plants and small soil animals such as beetles and nematodes.

This group also includes some of the most ecologically important fungi—the mycorrhizae, or root fungi. These fungi live in association with the roots of many plants. The fungi draw nutrition from the roots and, in return, provide the plants with usable forms of soil minerals such as nitrogen. The majority of domestic crops, as well as many trees (such as pines), depend on mycorrhizae for healthy growth.

Some small fungi, such as yeast (below), are single-celled organisms. These simple fungi are so tiny, in fact, that a strong microscope is required to view them.

Ascomycota—the Sac Fungi

Often called "sac fungi," the species in this group are aptly named for their pouchlike reproductive structures, called *ascocarps* (derived from the Greek *askos*, meaning "sac"), which bear spore sacs called *asci*. Ascomycota is also the largest of the three phyla of fungi. Each of its several subgroups is distinguished by its unique type of ascus.

The simplest of these groups includes the one-celled yeasts, several of which may fuse to produce a single ascus. The members of the most advanced group—the cup fungi—bear millions of asci on their mushroomlike fruiting

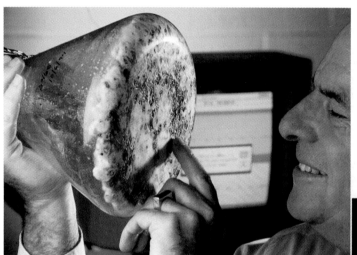

of the same species can reproduce by simply fusing their two cells together. The fused cell then divides to produce several (four or eight) spores within a simple ascus. These durable spores can remain dormant for many years before germinating. They constitute the contents of the packets of dry yeast that can be purchased in a grocery store.

When placed in a suitable growth medium—such as warm sugar water—the yeast spores germinate into living cells. These will then reproduce asexually, by budding. That is, a portion of each parent cell pinches off to produce a daughter cell that contains an exact copy of the parent's genes. Budding continues in this fashion to produce a large mass, or colony, of yeast cells. The colony is visible as a soft, creamy-white foam on the surface of the growth medium.

In nature, yeasts commonly occur wherever simple sugars are available—on the surface of fruits, on tree sap, and in flower nectar. Most are harmless, but not all. The yeast *Candida albicans*, for example, can cause thrush, a disease of the mouth

By studying fungi cultures (right), scientists have isolated fungal fragments called sclerotia (above, being pointed to) that contain compounds toxic to insects.

bodies. Familiar examples include the beautiful scarlet cup (*Sarcoscypha coccinea*) and the edible morels (*Morchella*) and truffles (*Tuber*) found throughout Europe. In between the yeasts and the cup fungi are a variety of sac fungi commonly called "mildews" and "plant blights."

Yeasts. The best known of the many ascomycetes yeasts is probably the baker's yeast (*Saccharomyces cerevisiae*). It is used worldwide, not only to leaven bread dough, but also to ferment grain and grapes to make beer, wine, and other alcoholic liquors.

The life cycle of a yeast is as simple as its tiny body—a single cell. Two yeast organisms

Classification of Fungi

Fungi are unicellular and multicellular organisms with cells that possess a distinct nucleus (eukaryotic) and cell walls made of chitin. They have stringlike body tissues (hyphae) that absorb nutrition from dead or living organic matter; all lack photosynthetic pigments. Fungi reproduce sexually, asexually, or both—via spores, budding, or fragmentation. This kingdom includes mushrooms, molds, mildews, yeasts, and lichens (a symbiotic association of green algae or cyanobacteria living in the tissues of certain fungi). They are found worldwide, primarily in damp places. The approximately 150,000 known species of fungi are classified into three phyla, as follows:

KINGDOM Fungi:

PHYLUM Zygomycota: *Multicellular fungi in which the hyphae (body filaments) are not divided, but open into one another. Characterized by the sexual production of thick-walled, long-lasting spores called zygosporangia, which germinate under favorable conditions. Most zygomycetes decompose dead plants or animals. Some parasitize plants, soil arthropods, and houseflies, occasionally infecting mammals, including humans. Many grow in symbiotic association with plant roots (mycorrhizae). Reproduce both sexually and asexually. Found worldwide, primarily in soil. About 770 known species. Examples: bread-mold fungus, glomus, and shotgun fungus.*

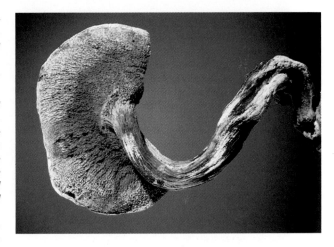

PHYLUM Ascomycota: *Unicellular and multicellular fungi in which the hyphae are divided by cross walls (septa) with one or more pores. Characterized by the sexual production of a saclike, spore-bearing structure called the ascus, which bursts when mature to release (typically) four to eight ascospores. Asexual reproduction produces dustlike spores called conidia. Many ascomycetes parasitize plants. This phylum also includes yeasts, morels, truffles, and the lichens, which represent a symbiotic relationship that occurs mainly between certain species of ascomycetes and green algae or cyanobacteria. Found worldwide, in both dry and aquatic environments. About 30,000 known species. Examples:* Cryphonectria parasitica *(causes chestnut blight), black morel, and baker's yeast.*

PHYLUM Basidiomycota: *Soil fungi in which the hyphae are divided by complete cross walls. Characterized by the sexual production of club-shaped, spore-producing cells (basidia), typically borne on aboveground fruiting bodies (basidocarps). Also includes species that cause plant diseases, such as smuts and rusts. Found worldwide, primarily in moist, shaded soil rich in organic matter. About 16,000 known species. Examples: field mushroom, stinkhorn, and* Ustilago maydis.

and throat in humans and other animals. Many other yeasts can cause respiratory infections.

Mildews. The fungi we commonly call "mildews" are among the most common and widespread of the kingdom. They grow on many organic substances, including food and cloth. Although some blue and green molds reproduce sexually, the majority lack any sexual stage, reproducing only by means of asexual spores, or conidia. The conidia grow in large numbers on upright, branched chains of mycelium. They give the mildews their characteristic colors—greenish, blue-green or blue, and sometimes yellow, tan, or black.

Ascomycetes commonly known as powdery mildews cause a variety of plant diseases

Like smoke from a chimney, spores spew forth from a puffball (above). The spores drift on air currents to new homes where, if conditions are suitable, they will grow.

Some sphere fungi parasitize plants, while others live on dead organic matter. Among the parasitic varieties is the chestnut-blight organism. Introduced into New York from Asia about 1900, it has almost completely destroyed the American chestnut tree. Other species of the sphere fungi cause Dutch elm disease, oak wilt, apple scab, dogwood anthracnose, and cereal ergot.

The genus known as *Neurospora* has been tremendously useful to science. The simple structure of its genetic material has enabled scientists to study it in great detail. Studies of *Neurospora* in the mid-20th century laid the foundation of modern genetics and genetic engineering.

Cup fungi. This large group of sac fungi are named for their cup-shaped fruiting bodies, which vary in size from that of a pinhead to several inches across. The largest forms tend to be fleshy cups or saucer-shaped bodies, often brightly colored. The majority of cup fungi live on dead wood, decaying leaves, and soil. Some cause destructive diseases. The brown-rot fungi, for example, attack peaches and other stone fruits, as well as apples and pears.

Some of the larger species are edible. Among the most popular are the mushroomlike morels, recognized by their conical, pitted caps. Closely related to the morels are the truffles. The truffle's fruiting body is unusual in that it grows underground. The truffle's thallus (main body) is mycorrhizal (symbiotically associated with plant roots), mainly on oaks and hazelnuts. Truffle hunters "sniff out" these highly prized delicacies using specially trained dogs and pigs.

Imperfect fungi. Also counted among the sac fungi is a miscellaneous collection of species, all of which appear to lack a sexual stage. So far as scientists can tell, they reproduce only by conidia. This so-called "defect" has earned them the name "imperfect fungi." Nonetheless, they make up a very large and successful group, found virtually everywhere.

Some cause mildewing of fabrics; others, molds of foods. The parasitic species are very destructive to crops and ornamental plants.

on grapes and fruit-bearing plants. Typically, these infections appear as a white powder over the infected plant, especially its leaves. This powder contains an enormous number of conidia. The spores develop through the summer, leading to an autumnal sexual stage that produces dark spots over the infected leaves. These dots are small ascospores (sexual spores). They survive the winter in a dormant state, then infect the plant anew in spring.

Plant blights. Sphere fungi, the largest group of ascomycetes, are characterized by fruiting bodies in the shape of small spheres or flasks. Each of these fruiting bodies has a small pore through which its spores escape. Many species also produce conidia.

One of the most successful partnerships in nature is the one that exists between a fungus and algae. Together, these two very different organisms create a unique, self-supporting life-form known as a lichen—able to thrive in places where neither organism could survive on its own.

Found growing on rocks, trees, fence posts, and other bare surfaces, most lichens superficially resemble green plants. But they are nothing of the kind. Seen under a microscope, the body of the lichen is a hollow network of fungus filaments filled with millions of photosynthetic algae. The algae supply both themselves and the fungus with energy-rich food. The fungus, in turn, provides the algae with a protective home, highly resistant to harsh weather. The fungus also supplies both itself and the algae with minerals, which it extracts from the rock or other surface on which it grows. Finally, the fungus can absorb and hold water in its filaments, keeping both itself and the algae moist in times of drought.

In a typical lichen, the fungus makes up some 90 percent of the organism; algae comprise the rest.

Thanks to this cooperative, or symbiotic, relationship, lichens can live in some of the harshest habitats on Earth. They thrive on windswept alpine peaks as well as the sunbaked rocks of the desert. They can even be found growing in the frozen and fractured rock of the seemingly lifeless Antarctic.

There are some 15,000 different kinds of lichens. Most often, the fungus partner is a member of the ascomycetes group, or sac fungi. They associate with some 40 genera of green algae and cyanobacteria. A few lichens contain more than one kind of photosynthetic algae.

Many lichens form beautiful "leafy" rosettes on rocks and other surfaces. Others form feathery drapes that hang from the branches of trees. Lichens adapted to the desert tend to be crusty in texture, growing just below the surface of the soil. Still other types of lichens are tiny—no larger than a pinhead.

In color, lichens range from white to black, through shades of yellow, orange, red, and green; their pigments have long been used as fabric dyes. They are also a traditional source of folk medicines. The lichen known as Iceland moss, *Cetraria islandica*, for example, has long been used to treat diabetes, kidney infections, and even the common cold.

Importantly, lichens are often the first plant to grow on bare rock. Their activities help break down the rock into small pockets of soil—paving the way for the first small plants. Lichens also provide food for animals in regions where little else grows. They play a significant role in the food chain since they are widely eaten by snails, slugs, insects, and other invertebrates. In arctic regions, they are an especially important fodder for reindeer and other caribou. One lichen, *Lecanora esculenta*, is reputed to be the "manna" that fell from heaven to feed the ancient Israelites on their flight from Egypt.

Many fungi that cause disease in humans also belong to this group. They are responsible for such ailments as ringworm and athlete's foot.

Other members of this group have proven themselves enormously useful. Among the most famous is *Penicillium notatum*, from which the antibiotic penicillin is derived. Another species of *Penicillium—P. roqueforti*—produces the distinctive marbled colors and sharp flavors characteristic of cheeses such as Roquefort and

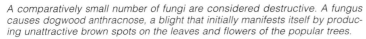

A comparatively small number of fungi are considered destructive. A fungus causes dogwood anthracnose, a blight that initially manifests itself by producing unattractive brown spots on the leaves and flowers of the popular trees.

Camembert. In the Far East, a variety of species in the genus *Aspergillus* are used extensively in the commercial fermentation of soybean products such as soy sauce, tofu, and miso.

Basidiomycota—the Club Fungi

This, the third phylum of Kingdom Fungi, contains the most highly developed species. Often called club fungi, they derive their name from their tiny, club-shaped spore-producing cells—the *basidia*. Typically, each basidium produces four spores, called *basidiospores*. Mycologists divide the basidiomycetes, or "club fungi," into three classes.

Class Hymenomycetes. This class contains the true mushrooms, jelly fungi, coral fungi, and shelf fungi. We know these species by their distinctive fruiting bodies, which bear millions—sometimes trillions—of basidia.

Mushrooms are easily recognized by their familiar fruiting body. It consists of a cap, or *pileus*, that sits atop a stalk, or *stipe*. Typically,

the lower surface of the cap consists of a frill of tissues, called *gills*. The mushroom's vegetative body, or thallus, grows underground, where it absorbs nutrients from decaying organic matter. In an uninterrupted area such as a lawn or open meadow, the thallus often spreads underground for great distances to form a large circle. It may then die at the center (after depleting the nutrients there), and produce a ring of mushrooms around its outer edges. When left undisturbed, these circles will grow larger each year. In Europe, they are affectionately known as *fairy rings*—a name derived from the superstition that the circles represent the paths of dancing fairies.

Extremely varied in size and color, mushrooms are among the brightest and most attractive of fungi. Many are edible—the best known being the common field mushroom, *Agaricus campestris*. But others are highly poisonous. Even a bite of the "destroying angel," *Amanita virosa*, can prove deadly.

Coral fungi produce branching fruiting bodies that bear a striking resemblance to pieces of coral. They are fleshy in texture and vary greatly in color. Coral fungi grow abundantly among fallen leaves in temperate, deciduous forests. Most are edible.

Bracket, or shelf, fungi commonly grow on the sides of dead trees and fallen logs. Their fruiting bodies grow in shelflike fashion, often with one shelf rising above the other. In texture, they are often leathery.

Class Gasteromycetes. This class includes the familiar puffballs and stinkhorns, as well as the unusual-looking earthstars and bird's-nest fungi. Puffballs typically grow on the forest floor, absorbing nutrients from decaying organic matter such as rotting wood. The fruiting body of a typical puffball, such as *Lycoperdon*, ranges in shape from a perfect sphere to that of a pear. Whitish at first, puffballs turn brown when mature. At this point, the slightest pressure from wind, rain, or animal will cause the puffball to expel its spores through a small opening. A single large puffball can contain millions to trillions of dustlike spores.

Stinkhorns, the close cousins to the puffballs, are well named for their odor—akin to that of rotting flesh! Most stinkhorns have a stalk, usually with a cup at the base, and a cap covered with a dark, slimy mass of spores. From this spore mass wafts the characteristic scent—a perfume highly attractive to flies, which then carry the sticky spores away on their feet.

Fungi include such edible mushrooms as the morel (top). Some fungi are identified by their shape or color (above), others by the kinds of spores produced.

Bird's-nest fungi produce small cups, each of which contains several round spore-bearing structures. The entire fruiting body resembles a miniature bird's nest filled with tiny eggs. These fungi grow on humus, dead wood, and the dung of plant-eating animals such as deer.

Class Hemibasidiomycetes. This class includes a variety of destructive plant molds commonly known as rusts and smuts. Unlike other club fungi, or basidiomycetes, rusts and smuts do not form fruiting bodies. Instead, they produce masses of tiny spores that cover the leaves of the plants that they infect. Basidiomycetes cause leaf spots and galls (swellings) on a variety of important crops and ornamental plants.

The rusts are named for their powdery, brownish-red (rusty-looking) spores. One of the most destructive of the rusts is the cereal rust, *Puccinia graminis*. This fungus must alternate between two host plants to complete its life cycle. It produces certain spore forms on wheat and different forms on barberry. Many rusts have such a *heteroecious*, or "two-host," life cycle. They cause great damage to cereals, vegetables, fruit trees, and others.

The spores of smuts cover infected plants with a blackish powder. Their life cycle, simpler than that of the rusts, involves a single host plant. Smut spores are dry and easily blown about from one plant to another, or from one field to the next. Among the most destructive smut fungi is corn smut, which appears as white blisters on the stems or fruit of grasses such as corn. When mature, these blisters burst to release millions of black spores. Other important smuts attack such commercially important plants as wheat, oats, barley, and rye.

THE ALGAE

by Jessica Snyder Sachs

Ever slip on a slimy rock while crossing a stream? Or have seaweed wrap around your legs in the surf? If so, you're familiar with algae. Chances are, you've also eaten plenty of it—often without even realizing it.

The algae are a large and varied group of simple plantlike organisms. Among the more familiar examples are the many kinds of microscopic algae that form patches of "scum" over ponds and other bodies of water. Seaweeds are also algae—and there are thousands of kinds, including the ropelike kelps and the delicate, frilly "sea lettuces." Algae also include the many tiny organisms that gather just below the sea surface as "phytoplankton." Together, this varied group of organisms forms the vast food base on which the world's aquatic life depends.

ALGAE VERSUS PLANTS

For many centuries, scientists lumped algae into the Plant Kingdom. Even today, most people think of them as "water plants." But in recent years, powerful microscopes and chemical tests confirm what scientists had suspected: despite many similarities, algae are not true plants. But why not?

First, algae are built differently than are plants. Algae lack specialized plant tissues such as roots, leaves, and stems. Nor are their cell walls always made of cellulose, as are those of all plants. Algae also possess a far greater variety of photosynthetic pigments than do plants. Many of these are designed to catch the wavelengths of light that penetrate the water in which algae live.

Second, algae reproduce quite differently than do plants. Most algae are equipped with animal-like sex cells that actively swim through the water with whiplike tails. Algae also lack the special egg- and sperm-producing structures found in all true plants.

For these and other reasons, scientists today place algae in the Kingdom Protista, along with other simple organisms such as slime molds, diatoms, and protozoa. Like algae, many

Some algae, like kelp (above), grow together in huge undersea forests. Others, like the single-celled Volvox, *link together by the thousands to form colonies (inset).*

of these organisms have both animal-like and plantlike traits. This is not to say that algae and plants are not closely related. In fact, the first true plants most likely evolved from some type or types of green algae—much as the first land animals evolved from some type of fish. True plants then evolved the many special adaptations (roots, stems, leaves, and the like) needed to conquer solid land.

SIZE AND DISTRIBUTION

In size, algae range from the tiny, one-celled swimmer Micromonas (0.0004 inch—0.010 millimeter in diameter) to giant ropes of sea kelp more than 200 feet (60 meters) long. Like Micromonas, many algae consist of just one cell. Others have two or three cells, and the largest have millions. The larger algae have simple tissues designed for specialized functions such as photosynthesis or anchorage. Unlike plant roots, algae anchors do not absorb water or nutrients from the soil.

A great many algae grow suspended, or afloat, in the water. These are called *planktonic algae*. Those anchored to the seabed are called *benthic algae*. *Neustonic algae* grow on top of the water surface, often forming a green or red scum. Some algae can survive, even thrive, in hot springs and the superheated water around deep-sea vents. These are called *thermophilic*, or "heat-loving," algae. Conversely, *cryophilic* ("cold-loving") algae can grow on snow and ice. Still other algae live on or in damp soil (*epidaphic* and *endedaphic*). *Epizoic* algae grow on animals such as turtles, polar bears, and tree sloths (sometimes producing a green tinge). *Epiphytic* algae grow on plants, fungi, and even other algae. *Epilithic* and *endolithic* algae live on and inside rocks, respectively.

In general, algae found on land are limited by their need for constant wetness and warmth. In contrast, algae that live immersed in water have boundless moisture and even temperatures. Their growth can be limited by lack of sunlight, which is filtered, or absorbed, by water, and by a scarcity of nutrients. This is why certain types of pollution—which supply nutrients—cause sudden overgrowths, or algal "blooms," which we see as green "scum" or "red tides."

THE ALGAL CELL

Algae cells come in a stunning variety of forms. The greatest diversity is seen among the one-celled algae. Diatoms, in particular, are known as the "jewels of the sea," for their intricate cell walls made of silica plates. Golden algae and dinoflagellates display their own distinctive arrays of star-shaped, fan-shaped, and boxlike skeletons. *Euglena* are well known for their pulsing green, pitcher-

Many millions of years ago, green algae adapted to habitats on land, becoming the ancestors of all land plants. Today green algae can be found clinging to rocks and trees, spreading across the surface of a pond (left), growing in colonies (above), and occasionally even covering the shells of turtles.

bound nucleus and a variety of membrane-bound organelles such as mitochondria, chloroplasts, and vacuoles.

ALGAE LIFE CYCLES

Unlike the other kingdoms of life (plants, animals, fungi, and monerans), it cannot be said of algae that they reproduce in similar ways. Their methods of reproduction range from some of the simplest known to some of the most complex. The simplest methods include those used by some one-celled algae, many of which reproduce by simply splitting in two after duplicating their chromosomes (genetic material). In contrast, the red algae produce several different kinds of spores and sex cells, making their life cycle one of the most complex. Like plants, many of the larger algae can also produce new individuals from fragments of their bodies.

Perhaps the most familiar brown algae is kelp (above), which can be found anchored to rocks by a structure called a holdfast (right). Brown algae are harvested for use as food and for their natural chemicals, which are used in paints, cosmetics, and drugs.

As mentioned, one of the important differences between algae and plants is the algae's motile (swimming) sex cells, called *gametes*. Most of the alga's gametes swim through the water with whiplike flagella. After fertilization, many algae can produce tough spores around the fertilized egg, or *zygote*. These "zygospores" contain a large store of food, and can survive for months, maybe years, until the right conditions (light, warmth, and nutrients) trigger their growth.

Similarly, some red and green algae produce large, asexual spores that can float great distances on ocean currents before germinating. The asexual spores of other algae can actively swim. They are called zoospores ("zoo" meaning animal-like). The life span of most microscopic algae is a few days, weeks, or months. These tend to "bloom" in great numbers during certain periods of the year. Then they become dormant, often in spores, for the rest of the year. In contrast, many seaweeds grow for years. After a season of active growth, they may "die back" to mere stems, then sprout anew with the next growing season.

shaped bodies, which lack any cell wall. Many one-celled algae form large colonies, which resemble spectacular spinning kaleidoscopes when viewed through a microscope.

As mentioned, many kinds of algae produce actively swimming cells during at least part of their life cycle. A few one-celled algae such as *Euglena* and the green alga *Chlamydomonas* remain active throughout life. Many also possess an eyespot that operates like a primitive eye.

Other algae have plantlike or funguslike cells with rigid walls made of cellulose or chitin. Still other algae have cell walls made of polysaccharide, a type of sugar. Internally, algal cells are much like those of any plant, animal, or fungi. Each cell contains a distinct, membrane-

THE ALGAE GROUPS

Scientists classify the larger algae into groups, called phyla, according to their colors: green, brown, red, and golden. These colors reflect the pigments most abundant in each specific group.

Also included with the algae are the one-celled photosynthetic organisms known as euglenoids, dinoflagellates, and diatoms. These are discussed below, along with the fungus-like organisms known as water molds and slime molds, which scientists place alongside the algae in the Kingdom Protista.

Red algae are always attached to rocks or other objects. Unlike other algae, they can photosynthesize in the dim light far below the water's surface. Many species, including Irish moss (above), are important food sources.

Green Algae

The common pond scum *Spirogyra*, sea lettuce (*Ulva*), and *Volvox* are just some of the 7,000 species of green algae that make up the phylum Chlorophyta.

The close resemblance of green algae and true plants is no coincidence. Scientists have little doubt that the first plants evolved from green algae. As evidence, green algae and plants use identical photosynthetic pigments—chlorophylls a and b, which produce their characteristic green color, as well as red, orange, and yellow carotenoids. Like plants, all green algae store their food as starch, and many have plant-like cell walls made of cellulose.

Most green algae grow in freshwater—typically as slime on submerged rocks and scum on the water's surface. These scums and slimes are actually colonies of thousands to millions of microscopic algae such as *Spirogyra*. *Spirogyra* is an example of a filamentous green algae. Each organism consists of a single, very long cell, or filament. Each colony consists of a mass of these intertwined unicellular organisms.

Other green algae, such as sea lettuce, or *Ulva*, grow in salt water. This green seaweed forms delicate, leaflike blades just two cells thick. It is most often seen growing in shallow water along the seashore, where it anchors itself to pilings and rocks.

Still others have made their way onto land, where they survive in wet places, from damp soil and leaves to the melting surface of snow. Several species of green algae have forged symbiotic (mutually beneficial) relationships with fungi to form lichens. A few even grow on the damp parts of animals, such as the fur of tree sloths, or cover the shells of turtles. The sloths and turtles benefit from the green camouflage!

A great many green algae are seldom seen. They are one-celled organisms that lead solitary lives. Some swim through the water like microscopic tadpoles. Others form spinning colonies made of tightly connected individuals.

The classic example of a one-celled green algae is *Chlamydomonas*, found in stagnant ponds and lakes the world over. Although small, it can move rapidly, darting through the water by beating its two whiplike flagella, or "tails." A single chloroplast fills most of *Chlamydomonas'* body. Near the chloroplast is a red eyespot, or stigma. *Chlamydomonas* reproduces both sexually and asexually. During asexual reproduction, its nucleus divides twice, producing four identical daughter cells. Sexual reproduction involves the fusion of two individuals belonging to different mating strains.

Volvox is an example of colonial green algae. Each colony is a hollow ball made up of 500 to 50,000 one-celled individuals. The cells share nutrients through openings in their cell walls. Together, the cells spin their colony through the water by each beating its flagella.

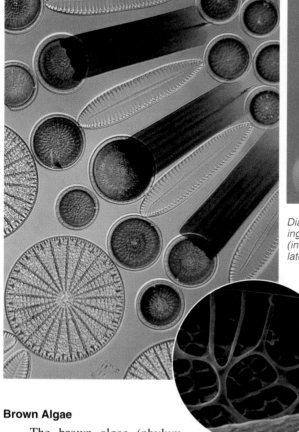

Diatoms (left) are the most numerous organisms making up marine plankton. Their hard, glassy cell walls (inset) give them a jewel-like appearance. Dinoflagellates (above) swim using tail-like flagella.

Brown Algae

The brown algae (phylum Phaeophyta) are multicellular organisms, many of them growing to more than 300 feet (90 meters) in length. Their characteristic color comes from fucoxanthin, a carotenoid pigment. This pigment absorbs light in the green range of the spectrum—namely the wavelengths that are most abundant below the water's surface. (In contrast, chlorophyll reflects green light, giving plants and green algae their color.) Brown algae store their food as an unusual sugar called laminarin. Their cell walls are a mixture of cellulose and complex sugars.

The best-known brown algae are the mineral-rich kelps so common in northern oceans. Some form enormous floating forests many miles wide and more than 200 feet (60 meters) deep. Many kelp have distinct parts such as holdfast (a rootlike anchor), stipe (a ropelike stem), and blade (a leaflike sheet). The blades and stipes can have air-filled bladders that act as floats. Dense forests of kelp provide lush habitats for many marine animals.

Red Algae

Red algae are the most common seaweed in tropical seas, and also occur in colder waters. Their distinctive colors come from their unique combination of pigments: chlorophyll a, carotenoids, and phycobilins. These pigments are similar to those found in primitive cyanobacteria (blue-green algae), which may be a distant relative.

Red algae always grow attached to rocks and other objects. Unlike other seaweeds, they cannot survive floating freely in the water. This is because they need the tug of tides and currents to move gases in and out of their tissues. Red algae such as dulse (*Rhodymenia palmata*) and nori (*Porphyra* species) are important foods. Red seaweeds are also processed into extracts used as gelatin substitutes in puddings, ice cream, and other food products.

Golden Algae

Golden algae (phylum Chrysophyta) make up the bulk of the world's phytoplankton—the food base for all ocean life. Like brown algae, the tiny golden algae get their color from the pigment fucoxanthin, which they use to catch sunlight filtering through the ocean surface. However, golden algae are much simpler than their darker cousins. Virtually all are simple one-celled organisms. They are unique for the beautiful and intricate designs of the silica plates in their cell walls (as seen with a microscope). This is especially true of the diatoms, a large class of golden algae often called the "jewels of the sea."

Euglenophyta

This small phylum of alga is named for the genus *Euglena*, its most common and familiar member. Many scientists consider *Euglena* the most versatile of all one-celled organisms. It can both produce its own food through photosynthesis and consume food like an animal. *Euglena* scoots through the water using a single flagellum. It also has a distinctive eyespot, or stigma, which it uses to find light.

Fire Algae

The fire algae, or dinoflagellates, are often called the "spinning flagellates." Each of these microscopic one-celled organisms has two flagella that beat inside grooves in its cell walls. One of these flagella wraps around the cell like a belt, and the other lies perpendicular to it. When the dinoflagellate beats its flagella, therefore, its entire "body" spins like a top as it zips through the water. Like diatoms, many dinoflagellates have cell walls laced with intricate plates of armor. But in the case of dinoflagellates, this armor, or skeleton, is made of hard cellulose rather than silica.

THE FUNGUSLIKE PROTISTS

Alongside the algae in the Kingdom Protista are classified four groups of funguslike organisms. They are the chytrids (phylum Chytridiomycota), water molds (phylum Oomycota), cellular slime molds (phylum Rhizopoda), and plasmodial slime molds (phylum Myxomycota). These plantlike organisms bear a considerable resemblance to fungi in that they grow by producing filaments (long chains of open-ended cells), and feed by absorbing nutrients from their unique environments.

Yet all but the chytrids greatly differ from fungi on the biochemical level. That is, they are made of fundamentally different materials. It is therefore unlikely that any but the chytrids are actually related to fungi.

Like fungi, chytrids have cell walls made of chitin and use similar chemicals (RNA) to direct cell activities. Many chytrids are simple one-celled organisms that swim through the water or the body fluids of their hosts. Some parasitize mosquitoes.

Water molds, as their name suggests, live primarily in water and wet soils. On a damp forest floor, the mold's funguslike mycelium can be seen wrapping around bits of rotting log, tall reeds and dying grasses, and other decaying matter. A few water molds are parasites, causing diseases in algae, plants, crustaceans, and fish.

Slime molds are primitive funguslike protists whose spores germinate into single-celled organisms. Some, like the red raspberry slime mold (Tubitera terryginosa) *shown below, have vividly colored fruiting bodies called sporophores.*

The Kingdom Protista, home of algae, slime molds, and protozoa, has long been a grab bag for organisms that do not quite fit anywhere else. Many have traits of both plants and animals. Most protists are one-celled organisms, although several groups have multicellular members. Even those that have many cells lack highly specialized tissues such as leaves, roots, and stems. The most animal-like of these organisms are discussed in the ANIMAL LIFE section of this volume. Below is the classification of those protists traditionally seen as more plantlike or funguslike in nature.

KINGDOM Protista: *Eukaryotic organisms (cells with nuclei) ranging in size from one cell to millions of cells. Reproduce sexually with gametes, asexually with spores, or both. Photosynthetic protists contain a wider variety of pigments than are found in the Plant Kingdom. Lack differentiated tissues such as true roots, stems, or leaves. Can absorb minerals and other nutrients directly into cells. Found worldwide, primarily in water.*

PHYLUM Oomycota: *Water molds. Heterotrophic (outside-feeding) organisms that absorb and store nutrition in a funguslike manner, but have plantlike cell walls composed of cellulose. Have motile (swimming) spores with flagella. Cause a variety of plant diseases such as downy mildew. Found worldwide in aquatic or moist environments. About 580 species.*

PHYLUM Chytridiomycota: *Chytrids. Funguslike, aquatic organisms with cell walls made of chitin. Have motile spores and gametes (sex cells) with flagella. Found worldwide in marine water and freshwater. About 575 species.*

PHYLUM Rhizopoda: *Cellular slime molds. Funguslike organisms with creeping, amoeba-like cells. Engulf and digest bacteria. Have plantlike cell walls made of cellulose. Found worldwide in moist, rich soil. About 70 species.*

PHYLUM Myxomycota: *Plasmodial slime molds. Funguslike organisms that form masses of protoplasm (cell contents unbound by cell walls) that creep in an amoeba-like manner. Engulf and digest bacteria, yeast cells, fungal spores, and bits of decaying plant and animal matter. Found worldwide in moist places. About 500 species.*

PHYLUM Chrysophyta: *Golden algae. Mainly autotrophic (self-feeding), one-celled organisms, many with silica plates in cell walls. Primary photosynthetic pigments are chlorophylls a and c, and the carotenoid fucoxanthin. Store food as chrysolaminarin. Found worldwide as plankton in marine water and freshwater. More than 6,500 species.*

Unlike true molds (a kind of fungus), water molds have plantlike cell walls made of cellulose. They need water to reproduce, since their gametes and asexual spores swim through the water using flagella.

Like the water molds, cellular slime molds have cellulose in their cell walls. But the similarities end there. These unusual organisms have amoeba-like cells that feed on bacteria by surrounding and engulfing them. When starved, cellular slime molds form a sluglike mass that moves to a new place before producing spores. The mold mass accomplishes its change of location by contracting molecules of myosin protein—the same protein that causes muscle contraction in animals. By undertaking this trip before producing spores, the cellular slime molds avoid starting a new generation in a place already depleted of food.

Plasmodial slime molds are a unique form of life that exists as a thin, creeping mass of protoplasm (cellular contents). This mass of protoplasm—undivided by cell walls—engulfs and digests bacteria, yeast, fungal spores, and small bits of dead and decaying matter. A plasmodial slime mold can grow to weigh as much as 10 ounces (280 grams). Because its "body" forms a thin film, an individual this size may cover several square yards. They are sometimes seen as "moldy"-looking films on dead tree trunks and other decaying matter.

IMPORTANCE OF ALGAE

Algae form the vast base of the aquatic food web—a role very similar to that played by plants on land. This is especially true of the tiny algae that make up phytoplankton. But the im-

PHYLUM Pyrrhophyta: *Fire algae, or dinoflagellates. Mainly autotrophic, one-celled organisms with cell walls made of cellulose. Primary photosynthetic pigments are chlorophylls a and c, and the carotenoid peridinin. Store food as starch. Swim using two beating flagella of different lengths. Found worldwide as plankton in marine water and freshwater. More than 2,000 species.*

PHYLUM Euglenophyta: Euglena *and kin. One-celled, mainly photosynthetic organisms recognized by elongated cell and eyespot. No cell wall. Primary photosynthetic pigments are chlorophylls a and b, and various carotenoids. Store food as paramylon. Swim with flagella and beating hairs. Found mainly in freshwater. About 1,000 species.*

PHYLUM Rhodophyta: *Red algae. Plantlike, many-celled organisms with cell walls made of galactans, cellulose, and calcium carbonate. Primary photosynthetic pigments are chlorophyll a, carotenoids, and phycobilins. Store food as floridean starch. Lack flagella (nonmotile). Found worldwide, mainly in marine water, often attached to plants near shore. More than 4,000 species. Example: Irish moss.*

PHYLUM Phaeophyta: *Brown algae. Plantlike, many-celled organisms with cell walls made of cellulose with polysaccharides. Primary photosynthetic pigments are chlorophylls a and c, and the carotenoid fucoxanthin. Store food as laminarin and mannitol. Sex cells swim using flagella. Often very large. Found mainly in cold ocean water. About 1,500 species. Example: bull kelp.*

PHYLUM Chlorophyta: *Green algae. One-celled and many-celled plantlike organisms with polysaccharide and cellulose cell walls. Primary photosynthetic pigments are chlorophylls a and b, and carotenoids. Store food as starch. Some have flagellated (swimming) sex cells. Found in freshwater and marine water. More than 7,000 species. Examples: sea lettuce and* Spirogyra.

Agar—a preparation containing up to seven types of red algae—is used by researchers as a substrate for laboratory cultures of microorganisms.

portance of algae reaches beyond the ocean realm. As photosynthetic organisms, algae produce 30 to 50 percent of the oxygen in our atmosphere. (Bear in mind that two-thirds of Earth is covered by water, and plants are virtually absent from this area.)

Algae have also produced some of the world's largest deposits of fossil fuels. The vast North Sea oil deposits are derived from the bodies of algae that sank to the ocean floor millions of years ago. The Colorado oil shales were produced by algae that thrived when shallow seas and swamps covered North America.

Algae also feed much of the world. In fact, people eat some 500 different kinds of algae, especially seaweeds. They are harvested from northern oceans by large, specially designed ships; throughout much of Asia, seaweed is actually cultivated in shallow waters.

Much of the world's harvested algae is processed into food extracts. These products are most commonly used to improve the flavor and texture of packaged foods. Algal extracts such as agar and carrageenan are ingredients in many "instant" puddings, pie fillings, and frostings. Algin, another algal extract, is often found in ice cream, candy bars, and salad dressings. These products are also used in hair and skin products to emulsify, or blend, ingredients.

A few algae can be toxic. Among the most serious are dinoflagellate algae of the genus *Gonyaulax*, which produce saxitoxin and other substances that can cause paralysis and death. People seldom eat these algae directly, but consume them in shellfish that have eaten them. Ciguatera, another example of algae poisoning, is caused by eating fish that have consumed toxic algal phytoplankton.

BOTANICAL CLASSIFICATION

At least 10 million different kinds of living things share our planet. Sorting them into categories is a challenging task we call *taxonomy*, the science of classifying organisms. And many consider the 18th-century botanist Carolus Linnaeus to be its "father."

Linnaeus, like modern taxonomists, tried to sort all organisms into a series of groups—broad to specific—based on common characteristics. His taxonomic system, still in use today, also assigns every plant and animal a two-part genus-species name, recognized by scientists the world over. By tradition, this name is in Latin, the universal language of science.

For example, the plant known in English as "pansy" is named and classified as follows:

- **Species:** *Viola tricolor*
- **Genus:** *Viola* (with 500 species)
- **Family:** Violaceae (with 22 genera)
- **Order:** Violales (with 19 families)
- **Class:** Dicotyledoneae (with 70 orders)
- **Phylum:** Anthophyta (with 2 classes)
- **Kingdom:** Plantae (with 12 phyla)

This classification system, devised by Linnaeus in 1753, has persisted essentially unchanged to modern times. The greatest changes have occurred in the number of kingdoms—the largest groupings of organisms. Early scientists such as Linnaeus recognized only two living kingdoms: Plantae and Animalia.

This simple "either/or" kingdom of life worked fine so long as the only known plants were those that grew fixed in one place and made their own food, and all known animals moved about and consumed food. But it began to fall apart in the late 19th century as scientists discovered microscopic "plant-animals" that moved about like animals, but produced their own food like plants. It further disintegrated in the late 20th century, as scientists discovered fundamental differences between plantlike organisms such as seaweed and green algae, and true plants such as moss, ferns, and seed plants.

Today most scientists recognize five distinct kingdoms of life. In addition to Plantae and Animalia, they are Monera (bacteria), Fungi (fungi and lichens), and Protista (true algae, slime molds, and protozoa). Following centuries of tradition, modern botanists still include monerans, fungi, and the plantlike protists in their area of study. These organisms are also included in the Plant Life section of this volume.

Botanists have begun to rely increasingly on genetic characteristics as the principal criteria for assigning a plant or other organism to a taxonomic classification.

KINGDOM Monera: *Bacteria: one-celled organisms lacking a distinct nucleus or any other membrane-bound cell structure (prokaryotic cell). Reproduce asexually. Found worldwide. More than 3,000 known species, with many times that number awaiting discovery. Examples: Bacillus (a bacterium) and Gloeocapsa (a cyanobacterium, or blue-green alga). (See also "Moneran Classification," page 29.)*

KINGDOM Fungi: *Unicellular and multicellular organisms with cells that possess a distinct nucleus (eukaryotic cells) and cell walls made of chitin. Have filamentous (stringlike) body tissues that absorb nutrition from dead or living organic matter. Lack photosynthetic pigments. Reproduce by spores, budding, or sexually. Include mushrooms, molds, mildews, and yeasts. Lichens represent a special symbiotic relationship in which photosynthetic algae live in the tissues of certain fungi. Found worldwide, primarily in damp places. About 100,000 known species. Examples: Penicillium species (mold); morel mushroom; and red crust lichen. (See also "Classification of Fungi," page 33.)*

KINGDOM Protista: *A broad kingdom best known for one-celled, animal-like organisms such as protozoa, but also including many one-celled or multicellular plantlike organisms such as euglenoids, and true algae. Plantlike protists possess a variety of photosynthetic pigments, including chlorophyll. Reproduce asexually by fission or spores, as well as sexually. Found worldwide, primarily in aquatic or damp places. About 23,000 known species of plantlike protists. Examples: Euglena, a one-celled organism; Physarum, a slime mold; bull kelp; and sea lettuce, Ulva. (See also "Classification of Plantlike Protists," pages 52–53, and "Classification of Animal-like Protists," page 211.)*

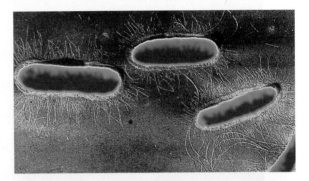

Several groups of "plantlike" organisms are traditionally considered within the realm of botany. Monerans (top), mushrooms and other fungi (above), and plantlike protists belong to their own kingdoms.

KINGDOM Plantae: *True plants: multicellular, photosynthetic organisms possessing chlorophyll a and b in chloroplasts within cells bounded by cell walls made of cellulose. (Some have lost photosynthetic pigments and abilities.) Develop specialized tissues such as roots and stems. Reproduce both sexually and asexually through alternating generations of spore-producing and gamete-producing individuals. Many also reproduce vegetatively, through growth of fragmented roots or stems. Found worldwide, primarily on land. About 275,000 known species. The major phyla and classes are as follows:*

PHYLUM Bryophyta: *Bryophytes: small, green, flattened plants that lack specialized conducting tissue, and therefore bear no true stems, roots, or leaves. Grow close to the ground, anchored by hairlike, rootlike structures called rhizoids. Lack seeds. Reproduce sexually and asexually. Gamete-producing generation is dominant, with spore-producing generation growing from and dependent on it. (In all other plants, spore-producing generation is dominant.) Require water for sexual reproduction. Found worldwide, primarily in damp soil, wetlands, and streams.*

CLASS Hepaticae: *Liverworts—the simplest of all true plants, with leaflike or flattened tissues that grow horizontally on the ground and spore capsule held atop stemlike structure. Found on moist, shaded soil, rocks, or trees, occasionally in water. About 8,000 species. Example: horned liverwort.*

CLASS Anthocerotae: *Hornworts—small, nonleafy plants that superficially resemble liverworts. Unlike liverworts, hornworts possess specialized breathing pores (stomata) and complex chloroplasts. Long, upright, spore-bearing structure splits along length to release spores. Although hornworts reach their greatest diversity in the tropics, they occur worldwide on moist, shaded soil and rocks, occasionally in water. About 300 species. Example: common hornwort.*

CLASS Musci: *Mosses—low-growing plants with many leaflike tissues arranged spirally on upright, stemlike shafts. Spores are contained in complex capsules. About 10,000 species. Examples: peat moss,* Sphagnum *species; and hair-cap moss,* Polytrichum *species.*

PHYLUM Psilotophyta: *Whisk ferns: small, upright plants with true conducting tissue. Considered the simplest vascular plants, with true stem but no true roots and often no true leaves. Lack seeds. The gamete-producing generation of most species grows underground and produces an aboveground spore-producing generation under favorable circumstances. Some grow attached to other plants. Require water for reproduction. Found in tropical and semitropical regions worldwide. Fewer than 10 species. Example: moa plant.*

PHYLUM Lycopodiophyta: *Club mosses, spike mosses, and quillworts: typically small, low-growing plants with true stems, leaves, and roots. The leaves are simpler than those of other vascular plants, in that they have only one vein and one vascular connection to the stem (leaf trace). Lack seeds. Require water for fertilization. Extinct orders included many small to large trees. Found worldwide in wet, shady habitats. Examples: running pine and resurrection plant.*

Plants have evolved numerous and ingenious ways of reproducing. The underside of a fern frond, for instance, is laden with reproductive structures called sporangia (left). The seed cone of a conifer grows large (above) after fertilization.

PHYLUM Sphenophyta: *Horsetails: vascular plants with two distinct types of shoots: fertile shoots, with ribbed and jointed stems and tiny leaves in whorls around stem joints; and vegetative shoots, with many small branches in whorls around stem joints. Lack seeds. Require water for fertilization. Extinct forms were treelike in size and abundant some 300 million years ago. Modern forms are less common and small in size, although several species in Central and South America have been known to exceed 30 feet (9 meters) in height. Found in moist soils worldwide except Australia and Southeast Asia. About 30 species. Example: common horsetail.*

PHYLUM Filicophyta or **Pterophyta:** *True ferns: tiny to treelike plants with true roots and creeping stems. Leaves, in the form of fronds, are typically divided; leaf maturation occurs progressively from the base to the tip. Spore structures are often found on the underside of leaves. Lack seeds. Found worldwide, primarily in the tropics. About 12,000 species divided among approximately 350 genera in 28 families. Examples: northern maidenhair fern and tree fern.*

PHYLUM Cycadophyta: *Cycads: palmlike, seed-producing plants, typically with short, thick, unbranched trunks and large, leathery, divided leaves. Stems sometimes grow entirely underground. Large seed cones are often born on tip of main stem. Pollen is brought to egg by pollen tube. About 120 species, mainly tropical or subtropical. Example: Florida cycad.*

PHYLUM Ginkgophyta: *Ginkgo: a tall, many-branched tree with well-developed woody trunk, stems with distinct long and short shoots, and simple, fan-shaped leaves. Sexes on separate trees. Lacks seed cones. Instead, seeds mature within strong-smelling fruit. Native to Asia, introduced around the world. One species:* Ginkgo biloba.

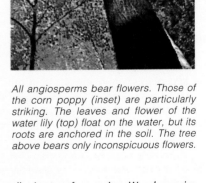

PHYLUM Coniferophyta: *Conifers: typically large trees with well-developed woody trunks; scaly, needlelike leaves; and large, well-developed cones. Pollen is transported to egg by pollen tube. Found worldwide. About 550 species. Examples: bristlecone pine, balsam fir, and Gowen cypress.*

PHYLUM Gnetophyta: *Gnetophytes: unusual group of three dissimilar genera classified together for their unique type of flowerlike reproductive structure (neither a cone nor a true flower). They are also the only nonflowering seed plants to possess vessels in their xylem tissue. Forms include trees, climbing vines, and herb plants.* Gnetum *found in moist tropics;* Ephedra *in arid and desert regions worldwide; and* Welwitschia *in coastal deserts of southwestern Africa. About 70 species. Examples: California ephedra; Namibian welwitschia; and common gnetum.*

PHYLUM Anthophyta or **Magnoliophyta:** *Flowering plants (angiosperms): highly developed plants in which eggs are enclosed within a flower, and mature seeds are enclosed within fruits. The gamete-producing generation is reduced to microscopic size and borne on the larger, independent spore-producing generation.*

CLASS Monocotyledones: *Monocots—flowering plants with one cotyledon (seed leaf). Flower parts typically come in set of threes. Leaf veins are usually parallel. Vascular bundles are scattered through stem. Found worldwide. About 65,000 species. Examples: coconut palm and rice.*

All angiosperms bear flowers. Those of the corn poppy (inset) are particularly striking. The leaves and flower of the water lily (top) float on the water, but its roots are anchored in the soil. The tree above bears only inconspicuous flowers.

CLASS Dicotyledoneae: *Dicots—flowering plants with two cotyledons (seed leaves). Flower parts are typically in sets of four or five. Leaf venation is usually netlike. Vascular bundles in stem form a ring. Woody species have vascular cambium and true secondary growth. Found worldwide. Nearly 200,000 species. Examples: apple tree, soybean, and saguaro cactus.*

MOSSES AND OTHER NONVASCULAR PLANTS

by Jessica Snyder Sachs

Picture a planet without plants. Vast, shallow seas lap at the margins of a few small continents. The only green is that of algae growing as seaweed in the ocean, or as scum on the surface of ponds and wet rocks. This planet is Earth—some 450 million years ago. It will be nearly another 100 million years before the first vertebrate animal crawls out of the sea. But before that happens, another kind of life must colonize the land.

Although barren by today's standards, the dry land of the Ordovician era had a lot to offer the first plants: abundant sunlight unfiltered by water, an atmosphere rich in carbon dioxide for photosynthesis, and lots of room to grow. But the land also presented one tremendous difficulty for a would-be plant. It was dry.

The first plants to conquer dry land likely did so in much the same way as did the first animals. They probably retained many traits of their aquatic ancestors (green algae) while pioneering new traits needed to survive in open air. In other words, they were "amphibians."

WHAT IS A BRYOPHYTE?

A small group of such amphibious plants has survived to modern times. We know them best as the mosses. Together with the less-familiar liverworts and hornworts, they make up the division of the Plant Kingdom known as bryophytes (from the Greek *bryos*, "moss," and *phytos*, "plants"). Truly "living fossils," they reflect how plant life may have first appeared on Earth some 450 million years ago.

Amphibians of the Plant World

Like all true plants, bryophytes are designed to live on land. Their reproductive organs and spores are coated with a protective layer of tissue that prevents drying. Likewise, most bryophytes are covered by a waxy "skin" layer, called the *cuticle*, that slows moisture loss from the entire body. But this cuticle is not so thick in bryophytes as it is in other true plants. Like the amphibians of the animal world, therefore, bryophytes may be able to "breathe" in part through their cuticle, or "skin." Most also have small pores in the cuticle, through which they can draw additional air.

In other ways, bryophytes have remained dependent on water—much more so than other plants. Like algae, they need water to reproduce. Their male sex cells (sperm) actually swim to the female's egg, using whiplike flagella, or tails. Bryophytes must also remain moist in order to grow. They lack true roots for absorbing water and minerals from the soil. Instead, they absorb water and minerals directly through the green parts of their simple bodies.

This is not to say that bryophytes cannot survive in dry environments. Mosses, in particular, are famous for their ability to survive long droughts by entering a "near-dead" state called *dormancy*. Although no growth takes place in dormancy, the moss is ready to resume "life" as soon as moisture returns.

The mosses and the other bryophytes also lack the vascular, or conducting, tissues that carry food and water up through the stems and leaves of other plants. For this reason, they are called *nonvascular plants*. And for the same reason, they remain small and close to the ground. Few grow more than 2 inches (5 centimeters) tall.

In these and other ways, bryophytes remain intermediate between the simpler green algae and the more highly evolved vascular plants. Bryophytes are clearly true plants. Yet, within the Plant Kingdom, they remain a group separate from all others.

LIFE CYCLE OF A BRYOPHYTE

The life cycle of plants, including bryophytes, differs from that of animals in a fundamental way. All plants undergo an *alternation of generations*, in which a spore-producing, or asexual, generation alternates with a gamete-producing, or sexual, generation. In all plants but bryophytes, the spore-producing generation is the dominant of the two. That is, it forms the main visible plant body. This process is reversed in mosses, liverworts, and hornworts.

In the bryophyte's unique life cycle, the gamete-producing generation, or *gametophyte*, forms the green plant body. The gametophyte produces sex cells (eggs or sperm) that unite to create a smaller *sporophyte*, or spore-producing generation. This sporophyte grows atop the green gametophyte, which supplies it with nutrition. When mature, the sporophyte produces a

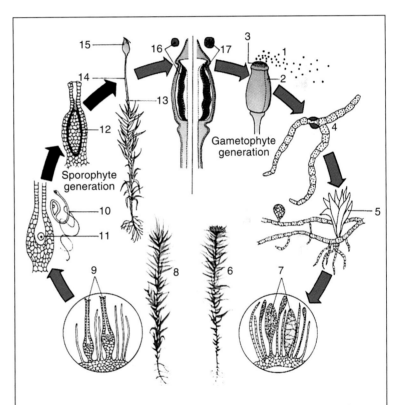

In the life cycle of a typical moss, spores (1) are released from the capsule (2) through two rows of teeth (3). The spores germinate into branched filaments called protonemata (4), which produce buds that develop into leafy green plants called gametophytes (5). Mature male gametophytes (6) bear reproductive structures called antheridia (7); mature female gametophytes (8) bear archegonia (9). Sperm (10), attracted into the archegonium, fuse with an egg cell (11), forming a zygote. The zygote, when mature, produces an embryo sporophyte, or spore-producing plant (12), which consists of a foot (13), a stalk (14), and a capsule (15). Spore mother cells (16) within the capsule undergo meiosis, producing spores with a single set of chromosomes (17). When the spores are released, the cycle repeats.

Nearly all mosses are short plants, rarely growing more than a few inches tall. The most common mosses have simple, unbranched shoots whose spore capsules extend straight up on stiff, slender "threads."

spore capsule. When ripe, the spore capsules release male and female spores, which scatter around the parent plant. Each spore can sprout into a new individual without the need for sexual reproduction (no fusion of sex cells). The cells of each spore simply divide to produce new male and female gametophytes. And so the cycle continues.

In some bryophytes, male and female parts occur on the same plant. In others, males and females grow separately. But in all cases, the two sexes must be close together, since the male's sex cells, or sperm, must be able to swim their way to the female's eggs.

THE MOSSES

Mosses can be found in most every healthy forest, often resembling patches of lush green carpet. Although they appear quite delicate, they are among the hardiest of all plants. Mosses grow in areas no other plants can — on the rocky slopes of high mountain peaks, and down in the frigid Antarctic. A few species can even live in deserts, where they survive by remaining dry and dormant for long periods, and then springing back to "life" when rains finally arrive.

Mosses are especially abundant and diverse in moist, unpolluted areas. Their greatest vulnerability (in modern times, at least) is their extreme sensitivity to air pollution, particularly sulfur dioxide. This may be due to their "amphibious" lifestyle—indeed, they absorb pollutants as well as mineral nutrients directly through their green tissues.

Mosses are often the first plants to "colonize" wet, crumbling rocks and logs. Importantly, they help form soil atop these solid surfaces by leaving an organic layer when they die. This layer ultimately paves the way for larger plants. Mosses are also important for their role in preventing erosion. By carpeting bare ground with their water-absorbing bodies, they help prevent its removal by rain and runoff.

True mosses all develop from spores. Each spore germinates into a green branching fiber called a *protonema* (from the Greek *protos*, "first," and *nema*, "thread"). The moss protonema is just one cell thick, and resembles a simple green alga. As it matures, the protonema produces buds. Each bud grows into an erect shoot with a spiral of leafy frill. These green, leaflike structures contain chloroplasts and produce food through photosynthesis.

Moss "Wanna-bes"

A surprising number of small plants are called "mosses" that are not mosses at all. The "moss" found on the north side of trees, for example, is actually green algae. Irish moss, the kind that grows on seashore rocks, is actually red algae. Beard moss, oakmoss, and reindeer moss are different types of lichens. Spanish moss is actually an air plant, and club moss is a kind of simple vascular plant called a lycopod.

But they are not true leaves, as they lack organized tissues. (See the box titled "Anatomy of a Leaf," page 70.)

Mosses also lack true roots. Instead, tiny threads called *rhizoids* anchor each green shoot onto the ground or other surface. Rhizoids do not conduct water or minerals into the plant, as true roots do. Instead, their function is to simply anchor the moss in place. While mosses lack true vascular, or conducting, tissue, a few species have a center core of water-carrying cells that resemble the tracheae of vascular plants. But they lack many of the special features of true vascular tissue.

Reproduction

The reproduction of mosses is typical of that of all the bryophytes. The green shoots of the moss plant are its gamete-producing generation, or gametophyte. The gametophytes produce sex organs at the tips of their shoots. In some mosses, male and female parts grow on the same plant. In others, they exist as separate plants. In either case, several egg-producing structures—called archegonia—grow on the tip of each female shoot, with a single egg at the base of each archegonium. A canal extends from its base to its open mouth.

The sex organ of the male shoot is called the *antheridium*. Each male shoot produces several, each of which contains many sperm. The antheridia discharge their sperm into water droplets that collect at the tip of their shoot. The sperm actively swim through the water using long, whiplike tails called *flagella*. There they wait until rain or running water splashes them onto a nearby female shoot. The sperm then make their way into the canal of the archegonia. The first sperm to reach each egg fertilizes it.

The fertilized egg then launches an entirely different generation—the *sporophyte*. It consists of a foot, the base of which becomes embedded in the green shoot of the gametophyte. From this foot rises a threadlike stalk (*seta*) bearing a spore capsule (*sporangium*) covered with a protective jacket (*calyptra*).

When the spore capsule is mature, its calyptra falls off. Soon after, the top of the spore capsule (the *operculum*) bursts. Now the capsule is ready to release its spores like salt from a shaker. It does so whenever the wind or animals jostle its long, thin stalks. A typical moss capsule may release up to 50 million spores. Each can germinate to produce a new gametophyte. And so the cycle begins anew.

Variety of Forms

There are more than 9,500 known species of mosses distributed around the globe.

Prevalent types. Typically, mosses grow in one of two forms. The so-called "cushiony" mosses tend to have simple, unbranched shoots with rings of leaflike frills. The shoots grow erect, and their spore capsules extend straight up on stiff, slender "threads." Examples include the *Polytrichum* mosses, probably the most familiar in North America.

By contrast, "feathery" mosses tend to have highly branched shoots that creep horizontally across the ground or drape in mats from the branches of trees. Examples include the fern mosses (*Thuidium*). Both cushiony and feathery mosses tend to hug the ground, seldom growing more than a few inches high. From a distance, they often resemble patches of thick green turf.

A third, less common type comprises the water mosses. They form thick tangles of underwater vegetation in woodland ponds. A familiar example is *Fontinalis*, a popular plant for freshwater aquariums.

Peat moss. Unlike any other moss is the genus known as *Sphagnum*, or peat moss. Larger than most, it can grow up to 12 inches (30 centimeters) in height, forming thick patches of branched stems with moplike heads. The living tissues of sphagnum moss also contain many dead cells, which can absorb great quantities of

In a peat bog (above, in Scotland), a mat of sphagnum moss and other plants becomes compacted, forming a carbon-rich deposit that, when dried, is used as fuel.

water. Indeed, sphagnum mosses can hold up to 20 times their dry weight in water—more than five times the amount that cotton does. For this reason, sphagnum was once used in bandages and surgical dressings.

In many parts of the Northern Hemisphere, sphagnum forms enormous mats of growth called peat bogs. The "peat" is formed by the compressed bodies of the moss itself along with the many reeds and grasses that grow among it. This material is especially high in carbon (some 60 percent). In Ireland and other northern regions, dried peat has long been harvested and burned as fuel. The world's coal comes largely from underground deposits of peat millions of years old.

OTHER BRYOPHYTES

The liverworts and hornworts are the simplest of all true plants. Like mosses, they lack true stems, leaves, and roots. Most have a small, simple body, called a *thallus*, that forms thin lobes of tissue on the ground. Even small-

er than the mosses, these flattened plants seldom grow to a width of more than a few inches.

The Liverworts

The first plant to emerge onto dry land some 400 million years ago may have looked like a liverwort. Indeed, the oldest liverwort fossil (*Hepaticites*) is thought to be nearly that old.

Liverworts get their name from their simple shape, which somewhat resembles that of a flattened liver. This tiny plant has the simplest of tissues and a little waxy covering (*cuticle*) over its body.

Liverworts are most common in the tropics, although they occur around the world. Typically, they grow on moist, shaded stream banks, forest floors, rocks, and tree trunks. Like mosses, liverworts play an important role in breaking down rock to form soil. Today there are more than 8,000 species. There are two basic types of liverworts: thallose liverworts, which have flattened, ribbonlike bodies that form several small, rounded lobes; and leafy liverworts, which produce small, fernlike fronds covered with rows of

Plant Spores

Chances are, you've seen millions of plant spores. They may have looked like grains of pepper around a moss plant or yellow "dust" near a fern. Many people think of plant spores as simple "seeds." But they are something else entirely.

A seed is a protective coating that forms around the fertilized egg, or embryo, of certain plants. That is, it results from sexual reproduction and produces a plant with a copy of both parents' genes.

A spore is also a reproductive cell—but an asexual one. A spore cell requires no fertilization, but simply divides and divides again to produce a new plant. But this plant has just a single copy of its parent's genes—it has only one parent. In other words, each spore produces an exact clone of its parent.

Spores are a key step in the unique life cycle that sets true plants (and a few algae) apart from all other forms of life. It is a life cycle that continually alternates between sexual and asexual phases, or "generations."

Spores are the products of the asexual phase, or sporophyte. They germinate into male and female plants, called *gametophytes*. When fertilized by the male, the eggs of the female produce another generation of sporophytes. And so on.

Although all plants produce spores, they are obvious only in "nonseed" plants such as mosses, ferns, and horsetails. In seed-bearing plants, the spores remain within the parent plant, inside the structure of a cone or flower. There they germinate into a microscopic generation of gametophytes that sexually produce seeds.

Unlike seeds, which tend to be scattered far and wide, most spores are designed to fall and germinate close together. Often the parent plant sheds its spores straight down from the underside of its leaves. In this way, the male plants that germinate from the spores sit close by the females—close enough for sexual reproduction and another turn of the life cycle.

Most species of liverworts inhabit tropical regions. In the leafy liverworts (above), the thallus divides in such a way as to suggest leaves of great delicacy. The sporophyte of Marchantia (inset), a common liverwort, looks somewhat like a miniature palm tree.

elaters. When the sporophyte opens to release its spores, the elaters twist and spin to help scatter them.

Many liverworts (and some mosses) also produce a special reproductive structure called a *gemma cup*. Within each cup are several small disks of green tissue, called *gemmae*. When gemmae are splashed out of their cups by water, each one can sprout into a new individual, genetically identical to its "parent."

The Hornworts

In outward appearance and size, hornworts greatly resemble the liverworts. In fact, they were long considered a type of horned liverwort. More recently, scientists have discovered that hornworts have chloroplasts and pigments that resemble those of green algae more than that of true plants. For this and other peculiarities, botanists place the hornworts in a class by themselves.

Hornworts derive their name from their distinctive sporophytes, which sprout like green horns from the flattened body of the main plant (the gametophyte generation). In all, there are more than 300 species, found on wet rocks and damp ground around the world. The male and female sex organs of hornworts (antheridia and archegonia) often occur on the same plant. They have no stalks, but lie sunken into the plant's flat surface. The hornwort's sperm therefore need only swim out of the plant's antheridium and into a nearby archegonium to fertilize an egg.

The fertilized egg gives rise to the spore-producing structure that gives the hornwort its name. It grows as a tapered cylinder, or "horn," sometimes attaining a height of up to 2 inches (5 centimeters). When mature, each spore case splits open into ribbonlike halves from the top down and releases millions of spores.

"leaves." Liverwort "leaves," like those of moss, are not true leaves, as they consist only of a single layer of cells (with no true leaf tissue).

The typical life cycle of these plants is well illustrated by *Marchantia*, a common thallose liverwort. Like all bryophytes, it goes through an alternation of generations, with the gamete-producing generation being that which we see as the green plant. This green gametophyte arises from the germination of male and female spores. When mature, it produces male or female sex organs that grow as small stalks from its flattened body. The male sex organ, or *antheridiophore*, bears a disk-shaped cap, looking much like a tiny mushroom. The female *archegoniophore* looks more like a tiny palm tree or ragged umbrella. Rain or heavy dew enables sperm from the antheridiophore to swim to a nearby archegoniophore and fertilize the eggs there.

Each fertilized egg produces a new generation, or sporophyte. The sporophytes remain attached to the underside of the archegoniophore "palm tree" like so many tiny coconuts. The inside of the sporophyte becomes filled with spores. It also contains threadlike cells called

VASCULAR PLANTS

by Jessica Snyder Sachs

Plants, like all living things on this planet, came from aquatic ancestors. And like other organisms, they conquered land in stages, adapting step-by-step to a brave new world of bright sunlight and open air. Most likely, the first land plants were tiny organisms. They grew in wet, shady spots where their small bodies were protected from drying. That is, they were amphibious—living on land, but remaining within reach of ample water.

Nonvascular plants such as mosses, liverworts, and hornworts never evolved beyond this amphibious stage. It was left to a second group of plants to wholly conquer dry land. These were the vascular plants. They appeared quite early in evolutionary history, about 410 million years ago. Their great advantage was a vascular system that could distribute water and nutrients throughout their bodies.

This system enabled vascular plants to separate the tasks of water absorption and food production into different body parts—namely, roots and leaves. It also enabled the first vascular plants to literally pick themselves up off the ground—by the stem, that is, which lifts the vascular plant's leaves into the sunlight.

As a result, the first vascular plants grew taller and bigger than their amphibious cousins. In essence, they grabbed the sun, shading out their smaller, nonvascular cousins.

Not surprisingly, the vascular plants flourished. As climates and landforms changed, they diversified into a dazzling array of forms. Today they comprise 95 percent of all plants. All flowering and seed-producing plants are vascular, as are the ferns, horsetails, and club mosses. From the tiniest fern to the giant sequoia, they carpet the land with well over 250,000 known species.

Many of the world's quarter-million species of vascular plants flourish in the year-round rains and perennial warmth that characterize the tropical rain forest (above).

WHAT IS A VASCULAR PLANT?

In its simplest form, the body of a vascular plant consists of two basic parts: the roots and the shoots. The roots specialize in the work of burrowing through the soil in search of moisture and minerals. The roots of the vascular plant do not need sunlight or photosynthetic pigments, because they are "fed" from above, through the vascular system.

The roots, in turn, supply the aboveground shoot with water and dissolved minerals from the soil. By comparison, the rootlike rhizoids of nonvascular plants (mosses and liverworts) and the holdfasts of algae (seaweed) are no more than anchors. They do not actively absorb water or minerals.

The vascular system that connects the roots and shoots is organized into two special types of tissue. *Phloem* distributes the foods produced by photosynthesis, primarily sugar and starch. It carries these foods away from the main site of photosynthesis—the leaves—and delivers them to areas where energy is needed for growth. Much nutrition is sent to the roots to fuel their expansion. Extra food is taken to storage areas for later use.

Xylem conducts water and dissolved minerals up from the roots to the aboveground parts of the plant. Because they are supplied with water from the inside, vascular plants can cover themselves with a thick waxy covering called *cuticle*. (The cuticle remains quite thin in nonvascular plants, which must absorb moisture through their entire surface.) Having such a waterproof covering enables vascular plants to grow quite large. Without it, a plant with a large surface area would lose too much moisture to the dry air.

SPECIAL TISSUES

The body of a vascular plant is much more complex than that of a moss or other nonvascular species. The cells of the more-primitive nonvascular plants are about the same. Like a jack-of-all-trades, each cell performs more or less the same function as the others.

By comparison, the cells of a vascular plant are specialists. That is, evolution has fashioned a variety of different cells inside the body of a vascular plant. These different classes of cells, in turn, have been organized into a variety of different tissues, tissue systems, and organs, each with its own special role to play.

Three basic types of tissue make up the vascular plant: *dermal* tissue (or epidermis); *vascular* tissue; and *ground* tissue. The dermal tissue protects the surface of the entire plant, from shoot tip to root cap. The vascular tissues run in bundles through the core of the plant. In between lies the ground tissue. It fills the greater part of the plant body, providing physical support and a storage place for food.

Ground Tissue

The bulk of a vascular plant is made of ground tissue, what we might call the "fleshy" part of the stem, leaf, and root. This is very simple tissue, made primarily of a single type of cell—*parenchyma*, the most abundant of all

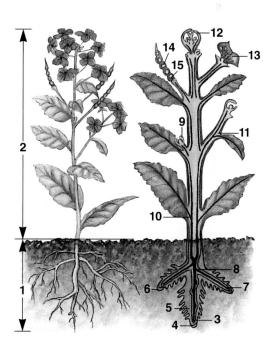

A typical vascular plant consists of a root (1) and a shoot (2). The root grows from an apical meristem (3), which is protected by a root cap (4). Both primary (5) and branch (6) roots contain water-conducting xylem (7) and food-transporting phloem (8). Leaves and auxiliary buds (9) occur at nodes (10) of the stem. Branch stems (11) arise from auxiliary buds if the terminal bud (12) is damaged. In angiosperms, the flower (13) is the reproductive structure that develops, when fertilized, into a fruit (14) that ultimately bears seeds (15).

plant cells. Parenchyma cells have thin walls with many irregularly shaped sides. They readily absorb water, swelling to support and shape leaves and young green stems. When parenchyma cells are filled with water, the plant looks lush. When they lose too much water, as in times of drought, young stems and leaves droop. The plant looks wilted.

Parenchyma cells can be found in all parts of the plant body. In the leaves, they tend to be filled with chloroplasts. Those in stems and roots serve as storage sites for food in the form of starch. Parenchyma also serves as a type of all-purpose cell, ready to produce new tissue to heal a wound or regenerate a lost branch.

In smaller amounts, ground tissue also contains cells known as *collenchyma* and *sclerenchyma*. These cells have thickened cell walls that help support the plant. Collenchyma cells occur as stretchy "strings" in green stems and along the veins of some leaves. They are important in the support of young, growing stems.

Sclerenchyma cells come in two types: *fibers* and *sclereids*. Fibers occur in long, tough strands that strengthen parts of the plant that have stopped growing in length. They often lay alongside vascular tissue in the stem, to give it extra strength. Hemp, flax, and jute are familiar examples of sclerenchyma fibers used in human-made products. Sclereids, or stone cells, tend to be shorter than fibers. They form the hard outer covering of seeds, nuts, and some fruits. The gritty texture of pears comes from that fruit's abundance of these grainy cells.

Vascular Tissue

Xylem is the "plumbing" of the vascular plant. Working against gravity, bundles of xylem tissue conduct water and dissolved minerals out of the plant's roots and up through the shoot. Xylem contains two types of conducting cells: *tracheids* and *vessels.* Both consist of long, narrow cells with walls hardened by lignin. When mature, these cells die, leaving behind their hollow, tubelike "skeletons."

Tracheid cells have closed, tapered ends that overlap with one another to form long, hollow strands. Water flowing up from one tracheid to another passes through thin patches, called *pits*, in their cell walls. All vascular plants have tracheid cells, the longest of which are more than 1 inch (2.5 centimeters) long.

The xylem of flowering plants also contains the second type of xylem cell, the vessel. These probably evolved from tracheids, which they resemble in shape. Vessels differ from tracheids in that they lay end to end, like so many sections of pipe. In addition, each end of the vessel cell is perforated with holes, facilitating the free flow of water from one cell to the next.

Phloem is the vascular plant's food-conducting tissue. The phloem extends into the leaves, where it picks up the sugar and other organic molecules made in photosynthetic cells. It carries this food primarily to actively growing, but nonphotosynthetic, tissues such as roots, flowers, and newly emerging buds. Extra foodstuffs get delivered to storage cells, primarily in the roots and stem.

The food-conducting cells of the phloem are called *sieve elements*. Like the tracheids and vessels of the xylem, sieve elements form long strands through the length of the plant. But unlike the xylem cells, sieve elements remain alive when mature. Pores in the walls of the sieve el-

Anatomy of a Plant Root

A protective covering called the root cap shields the root's growing tip as it pushes its way through the soil. Immediately behind the root cap is a zone of actively dividing cells, the *apical meristem*. Behind the apical meristem is a zone of cell elongation. There the young cells expand in length. The next zone contains mature cells ready to differentiate, or specialize, into mature tissues such as the epidermis, ground tissue, and vascular system.

The epidermis of the root does not produce waxy cuticle, as does the epidermis of the stem and leaves. Such a covering would interfere with the root's ability to absorb water. Instead, the young dermal cells produce fingerlike extensions called *root hairs*. They absorb most of the water and dissolved minerals taken in by the roots.

Why does water flow into, and not out of, the roots? Generally, it is because root cells contain a higher concentration of salts and minerals than does the water in the soil. So the water moves into the roots by *osmo-*

ements allow their cell fluids, or *cytoplasm*, to flow freely from one to another. Dissolved in this fluid are the sugars and other molecules created by photosynthesis.

Sieve elements come in two forms. Flowering plants have "sieve tubes" made up of sieve cells connected—end to end—by large openings called sieve plates. By contrast, the "sieve cells" of nonflowering plants have many small pores along the entire length of each cell. The cells overlap, allowing the cytoplasm from one to "leak" sideways into the next.

The xylem and phloem usually lie close together, forming long, parallel strands called *vascular bundles*. In most plants, these bundles occur in a central column called the *stele*. The stiff vascular tissue in the stele also helps support the plant, giving it a "backbone" of sorts.

Dermal Tissue

The dermal tissue, or epidermis, forms the plant's outermost layer of cells. Dermal cells tend to be flat and tightly packed. Otherwise,

they vary widely in form, depending on the part of the plant that they cover. Certainly the surface of a leaf feels and looks different from that of a root, blossom, fruit, or seed.

In general, the epidermis of a plant is just one cell thick. But the cells in this thin layer fit together tightly to form a tough, protective wall. The dermal cells also exude a waxy covering over their outer surface. This is the *cuticle*, responsible for maintaining a near-waterproof seal over the plant.

A thick cuticle prevents water loss. But it also prevents carbon dioxide and oxygen from flowing into and out of the plant. Vascular plants have surmounted this problem with special pores called *stomata*. Each stoma (singular of stomata) is surrounded by a pair of sausage-shaped *guard cells*. During times of ample light and water, the guard cells fill with fluid and bow outward. This opens the stomata and allows a free flow of gases into and out of the plant. At night and in times of drought, the guard cells lose water. This changes their shape. They go

sis (defined as the tendency of water to move from a less-concentrated solution to a more-concentrated one).

Water and minerals absorbed by the root hairs quickly pass through the thin epidermis to a large area of ground tissue called the *cortex*. The cortex contains many air spaces, which help conduct the water toward the vascular tissues at the root's core.

Running through the core of the root is an area of tightly packed parenchyma and vascular cells—the *endodermis*. Just inside the endodermis is another cylinder of cells, just one cell thick, called the *pericycle*. The pericycle produces lateral roots, which grow out through the cortex and epidermis.

Inside the pericycle lays the vascular system, composed of *xylem* and *phloem*. The xylem carries water and dissolved nutrients to the aboveground part of the plant. The phloem delivers food from the leaves to the roots. This food passes out of the vascular system and moves through the cortex, where much of it is stored as grains of starch.

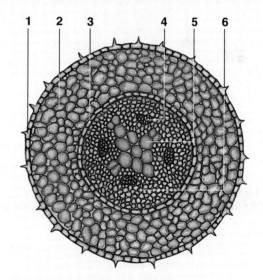

A cross section of an angiosperm root reveals several distinct tissue layers. The epidermis (1) absorbs water and minerals through root hairs. Cells of the cortex (2) store starch and other substances. A thin endodermis (3) encloses the vascular cylinder, which contains food-conducting phloem (4), water-conducting xylem (5), and a region of dividing cells (6).

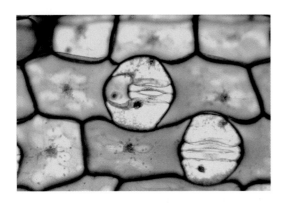

In vascular plants, the intake of carbon dioxide and the release of oxygen occurs through pores called stomata, which are mostly on the lower surface of the leaf.

tokinins that stimulate growth and development. These, too, are shunted above the ground through the vascular tissue when needed.

The work of the plant root is often aided by a relationship with certain types of beneficial fungi or bacteria. The root provides shelter for these organisms, which in turn help the roots absorb or use certain nutrients. The bacterium *Rhizobium* invades the roots of many legume plants such as peas, clover, and beans, and helps these plants obtain nitrogen in a form they can use for growth. Most plants also have one or more kinds of fungi growing on (or even in) their roots. The fungi increase the root's absorption of minerals and other nutrients. This beneficial relationship is called *mycorrhiza*.

Root Development

When a seed or spore germinates, it already bears its first root. This primary root, or *radicle*, penetrates the soil and begins to produce branches, or lateral roots, within a few days. At this point, the root system will develop in one of two basic ways.

In a *taproot* system, the primary root grows straight down. It produces smaller branches, or lateral roots, as it grows. But the primary root, or taproot, remains the largest and fastest-growing branch of the root system. A typical taproot is thick at the base, where it meets the aboveground stem, and tapers downward to a growing point. Familiar taproot plants include carrots, radishes, beets, and dandelions.

In a fibrous-root system, no one root is more prominent than the others. The primary root tends to be short-lived, giving way to a mass of slender roots and their network of tangled side branches.

Fibrous roots often develop from buds on the plant's lower stem. These are called *adventitious roots*, a name that refers to any root growing from a plant part other than the primary root. Sometimes adventitious roots extend above the ground to form props that brace the main stem. This can be seen in tree ferns, corn plants, and in banyan and mangrove trees.

"limp," so to speak, closing over the stomata and further slowing water loss. It also stops the flow of carbon dioxide, which eventually shuts down photosynthesis.

Together, vascular, ground, and dermal tissue form the different structures, or "organs" of the plant—namely, the leaves, roots, and stems. Their arrangement varies somewhat from one structure to the next, as may the shape, size, and function of their individual cells. The parenchyma cells in a leaf, for example, are usually packed full of chloroplasts. Those in the root lack chloroplasts, but may instead be filled with starch. Likewise, you can feel that the texture of a leaf differs from that of a stem or a root. The varying textures reflect differences in the dermal cells of these plant parts.

ROOTS

Roots constitute the underground portion of a vascular plant. Roots have two primary roles: to anchor the plant in place; and to absorb water and minerals from the soil. Most roots also play other roles. For instance, they store food manufactured by the photosynthetic parts of the plant, a function best seen in the starchy roots of carrots, sugar beets, and sweet potatoes. The roots use some of this stored food to fuel their own growth. But much of it is sent back up through the vascular tissues to the aboveground structures. This is especially important at the start of a new growing season, when plants draw on stored nutrition to produce new shoots. Roots also produce hormones such as cy-

STEMS

Stems produce and support the light-collecting organs we call leaves. Stems also serve as pipelines for the passage of water, minerals,

Anatomy of a Stem

The growing tip of the stem is organized much like that of a root, with a zone of cell division followed by a zone of cell elongation, and finally a zone of differentiation. As in the root, the outer layer of stem cells develops into a protective epidermis. The cells of the stem epidermis produce the waxy "sealant" called *cuticle*. Inside the epidermis is the stem's *cortex*, made up of storage and supporting cells. The cortex of the stem is not nearly so thick as that of the root.

The bulk of a typical plant stem is filled by its central column, or *stele*. It contains a number of special tissues arranged in cylindrical layers. The outermost layer is called the *pericycle*. Next comes a layer of *phloem*, the food-conducting tissue. Inside the phloem are bundles of *cambium* cells surrounding bundles of *xylem*, the water-conducting tissue. The very core of the stem is composed of *pith*, an area of parenchyma cells that serves chiefly to store food. Extending out from the pith, usually through both xylem and phloem, are a series of *vascular rays*. These vascular rays conduct food and

other materials between the core of the plant and its outer surface.

This type of arrangement best describes a stem in its first year of growth. In woody plants, the second growth season begins the process of outward expansion (*secondary growth*) that substantially changes the stem's anatomy. The xylem tissue expands to largely fill the stem, forming rings of dead cells that are visible to us as woody growth rings.

The stem of plants known as monocots differ in details from that of the typical stem described here. (See the article "Flowering Plants," beginning on page 98.)

1 2 3 4 5   **6**

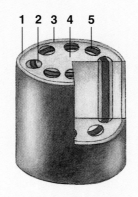 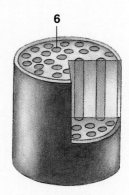

The stem of a typical dicot, such as that of the sunflower (left), is surrounded by epidermis (1) and contains bundles of vascular tissue (2) arranged in a ring. This ring separates the outer cortex (3) from the inner pith (4). A layer of dividing cells, the vascular cambium (5), produces tissue that thickens the stem. Grass (right), a typical monocot, has vascular bundles (6) scattered throughout the stem. The bundles lack a cambial layer, and therefore lack the capacity to grow.

and food between the roots, leaves, and other plant parts. Stems further serve as a storage place for food, and may themselves contain photosynthetic cells for the manufacture of additional food.

A plant's first stem, like its primary root, is already present in the embryo. When a seed or spore germinates, a slender stem unfolds. If need be, it pushes upward through the soil and into the open air. The stem continues to elongate from its growing point, called the *apical meristem* or *terminal bud*. The sides of the growing

tip produce clusters of *leaf primordia*, which then expand into true leaves.

As the stem tip grows longer, it also leaves behind small bits of growth tissue, called *meristem*. Often meristem is left just above the point where a leaf separates from the stem. Each patch of meristem can produce a *lateral bud*. These buds can give rise to structures such as flowers, runners (ground stems), or rhizomes (underground stems). If the stem loses its terminal bud, one or more of its lateral buds can produce a new main stem.

Despite their great differences in external appearance (size and shape), all leaves follow a similar internal pattern. As with stems and roots, the surface of each leaf is covered with a layer of epidermal cells, both top and bottom. These cells secrete a waxy coating, the *cuticle*, which slows water loss. Special cells in the epidermis form collapsible pores called *stomata*. These are most abundant on the leaf's lower surface. Each is enclosed by a pair of *guard cells*, which open and close over the opening in response to special cues such as sunlight and water.

The epidermal cells of some plants produce tiny hairs. These hairs can partly shade the leaf from extreme sunlight, as is the case with certain desert plants. So-called "air plants" use leaf hairs to absorb water and minerals. Still other leaf hairs may help protect the leaf from insect pests.

Sandwiched between the upper and lower epidermis of the leaf is a special kind of ground tissue called *mesophyll*, meaning "middle leaf." It is filled with two kinds of photosynthetic cells. A layer of long, thin cells called *palisade parenchyma* lies just beneath the upper epidermis—its cells packed tightly together like tiny pillars. These are the primary photosynthetic cells.

Beneath the palisade parenchyma and above the lower epidermis is a layer of loosely packed, irregularly shaped cells called *spongy parenchyma*. These contain fewer chloroplasts than do the palisade cells. Importantly, the spongy parenchyma contains many air spaces. These serve as a reservoir of carbon dioxide during times when the stomata are forced to close in order to preserve water.

Weaving throughout the mesophyll tissue are *vascular bundles*, or *veins*. *Xylem* cells in the veins deliver water and minerals to the photosynthetic cells. The *phloem* cells carry away the sugars and other products of photosynthesis.

Although leaves may vary in appearance, size, and arrangement, their internal structures (above) work together in a similar fashion to accomplish the tasks that are needed to ensure survival of the plant.

Lateral buds may grow spirally along the stem or in pairs, one bud opposite the other across the stem. The part of the stem where one or more leaves are attached is called the *node*.

After its first season of growth, a section of stem no longer increases in length except at its growing tip. However, the stems of many plants gradually increase in diameter. This is called *secondary growth*. The area of secondary growth is called *vascular cambium*.

Water Movement

Since water enters vascular plants almost entirely through the roots, a fundamental problem exists: making water "defy" gravity and flow up through the vascular tissues of the stem.

Common sense tells us that there are two ways to move water up through the plant: push from the bottom, or pull from the top. Some plants do build up enough pressure in their roots to push water a short distance up their stems. But clearly, this is not enough pressure to deliver water to the tip of a tall plant, let alone a tree.

As far as botanists can tell, plants pull water up through their stems. The pulling force is *transpiration*—the loss, or evaporation, of water from the surface of the plant, mainly its leaves. This continual loss (slowed but not stopped by the waxy cuticle) creates a negative pressure in the leaves that pulls water up and out of the plant's vascular tissues. That is, the water evaporated from the surface of the plant is replaced by water pulled up through the stem.

LEAVES

Broad and thin, the leaf of a vascular plant is designed to catch the maximum amount of sunlight possible. It is nature's ultimate "solar battery," the primary site of plant photosynthesis. By their very nature, leaves tend to be intensely green, for their cells are crowded with pigmented chloroplasts.

A typical leaf consists of a *petiole* (leaf stalk) and a *blade*. The blade's broad, thin surface allows for maximum sunlight exposure to power photosynthesis. An abundance of stomata (collapsible pores) on the leaf's surface maximizes the flow of gases into and out of the plant. Most important is atmospheric carbon dioxide—the raw material that photosynthetic cells use to assemble sugars and other foodstuffs.

The petiole contains a large strand of vascular tissue containing both xylem and phloem. In the leaves of most plants, the vascular tissue branches across the leaf blade in a series of veins. The veins form a fine network that reaches every photosynthetic cell in the leaf. The phloem carries away the cells' photosynthetic products. The xylem delivers water and dissolved minerals to the cells.

A leaf's shape, texture, and size are determined by its genes, or hereditary instructions. So all the leaves of all the plants in a given species share the same general pattern. Typically, this pattern reflects the environment in which the plant species evolved over many hundreds, thousands, or millions of years. Plants in a dry but sunny habitat, for example, tend toward small, leathery leaves (to minimize water loss). At the other extreme are plants in wet, shady environments such as the floor of a rain forest.

With ample moisture, they can produce enormously broad leaves (to collect as much dim light as possible).

Leaves also differ in arrangement. A leaf whose blade is divided into several distinct leaflets on a shared petiole is called a compound leaf; the frond of a fern is an extreme example. A simple leaf consists of a single blade on a petiole. The blades of some simple leaves are deeply lobed like those of an oak or maple tree. Leaves that lack petioles are called *sessile*. Their blades grow directly from the stem; most grasses fall into this category.

In addition to these differences, it is not unusual to find slight variation among the leaves of two plants of the same species or even the leaves of a single plant. Many plants, for example, tend to produce smaller, thicker leaves in bright light than they do in the shade. Some plants also produce one type of leaf in early growth and then another type of leaf when they mature.

Life Cycle of a Leaf

Leaves arise from the sides of a stem's tiny apical meristem, or bud. They begin as tiny bulges of growth called leaf primordia. Inside the leaf primordia, a tiny strand of vascular tissue forms and grows to connect the leaf with the stem's main vascular system.

In some plants, the leaf primordia arise in pairs opposite one another. In others, they form a circle, or *whorl*, around the terminal bud. At first, they are clustered together, one pair or whorl nearly on top of the other. But as the leaf primordia expand and develop into leaves, the growth of the stem spaces them along its length.

No leaf lasts forever. In fact, most leaves are designed to drop off a plant at a certain age (one to five years) or season (typically autumn). This normal separation of leaf from stem is called *abscission*. It is preceded by a series of changes that minimize damage to the plant.

The deep green of summer leaves comes from chlorophyll. As autumn progresses, the chlorophyll decomposes, and the red and yellow pigments reveal themselves.

Scotch pine   Willow   Maple

A simple leaf bears only one blade. Conifers bear leaves that resemble needles, like those of the Scotch pine (left). Willow leaves (center) are noted for their linear shape. A maple leaf (right) has palmate lobation.

First, many useful substances, such as minerals and sugar, flow back to the stem; at the same time, a separation layer forms at the base of the leaf. Typically, it consists of a line of short cells with poorly developed walls. A layer of dead cells, or *cork*, may form there as well. Finally, the leaf produces enzymes that weaken the separation layer, which then breaks. The leaf may dangle for a brief time, still attached to the stem by its threadlike vascular bundles. Eventually, they, too, break, and the leaf falls off.

The red and yellow colors of autumn leaves result from this gradual separation process. Once the abscission layer has formed, no more minerals or other nutrients flow into the leaf. So its cells die, and their pigments begin to decompose. The green pigment chlorophyll is usually the first to go, revealing the yellows and oranges of the carotenoid pigments.

Leaf Structure

It is no wonder that leaf collections are among childhood's most popular nature projects. Leaves come in a seemingly endless variety of shapes, patterns, and sizes. In fact, no two plant species bear exactly the same leaves. So botanists, like children, use leaves to identify the plants they study. In doing so, they use a variety of terms to classify a leaf's shape, structure, and other visible traits.

Shape. A botanist might begin by looking at a leaf's overall shape. Conifers, for example, have leaves that resemble needles—as in pines, spruce, and fir—or scales, as in junipers. Pine needles tend to be bundled in papery sheaths attached to the stem. The number of needles helps amateur botanists distinguish among different species of conifers. For example, the eastern white pine (*Pinus strobus*) bears needles in clusters of five. Ponderosa pine (*P. ponderosa*) bears clusters of three, and Scotch pine (*P. sylvestris*) bears clusters of two.

Venation. Most other vascular plants have broad, flattened leaves, which botanists distinguish by their vein patterns. The most common pattern is called *pinnate*, meaning "feather-veined." The pinnate leaf has a single large vein, called the midrib, that extends from the petiole through the center of the flattened blade. Smaller veins branch out from either side of the midrib like the barbs of a feather. Common examples of pinnate leaves include those of elm and oak trees.

Many other leaves have a venation pattern called *palmate*. In a palmate leaf, five or more major veins rise from the base of the blade and radiate out to its tip or tips. Familiar examples include the palmate leaves of geraniums, mulberries, and sweet-gum trees.

Both palmate and pinnate leaves have what is called *net venation*. That is, their veins form a web, or network, of veins extending in different directions. By contrast, grasses, irises, and some other plants have leaves with veins that run in the same direction. This is called *parallel venation*. In a parallel-venation leaf, all the veins arise at the leaf base and run, side by side, across the blade to its tip.

In the vascular plants, one more vein pattern can be found—that of the ginkgo tree

| Horse Chestnut | Ash | Honey locust |

A compound leaf is subdivided into leaflets attached to the same stalk. The horse chestnut (left) has a whorled leaf pattern; the ash (center) has an opposite attachment arrangement, while the honey locust (right) has an alternate pattern.

(*Ginkgo biloba*). Many equal-sized veins rise from the ginkgo leaf's base, and fork one or more times as they fan across the leaf blade. This is called *forked venation*.

Arrangement. Botanists also classify leaves as either simple or compound. A simple leaf bears only one leaf blade. A compound leaf is subdivided into two or more separate leaflets that attach to a shared leaf stalk.

When subdividing simple leaves, botanists recognize nearly two dozen distinct shapes. *Palmate lobed leaves*, such as those of a maple, are indented around several major veins that each arise from the leaf base. *Pinnately lobed leaves*—for example, those of oaks—have same-sized indents on either side of the midrib. Other common leaf shapes include *linear* (long and narrow like that of a eucalyptus or willow tree), *ovate* (more or less oval like that of an alder), and *lanceolate* (lance-shaped like that of a chestnut leaf).

Compound leaves, in turn, may be *palmately compound* or *pinnately compound*. The leaflets of a palmately compound leaf radiate from a single point at the base of the leaf stalk. The leaf of a horse chestnut provides a good example of this arrangement. In pinnately compound leaves, a row of leaflets forms on either side of the leaf stalk. Poison sumac is a classic example. Some pinnately compound leaves, such as those of the honey locust, branch a second time. They are called *bipinnately compound* leaves.

Margin outline. Botanists further describe a leaf by the general outline of its margin, or edge.

Leaves with a smooth edge are called *entire*. Those with coarse "teeth" are called either *dentate* or *serrate*. The teeth of dentate leaves point at right angles to the midrib. Those of serrate leaves angle toward the tip, or apex, of the leaf. Leaves with rounded "teeth," or scalloped edges, are called *crenulate*.

Attachment. Finally, plant scientists distinguish leaves by the manner in which they attach to the stem. Leaves can be arranged along the stem in one of three readily recognizable ways: opposite, alternate, or whorled.

Opposite leaves grow out from the stem in pairs, one on each side of the stem, directly across from one another. The leaves of zinnias and maples are two familiar examples. Alternate leaves occur singly along the stem—either in a left-right pattern or in an ascending spiral. Familiar examples include the leaves of elm trees and ficus plants. Whorled leaves form a circle around the stem, in equally spaced groups of three or more. A familiar example is the popular aquarium plant waterwort (*Elatine hexandra*).

Botanists also look to see if a leaf attaches to the stem via a leaf stalk, or petiole. Those that lack such a stalk are called *sessile*. The blade of a sessile leaf attaches directly to the stem, as seen in corn and other grasses.

Nature has mixed and matched these five leaf traits—shape, venation, arrangement (single or compound), margin outline, and attachment to the stem—to create some 250,000 different kinds of leaves. With the help of a plant field guide, these leaf traits can be used to identify nearly any vascular plant on Earth.

HORSETAILS AND CLUB MOSSES

by Jessica Snyder Sachs

The world of 300 million years ago looked much different than it does today. Much of North America and Europe was covered with vast swamps and shallow seas. Rising from the water were great expanses of forests—forests comprised of gigantic trees.

To the modern observer, this prehistoric landscape would look decidedly bizarre. After all, the trees bear no resemblance to oaks or pines or elms. Instead, they look like giant vegetables—colossal spears of broccoli and asparagus, to be exact.

The weird swamp forests of the Carboniferous period were filled with just such primitive vascular plants. These plants had internal conducting tissue to transport water, minerals, and food, enabling them to grow tremendously tall. But few had evolved the innovation we call a seed, and their leaves remained small and scaly.

The dominant trees included 65-foot (20-meter)-tall horsetails called *calamites* (the "asparagus") and 100-foot (30-meter)-tall club mosses called *lepidodendrons* (the "broccoli"). These trees formed a high understory, beneath which grew a dazzling variety of ferns.

These seedless vascular plants first appeared in the Devonian period, about 380 million years ago. They reached their peak in the warm, swampy Carboniferous period, 80 million years later. When cooler, drier conditions arrived, the vast swamp forests disappeared. Conifers and other early seed plants replaced the calamites and lepidodendron trees, whose remains were ultimately transformed into the vast beds of coal upon which we still draw today.

PRIMITIVE SURVIVORS

Fortunately, the curious majesty of calamites and lepidodendrons—in miniature form—survives in the form of modern-day horsetails and club mosses. These easily overlooked plants seldom grow very tall. Although they occur just about everywhere from the Arc-

Only 15 species of horsetails survive to modern times. Most, including the common horsetail above, grow all but unnoticed, tucked away in damp, shady areas.

tic to the tropics, nowhere do they dominate the landscape. Instead, they survive tucked away in small places—mainly wet, shady spots, along a stream or woodland edge or dangling from the dripping canopy of a rain forest.

Horsetails and club mosses are true vascular plants, although they share many traits with the more primitive nonvascular plants (true mosses and liverworts). They reproduce not with seeds, but with spores; they also require water for fertilization. Indeed, like nonvascular plants, horsetails and club mosses have sperm that swim through the water with whiplike tails (flagella). As with all plants, the life cycle of horsetails and ground mosses alternates between a sexual, or gamete-producing, generation, called the *gametophyte*, and an asexual, or spore-producing, generation, called the *sporophyte*. But, like vascular plants, in horsetails and club mosses, the plant we see is the sporophyte. The gametophyte is barely noticeable.

Like other vascular plants, horsetails and club mosses have true leaves, stems, and roots, although these structures are much simpler than they are in the seed plants and flowering plants. In seedless vascular plants, each tiny leaf has just one vein. The roots are small as well, and grow from the plant's stem instead of a primary root. The stems, in turn, lack wood, or secondary growth. So they do not expand in diameter after the first growing season. (Their ancient ancestors did have secondary growth, and so were true trees with woody stems.)

HORSETAILS

More than any other group of plants, the horsetails deserve the name "living fossils." In modern times, they number just 15 species, all of which belong to a single genus—*Equisetum*—that has survived virtually unchanged for 300 million years. *Equisetum* may hold the distinction of being the oldest living plant genus on Earth.

Today *Equisetum* is the only group remaining in the phylum Sphenophyta. The name is derived from the Greek *spheno*, meaning "wedged." Like modern-day horsetails, all the plants in this once-vast group had curiously wedged, or jointed, stems. Among its many now-extinct members were giant vines, leathery shrubs, and giant trees. The horsetail trees, or calamites, dominated the world's forests for nearly 60 million years, from 360 million to 286 million years ago.

Modern-day horsetails can be found on every continent except Australia. At first glance, they resemble rushes, or swamp grass. But closer examination reveals their truly unusual form. Many long, bumpy ribs run the length of their jointed, hollow stems. A long portion of the stem runs underground, as a rhizome, and it gives rise to circles of tiny roots at each joint.

The most common horsetail, *Equisetum arvense*, can be seen along stream banks and in wet meadows across North America and Eurasia. It produces two kinds of aboveground shoots from the same underground rhizome.

The first shoot to appear is deep green, with spirals of feathery branches growing out from each joint of the stem. These are the vegetative shoots. Typically, they appear in early spring, then give way to a very different type of fertile, or spore-producing, shoot.

The spore-producing shoots resemble flesh-colored asparagus sprouts. Their joints give rise to whorls of tiny brown leaves that resemble pointy crowns encircling the stem. The

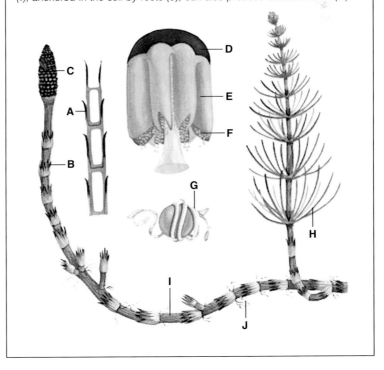

The common horsetail has a hollow, silica-rich stem (A) and leaves reduced to scales (B). The conelike reproductive structure (C) bears clusters of whorled sporangiophores (D), which have saclike sporangia (E) that bear spores (F) attached to their inner surfaces. Changes in humidity cause elators (G) coiled around the spores to uncoil and eject the spores. The rhizome (I), anchored in the soil by roots (J), can also produce a sterile shoot (H).

tip of each fertile shoot bears a conelike structure, called a *strobilus*, which produces spores. Both types of shoots stand between 1 and 4 feet (between 30 and 120 centimeters) high.

The horsetail's branching green stems reminded early Europeans of a horse's tail, earning the plant its common name. American pioneers called them "scouring rushes" for their usefulness in scrubbing out pots and pans. The plant's abrasiveness comes from the glassy mineral silica, which is very abundant in its epidermis, or surface cells.

The giant horsetail (left) can reach 30 feet in height, while the fir club moss (above) rarely grows even 10 inches.

A few kinds of horsetails can reach surprising heights. The giant horsetail of South America, *Equisetum giganteum*, can grow as high as 30 feet (9 meters) if partially supported by other plants. Such height is truly amazing in view of the fact that this plant's stalk is less than 1 inch (2.5 centimeters) in diameter. This is because horsetails—like other living seedless plants—do not grow in width after the first growing season. That is, they produce no wood. Moreover, horsetail stems are largely hollow. A large center cavity fills one-quarter to one-half of the stem. The exceptional strength of the horsetail stem lies in the thick, silica-hardened walls of its epidermal cells.

Horsetails are poisonous to cattle and other livestock, but they have been used in small amounts in many folk medicines. Horsetail tea is still used as an herbal diuretic—a remedy for water retention, or bloating.

Life Cycle of a Horsetail

Horsetails, like all true plants, undergo an alternation of sexual and asexual generations. The visible horsetail plant represents the asexual stage, or sporophyte. It produces spores that germinate into tiny green plants. These are the horsetail's gametophytes, or sexual-stage plants. Most are no larger than a pinhead; the largest are just 0.25 inch (0.6 centimeter) wide.

Each gametophyte has both male and female sex organs—*antheridia* and *archegonia*. When water is abundant, the sperm swim out of the antheridia using whiplike tails. They zero in on the archegonia, guided by hormones that act as a chemical lure. The first sperm to reach each archegonia fertilizes its single egg. The fertilized egg cell then multiplies to produce a new sporophyte. It begins life attached to the gametophyte, which supplies it with food.

Once it develops its own shoots and roots, the horsetail sporophyte detaches from its withering parent and becomes an independent plant. Horsetails also reproduce vegetatively. That is, many new shoots can arise from the nodes along a single underground rhizome.

CLUB MOSSES AND THEIR KIN

Club mosses and their relatives, the spike mosses, are true vascular plants. (True mosses—to which club and spike mosses bear no kinship—are nonvascular.)

A larger number of club mosses than horsetails have survived from their Carboniferous heyday. Remaining are some 400 species of small plants that grow as low creepers or upright herbs. Most are native to tropical mountain forests in South America and Asia. Many of these are *epiphytes*, plants that grow attached to trees, often high in the rain-forest canopy.

More familiar to North Americans are several dozen species of club mosses that grow on the shaded floor of cool woodlands. Scaly or needlelike leaves cover their creeping stems, which form evergreen mats across the ground. The stems fork repeatedly as they grow, producing more and more side branches. Most club mosses also produce upright stems with spore-producing structures (*strobili*) that resemble tiny green pinecones.

The most common of the creeping club mosses is the running pine, or stag's-horn moss (*Lycopodium clavatum*). Its ground stems grow up to 10 feet (3 meters) long. From these stems grow upright spikes, each crowned with three strobili. The stems are covered with deep-green, scalelike leaves.

Among the 700 species of spike mosses is the rain-forest selaginella (above), which grows in the jungles of Malaysia.

The club moss known as ground cedar (*L. complanatum*) is native to Canada and the northern states. It produces fanlike branches that resemble sprigs of juniper with needlelike leaves. Fir club moss (*L. selago*) forms long underground stems (rhizomes) that give rise to upright shoots some 10 inches (25 centimeters) tall. It grows in northern forests, high mountains, and cool, wet woodlands and bogs. The yellowish-gray Alpine club moss (*L. alpinum*) is one of the hardiest plants on Earth, capable of growing under the ice and snow of high mountain peaks and the Arctic tundra.

The name "club moss" is also used to refer to many species that belong in a separate but closely related group, the 700 species of spike mosses (family Selaginellacea). Like true club mosses, spike mosses are small, creeping evergreen plants, with long, thin stems bearing many tiny leaves. Some resemble ferns, with fans of tiny leaflets on long, delicate fronds. Still others form climbing vines, or trail from the branches of trees. In general, their leaves tend to be shiny and deeply colored, with hues ranging from dark green to peacock blue.

As with club mosses, the majority of spike mosses grow in damp forests, from the tropics to the taiga. But others survive in dry, rocky areas, so long as there is sufficient rain to aid in reproduction.

The most familiar spike moss is the lesser club moss (*Selaginella selaginoides*). Found in northern forests and bogs, its branches trail along the ground to form an evergreen mat of fernlike fronds. From this mat grow upright yellow-green strobili some 3 inches (7.5 centimeters) tall. The similar rock selaginella (*S. rupestris*) of North America has scaly leaves and grows on rocks or in sand. Among the most unusual of the spike mosses is the resurrection plant (*S. lepidophylla*) of the American Southwest. When dry, this aptly named plant forms a gray, lifeless ball; following a rain, the plant "resurrects"—unfurling itself and turning green.

Life Cycle of a Club Moss

Club mosses and spike mosses share a similar lifestyle. Spores arise in the conelike strobili, at the base of the tiny leaves. The spores of club mosses produce a hermaphroditic plant, with male and female parts on the same plant. Spike mosses produce two kinds of spores, which germinate into male and female plants.

In most North American species, the gametophyte grows underground, absorbing nutrition with the help of *mycorrhizal* (symbiotic) fungi. When mature, the antheridia open to release sperm, which swim to eggs in a nearby archegonium—female sex organ. The fertilized egg cell divides to produce the first green shoot of the new sporophyte generation. The young plant remains attached to the underground gametophyte for several weeks or more. During this time, the "parent" continues to absorb nutrients from the soil, passing them on to its growing "daughter." Eventually the new generation produces roots of its own and becomes independent.

Something about the feathery lace of a fern leaf evokes the peace of a quiet woodland and the comfort of a shady garden. Of course, there is no one fern, but more than 10,000 kinds. Indeed, ferns are second only to flowering plants in abundance and diversity.

Yet the array of ferns we see today is a mere shadow of a former glory. Like other seedless vascular plants, ferns reached their peak of diversity in the Carboniferous period, some 300 million years ago. Ferns were by far the most-abundant plants in that period—a time sometimes called the "Age of Ferns." A great many species have since disappeared. Among them, the ancient, treelike seed ferns, which may have given rise to the first flowering plants.

DISTRIBUTION

Despite these great extinctions, ferns have remained abundant. They are especially common to the warm, wet tropics. In fact, it is estimated that 1 acre (0.4 hectare) of tropical rain forest harbors up to 100 different species of

Ferns flourish in moist climates. Sword ferns (above, foreground) grow in abundance in the temperate rain forests of the Pacific Northwest.

ferns. Their numbers gradually decrease with distance from the equator. The small Central American country of Costa Rica, for example, is home to more than 900 species, while fewer than 400 occur north of Mexico. Most northern ferns grow in damp, shady forests. A few even survive on the frigid Arctic tundra. Because they thrive in low light, ferns also grow indoors. In fact, they are among the most easily cared for and popular of houseplants.

Most modern-day ferns are modest in size—with fronds 1 to 2 feet (30 to 60 centimeters) long. The smallest species are filmy water ferns less than 0.5 inch (1.25 centimeters) long. The largest include the so-called "tree ferns," with upright stems up to 80 feet (24 meters) tall.

About one-third of all fern species grow as *epiphytes*, or "air" plants, dangling from the trunks, branches, and crowns of trees. These ferns are not parasites, but merely anchor themselves to the trees, drawing minerals from rainwater and photosynthesizing their own food.

Unexpected Environments

Although most ferns thrive in moist, shady places, some can withstand prolonged periods of dry weather—and even drought. These tough ferns are often the first plants to grow in disturbed fields, where they help break up the soil and prepare it for larger plants. Other ferns have evolved in ways that allow them to survive in very "unfernlike" environments. The bracken ferns (*Pteridium* species) of North America, for example, grow fully exposed to sunlight in meadows and the open prairie.

Still other ferns grow only on bare rock and cliff faces, where they root in cracks and crevices. These ferns, together with many of those that grow dangling from other plants (epiphytes), share a need to conserve water and protect themselves from strong, direct sunlight. Typically, they possess an extra-thick layer of waxy cuticle on their stems and leaves. Some create their own shade with a covering of hairlike filaments or scales. The toughest of these species are called "sun ferns," and do not require any shade as mature plants.

The water ferns constitute a very different group, adapted to lead a rootless life floating on the surface of ponds and puddles. These plants include the miniature clovers (*Marsilea*), water spangles (*Salvinia*), and mosquito ferns (*Azolla*). As the name suggests, the miniature clovers produce four clover-shaped leaves, which float on the water surface above long, slender stalks. The simple, rounded leaves of the water spangle likewise float on the surface, but in groups of three. One leaf of each trio disintegrates into a mass of white filaments that bear the plant's spores.

Surprisingly, water ferns are most common in dry regions rather than in areas that are wet year-round. They tend to appear suddenly right after a heavy rain, in a temporary pond or puddle. They grow quickly, as they need to complete their life cycle before the water evaporates. Most water ferns produce especially tough spores. Those of some species can lie dormant for 100 years or more.

THE FERN BODY

In form, ferns are more complex than other seedless plants (horsetails, club mosses, and nonvascular plants), but simpler than the more highly evolved seed and flowering plants. Most ferns grow from underground stems, called *rhizomes*. A few species of ferns produce vertical stems supported by a girdle of aboveground roots. These plants are called *tree ferns*, although they have no woody tissue, and so are not real trees.

Leaves

The visible portion of most ferns consists entirely of leaves. The young fern leaves begin life as curled stalks, commonly called *fiddleheads*, that push out of the ground. The leaf gradually uncoils from the tip down, spreading as it lengthens.

Clearly, the fronds of a fern are among nature's most-elaborate leaves. A typical fern leaf has a long, central *petiole* (leaf branch) with many side-branching leaflets, called *pinnae*. In many species, the pinnae are themselves divided into lobes or even more side-branching leaflets called *pinnules*. These in turn may be divided yet again and again, with the final leaflets being as small and delicate as hairs. A few species of fern have simple leaves, meaning that they consist of a single petiole and blade. But this blade is deeply lobed to give the frond the appearance of a feathery, compound leaf.

The purpose of all this subdividing is to increase the leaf's surface area, thus maximizing the leaf's ability to capture solar energy even in dim light. As a result, ferns can thrive in places too shady for other plants to grow. In fact, most ferns require at least partial shade to survive.

As in other vascular plants, the upper surface of

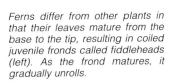

Ferns differ from other plants in that their leaves mature from the base to the tip, resulting in coiled juvenile fronds called fiddleheads (left). As the frond matures, it gradually unrolls.

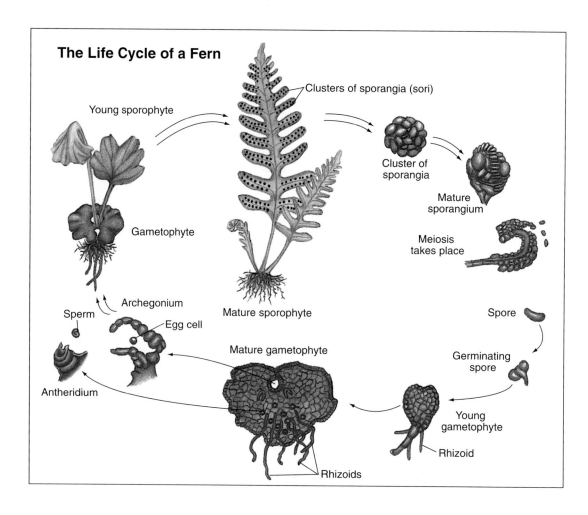

The Life Cycle of a Fern

Young sporophyte

Clusters of sporangia (sori)

Gametophyte

Cluster of sporangia

Mature sporangium

Meiosis takes place

Archegonium

Sperm

Egg cell

Mature sporophyte

Spore

Mature gametophyte

Germinating spore

Antheridium

Young gametophyte

Rhizoid

Rhizoids

the fern leaf is intensely green. Its cells are crowded with photosynthetic chlorophyll pigments. The underside of the leaf is pierced by microscopic *stomata* (pores) that open to allow carbon dioxide to flow into the leaf.

Roots

The roots of a mature fern are typically thin and wiry. They do not grow from a primary root, but arise directly from the fern's underground stem, a type of root called *adventitious*. Ferns do produce a true primary root early in life, but it disintegrates while the plant is still young. In this way, ferns are intermediate between the other seedless plants, which lack primary roots, and the more highly evolved seed and flowering plants, all of which possess them. Like true roots, the fern's adventitious roots not only anchor the plant in place, they also absorb water and dissolved minerals from the soil.

The roots of certain tropical ferns have beautiful "hairy" roots covered with locks of silky, golden-brown "fur." Many of these ferns are epiphytes, growing from the branches of trees and other large plants. Their many root hairs help them catch rainwater and absorb dissolved minerals.

LIFE CYCLE OF A FERN

The life cycle of a typical fern features both a sexual phase and an asexual phase, or generation. This type of life cycle is true of all plants, but it can be seen most clearly in the ferns. In all other plants, one or the other generation is small and grows attached to the other generation, making it barely noticeable. Only in the ferns can both the sexual and asexual generations be seen living independently of each other in nature.

The fern's sexual generation, or *gametophyte*, begins with the germination of a simple spore consisting of a single cell. In moist, warm conditions, the cell begins to multiply, cracking open the spore's hard wall. Emerging from it is a simple root that attaches to the soil. A single green mother cell produces the rest of the plant. Typically, the fern's sexual generation resembles a liverwort, a simple plant that lies flat against its growing surface. Depending on the species, it takes the shape of a heart or a ribbon.

The cells across the top of the fern gametophyte carry on photosynthesis. The bottom of its flattened body produces a mat of fine, hairlike cells, called *rhizoids*, that draw water and minerals from the soil.

Also on the bottom surface are two types of microscopic sex organs: the *antheridia*, which produce sperm; and the *archegonia*, which produce eggs. The presence of water—often in the form of rain or dew—triggers the fern's sex organs to open. Like those of other seedless plants, the sperm have whiplike tails, or flagella. They actively swim through the water to penetrate the archegonia, each of which holds a single egg. At this point begins the second generation—the *sporophyte*, or asexual plant.

The young sporophyte does not yet resemble a mature fern. It develops one true root, which penetrates downward, and a single, simple leaf that grows upward. (At this stage, the sporophyte remains attached to its parent, the gametophyte.) A series of larger and more-complex leaves grow from the base of the first leaf. Then the first fiddleheads appear and unfurl into mature fronds. Their bases give rise to a creeping underground stem, the rhizome. About this time, the parent gametophyte disintegrates, as does the first primary root.

The mature sporophyte has the familiar feathery form that most people recognize as typical of a fern. Ordinarily, this asexual generation can live for a surprisingly long time. Most of the familiar ferns of North America produce new leaves from their underground stems each spring. These leaves may die back the following winter. But many species—including the aptly named holly fern (*Polystichum*)—remain lush and green year-round, even when covered with a layer of snow and ice.

Fern Spores

When mature, ferns produce spores, typically on the underside of their leaves. Microscopic, the spores lie within round spore cases, themselves no larger than specks of dust. The spore cases (*sporangia*), in turn, lie in clusters called *sori*—grainy patches or lines, colored yellow, orange, brown, or black. In some ferns,

A mature fern bears spore cases, or sporangia, on the undersurface of its fronds (above). The sporangia often occur in clusters called sori.

the sori are themselves enclosed by special outgrowths of the leaf called *indusia*.

In most ferns, all the leaves can produce spores. But a few species produce special spore-producing stalks separate from their vegetative leaves. Examples include the southern grape ferns (*Botrychium*) and adder's-tongues (*Ophioglossum*) of North America. Such ferns produce just one leaf a year: it consists of a normal blade and a long, fertile petiole with two rows of spore capsules. In *Botrychium*, the spore capsules resemble clusters of grapes, giving this fern its common name. (An interesting aside: the adder's-tongue has the highest known number of chromosomes of any living organism—more than 1,200. By contrast, humans have 46.)

When mature, the dustlike spore capsules scatter to the wind. The wall of each spore capsule has a "zipper" consisting of a row of cells

Whisk ferns are not true ferns, but close relatives to them. Like true ferns, they lack seeds, reproducing instead by spores. Whisk ferns also lack leaves and roots. In essence, these plants are all stem, making them the simplest of all living vascular plants.

One portion of the whisk fern's stem does the work of a root. Colorless, it grows below ground, creeping just beneath the surface of the soil. Anchoring it in place are many hairlike threads called rhizoids. The green, visible portion of the stem does the photosynthesizing. Green scales growing from the sides of the stem help increase the stem's surface area, and so maximize photosynthesis. But they are not true leaves. The whisk fern's spore-producing structures, or sporangia, grow from its stem tips.

Fewer than a dozen species of whisk fern survive today. Botanists place them in two groups, or genera. The most familiar is *Psilotum*, called the moa plant in Hawaii.

Psilotum's aerial stem divides repeatedly into many small branches of equal size. This gives the plant the appearance of an upside-down whisk broom. Its stem scales are very small, barely visible. Its sporangia turn bright yellow when mature. Several species of *Psilotum* grow in tropical and semitropical areas as far north as Florida, Louisiana, and Texas. A few of these are sometimes grown farther north—as indoor houseplants.

Psilotum's only living relatives are a few species in the genus *Tmesipteris*. Very difficult to cultivate, *Tmesipteris* grows wild as an epiphyte, dangling from trunks of tree ferns in the tropical forests of Australia, New Zealand, and various islands of Oceania. The green scales on its stems are larger than those of the moa plant, giving them the outward appearance of true leaves. The rootlike portion of the plant's stem attaches itself to the roughened surface of the tree ferns on which it lives.

that forcibly contract and expand when exposed to dry air. This tears open the capsule and discharges the inner spores with a powerful blast. In this way, a single fern can fill the air around it with millions of spores. Yet only a fraction actually germinate to produce new plants.

By design, the spores of most ferns are long-distance travelers. They can be blown across entire oceans before reaching a suitable place to germinate. Fern spores can also remain dormant for many years, even a century, before germinating. When they do, the complex life cycle begins again.

Unusual Life Cycles

Many ferns can also reproduce vegetatively—producing clones of themselves from various parts of the parent plant. A familiar example is the walking fern (*Camptosorus*), which takes root and produces new plants wherever the parent's arching fronds touch the ground.

The resurrection fern (left), like all epiphytic ferns, grows on the trunks or branches of trees and derives its nourishment from rainwater and from its own photosynthesis.

Ferns native to tropical and subtropical climates add a certain exotic decorative element to many offices and homes. As a rule, ferns require very little care and need only low levels of light, making them ideal houseplants.

Other fern species produce special filaments called *gemmae* that break off to produce colonies around the parent plant. They can also be carried away by running water or by a passing insect to start new colonies some distance from their parents. Crickets, in particular, help distribute the tiny gemmae of certain ferns.

A few unusual fern species grow only as small, ribbonlike gametophytes. These plants never produce the familiar feathery fronds of the sporophyte generation. Instead, they multiply solely from gemmae, which scatter to create genetically identical colonies of still more gametophytes. Examples include the unusual bristle ferns (*Trichomanes*) and shoestring ferns (*Vittaria*), which grow in the cool, wet caves of western Ireland and the Appalachian Mountains in the eastern United States.

Still other ferns—such as the maidenhair—have developed an unusual life cycle known as *apogamy*. The maidenhair's heart-shaped gametophyte (sexual-stage plant) does not produce sex organs. Instead, the sporophyte (the asexu-al-generation plant) simply sprouts from the places where the sex organs would normally have been. As a result, maidenhair ferns do not need water to reproduce. Another advantage to apogamy is that the fern quickly grows through its delicate gametophyte stage. As a result, it can survive and multiply in areas considered too dry for most other ferns.

ECONOMIC IMPORTANCE

Like other seedless plants, ferns are little used for food or building material. Tree ferns are used locally as lumber in the tropics, and fiddleheads are sometimes eaten as vegetables. (Large amounts can be poisonous and may cause cancer.) More than anything else, people use ferns as ornamental plants for the house and garden. Among the most popular are the hardy, easy-care maidenhair (*Adiantum*) and holly ferns (*Polystichum*); the dramatic, 4-foot (1.2-meter)-tall ostrich fern (*Matteuccia*); and the delicate lady ferns (*Athyrium*).

CONIFERS

by Jessica Snyder Sachs

The first tender green plants appeared in an age when the world was a warm, swampy place and temperatures changed little from season to season. Although some plants grew tremendous in size, they remained simple in form. They reproduced with the help of water.

Then, some 280 million years ago, the world's climate underwent vast changes. The air grew dry, and the great swamps disappeared. Glaciers advanced over much of the land. In the Animal Kingdom, amphibians declined, largely replaced by tougher-skinned reptiles. In the Plant Kingdom, the tender seedless plants gave way to the *gymnosperms*, or "naked-seed plants."

By the time the first dinosaurs appeared during the Triassic period (248 million to 213 million years ago), the seedless swamp forests were all but gone. In their place were vast forests of gymnosperms such as conifers, cycads, and ginkgoes.

The most successful of these were the conifers. Some of the first were trees with long, strap-shaped leaves. Others resembled the modern-day Norfolk Island pine, with whorled, flattened branches and needlelike leaves. These were soon followed by redwoods, cypresses, junipers, and firs.

All the gymnosperms shared a great new innovation—the seed. Within each seed lay a fully formed young plant, or embryo, along with a generous supply of stored food from its parent. A tough outer covering, or coat, protected the seed and its precious cargo. So sheltered and supplied with food, the young seedling had a

Conifers are seed plants that characteristically bear cones and evergreen needles or scales. Douglas firs (above) reach towering heights in the Pacific Northwest.

much greater chance for survival than did the vulnerable spores of the seedless plants.

Seed plants also shared another great advantage. They did not need water for fertilization, thanks to another remarkable innovation: the pollen grain.

A TOUGHER PLANT

Of all the early seed plants, conifers were the best equipped for survival. Their thin, leathery leaves and tough, corky trunks protected their bodies from drying in summer and from freezing in winter. Many could even survive the forest fires that became more frequent as the land grew parched. As other early seed plants faltered, the conifers grew ever more successful.

Today conifers make up the largest division of gymnosperm plants. Three smaller and less-familiar divisions are the cycads (*Cycadophyta*), the unusual gnetophytes (*Gnetophyta*), and a single species of ginkgo (*Ginkgophyta*). (See "Ginkgo and Cycads," pages 94–97.) In total, modern-day gymnosperms number between 800 and 1,000 species. More than half of these, some 550, are conifers.

As the name gymnosperm, or "naked seed," clearly states, the seeds of these plants are not enclosed by a ripened ovary, or fruit. Instead, they lie exposed on the surface of a reproductive structure such as the bracts of a woody cone.

The development of fruit came later—an "invention" of the *angiosperms*, or flowering plants. This and other innovations enabled the flowering plants to surpass the gymnosperms in number and diversity during the Cretaceous period, 144 million to 65 million years ago. Nevertheless, the hardy conifers have remained relatively abundant, especially in cold regions where few other plants can grow successfully.

VARIED FORMS

Most conifers are trees. They include the world's tallest, largest, and smallest trees, all of which happen to grow in California. They are, respectively, the 350-foot (106-meter)-tall redwood, *Sequoia sempervirens*; the 4.4-million-pound (1.9-million-kilogram) giant sequoia, or "big tree," *Sequoiadendron giganteum*; and, tying for smallest, the 8-inch (20-centimeter)-tall shore pine, *Pinus contorta*, and natural Gowen cypress, *Cupressus goveniana*. The shore pine and Gowen cypress grow in the weird pygmy forests of the northern coast, just west of their towering cousins. The world's oldest trees are also conifers: the 5,000-year-old bristlecone pines (*Pinus longaeva*) that grow in the arid mountains of the North American Southwest.

The conifers also include a number of creeping bushes and upright shrubs, the most successful being the junipers. Like all conifers, junipers produce secondary growth, or wood, beginning in their second year.

The leaves of most conifers are leathery, long, and slender. Examples include the long, stiff "needles" of the pines, firs, and spruces. Typically, the needles grow in spirals around each young stem. In some species, the needles arise singly from the stem. In many, they grow in bundles of 2 to 10 needles.

Other conifers—such as cypresses, cedars, and some of the junipers—have small, scaly leaves that cover their stems like green armor. The unusual monkey-puzzle tree (*Araucaria araucana*) of Chile produces leaves that look

The conifers include the world's largest, smallest, tallest, and oldest trees. Few specimens survive long enough to reach the age achieved by the fallen sequoia above.

like thick, triangular wedges. Whatever their shape, conifer leaves are all designed to minimize water loss. Their leathery feel comes from an extra-thick, nearly waterproof covering of waxy *cuticle*. To further minimize water loss, the leaf's *stomata* (air pores) lie in sunken pits that reduce contact with dry air.

Virtually all conifers are evergreen. That is, they keep their needlelike leaves from season to season. Exceptions include the larches, bald cypresses, and dawn redwood. They drop their needles each fall, sprouting new ones the following spring. Most conifers produce their

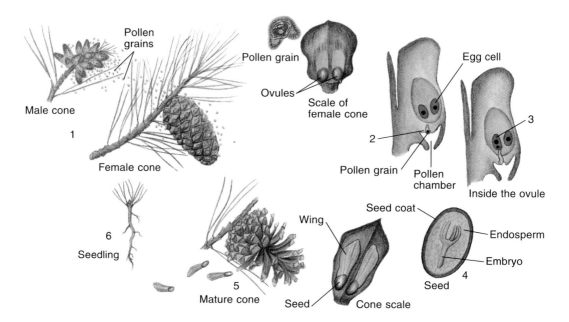

The sexual-reproduction process of a conifer begins when pollen grains from the male cone are carried by the wind to the female cone (1), where they enter the pollen chamber (2). A pollen tube grows from the pollen grain into the ovule, through which sperm travels to the egg cell. After the sperm cell and egg cell unite (3), the fertilized egg develops into a seed containing an embryo and an endosperm (4). Once the cone matures, it opens, and the wind scatters the winged seeds (5). The fallen seeds germinate, and a new plant begins to grow (6).

seeds in woody cones. These are not the same as fruits. A fruit is a ripened ovary, enclosing the seeds within it. The conifer cone, by contrast, consists of an open spiral of woody scales. On top of each scale lies an exposed, or "naked," seed, which eventually breaks free from its perch. A few conifers—notably the junipers and yews—produce fleshy cones designed to attract birds and other animals, which then distribute the seeds in their droppings.

In addition to seed cones, conifers have smaller cones that produce pollen. Often the seed and pollen cones grow on separate branches of the same tree. In yews, they are found on separate trees.

The wood of conifers and other gymnosperms is often called "softwood." On the whole, it is simpler and less dense in structure than that of flowering trees such as oak or maple. This is because gymnosperms lack the complex mixture of vascular tissues and fibers found in the stems of the more highly evolved flowering plants.

Conifer softwood supplies the bulk of the world's lumber, as well as most of the pulp used in making paper. The Douglas fir (*Pseudotsuga menziesii*) is North America's most valuable timber, logged throughout western Canada and the United States. The quality of pinewood is not as high as that of Douglas fir. But what they lack in quality, pine trees make up in quantity. With nearly 100 species, pine is the world's most abundant and widely distributed conifer. Some pine species make fine lumber. Others are made into utility poles and fence posts.

Spruces and true firs are also harvested for timber. A millennium ago, the cedars of the Mediterranean supplied the world's most valuable wood, until overcutting reduced the majestic cedar forests to scattered patches. Many conifers are also grown in nurseries, as seedlings for reforestation or as ornamental plants for the garden. Not to be forgotten is that always-popular seasonal item, the Christmas tree—traditionally a balsam or Douglas fir.

DISTRIBUTION

Conifers can be found on every continent but Antarctica. As mentioned, they are most abundant in cooler regions—throughout the Northern Hemisphere as well as tropical mountains. Conifers are especially suited to regions with freezing winters and dry summers, where their leathery leaves and heavy bark give them an advantage over more-tender trees. Thanks to their tough bark, some conifers such as red-woods can withstand fires that clear away other trees. Some conifers even require fires to open their tightly closed seed cones.

At the extremes of cold weather—on the slopes of high mountains and within the Arctic Circle—conifers often grow in large, pure stands. The best examples include the dense pine and spruce forests of northern Canada. So tightly packed are the trees in these forests that a hiker would find it all but impossible to pass through without a chain saw. At lower latitudes and altitudes, conifers grow in mixed forests, scattered among flowering trees such as oaks, maples, elms, and dogwoods.

The most widely distributed and familiar conifers are the pines and junipers, abundant throughout most of Eurasia and North America. Other familiar conifers include spruces, firs, larches, hemlocks, and cedars. As mentioned, the great redwood forests of the Pacific Northwest are home to the largest and tallest of all the world's trees.

The lesser-known conifers of the Southern Hemisphere include podocarpus, kauri, and rimu. These trees tend to grow only in scattered patches or hidden among flowering trees in mixed mountain forests.

LIFE CYCLE OF A CONIFER

To understand the great success of the conifers is to understand the evolution of the seed and the complex life cycle that produces it. The life cycle of the pine well illustrates that of most conifers.

First, bear in mind that all plants alternate between an asexual, spore-producing generation, called the *sporophyte*, and a sexual, gamete-producing generation, called the *gametophyte*. As in other vascular plants, the conifer sporophyte is the larger of the two generations—taking the form we recognize as a tree. In fact, the conifer's sexual gametophytes are so small that a microscope is needed to glimpse their form. Only those of the flowering plants are smaller.

The pine tree produces its spores in two types of cones. The larger, woody cones produce female spores, or *megaspores*. They are not visible to the naked eye, but lie hidden inside the cone's woody scales in structures called

ovules. Each scale contains one ovule, inside of which a megaspore germinates to produce a tiny female gametophyte (the sexual generation).

Each female gametophyte has several egg structures called *archegonia*. Over several months to a year, each produces a single egg. When the eggs are ready—typically in spring—the surrounding ovule produces a sticky liquid. This drips from a tiny opening at the ovule's tip.

Meanwhile, on another branch of the tree, the pollen cones are reaching maturity. Like seed cones, the pollen cones produce spores. The difference lies in the fact that the pollen cones produce many more—millions and millions more than seed cones do. Each male spore can germinate into a tiny male gametophyte called a *pollen grain*. Inside the grain, the ga-

The unusual appearance of the monkey-puzzle tree (below)—a tree native to South America—has made the conifer a popular ornamental tree in the United States.

metophyte produces two sperm cells. Unlike the sperm of seedless plants, these do not swim.

Sometime in spring, the pollen cone opens, releasing millions of pollen grains to the wind. So great is the release of pine pollen that it often covers woodland ponds and other surfaces with a thick yellow scum or dust. Eventually, pollen blows onto the surface of a female cone. Some of it reaches the gluey liquid at the tips of the ovules. As the liquid dries, it pulls the pollen into the neck of the ovule.

Now the pollen grain continues its development. It produces a tiny, hollow pollen tube, which grows through the tissue of the ovule to the egg. The sperm cells travel down the tube and enter the egg cell. One reaches the egg cell's nucleus and fuses with it. Fertilization is achieved.

It is important to note that fertilization in conifers and other seed plants does not require water. Instead of swimming to the eggs through water, the sperm cells of the conifer are delivered by the wind-borne pollen grains and their tiny pollen tubes. As a result, conifers and other seed plants can reproduce sexually in conditions too dry for the fertilization of seedless plants.

After fusing with the sperm cell, the fertilized egg divides to form a tiny embryo—a new plant, or *sporophyte generation*. Its embryonic stem is called the *epicotyl*. One end of the epicotyl develops embryonic leaves, called *cotyledons*. The other end develops an embryonic root, called the *radicle*.

As the embryo forms, the ovule surrounding it hardens to form the seed coat. In between the seed coat and the embryo are the remains of the gametophyte, which serve as a ready supply of food. In this way, every conifer seed contains three distinct generations: a seed coat produced by the "grandmother" seed cone, a food supply provided by the "mother" gametophyte, and finally the "daughter" embryo.

In pines and most other conifers, the seed coat forms a thin, flattened "wing" at one end. So equipped, each seed is ready to fly away from its cone, which by now has opened its scales. If and when the seed finds a suitable spot, it will germinate to produce a seedling, and perhaps eventually a tree.

Secondary Growth

In their first year of growth, conifers grow primarily in length. They produce a stem, leaves, branches, and roots by expanding from growing tips called *apical meristems*.

During their second season of growth, conifers, like other woody plants, begin to expand in width. This is called *secondary growth*. It takes place in a cylinder of special growth tissue called the *vascular cambium*.

Secondary growth is simpler in conifers and other gymnosperms than it is in the angiosperms, or flowering plants. In gymnosperms, the vascular cambium forms a cylinder through the plant's stem, branches, and main roots. The inside edge of the vascular cambium produces secondary *xylem*, or wood. (Xylem is made up of the long, hollow remains of dead cells called *tracheids* that conduct water through the plant.)

The vascular cambium produces more and more xylem each growing season. The xylem produced early in the growing season consists of larger, thinner-walled tracheids than those formed late in the season. As a result, each year's growth forms alternating light and dark rings through the wood of the tree trunk. In the science called dendrochronology, such "growth rings" are used to determine the age of fossils.

Vast stands of ponderosa, or yellow, pines (above) are found in the western United States. These trees are the most valuable source of lumber in the Rocky Mountains.

The Sitka is the largest species of spruce. Although native to the western coast of North America, huge plantation forests of Sitka spruces have been established in Britain (above) and other locales where maritime climates prevail.

The outer edge of the vascular cambium produces *phloem*, the long, tapering cells that conduct food up and down through the plant. As it expands in thickness, the phloem forms the inner layer of the tree's bark. Yet another growth area, just outside the vascular cambium, forms the corky outer bark. This outer growth area is called the *cork cambium*.

The wood and bark tissue also contain spaces surrounded by cells that secrete a sticky substance called resin, or sap. These are the resin ducts. When the wood or bark near a duct suffers a wound, the sticky resin flows out to form a bandage of sorts. This process also helps protect the inside of the tree from attack by harmful insects and fungal disease.

THE DIVERSITY OF CONIFERS

Botanists group the modern-day conifers into seven families. The largest by far is Pinaceae, that of the pines and their close relatives—the spruces, firs, larches, hemlocks, and cedars. These are the conifers most familiar to North Americans. All have long, needlelike leaves, woody cones, and winged seeds.

The cypresses, arborvitae, and junipers form the family Cupressaceae. Their leaves tend to be scaly in form, tightly hugging the branches on which they grow, to form broad, flattened fronds. With more than 50 species, the junipers are especially widespread, covering much of the Northern Hemisphere. Also found in North America is the yew family, Taxaceae.

The less-abundant and less-familiar conifers of the Southern Hemisphere include the podocarpus (family Podocarpaceae), with their unusual yellow wood and brightly colored, fleshy scales; and the damars (family Araucariaceae), with their massive seed cones.

Pines

Pines are among the most common and widely distributed of all trees, with 100 species. Most grow naturally in the Northern Hemisphere, although they have now been introduced to all parts of the world. Pines are recognized by their bundled evergreen needles, which grow at the tips of short shoots. A papery sheath wraps around the base of each cluster, which usually contains two to five needles, depending on the species. The needles generally remain on the tree several years, usually two to four.

Pine trees not only survive, but thrive, in some of the most-difficult growing conditions. They prefer dry, rocky, nutrient-poor soil. They can tolerate drought, but need full sunlight and clean air for healthy growth and reproduction. Their chief value is their wood, used for both lumber and paper pulp. Pine trees also yield turpentine, resin, oils, and wood tars. Some species produce edible seeds called pine nuts, or piñons.

The stately eastern white pine (*Pinus strobus*) is the tallest tree in the eastern states, reaching heights of 170 feet (52 meters). Its cones grow up to 8 inches (20 centimeters) long, and its leaf bundles contain five needles. The Ponderosa, or western yellow, pine (*P. ponderosa*) is the most valuable timber tree in the Rocky Mountains. It grows to some 200 feet (60 meters) in height, with three long needles in each leaf bundle. As mentioned, the bristlecone pine (*P. longaeva*) of the Rocky Mountains is the oldest known tree. A stand of bristlecone pines in the Rockies of eastern Nevada contains several trees more than 3,000 years old—the oldest specimen among them is nearly 5,000 years old. The largest species is the sugar pine (*P. lambertiana*) of California, growing to heights of more than 230 feet (70 meters), with a trunk some 10 feet (3 meters) in diameter.

The slash pine (*P. elliotii*) is the most important conifer in Central America. The Scotch pine, which grows throughout Europe and Siberia, has reddish-orange bark and bears dark bluish-green needles in clusters of two. The Aleppo, or Jerusalem pine, is native to the Mediterranean, where it has been an important source of turpentine, tar, and rosin for thousands of years. The hauntingly beautiful Japanese black pine (*P. thunbergii*) is known the world over from paintings on Oriental pottery.

Junipers

The junipers are second to pines in number and range, with about 50 species of evergreen trees or shrubs. They, too, are native to the Northern Hemisphere, although now cultivated worldwide. The leaves of the mature juniper are small, scaly, and highly scented with aromatic oils. Its seed cones are fleshy and berrylike with a waxy covering.

Common juniper (*Juniperus communis*) grows as a sprawling shrub in rocky areas. The fruity cone of this species is used to give a bittersweet flavor to foods and beverages. This species, along with the creeping juniper (*J. horizontalis*), has been developed into popular ornamental ground covers and shrubs. The species of juniper commonly known as the eastern red cedar (*Juniperus virginiana*) is valued for its fragrant wood, which is used in the making of cabinets, fence posts, and pencils.

Spruces

Spruces are pyramid-shaped conifers, with circles of branches that become progressively shorter toward the crown of the tree. Their bark is thin and scaly. Their leaves arise singly from the main branches, each on its own peglike stalk. The seed cones droop downward from the tips of the branches.

Spruces are important timber trees. Although their wood is not particularly strong, it is light, and this makes it ideal for ship masts, planks, and oars. The wood is also resonant, or able to vibrate with sound, making it useful for sounding boards in pianos, violins, and other string instruments.

About 40 species of spruces grow in the Northern Hemisphere. They are most abundant in far-northern regions such as Siberia and Canada, where they form vast, tightly packed forests. Among the most common are black

In a cherished holiday tradition, a freshly cut conifer is brought indoors, its branches are adorned with lights and ornaments, and gifts are placed beneath it.

The largest tree trunk in the world—its circumference exceeds 138 feet—reportedly belongs to the Montezuma cypress (above) in Mexico. As a rule, most species of cypresses are noted more for their height than for their girth.

spruce (*Picea mariana*) and white spruce (*P. glauca*), both valued for paper pulp and timber. The cones of black spruce are purple; those of white spruce, brown. Another timber spruce is the Engelmann (*P. engelmannii*) of western North America. The Colorado spruce (*P. pungens*) has become a popular ornamental, valued for its bluish-green leaves. The deep-green Norway spruce, although native to Europe, is now grown in North America for timber.

Firs

Firs have a striking pyramid shape, similar to that of spruces, with which they are sometimes confused. They can be distinguished by their needles, which do not grow from peglike stalks (as do those of spruces), but directly from the main branch from bases shaped like suction cups. Older branches are marked by circular scars in places where needles have fallen. The cones are held upright on short, woody spikes that remain on the branch after the mature cone falls apart.

Of the 40 to 50 species of firs, 10 are native to North America, primarily west of the Rocky Mountains. Several of these grow more than 200 feet (60 meters) tall. These towering giants include the white fir (*Abies concolor*), the noble fir (*A. nobilis*), the California red fir (*A. magnifica*), and the Pacific silver fir (*A. amabilis*). Few are used for lumber or paper pulp, since the wood of true fir is inferior to that of spruce or pine. North America's classic "Christmas tree" is the balsam fir of the eastern states and provinces. It can grow to up to 60 feet (18 meters) when mature, but is usually harvested at "living room" height.

Douglas Firs

The six species of Douglas firs (genus *Pseudotsuga*) are distinct from the true firs (genus *Abies*). Douglas firs can be recognized by their distinctive yellow-green or blue-green needles. Each needle is long and flat, with a groove down its center and a short stalk at its base. They grow in spirals attached directly to the tree's branches. The seed cones of the Douglas fir are long and slender, and hang from the underside of its branches.

Douglas firs grow throughout western North America and eastern Asia. They are named after their discoverer, Scottish botanist

David Douglas. (Douglas found many new animal and plant species when he explored British Columbia in the 1820s and 1830s.) As mentioned previously, Douglas firs are the most-important timber trees in North America. They are harvested and grown throughout the Pacific Northwest, where they reach heights of 330 feet (100 meters), with widths of 15 feet (4.5 meters) around the base of the trunk.

Douglas firs do not begin producing seeds until they are about 25 years old. Thereafter, they produce huge crops of cones every five to seven years. The long, drooping cones mature in one season and drop intact to the forest floor.

Larches

Larches are one of the few nonevergreen conifers. They lose their needlelike leaves each fall. An attractive light green, the short needles are considerably softer than those of other conifers. They grow in thick clusters of 10 to 30 needles on the tips of short spurs on branches and the tree's trunk. They also grow singly, in circles around young green twigs.

The larch's overall shape is that of a tapering cone. Its seed cones often hang from the tree for several years before falling to the ground. Larch wood is strong, hard, and heavy, and has long been used for telephone poles, mine braces, and railroad ties. Scientists recognize 10 to 12 species of larches, all of them native to the cooler parts of the Northern Hemisphere. One species, *Larix griffithi*, grows only in the Himalayas. The most widely distributed American larch is the tamarack, or eastern larch (*L. laricina*), distinguished by its gray to reddish-brown bark. Tamaracks mature slowly, growing up to 70 feet (21 meters) tall over a life span of 100 to 200 years. Their western cousin is the western larch (*L. occidentalis*) of the Pacific Northwest, which grows slightly faster and taller. Popular ornamental larches include the domesticated Japanese larch (*L. leptolepis*) and European larch (*L. decidua*).

Cedars

Three of the four living species of true cedars are native to the Mediterranean. Their fragrant, red-tinged wood was so valued in ancient times that cedars were all but annihilated thousands of years ago. Today they survive only in scattered groves. Cedars grow to be massive trees with thick trunks and gigantic crowns of irregularly shaped branches. A smooth, dark-gray bark covers the trunk of young cedars. With age, it turns brown and becomes deeply fissured and scaled. Unusual, three-sided needles grow scattered along young twigs. Older branches bear thick tufts of needles at the tips of short spurs. The large green or purple seed cones have overlapping scales, each with a clawlike spike.

The best-known species is the cedar of Lebanon (*Cedrus libani*), which reaches heights of more than 125 feet (38 meters). Also native to the Mediterranean is the Atlas cedar (*C. atlantica*) of North Africa, and the Cyprian cedar (*C. brevifolia*). The Himalayan deodar (*C. deodara*) remains an important timber tree in its native India. Cedar wood is especially popular for building (or lining) closets and clothes chests. Its fragrant resins and oils are said to discourage insect pests, such as destructive moths. Its oil is also used as perfume.

Cypresses

Cypresses cannot withstand freezing temperatures, and therefore grow only in the milder regions of the Northern Hemisphere. Most are graceful trees with fragrant, feathery foliage and large, spreading crowns. Many grow to be quite tall, up to 80 feet (24.5 meters). When young, cypresses tend to be shaped like a pyramid, with smooth bark. With age, they develop broad, spreading crowns, and the bark peels into thin strips. The young twigs bear teardrop-shaped leaves. Smaller leaves form a scaly covering along the older branches. The cypress' small, round cones resemble buttons, and remain on the tree for several years before opening to release their winged seeds.

Cypresses number about 20 species. They include the picturesque Monterey cypress (*Cupressus macrocarpa*), which grows on the craggy rocks of the central California coast. Cypresses are also popular as ornamentals, cultivated for their foliage and graceful forms.

Redwoods and Sequoias

The world's tallest trees grow in towering, fog-laced forests along the coast of northern California and southern Oregon. These are the coastal redwoods (*Sequoia sempervirens*), which often exceed 300 feet (90 meters) in height, over a life span of 400 to 500 years.

Sequoias are the largest organisms on Earth. The biggest of the biggest is the General Sherman Tree (above), which soars to a height of more than 275 feet.

When a redwood is young, its branches sweep down to the ground. With age, the lower branches drop off, leaving a massive, towering trunk—swollen at the base and deeply furrowed with reddish-brown bark. Huge upper branches stand out stiffly from the trunk at intervals. The leaves come in two forms: scaly spirals that wrap around the main branches, and needles that spread in two rows along the outer branches.

Surpassing the coastal redwood in sheer bulk is the massive giant sequoia, or "big tree" (*Sequoiadendron giganteum*), growing just to the east in California's Sierra Nevada. Slightly shorter than its coastal cousin, the massive trunk of a giant sequoia can weigh more than 2,000 tons, making it by far the largest organism on Earth. (The largest animal, the blue whale, weighs less than one-tenth as much.) The famed General Sherman Tree, a giant sequoia in California's Sequoia National Park, measures more

than 37 feet (11.3 meters) around its base and 275 feet (84 meters) in height. The leaves of giant sequoias are small, scaly, and pointed. The cones are egg-shaped, and remain on the trees for years before ripening.

Known only from fossils and thought to be long extinct, the dawn redwood (*Metasequoia glyptostroboides*) was discovered living in the remote valleys of central China in the 1940s. Since that time, its seeds and cuttings have been planted throughout the world.

Yews

Popular ornamental plants, the seven species of yews are recognized by their unusual flattened, dark-green leaves. These grow in spirals around the tree branches, twisting to form two distinct rows. The underside of each leaf bears two yellowish to gray-green stripes. The yew's pollen cones are small, round, and scaly. The female cones are even smaller, each forming a fleshy red cup around a single seed. Most yews have red, flaky bark that becomes deeply furrowed with age.

The English yew (*Taxus baccata*) and the Japanese yew (*T. cuspidata*) are valued as ornamental plants. Like all trees, they grow slowly but live long—some are thought to be more than 4,000 years old.

Hemlock

The hemlocks include 10 species of tall, feathery conifers with purplish to reddish bark; droopy, slender branches; and short, blunt leaves that grow from small cushions along young twigs. Small seed cones hang from the tips of older branches.

Among the most familiar is the eastern, or Canada, hemlock (*Tsuga canadensis*), which grows more than 100 feet (30 meters) tall, with a trunk about 4 feet (1.2 meters) in diameter. Its dark-green leaves have grooves on the upper surface and two white stripes on the lower. Its bark contains high amounts of tannin, used to cure leather. Its splintery wood is good only for inexpensive items such as disposable boxes. Many types of cultivated hemlocks are used as ornamentals. Among the most popular is Japanese hemlock (*T. diversifolia*). The "poison hemlock," the legendary plant used to kill Socrates back in ancient Greece, was not a true hemlock at all, but an herb related to parsley.

GINKGO AND CYCADS

The palmlike cycads and the graceful ginkgo tree are the "eccentric" relatives of the familiar conifers. Like conifers, they are *gymnosperms*, or "naked seed" plants—lacking the blossoms and fruit of the more-advanced *angiosperms*, or "flowering plants."

ANCIENT SURVIVORS

Modern-day cycads include some 100 species. Of the ginkgo, or "maidenhair tree," there is only one. But they once shared a far greater diversity. Appearing in the Permian period, approximately 286 million to 248 million years ago, they filled two large divisions of the Plant Kingdom. They reached their peak when dinosaurs roamed Earth during the Mesozoic era, 248 million to 66 million years ago. The cycads, in particular, were so abundant that some scientists refer to the Mesozoic era as the "Age of Cycads and Dinosaurs."

The ginkgoes, too, commonly appear in the fossil record alongside the bones of *Tyrannosaurus rex* and its kin. But living ginkgoes were entirely unknown to the Western world until the 17th century, when one species, *Ginkgo biloba*, was found cultivated in the temple gardens of China and Japan. Surprisingly, this primitive tree—possibly the oldest living seed plant—has proven to be one of the most pollution-tolerant trees ever known. As a result, it can now be found planted along some of the most traffic-choked streets in some of the smoggiest cities in the world.

So why did these remarkable trees—the ginkgoes and cycads—dwindle to next to nothing, while their cousins the conifers continued to multiply and thrive in large numbers? The fate of the cycads may be the easier to explain. Like the true palm trees that they resemble, cycads cannot survive freezing weather. So their worldwide range was greatly reduced by the series of Ice Ages that ended 10,000 years ago.

The ginkgo tree has glossy green leaves that turn a lovely golden-yellow color (top) before falling in the autumn. Its plumlike fruit (above) has a rancid odor when ripe.

Today they grow only in tropical and subtropical regions; a few species live in Florida.

The virtual disappearance of the hardy ginkgoes remains more of a mystery to scientists. The fossil record suggests that ginkgoes began to decline about the same time as the last dinosaurs disappeared from the face of Earth, approximately 66 million years ago. It may be that they were simply no match for their greatest competitors, the flowering plants, which appeared and became dominant at about the same time. The last natural ginkgo forests disappeared from China thousands of years ago, most likely cut down for firewood.

LIFE CYCLE

In many ways, the reproduction of cycads and the ginkgo is halfway between that of the primitive seedless plants and that of the conifers. Like club mosses and ferns, cycads and the ginkgo have swimming sperm that travel through liquid using whiplike tails. But like conifers, cycads and the ginkgo have pollen, which carry the sperm cells to the seed cones for fertilization. In conifers, a pollen tube actually injects the sperm into the eggs waiting inside the seed cone. By contrast, the sperm of cycads and the ginkgo must swim the last fraction of an inch to their goal. Specifically, they swim through a small amount of the fluid surrounding each egg inside its ovule.

THE GINKGO

The ginkgo, or maidenhair tree, is like no other. As tall and stately as an oak, it produces a thick covering of beautiful, fan-shaped leaves. These unique leaves have no midrib. Instead, the entire leaf surface is etched with parallel rows of delicately forking veins. Many of the leaves bear a distinctive top notch that divides the leathery blade into two shapely lobes. Any breeze sets the leaves aflutter, each one twirling and twisting on its long, thick stalk, or *petiole*. In fall, the leaves turn from gray-green to bright yellow. They cling to the tree long past those of other deciduous plants.

Illustrious History

In ancient times, the Chinese and Japanese brought this magnificent tree into their temple gardens, inadvertently saving it from total extinction in the wild. They called it "ginkgo," meaning "silver apricot," for the color of its seeds. Today, as in ancient times, traditional Asians consider roasted ginkgo seed a delicacy. Less pleasant is the foul-smelling flesh that covers the seed; its odor resembles that of rancid butter. Asian folk healers also use ginkgo leaves to make remedies said to strengthen the heart and lungs. In recent years, scientific studies have confirmed the ginkgo's medicinal usefulness. Today *Ginkgo biloba* extract (GBE) is widely prescribed by European physicians to treat asthma and poor circulation.

When the English visited Asia in the 17th century, they brought home many ginkgo specimens. They renamed the tree "maidenhair" for the leaves' resemblance to those of the maidenhair fern. Today botanists recognize the ginkgo as a "living fossil," for this single species has survived unchanged for nearly 300 million

The ginkgo's remarkable resistance to insects, disease, and air pollution has led to its frequent planting along the sidewalks of New York (below) and other cities.

years. The ginkgo was also greatly appreciated by the world's horticulturists. It thrives in crowded cities, where automobile exhaust kills most other trees. It is also tolerant of cold, and resistant to insect pests and fungal disease.

Characteristics

In overall shape, the ginkgo is tapering, with a thick, sturdy trunk. Its gray, corky bark develops many cracks and fissures with age. Like other gymnosperms, the ginkgo produces wood, or secondary growth, so its trunks and branches expand in width as well as in height.

During its first year, a ginkgo produces clusters of leaves directly from the surface of its branches. In later years, the branches produce short, thick shoots, each of which ends in a whorl of leaves. Ginkgoes grow very slowly, but can eventually reach heights of up to 100 feet (30 meters).

As in conifers and all other seed plants, the visible portion of the ginkgo—the tree—is asexual (neither male nor female). Only the tiny *gametophyte generation* (the pollen grains and ovules) comes in two distinct sexes. But ginkgo trees are often referred to as "male" and "fe-

The Gnetophytes

The gnetophytes represent a small grab bag of plants as unusual as their names: *Gnetum*, *Ephedra*, and *Welwitschia*. Together with the conifers, cycads, and ginkgo, they complete the group we know as *gymnosperms*, or naked-seed plants. Like cycads and the ginkgo tree, the gnetophytes can be described as "throwbacks"—the truly bizarre remnants from an age when dinosaurs ruled Earth. Like cycads, they bear their pollen cones and seed cones on separate "male" and "female" plants. But their sperm do not swim, and so more closely resemble those of conifers. Some botanists believe that the gnetophytes are the flowering plants' closest relatives. As evidence, only flowering plants and gnetophytes have *vessel elements*, a highly evolved type of vascular cell.

The genus *Ephedra* includes about 35 species of small desert shrubs and drought-resistant vines. With their small, scaly leaves and jointed stems, the ephedras somewhat resemble the primitive, seedless horsetails. They include the mahuang plant (*Ephedra sinica*), a Chinese herb whose dried stems are made into a potent medicinal tea for relieving congestion and stimulating the heart. North American species include the desert shrub known as the joint fir (*E. nevadensis*), which has also long been used in folk remedies such as Mormon tea.

The genus *Gnetum* contains 30 species that are found in the tropics of Africa, Asia, and South America. Most gnetums grow as large, woody vines that climb high into the trees of tropical jungles. The others are shrubs or trees. The melindjo tree (*Gnetum gnemon*) is grown throughout Asia for its tough fiber and edible seeds and young leaves. Like flowering plants, gnetums have broad, oval leaves, and fleshy seed coverings that somewhat resemble fruit.

Welwitschia (shown in the photo above) has been called the world's strangest plant. Native to the deserts of southwestern Africa, it grows largely underground like a giant radish 2 to 4 feet (0.6 to 1.2 meters) around. The trunk consists of no more than a massive sunken disk. It produces just two leaves, which emerge as a pair of broad, flat straps that rip into shreds as they grow. The leaves continue to lengthen, like endless green ribbons, throughout the plant's life. *Welwitschia* have large seed cones and smaller pollen cones, both of which produce a sticky, sweet nectar that attracts pollinating insects.

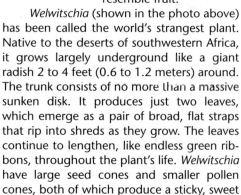

male" because pollen and ovules are produced on separate individuals. The so-called "male" trees bear short, dangling pollen fronds that resemble catkins. The "females" produce pairs of ovules, or egg-producing buds. Like conifers, ginkgo trees rely on the wind for pollination. Once they are pollinated, the ginkgo's ovules produce plumlike seeds about 1 inch (2.5 centimeters) long and wide.

THE CYCADS

If a giant fern married a palm tree, their offspring would look like a cycad. In fact, the ancestors of these remarkable plants were the treelike seed ferns, which disappeared along with the dinosaurs at the end of the Cretaceous period, 66 million years ago.

Characteristics

Cycads can be recognized by their circular crowns of arching fronds. Like the frond of a giant fern, each leaf consists of a long midrib with a row of smaller leaves, or *pinnae*, on each side. When it first emerges from the stem, the young cycad leaf is curled like the fiddlehead of a fern.

Once its large fronds have unfurled, the mature cycad looks like a palm tree, with a large, umbrella-shaped crown. The trunks of cycad trees likewise resemble those of palms. As in palms, the broken bases of the cycad's dropped leaves form a heavy armor of thick spikes.

Cycads produce pollen cones and seed cones, often at the upper tip of their trunks. As with the ginkgo, these male and female parts occur on separate trees. Both wind and insects help carry the pollen from the "male" trees to nearby "females." The majority of cycads stand less than 10 feet (3 meters) high. A few can reach 30 to 60 feet (9 to 18 meters) in height. Many grow primarily beneath the surface, with underground trunks that resemble gigantic turnips or carrots. Whatever their height, the trunks of most cycads remain soft and fleshy. Only a few species produce any significant amount of wood.

Cycads grow exclusively in warm climates. Encephalartas, a South African genus (above), produces remarkably massive cones (left).

Warm Weather Only

Cycads grow only in tropical and subtropical areas because their stems and roots cannot survive a hard freeze. Most North Americans know cycads only from botanical gardens, where they are cultivated in glass-enclosed conservatories. The only cycad native to North America is the Florida arrowroot (*Zamia integrifolia*), a short, stocky plant found in Florida's sandy woodlands. Florida's Seminole natives ground the arrowroot's roots and half-buried stems into a starchy food called *coontie*, or comfortroot. Other cycads, such as the sago palm (*Cycas* species), have been introduced to the southern United States.

Although limited to warm climates, cycads can be found in a variety of habitats, from rain forests to arid deserts. Yet, nowhere are they common. In fact, many cycads are endangered. At present, nearly 50 species can be found in Latin America. Another 40 grow in Africa, 16 in Australia, and 25 in Southeast Asia.

THE FLOWERING PLANTS

by Jessica Snyder Sachs

Sifting through the fossil record, looking back through time, it is astonishing to realize that Earth was covered with plants for more than 300 million years before the first flower bloomed. For all that time, there were no blossoms, no fruits, berries, or nuts, no vegetables as we know them today. Then, in a geologic "instant," they appeared. Scientists believe that fossils found in a lake bed in China in 2002 are the remains of the oldest flowering plant—dating back 125 million years. Around this time, di-

nosaurs were beginning to disappear and a few small, ratlike mammals were taking their place.

By no coincidence, the sudden appearance of flowering plants arrived hand in hand with a dizzying array of new insects—including the first butterflies and moths. The success and evolution of these and many other insects were in-

Flowers do much more than beautify the environment— they perform an essential biological function by making the seeds that will produce the next generation of plants.

extricably tied to the flowers that beckoned them with an astonishing variety of dazzling colors, fragrant oils, and sweet nectar. In return, the flowering plants gained their own private army of messengers. Dutifully carrying pollen from flower to flower, the insects helped ensure that flowering plants would surpass all others in diversity and abundance.

The flowering plants enlisted other animals to do their bidding as well. Through the patient process of evolution, these plants wrapped their seeds in delicious fruits. Birds and mammals that ate the fruit passed the durable seeds through their guts. They dropped them unharmed in new places, creating new colonies of plants wherever they roamed. It was as if the plant world had suddenly sprouted legs and wings—and in a way, it had.

So far as botanists can tell, the first flowering plants appeared in out-of-the-way places such as tropical mountains. At the time, the lowlands were already crowded with more-primitive plants. Patiently biding their time, the newcomers developed the special traits that would ensure their success: flowers, fruit, and a highly efficient vascular system.

Then they spread with amazing speed. Between 30 million and 40 million years after the first flowering plant appears in the fossil record, its kind had covered much of Earth, from the tips of what are now Africa and South America north to above the Arctic Circle.

THE ANGIOSPERMS

Scientists call the flowering plants *angiosperms,* from the Greek words meaning "vessel seed." The "vessel" in this case is the *carpel,* the flower part that encloses the seed and develops into a fruit. By contrast, conifers and their kin, with their unenclosed seeds, are called *gymnosperms,* meaning "naked seed" plants.

Today, angiosperms account for more than 80 percent of the world's plants. With some 250,000 known species—one recent estimate puts the figure as high as 421,968—just listing them would fill several volumes of an encyclopedia. Flowering plants supply us with all of our fruits and vegetables, as well as our grains, sugars, and cooking oils. We use the fibers of flowering plants to make clothing and textiles. We extract their natural chemicals to make lifesav-

The 120-million-year-old fossil of the Koonwarra (above) is among the earliest known example of a flowering plant. Botanists believe that it bore just one flower.

ing medicines and crop-saving pesticides, alluring perfumes, colorful dyes, and an array of flavor-enhancing condiments.

The angiosperms also include most of the world's trees. In form, angiosperms range from prickly cacti to broad-leaved tropical plants. In size, they range from duckweed no larger than a pinhead to towering eucalyptus trees more than 300 feet (90 meters) tall. Some live for only a season, others for hundreds of years.

For all their special qualities, the angiosperms share more similarities than differences with the simpler, nonflowering plants. Like all true plants, they photosynthesize, using chlorophylls a and b along with beta-carotene to make their own food from sunlight. Like other vascular plants, they have roots, stems, and leaves. A waxy, waterproof cuticle covers their skin, pierced only by breathing pores called *stomata.* They conduct food and water up and down through their bodies via a vascular system made of *xylem* and *phloem.*

Many flowering trees are planted for purely ornamental reasons. The "flowers" of the pink dogwood that burst forth each spring are actually the vividly colored bracts that surround the tree's inconspicuous greenish-yellow flowers.

But the vascular system of flowering plants is more complex and efficient than that of the gymnosperms and seedless plants that came before them. They possess special water-conducting cells called *vessel elements*. Many large holes perforated the ends of these long, hollow cells. Assembled end to end, like tightly fitting sections of pipe, they can quickly conduct water from roots to leaves. Nonflowering vascular plants lack vessel elements, but instead rely solely on water-conducting cells called *tracheids* that lack direct connections. (Flowering plants also possess tracheids, but rely primarily on their more-efficient vessels.)

Flowering plants evolved a similar "plumbing" system to conduct sugar and other dissolved foods through their stems, leaves, and roots. The food passes through "pipes" made of rows of long, interconnected cells called *sieve-tube members*. These, too, have large openings (called *sieve plates*) at their tips, to allow the free flow of nutrients from cell to cell. In contrast, the sieve cells of nonflowering plants lack direct connections. So food must seep slowly from one sieve cell to the next.

In addition to their highly evolved "plumbing system," angiosperms also developed the two great inventions mentioned earlier—the flower and the fruit. Most everyone appreciates these two "wonders of nature" for their beauty, fragrance, and flavor. But what are they? What is their purpose, and how did they come to be?

THE FLOWER

The first primitive flower was probably a spore-bearing leaf that folded in on itself. In doing so, it formed a simple ovary, or egg-bearing structure. Over the ages, evolution has elaborated on this simple plan to create the *carpel*—the centerpiece of the flower. (See "Anatomy of a Flower," facing page.)

The flask-shaped carpel contains eggs in its swollen base, called the *ovary*. Above the ovary is the carpel's slender neck, called the *style*. The tip of the style, called the *stigma*, is sticky—custom-designed to catch pollen. (Some older books refer to carpels as "pistils.") Most flowers have one or more carpels at their center. The carpels may be separate, as in blackberry blossoms, or fused, as in apple blossoms and lilies.

The flower's so-called "male" part is the *stamen*. Most flowers have several. Each consists of a long stalk, called the *filament*. At its tip is the *anther*, the organ that produces the pollen. In most flowers, the stamens grow in a whorl just beneath and surrounding the carpel. In other flowers, such as peas, mallows, and sunflowers, the stamens fuse together into a column. In still others, such as phlox and snapdragons, they fuse with the flower's colorful petals.

Flowers that contain both stamen and carpel are called *perfect*. *Imperfect* flowers contain one or the other, and so are sometimes called "male" and "female" blossoms. Magnolia and apple are familiar examples of perfect flowers. Those of corn and oaks are imperfect.

When male and female flowers grow on the same plant, as in oaks and corn, the species is called *monoecious* (Greek for "one house"). When the two types of flowers grow on separate plants, as in willows, the species is called *dioecious* (meaning "two houses").

Stamens and carpels make up the reproductive parts of the flower. Surrounding them, in most flowers, is a whorl of *petals*, and beneath it, a circle of *sepals*. Petals tend to be colorful and showy, designed to attract insects and other pollinators. The sepals tend to be green, resembling small leaves. But in some plants, such as tulips and lilies, the sepals grow just as colorful and large as the petals. The sepals' main purpose is to form a protective envelope, the *flower bud*, which opens before pollination.

Carpels, stamens, petals, and sepals all sit on the *receptacle*—the tip of the floral stem. A flower having all four parts is called *complete*. Those lacking one or more of these parts are called *incomplete*.

Flowers vary somewhat in the arrangement of their parts. Often the sepals, petals, and stamens grow separately from the receptacle, below the ovary. Such flowers are called *hypogynous*. Familiar examples include lilies, buttercups, and magnolias. In other flowers, the various flower parts fuse together at their base to form a small cup. Such flowers are called *perigynous*. Familiar examples include roses and

Anatomy of a Flower

A "perfect" flower, in the scientific sense, is one that has all four flower parts: carpel, stamen, petals, and sepals. In a typical flower such as this lily, the *carpel* is found at the center. The swollen base of the carpel is called the *ovary*, as it holds the eggs. Extending up from the ovary is the long neck of the carpel, called the *style*. The style's sticky tip, or *stigma*, is a pollen trap.

The so-called "male" portion of the flower is the *stamen*, which consists of a long filament bearing the pollen-producing anther. Most blossoms have several stamens surrounding a central carpel. Below the

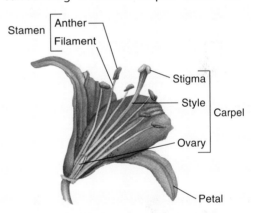

A Perfect Flower
(*cross section*)

stems is a whorl of *petals*, and below that a whorl of *sepals*. In flowers such as this lily, the petals and sepals are identical. In many other plants, the petals are large and colorful, while the sepals are smaller and green. Before the flower opens, the sepals form a protective envelope, called the *bud*, around the other flower parts.

Not visible here are the tiny nectaries and oil glands that produce the flower's nectar and fragrance. These glands may be found in any one or more of the flower's parts, depending on the species. Often the nectaries lie deep within the flower, so the nectar-feeding insect or other animal must pass over the stigma and anthers, picking up or transferring pollen with its body.

cherry blossoms. In the third type of flower, the ovary lies below the other flower parts, enclosed by a cup formed by their fused bases. These flowers are called *epigynous*, and they include asters and the blossoms of apples and pears.

In most flowers, the parts arrange themselves in a circle, usually with the carpel at the center. All the early angiosperm plants had such circular, or radially symmetrical, flowers. Evolution later produced irregular flowers such as orchids and snapdragons. Their unusual shapes are designed to precisely guide insects in and out of the blossom in ways that maximize pollination. Still other flowers rely on the wind for pollination. They tend to be small and drab, for they have no need to attract animal pollinators.

Many flowers pollinated by animals produce alluring scents from oil glands in the sepals, petals, stamens, or carpels. The fragrances, like the blossom's bright colors, advertise the flower's offering of nectar. Nectar is likewise produced by special glands in one or more flower parts. Nectar is rich in a variety of sugars, with trace amounts of amino acids and salts.

All flowering plants bear fruit. The woody fruit of the coconut palm (below) contains an oil that is used as an ingredient in margarine, cooking oils, and shampoo.

Flowers pollinated by moths, butterflies, and hummingbirds often hold their nectar in a small pouch, or *nectary*, at the end of a long tube formed by the sepals. In general, the nectary's location requires the pollinating animal to move over the stamens and stigma, where its body picks up and deposits grains of pollen.

Pollination

Most of us are somewhat familiar with pollination, if only because the dusty grains make us sneeze in spring and fall. A closer examination reveals a process that is especially complex in the flowering plants. In flowering plants, pollen develops from spores produced inside the anthers. Each pollen grain consists of a male *gametophyte* (the sexual generation of the plant life cycle) encased in a tiny capsule. This microscopic male plant has just three cells: two sperm cells and a tube cell. When the pollen grains mature, the anther opens.

As mentioned, a few flowering plants rely on the wind to distribute their pollen. (Wind pollination is more common in the gymnosperms.) Typically, though, the pollen of flowering plants is picked up by the bodies of nectar-feeding animals, be they insects, bats, or birds. If all goes according to plan, they carry the pollen grains to the carpel of the next flower they visit.

Most plants benefit from *cross-pollination*. That is, they produce the healthiest offspring when the pollen of one plant fertilizes the eggs of another of the same species. This encourages a healthy mixing of genes. By contrast, *self-pollination*—the fertilization of a plant's eggs with its own pollen—produces no such mixing, and can lead to unhealthy inbreeding.

Many flowers have evolved ways to avoid self-pollination. Some flowers do this by producing their pollen-bearing stamens at a different time than they produce their egg-bearing carpels. In others, the tissues of the carpel automatically reject pollen that is genetically identical to itself. (The carpel tissue also rejects pollen from plants of a different species.)

Fertilization

The sticky stigma of the carpel is designed to catch pollen grains. Once on the stigma, each grain produces a tiny, hollow pollen tube. It grows down through the carpel's style, carrying with it two sperm cells.

Peach   **Pear**   **Raspberry**   **Pea**

After fertilization, the wall of the flower's ovary develops into the fruit. The fruit may take the form of soft pulp like that of an apple, or it can be hard and dry, like the shell of a nut. In the botanical sense of the word, fruits also include all the "seedy" vegetables, from squash to tomatoes. The pod of a pea or bean, for example, is the leathery jacket of its ovary.

Many fruits have several distinct layers. The skin and flesh of the peach, for example, develop from the outer and middle layers of the ovary wall. The hard stone comes from the ovary's inner wall. Inside the stone lies the seed. Fruits such as peaches, plums, and tomatoes are called "simple" because each develops from a single ovary.

Fruits that develop from one or more flower parts in addition to the ovary are called "accessory" fruits. Examples include pears and apples. The skin and pulp of these fruits develop from the receptacle that held the apple or pear blossom to its stem. The ovary produces only the fruit's seedy core. The papery layer that divides the core and outer pulp is the mature ovary's outer wall.

Aggregate fruits consist of many mature ovaries, or fruitlets, clustered around a cone-shaped receptacle. Familiar examples include raspberries and strawberries.

Often many grains of pollen reach the stigma at the same time. Then the slender style becomes a racetrack; its length helps ensure that the strongest and fastest sperm reach the eggs first and fertilize them.

Meanwhile, inside the ovary, one or more female gametophytes are maturing. One sits in each of the ovary's compartments, called *ovules*. Each female gametophyte consists of just seven cells. Two of them are of special interest: one is the egg; the other, called the *central cell*, contains two nuclei.

When a pollen tube reaches an ovule, it discharges its sperm. One of the sperm fertilizes the egg cell. The fertilized egg then begins to divide to form an embryo. The second sperm unites with the gametophyte's central cell. It then begins to divide to produce a unique tissue called *endosperm*, which provides food to the growing embryo. The embryo and endosperm, together with the ovule wall around them, develop into a seed.

In some flowering plants, such as peas and beans, the embryo consumes all the endosperm before the seed ripens. In other plants, such as wheat, barley, and rye, the endosperm remains to nourish the seedling when it germinates. Indeed, the bulk of a grain seed is endosperm—the stuff of which flour is made. An example of liquid endosperm is found inside coconuts. It is the so-called coconut "milk." Coconuts also contain solid endosperm—the sweet, white, chewy material that we buy shredded.

Fruits

Few of us stop to think about plant anatomy when we bite into a juicy peach or crack open a nut. Scientifically speaking, a fruit is a ripened ovary—be it soft and juicy like a peach, or hard and dry like the shell of a walnut. In a botanical sense, fruits also include bean and pea pods, tomatoes, cucumbers, and squash.

Fruits develop as follows: after fertilization, the petals and stamens of the flower with-er, while the base of the carpel, or ovary, swells in size. The ripening ovary, or fruit, may contain a single seed, as in a peach, apricot, or almond. Or it may contain several seeds, as in an apple, pea pod, or cucumber.

Other parts of the flower can likewise contribute to the formation of the fruit. In apples and pears, for example, the bulk of the fruit develops from a tube-shaped receptacle. Unlike the endosperm, the fruit does not nourish the seed. It forms the seed's protective covering. In many cases, the fruit also serves as a vehicle for long-distance travel.

Some fruits, such as that of the mistletoe, simply burst when ripe—shooting their seeds far and wide. Many trees, such as maples, produce winged fruits designed to fly with the wind. The woody fruit of the coconut is designed to float away like a watertight ship, carrying its seed to new shores.

The most-familiar fruits are those that nature designed to be eaten. Such fruits are often brightly colored, as an advertisement to hungry birds and mammals. The seeds contained within them are designed to pass unharmed through the animal's gut. Hours or days after being eaten, the seeds exit the animal in its droppings, often miles away.

Burrs and thistles are also fruits. They are designed to adhere to the fur, feathers, or clothing of passersby, which then carry them unwittingly to new homes. In these and other ways, the seeds of flowering plants travel much farther and faster than can the seeds of simpler plants.

From Seed to Seedling

A seed matures and drops to the ground, or perhaps it is carried miles away in the gut of an animal that ate its fruit. Most seeds must wait through a period of dormancy before they can sprout, or germinate, into a seedling. Dormancy ends when a crack or other opening develops in the seed coat (1). Now the seed absorbs water, and the embryo within begins to grow. The young root, or radicle, is the first part of the seedling to emerge (2). It anchors the seedling to the soil and begins to absorb water and dissolved minerals. Next, the seedling's young shoot, or *hypocotyl*, begins to lengthen (3). If the seed lies beneath the soil, the hypocotyl will arch upward as it lengthens, pulling with it the cotyledons, or seed leaves. When the cotyledons break free of the seed coat, the seedling's growing tip, or *epicotyl*, begins to lengthen (4). Food stored inside the cotyledons nourishes the young seedling until it produces its first true leaves (5). Now through the biological process called photosynthesis, the young plant can manufacture its own food. Its cotyledons drop away, marking the end of the seedling stage.

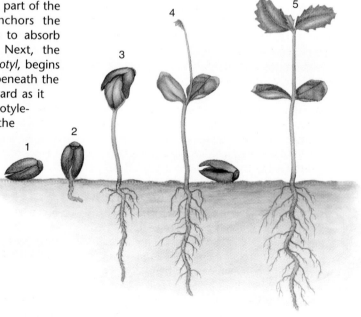

A seed is in an inactive state (1) until conditions are favorable for it to start to germinate. First, the root emerges from the seed (2), followed by the shoot with its seed leaves (3). As growth continues, the leaves begin to develop (4). Once several leaves are in place (5), photosynthesis can occur.

Not all flowers are showy. Oats and most other types of grains bear flowers similar in color to the rest of the plant. The edible seeds of the oat plant are tucked inside the spiky flower heads (below). Harvesttime occurs months later, when the plants are dry and yellow (right).

GERMINATION

Most seeds are not ready to sprout when they first fall or are carried away from their parent plant. First, they must go through a resting period called *dormancy*. This period varies from just a few days, as in a sugar maple (*Acer saccharum*), to 1,000 years, as in the sacred lotus plant (*Nelumbo nucifera*). A prolonged period of dormancy is especially important for seeds produced at the end of a growing season. In most cases, it is to their advantage to wait until the following spring or rainy season before sprouting and beginning the growth cycle.

The minimum amount of time that a seed must remain dormant is generally preset, according to its species. Many seeds, however, can remain dormant for much longer than this minimum period. That is, they can wait indefinitely until conditions become favorable for growth.

The longest known dormancy was set by a handful of 10,000-year-old seeds from a tundra lupine (*Lupinus arcticus*) found in frozen Arctic soil in 1966. Once thawed, it took the ancient seeds just two days to sprout with life. At the other end of the spectrum are tropical plants whose tender seeds remain viable for just a short time. Such is the case with many orchids: once their seeds drop to the ground, they must germinate within a few days, or die.

What signals a seed to end its dormancy? As a general rule, the embryo inside a seed needs ample moisture, oxygen, and warmth before it can grow into a seedling. Typically, it is the thickness of a seed's coat that determines how long it takes for moisture and oxygen to reach the embryo. Quick-germinating seeds tend to have thin, papery coats, like those of a pea or peanut. By contrast, the hard-walled Brazil nut must be opened by brute force.

Something, then, must wear down the seed coat before the seedling can emerge. It may take months to years of wear and tear from rain, sunlight, and wind. Some seeds need to be partly digested in the gut of an animal. Others must literally be scorched by fire before they will open.

Eventually a crack develops. Once it does, water can enter, swelling the seed and further splitting the coat. Reawakened by moisture and oxygen, the inner embryo resumes its active growth, or *germinates*.

The growth begins with the embryonic shoot, or *hypocotyl*. One tip of the hypocotyl becomes the seedling root, or *radicle*. It is the first part of the plant to emerge from the seed coat. The radicle anchors itself into the soil with root hairs and tiny branches, and begins to absorb water and minerals.

As the tiny root develops, the seedling's hypocotyl continues to lengthen. Attached to the hypocotyl, still inside the seed coat, are one or two *cotyledons*, or seed leaves. They supply nutrition to the growing seedling as it pushes out of the ground.

In some plants, such as beans, the hypocotyl arches up and out of the soil, pulling the cotyledons with it. In such cases, the cotyle-

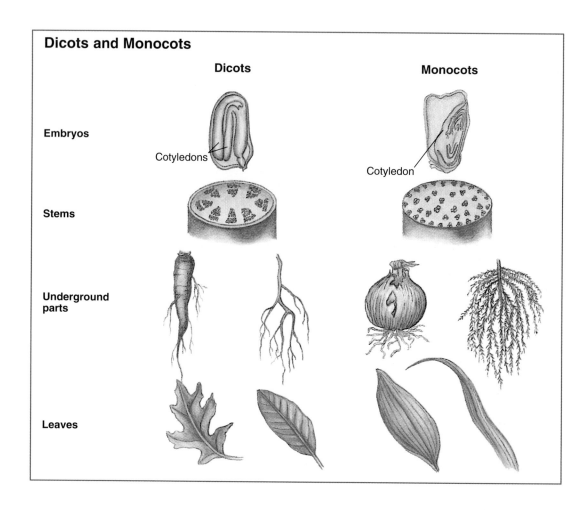

Dicots and Monocots

Dicots

Monocots

Embryos

Cotyledons

Cotyledon

Stems

Underground parts

Leaves

---

dons often contain chlorophyll and can manufacture food through photosynthesis for a short time. In other plants, such as peas and corn, the hypocotyl and cotyledons remain in the soil, while a growing tip, called the *epicotyl*, pushes up out of the ground.

In either case, the cotyledons and the seed's endosperm supply the new seedling with food until it produces its first true leaves. The cotyledons then drop away, marking the end of the plant's seedling stage.

If conditions are favorable, the young plant will mature to eventually produce its own flowers, seeds, and fruit. In reality, only a fraction of all seedlings survive that long.

MONOCOTS AND DICOTS

Botanists divide the flowering plants into two broad groups, or classes: the *dicotyledons*, or dicots, and the *monocotyledons*, or monocots.

The dicots are by far the larger of the two, with more than 175,000 known species. Examples include most common garden plants, shrubs, trees, and broad-leaved flowering plants from magnolias to hollyhocks. Monocots number about 65,000. They include all grasses, as well as palm trees, lilies, orchids, and irises.

These two great classes have far more similarities than differences. But their evolution clearly diverged early in the history of the flowering plants. All dicotyledons, for example, begin life with two cotyledons, or seed leaves, hence their name (di-, meaning "two," cotyledons). Similarly, all monocots begin life with a single ("mono") cotyledon. The two groups have several other basic differences, which makes them easy to tell apart.

Half of all dicots are woody, which means that their stems expand in diameter with secondary growth. All flowering trees, for example, are dicots. Most monocots, by contrast, do not produce wood. Their stems remain herbaceous, or green. A few monocots, such as palm trees and bamboos, do produce a kind of pithy wood, not as organized or sturdy as that of dicot trees.

Monocots and dicots can likewise be distinguished by their leaves. The leaf of a typical monocot has parallel veins running its length. A grass blade and a palm frond clearly illustrate this pattern. In contrast, the leaf veins in dicots tend to form a broad, intricate net, or mesh, like that seen in a maple or oak leaf.

Looking through a microscope at the leaf of a monocot, one can see that its *stomata* (leaf pores), like its veins, lie in neatly parallel rows. In contrast, the stomata on the surface of a dicot leaf are usually scattered, with no clear organization readily perceptible.

These two groups can also be distinguished by their flowers. Most often, monocots produce blossoms whose parts (sepals, petals, and stamens) come in multiples of three, seldom four, but never five. This can be seen best in the blossom of a lily, and also in the tiny blooms of rice and other grasses. Most dicots have flower parts in sets of fours or fives. The examples are endless, from cactus blooms to roses.

Most monocots form masses of fibrous roots, where no one root is larger or more important than the others. The matted roots of crabgrass are a good example. By contrast, many dicots produce taproots, as seen in dandelions and root vegetables such as parsnips, carrots, and radishes.

A more fundamental difference between the two groups can be seen in a cross section of their stems. In monocots, the vascular tissue (water- and food-conducting cells) lies in bundles scattered throughout the stem. In dicots, the vascular tissue is organized in a distinct ring around the stem's central core.

So far as they can tell, botanists believe that dicots are the older of the two groups. The first monocots probably evolved from a dicot well over 100 million years ago. Thereafter the two groups evolved separately.

ADAPTATION TO CLIMATE CHANGE

The flowering plants first flourished during a period when the world's climate remained warm and humid year-round. Over the ages that followed, the climate grew cooler and drier, es-pecially in the Northern Hemisphere. Many flowering plants became extinct. Others evolved lifestyles that avoided harsh weather while taking advantage of times when water and warmth were in good supply.

Today we can see plants do this in one of three ways. Plants called *annuals* complete their entire life cycle—from germination to seed production—in a single growing season. The parent plant then dies, and its seeds lie dormant until the next growing season begins. Annuals include most tender garden vegetables such as cucumbers, pepper plants, and corn. They also include pansies (*Viola* species), buttercups (*Ranunculus* species), touch-me-nots (*Impatiens* species), and other garden flowers that are generally replanted each spring.

Other flowering plants require two growing seasons to mature from seedling to seed-bearing plant. Examples of such *biennials* include vegetables such as potatoes and carrots, and garden flowers such as sweet William (*Dianthus barbatus*), common foxglove (*Digitalis purpurea*), and evening primrose (*Oenothera biennis*). In the first growing season, these plants establish a root, a short stem, and a few ground-hugging leaves. They then remain dormant through the winter or dry season. With the return of spring or rains, the plant resumes its growth, producing flowers, fruit, and seeds before dying at the end of its second year.

The third lifestyle adopted by plants is that of the *perennial*. Perennials can persist for many years, producing flowers, fruit, and seed many times over. In tropical and subtropical areas of the world, perennials tend to grow year-round. In less-favorable climates, perennials tend to die back to their roots, bulbs, or underground stems (rhizomes) at the end of each growing season. In this way, the perennial remains dormant until the following spring or the onset of the rainy season, when it produces new shoots and leaves. Many flowering trees and woody shrubs are likewise perennial. At the end of each growing season, they drop their leaves rather than die back to the ground.

Some plants can vary their lifestyles according to the climate in which they grow. Many garden flowers, for example, grow as perennials in the southern states, but survive only as annuals in the North, where winter temperatures plunge below freezing.

CARNIVOROUS PLANTS
AND OTHER UNUSUAL SPECIES

by Jenny Tesar

Most green plants absorb water and minerals from the soil, and oxygen from the air. Using these raw materials, they produce all the food they need in a series of processes that begins with photosynthesis. Some green plants, however, derive part or all of their food from other sources. These species include carnivorous plants, parasitic plants, and plants that form symbiotic associations.

CARNIVOROUS PLANTS

Carnivorous ("meat-eating") plants grow mainly in moist areas with highly acidic soils. This acidity severely limits the plant's supply of available nitrogen and other essential nutrients. To survive in this environment, carnivorous plants have evolved modified leaves that trap insects and other small animals. The plants then digest and partially absorb the animals to obtain the nutrients they need for photosynthesis. Chemically, the digestive process is quite similar to digestion in animals. Some carnivorous plants secrete digestive enzymes that break down the animal matter. Other species depend at least in part on enzymes produced by bacteria that live on their leaves.

General Characteristics

Most carnivorous plants are small, their height and diameter measured in inches (centimeters). The largest are members of the species *Nepenthes*. These tropical pitcher plants are essentially stout vines that climb rain-forest trees to heights of 50 feet

The Venus's-flytrap (top) has nectar-producing glands to lure a fly (middle) or other prey to its leaves. When the fly lands, the leaf snaps shut (above), trapping the prey.

(15 meters) or more. Depending on the species, the traps, or pitchers, may be 12 inches (30 centimeters) long. In contrast, the trap of a bladderwort (genus *Utricularia*) measures as little as 0.01 inch (0.25 millimeter).

As might be expected, the size of prey that can be captured varies with the size of the trap. The smallest aquatic bladderworts capture microscopic protozoa; bladderworts with bigger traps catch mainly rotifers and water fleas (*Daphnia*) as well as mosquito larvae and young fish fry. Crawling and flying insects are the main prey for most carnivorous plants that live on land. There have been reports that frogs, rodents, and small birds have been trapped in large *Nepenthes* pitchers; if true, the animals were most likely sick and therefore unable to escape quickly.

The various types of traps can be placed into two groups: active and passive.

Active traps. Active traps use movement to catch prey. The best-known example is the jawlike closing of a spring trap, as seen in Venus's-flytrap (*Dionaea muscipula*). The leaf blade is hinged along the midrib, which enables the two halves of the leaf to move toward each other, similar to the way the two halves of a clamshell can move together. The margins of the leaf are lined with sharp, bristlelike hairs and tiny nectar glands. On the upper surface of each half of the leaf are several smaller, finer trigger hairs that are extremely sensitive to touch. When a fly or other appropriate prey touches two or three trigger hairs—or touches one trigger hair two or three times—electrical signals pass from the hairs to special cells in the hinge, and the trap slams shut.

In approximately 30 seconds, the sharp hairs on the two margins mesh, forming a barred prison from which the insect cannot escape. Slowly, the margins themselves move together, until a slim, closed pouch is formed by the two halves of the leaf. Digestive juices then flow from glands in the leaf. Over a period of 5 to 10 days, the insect is digested and the nutrients are absorbed. Then the trap reopens. Dried bits of skeleton and other indigestible parts of the victim remain on the leaf's surface; they eventually fall out or are washed away by rain.

An even-more-rapid trap is found on the aquatic bladderworts, which have worldwide distribution. Some of the segments of their leaves bear small, usually transparent bladders. Unless a bladder contains prey, its walls are concave and a partial vacuum exists within it. Closing the entrance to the bladder is a flaplike trapdoor. One edge forms a hinge; the other is free-hanging. Near the free-hanging edge are

The sensitive hairs of the sundew plant actively move an ensnared insect to the plant's center. The plant then wraps itself around the insect and digests it (above).

several trigger hairs. When an animal touches the trigger hairs, the door opens inward. The victim and water are sucked into the bladder—which becomes bulbous, with convex walls—and the door swings back to a closed position. The whole process takes an infinitesimal fraction of a second—or less. The water then moves out of the bladder, restoring the partial vacuum. Digestive enzymes are released to break down the victim's tissues. Often a new victim is captured by the trap before the previous victim has been completely digested.

Passive traps. Flypaper traps, such as those of sundews (genus *Drosera*), are considered passive traps, which do not use movement to capture their victims. The upper surface of sundew leaves is covered with numerous long,

Insects in search of food become a meal themselves when, mired in water-lily secretions (above), they trigger the flower to close around them (right) and begin digestion.

pitcher by its vivid color or sweet nectar. Just below the nectar glands, the inner surface of the pitcher becomes very slippery. Insects lose their footing and tumble toward the bottom. Downward-pointing hairs within the pitcher make it almost impossible for the insects to crawl out. Eventually they become exhausted and fall into the liquid, where they drown and are digested.

Evolution

Scientists have identified nearly 600 species and subspecies of carnivorous plants. Their evolutionary history is still unclear, although it is apparent that different types of carnivorous plants evolved separately at different places and different times in history.

Many species have been known for centuries, but it was not until the late 1800s that British naturalist Charles Darwin and others performed various experiments to prove that the plants were carnivorous. For example, Darwin wrapped a piece of meat in sphagnum moss and put another piece on a sundew leaf. The meat in the moss rotted, but the meat on the sundew leaf slowly disappeared. Darwin concluded that the sundew had digested and assimilated the meat before it could rot. In recent years, scientists gave fruit flies food containing radioactive tracers, and then fed the flies to carnivorous plants to confirm Darwin's theory.

Darwin also showed that a sundew's tentacles bend in reaction to any solid stimulus. However, if the object is inorganic and does not contain nitrogen, the tentacles return to their normal position comparatively quickly. He noted that sundews do not react to liquid stimuli unless the liquids contain protein. And he observed that sundews grown in terrariums that contained no insects were smaller and flowered

spreading hairs, or tentacles; fewer tentacles are found on the lower surface of the leaves. The tentacles bear glands—often brightly colored—that secrete three kinds of substances: sweet nectar to attract insects; adhesive compounds to hold the insects; and enzymes to digest the victims. The glands also absorb much of the digested nutrients.

When an insect alights on a sundew leaf, it is held fast by the sticky secretions on the tentacles it touches. Nearby tentacles often are stimulated and slowly bend over to also adhere to the insect. In some species, the edges of the leaf fold inward, too, to further trap the insect. These actions are slow, taking minutes or even hours. After the insect has been digested, the leaf and tentacles return to an open position.

Another type of passive trap is seen in pitcher plants, which have leaves that are tubular or pitcher-shaped. In the base of the pitcher is a liquid containing digestive enzymes. At the top of the pitcher is a hood, which in at least some species appears to prevent rainwater from entering the pitcher and diluting the digestive juices. Insects are lured to the opening of the

less profusely than sundews grown under conditions where they could catch prey.

Distribution

Some types of carnivorous plants are widely distributed; for instance, the water-bug trap (*Aldrovanda vesiculosa*), a small aquatic plant with a spring trap, grows in acidic waters from Europe and Africa eastward to Japan and Australia. The five genera of pitcher plants include both tropical and temperate species. Sundews are even found in parts of the Arctic. While most bladderworts are aquatic, some live in wet areas on land. There also are epiphytic bladderworts that live on the trunks and branches of trees in South American rain forests.

Other types of carnivorous plants have very limited distributions. Venus's-flytrap grows only in the coastal plain of southeastern North Carolina and eastern South Carolina.

Species that live in warm, moist climates tend to grow year-round. Elsewhere, species have adaptations to survive periods of drought or low temperatures. The cistus flowered sundew (*Drosera cistiflora*) of South Africa normally grows during autumn, winter, and spring, when rain is plentiful. During the summer

Aquatic bladderworts derive their name from their bulbous bladderlike structures, which contain a suction "trapdoor" that permits prey to enter but not to exit.

drought, the aboveground parts of the plant die; only an underground rhizome and roots survive. When the rains return in autumn, new leaves grow from the rhizome.

Sundews that live in northern parts of the Northern Hemisphere form *hibernacula*, or winter resting buds, in autumn. A hibernaculum is a spherical mass of closely packed young leaves. After it forms, the rest of the plant, including the roots, die. In spring, new roots form, the hiber-

Prey, drawn to glands on the rims of the pitcher plant's pitcherlike traps (below), slip and fall into a tubal prison (inset), where they drown in digestive juices.

naculum opens, and the plant begins to grow again. Many temperate aquatic bladderworts overwinter by means of hibernacula called *turions*, which form at the tips of stems. When the stems die, the turions either float or sink to the bottom of the pond or stream. In spring, they rise to the surface and grow into new plants.

Many species of carnivorous plants are subject to severe overexploitation by collectors. Another threat is habitat destruction, as people drain wetlands for farms, housing, and other development. In some places, taking carnivorous plants from the wild is illegal.

PARASITIC PLANTS

Parasites are organisms that derive all or part of their food from the tissues of other living organisms. Parasitic plants absorb nutrients from their hosts via special structures that penetrate the hosts' tissues. For instance, the seed of a broomrape (genus *Orobanche*) will germinate only when it comes in contact with the root of

Any discussion of unusual plants should at least mention Titan arum, *which takes on a truly bizarre appearance (below) during its infrequent periods of bloom.*

an appropriate host, such as clover or tomato. The seedling sends rootlike *haustoria* into the roots of the host, establishing a connection with the host's vascular system. The only part of the broomrape that ever grows above the soil's surface is the flowering shoot, which has brownish, scalelike leaves devoid of chlorophyll.

Another root parasite is *Rafflesia arnoldi*, an Indonesian species best known for producing the world's biggest flowers. *Rafflesia*'s tissues circle the vascular tissues of the host, forming such a complete union that it is difficult for a human observer to tell where one set of tissues begins and the other ends. No stems or leaves are ever produced by *Rafflesia*; only the flower appears above ground—a reddish blossom that may be more than 3 feet (1 meter) across and weigh up to 25 pounds (11 kilograms).

Mistletoe, *Viscum album*, is a partial parasite that grows in globelike clumps high up on the branches of oaks, sycamores, and other trees. It obtains water and minerals through haustoria that penetrate the bark of the host tree, although it has chlorophyll-containing leaves that carry out photosynthesis.

MYCORRHIZAL ASSOCIATIONS

Some flowering plants that lack chlorophyll depend on fungi for their food. Indian pipe, *Monotropa uniflora*, which grows on forest floors, is one such species. It has a fleshy white or pinkish stem with colorless leaf scales and a single terminal flower. Its roots form a dense complex, called a *mycorrhiza*, with the hairlike filaments, or *mycelia*, of a particular type of fungi. The Indian pipe obtains all of its food from the fungus, which has enzymes that break down dead leaves and other ground litter.

Chlorophyll-containing plants may also have mycorrhizal associations. Many trees—including oaks and pines—photosynthesize but absorb water and nutrients from fungi that live in close association with their roots. The fungi, in turn, obtain sugar and other foods from the trees. This mycorrhizal association is not essential for the trees, but experiments have demonstrated the association's benefits. If seedlings of these trees are grown in sterile soil, their growth is slow and weak; if the soil is inoculated with the fungi, and the fungi infect the seedlings' roots, the growth rate improves rapidly.

PLANT BEHAVIOR

by Jessica Snyder Sachs

Plants can touch. They can feel. They can race across the forest floor in search of light or shade or water. They can fly through the air like jet-propelled rockets. They can warn one another of danger, or themselves launch a deadly attack. They can estimate time.

EXTRAORDINARY ABILITIES

Do such statements sound far-fetched? After all, we think of "action" and "reaction" as qualities unique to animals. But plants do move, and they respond to their surroundings. We seldom notice, perhaps, because we live on a vastly different timescale than they do.

To observe plant behavior takes tremendous patience—or a copious amount of film. Indeed, when viewed through a week's worth of time-lapse photography, a field of sunflowers looks like a crowd of tennis fans watching a fast-paced match. Each night, the plants turn east to face the sunrise, then track the Sun west on its journey across the sky.

Plants also have the extraordinary ability to reach out for what they need by growing to it. Unlike an animal, with its more or less fixed form, a plant retains the ability to extend itself in almost any direction from virtually any body part. Witness an ordinary kudzu vine (*Pueraria lobata*). Hacked to the ground, it will rise again to engulf an entire house in a single season, and then the next house, and the next, and so on.

Plants can also direct their growth with great precision. Witness the seedling that bends toward a shaft of light, or the thirsty plant that directs all its growth toward reaching underground water. Or consider the amazing sundew (*Drosera* species), an insect-eating plant found in European bogs. When a fly becomes snagged on one of the sundew's sticky leaf hairs, surrounding hairs literally grow toward the insect, engulfing it in less than a minute!

Tropical water lilies intertwine (above) as each plant seeks its place in the sun. The tendency of plants to grow toward light is a readily observed plant behavior.

Such behaviors tempt us to describe certain plants as "aggressive," while others, growing neatly in their beds, might be called "well-behaved." This is not to suggest any form of consciousness. Certainly, plants have no organ like a brain, no "central processing unit," so to speak (although scientists recently discovered that one kind of plant, the weed *Arabidopsis thaliana*, contains neurotransmitters similar to those found in animal brains). Yet evolution has produced plant behaviors as useful as those of any thinking animal. In recent decades, botanists have come to understand the mechanisms behind many, though not all, of these behaviors.

TROPISMS

A *tropism* is a growth response. Specifically, it involves a plant bending or growing toward or away from an external stimulus. The most familiar plant tropism is *phototropism*—the tendency to grow toward light. Since a plant has no eyes to literally "see" the light, nor a brain to "desire" light, what controls this movement? In a word: *auxin*, the primary plant growth hormone.

Auxin "tells" a plant tissue to lengthen. It is most abundant in a plant's growing tips, although its concentration there can change. Indeed, auxin can flow from one side of the growing shoot to the other, which is just what happens when one side of the growing tip is more shaded than the other. Auxin flows away from the side facing light to the side facing shade. This prompts the cells on the shaded side to lengthen more rapidly than those on the opposite side. As a result, the shoot bends toward the light as it grows.

Sometimes plants will grow away from light. This is called *negative phototropism*. A fascinating example is provided by the Swiss cheese plant (*Monstera deliciosa*), a philodendron that grows in the Central American rain forest. The cheese plant produces small seeds that rain down to the forest floor. There they sprout into green, wormlike shoots that rapidly grow toward the trunk of the nearest tree.

What guides them? Auxin in the growth tip of the cheese-plant seedling flows toward the side that faces light. So it grows toward the deepest shade—the base of the closest tree.

Just as remarkable, the cheese plant changes its growth pattern as soon as it touches a vertical surface. The flow of auxin reverses, flowing away from the lighted side of the shoot. So now the shoot bends toward the light—snaking its way up the tree trunk to reach the sunlight at the top of the rain-forest canopy.

Two other tropisms affect the growth of the young cheese plant. Like other plants, it responds to gravity—*geotropism*—and to contact with a solid object—*thigmotropism*.

It is easy to demonstrate geotropism by laying a potted plant on its side. Even if light reaches the growing tip equally from all sides, the plant bends to grow upward. In fact, if the pot is suspended completely upside down, the stem will make a complete U-turn. Geotropism has the opposite effect on roots, directing them to grow in the same direction as gravity. So the roots of a potted plant suspended upside down will eventually poke back out of the soil.

Scientists do not entirely understand geotropism. But it seems to result from an interplay of growth hormones, the mineral calcium, and the settling of starch grains in certain cells.

Still more complicated and less understood are the mechanisms behind thigmotropism. Like

In the plant behavior called thigmotropism, a grapevine that encounters a wire support (left) will respond by wrapping its "feelers," or tendrils, tightly around it.

A botanical clock "tells" the first-light cactus at right to bloom at dawn. Similarly, a night-blooming cactus somehow "knows" to bloom after dark, just in time to be pollinated by a bat (bottom).

the Swiss cheese plant, many species alter their growth pattern when they touch a solid object. A familiar example is seen in climbing plants. Such plants often send out long, wirelike "feelers" called *tendrils*. When a tendril touches a branch, fence, or other object, it begins to curl, wrapping itself around the support over and over again.

What causes this twining? Again the answer is auxin. Auxin in the tendril's growing tip flows away from the side that touches the solid object. This causes the cells on the opposite side to rapidly lengthen, curving the tendril around the support. So fast is this response that a climbing vine such as the garden pea plant (*Pisum sativum*) can lash itself to a support within an hour of touching it.

The tendrils of many plants, such as gourds, can even "decide" whether or not an object is worth climbing. They will simply unwind from any surface too smooth to provide a secure grip, then continue their search for something more appropriate. Once it has found a suitable support, the tendril of a gourd will begin to coil its length into a tight spring. In doing so, it pulls the rest of the plant closer to the support, encouraging other tendrils to latch hold.

Touch stimulates other plants, such as ivy and ficus, to produce root hairs, hooks, suckers, and other tools for latching onto a surface such as a tree trunk or a wall. A slightly different touch response goes by the tongue-twisting name of *thigmomorphogenesis*. Our understanding stems from studies in the 1970s, when botanists showed that touching and rubbing plants on a regular basis causes them to grow shorter and stockier than those not touched.

The researchers discovered that such stimulation caused a plant to produce a variety of growth hormones that promote branching at the expense of lengthening.

What is the purpose of this response? In nature, a plant frequently buffeted by rain and wind or brushed by passing animals is "wise" to develop a sturdy form that can withstand such rough "handling." This phenomenon also helps to explain why plants cultivated in a greenhouse tend to be taller and spindlier than those grown in gardens and other less-protected environments.

It is also thigmomorphogenesis that directs the sticky hairs of the sundew plant to grow toward a struggling insect on its surface.

CIRCADIAN MOVEMENTS

Many plants open their flowers each morning, only to close them again at dusk. Others, such as night-blooming cacti, open only at night. Some plants also fold or drop their leaves into a "sleeping position" each night. Take any of these plants into a windowless room, and they will continue their opening and closing like clockwork, regardless of darkness or light.

Such regular daily movements are called *circadian*. They are controlled by a mechanism that scientists often call a "biological clock." The nature and location of this "clock" in plants remain a great mystery. The usefulness of a biological clock is more obvious: night-blooming plants, for example, tend to be pollinated by moths and other creatures of the darkness, while flowers that open in the morning have pollinators that work by day. Similarly, plants that fold their leaves at night may benefit from reduced heat and moisture loss.

Photoperiodism

Plants can also measure changes in the length

of day and night, and use this ability to time the season in which they flower. The effect of day length on plants, discovered by scientists in the 1920s, is called *photoperiodism.*

Violets (left), poinsettias, and other short-day plants respond to the seasonal changes in the duration of light and dark periods by producing flowers.

Plants that flower only when days are shorter than a certain predetermined period are called short-day plants. They tend to flower in early spring, late summer, or autumn. Long-day plants, such as lettuce and spinach, bloom only when day length extends longer than a certain period. These plants usually blossom in late spring and early summer.

Working with plants under controlled conditions, botanists have discovered that it is the length of uninterrupted darkness rather than the length of light that triggers flowering in short-day and long-day plants. So how do these plants measure the night?

The process takes place in the leaves and involves a pigment called *phytochrome*. Phytochrome exists in two different and interchangeable forms—P(r) and P(fr). When P(r) absorbs red light, it turns into P(fr). When P(fr) absorbs far-red light, it changes back into P(r).

Daylight contains both red and far-red wavelengths. So, during the day, a plant contains an abundance of both P(r) and P(fr). But P(fr) breaks down in darkness. So the longer the night, the lower the level of P(fr) by morning. A short-day plant, then, requires levels of P(fr) to drop below a certain point before it will bloom. By contrast, low levels of P(fr) inhibit the flowering process in long-day plants.

With this understanding, flower growers have learned to use photoperiodism to their advantage. They can delay flowering in

potted chrysanthemums, for example, by simply switching on greenhouse lights in the middle of the night. As a result, consumers can purchase flowering chrysanthemums in midwinter, many months after they normally bloom.

Phytochrome also "tells" a plant when to shoot up in height and when to bush out with leaves. In dark or shady conditions, phytochrome exists mainly in the P(r) form. This directs the plant to concentrate all its energies on lengthening. A familiar example is a seedling germinating under the soil or in a dark room. It does not waste energy producing leaves, but directs all growth to stem elongation. For the same reason, sunlight-loving plants grow tall and spindly when placed in too much shade. In effect, the plants are "searching" for the light they need to survive. Once they reach ample light, the P(fr) in their tissues builds to a level that promotes branching and leaf production.

Phototracking

Plants can also move in ways that do not involve growth. Among the most familiar examples is the ability of many plants to change their

Much research has focused on how plants react to tactile stimulation. Excessive touching of young plants may result in short, stocky adults.

posture to face the Sun. This phenomenon is called solar tracking, and it can be seen quite dramatically in a meadow of lupine or in a field of sunflowers, cotton, or soybeans. These and many other plants begin each day facing east, then turn their leaves to follow the Sun as it arches overhead and sets in the west.

Such movements are controlled by a joint-like thickening at the base of each leaf. Water and minerals flow into and out of the cells on either side of this joint. As a result, one side or the other expands while the other contracts, turning the leaf. Phytochrome may play a role in controlling this movement.

Plants can also use solar tracking to avoid excess sunlight. Some plants lose too much water when they are exposed to the full force of the midday sun. Many others need to minimize solar exposure during times of drought. They do so by turning their leaves vertically, so that only the narrow edge of each blade faces direct sunlight.

NASTIC MOVEMENTS

Among the most fascinating of plant movements are those that can be seen with the naked eye. A delightful example is the leaf-drooping trick of the sensitive plant (*Mimosa pudica*), a common tropical weed. Its fronds are feathery, with a row of small leaflets on either side of the leaf stalk. Touch any one leaflet, and, within seconds, both rows collapse flat against the leaf stem. Shake the whole plant, and both leaflets and fronds will suddenly droop. This response is often enough to frighten or at least baffle a grasshopper or other leaf-eating pest.

How does it work? The slightest touch triggers a tiny electrical current that travels along sap ducts in the leaf stalks and stem of the sensitive plant. This signal triggers a sudden water loss from the swollen joints at the base of each leaf and leaflet, which causes them to droop.

In a classic example of passive defense, the leaves and other structures of the poison-ivy plant (above) contain oils to which humans are highly allergic.

A similar mechanism may be at work in the Venus's-flytrap (*Dionaea muscipula*). Like the drooping of the *Mimosa* leaf, the sudden closure of the flytrap's toothy snare is triggered by touch. But one might say that the Venus's-flytrap is "smarter" than the sensitive plant because it can distinguish between the touch of an inanimate object such as a leaf and a live one such as an insect. Namely, the flytrap's hair triggers must be touched twice before its snare snaps closed. (See also "Carnivorous Plants and Other Unusual Species," page 108.)

ATTACK AND DEFENSE

The quick snap of the Venus's-flytrap and the collapsing-leaf trick of the sensitive plant are among the Plant Kingdom's most dramatic examples of attack and defense. Other plant "battle tactics" are less obvious but equally fascinating.

Many plants produce chemical weapons to deter their enemies. Sometimes this method of defense requires no special action on the part of the plant. Poison ivy (*Toxicodendron radicans*), for example, contains stinging oils whether or not it is ever touched.

By contrast, many plants crank up production of their chemical defenses only in response to attack. In the Arctic, for example, low-growing plants such as sedges must withstand browsing by animals such as lemmings. The browsing stimulates the roots and leaves of these plants to produce chemicals such as tannin that block an animal's digestive juices. If the browsing is light, the plants stop producing this chemical after a few days—thus conserving their energy for growth. But when browsing is heavy, the sedges produce more and more of these chemicals. As a result, the browsing animals cannot digest any food, grow ever hungrier, and eventually (if all goes according to the sedge's "plan") die or migrate elsewhere.

Similarly, when gypsy-moth caterpillars strip an oak tree of its leaves, the tree will produce new foliage that is both high in tannin and

Lovely blossoms (above) belie the purple loosestrife's behavior underground, where it wages war with the roots of other plants. The tamarisk tree (below) absorbs huge amounts of water at the expense of other plants.

leathery in texture. As a result, caterpillars feeding on the replacement leaves grow more slowly, if at all. Often this is enough to ease future gypsy-moth outbreaks.

Botanists have recently discovered that plants can even "warn" their neighbors of impending attack. When an animal browses on the African acacia, for example, the plant both fills its leaves with distasteful chemicals and releases ethylene gas into the air. The gas stimulates surrounding acacias to produce distasteful chemicals of their own. Finding no plants fit to eat, browsing animals then leave the area. Scientists also have discovered similar behavior in lima-bean plants and sagebrush. When attacked, these plants also release chemicals that warn their neighbors to prepare themselves.

But plants can often be the aggressors. In their never-ending struggle for light, plants jockey with each other for a larger place in the Sun. Victory usually goes to whatever plant can grow fast enough to shade out its neighbors. Evolution has also produced thousands of climbing plants that clamber up and over larger individuals using tendrils, spikes, hooks, and adhesive pads. Many of these go so far as to kill their supports with encircling vines, as do strangler figs, honeysuckles, morning glories, and ivies.

Plants also battle out of sight, their roots competing for moisture and minerals. An extreme example of such underground combat can be found in the parched western heathlands of Australia. There, in the hottest and driest months of summer (December and January), the beautiful Christmas-tree plant (*Nuytsia floribun-*

da) bursts into bloom, its leafy branches loaded with golden-orange blossoms. The sight is all the more spectacular as, all around the Christmas tree, other plants have withered back to the ground for lack of water.

What is its secret? When one of its roots meets that of a neighbor, the Christmas-tree root produces a small white clamp that encircles its victim and pierces it with two sharp, woody pincers. The pincers then grow inside the wound, snaking their way into the neighboring plant's water-conducting tubes. The root of the Christmas-tree plant then becomes a siphon, sucking its victim dry. In this way, a single Christmas-tree plant can steal water and nutrients from thousands of plants in a circle measuring up to 300 feet (91.5 meters) from its trunk.

It may seem no surprise that the Australian Christmas tree is a member of the mistletoe family. The familiar mistletoes of North America and Europe "bleed" their hosts by attaching themselves directly to a trunk or branch.

TRAVEL

Although we think of plants as stationary, they all must travel at some point in their life cycle, if only as a seed. Most plants do this in a passive way—their seeds simply fall with gravity, ride the wind, or hitch a ride on (or in) a passing animal. A few plants, however, have evolved spectacular ways of dispersing their seeds using their own brute force.

The squirting cucumber (*Ecballium elaterium*) is famous for its small blue-green cukes, which fill to near-bursting with slimy juice. The pressure within builds until the mature cucumber finally bursts off its stalk. It literally flies

Plants have evolved various methods of seed dispersal to ensure that their species survive. For some plants, a gust of wind (top) is enough to carry seeds to a new destination. Sometimes humans help the cause (above).

through the air as far as 20 feet (6 meters), riding a jet spray of slime and tiny seeds.

Even more explosive is the seed dispersal of the dwarf mistletoe (*Arceuthobium minutissima*) of the Himalayas. Each of the mistletoe's bullet-shaped seeds grows enclosed in a small, juicy berry. Like the fruit of the squirting cucumber, the mistletoe berry fills with juice as it matures, building up tremendous pressure. When ripe, the skin of the berry violently ruptures, spewing its seed up to 50 feet (15 meters) away. Measurements show the seed to be moving at an impressive 60 miles (96 kilometers) per hour as it leaves its launcher! Thanks to a gluey coating, the seed sticks to whatever branch or trunk it strikes. Fortunately, most mistletoes grow fairly high in the canopy, keeping hikers out of their direct line of fire.

Many plants power their explosions in the opposite manner. Their launch energy comes from drying rather than fluid buildup. The spore cases of ferns and the seed pods of broom plants provide familiar examples. Uneven drying creates a tension across the surface of the capsule or the pod, which then splits violently along a line of weakened tissue.

The most dramatic example of all may be the explosive seed pods of the sandbox or monkey's dinner-bell trees (*Hura crepitans* and *H. polyandra*) of Central and South America. When ripe, their pumpkin-shaped pods explode with the sound of a rifle shot. Although sometimes used to line boulevards, these trees have some obvious disadvantages. Not only are they noisy, but passersby have to frequently take cover from their scattering seeds!

Plant succession is the orderly process by which plant communities evolve over time. A catastrophic forest fire (left) often gives ecologists the first-hand opportunity to study secondary succession (above), the succession process in an area where it has occurred at some point in the past.

PLANT SUCCESSION

by Matthew Longabucco

All that's left in the wake of a disastrous forest fire is a blasted landscape and a deep carpet of ash. And yet, within a year—or sometimes just a few months—fresh new grasses and wildflowers will spring from soil newly enriched by the recent catastrophe. In the years that follow, tall grasses will flourish, then gradually give way to hardy pines. Ultimately, an oak and hickory hardwood forest will establish itself, accompanied by the complex web of animal life characteristic of the region.

Hundreds of miles away, people in a large city drive each day past an abandoned lot. Some may notice, however, that the stone surfaces do not remain bare for long. Lichens take hold in a sunny corner, while grasses literally break through the old foundations. Before long, grasses several feet tall wave to passersby; if left undisturbed, the lot's flora will soon include young saplings.

Even the former swimming hole is covering up with a thick layer of surface algae. A few more years, and the fishermen must leave as well: the pond has grown shallow with soil and grasses, while the water has become too deoxygenated for fish to survive. The process continues for centuries, and, if conditions are right, a deciduous forest will one day take its place.

THE PROCESS OF SUCCESSION

The above are examples of plant succession, the process by which plant communities evolve along a predictable path in a given environment. The term for a complete arc of a particular succession is a *sere*, and each community in that succession is referred to as a *seral stage*. Plants and their environments change together through the process of succession: plants alter their surroundings (by affecting wind, temperature, humidity, and soil), and these changes permit the establishment of different plants, which will then further alter the environment, and so on in a repeating cycle.

Ecologists agree that the force driving this process is *autogenous,* or "community-controlled," meaning that the plants themselves determine the direction and progress of succession. Researchers also recognize, however, that variables present in the environment play a role in the pattern, speed, and limits of succession.

Plant succession will occur in virtually all terrestrial or freshwater environments (marine succession is difficult to study because the oceans have been stable for many millennia). Succession always proceeds in a number of natural directions:

- From severity to stability;
- From less organic matter to more;
- From linear food chains to weblike ones;
- From low species diversity to high;
- From small species to large ones;
- From high entropy to low;
- From short life cycles to long ones; and
- From open mineral cycles to closed ones.

Ecologists point out that succession represents a shift in energy flow in that, ultimately, more and more energy will be used for the maintenance, rather than for the proliferation, of increasingly complex communities. Interruptions in these progressions—be they natural catastrophes or from human intervention—can prolong or reverse succession.

Primary or Secondary?

The starting point of a given sere determines whether the succession is classified as primary or secondary. *Primary succession* occurs when living organisms arrive in an environment that has never before been colonized. Such a situation might occur on bare mineral soils, rock, volcanic ash, sand dunes, or new islands; a new dam or a diverted stream might set the stage for primary freshwater succession.

The first plants in a given primary succession constitute the *pioneer community*. The species that comprise the pioneer community depend on the climate, altitude, and a number of other environmental factors. Regardless of these conditions, all pioneer species must be hardy, equipped to survive in adverse climate and inhospitable edaphic (soil) conditions, and, most important, capable of altering the environment. During their brief stay, the pioneers will make an area "friendlier" for the species to come.

Secondary succession occurs in an area where succession has happened in the past. The community in such an area might have given way to climate changes, been wiped out by natural catastrophe such as fire or flood, or been removed by humans intentionally (a cleared forest) or inadvertently (a polluted area). Species

In a cooled lava flow, the hardy plants that first take hold gradually help crumble the rock, paving the way for increasingly complex plants to establish themselves.

Just because succession is natural does not necessarily make it beneficial. Plant and animal diversity reflects healthy, complex ecosystems, and diversity is a result of change and rejuvenation. Fire plays a key role in promoting that rejuvenation.

When fires of natural origin are allowed to burn, they remove dead brush and species that have come to dominate an environment at the expense of others. After a blaze clears an area, secondary succession gets a kick start that always impresses ecologists with its variation and vigor. A wealth of nutrients from burned organic material, along with sunlight that may be reaching the ground for the first time in decades, provides a growth opportunity for long-subordinated plants to make a new thrust toward a different climax—one that may create a niche for previously excluded plant or animal life, such as the bluebird at left.

Many plants need fire simply to begin growth; the lodgepole pine has seeds encased in resin that requires high heat to begin germination. Without fire and new chances for succession, the forest would lose the dynamic forces that give it vitality.

that initiate secondary succession do not necessarily emphasize hardiness, since previous succession has probably made the environment fairly hospitable. Rather, these species are noted for their ability to exploit a vulnerable area.

Climax Communities

The ultimate goal of all succession is the *climax community*—the point at which an ecosystem has stabilized, supporting the maximum amount of complex life-forms in a closed and efficient system. Nutrients are recycled within the community, symbiotic relationships among plants and animals function at peak levels, and few environmental extremes exist.

The plant-succession process shown here follows the transformation of an abandoned field into a forest. Essentially, the bare landscape gradually fills with grasses and weeds. As time passes, shrubs dot the grassy habitat. Finally, trees emerge among the shrubs, and, ultimately, large trees predominate.

PRIMARY SUCCESSION

Colonization of Bare Rock

By the process of succession, even bare rock can become a forest. As an example, consider a rock surface in a climate that experiences a moderate amount of moisture. Such a precipitation level will foster *mesarch succession*, an advantageous condition for the plants that will eventually thrive there.

The unavailability of soil nutrients makes bare rock a particularly harsh environment. However, lichens (a combination of algae and fungi) are able pioneers on such a surface. These organisms can endure exposure to the elements, thrive in direct light (which they photosynthesize into energy), and require no soil nutrients. The lichens immediately begin to alter the rock surface by fixing nitrogen (a key nutrient) from the atmosphere and by producing acidic waste materials. These acids break down the rock, liberating minerals that, together with the atmo-

| Abandoned field | Grasses (1 to 10 years) | Grasses and shrubs (10 to 25 years) |

spheric nitrogen, provide enough of a nutrient base to support the next community: mosses. The mosses that replace the lichens grow in webs, forming a mat of vegetation. As the mosses continue to break down the rock surface, their leafy structures also function to catch wind-borne soil and add it to the mat.

Hardy grasses come next in the succession process. They, too, can fix atmospheric nitrogen through a symbiotic relationship with microbial species in their roots. As the size of the vegetation grows, the amount of organic material added to the surface when organisms die and decompose increases as well. The lichens and mosses are gone now, their light source cut off by tall grasses, and their ability to compete for resources severely limited. Biennial grasses come and go, gradually replaced by perennial grasses. A grasslike broomsedge or alder might be dominant after 50 years. Eventually shrubs and sumacs establish themselves.

By this point, the soil layer is thick and rich, and pines are likely to take over. The nutrients are no longer so much in the soil, but are instead incorporated into the living trees and other plants. Eventually, over several centuries, taller hardwoods—ashes, elms, and birches—will shade out the pines, which require sunlight to thrive. Finally, an oak-hickory forest will emerge as the climax community.

By virtue of its unique composition, a sand dune (above) undergoes a specialized form of plant succession—one that is quite vulnerable to human activity of any kind.

Colonization of Sand Dunes

The process of succession unfolds on sand dunes as well, although thousands of years may be required to see it through. Ecologists have witnessed stages of such a succession on dunes left in the wake of the receding waters of Lake Michigan. *Xerarch succession* is the term used to describe plant growth in a sandy environment and in other biomes with minimal moisture. Xerarch communities will progress toward a point of average moisture, then follow the process of mesarch succession from that point.

Pioneers on dunes include various beach grasses. If wind blows sand over these pioneers, the succession may be halted. (Human activity can have a similar effect, which is why many

Emerging forest
(25 to 100 years)

Mature forest
(more than 100 years)

If left on its own, a pond will eutrophicate—gradually fill in with plants (above) until it loses its identity as a body of water and ultimately evolves into a forest.

beach areas request that visitors stay off sand dunes.) The grasses form deep, interconnecting roots that help hold the sand together.

As the grasses grow larger, windblown soil is added to the humus formed by decomposition. Scrub bushes will flourish and then give way to a jack-pine forest. Black oak will edge out the pine, and a shade-tolerant understory will take over beneath. A maple-beech forest is the probable climax. Over the course of the succession, the dry, sterile sand has given way to moist, rich, deep soil.

Colonization of a Pond

The process by which a pond or other body of water becomes a forest has its own name: *eutrophication*. Eutrophication is an example of *hydrarch succession*: it begins with a highly moist area and progresses toward a more-average moisture level. Like xerarch succession, the hydrarch process takes an extended period of time, since the communities expend great effort just to arrive at the starting point of mesarch succession.

Surface algae provide the initial nitrogen and organic material in the pond. Pollution often speeds up eutrophication at its outset by infusing nitrogen and phosphorous industrial by-products (which serve as nutrients) into the body of water. Below the surface, algae and submerged plants such as pondweed, tape grass, bladderwort, and water milfoil establish themselves. Airborne and waterborne sediments are important factors; they "silt

in" the pond or lake, reducing its depth and bringing submerged species closer to sunlight. Dead organic material from both the submerged plants and from the more-advanced water lilies and duckweed also fills up the pond. Eventually, emergent species arrive; cattails, bulrushes, wild rice, and saw grass grow out of the water. The vegetation is thickest along the edges of the pond, marching slowly toward the ever-shallower center as the years go by. Both the volume and rate of movement of the water affect the rate of succession.

Once the emergent species have created a marsh environment, a thicket of cottonwood, swamp rose, and alder will arrive, to be replaced in turn by basswoods, then tulip trees, white elm, and ash; eventually, a climax forest of beech and maple or oak and hickory is achieved.

SECONDARY SUCCESSION

A good example of secondary succession occurs on the unused farm fields in the uplands of North Carolina. While the soil may be too nutrient-poor to grow crops, it is far richer than most primary-succession environments. Thus, the first species to arrive is the one that can most quickly establish itself: in this case, crabgrass.

Species turnover then accelerates rapidly. Horseweed, with its efficient seed-dispersal system, proliferates quickly, and soon shades out the crabgrass. Wild aster, however, can grow be-

Secondary succession proceeds quickly on abandoned farmland. On the neglected Michigan farm below, junipers and red cedars took root almost immediately.

neath the horseweed, whose decomposition inhibits its own growth. Soon the aster, accompanied by ragweed (a plant that does not require many nutrients), becomes dominant.

In only the third year, broomsedge arrives. Within 15 years, pines 10 to 15 feet (3 to 4.5 meters) tall have formed a canopy, ironically preventing further shade-intolerant pines from flourishing. The herbs below die out as well and, together with organic material from decomposing pines, provide the deep, moist soil in which hardwood seedlings now sprout. Dogwood, red gum, and red maple trees will all help shade out the pines. After about 150 years, oak and hickory will dominate.

CLIMAX CLASSIFICATION

Why do temperate-zone climaxes favor oak-hickory or beech-maple forests? Why are hardwood trees more "successful" than, say, horseweed and aster? The answer is that these particular species seem to best fit the requirements of a climax community: sustained reproduction and nourishment.

One of the major factors that will determine the type of climax community is climate. In the United States, for example, Virginia might favor oak and hickory, while Wisconsin's cooler weather will lead to beech and maple. But even within distinct climatic regions, various factors will figure prominently in determining where succession ends up. Wet soil in a beech-maple area will result in a sycamore-tulip climax, while drier soil fosters an oak-chestnut community. A valley may have a local climate significantly different from the regional norm; climaxes will reflect this difference.

Ecologists have affixed the designation of *preclimax* to climaxes that occur in xeric, or drier, areas of a climatic zone. South-facing slopes, or regions at the southern fringe (in the

Northern Hemisphere) of a large zone, will experience warmer and drier conditions. "Preclimax" is a confusing term because the prefix "pre" would seem to suggest that this is a community that exists prior to a climax. In fact, preclimax is an arbitrary term, and it refers to a climax in its own right.

The same applies to the term *postclimax*—a successional end point occurring in a more *hygric*, or moister, portion of a given zone. Lowlands, deltas, and floodplains, north-facing slopes, or the northern fringes of the zone might display postclimax communities.

Still another special case is the *disclimax*, a situation resulting from repeated disruption of an area. A successful climax might be prevented by overgrazing, logging, or periodic fires. Even a front lawn is an example of a disclimax. A disclimax may be fairly uniform: always reaching a certain point, but never realizing its potential climax.

When environmental conditions simply prohibit complex communities, a *subclimax* is in effect. A prairie exemplifies a subclimax.

Ecologists have long debated whether preclimaxes, postclimaxes, disclimaxes, or subclimaxes are true climaxes. Some ecologists maintain that there is only one type of climax for each climatic zone. Their so-called *monoclimax* theory states that all climaxes in a zone will continue to struggle, no matter how long it takes, toward the one real climax for their climate. Supporters of the *polyclimax* theory argue that if a succession has progressed as far as local conditions will allow, the resulting community must be designated a climax for that environment. These ecologists feel that there are a number of possible stable end points for any given region.

This theory had become dominant in recent years, and field research bears it out. For example, ecologists in Guyana have identified five different stable climaxes in one climatic zone. Because conditions are so susceptible to local variations, it makes more sense to conceptualize climaxes as diverse and adaptable.

The climax of nearly every temperate-succession process is a hardwood forest (above) in which the nutrients are contained within the trees rather than the soil.

FORESTERS AND THEIR SCIENCE

by Matthew Longabucco

Since 1977, Wangari Maathai's Green Belt Movement has overseen the planting of some 30 million trees in 15 African nations. In addition to a program that compensates women for planting trees, Maathai's organization also coordinates efforts to protect existing forests. The Kenyan environmentalist was awarded the 2004 Nobel Peace Prize for her work. Meanwhile, in northwest Costa Rica, Daniel Janzen's Guanacaste National Park Project fights enemies as diverse as fire and funding problems in order to revitalize a section of tropical dry forest. Janzen plants trees and encourages nature's own growth processes to restore a habitat rich with spectacular species and biological mysteries. He predicts it will take 1,000 years for the dry forest to be as it once was.

Why do these people and organizations devote their lives to projects whose ends they will never witness? And how can they hope to replace and shape forests—one of nature's most complex creations? Indeed, the ecosystem of our planet depends on forests to prevent soil erosion, provide watershed sources, and serve as an important wildlife habitat. Foresters recognize the forest as a resource of unparalleled value to Earth and humanity.

WHAT IS FORESTRY?

Forestry is an enormously practical science. While laboratory analysis and academic research do represent important aspects of the discipline, most foresters can be found in the field, concerning themselves with the direct management of the natural systems they study. Forestry is the science of cultivating, managing, and protecting the world's forestlands.

To accomplish such goals, foresters must juggle the variety of demands placed on the resources of the forests. If these demands make physical use of the forest, they are classified as *consumptive.* Examples include timber cutting by private industry for lumber, pulp, paper, and chemicals, and by private individuals for use as a fuel source. Demands that do not physically deplete the forest are termed *nonconsumptive.* An example is the recreational use of natural areas by urban populations. Forestry professionals are trained to carefully balance consumptive and nonconsumptive demands as part of their efforts to preserve forests from the potential problems caused by excessive logging, careless exploitation, and the natural threats posed by fire, insects, and disease.

THE HISTORY OF FORESTRY

Forests were once so seemingly vast and plentiful that no one believed they could ever disappear. Trees were cut down to make room for agriculture or to clear space to build cities. Forests were also seen as "green gold," an inexhaustible resource pool to be exploited for building material, fuel, and other purposes. The Industrial Revolution that began in the 18th century required ever-increasing amounts of these resources, and forests provided them. Americans cut vast tracts of forests, although they took pride in their natural wealth. (The American folk hero Johnny Appleseed was a model of primitive forestry.)

Europeans were the first to face forest depletion, since they had a long history of agriculture and were enthusiastic proponents of industry. Because of this depletion, Germany, France, Sweden, and other countries were already planning and planting new forests in the 1700s. But in the United States, it was not until much later that forestry concepts took hold.

Concern in the United States for forest management arose in the early 1800s, when oak and pine, necessary for shipbuilding, were becoming seriously threatened in the Northeast. Consequently, the military insisted that care be taken in logging these particular varieties. But it was

not until 1891, after Americans had already cleared forests from coast to coast, that Congress passed a law creating forest reserves.

Visionaries such as Gifford Pinchot, who created the Society of American Foresters in 1901, realized that their generation must begin protecting the forests before one of America's greatest assets was gone forever. In 1905, Pinchot became chief forester of the newly formed Forest Service. He had a strong ally in President Theodore Roosevelt, an avid naturalist whose dedication to conservation added 128 million acres (51 million hectares) to America's fledgling forest reserves.

Forests with high aesthetic quality or important watersheds became the first national parks. By the mid-20th century, the United States was instituting reforestation laws and even planting trees on farmland that had become unproductive. Today, the United States possesses about 71 percent of the more than 1 billion acres (405 million hectares) of woodlands that once covered its breadth. Of this land, only 5

Whether in the trees (facing page) or on the ground (right), foresters bear the awesome responsibility of cultivating, managing, and protecting the world's woodlands.

percent is considered to be virgin forest, untouched since its ancient origin.

In 1945, the United Nations inaugurated its Forestry Division. Forestry became a worldwide concern, not only in terms of national parks (present in more than 100 countries) and other forest preserves, but also because world ecosystems were at stake. The recent history of forestry is particularly important in South America and Africa, where foresters fight for the very survival of the environmentally crucial rain forests, which contain a wealth of species, produce substantial oxygen, play a key role in world climates, and harbor untold natural medicines.

TECHNIQUES OF FORESTRY

Foresters deal with all types of woodland use by measuring the amount of trees, determining whether they can be cut and how, fighting

Some foresters develop strategic plans for preserving or rejuvenating rain forests (above) and other woodlands threatened with destruction.

natural hazards, and implementing realistic conservation techniques to preserve this renewable resource. To tackle such weighty tasks requires a wide breadth of methods and specializations within forestry. In these tasks, foresters are frequently assisted by specialists called *rangers*, men and women who serve an important custodial function in forests around the world, including woodlands throughout the U.S. national-park and national-forest systems.

Mensuration

The first step in managing a forest is to evaluate the quantity and quality of the trees that make up a particular system. The science of measuring forests is known as *mensuration*.

Foresters in the field first survey and map a given forest area, usually with a compass and simple pace measurements of distances, but sometimes with advanced technology such as satellite imaging. The maps are then used to divide the forest into *compartments*, or manageable units of area. These compartments are usually uniform rectangular shapes, but sometimes they follow natural boundaries such as streams or cliffs. Evaluation of the actual timber in these compartments is then accomplished by a method known as *cruising*. In a timber cruise, foresters either systematically or randomly (depending on the degree of accuracy desired) sample an area of forest, collecting data on the diameters, heights, and varieties of trees. Tree rings are also counted to determine ages and histories of the trees. Using these samples, foresters apply their knowledge of woodland systems to calculate an estimate of the volume of timber in the total acreage. Groups of trees are divided into units known as *stands* if they possess uniformity of age, species, structure, and/or growth conditions. Stands occupy areas ranging from 1 to 100 acres (0.4 to 40 hectares).

Mensuration also includes appraising forests in terms of the wildlife habitats they provide; the type of watersheds existing there; and the extent of damage from fires, insect pests, and disease. This information may be needed by environmental groups, timber companies, government agencies, or other parties.

Silviculture

When foresters want to grow a planned forest, stimulate the growth of certain desirable trees, remove undesirable species, or manipulate stands of trees in any other way, the techniques they use belong to the specialization known as *silviculture*. Silviculture is in essence a form of long-term agriculture; after all, it takes several decades to grow marketable timber.

Consider the example of a company that wants to cut timber in such a way as to be able to regrow trees on the land. Depending on the types of trees and the environment in general, foresters employed by the company might turn to any one of several silvicultural methods.

Clear-cutting. This method entails cutting all the trees in a section of forest. Conifers might be cut in this way, because these trees do not need shade or shelter from exposure to temperature changes to regrow on the bare land left behind. Foresters choose to clear-cut when seeking to regrow a stand of a uniform age.

Seed-tree cutting. This technique leaves only a few trees behind. The remaining trees provide seeds to regenerate a new stand that will be of uniform age except for the seed trees.

Shelterwood cutting. Such cutting removes an old stand in stages. In this way, enough shade is present at any one time to provide shelter for species that require it for growth.

Selection cutting. Here only a few trees (usually the more mature specimens) are removed at a time, creating an uneven-age stand of shade-tolerant trees.

Release cutting. This method eliminates overtopping trees whose shade is stunting the growth of desired species below. Undesirable species may also be cut to make more room or leave more nutrients for other trees.

Afforestation. In this practice, trees are grown where none exist—that is, without a seed source. To achieve this objective, foresters plant nursery-grown seedlings or saplings. Nursery trees may be used in any situation to supplement or replace natural regeneration.

Some foresters originally entered the field by building upon a general interest in the environment.

Careers in Forestry

Most foresters have a college degree, and it is not uncommon for forestry professionals to pursue a master's degree or doctorate as well. A forestry degree in the United States can be pursued at any one of 48 schools accredited by the Society of American Foresters. However, since forestry's emphasis on fieldwork calls for specific skills, many vocational and technical schools offer their own programs. Germany and other heavily forested countries have such a large market for forestry that they often employ nonprofessionals as well, mainly as field assistants who work under the supervision of well-trained professionals.

Of the 20,000 or so foresters in the United States, about two-thirds are employed by federal, state, or local government agencies, notably by the U.S. National Park Service, the U.S. Forest Service, and the U.S. Bureau of Land Management. In the private sector, many foresters work for paper companies, chemical manufacturers, and even railroads or mining companies (which own large tracts of land). Any organization in the public or private sector that owns or oversees forestlands needs to employ foresters to preserve its resources and to ensure compliance with environmental legislation. Other careers in the field include education or consulting.

Entry-level jobs in forestry include compassman (working with mapmaking crews), forest-fire spotter or dispatcher, or one of myriad positions assisting more-experienced scientists in cataloging, cutting, protecting, and maintaining forests. Experienced foresters supervise planting crews, evaluate timber, designate timber for cutting, inspect logging practices, serve as consultants for environmental agencies, work in public relations, or perform any of a host of other tasks. Salaries are competitive, especially now that the need for more forestry professionals is growing every day.

Fire prevention figures prominently in the duties of a forester. Foresters work closely with firefighters and government officials to bring major blazes under control.

and control fires, foresters first must find them. Foresters may consult the *fire danger rating and burning index* to gauge the risk for fires based on humidity levels, moisture content of trees, the slope of the land, elevation, and other data. Fire-spotting towers are common in virtually all high-risk forests, and aircraft also search the vast woodlands for "smokes." Global satellite systems are now used to detect outbreaks, and computer simulations have been developed that predict a fire's likely spread.

Communications systems play an essential role in reporting back fire spottings to dispatching stations. Specialists triangulate (calculate using several reference points) the location of the fire and send out highly trained crews to fight the blaze. This may entail the dispatching of aircraft to drop flame-retardant chemicals on the fire or ground crews to snuff out the fire using dirt or water.

Another way to fight fire is with fire itself; small, controlled fires in the path of a major conflagration can use up all the fuel and stop the larger blaze from spreading past the burnt-out

Silviculture experts choose which of these or other methods is appropriate. An uninformed choice of cutting methods could have adverse environmental consequences. Silviculturists also prune and trim trees; work with genetic engineering and hybridization; and use machinery, remote-control pruners, advanced fertilizers, or even controlled fires to manipulate stands. If they work for a timber company, their likely goal is *sustained-yield management*: setting up a system in which the harvest of trees equals the new growth.

FOREST PROTECTION

Three serious threats to any forest are fire, insects, and disease; foresters combat all three. Forest fires can occur naturally (lightning is often the culprit) or, as is overwhelmingly the case, because of human carelessness. To prevent

Pollution can cause great damage to trees. In Sweden (right), foresters use a special apparatus for monitoring acid rain and its effect on various species of trees.

boundary. Sometimes foresters will intentionally burn a particularly high-risk section of forest before a fire even starts, thereby protecting the larger forest around it. A North American forest that had 25 mature trees per acre a century ago could now have up to 1,000 mature trees on that same acre. Packed tightly together, the trees are not only weaker and more disease-prone, but the concentration of flammable material poses a significant threat, especially during drought. Experts advise the use of intentional, controlled fires to maintain a forest's health. Prescribed fires, also called controlled burns, can protect trees from future fire, disease, and insects.

Insects and the damage they wreak on a forest are generally controlled with pesticides. Unfortunately, the chemicals in pesticides can have serious repercussions. Insects necessary to the complex web of a forest ecosystem may be killed. The chemicals may also harm other wildlife or pollute watershed areas. Foresters, while always on the lookout for safer pesticides, also seek "natural" defenses, such as predatory birds to feed on pest insects, or the cultivation of insect-resistant trees.

Disease has wiped out many forests in the past. Usually disease is a necessary element of natural selection, ridding the forest of weak or old trees to make room for healthier specimens. But when trees or tree cuttings are transplanted among unfamiliar forests, diseases may be unwittingly introduced with which even the healthy trees in a forest may be unable to cope. The best way to prevent such occurrences is for foresters to carefully consider what transplants they introduce into a balanced system.

Foresters committed to forest protection also address the problems of acid rain and pollution, which can have devastating effects on woodlands. These battles are often fought in a courtroom or in the halls of government.

FORESTRY IN THE FUTURE

When foresters talk about the future, they use the term *multiple use*. The concept of multiple use acknowledges that many demands, both consumptive and nonconsumptive, vie for the resources of the world's forests. To strike a balance among these demands means compromise. Strict conservationists who champion animal habitats, watersheds, and biological research

Scientists are nowhere near identifying all plants that flourish in the rain forest. Foresters hope to discover species that have natural medicinal properties.

often conflict with tourists who need roads and parking lots to reach natural beauty; both of these groups may be at odds with logging companies that provide jobs and follow responsible silviculture practices. National parks are often in the eye of the storm when it comes to arguments over multiple use; in the United States, one-third of the timber comes from these parks, a figure some feel is too high. Sorting out the rights of all parties involved is a central and complex task for the future.

Improvements in forestry methods are also being explored for the future. Better protective methods need to be discovered, bare lands beg to be replanted, stands should be revitalized with healthy species; down the road, genetic hybridization can lead to forests of unimagined potential. New specializations such as agroforestry and urban forestry look to bring forests to new frontiers, reclaiming farmland and urban terrain. The future looks bright when one considers the 1.4 billion seedlings planted in the United States each year, but the 100,000 forest fires that take place in the same span of time demonstrate that much remains to be done.

PLANT COMMUNITIES

by Matthew Longabucco

In a human context, the term "community" can be defined as a unified body of individuals—people whose common social, economic, or political interests motivate them to strive for a common goal, all the time maintaining a continuous and harmonious relationship among themselves.

In a botanical context, the term "community" also refers to a unified body of individuals—in this case, plants. The individuals in a plant community inhabit and maintain themselves with reasonable permanence in a particular area, all the time working together to achieve maximum efficiency. When this goal is met, *emergent properties* manifest themselves—synergies of the group that are not necessarily properties of any given individuals. For example, a well-functioning plant community recycles nutrients far more efficiently than could any of its member species individually.

In southeastern Arizona (above), an unusual combination of geology and climate combine to create a complex of communities noted for their diversity of plants.

GENERAL CHARACTERISTICS

Some ecologists argue that no true plant communities exist, but rather, that species types merely blend together and change across any given geographic area. The prevailing view recognizes distinct boundaries between communities, but also acknowledges that blending occurs—and even applies the term *ecotone* to describe the areas between two communities that contain elements of both. Both schools of thought see a community as part of the environment that affects it, and the environment as being affected by the community.

At the very least, a plant community has in common the same physical requirements (soil type, water needs, temperature tolerance, and solar-energy levels, among other criteria). If a plant community contains many species, even if these species are represented by only a few individuals, it is said to enjoy *high species richness*. If numerous species are well represented in a community, it is said to have *high species diversity*. In general, larger communities, ones in warmer climates, or communities further along in the process of plant succession have more member species.

The dominant species of a community is typically used to describe the entire complex. For example, the preponderance of pine trees in a wooded area would lead the community to be called a coniferous forest, even though maples and oaks are present, albeit in smaller numbers.

TYPES OF COMMUNITIES

Terms such as "desert" or "pond" refer to *abstract communities*, which have certain universal characteristics. *Concrete communities*, by contrast, are the actual geographic sites of given communities. This distinction is necessary because no two concrete communities are exactly alike. Indeed, two communities may both be called ponds, but share only general common characteristics.

The largest communities that are still uniform enough to recognize are called *biomes*. Owing to their sheer size, some biomes can be viewed on a world map, where the largest of them appear in a series of belts more or less parallel to the equator. This belt configuration is indicative of the fact that biomes are mainly a function of climate, which varies with latitude and, in some areas, altitude. Biomes are, in fact, almost invariably identified by their climatic region (arctic, temperate, tropical, etc.) as well as by the climax state they achieve.

Separate articles on several of the biomes discussed below appear in this volume, immediately following this article.

Terrestrial Plant Communities

Tropical rain forests. Substantial areas of rain forests occur in the Amazon and Orinoco basins in South America, in West-Central Africa, and in much of Southeast Asia—all low-altitude equatorial regions. Rainfall exceeds 80 inches (2,000 millimeters) annually and is distributed over the course of the year, with intermittent dry seasons. The variance in temperature between daytime highs and nighttime lows is greater than the overall temperature difference between winter and summer.

Abundant moisture and the consistently warm weather endow the rain forest with the greatest variety of life of all biomes. Indeed, the whole of Europe supports fewer species of trees

than can be identified in just a few acres of rain forest. Rain-forest soil is termed *latosolic*: reddish, leached earth that is highly permeable, rich in clay, and frequently saturated—and therefore drained of its nutrients.

Favorable year-round growing conditions allow broad-leaved evergreens to thrive. These trees form a canopy under which little grows. The dark interior resembles a cathedral of branchless, tall trunks whose floor litter decomposes rapidly. Only where the upper stratum clears do shrubs, herbs, ferns, palms, and other plants grow densely.

Temperate deciduous forests. Sizable deciduous forests occur in the moderate climates of eastern North America, Europe, Japan, Australia, lower South America, and Central Asia. The 30 to 50 inches (760 to 1,270 millimeters) of precipitation is evenly distributed throughout the four distinct seasons. Soils are sometimes

Scientists recognize at least 10 different soil types. The properties of a given area's soil play a key role in the type of plant community that is likely to evolve there.

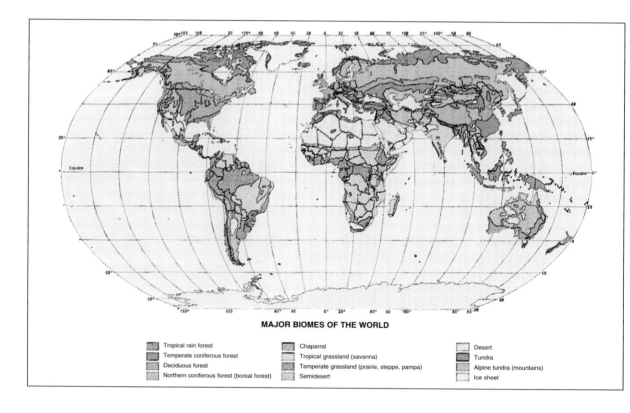

MAJOR BIOMES OF THE WORLD

Tropical rain forest	Chaparral	Desert
Temperate coniferous forest	Tropical grassland (savanna)	Tundra
Deciduous forest	Temperate grassland (prairie, steppe, pampa)	Alpine tundra (mountains)
Northern coniferous forest (boreal forest)	Semidesert	Ice sheet

latosolic, but predominantly *chernozemic*: dark ("chernozem" means "black earth"), fertile, and with a neutral pH level.

Deciduous forests have extensive ecotones and often support conifers during various stages of their evolution. For the most part, though, this biome consists of hardwood trees and shrubs (there is a well-developed understory), plants that lose their leaves in autumn and which require a dormancy period for seeds to ripen. Many of these plants produce pulpy fruits and nuts. The exact species present in a given forest depends on such varying factors as local temperatures, drainage, and elevation.

Coniferous forests. Biologists have identified numerous types (and subtypes) of coniferous forests. Some of the more familiar types are discussed here.

Southern pine forests occur along the Gulf of Mexico and in Florida, on the Iberian Peninsula, and sporadically elsewhere. The climate is subtropical, and the soils are rich with nutrients; some 40 to 80 inches (1,000 to 2,000 millimeters) of rain fall each year. Broad-leaved evergreens are the norm, although the famously stout live oaks thrive there, as do magnolias,

palms, and other warm-weather lovers. Vines are common, and ferns and orchids are plentiful in the understory of the forest.

In mountainous parts of the southwestern United States, the far drier climate and stony soils support piñon pines, junipers, and cedars.

The taiga, or northern coniferous forest, is a broad belt of evergreens that stretches across upper North America and Eurasia in what constitutes the world's most extensive continuous forest type—but one found only in the Northern Hemisphere. (Taiga may also occur at high altitudes—even in the tropics.)

This biome has a definite spring and summer, a brief (four- to five-month) growing season, and receives 10 to 30 inches (250 to 760 millimeters) of precipitation annually (including snowfall). The soil is *podsolic*—rich but acidic. Frequent fires stimulate nutrient cycling; otherwise, organic material decomposes slowly in the generally cold weather.

The taiga is characterized by needle-leaved evergreens, including spruces (white spruce is often dominant), firs, pines, hemlocks, and cedars. Local tree dominance is generally determined by variations in soil moisture. The dense shade created by these tree types all but prohibits shrub and herb growth, creating a fairly undeveloped understory.

The Pacific coast coniferous forest occurs along the western coast of North America from northern California to Alaska. Precipitation is high—from 50 to perhaps 120 inches (1,270 to 3,050 millimeters)—and fog and high humidity are common, leading the region to often be classified as a "temperate rain forest." The seasonal temperature range is slight and consistently mild. Soils are good, but vary in type.

Conifers dominate, although the specific species gradually change with increasing latitude. California oaks give way to redwoods and Douglas firs in Oregon, western hemlock in Washington, and Sitka spruce in Alaska. The thick undergrowth emphasizes moisture lovers: shrubs such as rhododendron and dogwood; ferns; and carpets of moss.

Tundra. The tundra is the northernmost biome, found worldwide adjacent to the polar ice caps, or in high-altitude mountain ranges such as the Andes and Himalayas (the so-called *alpine tundra*). Soils are poorly drained and poorly aerated, rendering the ground perennially wet—despite the fact that the tundra region receives less than 10 inches (250 millimeters) of precipitation annually. Some 12 to 18 inches (30 to 45 centimeters) below the surface lies *permafrost*—permanently frozen soil. Temperatures often fall below freezing at night—and remain there for weeks on end during much of the year—resulting in a very short growing season: only two to three months.

Tundra flora includes grasses, sedges, and rushes; scattered evergreen heath such as crowberry and bearberry; dwarf woody plants; and occasional wildflowers. Species flourish more in the "low tundra," the warmer regions of the biomes where a mat of vegetation and slowly decaying organic matter occupies water-saturated depressions in the landscape (decomposition is retarded by the cold). The "high tundra" represents the outposts of plant life on Earth; only lichens and sparse, hardy grasses can survive so close to the ice cap.

Grasslands. Grassland communities go by many names: steppe, llano, campo, pampa, prairie. They all spread widely across the interiors of temperate continents, where they are heavily exploited for pastureland. The 10 to 30 inches (250 to 760 millimeters) of precipitation in this biome exceeds desert levels, but falls erratically and is insufficient for forest growth. Fires are common and necessary for nutrient cycling; the soil is chernozemic. Seasons are alternately warm and cool, and plant life varies during the year as the temperatures fluctuate. Grass species minimize competition for moisture and nutrients by growing roots to many different depths. Environmental conditions generally determine the heights to which the grasses grow.

Chaparral. An extensive chaparral occurs in Mexico and Southern California, and similar systems are found on the Mediterranean and Black Sea coasts and in southern Australia. Dry summers alternate with winters of heavy rainfall. The soil is latosolic. Fire is a regular and integral occurrence: the community is a *disclimax*—constantly reborn from ashes (a necessity, since nitrogen would otherwise be scarce in this region).

Stunted, scrubby evergreens with thick, hard, broad leaves grow in the chaparral. Shrubs are hardy and short. Tree varieties include chamiso, coastal live oak, and manzanita.

Desert. Desert biomes occur in North America, Australia, and Asia, but the world's driest regions are in the Sahara, in Africa, and in South America, in northern Chile. Prevailing winds that have long since lost their moisture bring less than 10 inches (250 millimeters) of

Regardless of the latitude, the conditions high in the Himalayas (above) and in other lofty mountain ranges favor the development of tundralike plant communities.

By far, the oceans constitute the world's largest biome, albeit one with surprisingly little plant life. Seaweed, phytoplankton, and most other types of free-floating "plantlike" organisms are classified in Kingdom Protista.

rain to these environments. Soil is *desertic*—shallow and unstable. As a rule, days are hot, and nights are cold.

The amount of organic matter found in any desert is directly related to the moisture level. Plants are low to the ground and well spaced in order to reduce competition for scant resources. Annuals grow only after rainfall, when they bloom and reproduce with amazing rapidity. Desert shrubs readily shed their leaves if water must be preserved. Succulents such as cacti and yuccas store water; some cacti systems share shallow root reservoirs containing as much as 30 tons of liquid! Perennials have their survival methods as well; creosote bushes, for example, have waxy leaves to hold moisture, while mesquite sends roots as deep as 90 feet (27.5 meters) in search of water.

Savannas. India, South America, Australia, and especially Africa support savanna communities. From 20 to 50 inches (500 to 1,270 millimeters) of rain can fall, but soils are nevertheless desertic because of long dry seasons. The dearth of moisture during these periods leads to the frequent threat of fires.

Savannas are tropical grasslands dotted with clumps of trees. The species diversity is low and essentially limited to fire-resistant or-

ganisms. Acacias, palms, and baobabs are some of the more recognizable trees found on the African savanna, the landscape often associated with wildlife safaris.

Tropical deciduous forests. Between the often-dry savanna and the highly moist rain forest lies a tropical forest made up of deciduous trees. In Africa and Australia, these communities are called the *bush*; in Brazil, the *caatinga*; and, in tropical Asia, *monsoon forests*. Dry seasons alternate quite noticeably with wetter ones, although rainfall distribution can be erratic, even in the latter. (If precipitation distribution were uniform, a full deciduous forest would develop.) Soils are latosolic.

These forests consist of small, scrubby hardwoods, often so twisted and thorny as to be virtually impenetrable. The leaves, generally small, are shed in the dry season.

Shore Communities

Several types of communities establish themselves in the generally moist areas surrounding bodies of water.

Marshes. Marshes develop on river floodplains and around lakes in regions where wet and dry seasons alternate. Their early stages occur when depressions in the terrain fill with water and decomposed vegetation. The result is a moist, nutrient-rich habitat, one with the potential for high productivity. Water level is the variable that determines whether this potential will be reached: a developing community of shallow-water plants can be flooded, for example, or a deepwater community parched.

Soft-stemmed herbaceous plants dominate. Emergents such as cattails, sedge, and pickerel weed have stems partially in the water. Submergents such as milfoil and elodea survive entirely beneath the surface. Water lilies, pondweed, and other floaters have leaves and other structures that rest on the surface, but the plant itself is anchored to the marsh bottom. Saw grass is the characteristic species in Florida's Everglades National Park.

Swamps. These types of wetlands are sometimes transitional—a stage in plant succession. Periodic flooding, however, can maintain a permanent swamp community. These communities usually develop adjacent to sluggish rivers, where soil is black and highly organic, and where standing water saturates the ground during the growing season.

Woody trees and shrubs dominate, but climate and other factors decide whether hardwoods or evergreens will succeed. In the United States, there are red-maple swamps in the Northeast, and cypress swamps in the Deep South. Other common hardwoods include gums and ashes; cedars, firs, and spruces are swamp evergreens. These trees can form a canopy beneath which shade-tolerant shrubs—including alder, pussy willow, highbush, and sweetbush—thrive. Ferns, wildflowers, skunk cabbage, and moss are also part of the ecosystem.

Bogs. Bogs generally occur in once-glaciated areas. The distinguishing feature of a bog is its thick, spongy surface—a floating mat composed of sphagnum moss or other organic matter that forms a nonsoil surface with little visible water. The highly acidic conditions prevent bacteria from decomposing matter, causing the mat to thicken. Bogs support evergreen trees and shrubs, including spruces, larches, and cedars. The roots of the trees and shrubs help hold the mat together.

Estuary and sandy shore. Estuary plant communities occur where freshwater rivers meet the ocean, lending the soil a certain degree of *salinity*, or salt content, that varies with tides

and seasons. Water levels also shift considerably, affecting plant life by changing the amount of sunlight that reaches the estuary floor. Plant life is stratified across this type of environment, with the least-saline-tolerant plants found the farthest inland.

Along sandy shores, various forms of algae constitute the most successful flora. Such "holdfasts" attach themselves securely to rocks in order to cope with tidal activity. The type of rock, the minerals below the surface, and the water temperature of the region determine the species. Seaweeds, rockweeds, and red algae are common saline dwellers.

Aquatic Communities

Lakes and ponds. Lakes are large and deep. Water temperatures follow a stratified pattern, growing colder with depth. Ponds are smaller, their shallowness resulting in fairly uniform temperatures throughout. Both bodies of water are classified as oligotrophic, mesotropic, or eutrophic—being low-, medium-, or high-nutrient, respectively. Some ecologists declare that lakes and ponds are "born to die," regarding them as successional stages that will eventually be transformed into terrestrial communities.

No stem plants will grow in the deep center of a lake, where light is not available. Algae and phytoplankton form the basic organic aquatic community, while specialized vascular plants inhabit shallow waters or lake edges.

Rivers and streams. The rate of water flow—determined by the river's width and the steepness of its gradient—is the major factor for riverine communities. The direction of the current, the levels of oxygen and nutrients, and the composition of the riverbed also govern what plants establish themselves. The slower currents in pools and eddies make these areas hospitable to river bulrush, hornwort, and tape grass. In stronger currents, threadlike or boxlike algae attach themselves to rocks.

Ocean. The ocean is the largest biome, and the community about which scientists know the least. The communities in this biome are the least dense. Limiting factors include lack of nutrients and lack of light, although carbon dioxide (a necessity for plant respiration) is plentiful. Some submerged plants survive on the continental shelves, but algae constitute the majority of ocean flora.

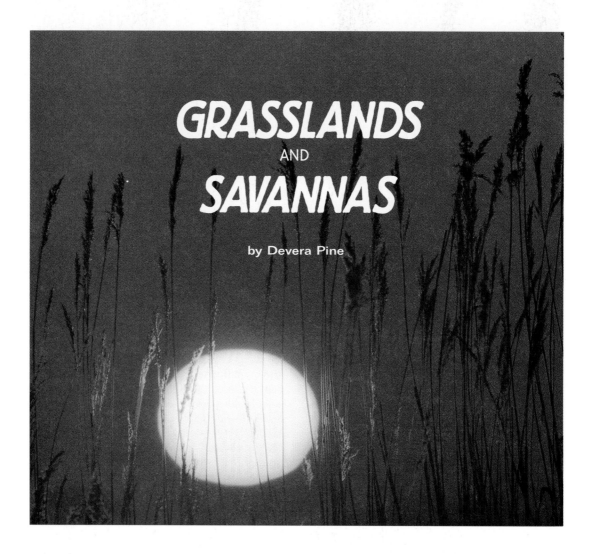

GRASSLANDS

AND

SAVANNAS

by Devera Pine

Grasslands are vast open tracts where the main vegetation is—not surprisingly—grass. In fact, grasslands are often described as a sea or an ocean of grass. Although trees and shrubs can grow on grasslands, they are sparse, existing primarily along the banks of streams.

GRASSLAND CRITERIA

Prairies, pampas, steppes, and savannas are all grasslands. They account for about 25 percent of the land surface on Earth. This biome occurs on every continent except Antarctica. Grasslands usually can be found in the middle of the continents and in what is known as a rain shadow—the side of a mountain range on which rain is less likely to fall.

Because grasslands usually receive from 10 to 30 inches (25 to 75 centimeters) of precipitation per year, they are too moist to be a desert but too dry to be a forest. Grasslands typically have a wet and a dry season, extreme temperatures, drying winds, and prolonged droughts—all of which shape the plants and animals that live on them.

Grasslands developed over the past 30 million years as Earth's climate became cooler and drier and as mountain ranges were pushed up, creating pockets of drier areas. As these new areas developed, new plants that could survive the extremes of life on the grasslands evolved.

Why Grasses?

Several conditions define plant life in the grasslands. First, plants must be able to tolerate a rainy season followed by a season of drought.

In North America, as many as 70 species of grasses flourish in the grasslands. Not so long ago, grasslands covered more than 40 percent of the continent.

Some grasses do this by entering *dormancy* (becoming inactive) until the rains return. Others rely on a far-reaching system of roots that can tap water deep beneath the surface. Still other grasses concentrate their root systems near the surface, where there may be less competition for water and nutrients with other species. Slim flower scurf pea *(Psoralea tenuifloral)*, for example, has a long root system that takes water from underground sources. But buffalo grass *(Buchloë dactyloides)* has a short root system designed for finding water in the upper layers of the soil. Buffalo grass is also able to survive the dry season because its short stems minimize water loss. The small flowers of the buffalo grass are easily pollinated via the wind.

Fires play a critical role in the plant life of grasslands. When a fire sweeps the land, it burns

A mixture of low shrubs, colorful wildflowers, and grasses of innumerable heights populate the grasslands biome.

and clears trees, shrubs, and herbs in its path. Grasses survive the fire, however, since their main growing parts are below ground. The burnt vegetation adds nutrients to the soil, helping the grasses and other plants to grow.

About half of all the living plant matter of a grassland can be found below ground, in the form of rhizomes (underground stems) and dense, fibrous root systems. These stems and roots not only provide water and nutrients to plants above the ground, they also help keep the grasslands highly fertile. Indeed, when the underground plant matter dies and decays, it acts as a fertilizer, adding nutrients to the soil. Because of the high fertility of the soil, many grasslands around the world are now utilized as farmland. In the United States, the vast grasslands in the middle of the country are often referred to as "America's breadbasket."

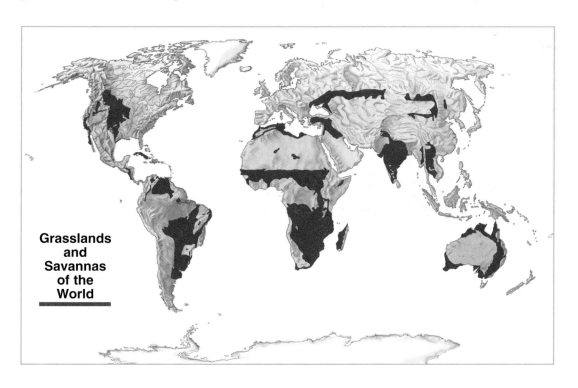

Grasslands and Savannas of the World

The wide-open spaces of the grasslands have encouraged the development of large herbivorous (plant-eating) mammals that roam the plains in large herds. In North America, bison (commonly called buffalo) once thrived on the prairies. Because the bison were able to roam the plains, no one area was overgrazed, and the soil was not eroded. They were eventually hunted down by European settlers and replaced by cattle.

Rabbits, rodents, and pronghorn cattle are also native to temperate grasslands. Rodents, along with insects, play an important role in making the land suitable for plant life by helping to improve the drainage of the soil and therefore restoring its fertility. Coyotes, badgers, bobcats, and snakes rely on rodents for food. Other herbivores on the plains of North America once included elk, prairie chickens, prairie dogs, wolves, and mountain lions. Many of these animals are now either extinct or endangered, and the area on which any remaining animals do roam is greatly limited. Birds on the temperate grasslands include meadowlarks, plover, lark buntings, and many species of predatory hawks and owls.

Although South America and Australia are both home to temperate grasslands, neither supports large grazing herds of hoofed animals, or ungulates. (Herds of ungulates did once roam South America.) However, in Australia, kangaroos and wallabies, though not ungulates, play the same ecological role by grazing the grasslands.

The steppes of Asia, however, do support large grazing herds of animals such as gazelles and antelope. Wild horses and wild asses used to be abundant there, but are now close to extinction. As in North America, rodents that burrow into the soil, such as marmots and ground squirrels, help improve drainage. Cranes, starlings, and bustards form part of the bird life of the steppes. Birds, in turn, feed on the steppe's abundant locusts and grasshoppers.

In tropical grasslands and savannas, the specific animals are different, but the pattern of animal life is essentially the same. The Serengeti Plain of Africa has more wildlife than any other grassland in the world. More than 1 million large animals populate this area, including giraffes, wildebeests, gazelles, impalas, zebras, and several dozen other species. They are preyed upon by cheetahs, lions, hyenas, leopards, and other carnivores. Birds, rodents, and insects also share in the life on the Serengeti Plain.

The savanna in Africa is also dominated by several types of large herbivorous mammals. Most of these animals, such as horses and cattle, graze—that is, they eat grass and low shrubs. Others consume a wider range of plant life. The giraffe, for instance, eats bark, leaves, and twigs, mainly of the acacia tree. Many of the grazing animals of the savanna have teeth specially adapted to resist being worn down by the dirt that they take in when they eat low plants or by the silica in grass stems. These animals also have longer legs, which helps them cover distances quickly as they move across the plains.

Smaller animals include grasshoppers and tortoises. Some small mammals survive by digging into the ground. Among them are gophers, mole rats, and tucotucos. Marmots and prairie dogs also live mainly underground, while kangaroo rats and jackrabbits survive because of their remarkable hopping ability. Some birds on the savanna—such as

Cooler Climes

Grassland plants vary according to their location. Temperate grasslands are found in central North America, and also in Argentina (where they are known as *pampas*), Russia (*steppes*), and China. Temperate grasslands have hot summers followed by cold winters.

North America has three types of grasslands, or prairies—the tallgrass, mixed-grass, and short-grass prairies. The tallgrass prairie is wetter than the other two, receiving approximately 30 inches of rain a year, and its soil is thick and rich in organic matter. Its grasses—such as bluestems, Indian grass, switchgrass,

the pheasant, grouse, bustard, and cariama (or seriema)—are ground dwellers. Other birds—ostriches, emus, rheas, cassowaries—are flightless.

Although savannas on the different continents developed separately, there were times through the ages that some landmasses were connected, allowing for an interchange of animal life. For instance, a land

On Africa's vast Serengeti Plain, the widely scattered watering holes are important gathering spots for zebras (above) and other savanna wildlife.

bridge across what is now the Bering Sea connected present-day Alaska and Russia. Thus, tapir ranged from South America to Asia, horses and camels spread from North America to Europe and Asia, and humans were able to spread from Africa to Europe and Asia and into the New World.

and needle grass—can grow as high as 5 feet (1.5 meters). In the United States, tallgrass prairie is found in the eastern Midwest.

The mixed-grass prairie—found in the middle of the Midwest—receives about 15 to 25 inches (38 to 63 centimeters) of precipitation per year, and the grasses grow 2 to 3 feet (0.6 to

1 meter) high. The short-grass prairie, in the western Midwest, receives only about 10 inches (25 centimeters) of rain a year and is made up of thinner soil than its tallgrass counterpart. Its grasses grow to about 2 feet tall.

On all the grasslands of North America, plant life is abundant. During the summer, as many as 70 species of grasses can flower at any given time. The sunflower and legume families are among the more common types of flowering plants on these lands. Both sunflowers and the legume Lambert crazyweed attract pollinating insects with their colorful flowers.

Although trees are for the most part rare on the grasslands, a few species have adapted to life in this biome. For instance, the boxelder tree, which belongs to the maple family; the silver maple; and the redbud tree (a member of the pea family) can all be found on the grasslands of the United States.

The grasslands of Argentina, Russia, and China are equally rich in plant life. In Asia, species of needle grass and fescue are abundant. In Argentina, Uruguay, New Zealand, and Australia, grasses grow *tussocks*, or bunches.

SAVANNA CRITERIA

Tropical and subtropical grasslands are known as *savannas*, although locally they may be called prairies, scrubs, chaparrals, pampas, or barrens. Compared to the open types of grasslands, savannas are more parklike, with deciduous trees and small evergreens widely spaced among the grasses and shrubs. Unlike temperate grasslands, savannas are hot year-round. Yet, like all grasslands, savannas are not quite a forest, but are too wet to be a desert. Forests generally change to savannas in areas that receive less than 40 inches (100 centimeters) of rain a year. However, if the conditions are right, savannas can sometimes develop in areas that are wetter. For instance, the savannas, or *llanos*, in Venezuela receive abundant precipitation, but only at certain times of the year.

Savannas are found most often in the middle latitudes of the world, generally where the

The farmers who cultivate the fertile soil of the Great Plains of the United States and Canada produce huge harvests of cereal crops each year. This region was primarily a temperate grassland when Europeans first explored it.

winds dry out the land. They are also common on the lee side of mountain ranges—that is, the side protected from the wind—often adjacent to deserts or the more open grasslands of the steppe. Savannas can also develop on either side of a rain forest. In South America, the savannas occupy an area of land about five times the size of France. Savannas and grasslands together extend over approximately 65 percent of the African continent.

The plant life of savannas is dominated by hardy plants: grasses, legumes (peas and beans), and composites (the largest family of plants in the world), all of which must survive four to eight months of drought a year, followed by a rainy season. Trees on the savanna are well suited to surviving the annual dry season. On the African savanna, for instance, trees include the baobab *(Adansonia digitata)*, the candelabra tree *(Euphorbia ingens)*, and the whistling thorn *(Acacia dreparalobium)*. As on the grasslands of North America, fires play a key role in managing the vegetation of the savanna. Plants on the savanna—and on all tropical grasslands—are adapted to the longer growing season of their area. In Africa, the major warm-season grasses are red oat grass, dropseeds, and bluestems. These grow not only in the savannas, but also in the grasslands of southern Africa, known as the *veld*. On another grassland in Africa, the Serengeti Plain, more than 100 species of grasses thrive, including—in the wet-

ter area in the west—tall red oat grass, elephant grass, and bluestems. Short grass, such as dropseed and Bermuda grass, is more common in the drier eastern sections of the plain. Plants in the mint and acanthus families represent two common types of broadleaf plants on the plains; and euphorbias (also called spurges) are also widely distributed.

HUMAN INFLUENCE

Humans have lived on grasslands since the beginning of our history: experts believe that the ancestors of *Homo sapiens* evolved on the savannas of Africa and the Old World. There they were able to develop crucial skills such as tool use, bipedalism (walking upright on two legs), and cooperative hunting.

Today humans still rely heavily on grasslands. Because of their typically rich soil, grasslands are often used to grow crops or feed livestock. In the United States, the prairie is now used mainly for farming corn, soybeans, and wheat. In South America, the savannas are used to produce meat, milk, and grains worth an estimated $15 billion a year.

Although grasslands can be very productive when farmed or grazed, they are easily de-

The common sunflower, a typical plant of the western prairies, sometimes reaches heights of 15 feet and bears flower heads exceeding 1 foot in diameter.

stroyed. Converting grassland into farmland can result in soil erosion, especially if crops fail during the yearly droughts, exposing the soil to the wind. One of the best-known examples of this was the "dust bowl" in the United States in the 1920s and 1930s. In the early 1900s, settlers began moving into the Great Plains, making a living by turning the prairie into farms. At first, these farms prospered, but by 1920, rainfall began to decrease and a drought began. Because the farmers had cleared the prairie's natural vegetation, and because the soil was now too dry for crops to grow, the bare soil was eroded by the wind. The result was huge dust storms that blackened the sky and spread across the country, ultimately reaching the East Coast.

Desertification (the process of turning productive land into land that cannot support plant life) continues today in other grasslands of the world. Overgrazing by pasture animals destroys the native plant life of the grassland, creating desertlike conditions when the dry season comes. As animals overgraze an area, nonnative plants may move in. The animals then ignore these plants as they continue to graze for food, allowing the nonnative plants to spread further. Eventually, nonnative plants are the main type of plant life remaining in the area. This makes living conditions for any surviving native wildlife very difficult. It is estimated that 5.6 million acres (2.3 million hectares) of African savanna are lost each year to farming, pastureland, or for use as firewood.

The destruction of the world's grasslands and savannas has a wide impact: some studies have found that savanna grasses help absorb carbon dioxide in the atmosphere by converting it into organic material. This storing of carbon dioxide may help slow global warming, since excess carbon dioxide in the atmosphere helps trap the Sun's heat, creating a greenhouse effect in which global temperatures rise.

Some efforts are being made to help prevent the destruction of grasslands. In the 1930s and 1940s, the U.S. government purchased approximately 10 million acres (4 million hectares) of land in the southern Great Plains. By replanting the land and installing devices to prevent erosion, the government was able to make the land productive; indeed, by 1945, grasses were once again growing in the area. Today, the U.S. Forest Service maintains 20 separate areas amounting to almost 4 million acres (1.6 million hectares) of prairie lands, known as the National Grasslands. This program helps conserve the prairie and provides a vital habitat for wildlife and an outdoor recreation area for people. The protected areas represent only a small portion of the prairies that originally covered vast sections of the North American continent.

Around the world, similar conservation projects are now under way. For instance, an ongoing international effort is focused on how to stop the destruction of the grasslands and savannas in Africa. In Canada, several projects are specifically aimed at preserving British Columbia's grasslands through education and preservation.

Representative Plants

Acacias
Bermuda grass
Bromegrass
Buckthorn
Buffalo grass
California buckwheat
Chokecherry
Coyote brush
Crazyweed
Deerweed
Elephant grass
Feather grass
Fescue
Foxtail barley
Green ash
Hackberry
Heath
Indian grass
Indian paintbrush
Mexican hat
Needle grass
Oak
Prairie alfalfa
Purple prairie clover
Red oat grass
Smooth sumac
Spurges
Sugarbush
Sunflower
Switchgrass
Timothy
White sage
Wild tulips

GRASSLANDS AND SAVANNAS   143

TEMPERATE FORESTS

by Devera Pine

The temperate forests of the world play a fundamental role in the overall ecological balance of nature. These forests support trees and other types of vegetation, and provide a home for a great variety of animal life.

TEMPERATE FOREST CRITERIA

The main types of plants in a temperate forest are broadleaf deciduous trees—hardwoods such as oak, maple, hickory, ash, and beech. These trees thrive in the frost-free growing season typical of temperate forests: from three to six months. This biome occurs most often in areas with well-defined seasons: summers are usually rather warm—although not as hot as a desert—while the winters are cold but not usually frigid. The temperature in the temperate forest averages about 50° F (10° C).

A temperate forest receives roughly 30 to 60 inches (760 to 1,500 millimeters) of precipi-tation each year, evenly distributed throughout the year. Of all the world's biomes, only the tropical rain forest averages more. In the winter, precipitation often falls in the form of snow.

Temperate forests occur in parts of Europe, in China, and in eastern North America. The temperate forest is the natural state of most of the U.S. eastern seaboard.

WHAT GROWS THERE?

The hardwood trees of the temperate forest are classified as deciduous because they lose their leaves at the end of the growing season (a pattern that helps the trees survive the winter, at least in part by lowering their wind resistance) and grow new ones each spring.

Temperate forests flourish in areas with four well-defined seasons. On a warm afternoon, visitors of all ages enjoy the sun-dappled trails that wind among the lovely trees.

As the weather turns colder in autumn, trees stop producing chlorophyll, the green pigment that is necessary to the process of photosynthesis. Once a leaf's chlorophyll production stops, the natural pigments (which are usually hidden by the green chlorophyll) begin to show through, and the leaves turn the lovely shades of red, yellow, and orange so closely associated with the beauty of autumn. The increasingly cold temperatures of the approaching winter also cause trees to shut down the water supply to their leaves. As a result, the leaves die and fall off, and the trees are essentially defoliated for the winter. A structure called a *bud scale* covers the area where each leaf falls off, setting the stage for a new one to grow in the spring.

In addition to producing leaves each year, a tree interacts with the environment around it. Trees draw from the soil the water they need for photosynthesis. Trees also play a prominent role in preventing water from running off the land during heavy rains. In areas stripped of trees, much soil that is rich in nutrients, and therefore essential for promoting plant growth, simply washes away.

During photosynthesis, trees take carbon dioxide from the air and release oxygen. This function helps keep Earth's atmosphere free of excess carbon dioxide, a "greenhouse gas" that many experts believe is increasing temperatures around the world—a process known as global warming. A forest that is young and growing adds more oxygen to the atmosphere than does one that is mature.

Finally, trees help keep minerals and nutrients in the forest biome by temporarily storing them in their roots. Many trees derive the nutrients they need from a root fungus, or *mycorrhiza*, through what is termed a symbiotic relationship. In such a relationship, all of the participants benefit. In this case, the tree obtains mineral nutrients from the fungus, and the fungus derives food from the tree.

Microorganisms play a key role in making forest soil suitable for a variety of plant life, especially by breaking down minerals and creating passages in the soil through which air and water can move unobstructed. The air and water help decompose the remains of dead plants and animals, allowing the return of their nutrients into the soil. This decomposition process proceeds more rapidly in warm, moist climates than it does in cold or dry ones. In the temperate forest, the soil is usually fertile, thanks in large part to the almost-constant infusion of decaying organic matter from falling leaves.

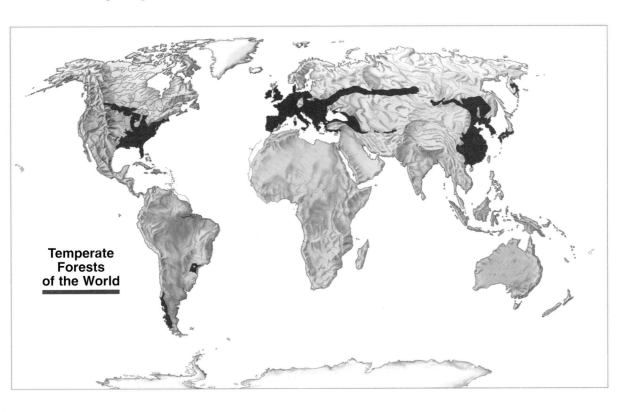

Temperate Forests of the World

In late winter, sap is drawn from the trunks of sugar-maple trees (above). Only after the sap is boiled does it attain the color and flavor associated with maple syrup.

PEOPLE AND THE FOREST

Humans have long relied on the abundance of plants and animals in the temperate forest for food and shelter. Unfortunately, years of overuse and mismanagement have placed these valuable resources in great peril. In the United States, only 5 percent of the forests that once covered the land now remain.

Logging

One of the obvious ways in which people have had an impact on temperate forests is through logging—the harvesting of trees. Worldwide, about half of all harvested wood is used for fuel. Wood is a popular fuel source in developing countries, where it is often less expensive than other sources of energy. Humans also use wood as lumber in the building of structures, and to make paper. Wood is used for some not-so-obvious purposes as well: its cellulose fibers are used in rayon, photographic film, artificial sponges, and even some plastics.

There are four techniques that are used to harvest trees from forests:

•*Clear-cutting*, in which all the trees in an area are cut down and removed at one time;

•*Seed-tree cutting*, in which all but a few trees are cut down. The remaining trees are left to reseed the area;

•*Shelterwood cutting*, which is the removal of an old stand (or group) of trees over the course of several years; and

•*Selection cutting*, which is the cutting down of a few mature trees repeatedly over a relatively short time period.

Each of these techniques has advantages and disadvantages. Timber companies prefer clear-cutting because it is the most-economical harvesting technique and allows sun-loving trees such as black cherry, Douglas fir, or southern pine to grow in an area that otherwise might be too shady. Unfortunately, this technique can easily be abused, leading to soil erosion and the loss of habitats for other native plants and animals. Seed-tree cutting allows the remaining trees to repopulate the forest. Shelterwood cutting leaves areas of shade so that trees that require some protection from sunlight will still be able to flourish. Selection cutting concentrates on removing weak and diseased specimens, while at the same time preserving areas of the forest where shade-loving trees can grow.

Trees are a renewable resource—a crop to be planted, harvested, and planted again. If any of these logging techniques is carried out improperly, the forest environment can be severely—and irreparably—damaged.

Forest Fires

Logging is not the only way in which people affect the forest. Fires started by careless actions—failing to extinguish a campfire is a prime example—can destroy thousands of acres of woodlands. There are about 100,000 forest fires in the United States each year.

Fires also play a positive role in the overall health of the forest. Fires started by natural means (a lightning strike, for example) can help maintain biodiversity—a wide range of different types of plants and animals—in the forest. Smaller, controlled forest fires also help rid the forest of dead leaves and wood, which could otherwise help fuel a larger, disastrous conflagration. This is especially true in North America, where forests are much more dense than they were in the past. An acre of woodland can contain up to 40 times as many trees today as it had a century ago. Prescribed fires can protect trees from future fire, disease, and insects.

Other Factors

Insects and diseases introduced by humans are a problem in many forests. Perhaps the most-notorious example of a destructive insect pest is the gypsy moth. In the late 1800s, a French naturalist brought specimens of this insect, native to Europe, Asia, and North Africa, to his Massachusetts laboratory in an attempt to develop disease-resistant silkworms. A few of the moths escaped and—with no natural enemies—quickly infested North America, feeding on the leaves of woody plants, especially oaks.

The Acorn Cycle

In the temperate forest, as in all the world's biomes, the lives of plants and animals are closely linked in complicated ways. In a typical oak forest in the eastern United States, for example, many plants and animals rely on the production of acorns for their survival, either directly or indirectly.

Oak trees produce large amounts of acorns, or seeds, every two to six years. In the "off" years, the trees produce few, if any, acorns. Scientists have found that a heavy production of acorns in the United States results in an increase in the rodent population—particularly white-footed mice, deer mice, and chipmunks. A similar phenomenon occurs in Europe's temperate forests, where the population of yellow-necked mice and other rodents also rises when acorn production is high.

Deer are also affected by these seed-producing cycles. In the year following a bumper crop of acorns, deer are more likely to give birth to twins. During years of heavy acorn production, deer are more likely to spend their time feeding in areas of the forest dominated by oaks than in areas where other trees, such as maples, are found. The end result is that deer spend less time eating young trees; therefore, more young trees are apt to survive.

The white-tailed deer is perhaps the most commonly seen large mammal of the North American temperate forest.

Rodents and deer, in turn, affect other animals in the forest. Mice, for instance, eat gypsy moths, helping to keep these insect pests under control. More acorns mean more mice to eat gypsy moths. During "low" production years, chipmunks—the world-champion acorn eaters—may resort to eating the eggs and even the young of ground-nesting birds for nourishment. During acorn famines, chipmunks and mice are also more likely to compete with birds in another way: the rodents eat seeds, which birds also rely on for food. Deer affect birds as well. When there are fewer acorns, deer, as mentioned, eat tree seedlings. As a result, fewer trees will survive, reducing the nesting sites available to songbirds in the forest. And since fewer acorns mean fewer mice to eat gypsy moths, the moths may consume an excessive amount of foliage, and those nests that are built may be more visible to predators.

Finally, even people are affected by acorn production. Deer, mice, and chipmunks all carry the deer tick in different stages of its life cycle. The deer tick, in turn, transmits Lyme disease. More acorns mean more deer ticks—and more chances that humans will be infected with Lyme disease.

During a severe infestation, gypsy moths can rapidly defoliate (take the leaves off, in this case, by eating them) large stretches of forest, causing countless trees to die.

In the early 1900s, a destructive fungal disease called chestnut blight was introduced to the United States from Europe. It has almost eliminated the American chestnut tree from U.S. woodlands. Although some young specimens continue to sprout in woodlands, these, too, will inevitably be killed by the disease.

The introduction of a new species of tree can also adversely affect a forest. In the southern United States, for example, forests that were once dominated by longleaf pine have now been taken over by slash pine, a fast-growing species that produces abundant seeds. Plants and animals that are dependent on the longleaf variety either died or were displaced.

Pollution is another way that human activity damages temperate forests. Air pollution and water pollution can weaken trees, making them more likely to succumb to disease and insect infestation. The effects of acid rain on trees have been especially severe in the forests of Canada and northern Europe.

THE QUESTION OF SURVIVAL

In the United States, laws were passed in the late 1800s and early 1900s to protect forests from fire, overharvesting, and overgrazing, and to set up a number of national parks and forests. In recent years, the U.S. government also began to convert some areas of farmland back to forests—programs instituted primarily to help stop soil erosion. At about the same time, logging companies in the southern United States created large-scale nurseries of tree seedlings

If allowed to revert to a natural state, most of the land along the East Coast of the United States would eventually support temperate forests not unlike those of the lush hills of eastern Tennessee (above). The brilliant autumnal colors of New England's temperate forests (right) have helped to make October an important tourist month in the Northeast.

and began replanting areas that they had deforested.

Today in the United States, the Forest Service, which is an agency of the Department of Agriculture (USDA), manages all public forestlands—191 million acres (77 million hectares) in 155 national forests and 20 national grasslands. (These include all types of forests—from tundra to temperate to tropical.) The job of the Forest Service is to protect the forests as homes for wildlife and as recreation areas for people—while still providing timber for industry. Meeting these goals has been a daunting challenge.

During and after World War II, the U.S. Forest Service attempted to meet industry's demand for timber by allowing clear-cutting—even in areas not well suited to the technique. In some places, the results were disastrous, with wildlife imperiled and runaway erosion causing landslides and other calamities. In 1976, new laws required the Forest Service to create a plan for each forest in the United States, with the aim of striking a balance between logging and other uses. But by 1992, a congressional report concluded that the agency still emphasized logging over other interests.

Today, the U.S. Forest Service is attempting to restore the natural ecosystems and biological processes of the forests wherever possible. For example, naturally caused "disturbances" such as fires, floods, drought, and disease are being viewed in a more favorable light as nature's way of maintaining the proper ecological balance.

In August 2002, President George W. Bush proposed the Healthy Forests Initiative to improve forest and rangeland health, which was followed by the Healthy Forests Restoration Act in 2003.

Temperate forests often occur in areas highly favorable for human settlement. Many trees are cut each year to clear land for housing, roads, and other uses.

Representative Plants

Black cherry
Black locust
Blue violet
Deerberry
Great laurel
Green ash
Hawthorn
Hickory
Indian pipe
Jack-in-the-pulpit
Lady fern
Pincushion moss
Primrose
Quaking aspen
Red maple
Royal fern
Shortleaf pine
Spicebush
Teaberry
Tree club moss
Tulip tree
White oak
Wood anemone

One of the goals of these programs is to reduce catastrophic wildfires by allowing loggers to harvest large trees and remove dense underbrush. This controversial practice is said to improve the health of the remaining trees. An estimated 19 million acres (7.6 million hectares) had been "treated" by 2006—up from 1.25 million acres (510,000 hectares) in 2000.

In another effort to protect the world's woodlands, known as forest certification, independent auditors check to ensure that a forest is managed according to environmentally responsible practices. (The Forest Stewardship Council, a nonprofit organization made up of members of the timber industry, conservation groups, indigenous peoples, and others, monitors the auditors.) Wood harvested from certified forests carries a special logo that consumers and businesses can look for when shopping for lumber and other wood products. The goal of the program is to increase demand for certified wood, thus providing an incentive for forest managers to use environmentally sound logging practices.

PLANTS
OF THE WETLANDS

Marshes and swamps are the two main types of wetlands, or areas in which the ground is saturated, or waterlogged, for a long or indefinite period of time. Open bodies of water, such as lakes, rivers, seas, or oceans, are not considered wetlands. Instead, wetlands have the distinction of sharing both features of bodies of water and features of solid land.

WHERE ARE WETLANDS?

Wetlands occur all over the world, although they are found most commonly in cool, damp areas where water remains in or on top of the soil even after a substantial amount of evaporation has taken place. Wetlands also form wherever water is slow to drain off; this can happen if the soil is primarily clay, or on large, flat expanses of land. In areas of the world that are simply very wet, wetlands form regardless of soil or topography. In such areas, the soil is so moist that the wetland just more or less covers the land. Finally, wetlands frequently form in areas regularly flooded by a river or, along the coast, by the tide.

From a geologic standpoint, wetlands tend to develop in areas where groundwater readily and frequently reaches the surface. Groundwater is water that seeps down through the soil until it is stopped by an impenetrable layer of rock or other nonporous material; the water then accumulates on this layer. The highest point to which this underground water accumulates is known as the *water table*. Depending on the

Colonies of reedy, soft-stemmed plants, such as cattails (above), compete with the fast-growing water hyacinth (inset) for nutrients in many temperate wetlands.

volume of groundwater available, the water table will rise or fall. In a swamp, marsh, or bog, the water table is close to, just at, or—in some cases—above the surface.

Wet but Happy

The plants that grow in wetlands share one overriding feature: they are all adapted to surviving in very wet conditions. The exact type of plant that grows in a wetland depends on a number of other factors, including the local climate, the mineral content of the area, and whether the water periodically drains or is present year-round. The source of the water that supplies the wetland is also a determinant: the more nutrients the water source brings in, the more plants will grow in the wetland. For instance, if the groundwater that supplies the wetland seeps through shale or limestone, it will carry an abundance of nutrients. If, on the other hand, it has seeped through granite, the water will contain few nutrients, and the wetland will be rather sterile. If the wetland's water comes directly from rain—that is, it doesn't first have to seep through mineral-rich ground—the wetland will likewise be relatively infertile.

TYPES OF WETLANDS

Geographic location seems to determine the name by which a wetland is known. Terms such as marsh, swamp, fen, moor, or heath each mean something different in different parts of the world. In general, though, scientists classify all wetlands into three categories: marshes, swamps, and bogs.

Marshes

The main type of plant life in marshes—which are also called emergent wetlands—are soft-stemmed, grasslike (herbaceous) plants; trees and shrubs are generally rare. Marshes can develop in relatively low-lying areas such as shallow depressions in the land, and in channels of rivers, floodplains, deltas, and the shores of lakes. In these areas, the marshes are often fed by streams or other sources of water that bring in both nutrients and silt (a type of very fine soil), which helps to make marshes very fertile. Indeed, marshes produce several tons of dead plant and animal matter that become available to the food chain every year. (Bacteria and fungi break down this material.)

Weird Lights over Wetlands

The folklore of cultures that developed near marshes or bogs invariably includes tales to explain the flickering, flamelike nocturnal lights that seem to hover above the surface of the local wetland. The strange lights have been given many fanciful-sounding names: will-o'-the-wisp, *ignis fatuus* ("fool's fire" in Latin), jack-o'-lantern, fox fire, corpse candle, ghost light, and friar's lantern, among others. Legends variously identify these lights as fairies, lost or punished souls, witches, or even omens of death. In virtually all cases, the lights were recognized as dangerous phenomena. Indeed, travelers groping through the dark in a marsh or bog might mistake the light for a friendly lantern or an illuminated window and follow it, only to watch the light mysteriously recede as they become ever more hopelessly lost. (Admittedly, a few tales tell of wanderers who were actually led to safety by a will-o'-the-wisp.)

What causes these lights, which rise from the ground in shades of blue, red, green, yellow, or purple? Scientists are not sure, but they hypothesize that they may be the result of burning methane gas—the gas produced by decaying organic matter in wetland environments. This theory makes some sense, since methane does escape from the ground periodically. Because methane does not spontaneously ignite, however, scientists have trouble explaining how the flame begins. One possibility is that hydrogen phosphide (another product of organic decay, one which may combust on its own) provides the spark that sets the methane burning. Another theory suggests that the natural phosphorescence that accompanies the decay of vegetable or animal matter creates the lights. It may be some time, though, before scientists can conclusively state what causes the phenomenon.

The salinity of a saltwater marsh changes with the tides. In Virginia (above) and elsewhere, many coastal wetlands are under strict government protection.

Plants that grow in marshes have evolved various adaptations to help them thrive. Cattails, rushes, arrowheads, pickerelweed, and bur-reed grow with their stems and leaves partially underwater. Other plants, such as water lilies, float on the surface even though their roots grow in the bottom of the marsh. Some plants, including the pondweeds and waterweeds, grow completely underwater.

The silt that supplies nutrients to a marsh can also help fill it in so that, ultimately, trees and shrubs invade the area, and the marsh becomes a swamp. If the water table is high enough, however, the marsh will never have the opportunity to begin the process of evolving into a swamp.

Salt marshes. Saltwater marshes (also called salt or tidal marshes) are found only in temperate coastal areas. Such marshes often form on the beaches of barrier islands (islands that act as a buffer between the ocean and the mainland), always on the side away from the ocean.

The inner area of a salt marsh is typically flooded; spartina, or cordgrass, is usually the most abundant plant there. As a general rule, the diversity of plant life in a salt marsh increases with distance from the ocean. Similarly, the proportion of freshwater in the marsh increases with distance from the sea. Brackish tidal marshes, for instance, are associated with rivers and are found upstream from a salt marsh. The salinity, or saltiness, of these marshes changes with the tides.

Swamps

In contrast to the herbaceous plants of a marsh, the main type of plants in a swamp are woody—usually trees and shrubs. Like marshes, swamps form in very wet areas; in some cases, swamps have a stream running through them. The soil is typically shallow and composed of organic silt and the mucklike layer of dead plants at the bottom.

Many different kinds of plants flourish in swamps. Near rivers and lakes, for instance, hardwood trees such as alder, willow, red maple, and white and black ash can be found. The bald cypress is found in the cypress swamps of the southeastern United States, and mangrove trees

The aerial roots of mangrove trees form tangled thickets that catch debris and soil. In large groups, mangroves help to stabilize and slowly extend the shoreline.

grow both in the southern United States and in other parts of the world. To help it survive in the swamp, the cypress tree grows what are known as "knees"—the more or less cone-shaped parts of its roots that grow near the base of the tree and extend above the surface of the water. Botanists do not understand the exact function of these knees, although they do know that cypress knees grow only when the tree is in a swamp, and not on dry land. The cypress tree itself is frequently home to orchids and bromeliads, which grow on the bark.

In a Massachusetts cranberry bog, the harvest begins with the flooding of the bog, which releases the ripe berries, causing them to float to the surface of the water.

The mangrove tree also uses a special adaptation, called *air roots*, to obtain the oxygen it needs to grow. The mangrove first produces roots that grow horizontally, into the mud of the swamp. Air roots that are about 10 to 15 inches (25 to 38 centimeters) long then branch off from the regular roots, growing up into the air. The mangrove also uses a root known as a *prop root* for support when it grows on the banks of tidal rivers or along the coasts of oceans.

Swamp plants tend to grow in layers, with "ground cover" such as skunk cabbage, purple-fringed orchid, cardinal flower, jewelweed, and marsh marigold covering the lowest level. Next come shrubs—highbush blueberry, swamp azalea, spicebush, and sweet pepperbush, among others. Trees constitute the top of the system.

Bogs

The third category of wetlands is a *bog* (also called moor, heath, or fen). Although the dominant plants are shrubs and evergreen trees, bogs are widely known for the deposits of peat that lie beneath them. Peat formation begins when plants in a wetland die, fall to the ground, and create a layer called *litter*. In order for this plant material to decay normally, it must be exposed to oxygen. In some wetlands, however, the litter is perennially covered by water, and very little oxygen reaches it. As a result, the decaying plant matter builds up in layers, forming a substance called *peat*. Peat is the first step in the very long process that leads to the formation of coal. Layers of peat can be as deep as 20 to 40 feet (6 to 12 meters).

As with all wetlands, the types of plants that grow in a bog vary with climate. Bogs in northern climates, such as the northeastern United States, are often home to trees such as black spruce and larch, and to shrubs such as leatherleaf, bog rosemary, bog laurel, and Labrador tea. In the southern United States, typical bog plants include the Atlantic white cedar tree. In some drier bogs, cranberries and blueberries are able to grow. Most of the peat in bogs is formed either from sphagnum moss or from sedges, a large family of grasslike plants, both of which grow on the bog in a floating mat of vegetation. Sphagnum moss (sometimes called peat moss) is often used by gardeners to help plants grow.

Most bogs are acidic and not very fertile, making them a difficult environment for plants to flourish in. As a result, some bog plants have developed unique adaptations for survival. One of the most unusual is the ability of certain bog plants to "eat" insects. These so-called carnivorous plants, such as the pitcher plant and the sundew, trap insects and digest them. (See also "Carnivorous Plants and Other Unusual Species," pages 108–112.)

The acidic, low-oxygen environment also helps make bogs "time capsules" of sorts. In the bog environment, the conditions impede bacteria from easily breaking down organisms. For this reason, the well-preserved remains of people and animals who lived thousands of years ago have been found in bogs. In Denmark, for example, peat cutters recovered the body of a man whose face was so well preserved that it was thought that he was the victim of a recent murder. Scientists ultimately determined that the remains—dubbed "Tollund man"—were from a man who had died nearly 2,000 years ago, probably as a sacrifice to a goddess of fertility. In England, the "Lindow man," also found in a bog, probably lived 2,200 years ago.

Bogs also preserve a record of ancient grains of pollen as far back as 12,000 to 15,000 years ago. By studying the microfossils of these pollen grains, scientists can determine on what type of plants they originally grew.

WHY CARE ABOUT WETLANDS?

Many people think of swamps as simply soggy breeding grounds for mosquitoes. But swamps and other wetlands actually play several important roles in the environment. First and foremost, wetlands are home to many different kinds of animals, including birds, fish, mammals, shellfish, reptiles, amphibians, and insects. (For more, see the box below.) For instance, around the world, marshes are the main breeding and feeding areas for ducks. Marshes also serve as crucial "rest stops" for many species of migrating birds.

In the environment as a whole, wetlands play a crucial role by storing water. In doing so, wetlands help to mitigate flooding by controlling how fast and when water flows over the land. Ultimately, therefore, the wetland protects

Beyond Mosquitoes

Wetlands are home to many different kinds of animals. In temperate marshes, many of the insects are aquatic—spending either all or part of their lives in the water. Dragonflies and damselflies are two notable examples. Various species of frogs and turtles also abound. Muskrats feed on the roots of cattail plants. In addition, swamps are usually home to raccoons and beavers, as well as to wood ducks, which use hollow trees for their nests.

Amphibians, especially frogs, are most commonly associated with bogs. A noteworthy mammal is the bog lemming.

Birds in the Everglades range from the snakebird, or anhinga, which uses a sharp bill to spear fish as it dives into the water, to wading birds such as the great blue heron, bittern, and egret. Other marsh birds include the everglade kite, the roseate spoonbill, and the American flamingo. Alligators abound during the dry season.

In the 1930s, nesting wading birds in the southern Everglades numbered roughly 300,000; their decline to between 10,000 and 15,000 by the early 1990s gave great urgency to the Everglades programs, which are now well under way. The dramatic bird decline may have occurred as a result of the draining of freshwater from the interior of the Everglades to meet drinking-water demand in south Florida.

Wood ducks have made a notable recovery since the 19th century, when demand for the male's striking plumage nearly led to the species' extinction.

the land against erosion. Wetlands can also help recharge the water table in an area. Indirectly, wetlands help keep water pollution-free: the vegetation traps sediment in the water, and the organic material is able to extract some metals and various other types of toxic materials from the water.

Wetlands also affect water in the air. They help to control local humidity levels by participating in the local cycle by which water falls as rain and then

Botanists, wildlife experts, environmental scientists, and government officials have devised a far-reaching plan to help restore the delicate ecology of Florida's Everglades (above)—perhaps America's best-known wetlands.

evaporates. The peat found in bogs plays a major role in storing carbon, helping to regulate the levels of carbon dioxide in the atmosphere and thereby playing a role (albeit minor) in the world's climate. Finally, wetlands produce methane, a so-called "greenhouse gas" that figures prominently in global warming.

Unfortunately, for centuries, wetlands have not been valued for their environmental role. Instead, people have drained wetlands to construct farms, houses, roads, and commercial buildings. Humans exploited peat for fuel and removed peat moss for horticultural applications. In the continental United States, there were once 215 million acres (87 million hectares) of wetlands; today it is estimated that less than half of the original wetlands still remain.

Fortunately, there is hope. In the United States, many projects aim at restoring wetlands to their natural state. Federal agencies coordinate many such conservation programs, often amid a great deal of controversy. In some cases, restoring a wetland simply means allowing the tide in a coastal area to wash over a marsh. In other cases, the approach to wetland conservation is substantially more complicated.

One major wetlands-restoration project— actually a series of projects over 20 years— focuses on the Everglades National Park in Florida. The dominant plant of the marshlands in this park is a type of sedge called saw grass. According to the U.S. National Park Service,

this so-called river of grass was once up to 60 miles (96 kilometers) wide. In the past century, however, much of this marshland was drained off. Today, the Everglades have been reduced to one-fifth of their original size. The Everglades are now considered the most endangered national park in the United States.

The Water Resources Development Act, submitted for congressional approval in July 1999, was signed into law in December 2000. The bill aims to restore and protect the Everglades through federal and state funding, and would entail several key efforts, including:

• Returning some of the natural flow of water through the Everglades area;

• Setting up several human-made marshes in the Everglades that can help filter out phosphorus—a pollutant that leaches into the water from fertilizer used on crops and lawns; and

• Educating the public about the importance of the Everglades.

In May 2003, the governor of Florida signed a bill that extended certain deadlines in the legislation from 2006 to 2016. The restoration—the largest project of its type ever attempted—is being studied by environmental scientists in hopes of using it as a model to save other endangered wetlands.

RAIN FORESTS

by Devera Pine

Rain forests are the most plant- and animal-rich biome on Earth. Although they make up less than 6 percent of the surface of Earth, rain forests are home to approximately three-fourths of all the known species of plants and animals in the world.

A rain forest is defined by the heavy precipitation it receives—upwards of 70 inches (1,800 millimeters) per year. There are two types of rain forests: tropical and temperate.

TROPICAL RAIN FORESTS

Tropical rain forests grow near the equator. More than half are found in Latin America; one-third of all tropical rain forests occur in Brazil alone. Other large tropical rain forests are found in West Africa, in Southeast Asia, and on various Pacific islands. Together, these rain forests contain more than half of all the plants and animals in the world—some 30 million species.

The term *jungle* is usually applied to the dense, scrubby vegetation that develops following the destruction of a true tropical rain forest.

A Layered Ecosystem

The dominant plants in the tropical rain forest are broadleaf evergreen trees. Unlike evergreens that grow in colder parts of the United States, those of the tropical rain forest have no protection against cold weather or droughts. These trees grow to heights of 90 feet (27 meters), forming a *canopy*—a tight, umbrella-like covering over the forest. The canopy is exposed to the Sun, but shades the plants that grow beneath it. Most of the organisms in this biome make their home in the canopy, one of the four

Tropical rain forests provide a home to approximately three-quarters of Earth's species. To study the canopy— the forest's uppermost reaches—some researchers simply climb a tree (facing page).

so-called "layers of life" in the tropical rain forest.

The branches of the trees that form the canopy are usually covered with vines and *epiphytes*, plants that grow on other plants. The vines, or *lianas*, are rooted in the soil, but use the surrounding trees for support, achieving heights of up to 200 feet (60 meters). As a result, the leaves of these vines form part of the canopy, and thus receive direct sunlight.

Rain-forest epiphytes include succulents, orchids, mosses, ferns, and bromeliads (which are related to pineapples). Epiphytes use the trees only for support, not for food; some can nonetheless harm trees. Epiphytes commonly called stranglers initially live on a tree, but eventually grow on their own. For instance, the strangling fig (or ficus) first takes root in a fork where a branch separates from the trunk of a tree. As the fig matures, it sends out long roots that find their way to the surface and begin growing in the soil. Other roots snake down the trunk of the tree, interweaving into a tight mesh. Eventually the roots of the fig completely cover the tree. Over time, this network of fig roots prevents the tree inside from growing, thus killing it.

Another stratum of plant life in the tropical rain forest is called the *emergent layer*. This layer is made up of trees that reach above the canopy, attaining heights of 100 to 165 feet (30 to 50 meters); a few trees grow as high as 200 feet (60 meters). These lofty trees receive more sunlight than even those in the canopy, but they are also exposed to higher temperatures, less humidity, and more wind.

The layer directly below the canopy, the *understory*, receives up to 15 percent less light than the canopy, so anything that grows there must be able to thrive in shade. Understory flora includes young trees and some herbaceous plants (that is, any plant that has a fleshy green

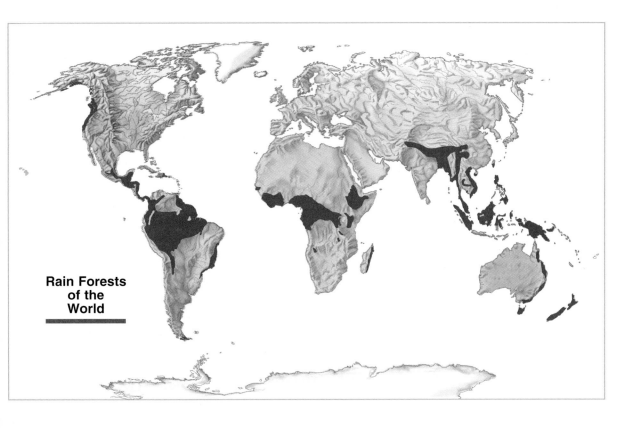

Rain Forests of the World

stem as opposed to a woody stem). Many popular houseplants originated in the understory.

Beneath the understory is the floor of the forest. Since little sunlight filters down to the floor, few plants are able to grow there. Instead, the floor is covered with a thin layer of plant matter (leaves, seeds, fruits, and more) that falls from the upper layers. Given the perennially

Animals and the Rain Forest

Tropical rain forests are home to a wide array of animal life, including parrots, monkeys, sloths, insects, bats, and more. In the temperate rain forest, wildlife includes hawks, owls, martens, wolves, and salmon. Alaska's Tongass National Forest is home to the greatest numbers of bald eagles and brown bears in the world.

In the tropical rain forest, little wind occurs to pollinate plants, and plants of the same species may be far apart. As a result, many plants in the tropical rain forest rely on animals to pollinate them.

Most flowers in the rain forest are pollinated by bees, which are drawn by the bright colors of the flora. Flowers that are pollinated by other types of insects have a different set of adaptations. For instance, flowers of the *Aristolochia* plant mimic the smell and the look of rotting meat (they are yellow, purple, or brown in color). This attracts flies, which, thinking they have found rotting meat, lay their eggs on the flower, pollinating it in the process. Some orchids produce a scent similar to that of a female bee or wasp. This attracts male bees and wasps, which pollinate the flower.

Other creatures also play an important pollinating role. Beetles are attracted to flowers such as those produced by the *Dieffenbachia*, which have a fruitlike odor and plenty of petals and other structures on which the beetles can feed. Hummingbirds can pick up pollen while feeding on one flower, and then deposit it on the next flower that they find. Plants that rely on birds for pollination—such as the hibiscus—usually produce flowers that are bright orange, red, or yellow, and that are strong enough to hold the bird while it is feeding. Because birds do not have a strong sense of smell, such flowers are rarely scented.

Some plants in the tropical rain forest even rely on bats for pollination. These species usually have scented flowers that bloom at night to attract these nocturnal flying mammals. Color does not matter to bats—they cannot see well—so the flowers are often pale. However, the flowers must stand up under the weight of the bat; they are often shaped like a ball or a bell.

Perhaps the largest predator of the Central American tropical rain forest is the jaguar (above), whose spotted coat blends in well with the dense vegetation.

Animals in the rain forest also help spread the seeds of plants. Some animals—including bats, tigers, pigs, and reptiles—expel seeds in their droppings, spreading them throughout the rain forest. The nutmeg tree, for example, relies on birds, which eat the fruit of the tree. Since the seed inside the fruit has a hard shell, it safely passes out of the digestive system of the bird. If conditions are right, the seed will grow wherever it was dropped. Other animals, such as primates, carry seeds on their fur from one area of the forest to another, thereby ensuring the next generation of plant species.

warm and moist conditions in the rain forest, this floor material decomposes quickly—even before the organic material is washed away. The nutrients of the decomposed matter are soon taken up again by living plants and animals. This means that most of the nutrients in a tropical rain forest are located in living plants and animals. In fact, despite the great variety of plants and animals that live in them, tropical rain forests actually contain less organic matter than do temperate forests.

Although tropical rain forests are rich in plant life, the soil in such areas is surprisingly poor—a phenomenon largely the result of the heavy rains that wash the nutrients out of the soil on almost a daily basis. Some studies have found that the diversity of life in the tropical rain forest is related to the changing and unstable nature of the forests over geologic time.

TEMPERATE RAIN FORESTS

Temperate rain forests occur at higher latitudes than do tropical rain forests—usually in wet coastal areas. The world's largest temperate rain forests grow along a 1,200-mile (1,930-kilometer) stretch of the Pacific coast of North America, from Oregon to Alaska. Other temperate rain forests are also found on the southeast coast of Chile; in Australia and New Zealand; and in some coastal areas of Norway, Japan, and Great Britain.

The timber from temperate rain forests is considered the most valuable in the world. Many of the temperate trees grow taller than do trees in the tropical rain forest, although there are many fewer species. In temperate rain forests in the Northern Hemisphere, conifers (trees that produce cones) such as redwoods and Sitka spruces are often the dominant trees. The redwoods, *Sequoia sempervirens*, grow as tall as 340 feet (103 meters), while the Sitka spruces grow up to 180 feet (55 meters) high. In the Southern Hemisphere, such evergreens as the eucalyptus, *Araucaria*, and *Nothofagus* (Antarctic false beech) are common.

THE EFFECT OF HUMANS

For centuries, humans have relied on rain forests for a variety of products. Foods such as tomatoes, peppers, corn, rice, coconuts, ba-

The Pacific coast of North America supports the largest temperate rain forest in the world. Some trees in Olympic National Park may be thousands of years old.

nanas, coffee, cocoa, tapioca, beans, and sweet potatoes all originally came from the rain forest. Many civilizations have exploited the timber in rain forests and cleared the land for farms. Some preliterate tribes have actually lived in the rain forests for thousands of years. Today people rely on tropical rain forests for a variety of everyday products: paper (7 percent of all paper pulp comes from the rain forest); rubber (used in tires and other products); wax (used in plastics); mahogany and teak (used in wood products such as furniture); and many other items.

Destructive Activities

Unfortunately, human activities have taken a toll on the rain forest. Some of the most-destructive practices are discussed below.

Farming. In some areas of the world, the practice of *shifting cultivation* has destroyed parts of the forest. In this type of farming, a farmer clears an area of the forest, plants crops for a few seasons, and then moves on to a new area. This can lead to a slow deforestation of the area. In many parts of the world, this type of farming has increased as people move out from overcrowded cities to farm small patches of land. On the island of Java, the forest has been almost totally cleared and replaced with rice or rubber plantations. Cattle ranching also poses a problem. In some areas, entire forests are cleared to create pastures for grazing.

Logging. The dramatic increase in the demand for exotic woods has led to the destruction of rain forests in Brazil, Central America, and Malaysia, and has endangered temperate rain forests in Alaska and British Columbia. Loggers in Alaska's Tongass National Forest have cut down more than 1 million acres (405,000 hectares) of virgin rain forest. A federal court ruled in 2001 that the USDA Forest Service failed to consider some roadless areas as eligible for wilderness designation within Tongass National Park. At the time, the Roadless Area Conservation Rule protected 58.5 million acres (23.7 million hectares) of roadless forests in 38 states. The Bush administration repealed the Roadless Rule two years later and replaced it with a voluntary state peti-

Representative Plants

Antarctic beech
Brazilwoods
Broadleaf evergreens
Bromeliads
Cassia
Epiphytes
Eucalyptus
Lianas
Mangosteen
Orchids
Redwood
Sapodilla
Shell seed
Sitka spruce
Strangler fig

tion process. In 2006, a lawsuit filed by four western states and 20 conservation groups won in court, and the Roadless Rule was reinstated—except in the Tongass. Efforts continue to reverse the exemption. Currently, 676,000 acres (275,000 hectares) of Tongass timber remain scheduled for logging.

Other activities. Rain forests are destroyed during the mining of their soils for iron, bauxite, or other minerals. Finally, wars, natural disasters, and construction projects (such as for dams and roadways) may destroy the forest.

Destruction Aftermath

The effects of rain-forest destruction are far-reaching and are often impossible for scientists to assess and to predict.

Soil and erosion. Because the soil in most rain forests is relatively infertile to begin with, once the plant layer is removed, the soil can quickly lose virtually all of its ability to support plant life. Some soils turn into a type of hard clay called *laterite*. Removal of a rain forest's vegetation can also lead to extensive erosion, as the soil, without plants to anchor it, is quickly washed away by rain and wind.

Flora and fauna. Destruction of the rain forests also limits biodiversity. As stated earlier,

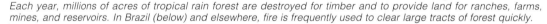

Each year, millions of acres of tropical rain forest are destroyed for timber and to provide land for ranches, farms, mines, and reservoirs. In Brazil (below) and elsewhere, fire is frequently used to clear large tracts of forest quickly.

Botanists are racing against time to preserve any as-yet-undiscovered species of plants, especially ones that might yield substances useful for treating diseases.

scientists believe that rain forests contain three-fourths of all the known species of plants and animals on Earth. Rain forests may also contain many species that have yet to be discovered, some of which could have medicinal value. Pharmaceutical companies are rushing to search rain forests for any species of plants that might be useful in treating diseases.

Climate. Rain forests play a role in the world's climate. They help regulate Earth's hydrologic (water) cycle, the process whereby water that evaporates from trees and plants falls back to Earth as rain. When a forest is destroyed, the cycle is changed. The result may be droughts, floods, and soil erosion in areas that would not normally experience such events. When forests are destroyed, the ability of the surface of Earth to reflect light also changes. This, in turn, alters the patterns of rainfall, and wind and ocean currents. In addition, scientists have found that old-growth trees in temperate rain forests are capable of holding astonishing amounts of carbon in the surrounding soil. When rain forests are destroyed, less carbon dioxide is removed from the atmosphere, further contributing to global climate change.

THE FUTURE

Conservation groups estimate that globally, the equivalent of two football fields of rain forest (about 2.5 acres or 1 hectare) is destroyed each second. A recent study concluded that the Amazon rain forest will be damaged beyond repair by 2016, or perhaps even earlier, if deforestation continues unabated. Furthermore, according to some estimates, the destruction of rain forests around the world could be causing the extinction of more than 130 species each day! This means that an estimated 20 percent of the biodiversity of Earth could become extinct within a generation. Some scientists estimate that nearly all tropical forest ecosystems could be destroyed entirely by 2030.

The best-received conservation programs aim to preserve the rain forests while still bringing economic rewards to the people and countries in which the forests are found. For instance, the Forest Stewardship Council—a nonprofit group made up of industry professionals, indigenous peoples, environmental groups, and others—has set up a forest-certification program. Under this program, accredited certifiers identify logging programs in which the harvesting of wood does not contribute to the mass destruction of the forest.

Efforts are also under way to help farms in rain-forest areas produce crops without damaging the rain forest. One such program, ECO-O.K., helps reward growers of crops for meeting environmental and social standards.

In addition, the Brazilian government pledged in 2003 to set aside 62 million acres (25 million hectares) of rain forest for permanent protection. The program would put 10 percent of the Brazilian Amazon under government protection. But budget constraints and other factors have delayed implementation of the plan, and the forest continues to lose acreage.

The ultimate effect of these and other efforts on the conservation of the rain forests is not yet certain. As a result, the survival of the world's rain forests—the richest, oldest, most productive, and most complex ecosystem on Earth—is still very much at risk.

TUNDRA AND TAIGA FLORA

by Devera Pine

The tundra and taiga can be considered the biomes at the top of the world. The tundra, which means "barren land" in Finnish, is the treeless biome that circles the North Pole. The taiga (a Russian word), found just below the tundra, is the world's largest terrestrial biome.

THE TUNDRA

The Arctic tundra, the most northerly biome, covers approximately one-fifth of the surface of Earth. Tundra that occurs on the tops of high mountains is known as *alpine tundra*.

The tundra is a treeless area characterized by *permafrost*—a layer of permanently frozen ground about 3 feet (1 meter) below the surface.

Because of its northern location, conditions are harsh: winters are long and cold, with temperatures dropping as low as –60° F (–51° C); summers are short and relatively cool, with temperatures rarely exceeding 50° F (10° C). Annually, the average temperature ranges between 10° and 20° F (–12° and –6° C).

These temperature ranges cause the top layer of soil (topsoil) to alternately freeze and thaw. In the warmer months, the thawed topsoil and snow create marshy areas, lakes, and streams. The cold temperature also means that

Neither the tundra nor the taiga supports a wide range of plant (or animal) species, a result of their perennially cold climates and exceedingly brief growing seasons.

organic matter decomposes slowly and water does not drain quickly from the land. As a result, bogs form as layers of decaying plant matter build up and turn into a substance called peat.

Overall, however, the tundra is fairly dry—in fact, it is sometimes called a polar desert. The average annual precipitation (snow and rain) is very low—less than 14 inches (350 millimeters), most of which falls during the warmer part of the year. Although, in winter, the average depth of the snow is not high, strong winds can create frequent blizzard conditions and substantial snowdrifts.

Owing to the extreme northerly location of the tundra, the Sun never sets during part of the summer, and the Sun never rises during part of the winter. The growing season on the tundra is very short—less than 60 days.

Tundra Flora

Most of the plants that grow on the tundra are relatively small and grow close to the ground, adaptations that help protect them from the cold. Even the trees—which are found only in the beds of lakes and streams—are small. Mosses, lichens, grasses, and dwarf shrubs are the main plants on the tundra.

Lichens grow on rocks, tree barks, decaying wood, and soil. Unlike other plants, lichens are a combination of two different organisms—algae and a fungus—growing together as one entity. There are more than 15,000 types of lichens, nearly all well adapted to survive extreme cold, dryness, or heat. The reindeer "moss" (genus *Cladonia*) is a common lichen in the tundra. These "pioneer plants" are among the first plants in the systemic ecological change known as succession (the process by which an area that was previously barren is occupied by an orderly series of plant communities). Lichens help prepare the way for the plant communities that follow by undergoing chemical reactions that help break down rock to form soil.

Mosses are another common tundra plant. Of the more than 9,500 species of mosses, many can be found growing on wet rocks, old logs, and in moist, shady areas. Sphagnum, or peat moss, is found in the tundra bogs. The granite mosses of the order Andreaeales are small, dark-colored plants found in Arctic and alpine areas.

Many of the plants on the tundra are colored in deep hues that help them to absorb maximum heat from the Sun. Examples include cotton sedge (*Eriophorum*); fireweed (*Epilobium*);

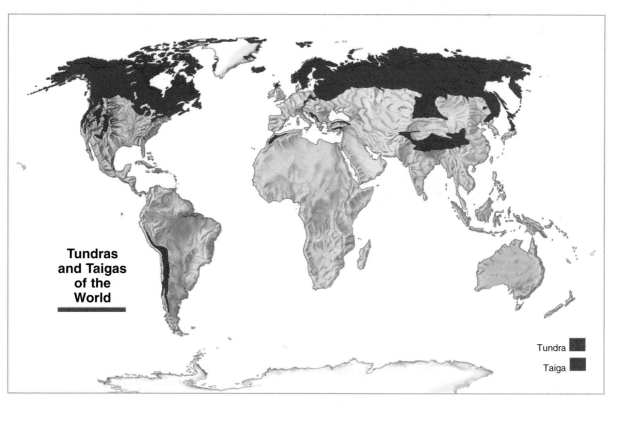

Tundras and Taigas of the World

Tundra

Taiga

saxifrage (*Saxifraga*), a type of herb that grows in rocky areas; and forget-me-nots (*Myosotis*).

Tundra flora exists in only a thin layer, and yet this vegetation helps insulate the permafrost. When the plant layer is destroyed, the permafrost can thaw, promoting serious erosion. The vegetation takes an enormously long time to grow back; some mosses, for example, may need 60 years to recover from damage. In certain areas of the tundra subjected to heavy machinery decades ago, the scars of erosion are still visible.

THE TAIGA

South of the tundra lies the taiga, the largest in area of all the biomes. The taiga, which is also called the boreal forest zone and the subarctic zone, occurs in North America, Europe, and Asia, in a belt that stretches around the globe.

As on the tundra, the weather in the taiga is cold, with very cold winters and cool summers. The average temperature in the summer is 50° F (10° C); in the winter, temperatures can drop to –40° F (–40° C) or even lower. The growing season is relatively short, lasting only 50 to 100 days. Precipitation is only slightly more plentiful than in the tundra: an average of 12 to 33 inches (300 to 850 millimeters) per year, mainly as rain in the summer.

Taiga Flora

Unlike the temperate deciduous forest or the temperate rain forest, the taiga does not have much biodiversity—that is, it is not home to a wide range of plants and animals. Instead, it is populated with groups of trees of the same species. Generally, these trees are conifers—evergreens that bear cones—especially spruces, larches, hemlocks, and firs. These trees are suited to the taiga in a number of ways. First, instead of broad leaves, most conifers have needles—thin, waxy-coated structures off which snow easily slides. Unlike deciduous trees, evergreens do not shed their leaves in the winter. Needles last for two to three years and are shed a few at a time, so the tree is never bare. Only the tamarack tree (larch), a conifer, sheds its leaves in the fall. The tree's general cone shape enables snow to drop from the branches in winter, thereby preventing excessive breakage.

In the fall or winter, conifers produce two types of cones—a pollen cone and a seed cone. The pollen cones are smaller, often bright red or yellow, and last only a few days. The woody seed cones are what most people would recognize as "pine" cones. Once the seed inside the cone is fertilized, it grows until it is fully developed. The cone then dries up, and, with luck, the seed falls into an area where it can germinate and ultimately flourish.

Animals in the Tundra and Taiga

Despite its bleak appearance and cold climate, the tundra is home to a wide variety of animals. Some of these animals, such as lemmings, live so successfully on the tundra that they form large herds. Some animals, including musk oxen and polar bears, live on the tundra year-round. Others migrate to the area during the short, cool summers. For instance, birds such as the whimbrel, or curlew; eider ducks; pintail ducks; and Canada geese spend the summer on the tundra. Golden eagles, hawks, gyrfalcons, and several types of owls can also be found there, as can moose and brown bears. The world's largest herd of caribou (also called reindeer) is found on the coastal plain of the Arctic National Wildlife Refuge. Every year, more than 150,000 animals come to this area. Caribou are important animals to native peoples around the world. The Kutchin Athabascan Indians in Alaska rely on caribou as their main source of food. In northern Scandinavia, the Lapp people use the meat, milk, and hides of the caribou.

Some animals divide their time between the tundra and the taiga—notably ptarmigan, snowy owls, and caribou. Birds on the taiga include loons, sandhill cranes, ospreys, hawks, and the peregrine falcon. Mammals include moose, wolves, lynx, and porcupines. Insects also live in these northern biomes. Every summer, millions of them fill the taiga, and every summer, birds migrate there to feast on the bugs.

The taiga is also home to a few species of deciduous trees, including the birch, poplar, alder, and aspen. Unlike the evergreens, these trees lose their leaves each fall, and are bare for the winter.

As does the tundra, the taiga has many lakes, ponds, and bogs. Sphagnum moss in the bogs dies and helps create peat, filling in the watery areas. Other plants—cranberries, blueberries, sedges, and sheep laurel, to name a few—can then begin to grow, starting the process by which watery areas are transformed into land. Eventually the area will be suitable for trees such as spruces and larches.

Many trees have developed a thick bark to protect them against wildfires. Fires are a natural part of the cycle of most forests, and, if not severe or frequent, they actually help keep the taiga healthy.

The tundra is by no means limited to the far north. In tall mountain ranges like the Rockies (above), the so-called alpine tundra offers botanists the opportunity to study tundra plants without traveling to a remote locale.

NEAR-TERM OUTLOOK

The isolated, dense woods and frozen lands of North America are not what most people envision when they think of endangered areas. For thousands of years, native peoples have lived off the bounty of these lands, depending on the health of these environments for their survival. Today the tundra and taiga in North America and throughout the rest of the world are facing the consequences of human development.

The main threats to the tundra and the taiga are posed by oil and gas drilling, logging, and fishing. The debate over oil and gas drilling in these areas has been especially controversial. For instance, it is likely that some area of Alaska contains still-undiscovered deposits of oil. Unfortunately, the deposits probably lie in a wildlife refuge—the coastal plain of the U.S. Arctic National Wildlife Refuge. The oil industry, the state of Alaska, and some energy officials argue that this

Representative Plants

Alpine bearberry
Bear grass
Bog bilberry
Bristlecone pine
Cotton sedge
Dwarf clover
Engelmann spruce
Fairy primrose
Fescue
Fireweed
Forget-me-not
Glacier lily
Goldenbush
King's crown
Moss campion
Mountain avens
Mountain heath
Mountain sorrel
Saxifrage
Sedges
Sheep laurel
White phlox
Willow

may be the last significant deposit of oil ever found in the United States. Environmentalists counterargue that the area is probably the last truly wild refuge in the country.

Elsewhere in the world, the trees of the taiga are under threat from logging. Traditionally, these forests were not attractive to the lumber industry because their slow-growing trees yield little lumber. Today, however, the boreal forests are increasingly harvested for use as pulp in making paper. Canada, for example, has leased 65 percent of its boreal forest for logging. Although the leasing arrangements require the development of parks and wildlife reserves, the logging is nonetheless widely opposed.

Other problems are more global in nature. Acid rain has contributed to the death of trees in the boreal forests, both through direct harm and by changing the makeup of forest soil. In the United States, the Environmental Protection Agency (EPA) is now taking steps to control acid rain by helping to limit the pollutants that industry and automobiles emit into the air. It is hoped that these and other steps will protect some of the last great areas of wilderness on Earth.

DESERT plants

by Devera Pine

Deserts around the world are home to a wide variety of plants, all adapted to living in the harsh conditions of a hot, arid ecosystem. Deserts and areas that are nearly deserts make up about one-third of all the land areas on Earth.

DESERT CRITERIA

Two characteristics define deserts: a lack of water and extreme temperatures. Deserts typically receive less than 10 inches (25 centimeters) of rain per year. This rain may come all at once in one storm or over the course of several months. Parts of the Sahara (the largest desert in the world) in Africa may go for years without a drop of water.

Desert temperatures vary from extremely hot during the day to freezing cold at night. In deserts that are considered "cold," precipitation falls mainly as snow. The Gobi in China and the Great Basin in the United States are two examples of "cold" deserts. In so-called "hot" deserts, such as the Sahara and the Mojave in the United States, precipitation falls in the form of rain.

There are many things that can cause an area to become dry enough to qualify as a desert. For instance, deserts sometimes form on the inland side of a mountain range—the so-called *rain-shadow* effect. As air rises to the top of the mountain range, it cools; as a result, it drops its moisture in the form of rain or snow. By the time the air reaches the top of the mountain range, it is very dry. Once the air heads back down the other side, it begins to grow warmer and regains its ability to hold moisture—making it less likely to rain or snow. Eventually, the lack of moisture causes a desert to form. Deserts are also likely to form in areas where there is little vegetation to absorb the heat of the Sun; where

The mighty saguaro cactus, the undisputed king of the Arizona desert, stands majestically among the thousands of other plants that thrive in the arid desert biome.

no lakes, streams, or other bodies of water exist to add moisture to the air; and in regions where persistently windy conditions cause any available water to evaporate quickly.

Scientists believe that the deserts on Earth today existed as far back as 3 million to 4 million years ago. As Earth's climate changed over the millennia, so, too, did the size and aridity (dryness) of the world's deserts.

THE GREEN DESERT?

Despite such unpromising conditions, plant (and animal) life flourishes in the desert. In fact, only tropical rain forests have a greater variety of life. In general, plants succeed in the desert by either devising ways to survive in the heat and dryness or avoiding those conditions as much as possible. Even though there is a wide

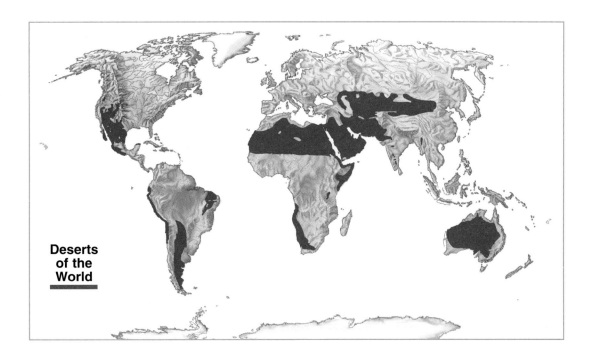

**Deserts
of the
World**

variety of plant life in the deserts, the plants tend not to grow close together as they would, for instance, in a rain forest. Desert plants also typically grow close to the ground.

Special Adaptations

Some plants are able to live in the desert because they have evolved special structures to help them store water. Cacti—such as the prickly-pear, saguaro, and barrel cacti—are among the best-known desert plants. Cacti are a type of succulent, or water-storing plant. Instead of leaves, cacti have a thick, waxy cuticle, or outer layer, that protects against water loss. Cacti are also able to store water in their stems.

The spines (thorns) on a cactus can help collect water, too—while also providing a bit of shade for the growing plant and a degree of protection from thirsty animals. In addition, the stomata (pores on the underside of leaves that allow the plant to take in air) on a cactus are usually sunken and can close during the day to prevent water loss.

Cacti have shallow roots that are far-reaching enough to quickly take up any available water when it rains. Plants such as the agave and the euphorbia use many of the same or similar mechanisms for capturing and storing water.

Other types of plants, such as perennials—plants that grow for several years—also have special adaptations for surviving in the desert. For instance, sagebrush *(Artemisia)* have tiny leaves to cut down on the amount of water the plant loses through transpiration (the evaporation of water into the air). Other plants have evolved waxy leaves—the chaparral bush *(Larrea tridentata)* is a notable example. This bush has other features that help it flourish in the desert, including an unpleasant smell and taste that discourage hungry or thirsty animals from visiting it. The stomata on its leaves open only at night, minimizing the moisture lost to the daytime heat. Like cacti, the chaparral bush has widespread shallow roots for catching rainwater; it also has roots that grow deep into the ground, tapping water from the water table. These features help the chaparral bush survive long periods without precipitation.

Another desert plant that relies on deep roots for survival is the mesquite tree *(Prosopis)*. Its roots can extend 30 to 100 feet (9 to 30 meters) in their search for underground water.

Representative Plants

Agaves
Barrel cactus
Brittle bush
Chaparral bush
Desert holly
Desert marigold
Desert paintbrush
Desert peach
Devil's claw
Giant wild rye
Gold poppy
Indian blanket
Indian rice grass
Joshua tree
Jumping cholla
Mesquite
Needle grass
Ocotillo
Organ pipe cactus
Paloverde
Prickly pear cactus
Pygmy cedar
Sagebrush
Saguaro
Seep willow
Spurges
Yuccas

Desert rains often presage the arrival of colorful wildflowers, including scarlet-blossomed ocotillos and lemon-yellow cholla blooms (above), and ground-hugging woolly daisies (right).

tion—in a matter of weeks. For example, winter rains will generally spur such plants as the Mojave aster or the desert paintbrush to begin growing in the spring. Exactly when annuals begin to grow and flower depends on the rainfall, temperature, light, and elevation. Plants that grow at higher elevations tend to bloom later in the season.

Although annuals produce seeds quickly, the seeds may not germinate (begin to grow) for a year or even more. The seeds will begin the growth process only when the temperature and the amount of rainfall are just right.

The seeds of the paloverde tree *(Cercidium)* also need just the right combination of conditions to germinate. The very hard seed of this tree must be cracked open for the tree to germinate. This may happen during a rainstorm, when rushing water and debris strike the seed.

Botanists believe that the seeds of some desert plants may not germinate immediately because of a seedling-inhibiting substance that some mature plants produce. Such a substance would prevent young plants from growing near the mature plant, and therefore would eliminate a potential competitor for precious water.

In the desert's harsh environment, plants and animals often depend on each other for survival. Many plants rely on animals to pollinate them and to disperse their seed. The plants, in turn, offer the animals food, shelter from the sunlight, and protection.

DESERTS AND PEOPLE

Around the world, humans have been able to adapt to desert living. Nomadic tribes, for example, survive in the deserts by traveling from oasis to oasis for water. Such is the case in certain African, Asian, and Australian deserts.

Irrigation systems and, in the case of modern cities in the desert, air-conditioning and other technologies have made the desert livable for people accustomed to temperate climes. The changes that humans bring to the desert can cause problems, however. If irrigation is not implemented correctly, salt and alkali from the sur-

Dormancy

Some desert plants survive the harsh environment by entering *dormancy*—a cessation of growth during dry spells. Such plants come to life suddenly when it rains, often producing flowers and seeds in very short order. The ocotillo plant *(Fouquieria splendens)* sheds its leaves and stops growing during periods of dry weather, but grows leaves, sprouts flowers, and bears seeds in the weeks after a precipitation event. After the seeds fall off, the plant becomes dormant again until the next time it rains. Depending on the weather, the ocotillo can go through this process several times a year.

Desert plants that belong to the lily family enter dormancy during dry times, too, losing their leaves so that only the bulb of the plant remains in the ground, unseen. Some desert plants remain green the entire year. Schott's pygmy cedar *(Peucephyllum schottii)* stays green because it is able to absorb dew.

Annuals

Annuals, or plants that live for only one growing season, also take advantage of the rains. Annuals in the desert can go through their life cycle—growth, flowering, and seed produc-

Animals in the Desert

Like plants, animals have had to evolve special features that allow them to survive in the desert. And also like plants, they have done this in a variety of ways.

Some animals cope with the heat and lack of water by living in underground burrows during the day. Skunks and badgers are two such nocturnal animals. Other animals, including rattlesnakes, are active in the cooler parts of the day—dusk and dawn. Such animals are said to be *crepuscular*.

Animals that are too big to burrow underground seek shade during the day. However, cold-blooded animals (those whose body temperature is controlled by the temperature of their environment), such as reptiles, must alternate between sunlight and shade to maintain a comfortable body temperature. Some animals avoid the heat completely by estivating through the summer.

Animals have developed a variety of mechanisms for retaining water in their bodies. Rodents and other small mammals excrete only concentrated urine and dry feces and keep perspiration to a minimum. Still, most mammals need water at least every few days, and some need water every day to survive. To get water, mammals eat either other animals or succulent plants. Camels are widely known for their ability to survive in the desert: camels can tolerate a body temperature of 105° F (40.5° C), and can lose 30

In an example of desert symbiosis, the yucca plant depends upon the yucca moth for pollination, and the moth larvae rely on the plant's seeds for food.

percent of their body weight and then replace it in a single session at the water hole.

Other animals have special physical structures for living in the desert. Many insects stay off the hot ground with their long legs. The feathers, scales, and skin of desert animals are often pale in color, to reflect heat and to make it more difficult for predators to see them on the light-colored land. The turkey vulture and the black vulture, which have dark-colored feathers, use a special process called *urohydrosis* to cool off: they urinate on their legs! The urine evaporates, cooling the legs, and the cooled blood then circulates through the rest of the bird's body.

Finally, the eggs of some animals are able to stay dormant until conditions are right. This explains why freshwater shrimp and some amphibians can sometimes be found in the temporary pools that form in deserts after rains.

face water and groundwater can render the soil sterile and unable to grow plant life. On semi-desert lands that are cleared in order to plant crops, the exposed soil is likely to erode.

Desert plants are threatened by overgrazing livestock. People may carelessly trample or drive over desert plants, or they may cut the vegetation for use as fuel or to sell to gardeners and others eager to raise exotic plants.

All these actions threaten to make existing deserts and semidesert lands less able to support plant and animal life, a process called, ironically, *desertification*. Generally, as desertification spreads through an area, the groundwater tables decrease, the topsoil and water become more

saline (salty), surface waters, such as streams and lakes, dry up; soil erosion increases; native plants disappear; and biological diversity—the wide array of plants and animals that an area such as a desert can sustain—is lost. Around the globe, desertification is a major problem, particularly in Africa. An estimated 10 billion acres (4 billion hectares), or approximately one-third of the world's land surface, are impacted by desertification, directly affecting more than 250 million people. The combination of high temperatures and lack of water make the desert environment one that is easily disturbed. Careful planning may be able to save these unique ecosystems, but for now the future seems uncertain.

HORTICULTURISTS AND AGRONOMISTS

AND THEIR SCIENCE

by Peter A. Flax

Norman Borlaug never thought he'd start a revolution with wheat. For years, he had crossed different types of wheat with the hope of creating strains that would grow faster, flourish in more-extreme climates, or otherwise be endowed with desirable traits.

Finally, in the 1950s, after many attempts at crossing native Mexican wheat with strains from around the world, Borlaug had promising results with a dwarf Japanese variety. After several years of experimentation, his creation—a short-stemmed plant with a large head—was thriving throughout Mexico. The strain showed great resistance to disease and pests. Using the new strain, Mexican farmers increased their yields by more than 50 percent in just two years—a welcome development in a nation struggling to feed its growing population.

Seemingly overnight, Borlaug's adaptable dwarf wheat was sprouting in Turkey, India, South America, and North Africa. In the follow-

ing decade, scientists copied his breeding methods to create new varieties of corn and other crops, including a dwarf rice strain that flourished in Southeast Asia. The worldwide exportation of Borlaug's techniques—which created what became known as the Green Revolution—ended famine for tens of millions of people. For his work, Borlaug was awarded the Nobel Peace Prize in 1970.

A generation later, the fruits of Borlaug's labor are still being reaped. India is enjoying its third decade without a major famine, Southeast Asia has experienced a historic economic boom, and much of Latin America is agriculturally self-sufficient. Without Borlaug's groundbreaking research decades earlier, the news today might not be so rosy.

The horticulturist above is comparing batches of fruit stored under various thermal and atmospheric conditions to determine which combination works best.

CLOSELY LINKED FIELDS

Few can argue with Borlaug's contributions to humanity. But there might be some disagreement as to how Borlaug should be identified: as a horticulturist or as an agronomist. Indeed, drawing distinctions between horticulture and agronomy is almost a science of its own. Both of these closely linked fields are concerned with the science of growing agricultural plants. Their basic difference lies in the scale of cultivation and the type of plants being grown. Simply put, horticulture deals with the growing of fruits, vegetables, and ornamental plants; agronomy is restricted to the large-scale cultivation of crops. Borlaug would therefore fall into the agronomist category.

In the past, horticulture was confined to plants raised in small gardens; today the definition has expanded to include produce grown on large orchards and farms; ornamental trees and bushes grown commercially; and flowers cultivated in fields or in greenhouses. Under the heading of horticultural crops fall a number of unusual species: coffee, tea, and other so-called "beverage crops"; plants grown for medicine; spice plants; and tree crops grown for oils.

Agronomy focuses on crops traditionally cultivated in large fields. Of particular importance to agronomists are such cereal crops as wheat, rice, soybeans, and sorghum, which form the nutritional backbone for nearly everyone on Earth. Agronomists also study the cultivation of plants for livestock and poultry feed, fibers such as cotton, and most vegetable oils.

The line between the two sciences can sometimes be so fine that one plant can fall into either science, depending on its use. Sweet corn, for example, is a horticultural crop when grown for human consumption, but it is an agronomic plant if cultivated as a feed crop for animals. Likewise, beets are horticultural when grown as food, but agronomic when grown for sugar production.

An Ancient History

The dawn of scientific agriculture arrived with the rise of advanced civilizations, particularly those in Mesopotamia, Egypt, Greece, and Rome. In these societies, people began to study and catalog plants, improve production techniques, and create new tools. Such advancements allowed the cultivation of large crop fields that could feed many people.

Agriculture remained essentially unchanged until comparatively recent times. When the Pilgrims came to the New World in 1620, they brought farming techniques and tools that largely resembled those used by the Romans. These new American farmers learned many new and valuable techniques from the native Indians, and later from Africans brought to the New World as slaves.

In the 18th and 19th centuries, inventions such as the grain drill (which distributes seeds into the ground), the cotton gin (which separates the seeds, hulls, and foreign material from cotton), the mechanical reaper (which speeds grain harvesting), and the steel plow (which allows for the cultivation of vast plots of land) transformed agriculture. Then, in the 20th century, thanks to the success of plant breeders—particularly with the interbreeding of corn in the

Early horticultural intervention may help prevent a pest problem that besets a backyard gardener from eventually afflicting nearby large-scale agricultural operations.

In Kazakhstan, U.S. horticulturists collected seeds and cuttings from wild apples that can withstand temperatures of −40° F. If crossbred with domestic strains, the resultant hybrid might be cultivatable north of the current "apple limit."

1930s and with the 1960s Green Revolution—farmers could produce far more on an acre of land. The development of new pesticides, more-effective fertilizers, more-advanced machinery, and efficient irrigation methods further changed the face of farming.

The results have been truly astonishing. In the United States, the population more than doubled between 1930 and 2005. During this same period, U.S. farmers were able to raise their productivity by far greater amounts. Per-acre yields of wheat have grown by more than 330 percent, tomato yields have risen 400 percent, and per-acre harvests of corn have improved more than sixfold. Such amazing productivity has allowed millions of Americans to give up sustenance farming for other pursuits, transformed the United States into an industrial giant, and greatly elevated the standard of living.

HORTICULTURE AND AGRONOMY TODAY

Horticulture is traditionally divided into four branches that represent major groups—fruits, vegetables, flowers, and ornamental plants. Modern horticulturists apply principles and techniques from genetics, ecology, plant physiology, entomology (the study of insects), pathology, or biotechnology to their work.

While horticulturists tend to specialize in a particular group of plants, agronomists usually work within an applied discipline that relates to a specific aspect of growing crops. Major areas of focus include crop management, crop breeding, soil science, and pest control.

Horticultural Disciplines

Pomology. The term "pomology" is derived from the word *pome*, which refers to tree fruits (such as apples and pears) with a distinctive central seed core. In reality, though, pomology deals with the cultivation of all fruits and nuts. Most fruits are harvested from trees, shrubs, and vines. An important subspecialty within this group is *viticulture*, the cultivation of grapes.

In recent decades, pomologists have made great strides in reproducing and improving fruiting plants using a technique called *grafting*. In grafting, parts of two plants are united to form a single specimen. Most fruit trees are propagated by grafting. The refinement of the technique has allowed the development of seedless fruit, such as navel oranges; the production of dwarf trees, which bear fruit faster and in greater quantity than do standard trees; and the emergence of hardier varieties. Scientists also regulate the growth of fruiting plants through the use of plant hormones, called *auxins*, to stimulate budding and fruit growth.

Olericulture. Scientists in this specialty deal with the cultivation of vegetables, the edible parts of herbaceous (nonwoody) plants. Vegetable crops are highly varied because much of an herbaceous plant can be eaten. Examples of the edible parts of vegetable plants include the root (sweet potato, beet), stem (asparagus, potato), leaf (spinach, lettuce), flower bud (asparagus, broccoli), and seed (pea, corn).

Horticulturists have created hundreds of valuable new plant strains using *hybridization*, a method in which two plant strains are crossed to produce a superior variety. Thanks to plant breeding, many of the vegetables sold at markets are larger, more attractive, more nutritious, hardier, and less prone to spoilage than their predecessors. More recently, scientists have developed improved vegetables through genetic engineering. Since 1994, for example, the U.S. government has approved the sale of genetically enhanced tomatoes, cotton, corn, soybeans, and other plants.

Floriculture. The cultivation of flowers and foliage plants falls under the heading of floriculture. Scientific advancements have helped create an enormous flower-growing industry. Many flowering and foliage plants are grown on large, mechanized farms or in sophisticated greenhouses, where every conceivable environmental factor can be controlled. For example, floriculturists use computerized lighting systems that can mimic the changing seasons or stimulate a plant to bloom faster than it would normally. Chemicals and hormones are also used to manipulate every aspect of a plant's growth.

Botanical breeders have helped develop new plant varieties, or *cultivars*, that have at-

Careers in Horticulture and Agronomy

Today, many employment opportunities are available to horticulturists and agronomists. Aspiring specialists must undergo intensive scientific education before they can enter the workforce. At the undergraduate level, most students opt to pursue a degree in one of these two sciences, or in a related discipline, such as biology or botany. These studies must include substantial coursework in chemistry, physics, and mathematics.

Horticulturists interested in research and most career agronomists also must generally hold advanced graduate degrees in their respective fields. For the majority of research and teaching positions, a doctorate degree is necessary—a course of postgraduate study that can take more than six years to complete.

Professionals in these fields have a wide range of employment options. Many horticulturists and agronomists find work at colleges and universities, where they can conduct their research and teach a new generation of students at the same time.

Many others are employed by nonacademic organizations: agricultural institutes, regional experiment stations, and government agencies, for example, often employ horticulturists and agronomists to conduct research on improving crop production or fighting pests. Others find work at arboretums, museums, scientific publishers, and botanical gardens. Many horticulturists pursue careers in the private sector, especially in the nursery, plant-growing, and seed-producing industries. Agronomists can also find jobs working at chemical, seed, and equipment-manufacturing companies.

Many believe that the opportunities for horticulturists and agronomists will grow rapidly in the future. As the world's population and its demand for food continue to increase, horticulturists and agronomists will be called upon to help lead the way.

Budding horticulturists and agronomists are often advised to keep a diary in which to record the names and characteristics of plant species they encounter.

tractive colors, long-lasting flowers, and can grow despite cool nighttime temperatures. The hundreds of rose cultivars now available have an amazing range of colors, sizes, scents, and flowering seasons.

Ornamental horticulture. This specialty deals with the growth of aesthetically pleasing outdoor plants. The products of this field—whether shrubs, trees, or grasses—can be seen in backyards, parks, gardens, golf courses, and even highway medians. Many of the people who work in this discipline are involved in applied fields such as landscape design, although basic research remains important. Horticulturists, for example, use their knowledge about hybridization and seed dormancy to cultivate grass specimens that germinate quickly and look beautiful but require little water and care. Others have developed varieties of trees that can thrive in urban and suburban settings.

Ornamental horticulture overlaps with landscape design when the shapes being created with shrubs and trees are intended to beautify a park or other grounds.

Agronomic Disciplines

Crop management. Agronomists specializing in this field are concerned with developing and improving methods to help farmers reap large harvests of desirable crops. One such practice is *crop rotation.* Farmers have known for centuries that growing different plants in sequence could produce better harvests; agronomists have transformed this age-old practice into a science. Agronomic research has enabled farmers to dramatically improve yields, to better control plant diseases and pests, and to improve soil health. Thanks to such work, farmers growing corn now know, for example, that rotating in bean plants can restore the nitrogen content of the soil; rotating in an alfalfa crop can control aggressive weeds.

Another important area of research is irrigation. Productive farming cannot occur in places where there is an insufficient or sporadic supply of water. In the United States, tens of millions of acres of valuable farmland are irrigated, including arid regions of California, Arizona, and Texas that are far from natural water sources. New irrigation systems deliver water underground—directly to the roots of plants—rather than wastefully sprinkling it over the surface of the soil where it quickly evaporates.

Other land-management subjects studied by agronomists include specialized tillage and cultivation techniques for battling weeds; the development and use of fertilizers; and seeding techniques. In recent years, scientists have even begun using satellite technology and powerful computers to help farmers track their yields with newfound accuracy.

Crop breeding. Many agronomists are involved in improving the genetics of crop plants. Scientists have been able to enhance such characteristics as yield, speed of maturity, disease and insect resistance, winter hardiness, and drought resistance. Such breeding has created new hybrids of corn, rice, wheat, soybeans, and other crops that outproduce their predecessors and offer extra nutritional benefits.

In some cases, plant breeding leads to the creation of an entirely new crop. In the 1960s, for example, scientists successfully crossed wheat and rye to produce the first human-made cereal, a grain called *triticale.* It combines the high protein and other nutritional benefits of rye with the superior milling and baking qualities of wheat. Scientists are working to develop triticale strains that do not grow to awkward heights and are disease-resistant as well.

Soil science. Many agronomists study soil, a key resource for crop production. Soil serves as a medium to anchor roots and support plants, as a reservoir to store moisture for plants, and as a source of elements essential for plant growth. The subdiscipline of soil chemistry concerns itself with studying substances in the ground that can boost or retard plant growth. Agronomists trained in this area can assess the fertility, the acidity, the level of nitrogen and other nutrients, and a number of other soil characteristics to help farmers make informed decisions about fertilizers and crop choice. Many soil chemists measure and assess damage caused by pollution.

Other scientists study the physical characteristics of soil. By examining the geography of an area along with the texture, depth, and the moisture-holding capacity of its soil, an agronomist can help farmers protect their land from erosion and poor crop choice. Such advice is certainly valuable: some scientists believe that soil erosion poses a larger environmental threat than do air or water pollution. There are many places in the world where it is now impossible to grow crops, even though in the past the soil was productive.

Pest control. Many agronomists work to help protect crop plants from insects, plant diseases, and weeds, which cause billions of dollars' worth of damaged or lost crops each year. Chemicals known as pesticides are widely used, although scientific and public concerns about the danger that they pose to humans and the environment has led to the formulation of less-toxic products. At the same time, other methods of control have gained wider use. For example, biological control—the application of living organisms such as wasps and ladybugs to fight unwanted insects and weeds—has become increasingly popular. Similarly, scientists have improved their understanding of how crop-rotation, cultivation, and irrigation techniques can repel crop pests.

Agronomists have also introduced novel approaches to combating crop enemies. Ad-

Using computer-equipped tractors, farmers can generate a unit-by-unit productivity profile of their land—with each unit representing only a tiny fraction of an acre.

vances in genetics have allowed scientists to develop cultivars that resist plant disease and certain insects. Scientists have successfully disrupted the reproductive cycle of some insects by applying natural hormones. Other advances include using microwaves to kill weeds and disease-causing fungi; utilizing infrared sensors to track crop infestation; and designing machines to recover and recycle herbicides.

THE FUTURE

Since the need for food and other valuable plant products is expected to grow, the work of horticulturists and agronomists will always be called upon to make plants more productive, more beautiful, and hardier. The fields of biotechnology and genetic engineering will likely provide researchers with powerful ways to accomplish such goals, as well as to battle new plant diseases and pests that will undoubtedly emerge in the future. Scientists must also develop plant varieties that need little water and can grow in harsh soil, and fertilizers that are less costly and not as toxic as those used today.

Finally, horticulturists and agronomists will figure prominently in solving important environmental problems. They will need to devise ways to protect food crops and valuable horticultural products from the effects of air and water pollution; to help agriculture thrive despite heightened competition over water and land; and to develop farming practices that do less harm to the environment.

ANIMAL LIFE

Animals have evolved an extraordinary variety of forms and adaptations. The brilliantly colored spine-cheek anemonefish (facing page), for example, swims among the tentacles of poisonous sea anemones. The fish is apparently protected from the plantlike creature's toxins by a unique mucous covering. Closer to home, it's not unusual to see a multicolored butterfly flitting about a garden (above), searching for just the right flower to visit.

ZOOLOGISTS AND THEIR SCIENCE

Few modern scientists would define themselves as simply "zoologists." More than likely, they would identify themselves with a specific area—one or another of the many subdisciplines that comprise the science of zoology.

And the subdisciplines (and their specialists) are myriad. For example, the area of zoology concerned with animal behavior is called ethology; scientists who study animal behavior are called ethologists. An ornithologist is a zoologist who studies birds. An ecologist studies the relationships between animals and their environment. A physiologist studies the function of organ systems. A geneticist studies heredity and genes. Ichthyologists study fish; herpetologists, snakes; entomologists, insects, and so on.

It bears mentioning that humans, too, are animals. Over the centuries, many important discoveries about human reproduction, growth, health, and behavior have come from the work of zoologists. Zoologists do not experiment directly on people; that work is generally left to medical researchers. Instead, zoologists often apply to humans what they learn from studying other animals.

ZOOLOGY THROUGH THE AGES

Zoology is one of the oldest life sciences. In a fundamental way, people have been studying animals since they began hunting them in prehistoric times. The need to understand ani-

Zoology encompasses much more than zoo science. Nevertheless, many associate the field exclusively with professionals who work at zoos and nature centers.

mal life increased as people began raising their own animals for meat, milk, and hides.

Still, early beliefs about animals were more superstition than fact. The first glimmerings of animal *science* appeared among the ancient Greeks 2,300 years ago. The Greek naturalist Aristotle was an avid collector and dissector of animals. He wrote extensive descriptions of their bodies, both inside and out. He also tried to relate differences in body parts to different ways of living. After Aristotle's time, Egyptian scholars continued dissecting animals and examining their parts. They elevated *anatomy*, the study of external form and internal organization, into one of the first true sciences.

Animal Sciences

Zoologists recognize a number of sciences as distinct disciplines. Although each is a specialty, cutting-edge research is likely to overlap two or more fields.

Taxonomy. The science of animal *taxonomy*, or classification, deals with the description and the naming of new animal species. Taxonomists also try to define the relationships between known species based on common traits. In the mid-18th century, Swedish scientist Carolus Linnaeus created the basic system of animal classification still used today. Linnaeus also established *binomial nomenclature*, a scientific naming system for living things.

Beginning in the 16th century, the Age of Exploration kept scientists busy describing, naming, and classifying the many new animals discovered each year. With the introduction of the microscope in the 17th century, taxonomy grew more sophisticated. This invention enabled scientists to examine ever-smaller physical traits. In doing so, they discovered previously hidden relationships between certain species and groups of animals. Today animal classification is undergoing yet another revolution as taxonomists compare the genes, or DNA, of different animals.

Physiology. The 18th century saw the rise of *physiology*, the science of such body functions as digestion, respiration, circulation, and excretion. Then, as now, experiments with animals advanced our understanding of human physiology. In the late 1700s, scientists came to recognize the chemical nature of physiology when French chemist Antoine-Laurent Lavoisier determined that animals "burn," or consume, oxygen to fuel their body functions. Today such studies are within the realm of *biochemistry*, the study of the chemical processes of life.

Embryology. In the 18th century, most scientists still believed that the

Zoology includes innumerable subspecialties. A taxonomist (left) focuses on describing, naming, and classifying new species of animals. The physiologist below gains insights into a guinea pig's cardiopulmonary system by examining the animal with a stethoscope.

Career opportunities for zoologists are many and diverse. But anyone considering such a career should know that competition is great for most jobs, so a high level of education is important. Experience, which may start with volunteer work or summer employment, also makes a big difference. A minimum of a bachelor's degree in biology or zoology is necessary for entry-level jobs. Most professionals continue their education toward a master's or doctorate degree in a chosen specialty. Today most zoologists work in one of the following areas:

•*Colleges, universities, and high schools.* Most large colleges and universities employ professors who work in departments of biology or zoology, or one of their many subdisciplines. Most university zoologists pursue research in addition to teaching. Such positions require a master's or doctoral degree. A bachelor's degree in science with additional teacher training is typically required for teaching science at a high-school level.

•*Government agencies.* Many zoologists work for government agencies such as the National Park Service (NPS), Fish and Wildlife Service, Department of Agriculture (DOA), and the Environmental Protection Agency (EPA). They include general zoologists, ecologists, and wildlife biologists who conduct field research; geneticists and physiologists who develop breeding and feeding meth-

Wildlife organizations hire a great number of young zoologists. Some specialize in the care and revitalization of endangered species.

ods; and interpretive naturalists who educate the public. State fish-and-game agencies hire zoologists to help develop environmental-protection programs and to enforce wildlife-protection and game laws.

•*Research institutes and private industry.* Independent research institutes employ zoologists to conduct research projects in such fields as marine biology, genetics, or biochemistry. Environmental-consulting firms and certain large private industries need zoologists who can study the effects of pollutants, heat, and other industry by-products on surrounding wildlife and their various habitats.

•*Wildlife organizations.* Organizations such as the Nature Conservancy and the National Wildlife Federation hire a limited number of zoologists to help maintain their sanctuaries, educate the public, and lobby the government. Such institutions often sponsor research with grant money.

•*Museums.* Natural-history and science museums employ a variety of zoologists as curators. In addition to collecting and preparing specimens and creating public displays, the museum curator may pursue research in his or her specialty.

•*Zoos and aquariums.* Large public zoos and aquariums employ zoologists to work as curators, directors, and high-level keepers who study as well as care for the animals.

---

adult existed fully formed but in miniature within the material that develops into an embryo and then a newborn. This faulty belief was changed forever in 1827, when Estonian zoologist Karl von Baer discovered ova, or egg cells, inside female mammals. He proved that all animals, including humans, arise from a single-cell egg

that develops into tissues and then organs. Baer also compared the embryos of different animals, and showed that they are quite similar to each other in the early stages of development.

Evolution. Zoology took another great step when English naturalist Charles Darwin developed his theory of evolution in the mid-19th century. Darwin, although not the first to propose that animals change from generation to generation, was the first to explain how and why. Darwin proposed that any new trait that improves survival and reproduction would naturally increase in a population. An accumulation of these new traits could produce new forms of animals, or species.

Although extremely controversial at the time, Darwin's evolutionary ideas changed zoology forever. Taxonomy could now be viewed as a description of the evolutionary relationships between different animal groups. In this view, simpler animals evolve into more-complex and more-efficient forms. At the same time, zoologists began comparing the anatomy of living animals to that of ancient fossils and found further evidence of evolutionary change.

Cell biology. About the same time, zoologists armed with microscopes were establishing that cells were the basic unit of life. The new science of *cell biology* concerned itself with the study of cells and their reproduction. *"Omnis cellula e cellula"* (all cells come from cells), wrote German cell biologist Rudolf Virchow in 1858. His dictum expressed the new idea that cell reproduction is the basis of life.

Genetics. With the dawn of the 20th century, a new breed of zoologists, called *geneticists*, focused on biological structures even smaller than the cell. They studied *chromosomes*, the hereditary units passed from cell to cell and generation to generation. In 1909, the American zoologist Thomas Hunt Morgan established that structures he called *genes* lay in a line along each chromosome. Each gene appeared to code for a particular trait, such as eye color or antenna shape in flies.

In 1933, another American zoologist, Theophilus Painter, found the first actual genes. He used the unusually large chromosomes in the salivary cells of *Drosophila* fruit flies. Under the microscope, *Drosophila* chromosomes show visible bands, which Painter demonstrated were the precise loci, or positions, of genes.

To study the impact of pollution on animals, the zoologist above measures the effect of dioxin on fish embryos. Computers enhance the ability of zoologists to conduct insect studies (below) and other research.

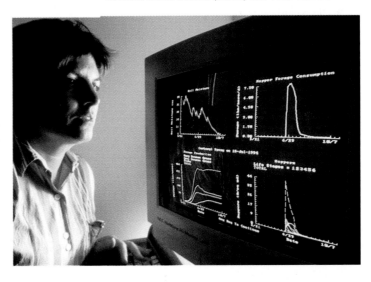

Ecology. While many 20th-century zoologists were focusing on smaller and smaller details of animal life, another group was stepping back to see how animals fit in with the larger world. These were the first *ecologists*, scientists who study communities of animals and their relationship to their environment. Zoologist Victor Shelford helped establish this new science with pioneering work on animal communities in North America. Shelford studied how changes in the availability of food, water, and other resources led to increases or decreases in animal populations. He also developed the concept of *biome* for the unique combinations of plants and animals that characterize large geographic areas such as tundra, forest, and desert.

Ecological studies also showed the interdependence of the three great divisions of life: the producers (plants), the consumers (animals), and the decomposers (primarily fungi and bacteria). Ecologists also awakened humanity to its own tremendous impact on Earth and on Earth's ability to sustain life.

Animal behavior. The 20th century also brought *ethology,* the study of the mechanisms behind types of behavior seen in many animals (aggression, submissiveness, parental care, etc.). Zoologists had long made observations about the behavior of animals, but it was not until the 1920s that the study became its own scientific field. Many consider the "father" of ethology to be the Austrian zoologist Konrad Lorenz. (See the article beginning on page 188.)

MODERN METHODS

Zoology has always advanced with the invention of new tools and the discovery of new techniques. But nothing can compare with the technological revolution that has occurred during the past few decades.

Computers can quickly complete calculations that once took weeks, months, or even years for an animal biologist to tackle. Ecologists use field observations, historical information, and satellite data to create complex computer models of habitats. These programs allow the scientists to pinpoint where certain species are most likely to be found, as well as to predict how changes to the environment might affect wildlife. Computers' lightning-quick processing speed allows users to include more information in their models and get results almost immediately.

Computers have become indispensable in other animal sciences as well. Biochemists use them to determine enzymatically controlled reaction times. Geneticists use computers to scan hundreds, even thousands, of chromosome samples at a time. Animal biologists of all types electronically store, retrieve, and organize their data, observations, and other information.

Modern biochemists also use special radioactive compounds to trace biological pathways in living organisms. Radioactive compounds introduced into the body through food or injection travel into cells and become incorporated in tissues. By following the paths of these compounds, biochemists are able to learn about where different biological activities take place inside the body.

Another revolutionary technique is *gene amplification.* Zoologists can now study an animal's genetic material by multiplying a tiny bit of it millions of times over. This enables geneticists to study individual genes and mutated versions of those genes. It also enables taxonomists to compare the genetic sequences of different species and trace the ancestry of various animal groups with great accuracy.

APPLIED ZOOLOGY

The impact of zoology cannot be underestimated. Zoologists have greatly enhanced the quality of life for humans, most especially in the past century. In particular, they have applied their science to problems in medicine and agriculture. To give a few examples: in the early 1900s, zoologist Ross Harrison pioneered organ-transplant techniques, with work on amphibians at Yale University. In the 1940s, zoologist Marston Bates of Harvard University helped win the war against yellow fever by studying the mosquitoes that carried the disease. Zoologists continue to work on the front line in the battle against cancer and other diseases that affect both humans and animals.

Animal physiologists and geneticists have greatly improved ranching and dairy farming by advancing our understanding of animal nutrition and selective breeding.

Ichthyologists and marine biologists have helped guide the commercial fishing industry to more wisely harvest the ocean without destroying its resources.

Entomologists have increased crop production through their understanding of insect pests and how to thwart them. Biochemists aide in this work by developing pesticides that do not harm surrounding wildlife or people.

Clearly, zoology is of great importance to both human and animal life today. Zoologists continue to learn more about how all life operates and how we affect and are affected by our fellow humans.

What Is an Animal?

"I eat and move, therefore I am." That might be the simplest answer to our title question. At least it distinguishes plant from animal on a superficial level. Dogs and cats gobble their food with great animation. Magnolia trees and marigolds do not.

But nature is seldom simple. Come to think of it, you've probably seen pictures of carnivorous plants closing their "teeth" around insects. And you'll never see a sea sponge chomp its prey—although the sponge is, in fact, an animal. Indeed, our concept of what is and is not an animal has changed somewhat since Aristotle divided up the world into Animal, Vegetable, and Mineral in the 3rd century B.C. In the past two decades, powerful microscopes and biochemical tests have deepened our understanding of what it means to be an animal.

A defining trait of animals is the presence of a nervous system. Animals derive their capacity to move and their instinct to search for water from the action of nerves.

EARLY BELIEFS ABOUT ANIMALS

It is easy to dismiss the early scientists as naive. Yet, with no instruments but their eyes and hands, they were able to categorize living things with remarkable accuracy. By early definitions, an animal was an organism that moved, ate, breathed, and stopped growing after reaching a certain size and shape. Plants, by contrast, did not move, eat, or breathe, but could make their own food and continue growing throughout their lives, sometimes changing shape as they did so.

This simple division worked for a long time. When microscopes were invented and scientists discovered one-celled organisms, the scientists simply divided the newly discovered lifeforms between the two established kingdoms. Bacteria, algae, and fungi—which did not appear to eat or move—were lumped with the plants. Protozoans—which did seem to eat and move—were dubbed animals.

Some animals—including the frog and dragonfly—reach adulthood only after passing through a process called metamorphosis.

Modern-day blue-green algae and bacteria are probably quite similar to these first living things. Today we call them *prokaryotes*, and place them in their own kingdom—Monera. There are no male or female prokaryotes. When it comes time to reproduce, these organisms simply split in two—each "daughter" an exact copy of its "mother."

From the early prokaryotes, there evolved a group of more-complex one-celled organisms. In these organisms, the genetic material, or DNA, of each cell is organized inside a distinct nucleus bound by a nuclear envelope. Cells with this more sophisticated structure are called *eukaryotic*.

The first single-cell eukaryotic organisms were similar to the green algae and protozoans found in pond water today. Scientists call them protists, and place them in the second kingdom of life—Protista. Some can make their own food, like plants. Others can move about in search of food, like animals. Still others are something in between.

From different protists, there evolved the final three kingdoms of life we know today: plants, fungi, and animals. All three types of organisms have bodies made of many eukaryotic cells. This is important, because eukaryotic cells, which have enclosed nuclei, can *differentiate*, or grow differently, to form different kinds of tissue. This is more or less where the similarities among plants, animals, and fungi end, and their important differences begin.

This system was never perfect. Already in the 18th century, scientists such as Carolus Linnaeus were stumped by such "animal-plants" as corals and sponges. They looked like flowers and did not move. But they fed on tiny prey filtered out of the water. To which kingdom did they belong? And what about fungi such as mushrooms? They did not move or actively feed. But neither did they make their own food, instead drawing nutrients from the bark or soil on which they grew.

Things grew still more confusing in the early 1900s, when scientists discovered microorganisms such as *Euglena*, which makes its own food like a plant, but actively swims about like an animal.

Today we recognize five kingdoms of life: plants, animals, fungi, protists, and Monera. Understanding their differences and their evolutionary relationships (how certain kingdoms grew out of others) helps us understand what makes animals truly unique.

THE ORIGIN OF ANIMALS

Life began on Earth some 3 billion years ago in the form of simple one-celled organisms. The first animals appeared more than 2 billion years later. What happened in between?

The first forms of life were very simple. Each individual consisted of a single cell with no enclosed nucleus or other cell structures.

WHAT MAKES ANIMALS UNIQUE

First and foremost, the eukaryotic cells of an animal lack the rigid cell walls found in plants and fungi. Animal cells are elastic, adaptable, and glued together with a strong but pliant protein called *collagen*.

Indeed, if there is any one thing that clearly divides the Animal Kingdom from all others, it is collagen. All animals make collagen. It is the primary building block of bones, tendons, ligaments, and skin. Collagen does not exist in the plant or fungi kingdoms; nor is it found in protists, the kingdom from which animals arose. This suggests that all animals may have evolved from a single common ancestor.

Movement and Support

Because their cells were elastic instead of rigid, the first animals were able to develop a great variety of cell types: nerve cells, muscle cells, bone cells, and the like. These cells then became organized into tissues and organs. The most important of these were muscles and nerves, which allow animals to move in a coordinated and deliberate way.

So it is true, as Aristotle first observed, that all animals move. And they do so primarily to find food for growth and reproduction. We now know that even stationary animals such as sea sponges do in fact move.

Although it is true that a few plants and fungi can move, their movements are very limited and different from those of animals. Fungi and plants (such as the Venus's-flytrap) move by changing turgor, or fluid pressure, in key cells. This limits their movement to one plane, like a door swinging open and closed on its hinge.

By contrast, animal movement is adaptable, finely controlled, and astonishingly variable: a flamingo takes flight; a sidewinder whips across the sand; an impala leaps over a 10-foot (3-meter) fence; a yellowfin tuna torpedoes through the water.

Presumably, animal movement started out simply. The fossil record shows that the first animals on Earth (600 million to 700 million years ago) were invertebrates. Invertebrates, by definition, lack backbones, and the first invertebrates lacked bones altogether. They were squishy, soft-bodied creatures similar to the jellyfish and sea worms we find today. Their movements consisted of elastic bending and relaxing.

Soon after came animals with hard shells such as mollusks, trilobites, and the first crustaceans. They could open and shut their valves or scoot along the ocean floor. Creatures with bony skeletons came last. They could bend, straighten, and rotate their bodies and limbs. As a result, a frog can plop into the water . . . and a baseball pitcher can deliver a curveball.

The Nervous System and Senses

Movement in animals is controlled by a nervous system. This system consists of millions of specialized cells, called *neurons*, that react to input from the outside environment. Bundles of neurons are called nerves.

In animals, nerves in organs such as the skin and eyes collect information from the environment. Associated nerves, primarily in the brain, evaluate this information and decide on a response. The chosen action is conveyed to the muscles by motor nerves. All animals have this three-part nervous system. But, as might be expected, its complexity varies tremendously between the simple invertebrates—such as jellyfish—and vertebrates such as fish, reptiles, and mammals.

Respiration

Animals need oxygen for the chemical reactions that liberate energy from their food. The end product of these reactions is carbon dioxide, which animals exhale, or otherwise discharge,

Animals instinctively seek food and seek mates. Orioles (above) and other songbirds do not hesitate to eat food left out for them. To reach their breeding grounds, salmon (below) will even leap over waterfalls.

Most animals have specialized sensory apparatuses. The walrus' touch-sensitive whiskers (left) double as food filters. Many higher animals—especially birds and mammals—devote much time to their young (bottom).

back into the environment. This process is called *respiration*. All animals do it. But they do so in a delightful assortment of ways.

Insects breathe through fine tubes leading from their body surfaces. Many aquatic animals extract oxygen from the water through special organs called gills. Other animals have organs for respiration—gills and lungs, respectively. Most amphibians begin life in the water, with gills, then develop lungs and move to land.

Circulation

It has been said that all animals live in water, even when they live on dry land. This is because animals have circulation systems that continually bathe their cells in fluid. This fluid, called *blood*, carries oxygen and nutrients to the cells and carries waste products away.

Except for very small creatures such as water fleas, animals need some type of pump to keep their blood moving around the body. This pump is the heart. In its simplest form, a heart may be little more than a blood vessel with a ring of muscle. Birds and mammals have the most-elaborate hearts, with four separate chambers for receiving and pumping blood.

Large, active animals such as vertebrates have what is called a "closed" circulation system. Their heart pumps blood through a network of large and small blood vessels. Simpler animals, such as many insects and crustaceans, have "open" circulation systems with few or no vessels. Their heart pumps blood directly over tissues and into body cavities.

Digestion

In contrast to plants, which manufacture their own food, animals get the energy they need by eating things. Digestion is the process of extracting the energy from food. The manner in which animals do this is nearly as varied as their different diets. Sponges, for example, have no visible digestive system. Their food (dissolved organic matter) is so simple that it can pass directly into the sponge's cells.

Animals that eat larger "chunks" of food need an internal cavity, or *gut*, for digestion. Here digestive chemicals called enzymes break down large food items into molecules that can be absorbed by the blood. In vertebrates, the digestive tract includes a stomach—a collapsible bag where food is partially broken down—and intestines, where the food molecules are actually absorbed into the body. Some animals have stomachs with several chambers or special pouches to break down extra-tough food.

Other animals partially digest their food before they eat it. Spiders, for example, inject digestive enzymes into their prey and suck the resulting juice. Starfish actually push their stomachs out of their mouths and digest their prey entirely outside of their bodies.

Reproduction

For any animal to endure on Earth, it must reproduce its kind. Protists, the ancestors to animals, reproduce asexually. That is, they simply split into exact copies of themselves. By contrast, most animals reproduce sexually

Animals Versus Plants

No doubt, you have no problem distinguishing a crab from crabgrass. Even a small child comprehends the basic differences between plant and animal. But some of the most important differences between these two kingdoms are not so obvious. Here are their distinguishing characteristics.

Characteristic	Plant	Animal
Hereditary material	DNA	DNA
Cell type	Eukaryotic (nucleus with nuclear envelope)	Eukaryotic
Cell wall	Present	Absent
Chloroplasts	Present	Absent
Primary structural compound	Cellulose	Collagen
Growth	Primarily at tips	All body parts expand at generally the same rate
Size and shape	Continually changes	Remains generally the same throughout adult life
Nervous system	Absent	Present
Muscles	Absent	Present
Nutrition	Makes own food (autotrophic)	Eats food (heterotrophic)
Mobility	Generally immobile	Generally active
Reproduction	Sexual and asexual reproduction	All species reproduce sexually at some time during life cycle

at some point in their life cycle. Sexual reproduction involves the mixing of hereditary material, or DNA, from two individuals. Generally this involves fertilization of an egg from a female with the sperm of a male. (Some invertebrates such as barnacles and snails are hermaphroditic, or both male and female.)

In many invertebrates, fish, and amphibians, fertilization takes place externally, and the parents provide little or no protection for the fertilized eggs and young. By contrast, fertilization in birds, mammals, and reptiles takes place inside the female's body. Mammals and some reptiles and amphibians allow the fertilized eggs to develop within their bodies.

Growth and Life Cycles

In contrast to plants, which grow primarily at their tips, animals generally expand all parts of their bodies as they grow. So every limb and organ system increases in size roughly in proportion to all other body parts.

Another important difference between animals and plants: animals can rarely regrow body parts lost to predators or accident. Exceptions to this rule include some types of invertebrates, such as lobsters and starfish, which can easily regrow lost limbs.

Some of the simplest life cycles are found in the most-complex animals. Most mammals and reptiles, for example, are born looking more or less like small adults. They mature by simply growing in size and developing appropriate sexual characteristics.

Life cycles are considerably more complex among insects, crustaceans, and other arthropods. They generally pass through several different physical forms on their way to adulthood. This is called *metamorphosis.*

A simpler form of metamorphosis is seen among amphibians. Many hatch as aquatic animals adapted to moving and breathing in water. After growing in size, they transform into air-breathing adult forms that can survive on land.

ANIMAL BEHAVIOR

In truth, all of us are experts on at least some aspects of animal behavior. As members of the species *Homo sapiens*, we are masters at interpreting the subtle turn of a smile ("come closer"), the clenching of a fist ("back off"), or the look of terror ("let's get out of here!").

Far more mysterious is the behavior of animals beyond our species. Why do birds sing in the morning and fireflies blink at night? Why do some animals migrate thousands of miles each year? And how do they find their way?

Such mysteries have long fascinated the human race. In the 3rd century B.C., the Greek philosopher Aristotle puzzled over the honey-making abilities of bees and the winter whereabouts of birds. He concluded that bees made honey by distilling dew under a rainbow-filled sky. And he thought swallows wintered in the mud at the bottom of ponds.

Aristotle's speculations sound silly today. Still, he broke new scientific ground by trying to observe the animals he wished to understand. Today direct observation remains the foundation of *ethology,* the study of animal behavior.

Like Aristotle, modern ethologists try to puzzle out how animals meet such common challenges as protecting themselves, finding food and mates, and rearing their young. How-ever, most ethologists today do more than just observe animals in the wild. They also try to determine the purpose of different animal behaviors. To do so, they may perform laboratory experiments to find exactly what triggers, or provokes, a particular reaction. They also employ chemical analyses to study the genes and hormones that profoundly influence how all animals behave.

ORIGINS OF BEHAVIOR

In the 1920s and 1930s, the Austrian zoologist Konrad Lorenz demonstrated the "instinctive" nature of many important animal behaviors. In his most famous experiment, Lorenz appeared before a gaggle of newly hatched goslings, quacking as their mother might have done. The goslings immediately adopted Lorenz as their "mother," and showed no interest whatsoever in other geese.

Lorenz observed that, at a certain critical stage soon after birth or hatching, many animals learn to follow their parents—or whatever sub-

Konrad Lorenz (above) coined the term imprinting *to describe the animal behavior demonstrated by goslings, which adopt whatever they see first as their "mother."*

stitute is offered to them. It is not a conscious decision, Lorenz explained, but an automatic response. Lorenz called the response *imprinting*, and used it as a dramatic example of the many unlearned, or instinctive, behaviors seen in animals.

About the same time, other scientists were discovering the automatic nature of other complex behaviors. A migratory bird hatched in a laboratory, for example, knows when and in which direction to migrate—despite never having been outside. Similarly, a hare raised apart from its kind somehow knows how to perform the appropriate courtship rituals when placed with a potential mate.

But if such behaviors are not learned, from where do they come? Today we understand that many, if not all, behavior patterns are inherited in much the same way as physical qualities such as height and weight. At birth, each animal holds an entire repertoire of behaviors coded in its DNA, or genetic material. So a baby gull automatically pecks at the red spot on its moth-

er's beak (and she instinctively regurgitates food in response). But the baby bird will likewise peck at any other red spot it sees. Such behaviors are predetermined and automatic. In the right situations, they help ensure an animal's survival or reproductive success.

Like any important trait, animal behavior is subject to natural selection. The bird that knows instinctively when to migrate and how to sing a courtship song will likely survive to adulthood and mate. So its genes, which determine these behaviors, get passed on to a new generation. Animals that do not perform acceptably leave no descendants, and so their behavior genes tend to disappear.

Like other traits, behavior can also be changed by natural selection. Thus, the way a species behaves can adapt to suit changes in its environment. Such evolutionary changes are difficult for scientists to study. After all, behaviors leave no fossils. But similarities between related species can hint at which behaviors they inherited from a common ancestor.

A basic instinct of every animal is self-preservation, a drive that manifests itself both as the desire to seek food and the need to defend oneself. The rattlesnake below could be set to pounce on prey or trying to scare off an intruder.

Each fall, hormones help trigger millions of monarch butterflies to set out on the grueling trek from the eastern United States and Canada all the way to Mexico.

For example, both a lion cub and a domestic kitten will practice hunting behaviors such as stalking and pouncing. Presumably, they do so in much the same way as did their common ancestors. But unlike the lion, the domestic cat has lost much of the aggressiveness that its wild ancestors needed to survive in the wild. Over many generations, its behavior has changed to suit its new environment—your living room.

Hormones

Research in the 1950s made clear that behavior is determined largely by the genes an animal inherits from its parents. But only recently have scientists begun the exciting work of explaining how genes translate themselves into action.

Much of this work concerns *hormones*, chemicals produced by the body at the direction of various genes. It has long been known that hormones control a vast number of body functions concerned with growth and reproduction. We now know that hormones profoundly affect behavior as well. The hormone prolactin, for example, encourages nurturing behavior in mammals. Adrenaline, on the other hand, stimulates the classic "fight or flight" response.

While genes tell the body how to make various hormones, it takes some type of trigger, or *stimulus*, to set the hormone-making machinery in motion. So a female cat's body produces prolactin when her kittens knead her belly. And the sight of an approaching lion will trigger a surge of adrenaline in almost any mammal!

All types of animals produce hormones, from lowly invertebrates to humans. Scientists believe that these chemicals appeared early in the evolutionary history of animals. However, different hormones serve different purposes in different species. For example, the same hormone that stimulates milk production and nurturing behavior in mammals—prolactin—spurs certain young salamanders to leave dry land and seek water.

Schooling behavior serves a defense function by creating a scene so confusing that a predator either hesitates or gives up.

In its drive to create a lodge for itself and its young, the beaver (inset) builds a dam (above) out of sticks, mud, and various other materials—and essentially redesigns the landscape in the process.

Migration is another behavior influenced by hormones. In many birds, changes in day length and temperature trigger the production of hormones that prepare their bodies for long flights. In certain mammals such as lemmings, overcrowding raises the level of hormones associated with restlessness and the driving desire to travel to lower ground.

Pheromones

Hormones can also serve as chemical signals to other animals. Such communication hormones are called *pheromones*. They can be seen to work most powerfully in the insect world. The female silkworm moth, for example, releases a particular pheromone when she is ready to mate. As a result, every male silkworm moth for miles around will fly to her side.

Social insects such as ants, bees, and termites use a variety of pheromones to communicate with their brothers and sisters. An ant that discovers food, for example, lays down a pheromone trail for its colleagues to follow. It uses another, foul-smelling pheromone to discourage its predators. Still other pheromones serve as identification tags for members of each ant colony. If an ant with the wrong "ID tag" tries to enter the colony, it is quickly recognized as an intruder and attacked.

To one degree or another, pheromones probably affect the behavior of all animals. Perhaps you have noticed how excited male dogs become when there is a female dog "in heat" somewhere in the neighborhood. Dogs also deposit pheromones in their urine to mark the boundaries of their territories. The odor is designed to tell other dogs, "Stay out!"

Special Senses

Each animal's genetic "blueprint" likewise determines its particular sense of sight, smell, hearing, touch, and taste. Certain fish can also sense electrical fields. Other animals, such as snakes and mosquitoes, are sensitive to slight changes in heat, or thermal radiation.

An animal's special senses profoundly affect its behavior, and in ways that can seem

The honeybee at left and other insects can perceive special ultraviolet patterns that indicate when a flower is ready for pollination and full of nectar.

mysterious to less-sensitive humans. Insects, for example, see a different spectrum of light than do humans. Many plants have evolved to take advantage of this. When their flowers are ready for pollination and full of nectar, they present special ultraviolet patterns visible only to insects. So the butterfly that appears to be randomly flitting from flower to flower may actually be responding to ultraviolet cues. Birds and bees can also see polarized light (reflected light with parallel waves) and use it to determine their direction on overcast days.

A rattlesnake, in turn, somehow senses direction using the heat-sensitive pits on its head. It likewise uses its heat sensors to hunt warm-blooded prey such as mice. Bats locate their prey by emitting high-pitched sounds and listening for the echoes. Certain predatory fish can find prey in muddy water by generating an electric field and sensing disturbances in it.

No doubt many special animal senses remain undiscovered. As a result, we remain baffled at the many "superhuman" abilities seen in the animal world.

Learning in Animals

Clearly, not all animal behavior is instinctual. Like humans, most animals can learn through trial and error. Even a creature as simple as an earthworm can be "trained" to avoid a wire that delivers an unpleasant shock.

Similarly, a bird that bites a nasty-tasting monarch learns to avoid all orange-and-black-striped butterflies. Animals are likewise quick to learn what tastes "good." A lion cub that discovers a mouse may initially consider it a toy or even a playmate. But soon the cub learns that this "plaything" is also quite tasty.

Like other traits, learning abilities seem to be determined largely by heredity. By interbreeding rats that learn to navigate mazes quickly, researchers can produce a "maze-smart" population. They can likewise interbreed rats that pass through with difficulty to produce "maze-dumb" groups.

Animal aptitudes, or learning abilities, vary greatly from species to species. So do the areas of interest. A mockingbird, for example, will pay keen attention to a melody and learn to copy it. A dog, by contrast, will ignore a melody but show keen interest in identifying a smell. A chimpanzee, in turn, may delight in learning how to use a simple tool such as a hammer.

No doubt, each species has inborn curiosities that guide its learning in ways that increase chances of survival. Predatory mammals such as wolves and cats, for example, show a passion for exploring their surroundings. When placed in a new environment, they will diligently investigate every nook and cranny. This natural curiosity enables a predator to learn the layout of its territory, including the whereabouts of prey and water and the quickest paths to and from its den.

Although an animal's general interests and abilities are inborn, its environment greatly influences how these inborn interests and abilities develop into useful knowledge and skills. As a rule, challenging surroundings foster learning. Aware of this fact, modern zookeepers often provide "toys" for the animals in their care. They may likewise hide an animal's food or set it in hard-to-reach places to present challenges like those found in nature.

Are Animals Intelligent?

While animals can no doubt learn, scientists still argue over whether this means they are intelligent. The problem may lie in our definition of the word. By intelligence, do we mean the ability to solve problems by purely mental processes? So far as we know, animals do not think with words, as humans do. But perhaps they can appreciate a problem and solve it mentally in other ways.

Most research on this type of intelligence has focused on our closest relatives in the animal kingdom: chimpanzees and apes. In 1916, the German-American psychologist Wolfgang Köhler performed experiments in which he presented chimpanzees with bananas placed just beyond arm's reach. He also provided a number of sticks that could be fitted together to make a pole that reached the bananas, and boxes that could be stacked so the chimps could climb to the fruit. After sitting quietly for some time—as if contemplating the objects—the chimps suddenly set about assembling the sticks and piling the boxes and eventually reached the bananas.

Did the chimps actually think about the problem and come up with an insightful answer? Köhler thought so. But others argue that chimpanzees tend to play with boxes and sticks just for the fun of it. So perhaps the chimps solved the problem unintentionally.

HOW ANIMALS BEHAVE

Thanks to the science of ethology, we have a basic understanding of the origins of animal behavior—the many triggers that prompt an animal to behave as it does. We also understand that each of these behaviors in some way helps ensure an animal's survival and reproduction. So now let's take a fascinating look at how animal behavior actually unfolds in the wild.

The Need to Feed

Survival in the animal kingdom very much depends upon getting food while avoiding becoming food. The simplest "hunting" behaviors are seen among the filter-feeding invertebrates. Creatures such as coral polyps and sponges do little more than passively filter nutrients from the water around them. Indeed, early naturalists mistakenly labeled these creatures "plants." Only with the invention of magnifying glasses could scientists see their tiny, animal-like movements.

The feeding behavior of many grazing animals seems nearly as idle. From outward

The archerfish (left) procures its next meal—a spider—by blasting it with a stream of water bullets. With similar precision, an African chameleon (below) whips out its long, sticky tongue and seizes its prey.

appearances, ruminants such as cattle and oxen look like slow-moving chewing machines. After all, when their food is abundant, it simply spreads out beneath their feet like a carpet. But the real activity is going on inside the ruminant's body. Since most grass and leaves are extremely difficult to digest, grazing animals must digest their food several times to get any nutritional value from it. They do so with a four-part stomach. After filling the first stomach chamber with food, the ruminant regurgitates the food and chews it again. This twice-chewed "cud" then passes through three other stomach chambers, where microorganisms help break it down further.

Grazing animals become more active when their food grows scarce and they must seek new pastures. The wildebeests of Africa's Serengeti Plain migrate for hundreds of miles when the dry season shrivels their food supply.

Other animals actively hoard food during seasons of plenty in order to have supplies for leaner months. Small mammals such as mice and chipmunks stockpile seeds in their burrows. Western woodpeckers drill thousands of holes in dead trees and fill them with acorns. Even predators such as wild dogs and cats will bury meat and bones for a short period of time.

More fascinating perhaps are animals that raise their own food. Certain species of ants and ladybugs, for example, will guard flocks of aphids, "milking" the tiny insects to get a sweet-tasting liquid. Other types of ants use special nest chambers to grow fungi for food.

Some of the most dramatic feeding behaviors can be seen among predatory animals: The

A porcupine fish keeps predators at bay by gulping water—a behavior that causes its flat-lying spines to swell up, making the fish look like a thorn-covered balloon!

unmatched speed of a cheetah, the silent swoop of a barn owl, the "sharpshooting" tongue of a frog, the eerie camouflage of a praying mantis.

Several species of anglerfish sport "fishing rods" that dangle wormlike flaps of skin in front of their mouths. When a small fish tries to eat the "worm," it quickly becomes a meal itself. And what can match the cunning beauty of a spiderweb? Ounce for ounce, its silk thread is stronger than steel.

Yet every predator's trick is matched by an equally impressive defense behavior on the part of its prey. At the sight of an approaching cheetah, a baby gazelle knows to "freeze"—disappearing, as if by magic, in the tall savanna grass. The young gazelle's dappled fur is an excellent example of camouflage—an especially popular animal defense. Certain reptiles and fish can even change color to match their surroundings.

Other animals escape predators by making themselves inedible or distasteful. When frightened, the porcupine fish inflates itself like a spiny balloon. The armadillo curls into an armor-plated ball. Certain ants and butterflies coat their skin with foul-tasting chemicals. Animals such as opossums become unappealing by playing dead.

Still other animals survive by daring to be

Among the animals that use chemicals to defend themselves is the stonefish (left), a creature whose jagged spines contain the deadliest of all fish poisons.

as fierce as the animals that would eat them. With its long fangs and powerful muscles, the male African baboon is quick to attack any creature that threatens its family. Indeed, male baboons have been known to kill leopards.

Fighting and Biting

Many animals likewise fight with members of their own species. Typically, they do so over food, territory, or breeding rights. Male elephants, for example, sometimes gouge each other to death over access to a particular water hole. Hens will viciously peck each other to establish who's boss of the henhouse. Male deer and goats butt and lock horns to vie for the chance to mate. Not surprisingly, some of the fiercest battles in the animal kingdom occur among predatory animals—creatures well equipped with deadly teeth and claws.

In most species, it is the male who is larger and more quarrelsome. But this is not always the case. Female hyenas, squirrel monkeys, and spiders tend to be both bigger and more aggressive than their male counterparts.

No matter who is doing the fighting, few species can survive constant battling among their members. For this reason, many animals have developed behaviors that demonstrate their prowess without risking injury. Deer stags bellow before fighting because the sound of a mighty roar is often enough to discourage a smaller rival. Other animals bare their teeth to scare off a competitor, or bristle their fur or feathers in order to appear larger.

In such situations, the lesser animal may signal its surrender with submissive behavior. A green chameleon, for example, will turn white when confronted by a larger or more aggressive male. A dog shows submission by rolling on its back to expose its belly and throat. These behaviors signal an animal's willingness to yield to its rival. And this may be enough to reestablish peace.

Meeting and Mating

More agreeable is the meeting of male and female during mating season. In some species, courtship and mating is a brief affair. Others court and mate with a fury of activity or a lengthy and elaborate ritual.

Some of the most spectacular courtship displays occur among birds, especially those of the pheasant family. Typically it is the male who "struts his stuff" to impress as many females as possible. Male pheasants, for example, display their colorful plumage by fluffing, spreading, and quivering their feathers while parading to and fro before a female audience. The emerald-green peacock is one of the most familiar and dramatic

The male bowerbird, perhaps aware of his drab plumage, carefully gathers an array of tantalizing baubles in hopes of attracting curious females.

examples, proudly lifting its showy long train vertically and spreading it for all to admire.

Bordering on the comical is the courtship display of the greater prairie chicken of North America. The prairie cock stamps in the dirt and bounces into the air. It inflates bright orange sacs on either side of its neck and erects a collar of bristly breast feathers. To make the display even more impressive, the cock "pops" and "booms" with an amazing call, loud enough to be heard a mile away.

But dramatic courtship behavior is not restricted to birds. Male anole lizards attract

females by bobbing and bowing their heads and inflating a large, colorful neck pouch. The familiar springtime chorus of frogs is likewise a courtship display. In this way, the males call females to mate, usually in a pool of water. Once a mate draws near, the croaking male clasps her in a tight embrace. She then releases her eggs, and the male fertilizes them.

Among fish, the stickleback is most famous for courtship behavior. The male dances around the female, fins whirring, nudging and guiding her into his nest. Just as she enters, he nibbles her tail—her signal to release her eggs.

To the human observer, spider courtship may seem the most frightening. In many spider species, the tiny male must perform a special dance to convince the larger, deadlier female not to consume him. In some cases, she eats him anyway after mating.

A more serene courtship ritual can be seen on summer nights in eastern North America. That is when male fireflies take flight, blinking a distinctive pattern of flashes with a special light-producing organ. Wingless females on

Many (but not all) animals care for their eggs and young. In an interesting case of role reversal, the male giant water bug (right) carries around the eggs on his back until they hatch.

the ground "reply" with their own sequence of flashes.

More commonly, insects' readiness to mate is communicated with chemical signals, or pheromones. Many female moths and butterflies secrete such odors, which males follow to the source.

To ensure reproductive success, each animal must take care to mate with members of its own species. This is not always easy. For example, many different species of frogs often crowd together in a small pond on a summer night. Their multitude of croaks and peeps can create a tremendous din. So how does each female find just the right male?

Research suggests that animals are amazingly sensitive to the specific mating signal of their own species. A female frog, for example, is all but deaf to calls of a pitch different from that of her own species. Similarly, some of the sensors on the antennae of a male moth respond to one and only one chemical. That chemical is the pheromone emitted by females of his species. Such extreme sensitivity to mating signals can be found throughout the animal kingdom.

Bringing Up Baby

To one degree or another, virtually all animals provide some care for their young. At the very least, a mother provides nutrition for her developing young—either inside her body or in the form of yolk inside an egg.

As a general rule, the more eggs or young an animal produces, the less care it lavishes on them. At one end of the scale are invertebrates such as sea urchins. A mature sea urchin spews millions of eggs or sperm into the sea. But only chance mixing determines which of these will fertilize and develop. (In truth, few do.)

By contrast, primates, including humans, typically give birth to just one or two young at a time, and care for them for many years.

Parental care often begins before birth. Nest building is the prime example. (In this context, a nest is a shelter built strictly for the protection of young.) Many kinds of animals build nests. But nest building is probably most elaborate among birds. Some, such as pheasants, scratch out simple nests on the ground. But most build their nests off the ground, out of the reach of predators. The most familiar is the woven, cup-shaped nest made by many perching birds.

An especially spectacular nest is built by the monk parakeet, native to South America and now found in much of the United States. Using sticks and small branches, flocks of monk parakeets work together to build enormous treetop nests. Some are as large as automobiles. Within this huge complex, each mated pair has a compartment for the care of its eggs and chicks.

Other birds weave baskets that they hang from branches, or daub mud nests against the side of a cliff or building. Still others nest in tree hollows, or excavate their own tree holes.

In every case, nest building appears to be a combination of instinct and learning. A nest-building bird will instinctively gather construction materials and attempt to piece them together. But its choice of materials and its weaving or daubing skills seem to improve with experience.

As mentioned, many animals continue to care for their young for days, months, or even years after birth or hatching. Most invertebrates and fish show little care for their eggs and young. Among the exceptions is the centipede. She remains curled around her eggs for nearly two months—guarding them from enemies and keeping them free of fungus.

Aside from mammals, birds are most noted for the care they lavish on their young. Above, a mother emperor penguin nudges its youngster to accept some food.

Insects such as ants, termites, and bees go even further. Their nests include special chambers where eggs, grubs, and nymphs are tended by special nursery maids.

Most birds and mammals take active care of their young for weeks, months, or even years. It was once thought that only mammals produced milk for their young. But now we know that some birds such as pigeons feed their young "crop milk" regurgitated from their gullets.

The fascinating ways that animals care for their young could fill many volumes. The broader subject of animal behavior could fill entire libraries. The important point to remember is that behavior, like any important trait, enables an animal to survive in its given environment. So cats are good at sneaking through the grass. Bees excel at finding nectar on sunny days. And songbirds fill the spring with melody. In truth, is human behavior any more difficult to explain?

ZOOLOGICAL CLASSIFICATION

Is there any order to the bewildering diversity of animal life? No sooner had the early naturalists decided what is and is not an animal than they set out to answer this question.

The Greek philosopher Aristotle may have been the first to classify animals in a logical way, more than 2,300 years ago. He grouped animals according to certain shared characteristics, such as two-footed animals or shelled animals. He then attempted to arrange these groups on a great natural scale, his *scala naturae*. Aristotle placed humans, whom he considered the "most perfect" animal, at one end of the scale. At the other end were those that he considered "least perfect"—those that barely moved.

Although Aristotle's *scala naturae* was rather arbitrary, it established the science of *taxonomy*—the classification of living things. More than 2,000 years would pass before taxonomy took its next major leap.

European scientists of the 17th and 18th centuries were astounded at the variety of plants and animals brought to them by seafaring explorers. So inspired, the Swedish biologist Carolus Linnaeus set out to arrange all the world's animals in a single grand classification system.

His system, introduced in 1753, divided animals into six classes: mammals; birds; amphibians and reptiles; fish; insects; and "vermin" (other invertebrates). Although it has been expanded and refined, Linnaeus' scheme remains the classification system that scientists still use—an amazing fact considering that Linnaeus knew nothing of evolution, the process by which distinct species arise from common ancestors. Yet his classification system reflects the evolutionary history of Earth's creatures. In essence, this taxonomic system classifies animals in groups arranged from most general to most specific. The main groups are as follows:

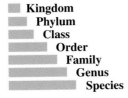

Kingdom
 Phylum
  Class
   Order
    Family
     Genus
      Species

To use humans as an example, the groups are named as follows:

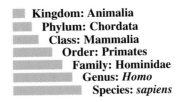

Kingdom: Animalia
 Phylum: Chordata
  Class: Mammalia
   Order: Primates
    Family: Hominidae
     Genus: *Homo*
      Species: *sapiens*

Each category down the scale is defined by a narrower set of characteristics than the category before it. The class Mammalia, for example, includes all animals whose young are nourished by milk glands, and that possess skin with hair. But the order Primates would include only those mammals that "are descended from tree dwellers and have fingers, usually with flat nails, and a reduced sense of smell." Taken together, the two most specific groupings—genus and species—constitute an animal's *scientific name*. Today this agreed-upon naming system is referred to as the binomial system of classification, or *binomial nomenclature*. It enables scientists around the world to overcome the confusion of popular names, which often differ from region to region and language to language.

By tradition, all scientific names are expressed in Latin. They are written with the first word capitalized, but never the second, and both italicized. When someone discovers a new species, scientists study its physical, biochemical, and behavioral traits to place it in the proper phylum, class, order, family, and, if possible, genus. The person who discovers the species has the privilege of assigning its species name.

The following classification system describes the major divisions of the Kingdom Animalia, or Animal Kingdom, and the Kingdom Protista. Scientists now recognize that protists are a form of life quite distinct from animals. Yet most protists do have animal-like qualities, and for that reason they are included here. When examining this system, bear in mind that Earth's animals are not evenly distributed across its divisions. Indeed, two-thirds of all known species belong to just one class: Insecta.

KINGDOM Protista: *One-celled organisms with an organized nuclear envelope. Some feed on organic matter. Others photosynthesize or otherwise manufacture their own food.*

SUBKINGDOM Protozoa: *Generally microscopic organisms that sometimes organize into colonies. Reproduce by fission, budding, spores, or sexual recombination. About 30,000 species. Examples: amoeba, stentor, and paramecium.*

PHYLUM Chrysophyta: *Photosynthetic, single-cell organisms with food stored as oil droplets or leucosin. About 10,000 species. Examples: diatom and golden brown alga.*

PHYLUM Pyrrophyta: *Photosynthetic, single-cell organisms, often with flagella for movement. Store food as starch. About 1,100 species. Examples: dinoflagellate and fire alga.*

PHYLUM Euglenophyta: *Photosynthetic, single-cell organisms that store food as paramylum. Typically have single flagellum for movement. About 450 species. Example: euglena.*

PHYLUM Gymnomycota: *Nonphotosynthetic, amoeba-like organisms that lack a cell wall and form spores. About 500 species. Example: slime mold.*

KINGDOM Animalia: *Multicellular organisms that feed on other organisms or decayed organic matter. Animals are generally active and lack the rigid cell walls seen in the plant kingdom. Generally reproduce sexually.*

The Greek philosopher Aristotle (384–322 B.C.) made the first attempt to classify animals according to a unified scheme. He originally distinguished creatures as either blooded or bloodless, and then subdivided them further based on such characteristics as hairiness or hairlessness.

PHYLUM Porifera: *Pore-bearing animals, or sponges. About 4,200 species.*

CLASS Calcarea: *Lime animals—marine sponges with an internal skeleton of lime spicules. Example: scypha.*

CLASS Hexactinellida: *Animals with six-pointed spicules—marine sponges with inner skeleton of siliceous spicules. Example: glass sponge.*

CLASS Demospongiae: *Common sponges, or sponges with spicules of silica or spongin or with no internal skeleton. Example: common bath sponge.*

PHYLUM Coelenterata, or **Cnidaria:** *Aquatic animals with radially symmetrical, jellylike bodies with tentacles and stinging capsules. Reproduce sexually or asexually. About 11,000 species.*

CLASS Hydrozoa: *"Water animals"—often colonial, with generations that alternate between sexual and asexual reproduction. Polyp stage is dominant. Example: hydra.*

CLASS Scyphozoa: *"Cup animals"—often large jellyfish, alternate between sexual and asexual generations with reduced polyp stage. Example: aurelia.*

CLASS Anthozoa: *"Flower animals"—attached marine polyps with no medusa stage. Some have hard external shell or skeleton. Examples: coral and sea anemone.*

PHYLUM Ctenophora: *"Comb-bearers"—body spherical to cylindrical, with bilateral or radial symmetry; stomach and internal tubes present. Moves by means of eight platelike bands of fused cilia; often has pair of tentacles; not colonial. Reproduces sexually, although sexes not separate. About 80 species. Examples: comb jellyfish and sea walnut.*

PHYLUM Platyhelminthes: *"Flatworms"—unsegmented, flattened worms with no distinct head or legs; body has bilateral symmetry; paired nerve centers; no circulatory system. Reproduce asexually or sexually; sexes not separate. Often parasitic. About 15,000 species.*

> **CLASS Turbellaria:** *"Wrigglers"—small, aquatic; move by epidermal cilia; not parasitic. Example: planarian.*
>
> **CLASS Trematoda:** *"Hole animals"—young are independent; adults parasitic and attached to host. Example: liver fluke.*
>
> **CLASS Cestoda:** *"Girdle animals"—long, narrow flatworms with hooks or suckers that anchor to the host; no digestive tract; all parasitic. Example: tapeworm.*

Swedish physician and botanist Carolus Linneaus (1707–78) invented the now universally used system of binomial nomenclature, in which every organism has a Latin genus name and a Latin species name. Many of the names Linneaus gave to the insect order are still used by scientists today.

PHYLUM Nemertea: *Flattened worms, usually marine, with simple circulatory and reproductive systems and a tubelike gut. Bilaterally symmetrical with brain in head. Move by means of cilia; capture prey. Reproduce sexually or asexually with separate sexes and larval stage. Not parasitic. About 600 species. Examples: nemertine, or proboscis worm.*

PHYLUM Mesozoa: *"Middle animals"—small, wormlike marine animals with bilateral symmetry and two-layered solid body. Reproduce by fission or sexually. Parasitic on other marine life. About 50 species. Example: dicyemid.*

PHYLUM Aschelminthes: *"Sac worms"—small, slender, often microscopic worms found free or attached in freshwater or marine water. Body has bilateral symmetry; digestive tract and other organs present. Reproduce by eggs with separate sexes and no larval stage. About 600 species. Example: spiny-headed worm.*

PHYLUM Rotifera: *"Wheel-bearers"—microscopic, wormlike or spherical animals with complete digestive tract. Most free-living, some parasitic. About 1,500 species. Example: rotifer.*

PHYLUM Gastrotricha: *"Hairy-stomach animals"—microscopic, wormlike animals that move by longitudinal bands of cilia. About 140 species. Example: chaetonotus.*

PHYLUM Nematomorpha: *"Thread-shaped animals"—long, very thin worms whose larvae infest insects. About 250 species. Example: horsehair worm.*

PHYLUM Nematoda: *"Thread animals"—round, tapered, thin worms; not segmented; may be parasitic. About 80,000 species. Examples: roundworm and hookworm.*

PHYLUM Acanthocephala: *"Spine-headed animals"—parasitic creatures with no digestive tract. Head armed with many spines. About 300 species. Example: echinorhynchus.*

PHYLUM Phoronida: *Long, wormlike marine animals that secrete and live in a leathery tube. Feed by means of a crown of tentacles. About 15 species. Example: phoronis.*

PHYLUM Bryozoa: *"Moss animals"—microscopic aquatic animals that form mosslike colonies and feed with U-shaped rows of tentacles. Retain larvae in special brood pouch. About 4,000 species. Example: hornera.*

PHYLUM Kamptozoa or **Endoprocta:** *Aquatic animals with interior opening and small, mosslike forms. Body with bilateral symmetry and various organ systems including U-shaped digestive tract. Tentacles with cilia surround mouth and waste opening. Colonial or individual; reproduce by eggs; sexes separate. More than 100 species. Example: urnatella.*

PHYLUM Brachiopoda: *"Arm-footed animals"—attached shellfish with bivalve shell and bilateral symmetry. Feed with ciliated tentacles. About 260 living species; 3,000 extinct. Example: lampshell.*

Johann Wolfgang von Goethe (1749–1832), now considered to be among the greatest German writers and philosophers, expected to be remembered more for his work as a scientist. Goethe developed the science of morphology—the study of form and shape—a concept fundamental to the theory of evolution.

PHYLUM Chaetognatha: *"Bristle-jawed animals"—predatory marine worms with small, long, bilaterally symmetrical bodies with finlike appendages, bristles around mouth, nervous system and brain, but no developed circulatory, waste, or breathing systems. Reproduce by eggs without separate sexes. About 50 species. Example: arrowworm.*

PHYLUM Annelida: *Ringed or segmented worms with bilateral symmetry. Possess developed organs, brain, nerves, and closed circulatory system. Often move using bristles or other paired appendages. Reproduce sexually or asexually, often with larval stage. Found in seas, streams, and soil. Some species parasitic. About 8,800 species.*

CLASS Polychaeta: *"Many-bristled animals"—marine annelids using bristles for movement and possessing head tentacles. Some forms free-swimming. Example: sea mouse.*

CLASS Oligochaeta: *"Few-bristled animals"—soil, freshwater, and marine annelids with few bristles or appendages. Example: earthworm.*

CLASS Hirudinea: *Parasitic, flat-bodied annelids with sucker at each end and typically no other appendages. Found in streams. Example: leech.*

PHYLUM Mollusca: *Soft-bodied unsegmented animals with head, mantle, and muscular foot, often with one or more hard shells and a three-chambered heart. Reproduce by eggs with separate sexes and larval stage. About 110,000 species.*

CLASS Polyplacophora, or **Amphineura:** *"Many-plated animals"—simple marine mollusks with elongated body covered with mantle and eight shell plates or spines. Move by creeping. Example: chiton.*

CLASS Bivalvia, or **Pelecypoda:** *Two-shelled mollusks, often with hatchet-shaped foot and no distinct head. Examples: oyster, clam, and scallop.*

CLASS Scaphopoda: *Elongated marine mollusks with tubular shell open at both ends with foot and tentacles but no head. Example: tooth shell.*

CLASS Gastropoda: *"Belly-footed animals"—aquatic and land animals, typically with single spiral shell that serves as a portable retreat and a head with one or two pairs of tentacles. Examples: snail, slug, and conch.*

CLASS Cephalopoda: *"Head-footed animals"—actively swimming marine animals with or without inner or outer shell and possessing many tentacles and distinct head and eyes. Move by propulsion of water jets. Can reach tremendous size. Examples: cuttlefish, octopus, squid, and pearly nautilus.*

PHYLUM Arthropoda: *"Joint-footed animals"—segmented animals with paired, jointed appendages and hard, jointed exoskeleton. Possess nerve cord and brain. Typically reproduce by eggs with separate sexes and larval stage. About 800,000 species.*

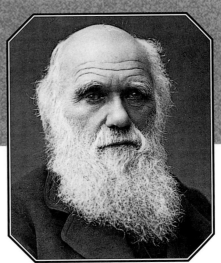

Few people have impacted the science of taxonomy more than Charles Darwin (1809–82), the English naturalist. Through Darwin's theories, biologists realized that an organism's origin and evolutionary history are more accurate than outward traits as criteria for scientific-classification systems.

CLASS Crustacea: *"Shell animals"—mainly aquatic, hard-shelled animals with one pair of mandibles, two pairs of antennae, and other appendages. Head and thorax fused. Examples: crab, lobster, and shrimp.*

CLASS Arachnida: *Mainly terrestrial, air-breathing animals with four or five pairs of appendages, the first of which is used for grasping. Often possess poison gland. Bite or suck prey or host. Examples: spider, scorpion, and tick.*

CLASS Merostomata: *Marine animals with broad, horseshoe-shaped shell and unsegmented belly with 12 legs. Example: horseshoe crab.*

CLASS Chilopoda: *"Lip-legged animals"—typically terrestrial animals with antennae, many legs, and long, segmented body. Example: centipede.*

CLASS Diplopoda: *"Double-footed animals"—typically terrestrial animals with short head and thorax and many legs. Roll into defensive ball and emit foul substances. Example: millipede.*

CLASS Onychophora: *"Claw-bearing animals"—long, wormlike animals, without distinct head and with many short, unjointed legs. Live on damp soil. Example: peripatus.*

CLASS Pycnogonida: *"Thick-kneed animals"—small-bodied marine animals with head appendages but no jaws, and 8 to 12 long legs. Example: sea spider.*

CLASS Pentastomida: *"Animals with five openings"—small, wormlike, unsegmented parasites with fused head and thorax, no appendages, and no hard covering. Internal organs absent or reduced, mouth equipped with hooks. Example: linguatula.*

CLASS Symphyla: *"Grouped-together animals"—long, colorless, wormlike animals with 24 legs, antennae, and jaws, but no eyes. Inhabit damp ground, primarily in cultivated vegetable gardens. Example: garden centipede.*

CLASS Pauropoda: *"Small-footed animals"—small, segmented, wormlike animals with antennae, 18 to 20 legs, but no eyes. Inhabit damp soil under rocks and logs, particularly in forests. Example: pauropus.*

CLASS Insecta: *"Cut-in animals"—most successful and advanced of the invertebrates, with nearly 1 million species. Possess distinct head, thorax, and abdomen with six legs, antennae, jaws, and mouth. When present, wings typically attached to thorax. Eyes simple to compound or absent. Lay eggs. Found everywhere. Examples: ant, beetle, and fly.*

PHYLUM Tardigrada: *"Slow-moving animals"—tiny, sluglike, unsegmented aquatic animals with eight stumpy legs ending in claws, pegs, or adhesive disks, and no blood vessels or breathing organs. Move with a lumbering, bearlike gait. About 350 species. Example: water bear.*

During his reign as Japanese emperor, Hirohito (1901–89) conducted a great deal of research into marine biology—work that contributed to the development of classification schemes for various marine coelenterates. Many modern taxonomists limit their research to a single order or family.

PHYLUM Echinodermata: *"Spiny-skinned animals"—radially symmetrical marine-dwelling animals, typically with five arms and internal shell-like case of lime plates or spicules. Possess specialized organs, tubes for circulating water, and tube feet for movement. Reproduce by eggs with separate sexes and larval stage. About 6,000 species.*

CLASS Stelleroidea: *Starlike animals with five or more flexible arms, or rays. Actively prey on other animals. Example: starfish.*

CLASS Echinoidea: *Spiny, free-living animals with round to flattened body and no projecting arms. Free-living. Examples: sea urchin and sand dollar.*

CLASS Holothurioidea: *Long, soft, sausage-shaped body with 10 or more branched tentacles around mouth. Example: sea cucumber.*

CLASS Crinoidea: *"Lilylike animals"—creatures usually attached to sea bottom by stalk with 5 to 10 branched arms extending from body shell. Examples: sea lily and feather star.*

PHYLUM Hemichordata: *"Animals with half chords"—wormlike animals with gill slits and bodies divided into three regions. Head region contains a notochord-like structure and solid nerve cord. About 91 species. Example: acorn worm.*

PHYLUM Chordata: *"Animals with notochord"—animals with bilaterally symmetrical bodies. Nerve cord with supporting notochord along back. Most forms possess brain and well-developed nerves and organ systems. Reproduction typically sexual, although asexual in lower forms. About 45,000 species.*

SUBPHYLUM Tunicata: *"Tunic animals"—marine animals whose saclike adult forms often generate branching colonies that feed by ciliary currents, possess gill slits and simple nervous system with no notochord. Active larvae do possess notochord and well-developed nervous system. Reproduce sexually or by budding. Examples: ascidian and salp.*

SUBPHYLUM Cephalochordata: *"Head-notochord animals"—fishlike marine animals with complete notochord and nerve cord, gill slits, and fins, but no true head. Example: lancelet.*

SUBPHYLUM Vertebrata: *"Animals with backbone"—aquatic and land animals in which the notochord is replaced by segments of cartilage or bone (vertebrae) to form a spinal column or backbone. Possess internal skeleton, brain, well-developed senses, and gills or lungs. Reproduction typically sexual, producing eggs or live young.*

SUPERCLASS Agnatha: *"Jawless fish"—fish without jaws or scales. Have cartilaginous skeleton and simple spinal column. Typically parasitic. Examples: lamprey and hagfish.*

The National Museum of Natural History in Washington, D.C., is among the world's leading institutions for taxonomic research. Its spider collection alone contains more than 116,000 specimens representing some 36,000 species; perhaps another 100,000 species of spiders remain to be identified.

CLASS Chondrichthyes: *"Soft-boned fish"—jawed marine fish with cartilaginous skeleton, scales, and paired fins. Examples: shark and ray.*

CLASS Osteichthyes: *"Hard-boned fish"—true jawed fish with bony skeleton, scales, paired fins, gills, and air bladder. Examples: bass, perch, and trout.*

CLASS Amphibia: *Typically breathe by gills in aquatic larval stage and by lungs in adult stage; also breathe directly through skin. Mainly four-legged, although some limbless. Lay eggs in freshwater. Examples: frog and salamander.*

CLASS Reptilia: *"Creeping animals"—typically terrestrial animals with naked or scaly skin. Possess bony skeleton, incompletely four-chambered heart, and lungs. Some have four limbs, others have vestigial limbs or are legless. Lay eggs. Example: snake and lizard.*

CLASS Aves: *Birds—warm-blooded animals with four-chambered heart, lungs, and skin with feathers. Typically, forelimbs serve as wings, although some are flightless. Walk on hind legs. Jaws developed into beak, usually toothless. Lay eggs. Example: ostrich, flamingo, robin.*

CLASS Mammalia: *"Animals with breasts"—warm-blooded animals with four-chambered heart and fused skull. Brain highly developed. Skin covered by hair or fur. Typically four-legged, bearing live young, which they suckle with milk from mammary glands. Sexes separate. Examples: whale, elephant, dog, mouse, and human.*

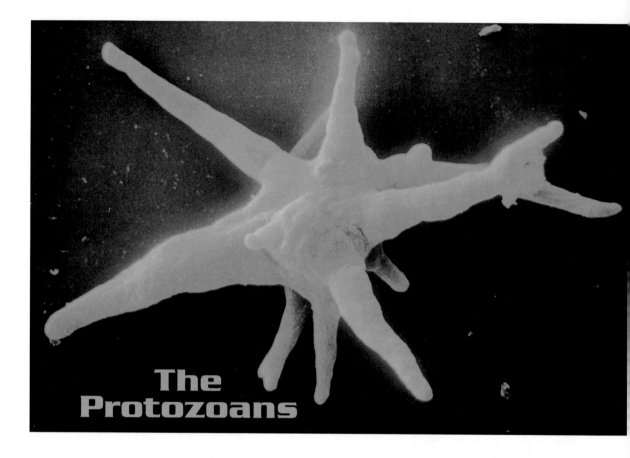

The Protozoans

When a drop or two of pond water is viewed through a microscope, a fascinating world in miniature is revealed—a world populated by a host of minute organisms. Many of them are tiny creatures called protozoans, which range in size from several microns to a few millimeters. (A micron is equal to 1 thousandth of a millimeter, or 0.00004 inch.)

WHAT IS A PROTOZOAN?

The answer to the above question depends upon what book you check, when the book was written, and by whom the book was written. Until the 1970s, the prevailing school of scientific thought held that protozoans were animals, and thus classified in the Animal Kingdom as phylum Protozoa. This system of classification created innumerable problems. To begin with, protozoans that carried photosynthetic pigments were classified as animals despite their obvious plantlike characteristics. The confusion was reduced to some degree by the creation of King-

dom Protista, to which a wide variety of entirely unrelated animal-like and plantlike unicellular organisms belong. Under this taxonomic system, Protozoa is now usually regarded as a subkingdom of the Protista.

In keeping with the grab-bag nature of Protista, it should be noted that the subkingdom Protozoa was set up to represent organisms of a certain level of organization rather than of a common evolutionary heritage. In other words, protozoans are single-celled eukaryotic organisms with animal-like characteristics. However, scientists have not presumed to suggest that all (or even most) protozoans have a common ancestor in their evolutionary past.

It should also be mentioned that even with the creation of Kingdom Protista, controversy continues to surround protozoan taxonomy. Some scientists still insist that all single-celled

The term "protozoan" generally refers to single-celled eukaryotic organisms with animal-like characteristics. Amoeba (above) is perhaps the best-known protozoan.

organisms are animals. Others further subdivide Protista, or create still new kingdoms. And every day, biologists are discovering microscopic creatures that fit none of the criteria that contemporary taxonomists use. Just about the only thing that everyone agrees upon is the fact that the definition and classification of protozoans are in a state of flux.

PROTOZOAN CHARACTERISTICS

Most protozoans consist of a single unit surrounded by a membrane, although some have a great many nuclei. Others consist of colonies of a number of individuals.

Protozoans can hardly be called simple organisms, a fact that becomes evident when they are compared with the specialized cells in the bodies of multicellular (many-celled) animals. In the latter, each type of specialized cell forms a different kind of tissue. The tissues make up the different organs by means of which the animals move about; catch, chew, and digest food; circulate body fluids; breathe; eliminate wastes; reproduce; and so on. In the protozoan, all of these activities occur within the tiny blob of protoplasm that comprises its body. Some of these processes take place in special structures called *organelles*. The specialized cells of multicellular animals have no independent life of their own. The protozoan, by contrast, is completely self-sufficient.

By virtue of their comparative complexity, protozoans can adapt themselves to a wide range of environments. Many species of protozoans are free-living organisms; others live as parasites in the body cavities, tissues, and cells of animals and plants.

There are more than 40,000 species of protozoans, most of which have not yet been adequately classified. Traditionally, the most-familiar protozoans are divided into four groups based on their methods of locomotion. They are the flagellates; the amoeba-like organisms; the sporozoans; and the ciliates.

THE FLAGELLATES

Members of the subphylum Mastigophora, called flagellates, possess one to several long filaments called *flagella* (singular: *flagellum*) that are usually attached to the front end of the body.

A flagellum may be used for swimming or for creating water currents that bring in food. It may also serve as a sensitive organelle for exploring the environment. In swimming, the flagellum ordinarily makes first a sidewise or backward beat, and then a relaxed recovery stroke to the forward position again. This causes the organism to move forward, often in a more or less spiral path.

The body of the flagellate usually assumes a definite shape and is covered by a firm *pellicle*, or skin. Some species may be encased in a shell, a cover of plates, or some other kind of armor. Often a flagellate will develop structures called *pseudopods*, or "false feet," which are formed by a flowing of the organism's protoplasm. Such a flagellate moves as its protoplasm streams into the newly formed pseudopods. These "false feet" represent only temporary extensions of the protoplasm.

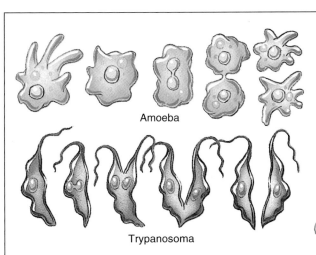

Amoeba

Trypanosoma

Asexual Reproduction in Protozoans

During asexual reproduction, or fission, a protozoan splits in two, each half forming a separate individual. Some protozoans, such as *Amoeba*, divide across the cell's width; others, such as *Trypanosoma*, divide across the cell's length. Inside a host cell, *Plasmodium* reproduces by multiple fission.

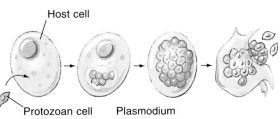

Host cell

Protozoan cell　　Plasmodium

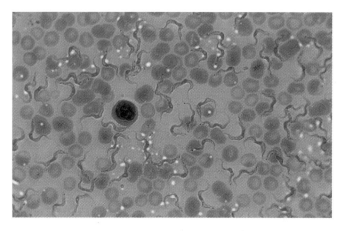

When the tsetse fly (below) bites a human, it sucks out blood while simultaneously transmitting to its victim parasitic protozoans of the genus Trypanosoma (above), which cause sleeping sickness, a serious tropical illness that can lead to coma and even death.

Flagellates cannot manufacture their own food. Some forms, especially the parasitic ones, absorb dissolved food materials from the medium in which they live. Most species, however, feed on microorganisms or nutritious particles in the water. This material is digested in food vacuoles that form within the flagellate's protoplasm. In general, the body shape of the animal like flagellates is rather plastic.

Representative Genera

Among the most-important flagellates, as far as people are concerned, are several species of the genus *Trypanosoma*. *Trypanosoma brucei gambiense*, the cause of sleeping sickness, has a slender, curving body that tapers at both ends. The single flagellum is attached throughout the length of the body by a thin layer of pellicle.

This forms a membrane that undulates when a wave passes down the flagellum. Trypanosomes (members of the genus *Trypanosoma*) are sucked up with the blood when a tsetse fly bites an infected host. The trypanosomes undergo development first in the gut and then in the salivary glands of the fly. Finally, when the fly bites another victim, the flagellates are introduced into the bloodstream of the new host. They invade the lymph nodes and sometimes the cerebrospinal fluid (a fluid in the brain and spinal cord), causing the disease called sleeping sickness.

Trypanosoma cruzi is the cause of Chagas' disease, or South American trypanosomiasis, which affects the muscles, heart, and nervous system. Other trypanosomes are found in the blood of fish, amphibians, reptiles, birds, and mammals.

Bodo, a somewhat different flagellate but apparently related to the *Trypanosoma*, is a small, oval-shaped organism that inhabits stagnant freshwater. It has two flagella, one of which is trailed in swimming.

In freshwater occur two other unusual types of flagellates, *Codosiga* and *Protospongia*. These organisms have an oval-shaped body surmounted by a collar that encircles the base of the single flagellum. The collar, a membrane made of protoplasm, is a device for obtaining food. Food particles or bacteria adhere to the collar and slowly pass down it to the body proper. In *Codosiga*, a number of these transparent collar cells, as they are called, cluster at the end of a simple or branching stalk.

Protospongia is comprised of a colony of from 6 to 60 organisms embedded irregularly in a gelatinous mass. The collar cells occur at the surface of the mass. The organisms on the inside are collarless. The only other animals with collar cells are sponges. It may be possible, therefore, that sponges evolved from organisms similar to *Protospongia*.

Various flagellate species belonging to the genus *Trichomonas* inhabit the intestines of vertebrates. They feed mainly on bacteria and yeasts found in this environment. In human beings, different forms of *Trichomonas* are found in the mouth, colon, and vagina. A typical *Trichomonas* is small, oval-shaped, and has four free flagella; a fifth flagellum is attached to an undulating membrane.

The large flagellate *Trichonympha* lives in the intestines of termites. There it digests wood fragments swallowed by the termite and makes some of the products of this digestion available to the insect. If for some reason the termite loses its flagellates, it will ultimately die of starvation, even though it continues to swallow large quantities of wood. *Trichonympha* is a bell-shaped organism covered with a great number of flagella; indeed, it is one of the most complex of the flagellates. Closely related forms of this flagellate inhabit the alimentary canal of cockroaches and woodroaches.

THE SARCODINES

Members of the subphylum Sarcodina, the amoeba-like protozoans, float or creep about in a liquid environment. A thin membrane surrounds the protoplasm of the body, allowing for the formation of pseudopods. These "false feet" are used both for movement and for capturing food. Some species are plastic, naked organisms. Others develop internal or external skeletal structures that protect the body and give it some rigidity. Sarcodines live almost entirely on small organisms, including other protozoans, tiny multicellular animals, and algae.

Perhaps the best-known sarcodine is *Amoeba*, a genus of freshwater organisms. They are quite large for protozoans, ranging up to 0.02 inch (0.5 millimeter) in size. A typical *Amoeba* has one to several fingerlike pseudopods. Its protoplasm contains a nucleus, numerous food vacuoles, granules, crystals, and a *contractile vacuole*—a sort of water pump. Since water diffuses into its body from the external environment, the contractile vacuole functions to pump out the excess, thus preventing *Amoeba* from swelling unduly and perhaps bursting. (Contractile vacuoles are found in all freshwater protozoans.)

The giant amoeba, *Chaos*, has several hundred small nuclei. This organism may grow to be as wide as 0.2 inch (5 millimeters) across—visible to the naked eye.

Various amoebas are found in people. *Entamoeba histolytica* occurs in the human large intestine and is responsible for the disease known as amoebic dysentery. This amoeba secretes a substance that dissolves the intestinal lining. The amoeba then enters the connective tissue and muscular layers, where it feeds on blood cells and tissue-cell fragments. It may invade the liver, where it does great damage by causing abscesses. Another *Entamoeba* species seems to contribute to pyorrhea, a serious disorder of the teeth and gums.

Termites feasting on a rotten log (above) are able to derive nutrients from the wood only if Trichonympha *protozoans are present in their intestines. These flagellates break down the wood's cellulose into glucose, a simple carbohydrate that the termites can digest.*

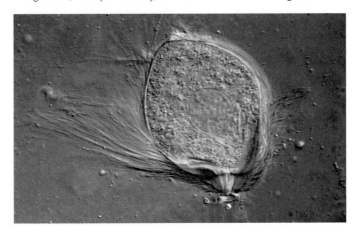

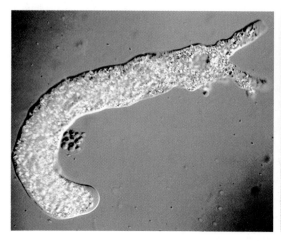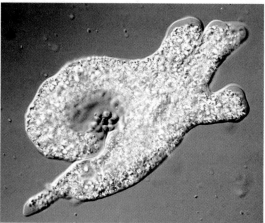

Members of the genus Amoeba *move in a creeping or gliding fashion by extending their protoplasm in projections called pseudopods. The organisms also use their pseudopods to surround (left) and engulf (right) food particles.*

Arcella and *Difflugia* are amoebas that house themselves in single-chambered shells. *Arcella* secretes a transparent to yellowish-brown shell that is made of tiny prisms, fitted together. The shell, formed of siliceous (silica-containing) substances, is domelike above and concave below, with a central opening through which the pseudopods extend. *Difflugia* fashions a globular or flask-shaped shell out of sand grains, which it "glues" together. Both of these shelled amoebas occur in freshwater and moist soils.

The *foraminifers* are shelled amoebas that live almost exclusively in the sea. The shells usually contain many chambers; the young organism starts life with one chamber and adds new chambers as it grows. Many foraminifers secrete siliceous or calcareous (containing calcium carbonate) shells. Others use foreign materials that are picked up by the pseudopods and pulled into the body, where they are held together in the shell wall by a secreted cement. The chambers of the shell assume a variety of configurations: they may be connected like a string of beads; they may be coiled in a flat or conical spiral like a snail's shell; they may be in two or three alternating rows like a braid; or they may be arranged irregularly. The shell is just inside the body of the foraminifer, so that a layer of protoplasm covers it. The pseudopods form a meshwork,

Through a long and complicated geologic process, the fossil remains of certain shelled amoebas, or foraminifers, were gradually transformed into such noted chalk deposits as the White Cliffs of Dover (left), in England.

Classification of Animal-like Protists

Many protists have traits of both plants and animals. The plantlike protists are discussed in the PLANT LIFE section of this volume. Below is the classification of protists traditionally seen as more animal-like in nature; several phyla are only marginally related to other protozoans.

KINGDOM Protista: *Eukaryotic organisms (cells with nuclei) ranging in size from one cell to millions of cells. Reproduce sexually with gametes, asexually with spores, or by both methods. The animal-like protists lack photosynthetic pigments, and therefore cannot manufacture their own food. Found worldwide, primarily in water and soil.*

SUBKINGDOM Protozoa: *Single-celled organisms with animal-like characteristics. A few are macroscopic; most are microscopic. All have formless bodies that gently flow from one shape into another as they move. Protozoa have a thin outer covering called a cell membrane. Inside the cell are found specialized structures surrounded by organelles, or little organs, within which essential functions occur. All protozoans hunt, digest, and store food. Classification is the topic of much controversy.*

PHYLUM Sarcomastigophora: *Single-celled organisms with one type of nucleus (although some may be multinucleated). Sexual reproduction not widespread. Flagella or pseudopodia occur during some point in life cycle.*

SUBPHYLUM Mastigophora: *The flagellates. Move by using one or more long, thin, whiplike structures called flagella. Some live freely in water; most subsist within the bodies of plants and animals. Nutrients are obtained by eating other organisms or by absorbing food molecules through cell membrane. Some maintain a symbiotic relationship with the organism in which they live; others are parasitic. Examples:* Trypanosoma, Trichomonas.

SUBPHYLUM Sarcodina: *The amoeba and kin. Move primarily by means of temporary fingerlike extensions of the cell called pseudopodia (false feet), which are also used to engulf molecules of food. Most occur in fresh- and saltwater; some ocean-living species make a hard, external shell. A few species are parasites of humans and other mammals. Example:* Amoeba.

PHYLUM Apicomplexa: *The sporozoans. Most species do not move, as they lack flagella, pseudopodia, or cilia. All are parasites with special organelles for invading host cells. Some species require two or more hosts to complete their life cycle, reproducing sexually in one host, asexually in the next—creating spores at one stage or another. Example:* Plasmodium.

PHYLUM Ciliophora: *The ciliates. Move and capture food by means of many short hairs, or cilia, that cover them. Some species have different sizes of nuclei: a single macronucleus and numerous micronuclei. Except for some sedentary forms, all reproduce sexually; most are free-living. More than 7,000 described species. Example:* Paramecium.

PHYLUM Labyrinthomorpha: *Spindle-shaped or spherical uninucleate colonial organisms that secrete a network of filaments called slime tubes within or along which individuals glide. Some species are known to reproduce by fission; in certain species, aggregations of individuals form spores. Some absorb nutrients by osmosis; most are parasitic on algae. Relationship to other protozoans obscure.*

PHYLUM Microspora: *Intracellular parasites that produce spores at some stage in their life cycle. They live in a wide variety of animals; all active stages occur in host tissues, specifically in the cytoplasm. No known relation to any other protozoan group. Example:* Pleistophora typicalis.

PHYLUM Myxozoa: *Spore-producing parasites of the tissues and organ cavities of various cold-blooded vertebrates, most especially fish and segmented worms. Example:* Myxidium giardi.

which traps the small organisms on which the foraminifer feeds. Among the best-known foraminifers are those belonging to the genus *Globigerina*. Their shells form a thick deposit, called globigerina ooze, on the seabed.

Other sarcodines include the *heliozoans* and *radiolarians*. The heliozoans are freshwater organisms with spherical bodies that are almost frothlike in appearance. Numerous stiff, long, and thin pseudopods radiate from the body.

The radiolarians are floating marine animals that differ from heliozoans in that the body is divided into an inner central capsule and an outer layer, both of protoplasm. They also have radiating and stiff pseudopods. The radiolarians secrete skeletons of silicon or strontium sulfate, which take the form of radiating spines or latticed networks. The skeletons assume shapes reminiscent of spheres, helmets, disks, bells, and other objects. They form a mud deposit on the ocean floor known as radiolarian ooze.

THE SPOROZOANS

These creatures make up the phylum Apicomplexa. All are parasitic protozoans, and all are noted for very complicated life cycles, during which spores are produced at one stage or another. The spore—a cell usually surrounded by a resistant membrane—is called a *sporozoite*.

In general, the sporozoans are incapable of locomotion, although the young sometimes move by means of flagella or pseudopods. These protozoans absorb from their hosts such food materials as dissolved protoplasm, body fluids, or tissue fluids.

The best-known sporozoan is *Plasmodium*, the malarial parasite. Naked sporozoites, exceedingly small and spindle-shaped, are inoculated into a person's bloodstream by the bite of an infected female *Anopheles* mosquito. Eventually the parasites enter the red blood cells. *Plasmodium* also causes malaria in birds, reptiles, frogs, monkeys, apes, bats, squirrels, buffalo, and antelope.

Babesia bigemina, whose sporozoites are inoculated by the bite of the tick, is responsible for Texas cattle fever. *Nosema bombycis* brings about pebrine, the fatal disease of silkworms. *Eimeria* infects chickens, causing coccidiosis. Sporozoan parasites are, in fact, found in almost any animal imaginable.

THE CILIATES

The ciliates, members of the phylum Ciliophora, are so named because at some point in their life cycle, they are equipped with well-ordered hairlike structures called *cilia*, which serve for locomotion.

The cilia are shorter and much more numerous than flagella. They are arranged on the ciliate's body in diagonal or horizontal rows. Their action suggests that of the oars in a multioar racing hull. The cilia push backward for the

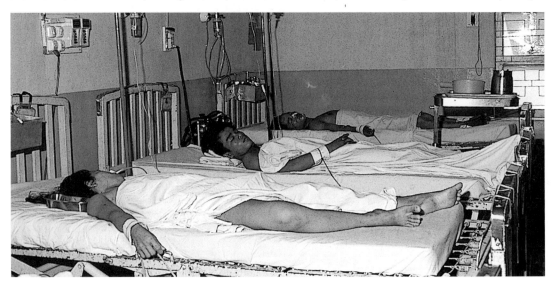

The *Anopheles* mosquito (above) transmits four species of *Plasmodium* protozoans to humans, each of which carries a form of malaria. In some tropical regions, hospitals are crowded with patients acutely ill with the disease (below).

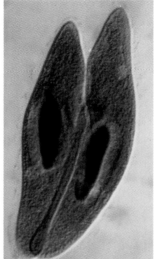

The reproduction process in Paramecium *begins with two individuals conjugating—temporarily uniting (right) to exchange genetic material. The individual cells later undergo binary fission—splitting into two separate organisms (below).*

power stroke. In the recovery stroke, they return to the forward position. At any given time, some of the cilia are engaged in the power stroke and some in the recovery stroke, resulting in a continuous flow of power that propels the animal ahead smoothly.

Although the body of a ciliate may twist or turn to some extent, or lengthen or shorten, it still retains a more or less permanent shape. The ciliates feed on dead organic matter or on various live microorganisms.

Opalina is a very much flattened ciliate possessing many nuclei of the same size. It is found in the intestines of frogs. The rest of the ciliates possess two kinds of nuclei: small ones, or micronuclei; and large ones, or macronuclei. The macronucleus seems to control many of the metabolic activities of the animal; the micronucleus is concerned with the reproductive process. Most ciliates have a mouth. All freshwater species have contractile vacuoles.

Paramecium is a well-known slipper-shaped ciliate found in freshwater. It has a uniform covering of cilia and a long groove leading into the mouth. Some species of *Paramecium* may reach a length of 0.01 inch (0.2 millimeter). *Paramecium* often falls victim to one of its relatives, *Didinium*—a barrel-shaped organism equipped at the front end with a projecting cone that terminates in its mouth.

Members of one group of ciliates—order Peritrichida—have a disk-shaped head end, with two or more rows of cilia surrounding the mouth. The movements of these so-called oral cilia create water currents that bring food into the mouth; few, if any, cilia occur on the rest of the body, and any that do are distinct from the oral cilia. Most species of this group are fixed to some attachment point by means of a stalk. *Vorticella*, a bell-shaped organism, is a common ciliate of this type.

Blepharisma is a typical representative of the ciliate class Spirotricha. Its elongated-oval body is covered with cilia for swimming. Rows of fused cilia surround the mouth and help push food toward it. *Spirostomum*, a common freshwater relative of *Blepharisma*, has an elongated, cylinder-shaped body from 0.04 to 0.12 inch (1 to 3 millimeters) in length—a giant among protozoans. *Stylonychia*, another freshwater form, has an oval body that is flat on the bottom and convex on the top. This ciliate has *cirri*—large, stiff bristles composed of fused tufts of cilia; when in motion, the cirri resemble walking legs.

Epidinium, a related form, is found in the digestive tracts of cattle and reindeer. It has special structures for moving about, feeding, swallowing, digesting, excreting, and contracting, and nuclei for maintaining metabolism and controlling reproduction. There is also an anus and special skeletal plates for maintaining the body's form.

The protozoans known as *suctorians* are ciliates that are highly specialized for food capture. These organisms are common in both fresh- and saltwater. The young are ciliated and free-swimming. Adults entirely lack cilia and are sessile: attached by stalks to inanimate objects, plants, or small animals. Although they lack a mouth, the suctorians have tentacles with which they seize their victims—small ciliates—whose protoplasm they feed upon. Suctorians may be spherical, conical, or branched in shape. Some species are known to have evolved a parasitic lifestyle.

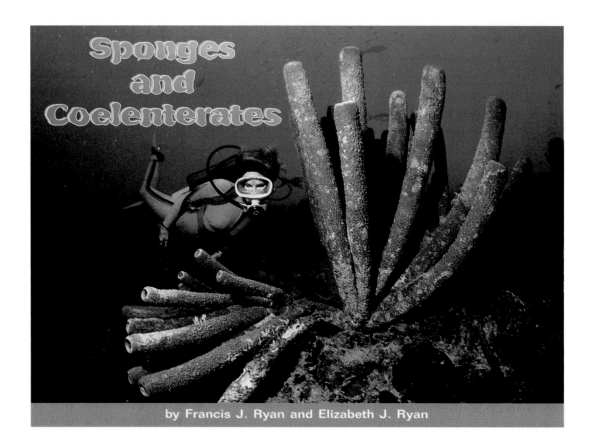

Sponges and Coelenterates

by Francis J. Ryan and Elizabeth J. Ryan

The sea-serpent stories spun by sailors of yore may well have had some basis in fact. Over the centuries, countless seafarers have attested to seeing mysterious creatures—some orange, others blue, many with oddly shaped body parts trailing behind them. Zoologists now know that at least some of these "serpents" were actually giant lion's-mane jellyfish—creatures whose 7-foot (2-meter)-diameter bodies bear awesome curtains of tentacles. Any sailor who came in direct contact with these tentacles was unlikely to tell any more tall tales. Indeed, the sting of this jellyfish is quite dangerous—and often fatal—to humans.

Fortunately, relatively few people come in contact with these creatures. But just about anyone who has swum in the ocean or walked along its coast has seen other, smaller jellyfish and their relatives, the anemones. Sponges are also spotted from time to time, but they often go unrecognized, since most living sponges bear little or no resemblance to the bath and kitchen sponges sold in stores.

Sponges, jellyfish, and anemones are among the simplest of the multicellular, or many-celled, animals. As in all multicellular creatures, different cells in each organism have different functions. Some are responsible for getting food, others for protection. Some specialize in movement, others in reproduction.

SPONGES

At first glance, sponges would appear to be odd gelatinous plants. They are fan-shaped or dome-shaped; formed like vases, bowls, goblets, or trumpets; branched like trees; or flattened out in lichen fashion. Sponges are, nonetheless, marine animals—albeit unusual ones. Basically, the sponge is a hollow tube, attached at one end to a support and open at the other end. Some sponges exist in colonies of many individuals united at their bases.

Although multicellular, sponges lack specialized organs and cannot move. The surface of a sponge is covered with a layer of flattened, protective cells perforated by tiny pores. This feature is responsible for the phylum name, Porifera, which means "hole-bearing."

Most divers who happen across a giant tube sponge (above) believe the structure to be some sort of underwater plant—and not the primitive animal that it actually is.

The pores open to canals that run through the jellylike substance, or *mesenchyme*, of the body. The canals, in turn, open into a large central cavity. In the more complex sponges, these canals lead to spherical chambers and pass from them into the central cavity.

Lining the chambers or central cavity are *collar cells*, or *choanocytes*. Each of these cells has a collar of protoplasm, which encircles the base of a whiplike structure known as a *flagellum*. As the flagellum undulates, it creates a current of water. The waving of many flagella causes water to enter through the sponge's pores, circulate in the canals and chambers, and flow into the central cavity. Microscopic plants and animals and organic debris are brought in with the water. The food particles are drawn to the collar cells, where they are engulfed and then either digested or passed on to cells that creep about like amoebas in the mesenchyme. The incoming water currents also bring oxygen to the cells.

After water circulates in the central cavity, it passes out through a large opening, the *osculum*. The water is often ejected with considerable velocity. Carbon dioxide and other waste products discharged by the cells are eliminated in the escaping water.

A skeletal framework supports the soft mass of the sponge. This prevents the canals from collapsing and allows considerable growth. (Some sponges may be almost 7 feet—2 meters—high.) Special mesenchyme cells secrete this skeleton, which consists of needles, called *spicules*, or of protein fibers, known as *spongin*.

Spicules may be straight or curved, and are often pronged; they may be sharply pointed, knobbed, or frayed at the ends. Often they project beyond the body, making the sponge appear bristly. The spicules, together with the unpleasant secretions and odors produced by the sponge, play an important role in protecting the creature from enemies.

Sponges probably evolved from an aggregate of individual protozoans, perhaps the choanoflagellates, which are much like the sponge's collar cells. Although the sponge has neither sensory receptors nor a nervous system, it can nevertheless close its pores and osculum and contract its body cells when harmful substances are in the water. A unique animal indeed, the sponge is set apart from all other multicellular creatures by its simple structure and the somewhat specialized but uncoordinated cells of its body.

Reproduction

Sponges can reproduce either sexually or asexually. In sexual reproduction, special mesenchyme cells increase in size and become egg cells, while others divide into sperm cells,

The Portuguese man-of-war's long, potent tentacles can attain a length of up to 165 feet. The tentacles are equipped with highly poisonous sting capsules capable of paralyzing fish (above) and causing great distress to humans.

which are discharged into the water. The egg remains in the mesenchyme, where it is fertilized by a sperm from another sponge.

The fertilized egg becomes a flagellated larva (a larva with flagella), which escapes through the osculum and swims away. Soon the tiny larva attaches to a support and begins to grow as a young sponge.

Asexual reproduction occurs through *budding*. Cells grow out from the body and develop into miniature sponges. Depending on the species, these either remain attached as members of a branching colony or drop off from the parent to lead an independent life.

Coelenterates display a somewhat higher organization than do the sponges, particularly in the development of a true digestive cavity and in the elaboration of special sensory cells, a nerve net, and muscle fibers. External stimuli affect the sensory cells, and impulses are conducted by way of the nerve net to the muscle fibers. Longitudinal muscles cause the polyp to shorten; circular muscles cause it to lengthen. Muscle fibers circling the mouth can close it off when harmful substances are in the water or when a falling tide leaves the animal high and dry. The various muscle fibers, coordinated by the nerve net, also allow polyps to bend in one direction or another and move their tentacles. The muscles of the medusa provide contractions of the bell for swimming.

It has been commonly held that coelenterates evolved from colonial protozoans, much as did the sponges. But a revolutionary theory that has gained considerable support assumes that the coelenterates evolved from a primitive flatworm. If this theory is true, then the sea anemones—with no medusa life-cycle stage—are the most primitive of coelenterates, and the jellyfish and hydroids, with their life cycles of alternating polyps and medusae, are a secondary development.

The coelenterate known as a sea pen (left) consists of an anchoring polyp whose upper portions bear leaflike clusters of small polyps.

Some sponges form internal buds called *gemmules*—small masses of food-enriched mesenchyme cells with a protective coat that is often strengthened with spicules. Gemmules are commonly produced by freshwater sponges—the dull-colored or greenish, irregularly shaped blobs that grow on submerged leaves and water-soaked logs in lakes, ponds, and streams. When the parent sponge dies, the gemmules—which can withstand freezing and drying—survive. They grow into adults when conditions become favorable once again.

Types of Sponges

Sponges are grouped into three classes, depending on the type of skeleton. Members of the class Calcarea secrete spicules of calcium carbonate. Members of the class Hexactinellida, called glass sponges, have siliceous spicules—that is, spicules made of silica. Deep-sea glass sponges form a skeletal network suggesting spun glass.

Sponges of the third class, Demospongiae, have either siliceous spicules, a skeleton of spongin, or a framework made of both spicules and spongin. Some have no skeleton at all. The Demospongiae are the most common sponges. They include the freshwater sponges and the boring sponge, which protects itself by etching its way into rock or mollusk shells. The so-called "natural" sponge sold in stores is not the whole animal, but only its framework of spongin, which is elastic, chemically inert, and similar to silk and horn.

One genus of sponge, *Suberites*, grows on empty snail shells that house hermit crabs. The sponge ultimately absorbs the shell, and thereafter serves as a covering for the crab as the crustacean moves about. This arrangement is mutually beneficial; the crab gains protection, while the sponge is transported from one place to another, and thus comes in contact with new sources of food.

Most sponges are veritable "apartment houses" for a host of animals. Marine worms, pistol crabs, shrimps, and slender fishes find a haven in the canals and chambers; barnacles attach themselves to the surface. All of these creatures obtain food from the water passing through the sponge's body.

COELENTERATES

The phylum Coelenterata, or Cnidaria, includes the hydroids, jellyfish, and sea anemones. The phylum name is derived from Greek words meaning "hollow intestine."

Like sponges, coelenterates (pronounced si-LEN-ter-ayts) are essentially tubular animals with a central cavity. Here food is digested as well as circulated; therefore, the structure is called the gastrovascular (digestive and circulating) cavity.

Food, which enters these creatures via the mouth at the upper end of the body, is broken down by enzymes secreted by gland cells, allowing the food's nutrients to diffuse into the body. Often the food is reduced to only particles, which are engulfed and fully digested, as with the sponges, by specialized cells lining the cavity. The beating of flagella gives rise to water currents, which bring in food particles and oxygen. Countercurrents carry wastes out through the mouth.

The outer surface of the body is covered by a layer of tightly packed protective cells. Interspersed in this layer are highly sensitive sensory cells and specialized cells called thread capsules, or *nematocysts*. Each nematocyst contains a fluid under pressure and a spirally coiled, hollow thread. When the capsule is stimulated by touch (and possibly by chemicals as well), the thread is forcibly ejected. Some of these threads pierce the coelenterate's prey and then inject a benumbing poison into it. Other threads either stick to the prey or wrap around its appendages. Nematocysts are especially abundant on the coelenterate's tentacles, which grow as a crown around the mouth. Once prey is paralyzed and held fast by the threads, the tentacles enfold it and draw it into the mouth.

Between the surface cells and those lining the gastrovascular cavity is a layer of supporting jellylike substance in which are found mesenchyme cells. These unspecialized cells form nematocysts and sex cells.

The animal just described—a sort of living tube crowned with tentacles—is a *polyp*. The different types of coelenterates are variants of this polyp form. They are grouped into three classes: Hydrozoa, the hydroids and freshwater hydras; Scyphozoa, the jellyfishes; and Anthozoa, the sea anemones and corals.

The Hydroids

Hydroids consist of hundreds of tiny polyps united by a stalk to form a branching colony. The gastrovascular cavity of each polyp joins with that of the stalk, forming a cavity common to the entire colony. Often the stalk and polyps are held erect and protected by a horny sheath. Hydroids feed on minute worms and various small crustaceans.

The fernlike hydroid colonies are commonly found attached to submerged objects such as wharf pilings, rocks, and kelp. The colony usually reproduces asexually by giving off buds. Some buds form a mouth and a circlet of tentacles at the tip to become what are known as feeding polyps. Others develop into reproductive polyps; they have neither mouth nor tentacles, but produce tiny saucerlike appendages. When mature, these saucers, called *medusae*, break off and swim away. They look

The body of a jellyfish is little more than a bag of jelly with a hollow interior. Divers have encountered some particularly gigantic specimens off the Australian coast.

very much like miniature jellyfish with tentacles hanging from the rim of the saucer.

The function of the medusa is to reproduce sexually. Sex cells, on the underside of the saucer, produce eggs or sperm, which are shed into the water, where fertilization takes place. Each fertilized egg becomes a ciliated larva—a larva provided with hairlike structures called *cilia*. The larva swims about for a time before attaching itself and forming a polyp. The polyp then buds, and a new hydroid colony is produced. The process whereby the colony forms asexual buds that give rise to sexually reproducing organisms is called *alternation of generations*. This behavior—also found in plants—serves to spread the species into new localities.

Some species of Hydrozoa have insignificant polyps; the medusa is the conspicuous stage in their lives. Others flourish as hydroid colonies, producing only attached, degenerate medusa-like structures that shed eggs and sperm into the water.

The freshwater hydra, a minute individual polyp, does not go through a medusa stage. Instead, the fertilized egg remains affixed to the outside of the parent's body until a heavy membrane forms around the embryo, at which point it separates from the parent and eventually develops into a young hydra. The hydra also produces asexual buds that grow from the body, form a whorl of tentacles, and finally pinch off from the parent.

Hydras prefer the clean waters of lakes and ponds, where they feed on tiny worms, insect larvae, young fish, and microscopic crustaceans. They glide along the bottom and on submerged plant stems by means of creeping movements of the cells at the base of the body. They can also move by somersaulting. First, they bend over and attach their tentacles to a support while releasing the base. Then they swing the base over and attach it, freeing the tentacles, and so on.

The coelenterate known as the Portuguese man-of-war is related to the hydroids and hydras. It is a complex colonial animal supplied with a crested, gas-filled float, from which hang feeding polyps, clusters of attached medusae, and long, trailing tentacles armed with stinging thread capsules. Some of these tentacles may attain a length of 165 feet (50 meters).

Bioluminescence occurs frequently in the ocean, but is usually limited to species of marine life that dwell at great depths. Nevertheless, a substantial number of surface-dwelling jellyfish are capable of producing "living light" (below).

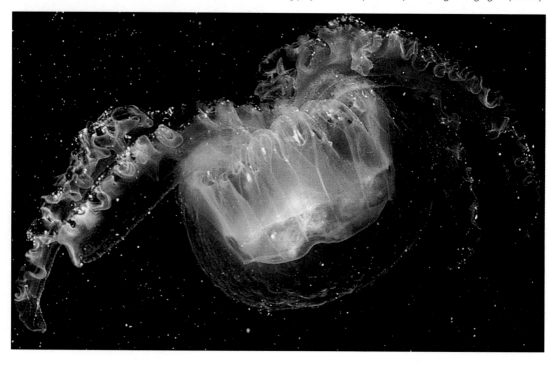

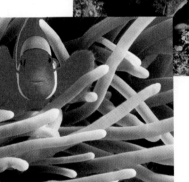

The external skeletons of stony corals act as the foundations of the world's tropical reefs (right), which serve as homes to thousands of marine plants and animals. Scientists do not entirely understand how the clown fish (below) manages to swim among the deadly tentacles of a sea anemone without getting stung.

Jellyfish

The typical jellyfish has a bell-shaped, gelatinous body. Under the central part of the bell is a short structure bearing the mouth. The corners of the mouth are pulled out into grooved oral arms. These appendages carry nematocysts that entangle and paralyze small aquatic animals. The prey is swept along the ciliated grooves of the arms, through the mouth, and into the spacious gastrovascular cavity, which has branched radial canals going to the margin of the bell. Numerous tentacles fringe the edge of the bell, as do sense organs that are sensitive to light, chemicals, and the directions of movement. The jellyfish weakly swims by rhythmically contracting its bell.

Ovaries or testes, as the case may be, lie on the floor of the gastrovascular cavity. Sperm are released into the water and fertilize the eggs in the cavity of another jellyfish. Each fertilized egg then lodges in a fold of an oral arm, where it develops into a ciliated larva. This larva escapes and grows into an inconspicuous polyp. Eventually the polyp develops a number of horizontal constrictions until it looks like a pile of saucers. The saucers break away as medusae and develop into adult jellyfish.

Sea Anemones and Their Kin

The stout-bodied sea anemone is a noncolonial polyp that attaches to rocks or shells and rarely changes its place. Tentacles rim the upper part of the animal and surround the mouth, which leads to a gullet. Below this is the gastrovascular cavity, whose partitions increase the digestive capacity of the animal such that large prey can be consumed.

The sea anemone can reproduce itself by dividing its body in half longitudinally. Sometimes, too, as the animal slides along on its slimy basal disk, or foot, fragments of its body are left behind. Small anemones are regenerated from these pieces. Eggs and sperm are produced on the partitions of the gastrovascular cavity and are released through the mouth. Ciliated larvae develop from the fertilized eggs and form single anemones.

The stony corals are colonial animals similar to anemones. They remain attached to one spot and secrete cups of calcium carbonate into which they can retract. Stony corals are found in deep, cold water, but it is only in the tropical and subtropical seas that they contribute to the building of reefs.

Many creatures can claim kinship to the anemones and stony corals. These include the organ-pipe corals, which live in calcareous tubes joined together by platforms, and the precious, or red, corals, which are stiffened by calcareous spicules and are used in making jewelry. The related sea whips, sea fans, and sea plumes are branching colonies of polyps supported by a flexible horny material.

STARFISH AND OTHER ECHINODERMS

by Francis J. Ryan and Elizabeth J. Ryan

A starfish is not a fish. A sand dollar is not a form of money. And a sea cucumber is not a vegetable. All of these misleadingly named animals are echinoderms, or "spiny-skinned" marine animals that live on the ocean floor. The phylum name, Echinodermata, comes from two Greek words: *echinos*, meaning "hedgehog," and *derma*, meaning "skin."

The echinoderms are not closely related to any of the other invertebrates. And in one very obvious way, the creatures in this phylum differ from other animals, vertebrates or invertebrates. Most animals, including human beings, have *bilateral symmetry*—their bodies can be divided into more-or-less-identical right and left halves. Echinoderms, by contrast, are endowed with *ra-*

Starfish occur in an infinite variety of vivid colors. Using its hundreds of well-coordinated tube feet, the starfish above can slowly crawl along the ocean floor.

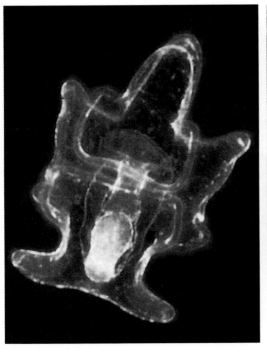

The stages in the life cycle, or metamorphosis, of an echinoderm bear no apparent resemblance to one another. A starfish larva (left) has bilateral symmetry. As an adult, the starfish has radial symmetry (above).

dial symmetry. Their bodies are built on a circular, or radial, plan. In the center of the body is the mouth. From that hub, the arms or other structures extend outward at regular intervals, much like the spokes of a wheel.

Biologists find the larval forms of echinoderms particularly fascinating because of their close affinities with the larvae of the protochordates—tunicates and other primitive animals whose ancestors gave rise to backboned animals.

ANATOMY OF ECHINODERMS

The skin of a typical echinoderm covers an internal skeleton of calcareous *ossicles*, or small bones, from which the creature derives a more or less rigid structure. Projecting outward from the ossicles are numerous calcareous spines.

Inside the skeleton is the large body cavity, or *coelom,* in which lie the internal organs. The

coelom contains a lymphlike fluid that bathes the organs. Amoeba-like cells creep about in the fluid, removing wastes and carrying nutrients to all parts of the animal's body.

Echinoderms have a complete digestive system leading from the mouth, on the underside of the body, to the anus. Digestive glands pour their secretions into the stomach. A unique arrangement called the *water vascular system* allows water to enter a sieve plate on the body's surface and then circulate by way of another canal to a ring canal, which branches into radial canals. Each radial canal gives off many pairs of *tube feet*. When these tube feet are distended with water, they are used for locomotion and serve as respiratory surfaces.

The tube feet of a starfish are powerful enough to pry open the shell of a mussel (above). The starfish digests its prey right in the shell—and then creeps away.

Some species of starfish have up to 20 rays, or arms, although the average number is five. The creature is well known for its remarkable powers of regeneration. Indeed, in a matter of months, missing arms can be completely reconstructed.

Encircling the echinoderm's mouth is a *nerve ring*. Five branches radiate from this ring, extending tiny nerves to the internal organs, the skin, and the tube feet. There are no well-developed sense organs, although the tube feet may play a role in sensory perception.

Echinoderms have sex glands that shed their products into the water, where fertilization occurs. Fertilized eggs give rise eventually to larvae, which swim freely by means of ciliated bands. The larvae go through many stages of development—some in which they have bilateral symmetry—before they begin to resemble miniature versions of their parents.

TYPES OF ECHINODERMS

There are more than 6,000 known species of echinoderms, grouped by zoologists into five classes. All live in either marine or brackish waters in the world's warmer seas.

Starfish

Starfish (also called sea stars), which make up the class Stelleroidea, are perhaps the most familiar of the echinoderms. The body is a central disk from which radiate five or more arms. Between the blunt spines on the upper surface project skin gills—fingerlike extensions of the coelom; they serve as excretory and respiratory organs. Small pincers interspersed among the spines protect the skin gills and help to clear the surface of foreign matter.

On the underside of each arm is a groove from which protrude the slender tube feet. A light-sensitive eyespot and a short tentacle, which may be sensitive to chemicals, are located at the tip of each arm. Starfish prey on tube worms, crustaceans, and mollusks.

The spherical sea urchin (above) is covered with brightly colored spines. Some of the small pincerlike organs that lie between the spines are poisonous to humans.

A sand dollar (above), its disk-shaped body marked with petal-shaped areas called *petaloids, lives in shallow water. It is not uncommon to find the skeleton of a sand dollar (right) on the beach after a storm.*

The starfish has a unique way of capturing and eating prey. When it happens upon a clam, for example, the starfish uses the hundreds of tiny tube feet on the underside of its body to creep over the clam. Then, again using its feet, it pulls apart the two valves of the clam's shell. When the shell is open, the starfish turns its own stomach inside out through its mouth and into the opening between the valves, surrounding the clam like a sandwich bag. Chemicals secreted by the starfish's stomach digest the clam—right in the shell! Once its meal is digested, the starfish swallows its own stomach and then slowly creeps away.

Commercial clam and oyster operations have for years fought a losing battle with starfish. At one time, people tried to eliminate troublesome starfish by chopping them up into several pieces. Assuming that this killed the creatures, the people tossed the pieces back into the sea. Unfortunately for the commercial interests, this tactic caused a great increase in starfish. Indeed, like many other animals with-

out backbones, starfish have the ability to regenerate themselves. If a starfish is cut into a number of pieces, any piece that includes at least a tiny part of the central disk will grow into a new, complete animal, thus producing several individuals from the original starfish.

Brittle stars and serpent stars (subclass Ophiuroidea) have a small, flattened body disk

Unlike most echinoderms, the aptly named sea cucumber (right) lacks hard skeletal plates. These soft-bodied creatures shovel into their mouths vast amounts of mud from which they extract organic material for nourishment.

with five or more arms. In some cases, as in the basket star, the arms repeatedly branch. The stomach is saclike, and there is no anus.

These animals use their flexible arms to move jerkily about on the ocean floor and to swim. The creature also uses its arms to catch worms, mollusks, and other animals and to bring the prey to its mouth.

As its name suggests, the brittle star is very susceptible to damaging its arms. When floating near the surface of the water, it defends itself by curling its arms around its body—like a big hug. In this position, the brittle star quickly sinks to the bottom of the water. This is an important escape tactic, because hungry seabirds and other creatures would quickly eat a brittle star floating near the ocean's surface.

Sea Urchins and Sand Dollars

Sea urchins and sand dollars (class Echinoidea) are globular-shaped, oval-shaped, or flattened into thin disks. Five teeth surround the mouth. The skeleton forms a hard shell of flattened, immovable ossicles; the spines are numerous, stiff, and movable. Five rows of tube feet radiate over the surface, converging at the upper and lower centers of the body.

Feather stars bear an uncanny resemblance to plants. These echinoderms sometimes live in dense clusters on the seafloor, their arms swaying in search of food.

Most sea urchins live near rocky shores, where they feed on algae, small marine animals, and decaying matter. Many people, particularly in Mediterranean countries, consider sea-urchin eggs a delicacy.

Sand dollars, sometimes called sea cakes, usually live partly buried in sand on the ocean floor. They have very short spines and tube feet that give the creatures a furry appearance. Sometimes hundreds or even thousands of sand dollars live packed together in a small area.

Closely related to sand dollars are the heart urchins. These creatures also burrow into the seafloor, where they feed on microscopic plants and animals.

Sea Cucumbers

Sea cucumbers (class Holothuroidea) are elongated animals with a mouth surrounded by tentacles at one end and the anus at the other. The skin—either leathery and muscular or delicate and transparent—has only microscopic calcareous ossicles. Sea cucumbers move by muscular contractions or by using the tube feet, which extend in five rows along the length of the body. Their diet consists of organic material taken from mud, and of small animals that become entangled by the tentacles at one end of the sea cucumber's body.

Sea cucumbers have an unusual protective device: if disturbed by an enemy, the sea cucumber may eject, or disgorge, its internal organs. The predator eats these, forgetting about the sea cucumber itself. Later the lost organs regenerate themselves.

In certain parts of China, the people consider sea cucumbers a delicacy. The animals are dried and used in making soups.

Sea Lilies

Sea lilies and feather stars (class Crinoidea) are flowerlike, brilliantly colored animals with flexible, branching arms. Many are attached, mouth upward, to the sea bottom by means of a horny stalk. Others have no stalk and swim freely by using their arms. Microscopic plants and animals, caught by the arms and swept to the mouth, constitute the diet of these unusual creatures.

Sea lilies and feather stars inhabit all ocean depths from just below the low-tide line to more than 2 miles (3.2 kilometers) below the surface.

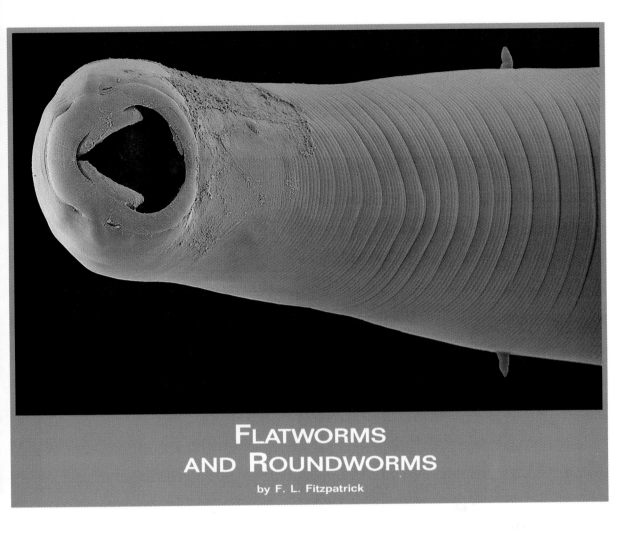

FLATWORMS
AND ROUNDWORMS
by F. L. Fitzpatrick

The word "worms" is popularly applied to a great variety of long, slender, and limbless animals: earthworms, tapeworms, hookworms, shipworms (which are mollusks), blindworms (which are lizards), and the larvae of various insect species.

To a zoologist, however, "worms" has a much more restricted meaning. It is applied particularly to three distinct groups (phyla) of animals: the flatworms, or platyhelminths; the roundworms, or nematodes; and the segmented worms, or annelids. The creatures belonging to these groups are found almost everywhere in the world. Some of them burrow deep into the earth. Others crawl along the ground. Still others swim in the water. A considerable number are parasites on other animals or on plants. Some worms are considered to be benefactors of humanity. Others, including tapeworms and liver flukes, rank high among the dangerous pests that afflict humans and other mammals.

FLATWORMS

The approximately 10,000 known species of flatworms make up a phylum called Platyhelminthes, a name derived from two Greek words: *platys*, meaning "flat," and *helmins*, meaning "worm." Flatworms are the simplest worms. Some species have an outer layer of hairlike structures called *cilia*. In others, the outer layer is smooth or spiny.

Tapeworms

Perhaps the best-known flatworms are the tapeworms, or cestodes. Many species are parasites of people and domestic animals.

The body of a typical tapeworm consists of a rounded head, or *scolex*, and a number of flat-

Many species of flatworms and roundworms are noted for their parasitic lifestyles. The hookworm (above, greatly magnified) causes disease in millions of people every year.

tened segments, or *proglottids*. The head bears hooks or suckers (or both), with which the worm attaches itself to the host—usually to the lining of the intestine. Growth in a tapeworm occurs through the formation of new segments next to the head. As the older segments keep on growing, the largest of all, naturally, are to be found at the tail end of the body. A fully grown tapeworm looks like a long, narrow ribbon—a ribbon that can reach 33 feet (10 meters) in length!

The tapeworm's head acts as an anchor, keeping all of the segments within the body of the host. Each segment functions more or less as a self-contained unit. There is no digestive system; each segment absorbs, through its walls, digested food from the digestive cavity of the host. As a segment grows older and larger, it becomes filled with eggs. When the segment finally matures, it breaks off from the rest of the tapeworm and passes out of the host through the host's excretory system.

One species notorious for its parasitic activities in human beings is the beef tapeworm, *Taeniarhynchus saginata*. This creature must live in the bodies of two different hosts to complete its life cycle. The adult beef tapeworm is found in the human intestine, where it sometimes exceeds 30 feet (9 meters) in length. When the egg-filled segments at the tail end of the tapeworm break off, they pass out of the human host with his or her solid wastes.

If the wastes are not disposed of in a sanitary manner, the eggs may end up in a field or someplace else where they are eventually ingested by cattle. Boring larvae are then freed from the eggs and migrate into the muscle tissues of the new host, where they form cysts. When a human eats raw or undercooked meat from one of these infected animals, the cyst, which encases a young worm, dissolves in the stomach of the human host. The worm then takes up its place of abode in the intestine, and the cycle begins anew.

The presence of a beef tapeworm in the human intestine is likely to prove neither fatal nor even terribly dangerous, because the creature cannot fill human muscle tissues with cysts. Its eggs must always pass out of the human body before they can hatch. A tapeworm is nevertheless a decidedly undesirable boarder, primarily because it deprives the human host of a portion of the nutrients that are normally derived from food.

Fortunately, a beef tapeworm can be eliminated from the body quite readily by means of simple drugs administered under the direction of a physician.

The pork tapeworm, *Taenia solium*, is far more dangerous to humans. In a typical life cycle, an adult worm living in the human intestine develops mature, egg-filled segments, which break off and pass out of the host from time to time. If any of the eggs are swallowed by pigs, the larvae that subsequently hatch from them will form cysts in the pig's muscle. When undercooked infected pork is eaten by a human being, the cysts dissolve and the adult worms become established in the human intestine. The pests can be disposed of, as in the case of beef tapeworms, by prescribed drugs.

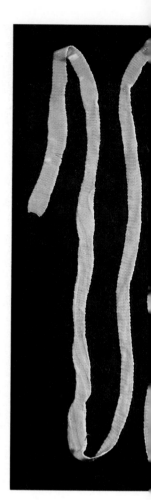

Unfortunately, some of the pork-tapeworm eggs may develop into young before they have the opportunity to pass out of the human host with the body wastes. When this happens, the young ultimately penetrate into muscle tissues, causing inflammation. The consequences are particularly serious when the encysted larvae lodge in such vital areas of the human body as the eye or the brain.

Dogs and rabbits also act as hosts for many kinds of tapeworms. Most of the parasites form their cysts in fish, mice, rats, rabbits, sheep, cows, and pigs. One species of tapeworm, *Echinococcus granulosus*, which occurs as an adult in dogs, forms cysts in human muscle as well as in liver, lung, brain, and bone tissue.

Humans become infected by eating unwashed vegetables that have been contaminated by dogs, by drinking contaminated water, or by kissing dogs on whose fur the eggs are clinging.

Domestic birds are also subject to infection by parasitic tapeworms. Adult worms develop in

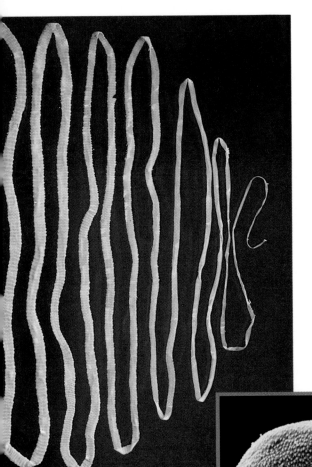

shaped larval form from freshwater snails and swims about, searching for a human host. Once the larvae penetrate the skin of a human, they move in the bloodstream to the lungs, liver, bladder, or intestine, where they mature and can cause life-threatening damage.

The liver fluke, *Fasciola hepatica*, infects the liver of sheep, cattle, and pigs. A single sheep's liver may house 200 adult flukes, which in turn produce an astounding number (upwards of 100 million!) of eggs. After the eggs have begun to develop, they pass through the bile duct of the liver into the intestine, and ultimately to the exterior with the sheep's wastes.

The egg of a sheep liver fluke needs to find itself in water of a certain temperature to continue its development. When these conditions are met, the egg gives rise to a tiny ciliated embryo. For this minute creature to survive, it needs to find a certain type of snail to serve as a

A human who eats raw or undercooked meat runs the risk of incurring tapeworms. Some tapeworms (above) ultimately exceed 30 feet in length. Schistosomiasis, caused by the liver fluke at right, is a dreaded disease in the world's tropical regions.

the bodies of birds when the birds eat infected earthworms or insects.

Flukes

The flukes, or trematodes, constitute another important group of flatworms. Perhaps the most medically significant fluke is the *schistosome*, which causes the debilitating disease known as schistosomiasis. Experts estimate that this disease affects about 200 million people worldwide, primarily in tropical regions of Africa, the Middle East, the Caribbean islands, and South America.

This fluke, after already having undergone a complicated life cycle, emerges in a tadpole-

host. If this host is forthcoming, the embryo burrows into it. Within the snail, great numbers of young flukes are produced by a complicated budding process. The young escape from the snail and swim about freely for a time. Then they climb upon blades of grass at the water's edge and form cysts around themselves. If a sheep swallows the cysts, the young flukes will gradually work their way into the liver.

Very few sheep liver flukes are likely to meet all the conditions set by such an exacting life cycle. These worms continue to thrive

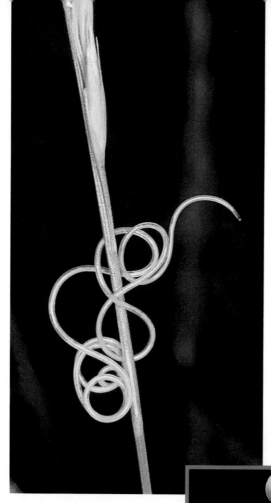

opening on the underside of the body. The cilia that cover their bodies can be used to produce swimming movements.

These worms are found in the sea, in freshwater, and in some moist places on land. They feed on worms, insects, tiny mollusks, and microscopic organisms.

Turbellarians belonging to the genus *Planaria* have the ability to regenerate, or regrow, lost parts of their bodies. If the head or tail end is removed, a new head or tail will develop. If the body is cut in two, the head end will grow a new tail and the tail end will develop a new head. This ability has made *Planaria* a favorite of biology teachers.

ROUNDWORMS

There are approximately 20,000 species of roundworms, also called nematodes. A number of these creatures are parasites on people and animals; some species attack plants. Countless numbers of nematodes inhabit the upper soil layers and the bottom muds of lakes and streams. In appearance, roundworms are slender, unsegmented worms without cilia.

Trichina Worms

At least from the human standpoint, the most notorious roundworm is the trichina, *Trichinella spiralis*, a parasite of human beings, pigs, house rats, and probably other animals. It is a tiny creature: adult males average only 0.05 inch (1.3 millimeters) long, while adult females range from 0.1 to 0.15 inch (2.5 to 3.8 millimeters) in length. The presence of the trichina worm in the human body causes the disease known as *trichinosis*. People are infected when they eat raw or undercooked pork from pigs that have adult trichina worms in their intestines.

While in the pig host, the female trichina worms bear tiny young, which penetrate the walls of the intestine, enter the blood vessels, and work their way into the pig's muscle tissues.

The eelworm (above), noted for its snakelike movements, is primarily a parasite of beets and other plants. Another nematode, Ascaris lumbricoides (right), is a prominent parasite of humans in areas of poor hygiene, particularly in the tropics.

because of the enormous number of eggs they produce.

Sheep may be seriously injured, and sometimes killed, by liver flukes, although drugs are available to effect an early-stage cure.

There are many other species of parasitic flukes that live in the intestines, lungs, and blood vessels, among other organs and structures. Several species of human liver flukes infect people in Africa and eastern Asia.

Turbellarians

The turbellarians, or true flatworms, are generally free-swimming animals that do not lead parasitic lives. They have short, flattened bodies and a digestive system with a single

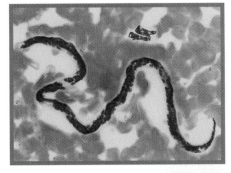

Once there, each tiny worm embryo forms a cyst around itself. Life in the muscle tissues of the host represents a dead end for the trichina worm unless a person or some other carnivore eats the infected tissue. If the host is not eaten, the cyst wall will begin to harden after about six months, and the embryo within the cyst will eventually die.

An entirely different scenario may arise if the infected pig is butchered and used as human food. The meat looks perfectly wholesome, because the cysts are too small to be seen by the naked eye. Thorough cooking will kill the trichina embryo within the cyst. But if the meat is eaten raw or is only partially cooked or smoked, the person who eats it is in acute danger of infection.

By the time the meat containing the parasites has reached the person's intestine, the cyst walls have dissolved. The young worms soon grow to adult size. The human victim may suffer from digestive disturbances—including nausea, diarrhea, and abdominal pain—if enough of the worms are present. If the disease is diagnosed at this stage, a physician can prescribe drugs that will expel the parasites from the intestines, and no lasting harm is done.

If the worms remain unchecked, the females will bear a new generation of young, which bore into blood vessels of the intestinal wall. The bloodstream carries the larvae to all parts of the body, where they form cysts in the muscle tissues. Muscle soreness and fever are typical symptoms of the disease at this stage. Breathing, swallowing, and chewing movements are likely to be painful for a period of three or four weeks; full recovery may take several months. The consequences of the disease are particularly serious when the trichina larvae damage vital areas of the body, such as the heart and diaphragm.

Once the young trichina parasites have made their way into the muscle tissues, they cannot be disposed of by means of drugs. It is possible to kill adults remaining in the intestines, thereby ending the production of any more young; otherwise, little can be done. Over

Dogs, cats, and various types of domestic livestock are vulnerable to a number of parasitic nematodes, including heartworms. Dirofilaria immitis *(left) is the species that most frequently attacks dogs, living in the animal's heart (below) or in the arteries that lead from the heart to the lungs.*

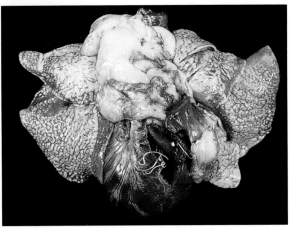

time, calcareous matter is laid down in and around the cyst, which is ultimately transformed into a granule of lime in the muscle.

Experts estimate that some human hosts may harbor as many as 100 million trichina cysts. In other cases, the number of cysts can be comparatively small, making it possible for people to be infected without serious consequences to their health.

Hookworms

The hookworms, another type of roundworm, are abundant in tropical and subtropical regions. The species known as the American hookworm, *Necator americanus*, is about 0.4 inch (1 centimeter) long—considerably larger than the trichina worm.

Adult American hookworms suck blood from the wall of the host's small intestine. The female produces large numbers of eggs, which pass out of the host though the excretory system. When these eggs are deposited on warm, loose, moist soil, they develop into tiny larvae.

The larvae generally gain entry into a human body through the soles of the feet—boring through the skin and producing a sensation known variously as ground itch, dew itch, or skin itch. Once they enter the blood vessels, the larvae embark on an amazing journey through the body. First they are transported by the bloodstream through the heart to the tiny blood vessels of the lung tissue. They then bore their way out into the air spaces of the lungs and eventually move upward through the bronchial tubes and windpipe to the back of the mouth cavity. They then pass down the esophagus and through the stomach, reaching the small intestine. There the hookworms settle down for perhaps six or seven years.

Hookworm victims usually suffer from loss of blood and become thin and anemic; their skin takes on a waxy appearance. They often suffer from heartburn and constipation and are easy prey to various diseases.

The first line of defense against hookworms is to wear shoes. Footwear will prevent most of the parasites from entering the body, even in areas where they are abundant. Another effective measure is to arrange for the sanitary disposal of human wastes.

Adult worms may be driven out of the human intestine by certain drugs administered under the direction of a physician. If left untreated, hookworms in the human body will eventually die in six or seven years.

The Filarial Worm

Another parasitic nematode of tropical and subtropical regions is the filarial worm, *Wuchereria bancrofti*, which is transmitted from one human to another by various species of mosquitoes. The adult female worms measure between 2.75 and 4 inches (7 and 10 centimeters); the males are half that size. They usually occur in the lymphatic vessels and lymph nodes.

In an infected human, female filarial worms produce eggs that develop into embryos called microfilariae, some of which reach the blood circulating near the host's skin. There the embryos are taken up by a mosquito as it feeds on its human victim. Within the tissues of the mosquito, the young filarial worms develop into infective larvae. These larvae enter the next human on which the mosquito feeds and eventually find their way to the new host's lymphatic system, where they mature.

The condition known as *filariasis*, which affects about 120 million people worldwide,

results from inflammation and from the obstruction of lymphatic channels by both the bodies of the mature filarial worms and by scar tissue caused by the worms' presence. A further complication, in which the limbs and other regions of the body swell to enormous size, is known as *elephantiasis*.

Other Parasitic Roundworms

The Guinea worm, *Dracunculus medinensis*, another parasitic roundworm of human beings, is found in Africa, parts of the Middle East, and India. People become infected by drinking water containing copepods (crustaceans) that carry the infective stage of the worm. After the infected copepods are swallowed, the worms mate and the female migrates through the tissues of its human host. About 10 months later, the fertile female, which by now may have achieved a length of 3 feet (1 meter) or more, comes to lie just under the skin, through which it frees its young. To extract the worm, one end of the animal is rolled up on a stick. Each day, the stick is given a few turns until the entire worm is drawn out.

Dogs, cats, poultry, cattle, sheep, horses, pigs, and goats are also attacked by parasitic roundworms. The heartworm, *Dirofilaria immitis*, lives as an adult in a dog's heart or in the arteries that lead from the heart to the lungs. The tiny young of the heartworm are transmitted via the bites of mosquitoes.

The stomach worm, *Haemonchus contortus*, attacks both sheep and cattle. Eggs produced by the female pass out of the host with the wastes and hatch within a very short time. The young pass through several stages of development. As larvae, they crawl up on blades of grass, where they are apt to be swallowed by grazing sheep or cattle.

Various species of roundworms attack plants. The sugar-beet eelworm, *Heterodera schachtii*, is a good example. It is never more than 0.04 inch (1.02 millimeters) in length. Its small size, together with the fact that it lives in the roots of the sugar beet, make control a difficult problem. This worm has been present in European beet fields for many years; it was accidentally introduced into the United States sometime after 1900. When sugar-beet nematodes appear in a beet field, the most effective control measure is to change to another crop.

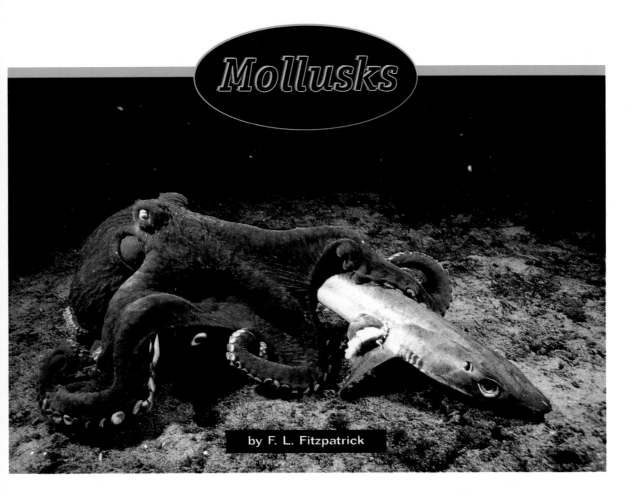

Mollusks

by F. L. Fitzpatrick

When zoologists decide upon the classification of an animal, it is often easy for the non-scientist to understand their rationale. After all, is there any question that butterflies and moths are closely related? And isn't it a given that dogs and cats have enough obvious similarities to justify their taxonomic relationship? But a tiny snail and a carnivorous octopus? A giant squid and a sea scallop? A delicate oyster and a troublesome zebra mussel? What possible thread could connect these six creatures—and more than 65,000 other species—so strongly that scientists assigned them to the same phylum, the one whose members are called mollusks?

CHARACTERISTICS AND CLASSIFICATION

The common bond among all these species is the presence of a soft body. (The phylum name Mollusca is, in fact, derived from the Latin *mollis*, meaning "soft.") In many (but not all) mollusks, this soft body is protected by a shell secreted by the body covering known as the *mantle*. The shell itself is made largely of calcium carbonate.

Another common feature of many mollusks is the presence of a *foot*, an unusual structure that takes different forms in different species. In clams, for example, the foot is a muscular extension that the creature uses to plow its way through mud and sand. In snails, it is flat and used for creeping. In squids and octopuses, the foot is divided into "arms," which the animals use to seize prey.

The phylum Mollusca is divided into six distinct classes: Cephalopoda, which includes squids, cuttlefish, octopuses, and the chambered nautilus; Bivalvia, which includes oysters, clams, scallops, mussels, and teredos; Gastropoda, which includes snails, slugs, limpets, abalones, and conches; Scaphopoda, the tooth shells; Polyplacophora, chitons, the most primi-

Despite its notorious reputation, the giant octopus, while not hesitating to scavenge on a dead dogfish shark (above), usually flees when it encounters a human.

Many species of squids live far beneath the surface of the ocean. The deep-dwelling squid above uses its ability to bioluminesce primarily to confuse potential predators.

making the water turbid and thus confusing the foe. Most cephalopods are capable of chameleon-like color changes as well. On their skin, specialized cells called *chromatophores* ("color-bearers") contain different pigments. When these cells expand or contract, the color of the skin changes rapidly.

Squids

The champion swimmer of the cephalopods is the squid, a streamlined, spindle-shaped creature sometimes called the "arrow squid" for its ability to dart through the water. The squid's foot is divided into 10 arms. Two of the arms are longer than the rest; these longer appendages bear suckers and are used to seize and hold prey. The eyes have no lids, but otherwise look startlingly human.

The squid draws water through a central body cavity—the *mantle cavity*—and forces it out through a flexible tube, the *siphon*, when the mantle is contracted. The siphon is located just behind the arms. The jet of water that spurts through the animal propels it swiftly backward. Ink is also discharged through this siphon.

tive mollusk class; and Monoplacophora, represented by the living *Neopilina* and numerous extinct forms of the phylum.

SQUIDS, OCTOPUSES, AND THEIR RELATIVES

The cephalopods (which means "head-feet" in Greek) include such striking creatures as squids and octopuses. These animals are so called because the foot, which is separated into a number of "arms," encircles the head.

Unlike most other mollusks, living cephalopods generally do not develop shells. Instead, the mantle forms the outer part of the body. In some species, there is an inner skeleton. Numerous extinct forms of cephalopods resembled the living pearly nautilus in that they formed a coiled, chambered shell.

All cephalopods dwell in the sea. They have arms, often called *tentacles*, that are equipped with suckers or hooks or both. Almost all cephalopods secrete an inklike fluid, which is stored in a special sac. When a cephalopod wishes to escape a pursuer, it squirts out the ink,

Some of the tinier mollusk species are no bigger than a grain of sand. Others, like the gigantic clam known as a tridacnid (below), can grow to a width of 3 feet or more.

The fins—two flaplike extensions of the mantle—function chiefly for steering and to propel the squid slowly forward or backward.

One of the most familiar species is the North American common squid, *Loligo pealei*, found primarily in the Mediterranean, in East Asian waters, and along the east coast of North America. Some fishermen use the creature as bait. In many parts of the world, this squid serves as human food.

Another species, the flying squid (*Ommastrephes bartrami*), has been compared to the flying fish. It often shoots out of the water, particularly when the weather is rough, and has been known to land on the decks of ships.

One of the most formidable species is the giant squid, *Architeuthis princeps*. Until recently, the giant squid was considered the largest of all invertebrates (animals without backbones), with a total length—including its body and arms—of 50 feet (15 meters) or more. But scientists have recovered an intact specimen of a "colossal squid," *Mesonychoteuthis hamiltoni*, which exceeds by more than 10 percent the size of the largest known adult *A. princeps*. The rare *M. hamiltoni*, an aggressive predator equipped with two razor-sharp beaks and swiveling talonlike barbs at the ends of its tentacles, lives far beneath the ocean surface, and is seldom encountered by seafarers.

Octopuses

Few dwellers of the deep stir the human imagination the way the octopus (genus *Octopus*) does. Many tales have been told of these creatures attacking hapless waders or divers. Such tales are grossly exaggerated—and probably not true. Certainly, a large octopus—with its eight long, powerful arms, its two large staring eyes, and a vicious-looking beak—would be a rather unpleasant creature to encounter underwater. But however threatening an octopus may appear, there is scant evidence to suggest that even the largest species attack—let alone bother—humans.

The foot of the octopus is divided into eight arms, the feature that gives rise to its name, which means "eight feet" in Greek. The animal has a parrotlike beak with which it rends its prey. Octopuses range from 2 inches to 30 feet (5 centimeters to 9 meters) in arm-and-body length. The larger species, sometimes called "devilfish," may attain a weight of 77 pounds (35 kilograms). The octopus can crawl along the sea bottom on its arms. Sometimes the creature swims about by sucking water into the body and then squirting it out.

The magnificent shell of the chambered nautilus is spirally coiled and divided into compartments, each one a "room" in which the nautilus lived at some stage of its growth.

Most octopuses are shy and retiring, passing their days hidden in crevices. At nightfall, they set out in search of prey. Stealthily, an octopus creeps up on some unsuspecting fish or crab. Once the powerful arms entwine the victim, there is no escape. The beaklike jaws quickly end the captive's struggle, and the octopus feeds upon the prey. With the approach of dawn, the animal retreats to its lair. The octopus is itself the prey of eels, whales, and sharks.

Humans dine on octopus in coastal areas of Europe, North America, in various parts of the Far East, and on the islands of the South Pacific.

Cuttlefishes and Nautiluses

A close relative of the squid is the common sepia, or cuttlefish, *Sepia officinalis*. This small creature, ranging from 6 to 10 inches (15 to 25 centimeters) in length, secretes a calcareous inner shell known as *cuttlebone*. Pieces of this substance are often placed in birdcages for the pet bird to peck at—and thereby derive its required allotment of certain minerals. Another cuttlefish product is sepia, a pigment prepared from the deep brown fluid (ink) that the creature ejects as a defense mechanism.

The pearly, or chambered, nautilus (genus *Nautilus*), found in the South Pacific and the Indian Ocean, is a member of an ancient group of cephalopods. Its shell is spirally coiled and divided into compartments, each one a chamber in which the nautilus once lived at some stage of its growth; the animal resides in the outermost chamber. About 90 tentacles are set around the mouth. Although the tentacles lack suckers, they can nevertheless cling tenaciously to solid objects. The head can be withdrawn into the shell. A hood at the back of the head partly closes the opening.

The female of the paper nautilus, or argonaut, *Argonauta argo* (a form closely related to the octopus), secretes a spirally coiled and symmetrical white shell each year before mating. This delicate shell serves as an egg case; the argonaut can drop it at will. The female may reach

Pearls: The Organic Gem

Certain species of saltwater oysters, saltwater and freshwater mussels, clams, and abalones produce pearls—undoubtedly the most glamorous products yielded by mollusks. Pearls are derived from the secretions of the mantle that envelops the mollusk's body. These secretions are the same lustrous substance—mother-of-pearl, or nacre—that lines the inner surface of the mollusk's shell. Pearls hold the distinction of being the only gem produced by animals.

How a pearl is produced. When a foreign body, such as a grain of sand, an undeveloped egg, or a parasite, finds a lodging place between the mantle and the shell, it serves as an irritant, and greatly stimulates the mollusk to produce secretions of nacre at that point. As the grain or egg or parasite is slowly encased in the nacreous coating, it may be rolled about by slight contractions of the mantle. It thus remains free from the shell and takes on a rounded form. In time, the little spherical object will be enclosed in many layers of nacre until it becomes a full-fledged pearl. By far the greatest number of pearls used in commerce are

Few things delight a diver more than opening an oyster and finding a pearl—the only gem created by an animal

produced by the so-called pearl oysters, belonging to the genus *Pinctada*.

Perfectly formed spherical pearls are few and far between. In many cases, such pearls originate when parasitic worms form cysts in the mantle layer. As the cysts are more or less rounded in form, they make ideal development centers.

The majority of pearls, called *baroque pearls*, are generally irregular in form. They may be pear-shaped, dome-shaped, or rather flat. Baroque pearls are often made into pendants, brooches, and rings. Baroque pearls are not nearly so valuable as the spherical varieties.

Pearls are of many different colors, including white, cream, rose, brown, blue, yellow, green, and black. The color depends on the oyster's diet and the temperature of the water, among other factors. The most-sought-after colors for pearls are white, cream, rose, steel blue, and black.

The matching of pearls has much to do with their commercial value. When large pearls of the same size and shape are matched to form a necklace, they bring a far

a length of 8 inches (20 centimeters); the male is much smaller—only about 1 inch (2.5 centimeters) long—and never secretes a shell.

CLAMS AND OTHER BIVALVES

Clams, oysters, mussels, and teredos belong to the class Bivalvia, or Lamellibranchia. They are called *bivalves* because their shells are divided into two parts, or *valves*. The inner surface of the shell is coated with a substance called *nacre*, or *mother-of-pearl*. This fine-grained layer may be white or may be as multi-hued as a rainbow.

The two valves are joined by one or two muscles strong enough to hold the shell tightly closed; it is these muscles that are cut when a mussel or clam is opened. Some bivalves, such as clams, have a well-developed foot, which the animal extends beyond the shell to move from place to place. As adults, true oysters cannot move about; instead, they remain firmly attached to solid objects on the bottom of the sea. Bivalves lack a specially differentiated head.

Some bivalves have two tubes, or *siphons*, through which water is drawn in and forced out. The incoming water contains tiny organisms that serve as food: protozoans, eggs, larvae, the

higher price than if the individual pearls were sold separately. Necklaces made up of pearls that are matched in a perfectly graded series—smaller to larger to smaller—are also considered valuable.

Pearl fisheries are found in various parts of the world. The most-valuable pearls come from the pearl oysters that grow in the waters of the Persian Gulf and the Red Sea and off the coasts of India, Australia, certain South Pacific islands, and Central America.

Pearl collecting is an uncertain business at best. For instance, a week's catch of 35,000 pearl oysters might yield only 21 pearls, of which only three are suitable for commercial use. Pearl collecting is frequently carried on in conjunction with the more dependable business of collecting mollusk shells and preparing them for market. In some areas, diving for pearls is conducted with much showmanship for the entertainment of tourists.

Pearls come in a variety of colors, including rose, blue, and yellow; jewelers tend to prefer white and black.

Cultured pearls. Humans have succeeded in "growing" pearls by deliberately inserting a foreign substance within the shell of an oyster or mussel. A pearl produced in this way is called a *cultured pearl*. It is very different in origin from the artificial pearl created by the chemist and used in costume jewelry.

Chinese Buddhists were pioneers in the production of cultured pearls. Between the shell and mantle of marine clams, they inserted small plates bearing the image of Buddha. These plates gradually became coated with nacre. They were sold as souvenirs and also as objects of religious veneration. This practice continues today.

It was not until the 1890s that the Japanese succeeded in producing spherical cultured pearls on a commercial scale; they now almost entirely monopolize the cultured-pearl industry. Typically, a mother-of-pearl bead is carefully inserted in the mantle of a pearl oyster, which proceeds to cover the bead with a thin coating of nacre. The original bead inserted in the oyster makes up most of the finished product. The nacre coating is generally only about 0.04 inch (1 millimeter) thick. The longer the pearl is permitted to develop, the thicker the coating—and the thicker the coating of nacre, the more valuable the pearl.

spores of algae, and minute plants called diatoms. Food is taken into the digestive canal by way of a mouth opening. Oxygen enters the blood through the two gills. Wastes are eliminated with the outgoing water.

Oysters

The true, or edible, oysters (genus *Ostrea*) lead sedentary lives attached to an underwater object. The shell is quite asymmetrical. The valve that is fastened to a submerged object is large and quite thick; the other one is smaller and thinner. The two parts of the shell are closed by a single muscle, popularly called the "heart," which extends from about the center of one valve through the animal's body to the other valve. True oysters occur in many parts of the world, but especially along the coasts of Europe, North America, and Japan.

When the first European settlers came to North America, they found that Indian tribes along the coast depended on oysters for a considerable part of their diet. Evidently they had been eating these mollusks for generations, because large piles of oyster shells had collected around Indian towns and encampments. The first settlers and those who followed picked and dredged oysters from the shallow bays. It was long thought that the supply was inexhaustible.

Increasing demand, however, led to overfishing in the late 19th century. It soon became necessary to supplement the natural supply by planting barren areas with young oysters, thus starting new beds. Today a considerable portion of the oyster supply in North America comes from privately owned beds. Oysters are also raised in Japan and in various European countries, particularly France and the Netherlands.

Successful oyster cultivation requires a familiarity with the life cycle of these shellfish. The female of a typical species, such as *Ostrea virginica*, an oyster found along the eastern coast of North America, produces millions of eggs each year. The eggs are discharged into the water, where many are fertilized by sperm cells ejected by the males. A fertilized egg develops into a tiny larva, which swims about freely for a few days and then begins to develop a shell. Within a week, the creature is entirely enclosed. It drops to the bottom, where it becomes attached to a rock or other solid object. The *spat*, as the young oyster is called, grows rapidly and in time becomes a mature oyster.

Despite the vast numbers of eggs produced by female oysters, the oyster population is not constantly on the increase. Many of the eggs are not fertilized; vast numbers of the little larvae are eaten by fish during their brief period of swimming. Even after they drop to the bottom and become securely attached, the oyster larvae are by no means safe. They may be suffocated by shifting sand and mud, or devoured by starfish, drumfish, or other natural enemies. And then, of course, once oysters reach the adult stage, they are sacrificed by the millions to meet the demands of the market.

During the breeding season, oyster cultivators locate places where the surface of the sea is covered with oyster larvae. The cultivators pave the seafloor of such places with various hard materials, such as old bricks, tile, empty bivalve shells, brush, and discarded metal parts. When the spat drops to the bottom, it becomes attached to the paving materials. These materials are then dredged up and planted in spots that have been selected as favorable for the development of oyster beds.

Oysters are often planted in moderately shallow water with hard-mud seafloors. In such places, there are likely to be marine plants, which will provide food for the microscopic organisms upon which oysters feed. Oyster cultivators avoid places where there is shifting mud and sand, or where starfish or other natural ene-

Zeroing in on Zebra Mussels

Alien species have been invading the Great Lakes since the 1830s, when canals around Niagara Falls made it possible for alewives and sea lampreys to swim upstream from the Atlantic Ocean. More recently, with the proliferation of shipping in the Great Lakes and the St. Lawrence Seaway, another wave of invaders have hitched rides in the ballast tanks of transoceanic ships.

Two of the most tenacious invaders are the zebra mussel *(Dreissena polymorpha)* and its close relative, the quagga mussel *(Dreissena bugensis)*. These small zebra mussels, found throughout Europe, were first discovered in the Great Lakes in 1988. They were discharged into Lake St. Clair, probably by an ocean vessel. By 2007, zebra mussels had spread to such rivers as the Arkansas, Hudson, Mississippi, Ohio, and Tennessee and had been reported in 24 states.

The quagga mussel, indigenous to the Dneiper River drainage of Ukraine, was first sighted in the Great Lakes in 1989. It later was distributed to all of the Great Lakes, Saginaw Bay, and throughout the St. Lawrence River north to Quebec City. In 2007, quagga mussels were found in Lake Mead, near Boulder City, Nevada, and Lake Havasu and Lake Mohave, along the California-Nevada border.

The zebra mussel's rapid colonization of North American waters can be attributed, in part, to its reproductive cycle. Both zebra and quagga mussels are prolific breeders. A mature female mussel can produce up to 1 million eggs per year. The eggs hatch into tiny free-swimming larvae known as veligers, which spend their first three to four weeks swimming about in search of firm objects to grasp onto. Once attached to an object, the veligers develop shells and grow.

Unlike the zebra mussel, which can adapt to temperature extremes and a range of water types, the quagga mussel seems to prefer the deep, cool waters of the Great Lakes. This may explain why the quagga mussel has not been found in large numbers outside the Great Lakes region.

Both zebra and quagga mussels form dense, layered colonies on submerged surfaces such as boat hulls, navigational buoys, piers, docks, and water-intake pipes—congregating in large beds. Within a few years of their discovery, they began clogging intake pipes to power plants and factories, forcing expensive cleanup efforts. Their effect on indigenous species is more difficult to determine, but is potentially more destructive. Zebra and quagga mussels feed by filtering microorganisms from the water, removing the food sources for many small fish and other organisms.

The challenge to find environmentally safe means to control the mussels' populations is ongoing. Water users have had to retool their water intake systems or apply chemical treatments.

Jerry Dennis

mies of oysters abound, or where the waters may be subject to pollution.

Oysters that are ready for market are collected in shallow waters by means of oyster tongs—instruments akin to two long-tined rakes, hinged so as to open and close like shears. In deeper waters, the oysters are taken by means of a dredge.

In France, young oysters are removed to partially enclosed "growing" ponds where the tides are admitted through sluices and floodgates. When fully grown, the oysters are fattened in small enclosed ponds called *claires*.

Japanese oyster farms are generally placed in shallow, brackish water. Each farm is enclosed by a bamboo fence or hedge. The young oysters are collected and held on bamboo stakes thrust into the bed. When the oysters are fully grown, the stakes are pulled out and the oysters harvested.

Clams

Many of these bivalves are also eaten by people. One of the most sought after is the soft-shell clam, *Mya arenaria*, so named because of its rather thin and fragile shell. It is found in Europe and along the Atlantic and Pacific coasts of North America. The soft-shell clam is also called the long-necked clam because of the unusual length of its "neck"—actually, two tubular siphons joined together and covered with tough skin.

The soft-shell clam uses its tongue-shaped foot to burrow into mud or sand to a depth of 3 to 4 inches (7.6 to 10 centimeters). The "neck" extends just out of the sand at high tide, as the animal feeds. At low tide, small holes in the mud or sand betray where the clam is buried. It is then a simple matter for a clammer to walk along the beach and dig out the desired amount of the bivalves.

The hard-shell clam, *Venus mercenaria*, differs in various respects from the soft-shell variety. Its thick, solid shell is a rather dirty-white color marked with concentric rings. The inner part of the shell is whitish, turning to purple at the outer edges. In the Americas, this purple section was used by coastal Indians for the money known as wampum. The hard-shell clam is also known as the quahog and as the littleneck clam, since its siphons are much shorter than those of the soft-shell variety.

The hard-shell clam is found in great numbers along North America's Atlantic coast, where it dwells on sandy or muddy seafloors at depths ranging up to 50 feet (15 meters). The creature slowly moves through sand or mud using its large foot. Clammers usually go out in boats to fish for hard-shell clams, gathering them with a rake or dredge. The clams are served raw on the half shell or are used for clam fries and in chowders.

Perhaps the most remarkable member of the clam group is the giant clam, *Tridacna gigas*, found in the coral reefs of the Pacific. This is the largest known of the living bivalves. Its shell may be almost 3 feet (1 meter) long and weigh more than 440 pounds (200 kilograms), with the edible portion accounting for 20 pounds (9 kilograms) or more.

Scallops

The bivalves known as scallops are found in many parts of the world, with a range extending from shallow water to fairly deep water. The shell is fan-shaped, and the valves arched and rounded. Two winglike projections occur at either end of the hinge of the shell. About 20 ridges radiate from the hinge, increasing in width as they extend outward.

Scallops are good swimmers, especially when young. The jets of water they spout as they alternately open and close their shells propel them through the water in a series of jumps.

Several species are highly esteemed as food. One of the most common species is the Atlantic bay scallop, *Aequipecten irradians*, found along the eastern coast of the United States. The only portion of the body considered edible is the single large muscle that in life serves to hold the two valves of the shell together.

Mussels

The marine mussel has a wedge-shaped black or bluish shell. A tuft of threads, called a *byssus*, is secreted by a gland located immediately behind the foot. These threads harden when they come in contact with seawater, causing the animal to be firmly attached to solid objects such as rocks. The byssus can be discarded and a new one secreted. The animal can thus move to new surroundings if unfavorable conditions arise.

The blue or edible mussel known as *Mytilus edulis* is popular in various parts of Europe and the United States. It abounds in Atlantic coastal waters and in the Mediterranean Sea.

Recently the zebra mussel, *Dreissena polymorpha*, commonly a marine mussel, has reproduced at astonishing rates in the fresh waters of the Great Lakes. These prolific mussels have damaged water-supply systems and navigational buoys, and threaten native wildlife in the area (see box on page 237).

Teredos

The teredo, or shipworm, excavates burrows in wood that is submerged in salt water. The two valves of the teredo have fine ridges, much like the teeth of a file. Soon after it hatches from the egg, the teredo begins rasping with its double file at the wood of a pile or ship bottom. As the burrow deepens, it is lined with a pearly coating. In time, the teredo becomes a long, wormlike creature, its tapering body dwarfing the tiny valves, which are at the innermost part of the burrow. Siphons protrude from the opening of the burrow to draw in water and food and force out wastes. When the siphons are drawn in, the hole is closed by means of two plates attached to the rear of the body.

Outwardly, a piece of timber attacked by teredos shows only a number of small holes. Inwardly, it may be honeycombed with teredo burrows, sometimes so close together that the wood between them is as thin as paper. In time, even the most-solid timbers become so burrow-riddled that they collapse. Metal or concrete sheathing protects timber from the attacks of teredos. Heavy impregnation with creosote has also proved effective.

SNAILS AND RELATED FORMS

Snails, slugs, limpets, abalones, and conches are included in the large class of mollusks known as gastropods. These animals have a foot and mantle cavity, like other mollusks. They also have a well-developed head region and generally sport a spirally coiled, one-piece shell.

Snails

Snails are ubiquitous. Some dwell in the ocean, others in the freshwater of rivers, ponds,

Gastropods comprise the largest class of mollusks. Many, like the snail below, have a single external shell with a coiled structure. Some species of gastropods have internal shells.

and lakes. Land snails abound in tropical jungles and in damp temperate regions.

The snail's head bears the mouth opening and one or two pairs of tentacles. The eyes are set upon or at the base of the tentacles. The animal uses its flat foot to creep from place to place. Specialized gland cells of the foot secrete mucus, which lubricates the path over which the snail crawls. This accounts for the slick trail that the animal leaves as it passes over a more or less flat surface. Both the head and foot of a snail can be withdrawn into the shell.

Freshwater snails and land snails have been eaten by people since prehistoric times. Today they are still regarded as delicacies in many countries. The market supply comes largely from snails that are raised in captivity on special farms in southern France, Italy, and

One of the least appealing mollusks is the common slug (above), a slime-covered creature with a voracious appetite for cultivated leaves and flowers.

Spain. About 10,000 snails can be kept in a 100-square-foot (9-square-meter) pen, where they are fed meal, vegetables, and bran.

In many areas, snails are considered pests because they feed voraciously on garden crops. The giant African snail, *Achatina fulica*, has become a particularly serious menace. This creature, a native of East Africa but now found in many other lands, is sometimes more than 6 inches (15 centimeters) long and as big around

as a tennis ball. Its diet is varied, including garden plants, flower petals, decaying tissues, and manure. It is long-lived and fertile and can thrive under the most unfavorable conditions.

Whelks and *periwinkles* are marine snails commonly used as food by Europeans. The whelk is widely distributed in the North Atlantic. Besides serving as food, it is used as bait in cod fishing. Periwinkles are found in temperate and cold seas in many areas. They abound on rocks and in seaweed, on which they feed. The long tongue, or radula, of the periwinkle is a remarkable structure equipped with many rows of sharp, curved teeth.

The rasping radula of the snail known as the oyster drill, *Urosalpinx cinerea*, is particularly well developed. This tiny creature, less than 1 inch (2.5 centimeters) long, drills a hole through the shell of an oyster near the hinge and then sucks out the soft body of the victim through the hole. The oyster drill is one of the chief foes of those who cultivate or fish for oysters.

Slugs

Among the snails' kin are the curious animals called slugs. These mollusks, which range in length from 1 to 4 inches (2.5 to 10 centimeters), have no external shell. Land slugs live in moist places, often under stones and in holes in the ground. At night, they emerge from their retreats to feed on plants, sometimes in a nearby vegetable garden. Sea slugs crawl on rocks or seaweed in shallow water along the coasts of North America, Europe, and Asia; they also feed on plant matter.

Limpets

The limpet has a rounded or oval shell that looks like a diminutive volcanic cone. Some limpets even have a small opening at the top of the shell, suggesting a crater! Thanks to their suckerlike foot, limpets adhere well enough to rocks near the low-water mark that they can withstand the beating of the surf. At high tide, they move about in search of the algae on which they feed. After their feeding forays, they again

Scaphopods, commonly called tooth or tusk shells, constitute a class of mollusks characterized by long, tubelike shells (right) open at both ends. Polyplacophorans, better known as chitons, have flat oval bodies covered by eight overlapping shell plates (lower right).

attach themselves to the rocks. Limpets are found in many parts of the world.

Abalones

The shell of the abalone has a rather startling resemblance to a human ear, leading to this gastropod's nickname of *ear shell*. The large shell is very ornamental, particularly after the rough outer surface has been polished. Abalones are found in the Far East and on the Atlantic and Pacific coasts of the Americas. They live on rocks near the shore, feeding on seaweed. When disturbed, they cling with surprising tenacity to rocky surfaces. The flesh is often used in stews and chowders, or is prepared in the form of a steak; in the Far East, it is generally dried or smoked.

Conches

The conch is a large gastropod especially common along the coasts of the southern United States and the West Indies. The shell—sometimes 10 inches (25 centimeters) long and weighing as much as 5.5 pounds (2.5 kilograms)—has a small spire with a large lower whorl. The foot of the conch is equipped with a clawlike appendage. The animal moves in a series of leaps, sometimes turning quickly to avoid capture. Conch shells are often made into horns, cameos, and buttons. The flesh is a popular food, particularly in chowders.

TOOTH SHELLS AND CHITONS

The mollusk class of the scaphopods, or tooth shells, is a small one, numbering only about 200 species. In most species, the long, curved, tapering, ivory-colored shell looks something like a boar's tusk. In some varieties—those known as elephant-tusk shells—the shell is not curved. Tooth shells generally live in fairly deep coastal waters.

The chitons and their kin make up the class Polyplacophora. They are found everywhere except in the polar regions. Most chitons have a shell consisting of eight overlapping plates.

Neopilina is the sole surviving genus of the class Monoplacophora. Its shell is caplike, and its body shows segmentation, a primitive feature relating mollusks to the segmented worms.

ECONOMIC IMPORTANCE

The mollusks are useful to humanity in a number of ways. Mollusk shells, for example, have many human applications. The beautiful shells of abalones, conches, and other varieties are commonly sold as souvenirs. The mother-of-pearl inner layer of various shells is used for pearl inlays and knife handles and in hundreds of other ways. Tons of bivalve and other mollusk shells are ground up every year and used as material for surfacing roads. Because of their lime content, the ground-up shells are used as fertilizer and are also fed to domesticated birds, such as chickens. Certain mollusks also produce pearls (see the box on pages 234–35).

THE SEGMENTED WORMS

by F. L. Fitzpatrick

The term "worm" conjures up different images to different people. A doctor hearing that term might think of tapeworm or hookworm infestation. A veterinarian worries about heartworm. A young fisherman dreams about night crawlers. Others imagine caterpillars or maggots. The truly squeamish simply shut their eyes and squeal!

Most of this confusion can be eliminated by simply placing the word "segmented" in front of "worm." Then the mental image gradually focuses in on the earthworm, its grooved body clearly divided into more than 100 segments. Further investigation reveals that earthworms are just one type of annelid, a group of animals that includes more than 7,000 species.

ANNELID CHARACTERISTICS

The segmented worms are slender, generally cylinder-shaped creatures. They have a complete digestive tract: a mouth at one end, an anus at the other. Most species are equipped with *setae*—short, bristlelike hairs that extend from the body wall and function in locomotion. Setae also help the creature cling tenaciously to whatever surface it is on. In the case of the earthworm, setae help it hold on to the walls of its burrow, making it difficult for a robin to pull the worm out of the soil.

TYPES OF ANNELIDS

Technically, segmented worms comprise Annelida, a phylum whose scientific name is

Earthworms, like all annelids, have bodies comprised of a great many segments, each of which is delineated by a groove that extends around the body.

derived from the Latin word *anellus*—"small ring"—a reference to the conspicuously segmented bodies of the group's members.

Annelids are divided into three main classes: the oligochaeta, which include the earthworms; the hirundinea, which include the leeches; and the polychaeta, or bristle worms.

Earthworms and Kin

Being the class that includes earthworms, the oligochaeta, or "few-bristled worms," are certainly the most-familiar annelids. They come in a variety of colors, including brown, purple, blue, green, and a nondescript pallid color. The body of the common earthworm (genus *Lumbricus*) is divided into dozens of segments, each delineated by grooves extending around the body. Each segment, except the first and the last, bears setae, which are controlled by muscles within the body wall.

An earthworm's body is covered by a thin, transparent membrane called the *cuticle*, which is secreted by the skin layer just beneath it. Further glandular secretions keep the cuticle moist at all times. It is through this membrane that an earthworm breathes.

The hundreds of different earthworm species are distributed all over the world—except in localities that are very cold or very dry. Earthworms come in an almost infinite variety of lengths. Some are very small—barely visible to the naked eye. Others, such as the giant earthworm (*Megaseolides australis*) of Australia, are imposing animals 7 feet (2 meters) or more in length—so long, in fact, that they are sometimes mistaken for snakes!

The common earthworm is exceedingly valuable to humans, a quality eloquently expressed by the English naturalist Charles Darwin in his work *Formation of Vegetable Mould Through the Action of Worms,* published in 1881. "The plough," Darwin observed, "is one of the most ancient and most valuable of man's inventions, but long before he existed the land was, in fact, regularly plowed and still continues to be thus plowed by earthworms." Darwin noted that a certain field had once been covered with stones, stones that had entirely disappeared over the course of 30 years. They had been, as it turned out, completely covered by the castings, or wastes, of earthworms.

Earthworms literally eat their way through the soil, obtaining nourishment from the organic matter contained in it. But their most important activity, interestingly enough, is also perhaps their most inelegant: they bring their waste products to the surface. It is through this process that earthworms turn over the soil. It has been estimated that more than 40,000 worms may be found in just 1 acre (0.4 hectare) of land. The earthworm population in black loam will bring a 1-inch (2.5-centimeter) layer to the surface, on the average, in a span of about 4.5 years. The worm burrows help make soil porous and enable rainwater to penetrate it.

During and following heavy rains, large numbers of earthworms are often seen crawling about on the surface of the ground. This occurs because the rainwater has literally flooded the creatures out of their burrows. People looking for fishing bait venture out on rainy nights in order to collect some of the larger worms, which are called night crawlers.

Earthworms serve as food for other animals, most notably birds and mammals (including people). Some scientists think that earthworms have the potential to do harm by spreading disease. If the worms have previously burrowed through the decaying bodies of deceased animals, for instance, they may transmit diseases to domestic animals that feed upon them. Some earthworms contain the young of parasitic roundworms that live as adults in domestic poultry.

Certain popular beliefs about earthworms are either entirely erroneous or only partially true. For example, some people maintain that the worms turn into fireflies—an absurd notion, based perhaps on the fact that the firefly (a beetle) passes through a wormlike larval stage.

Another belief, which is only partly true, holds that if an earthworm is cut in two, both parts will continue to live and ultimately develop new segments to replace those that have been lost. It is true that the head part of an earthworm that has been cut in two often continues to live and may add, or regenerate, tail segments over time. If the cut has been made too near the tail, however, the tail part never succeeds in redeveloping the important internal organs in the for-

The anatomy of the earthworm is typical of that of most ground-dwelling annelids. The drawings below show the external features of the earthworm (A) and organs of its various bodily systems (B, side view, and C, cross section).

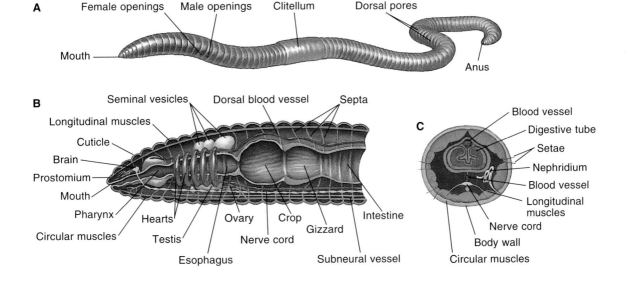

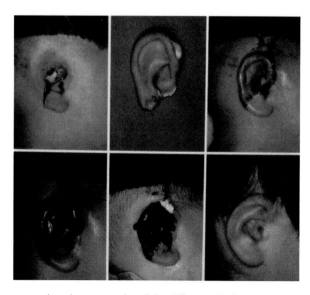

Leeches can make all the difference in the success of an ear-reattachment operation. Used postoperatively, leeches help maintain blood circulation to the area until crucial veins that nourish the ear have time to reconnect.

ward part of the body. It dies after a relatively short period of time.

Earthworms reproduce hermaphroditically—that is, each worm has both male and female sex organs. When copulating, paired earthworms exchange sperm. The eggs develop in cocoons for about two or three months. Earthworms may live more than 10 years.

Leeches

Leeches resemble worms in having segmented bodies, but there most similarities end. With the exception of just one species, leeches lack setae; instead, they are equipped with suckers. All species have a sucker at the rear end of the body; many have a second sucker surrounding the mouth at the head end. Some species are found in the sea, some in freshwater, and some on land. Most are parasitic.

A parasitic leech attaches itself to a host by means of its suckers. Once this is accomplished, the creature makes an incision in the host's skin and gorges itself with blood. Then it drops off. Leeches also use their suckers for locomotion— they make looping movements over solid surfaces. In the water, they swim along with undulating movements. Some nonparasitic forms feed on small forms of life that live in the water.

During medieval times and for several centuries thereafter, bloodsucking leeches were used by physicians to draw blood from patients. Then, for some time, the practice was largely, although not entirely, abandoned. In recent years, though, the status of leech therapy has risen somewhat, thanks largely to the valuable substances that occur only in leech saliva.

Most people nonetheless find leeches disgusting. In temperate regions of the world, these creatures annoy people who swim in rivers and lakes, even though leeches rarely cause any real harm to humans. Sometimes they get into the throat and nasal passages of certain forms of wildlife and cause fatal injuries.

Certain species, such as *Limnotis nilotica* in southern Europe, live in springs or wells. When a person or animal drinks from these sources, the possibility of ingesting leeches along with the water is high. Should a leech attach itself to the walls of the nasal passages, it can obstruct respiration and cause hemorrhages.

Bloodsucking land leeches, found in great numbers in tropical rain forests, may also enter the nostrils, which they block until they have had their fill of blood. It becomes a very dire matter should the leeches enter the sinuses, because once they become engorged with blood, exit becomes impossible.

Worms have a high protein content; in some places, they are considered delicacies. Nevertheless, few Americans would select an annelid topping for their pasta.

Earthworms and Composting

For many years, farmers and gardeners have recognized that earthworms perform important functions in the soil. Earthworms churn up and aerate the soil with their burrows, allowing easier penetration of water and fertilizers, and enrich it with their castings (waste products). Aided by bacteria, earthworms—particularly the type called red worms—can quickly convert many waste materials such as manure and organic garbage into fertile compost. The "compost heap" behind many barns and in backyard gardens has long been a source of rich soil.

Indoor gardeners can also put worms to work in making compost out of such household wastes as vegetable and fruit peelings, eggshells, and coffee grounds. With a relatively small container filled with damp bedding material (such as shredded newspaper and sphagnum moss) and a few thousand earthworms (available through mail-order catalogs), it is possible to reduce household waste and produce a steady supply of fertile compost for outdoor vegetable gardens, houseplants, and patio containers of flowers and vegetables. Such composting can be done indoors, even in schools and offices.

Many families make a project out of setting up a worm composting bin. The worms help transform kitchen garbage into rich new soil called compost.

With approximately 2,000 red worms, 1 pound (0.5 kilogram) of food waste per day can be converted into compost. These small worms—*Eisenia foetida* and *Lumbricus rubellus*, the species of earthworms most often found in leaf piles, compost heaps, and aged manure—will reproduce in this artificial habitat, reaching a population that remains in balance with available food.

Jerry Dennis

Bristle Worms

Among the most interesting of the annelids are those living in the sea. Some of them, such as the clam worms (genus *Nereis*), are free-swimming animals that prey on other marine creatures. Certain marine forms have beautifully colored gills—large, plumelike projections on the head or sides of the body. The curious-looking sea mouse (*Aphrodite*) has an oval body covered on top with a thick mat of long, silky, iridescent, hairlike setae.

Several of the marine annelid families are well-known tube builders. Some line the burrows in which they live with a thin, limelike secretion. Others build tubes in the sand. The parchment worm (*Chaetopterus*) constructs a parchmentlike, U-shaped tube that is buried in the sandy mud with only the openings jutting above the surface. The appendages of the middle segments of this worm are combined to form three pairs of circular fans that draw water in through one opening of the tube and force it out through the other. The numerous tiny organisms carried into the tube by this water current serve as food for the worm.

The Samoan palolo worm, *Eunice viridis*, found in the South Pacific, is famous for its breeding habits. During most of the year, the worm lies coiled up in its burrow, generally in a coral reef. As time goes on, eggs or spermatozoa develop in the hind-end segments of the animal. In the last quarter of the October-November moon, the hind ends of the palolo worms are cast off. They make their way to the surface of the sea in swarms, and the eggs and spermatozoa are then discharged into the water. The local people collect the worms and use them as food. A related species, the Atlantic palolo worm, *Eunice fucata*, of the West Indies, breeds similarly in the third quarter of the June-July moon.

Arthropods

by Kathy Svitil

Crabs, lobsters, spiders, insects, centipedes, and millipedes—these creatures all belong to the phylum Arthropoda, the most successful group of animals on Earth. Indeed, arthropods far outnumber all other types of animals combined, with an estimated 1 million species. Insects alone number more than 900,000 species, accounting for some 80 percent of all animals on Earth. Scientists predict that nearly as many await discovery.

The arthropods, or "joint-footed" animals, also fill every imaginable environment, from the deepest ocean trenches to the highest mountain peaks, from the frozen wasteland of Antarctica to the broiling Mojave Desert in the western United States. Arthropods such as mites and lice flourish on the bodies of almost every kind of animal on Earth.

A BASIC BODY PLAN

Despite their vast number and varied existence, all arthropods share certain characteristics. The most important may be their stiff covering, or *exoskeleton*. This development set the first arthropods apart from their soft-bodied ancestors, and may be what allowed some early arthropods to crawl out of the water without drying out in the open air or sagging under their own weight. Thanks to their exoskeletons, arthropods became the world's first land animals some 300 million years ago.

This all-important exoskeleton is secreted by the outer layer of the arthropod's three-layer skin. The outer coating is a waxy protein. The middle horny layer and an inner flexible one are made of *chitin*, a tough polysaccharide, or complex sugar. The union of these three layers creates a tough covering that protects the arthropod's soft body like a suit of armor. For added protection, the exoskeleton of ocean-dwelling arthropods (the crustaceans) is strengthened by the addition of the mineral calcium carbonate. The result is a rock-hard outer shell, familiar to anyone who has ever cracked open a lobster or crab leg.

The arthropod's exoskeleton conveys still another great advantage: its inner surface provides an anchoring place for muscles. This enables the complex movements that power the arthropod's many jointed appendages.

All arthropods have an exoskeleton, and every arthropod—including the dragonfly above—periodically sheds and discards its old exoskeleton for a new, better-fitting one.

For all of its wonders, the arthropod's exoskeleton comes with one rather serious drawback: it does not stretch or expand. Arthropods must therefore periodically replace their shells as they grow or change shape. They do this through a process called *molting*. When it molts, the arthropod literally bursts its old shell at the seams and backs out of it. This reveals a new, better-fitting exoskeleton that must then thicken and harden. No doubt this process requires a lot of energy. In addition, molting leaves the arthropod temporarily soft and vulnerable, until its new covering hardens.

All species of arthropods also share a basic body plan. Their bodies are segmented, or divided into distinct parts. The exact number of these segments varies from species to species; the segments tend to be fused together in groups to create distinct body regions such as head, thorax, and abdomen.

Arthropods have a large number of segmented appendages, or limbs; a pair of each can arise from each body segment. Evolution has fashioned these appendages into a brilliant array of forms. In addition to walking legs, arthropod appendages include antennae, mandibles (mouthparts), claws, swimming paddles, wings, and reproductive structures.

A typical arthropod has a simple brain, an amazing set of sense organs, and a nervous system that connects the two. Colorless blood flows through the

Arthropods constitute about 75 percent of all animal species. Representative arthropods include, from top to bottom: the shorthorned grasshopper (an insect); swimming crab (a crustacean); jumping spider (an arachnid); and centipede (a chilopod).

arthropod's body to nourish these as well as the other organ systems. In the simplest arthropod species, this fluid simply squishes to and fro. Larger crustaceans such as lobsters and crabs have a true heart and a few simple blood vessels.

Like all animals, arthropods need oxygen to survive. Some small arthropods simply absorb oxygen through their thin body coverings. Larger aquatic species breathe through feathery, fishlike gills. Insects and some other land arthropods breathe through a system of tiny body tubes called *tracheae*. Others, such as spiders and scorpions, breathe through "book lungs"—air-filled cavities that contain thin tissues resembling the pages of a book. Both tracheae and book lungs are unique to the arthropods.

Typically, arthropods have reproductive systems that are either distinctly male or female, and therefore reproduce sexually. Exceptions include the barnacles, many of which have both male and female parts in each individual.

GROUPS OF ARTHROPODS

The arthropods are often classified, or divided, into four distinct groups, or subphyla. They are Chelicerata, Crustacea, Uniramia, and Trilobita. These subphyla in turn are divided into several classes. The largest of these classes are the crustaceans (within Crustacea), the insects (within Uniramia), and the arachnids (within Chelicerata). Within these classes are an almost infinite number of species. The members of Trilobita, the trilobites, are all extinct.

The Chelicerates

The chelicerates include horseshoe crabs, sea spiders, and the arachnids. The most familiar arachnids are the spiders, scorpions, and ticks. All these animals share a common body plan. The head and mid-body are fused together to form the cephalothorax. Behind it is a distinct abdomen, which has a tail-like appearance in many species.

Unlike other arthropods, cheliceratids lack antennae and jaws. Instead, the first pair of appendages is a pair of pincers, or fangs, called *chelicerae*. Behind these are five more pairs of appendages: a set of touching organs called *pedipalps* and four pairs of walking legs.

The most abundant and familiar chelicerates are the arachnids, a class of 30,000 species that includes spiders, scorpions, mites, ticks, and daddy longlegs. In spiders, the sharp chelicerae connect to a pair of poison glands used to subdue prey and ward off attackers. Spiders also bear a set of special abdominal limbs that they use to spin silk.

Horseshoe crabs are unique among the chelicerates. The last surviving members of the class Merostomata, they appear much as they did 400 million years ago. The horseshoe crab's body is divided into three parts. The *prosoma*, or head, bears chelicerae and five pairs of walking legs. The trunk bears breathing appendages called *opisthosoma*. Last comes the horseshoe crab's unique spikelike tail, or *telson*. There are as few as five species alive today.

Sea spiders also evolved from an ancient class. Their bodies are divided into a head, a cylinder-shaped thorax with legs, and a small abdomen. The 600 species of sea spiders that still exist today are especially common in cold, polar waters, although they occur in all seas except the Caspian. Some live an astonishing 21,500 feet (6,550 meters) beneath the surface!

The Crustaceans

Crustaceans are found primarily in water. Unlike the two-part body of the chelicerate, the crustacean body is divided into three parts: head, thorax, and a tail-like abdomen. Covering the entire body is a "crusty" exoskeleton reinforced with calcium extracted from the water. The body appendages of the crustacean are jointed and branched. This can be seen best in the large claws of lobsters and crabs. When one of these appendages is damaged or lost, the crustacean has the remarkable ability to simply grow a replacement.

Instead of pincers, or chelicerae, the crustacean's mouth is equipped with three pairs of mandibles. These jawlike appendages move side to side, like a pair of tongs, rather than up and down as do human jaws. As an adult, the crustacean also sports two pairs of antennae in front of the mouth. These antennae serve as sense organs for touching, tasting, smelling, and sometimes hearing. The crustacean's eyes are compound, which means that each one contains many small lenses.

Crustaceans make up an extremely large class. With more than 25,000 species, they rival the arachnids in abundance. Aquatic forms include lobsters, crabs, and shrimp, as well as the many tiny species that make up oceanic plankton. Terrestrial crustaceans include the land crabs as well as the pill bugs, or sow bugs, found in damp basements and gardens.

The Uniramia

The Uniramia take their name from the Latin word for "unbranched," which refers to the fact that their appendages—legs, antennae, and the like—are not branched and jointed as are those of other arthropods. This group includes five classes of animals: insects, centipedes, millipedes, symphylids, and pauropods; the latter four are collectively known as myriapods, or "many-legged" animals. All have well-formed heads and long, flexible bodies, typically with 30 or more legs. All live on land, usually in damp, dark places such as the underside of rocks and logs.

By far the single largest group of arthropods is class Insecta, with an estimated 700,000 to 1 million species. Adult insects have one pair of antennae, one set of mandibles, and two compound eyes. Their compound eyes are often so large as to cover most of the head. These enormous structures often are accompanied by a pair of simple eyes called *ocelli*.

The insect thorax has just three segments, each bearing a pair of legs. (Most other arthropods have four pairs.) In addition, most insects bear one or two pairs of wings—making them the only flying arthropods. The insect's abdomen is devoid of limbs, but can bear a structure such as a stinger on the tip.

Despite this common body plan, insects are found in a bewildering array of forms, from the primitive silverfish to the sophisticated bees and butterflies. Like some crustaceans, most insects undergo metamorphosis. That is, they pass through one or more complete body changes as they mature from larva to adult. The classic example of metamorphosis is the caterpillar that changes into a butterfly or moth.

The horseshoe crab is a primitive arthropod more closely related to the spider than to the true crab. Fossils of horseshoe crabs date back some 545 million years.

The Trilobites

We know the fascinating trilobites only by their abundant fossils. They appear to have evolved in the early Cambrian period, some 545 million years ago. During their heyday, trilobites dominated the world's oceans. Some were as long as 18 inches (45 centimeters) and may have weighed 10 pounds (4.5 kilograms). Their bodies were divided into three side-to-side lobes as well as a head, a thorax, and a tail region (pygidium). They swam and crawled with an abundance of jointed appendages. Although successful for many centuries, the trilobites had entirely vanished by the Jurassic period, some 250 million years ago. Their extinction remains one of the great mysteries of paleontology.

ARTHROPOD EVOLUTION

Many biologists suspect that the arthropods evolved from the annelids, a phylum of segmented worms that includes the familiar earthworm. From their ancient annelid ancestor, the early arthropods inherited the segmented body plan that all arthropods share today. Some annelids also bear pairs of appendages on each of their segments, a trait shared by adult arthropods. And like annelids, arthropods are bilaterally symmetrical. That is, their right and left halves are mirror images of each other.

Fossils of these first arthropods can be found in rock dating to the Cambrian period, which began 545 million years ago. They included trilobites, horseshoe crabs, and crustaceans. Centipedes, millipedes, and scorpions were among the first arthropods to reach dry land. They appear in the fossil record about 450 million years ago. The insects arrived later, about 350 million years ago.

If sheer numbers be the judge, arthropods are by far the most successful group of animals ever to swim, fly, or crawl across the face of Earth. The secret to their success? The arthropod's tough, waterproof exoskeleton is no doubt part of the reason. It afforded the early arthropods unprecedented protection from predators. It also enabled the first terrestrial arthropods to survive on dry land without themselves drying out in the process.

Those who study insects, the most successful arthropods of all, also point out the great advantage of each species' specialized diet. This has enabled an abundance of different insect species to evolve and survive in small areas, some no larger than one cubic foot of soil. The insect's short life span and amazing egg-laying capacity also enable it to adapt to environmental changes that would drive other species to extinction.

Whatever the reason for arthropod success, the rest of the Animal Kingdom should no doubt be thankful. Insects form the broad base of the food pyramid on which all land animals depend for nourishment. A similar story occurs in the world's seas, where swarms of tiny crustaceans provide food for larger arthropods, small fish, and gigantic whales.

CRUSTACEANS

More than 500 million years ago—in the warm, murky soup that was the Cambrian sea—there arose a strange class of creatures. They skittered sideways across the ocean floor. They paddled backward through the water. They may, in fact, have been the first creatures ever to skitter or paddle on Earth.

These were the early crustaceans, the direct descendants of the wormlike creatures known as annelids. And they represented a huge leap forward in animal evolution. They not only had legs (an evolutionary first), but their legs had joints (*very* useful)! Moreover, their bodies had distinct parts, or segments, including a head, thorax, and abdomen.

Alongside their close cousins, the ancient trilobites, the first crustaceans filled the Cambrian oceans with life. Both were early members of the important phylum Arthropoda, or arthropods. But over the next 100 million years, the trilobites faltered and disappeared. The crustaceans, meanwhile, exploded with a diversity of new species. Today they are one of the most successful classes of animals on Earth. Indeed, if sheer numbers show success, they are second only to insects. With more than 25,000 species of crustaceans alive today, they easily outnumber all mammals, birds, reptiles, and amphibians combined. They vary in size from the almost-microscopic scuds and copepods to the giant Japanese spider crab, with its eight 12-foot (3.6-meter)-long legs.

The most familiar crustaceans, no doubt, are the many kinds of lobsters, crabs, and shrimp that end up on dinner plates. Together, they make up a crustacean group called the decapods, meaning "10-footed" crustaceans. The class Crustacea also includes the jagged barnacles found on beach rocks, and the water fleas seen popping about the sand at low tide.

In general, crustaceans live in water, although there are exceptions. In fact, many peo-

Perhaps the most familiar crustaceans are the decapods—a group of 10-footed creatures that includes lobsters, shrimp, and crabs in a whole rainbow of colors.

ple would be surprised to learn that they have crustaceans in their basements. The crustacean order Isopoda includes the familiar pill bugs, or sow bugs, that live in damp corners.

In all, there are 10 major orders, or subclasses, of crustaceans alive today. Some, such as the destructive "gribble," are serious pests, destroying millions of dollars' worth of wharves and piers each year. Others, such as the delectable decapods, are the basis for a multibillion-dollar fishing industry.

But the most important crustaceans of all may be the very smallest. Tiny floating crustaceans such as copepods form the bulk of sea plankton—the first link in the ocean food chain. Plankton provides valuable nourishment for larger crustaceans, fish, and other animals, which in turn are eaten by larger predators. Should the copepods disappear tomorrow, all other ocean life would likely follow.

ANATOMY OF A CRUSTACEAN

Hard Bodies

Crustaceans are the oldest surviving members of the phylum Arthropoda, which means "jointed" in Latin. The name *crustacean*, or *Crustacea*, is Latin for "crust." These two names provide a good, basic description of what it means to be a crustacean. True to their name, all crustaceans have an outer covering of a crusty, or shell-like, material called chitin. In some species, such as lobsters and crabs, the chitin over the head and back forms a thick, armorlike shield called a carapace. By contrast, the flexible covering of the water flea is thin enough to be transparent.

Like insects and other arthropods, crustaceans have no bones. Instead, their hard covering acts as an external skeleton, or exoskeleton. The crustacean's tough exoskeleton protects it from enemies. More important, the inside of the exoskeleton serves as a solid anchor for muscle. This may have enabled the first crustaceans to develop sophisticated legs that bend, pull, and push with muscular contraction.

The main drawback to the crustacean's exoskeleton is that it does not expand as the animal grows. The crustacean therefore must periodically molt, or shed, its old shell and grow a new and larger one. As you might expect, young crustaceans must molt frequently as they grow

to adult size. A young blue crab, for example, molts 20 times in 14 months before it stops growing. Other crustaceans, such as lobsters, never stop growing. But after five years, their growth slows to the point where they molt just once a year or less.

Typically, when a crustacean is ready to molt, it develops a crack down its thorax, or midsection. When this split is large enough, the crustacean literally backs out of its old shell. The newly emerged crustacean is not entirely naked. Its flesh already has a new covering, which is still very thin and soft. (This is when crabbers harvest the "soft-shell" blue crab.)

As soon as the crustacean slips out of its old shell, it begins to absorb water into its flesh. This stretches the new covering to provide some growing room before it hardens. Over the next several weeks, the crustacean's soft exoskeleton thickens and stiffens. Until its armor has hardened, the crustacean is very vulnerable to predators. Some species retreat into hiding places for several weeks after each molt.

Crustaceans occasionally lose a leg or claw while molting, or even as a result of an enemy attack. They then simply replace the limb, beginning at the next molt. The new appendage enlarges with each subsequent molt until it is completely restored.

Lots of Limbs

A crustacean's exoskeleton has many joints that give its body flexibility and divide it into distinct segments. Depending on the species, a crustacean may have anywhere from 9 to 60 body segments. Each body segment can produce a pair of segmented limbs, or appendages. Some are jointed legs. Others perform special functions related to feeding, sensing, or reproduction.

Most of a crustacean's sensing and feeding appendages are concentrated on its head. Using an adult lobster as a typical example, the first two pairs of appendages are long, sensitive antennae. Just behind these comes a pair of flexible stalks with eyes at their tips. Next is a set of mandibles, or jaws. Like those of insects, a crustacean's mandibles move from side to side, like a pair of tongs, rather than up and down like the jaws of a bony animal. Behind these are appendages called maxillae, which sweep food into the lobster's mouth.

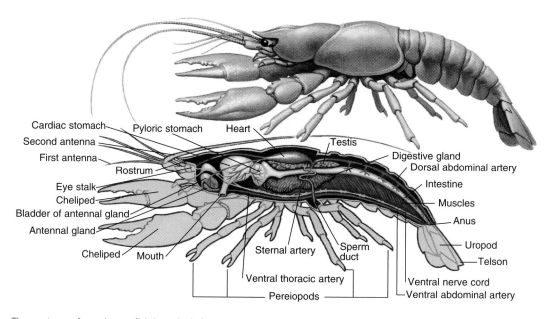

The anatomy of a male crayfish is typical of many crustaceans. The head has two pairs of sensory antennae and a pair of eyes on movable stalks. Appendages include four pairs of walking legs and one pair of claw-bearing chelipeds.

The segments of the lobster's thorax, or midsection, each give rise to a pair of jointed legs. Evolution has fashioned the first pair into claws of unequal size. The lobster uses the larger one for crushing, the smaller for grabbing and tearing. Behind these are the lobster's walking legs, or pereiopods. The first two pairs have small pincers that can snap at prey. The lobster uses its hind pair to clean its abdomen.

The lobster's muscular abdomen, or belly, is what we commonly call its "tail." It has several

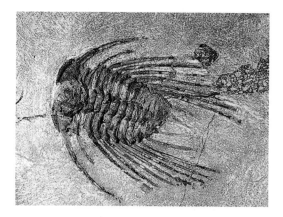

The trilobites are extinct marine arthropods that teemed in the world's oceans for millions of years. By studying fossilized remains, scientists have determined a relationship between trilobites and modern crustaceans.

segments, each with a pair of paddlelike limbs used for slow swimming. When the lobster needs to move fast—say, to escape an enemy—it snaps its powerful abdomen forward beneath its body. This shoots the animal backward through the water with considerable speed and force.

Compare this body plan with that of a very different crustacean: the barnacle. This tiny oval animal glues itself to a hard surface by its head, grows a rock-hard crust around its body, and kicks food into its mouth with six pairs of feathery legs. When stranded above water, barnacles can snap their shells closed, sealing in enough water and food to survive for several weeks. Most barnacles are small, just a fraction of an inch tall. But the shell of the giant Pacific barnacle reaches up to 3 inches (7.6 centimeters) high and 6 inches (15 centimeters) across.

Senses and Nervous System

Crustaceans possess a number of special senses that enable them to react with lightning speed to predators and prey. Like insects, crustaceans have compound eyes, with hundreds to thousands of multisided lenses called *ommatidia*. Each ommatidium is essentially an individual eye. Together, they deliver a mosaic image to the crustacean's brain. This enables the crustacean to see in dim water and detect incredibly small movements.

Crustaceans likewise have keen senses of smell and taste. Tiny hairs sticking out of the exoskeleton react to chemicals in the surrounding water. These hairs are especially abundant on the crustacean's antennae and mouthparts. Crustaceans such as lobsters also have sensory hairs on their feet. Some have the specific job of detecting food. Others are attuned to the chemical trails that lobsters leave in their wake. This enables the creatures to find their way to and from their dens.

Crustaceans can also feel their way in the dark using their long antennae and a variety of movable hairs sensitive to touch. Crustaceans have no ears. But they probably use their touch hairs, which are hollow, to sense sound vibrations around them in the water.

Decapods (lobsters, crabs, and the like) also have special organs for balance. Called statocysts, they are tiny, fluid-filled sacs at the base of the antennae. Projecting from these sacs are tiny hairs lightly coated with grains of sand. Depending on whether the crustacean is upside down or right side up, the grains of sand press

Lobsters are large crustaceans whose tasty white meat is considered a delicacy. In most species, one pair of legs forms two oversized, differently shaped claws.

against different hairs. This sends a signal to the brain, telling it which way is up.

Although the crustacean possesses many keen senses, the nervous system that conveys this information to the brain is very simple. The brain itself is little more than a circle of nerve cells in the creature's head. The brain connects to a large nerve cord that runs through the crustacean's body, from the back of its head to the base of its tail. Smaller nerves connect the crustacean's brain to its eyes, antennae, and statocysts. This simple system enables the crustacean to react automatically to incoming messages such as "danger" or "food."

Circulation

The crustacean's circulation system is also quite simple. Its heart is in its thorax, which is similar to the human chest. Little more than a muscular tube, the heart rhythmically squeezes colorless blood out through six short arteries. The arteries empty into open spaces in various parts of the body. There the blood washes over organs and tissues to deliver oxygen and pick up carbon dioxide and other waste products. The waste products are delivered to a simple bladder that secretes waste from a pore at the base of the animal's antennae.

Blood also pools near the crustacean's gills, where it picks up fresh oxygen and releases carbon dioxide. Finally the blood seeps back to a space surrounding the heart, which pumps it

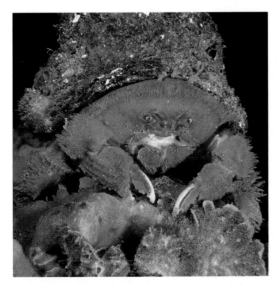

The sponge crab disguises itself by placing a piece of living sponge on its back. Predators, thinking the crab to be just an unappetizing sponge, swim right by.

Crustacean Classification

Scientists have identified more than 25,000 species of crustaceans. Thousands more no doubt await discovery. Taxonomists—scientists who classify living things—differ over the way these species should be grouped. But in general, they recognize the following 10 major orders.

ORDER	FEATURES	EXAMPLES
Anostraca	Stalked eyes, no carapace	Fairy shrimp
Conchostraca	Clamlike shell, fixed eyes	Clam shrimp
Cladocera	Tiny, branched antennae	Water fleas
Ostracoda	Hinged shell, two trunk limbs	Seed shrimp
Copepoda	No carapace, simple eye, swim with antennae	Copepods
Cirripedia	Encased in shell, feathery limbs	Barnacles
Isopoda	Many legs of similar length	Pill bugs, wood lice
Amphipoda	Body flattened side to side with no carapace	Scuds, beach fleas
Stomatopoda	Long forelimbs for grasping prey	Mantis shrimp
Decapoda	Ten legs on thorax	Lobsters, crabs, true shrimp, crayfish

out again. This type of circulation system is called "open" because blood washes freely through the body. By contrast, higher animals such as vertebrates have "closed" circulation systems, in which blood remains within a network of blood vessels and capillaries.

Even simpler is the circulation system of barnacles and the tiny plankton copepods. They have no heart, and instead keep their blood in motion with rhythmic body movements.

Breathing

Like all animals, crustaceans need oxygen to survive. Typically, they get the oxygen they need from the surrounding water through feathery gills, somewhat like those of fish. Lobsters and crabs have many pairs of gills, located beneath the thorax, near the base of the legs. Some crustaceans, such as the mantis shrimp, have gills on their feet. Many of the smallest crustaceans have no gills at all, but simply absorb oxygen through their thin body coverings.

How do land crustaceans breathe? Some, such as land crabs, have developed primitive lungs. Pill bugs and sow bugs breathe through gill-like openings in their legs.

Digestion and Feeding

Most crustaceans eat other animals, although they do not seem to care whether their food is alive or dead. Lobsters, for instance, are great scavengers, eating dead fish as well as worms and other bottom-living creatures. Crabs can be especially fearsome predators, and clams are among their favorite foods. Scientists believe that many of the sea's largest clams developed their thick shells as a defense against crabs. But crabs, in turn, have evolved ever-more-powerful claws to crush the thick shells of their prey.

Some of the tiniest crustaceans filter bacteria, mold, and bits of decaying matter from the water. Some flealike amphipods scrape scum off the leaves and stems of underwater plants. Others, such as the "beach fleas," feed on dead fish in or near the water. On the whole, such "cleanup" duties greatly benefit the environment.

But crustacean feeding habits can also be highly destructive. The mud-eating Thalassina shrimp undermines the foundations of rice paddies in southeast Asia. In the Americas, both land crabs and freshwater crayfish attack tomato and cotton crops. Gribbles and other wood borers destroy millions of dollars' worth of piers and other seaside structures each year. These tiny crustaceans do not actually eat the wood through which they bore. Rather, they feed on the bacteria and algae they find there.

Whatever their food, most crustaceans digest it in the same basic way. Their gut, or digestive system, consists of a simple tube that passes through the body from mouth to anus. Along the tube are pouches with digestive enzymes. The enzymes break the food down into small molecules that can be absorbed by the crustacean's blood.

The digestive system of the most complex crustaceans, the decapods, includes a two-part stomach. The first chamber has a toothlike structure called a gastric mill that grinds food into smaller bits. The smallest bits pass through a sieve of hairs to enter the second stomach chamber with its digestive pouches. There enzymes complete the digestion process, and nutrients pass into the decapod's body. Waste mat-

ter squeezes through the remainder of the tube and exits the anus.

Reproduction and Life Cycles

For most crustaceans, there are two distinct sexes that mate to produce young. Exceptions include the barnacles, which typically produce both eggs and sperm in one individual. This adaptation makes evolutionary sense for barnacles. Being cemented into place as adults, they are unable to move around to find mates. Some shrimp, on the other hand, change sex at midlife. The reason for this is less clear. Still other, very primitive, crustaceans produce eggs that need no fertilization to develop. This is true among some brine shrimp and water fleas.

Other types of crustaceans have dramatic differences between the two sexes. In the parasitic copepods, some males are so much tinier than their mates that they live in special pouches near the female's sex organs. Among decapods, however, the male tends to be much larger than the female. The male lobster, for example, must be large enough to flip his mate onto her back before fertilizing her. Male crabs tend to have very large claws, which they wave to attract the attention of females.

Some crustaceans, such as the lobster, can mate only when the female has shed her hard exoskeleton. Just after molting, a fertile female will release into the water a chemical that attracts nearby males to her den. The first male to arrive becomes her mate—if he is large enough to flip her onto her back. He then transfers a packet of sperm into her body using a pair of specially adapted legs. The male then remains in the female's den, guarding her until her new shell has hardened.

The next time the female lobster molts, she releases her eggs into a pocket on the underside of her abdomen. For the next 10 to 11 months, she keeps her abdomen curled beneath her to protect the developing eggs.

When the young lobsters hatch, they resemble tiny shrimp. Like most crustaceans, lobsters pass through several very different stages before assuming adult form. Lobsters go through three shrimplike stages in their first few weeks, followed by three stages that more and more closely resemble adults. Shrimp go through eight insectlike stages on the way to adulthood. Crabs pass through six.

Most barnacles live on shells, ship bottoms, and other usually submerged objects. They are the only group of crustaceans that exist permanently attached to a surface.

ARACHNIDS

Back in 1933, a gigantic gorilla, *King Kong*, terrified audiences. In 1956, Americans flocked to see *Godzilla, King of the Monsters*. In 1963, the avian world sought revenge against humans in Alfred Hitchcock's *The Birds*. And then there were the *Anaconda* movies, featuring a fearsome 40-foot (12-meter) snake.

By today's standards, these classic films seem altogether tame. Indeed, most of the so-called monster movies released over the past few decades appeal to the audience's sense of humor more than anything else. Perhaps that's why the film *Arachnophobia* received such good reviews upon its release—it successfully exploited a subject that still makes most people squeamish: spiders, the most common type of arachnid.

Spiders, scorpions, ticks, and mites—they are all arachnids, and they give just about everyone the creeps. And yet their bad reputation is not entirely deserved. Unlike most arthropods, arachnids often dote upon their young. Expert engineers, they create fantastic structures out of silk threads. And they eat harmful insects.

UNUSUAL ARTHROPODS

Like insects and crustaceans, arachnids belong to the huge phylum Arthropoda. Like all arthropods, arachnids have segmented bodies encased in an outer shell, or exoskeleton, which they shed and replace as they grow. Yet, in many ways, arachnids differ dramatically from their arthropod cousins. For example, the bodies of most arthropods are made up of three parts: head, thorax, and abdomen. By contrast, the arachnid's head and thorax are fused into one major body part, the *cephalothorax*.

Other arthropods have antennae, but not the arachnids. Instead, they "feel" their surroundings through a cover of sensitive body hairs. Other arthropods grind and chew their food with mandibles. Most arachnids, on the other hand, use fangs to pierce their food, inject

A spider produces silk from special structures called spinnerets. The spider then uses the silk to spin webs, line its burrows, or wrap its eggs in cocoons (above).

liquefying chemicals into it, and then suck the "soup" through a strawlike mouthpart.

Of all its arthropod kin, the extinct trilobite may be the arachnid's closest relative. Its closest living kin is the horseshoe crab, a primitive crustacean. Arachnids seem to have diverged along their own evolutionary line some 400 million years ago, some 50 million years before the first insects appeared.

Despite such curious features—or perhaps because of them—the arachnids are a tremendously successful class of animals. Indeed, the class Arachnida is second only to Insecta in number and diversity. With more than 75,000 species, arachnids can be found in every terrestrial environment from the Great Basin Desert to the frozen peaks of Mount Everest. They range in size from near-microscopic mites to the 7-inch (17.7-centimeter)-long black scorpion of Africa. More than half of all arachnid species are spiders, the most highly evolved and sophisticated order in their class.

ARACHNID ANATOMY

Unlike other arthropods, most of which pass through several life stages, arachnids change little during development, except to grow larger. As mentioned, the arachnid's body is divided into two main parts: the cephalotho-rax, to the front, and, to the rear, the abdomen. In spiders, these two parts are separated by a narrow waist, called a *pedicel*. In other arachnids, cephalothorax and abdomen join along a joint. Typically, a hard shield, or *carapace*, covers the arachnid's back, or upper surface.

Six pairs of appendages grow from the arachnid's cephalothorax. The first is a pair of fanglike feeding organs called *chelicerae*. The arachnid uses them to spear its food, and, in the case of a spider, to deliver a poison sting. Behind the chelicerae is a pair of food-handling limbs called *pedipalps*. The pedipalps of many arachnids take the form of pincers—an adaptation most noticeable among the scorpions. Next come the arachnid's four pairs of walking legs (not three, as in insects).

In spiders, ticks, and mites, the abdomen is short and rounded. In the scorpion-like orders, it is elongated, ending in either a stinger or a whiplike tail.

As mentioned, arachnids have no antennae. Instead, they sense their surroundings with tactile hairs and simple eyes. Long, spinelike bristles on the legs sense motion, including the movement of air currents and the vibration of approaching prey. Shorter, finer hairs, called *setae*, give the arachnid its slightly furry appearance. These hairs are likewise sensitive to touch. Some also detect temperature, humidity levels,

The anatomy of a spider (below), perhaps the most familiar arachnid, includes four pairs of legs and a body divided into two regions, the cephalothorax and the abdomen, separated by a narrow waist called a pedicel (not labeled).

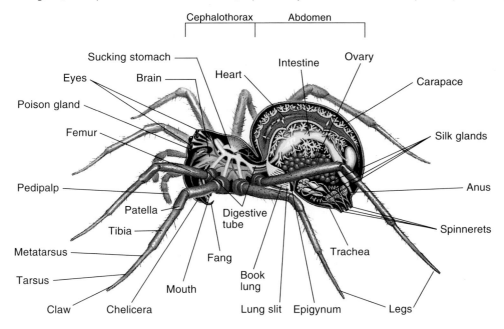

Cephalothorax   Abdomen

Sucking stomach — Intestine — Ovary — Eyes — Brain — Heart — Carapace — Poison gland — Femur — Silk glands — Pedipalp — Anus — Patella — Digestive tube — Tibia — Spinnerets — Metatarsus — Fang — Trachea — Tarsus — Book lung — Claw — Chelicera — Mouth — Lung slit — Epigynum — Legs

Scorpions have adapted to many habitats. A particularly unusual species of water scorpion is found in just a single cave in Romania, where it preys upon a species of equally rare pill bug (above).

the body chemicals of prey, or the pheromones of a fertile mate.

Most arachnids have eight eyes, although some are eyeless. The daddy longlegs has two. As a general rule, one pair of main, or direct, eyes faces forward, and the secondary eyes face sideways. All arachnids are quite myopic, or nearsighted. Only the farsighted jumping spider has the ability to see prey more than a few inches away.

The information from the arachnid's eyes and tactile hairs travels a short distance to its simple brain. The arachnid brain is more or less a circle of nerves, or *ganglia*. The ganglia to the back of this circle are notably larger in spiders that weave particularly intricate webs.

Digestion in most arachnids occurs outside the body. After piercing its prey, the arachnid regurgitates digestive juices that turn the victim's tissues to broth. The arachnid then sucks the liquid through a strawlike tube in front

Spiders have evolved clever ways of catching prey. The trap-door spider (right), waiting to ambush its next victim, peeks from beneath the camouflaged lid of its burrow.

of its mouth. It flows into a simple gut that can expand to fill the arachnid's entire abdomen.

Arachnids breathe in a variety of ways. Some of the tiniest species simply absorb oxygen through the surface of their thin bodies. Ticks, mites, and daddy longlegs breathe through simple tubes, called *tracheae*, in their exoskeleton. Scorpions breathe through *book lungs*—thin tissues stacked like pages in a book, with air spaces between. Most spiders use both book lungs and tracheae to breathe.

Near the arachnid's gut is a tube-shaped heart with a number of openings, called *ostia*, and two short arteries. Each time the heart contracts, the ostia close, and colorless blood squirts out through the arteries. One stream flows toward the front of the body, one stream toward the back. The blood empties into open spaces. As it flows against the gut, the blood picks up nutrients. As it flows near the arachnid's tracheae or book lungs, the blood picks up oxygen and discharges carbon dioxide. The blood then flows back into the heart through the open ostia, and the cycle begins again.

ARACHNID BEHAVIOR

Although they can vary tremendously in appearance, virtually all arachnids share one common trait: they are voracious predators. Except for some parasitic ticks and mites, nature has fashioned Arachnida into a class of fast-moving hunters, each one equipped with an amazing bag of predatory tricks. Although all these behaviors are instinctual, or automatic, it is rather difficult not to consider them devilishly ingenious.

The scorpion's success lies in a combination of patience and lightning-quick response. Typically, a scorpion will emerge from its hiding place at dusk and assume a motionless stance on the open ground.

Tick-borne Diseases

Most people know that ticks transmit Lyme disease, a potentially dangerous but rarely fatal illness distinguished by fever, headache, aching muscles, and other flulike symptoms. Less widely known is that the tiny arachnids—relatives of spiders, scorpions, and mites—can also spread about 20 other serious diseases, including babesiosis, five kinds of encephalitis, and at least seven varieties of fever.

Ticks are parasites that feed on the blood of other animals. They begin their lives as eggs, which hatch into larvae during the summer and crawl to the tips of grasses and other low-growing plants. They wait until the next animal happens past, then latch on, burrow into the skin, and begin sucking blood. When they are engorged to up to 10 times their normal size, they drop off their host and spend the fall and winter resting. In the spring, they metamorphose into nymphs and again wait for a warm-blooded meal. This time when they feed, they drop off and become adults, which climb higher in the underbrush and wait for a larger host—often a deer, moose, or human. While on the host animal, male and female ticks find one another and mate. The male tick soon dies, while the female, laden with ova, lays her eggs the following spring.

The deer tick transmits a number of diseases. The creature can more than triple its size when engorged with blood.

Diseases can be spread by a feeding tick in any stage of its life. After it burrows its head into the skin of a host, the tick glues itself into place and exudes an anticoagulant to keep blood flowing. While the blood flows from the host into the hungry tick, microbes and bacteria are exchanged.

Recently, researchers identified a tick-spread disease known as human granulocytic ehrlichiosis (HGE). The disease is transmitted by deer ticks, the same species responsible for Lyme disease, and shares some of the same symptoms, such as body aches, fever, headache, and nausea. HGE also causes a significant drop in infection-fighting white blood cells and is potentially life-threatening if not treated quickly with the antibiotic doxycycline.

The best protection against ticks is to wear light-colored clothes (to make the ticks more visible) with tight-fitting sleeves and cuffs. Insect repellents containing DEET help keep ticks off, but should be used sparingly on children. Careful inspection of clothes and body when returning indoors can eliminate most ticks before they attach themselves. Once attached, ticks can be removed with tweezers directed at their heads. Consult a health-care provider immediately if any symptoms develop.

Jerry Dennis

With its tactile hairs, it can sense the vibrations of insects and other small animals. It then turns toward the prey and rushes forward with open pincers. So quick is the scorpion's grab that it can even catch flying insects. For the most part, scorpions sting only prey too large to subdue with their pincers.

Even the parasitic ticks have evolved impressive ways to "capture" their food. After hatching, they instinctively climb toward light, usually to the tip of a grass blade or the end of a branch. There the tick waits—for years if need be—for a suitable host to approach. Recognizing the right host is key to the tick's success. Ticks that feed on mammals do so by detecting the scent of butyric acid, a chemical all mammals exude from their skin. Special hollow hairs on the tick's body can detect even a few molecules of butyric acid in the air. In response, the tick releases its grip and falls onto its host. The warmth of the host's body then signals the tick to insert its feeding organ to strike blood.

For its weight, the silk that forms a spiderweb is stronger than steel—and so sticky that any insect that flies into the web has very little chance of escaping.

Master Hunters

The greatest predators of all may be the spiders. This order of arachnids displays a stunning variety of hunting methods; the simplest is ambush. But even here, spiders have developed the tactic into an art. The trap-door spider, for instance, lays in wait within a burrow covered by a lid made of dust-colored silk. The spider holds the lid closed with its fangs until it senses the vibrations of an approaching insect. Some trap-door spiders booby-trap the area around their burrows with a series of silk trip lines. Any insect that blunders into the lines is quickly detected and eaten.

The purse-web spider of Europe weaves a thick silken tube up out of its burrow and camouflages the outside of the tube with bits of plant material. It then waits inside until an insect walks across the surface. Rather than rushing out to capture the prey, the purse-web spider simply spears the insects through the tube with a jab of its powerful fangs.

A few ambushing spiders simply chase after or pounce upon their prey. These include the wolf and jumping spiders, species with the best long-distance vision in their class. Some of them can spring as far as 40 times the length of their body. Nursery-web spiders (whose webs are used solely as "cribs") can be seen running over the surface of ponds and streams, where they catch insects, tadpoles, and small fish.

Among the most novel of hunting weapons are the sticky spitballs of the bola spider. The bola flings the globule at a passing moth, then reels it in with an attached thread. A similar tactic is used by the appropriately named spitting spiders. With excellent aim, they can squirt their sticky saliva nearly 1 inch (2.5 centimeters).

The Spiderweb

The most familiar spider traps of all are those set by the web-spinning spiders. The simplest webs are little more than flat mats spread across the ground that enable a spider to feel the vibrations of passing insects. Spiders that live above the ground produce a variety of three-dimensional webs. Some are mere tangles of thread that ensnare flying and jumping insects. Generally, these delay an insect just long enough for the resident spider to rush out and bite. Familiar examples include the messy "cobwebs" of the common house spider.

The comb-footed spiders add sticky strands to their webs and encase struggling cap-

The notorious black-widow spider is identified by its hourglass-shaped marking—and noted for its alleged practice of killing the male immediately after mating.

tives by flinging on more silk. Some comb-footed spiders, such as the black widow, add an enclosed retreat, or "parlor," at the web's edge.

Funnel-web spiders weave expanding tubes and sheets through crowded vegetation, crevices, and other small spaces.

The most beautiful spiderwebs, at least to human eyes, are those of the orb weavers. The foundations of their webs are support lines that radiate out from the web's center like the spokes of a wheel. Across these, the orb weaver attaches many spiral lines. Some orb weavers eat their web each evening and replace it with a new one in the dark of night. The garden spider spins one of the largest orb webs, some 20 inches (50 centimeters) across. The tiny shamrock spider spins one of the tiniest, hanging it between two blades of grass. Like all spiders, orb weavers need no instruction in their craft. Each can spin a perfect web on its first try.

Arachnid Courtship

The arachnids were the first creatures to develop elaborate patterns of courtship behavior—and for good reason. When an arachnid perceives even the slightest movement, the tiny motion is enough to trigger the arachnid's simple brain to launch an immediate and deadly attack. The male arachnid must therefore take extreme care to signal his intentions before approaching his ever-hungry mate. In scorpions, this behavior takes the form of a dizzying waltz. The male scorpion seizes the female by her front claws and begins spinning her in an elaborate dance, while stinging her in a special joint at the base of her claw. The dance can range over several yards and take as long as an hour. By its end, the female allows her partner to drag her over a packet of sperm he has dropped on the ground. He then beats a hasty retreat.

The male whip scorpion likewise grabs his mate, leading her through a dance until her resistance is worn down. The waltz may take as long as three hours, before the pair unite in a body-curling hug. The male wind scorpion gets the female's attention by digging near her burrow. When she rushes out to attack, he grabs her abdomen with his pincers and massages her cephalothorax with his pedipalps. This stroking sends the female into a kind of trance. She curls up and allows the male to deposit his sperm.

Male spiders tend to be especially cautious in their approach, since they are often smaller than their mates. In many species, the male taps out an elaborate coded message of love on the edge of the female's web. The female responds

Almost alone among the arthropods, spiders care for their eggs. The wolf spider (above) makes a particularly devoted mother. She wraps her eggs in a silken cocoon that she attaches to her belly and carries with her wherever she goes.

to the vibrations by rushing to meet him. At first, she may spar with her suitor, as if to test his strength and make sure he is of her own species.

Despite popular belief, most female spiders do not harm their mates. But a few, such as the black widow, eat the male right after mating.

The one arachnid order in which courtship is wholly absent is that of the daddy longlegs, or harvestmen. However, male suitors often fight with each other. In such battles, the largest male often pulls off one or more legs of his rivals.

Care of Eggs and Young

Like insects, many arachnids produce large numbers of eggs and young. Unlike insects, many arachnids expend great efforts to care for

Of all the classes of animals, the class Arachnida is second only to Insecta in size, with some 75,000 species. These species, in turn, are divided into 11 orders. The most successful of these are the spiders (order Araneae) with 35,000 species named so far. Close behind are the mites and ticks (order Acarina), with 31,000 species.

CLASS Arachnida: *Found in all habitats. Most are predators. Body divided into two parts (cephalothorax and abdomen) with six pairs of appendages, including eight legs. Most have eight simple eyes. Lack antennae and wings. Have fanglike appendages (chelicerae) in front of mouth.*

ORDER Araneae: *True spiders. Distinguished from other arachnids by a narrow "waist," or pedicel, which divides the cephalothorax from the abdomen. Most species have poison glands in chelicerae (fangs), silk-producing glands on abdomen, and eight simple eyes. Feed on insects and other small animals. Found in all habitats except Antarctica. About 35,000 known species. Examples: tarantula and black-widow spider.*

ORDER Opiliones: *Daddy longlegs, or harvestmen. Medium-sized, oval-bodied arachnids, most with very long, stiltlike legs. One pair of eyes on raised knob. Unique among arachnids in that male has penis for internal fertilization. Prey on worms, snails, insects, and other arachnids, including smaller daddy longlegs. Some scavenge dead organic matter. Nocturnal. Found in dry habitats. About 3,500 species. Example: harvest spider.*

ORDER Acari: *Mites and ticks. Small arachnids (from 0.003 to 1.2 inches—0.0076 to 3 centimeters) with cephalothorax fused to abdomen. Some eyeless. Chelicerae modified into pincers for biting, sucking, or piercing. Ticks parasitic; mites predatory or parasitic on a variety of animals and plants. Found in all habitats. About 31,000 species, 30,000 of them mites. Examples: spider mite and wood tick.*

ORDER Scorpiones: *Scorpions. Medium to large arachnids recognized by lobsterlike pincers behind mouth and stinger at end of long, upturned abdomen. Have four to seven eyes. Females give birth to live young, which they brood on their backs. Nocturnal. Prey on insects, spiders, and small reptiles. Found in most dry habitats. About 1,500 known species. Example: Sahara scorpion.*

them. The female scorpion, for example, retains her eggs inside her body and gives birth to live young. The newborns then scramble onto their mother's back, often with her help. There they ride until their first molt, when they disperse to fend for themselves.

In most species of whip scorpions, the eggs are glued to or hung from the female's abdomen. The tropical ricinuleid lays but one or two eggs, which she holds between her pedipalps until they hatch. In some species of daddy longlegs, the male builds a round nest of mud, bark, and saliva on top of a log or tree root. After inviting one or more females to deposit their eggs, he guards them until they hatch.

Although a few primitive types of spiders simply lay their eggs and abandon them, most spin elaborate silken egg sacs. The females of some species make a number of egg sacs, up to 20 or more, and hide them in crevices or camouflage them with plant material. Spiders that produce just one egg sac tend to remain nearby to guard it and the emerging spiderlings.

The female wolf spider attaches her egg sac at the tip of her abdomen and will defend it to the death. When her spiderlings hatch, they cling to her body for about a week. The nursery-web spider carries her egg sac in her mouth. Just before hatching time, she attaches the egg sac to a plant and surrounds it with a protective silk tent where the spiderlings live until they molt.

The daddy longlegs (above), although often thought of as a spider, is classified by scientists into an order distinct from spiders, scorpions, and other arachnids.

ORDER Pseudoscorpiones: *Pseudoscorpions, or false scorpions. Small arachnids with flattened bodies. Lack long abdomen and stinger of true scorpion. Have enlarged, scorpion-like pincers, often with poison glands. Some eyeless, others with two to four eyes. Silk glands near mouth. Prey on small invertebrates. Found under bark and leaf litter, in bird nests, moss, and compost heaps. About 2,500 known species. Example: chernetid.*

ORDER Solifugae: *Wind scorpions, or sun spiders. Medium-sized arachnids with large, scorpion-like pincers. Walk on six legs, using long front pair as feelers. Mainly nocturnal, preying on insects and small vertebrates such as lizards. Found in dry regions, often under stones. About 900 known species. Example: camel spider.*

ORDER Uropygi: *Whip scorpions. Medium to large arachnids with large, scorpion-like pincers. Long abdomen has whiplike tail instead of stinger. Walk on six legs, using long front pair as feelers. Nocturnal, preying mainly on small insects and arachnids. Found in tropics and southern United States. About 70 known species. Example: American whip scorpion.*

ORDER Amblypygi: *Tailless whip scorpions, or whip spiders. Medium-sized, wide-bodied arachnids with large, spiny pincers. Walk on six long legs, often scurrying sideways. Use extremely long front pair of legs as feelers. Nocturnal, preying mainly on small insects and arachnids. Found in warm regions, often under stones and logs. About 60 known species. Example: side-spotted tailless whip scorpion.*

ORDER Palpigradi: *Microwhip scorpions. Tiny, rare arachnids with whiplike tail that bears long, tactile bristles. May prey on smaller insects and arachnids. Found in warm regions in caves, under stones, and in soil. About 60 known species. Example: palpigrade.*

ORDER Schizomida: *Short-tailed whip scorpions. Tiny arachnids with segmented carapace; short, whiplike tail; and scorpion-like pincers. Prey on small insects and arachnids. Found in warm regions, usually in soil. About 80 known species. Example: schizomid.*

ORDER Ricinulei: *Ricinuleids. Small, thick-shelled, eight-legged arachnid with six-legged larval form. Possess a unique hinged flap over the mouthparts. May prey on termites. Found in warm regions, typically under leaf litter. About 35 known species. Example: ricinuleid.*

A few species of spiders actually feed their young. In some species, the mother regurgitates a nutritious liquid. As her spiderlings get older, they share her prey. In some funnel-web weavers, the mother dies near the spiderlings, and her body becomes their first meal.

DANGER TO HUMANS

No discussion of arachnids seems complete without discussing their dangers to humans. The vast majority of arachnids are not at all dangerous. Indeed, their huge appetite for insect pests is a great boon for humanity.

Still, there is no denying that this class also includes some of the world's most poisonous creatures. The painful sting of Arizona's centruroides scorpion delivers a nerve toxin that can cause paralysis, irregular heartbeats, and death. Equally dangerous is the venom of the black-widow spider, which can paralyze the muscles used to breathe. Perhaps one of the deadliest is the Sydney funnel-web weaver of Australia, whose venom causes severe pain, irregular heartbeats, and extremely difficult breathing, sometimes progressing to coma and death. Yet even these dangerous species will usually flee rather than attack.

More harmful overall may be parasitic species of mites and ticks. Ticks carry a variety of microscopic disease organisms, which they transmit with their bloodsucking habits. The wood tick of the western United States carries the bacteria that causes Rocky Mountain spotted fever. The deer tick common to the Northeast can transmit the bacteria that causes Lyme disease. Other diseases associated with ticks include babesiosis, encephalitis, and hemorrhagic fever. Mites, in turn, can cause skin infestations and irritations such as scabies and dermatitis. And tiny species such as the dust mite can trigger allergies and asthma.

Although the term "millipede" implies 1,000 pairs of feet, the maximum number of pairs yet discovered on any millipede is 355. Even with all those legs, most millipedes are too slow to escape from enemies by running away.

Scoop up a jar of pond water and you may see an abundance of scuds—tiny crustaceans that whir through the water on an abundance of legs. Some 450 million years ago, just such a creature may have spawned one of the first animals to walk on land—a myriapod, or "many-legged" one. This first, primitive myriapod eventually disappeared. But before it did, it gave rise to two related classes of invertebrates—class Chilopoda, the centipedes, or "hundred-legged" ones; and class Diplopoda, the millipedes, or "thousand-legged" ones.

Today millipedes and centipedes are abundant wherever there are dark, damp places to hide. They belong to the great phylum Arthropoda, alongside their cousins, the crustaceans, insects, and arachnids. Like other crustaceans, millipedes and centipedes have segmented bodies covered with a stiff covering, or exoskeleton. Like insects, they breathe through holes, called spiracles, in this covering. But unlike insects, millipedes and centipedes cannot close their spiracles to prevent water loss. As a result, they dry out easily. This is why you are most likely to find them in damp, dark places such as the underside of logs.

When it comes to distinguishing centipedes from millipedes, many people are understandably confused. Both look similarly bizarre, with wormlike bodies, insectlike heads, and an astonishing number of legs. Despite these mutual oddities, centipedes and millipedes could hardly be more different in temperament and lifestyle. The most important difference is the centipede's poisonous bite.

MILLIPEDES

Turn over any stone, log, or patch of damp leaves, and you are likely to find a few millipedes. Not appreciating the intrusion, they will likely glide away slowly and gracefully, on an undulating frill of delicate legs.

The millipedes common to North American gardens and woodlands are among some 8,000 species worldwide. The smallest burrow around plant roots, so tiny they can barely be seen. The largest include boldly colored tropical species that measure over 12 inches (30 centimeters) long.

Most millipedes feed on decaying plant matter. Others are garden pests, chewing away at roots or emerging at night to feed on leaves. A few large species gnaw at the bark of trees.

Anatomy of a Millipede

The sight of a millipede frightens many people, who mistake it for the poisonous centipede. Fortunately, the two cousins are easy to distinguish.

Before it begins to move, the millipede's most distinctive feature is its dark, cylindrical body. Each of its many segments forms a near-circular ring. Millipedes also appear to have two pairs of legs on each body segment. In truth, the segments are fused into pairs. (By contrast, centipedes have one pair of splayed legs on each distinct body segment.)

As their name suggests, millipedes have more legs than do centipedes of similar size. Depending on the species, they number between 9 and 355 pairs. The millipede holds these delicate-looking legs beneath its body. So when the creature moves, the legs produce a graceful, wavelike movement.

Despite their greater number of legs—or perhaps because of it—millipedes move less quickly than do centipedes. Too slow to escape enemies, they typically defend themselves by coiling up with their head and legs tucked in the center. Some millipedes also produce distasteful chemicals when attacked.

Reproduction

Millipedes are solitary creatures, fleeing even from one another when meeting by chance. To calm a fertile female, the male may drum on the ground or rub his legs together to produce a special sound. Such signals coax the female to approach. The male then caresses her head with his antennae as he places a packet of sperm in a special opening on her body. Some millipedes make a nest for their eggs, and a few even guard them. The young emerge looking like small versions of their parents, but with fewer segments.

CENTIPEDES

Somewhere in a damp basement, an unwary cockroach meets a gruesome end. Spearing the insect with deadly fangs, a centipede injects venom deep into its victim's body.

The common house centipede, *Scutigera coleoptrata*, is one of about 3,000 species of centipede found in temperate and tropical regions around the world. The largest may be the highly poisonous, 10-inch (25-centimeter)-long *Scolopendra gigantea* of Central America. The tiniest include the harmless, threadlike centipedes found in garden soil. All are quick and aggressive predators, able to catch insects slightly larger than themselves. Seldom deadly to humans, the medium-sized centipedes of North America can nonetheless deliver a painful bite. Fortunately, they are easy to recognize.

Anatomy of a Centipede

Unlike the wormlike millipedes, most centipedes are quite flattened and have large legs that splay out to the sides. The number of legs varies from 15 to 173 pairs, depending on the species. Rather than flowing up and down in

unison, the legs on each side step alternately. This produces a wriggling motion of the body.

If you look very closely, you can also see that each centipede leg is slightly longer than the one in front of it. This enables the speedy centipede to avoid tripping over itself. Each leg steps over and outside the one before it.

Another noticeable difference is the centipede's threadlike antennae, considerably longer than the millipede's. Just behind the antennae are the centipede's all important "fangs." In truth, they are a modified pair of front legs,

Centipedes have adapted to a number of unusual habitats. The blind, 2-inch-long centipede above belongs to a species found only in Romania's Movile Cave.

sharpened to a point and equipped with poison-injecting glands.

Reproduction

When centipedes mate, they never actually copulate, or touch sexual organs. After circling around each other in a lengthy courtship dance, the male spins a small web and deposits his sperm within it. The female then retrieves it to fertilize her eggs. Most female centipedes are fiercely protective mothers, guarding their eggs and hatchlings until they are large enough to fend for themselves.

ENTOMOLOGISTS
AND THEIR
SCIENCE

by Jessica Snyder Sachs

In 1962, an insect expert from the Natural History Museum in Budapest stepped up to the witness stand in a Hungarian courtroom. He had come to clear the name of a Hungarian ferry captain serving time for murder. The skipper had been convicted of a brutal murder committed at the ferry dock where he worked the night shift. Now the insect expert, or entomologist, was explaining to the judge that the skipper was innocent. He pointed to the victim's autopsy report, which noted the presence of newly hatched fly larvae. The entomologist had calculated how long it would take for this type of insect egg to hatch into larvae. He explained that the eggs must have been laid on the corpse during the day. So the victim must have been dead before the skipper arrived at the docks the evening of the murder. Combined with other evidence, the entomologist's testimony convinced the court to overturn the skipper's conviction. Soon after, police caught the real killer.

WHAT IS ENTOMOLOGY?

Few people associate studying bugs with fighting crime. But forensic sleuthing is one of the many types of work performed by modern entomologists, scientists who study the classification, life cycle, behavior, distribution, or control of insects.

Be it for work or for pleasure, the study of insects and their relatives is as fascinating as it is bizarre. Indeed, with their hardened bodies, multiple legs, bulging eyes, and antennae, these creatures may seem more like space aliens than fellow Earthlings.

Yet our intimate acquaintance with insects goes back to prehistoric times. The first *Homo sapiens* were no doubt already infested with a

Hands-on exhibits and three-dimensional displays engage entomologists of all ages at the Smithsonian Institution's Otto Orkin Insect Zoo in Washington, D.C.

variety of fleas, mites, and ticks. Then, as today, insects were also our biggest competitors—feeding on every natural food eaten by humans.

HISTORY OF ENTOMOLOGY

Despite insects' vast importance and intrigue, early scientists paid them scant attention—except perhaps with a flyswatter. The insect's late arrival on the science scene most likely has to do with its size. It was not until microscopes became available in the early 1600s that scientists could get a good look at an insect's tiny body parts.

Through such a lens in 1667, the Dutch naturalist Jan Swammerdam became the first to seriously study and draw insects, from their tiny hearts to their even tinier brains. He was likewise the first to accurately observe and record how various insects transform themselves from juvenile to adult forms. In 1668, Swammerdam published his historic *General History of Insects*. Its beautiful drawings and fascinating insect life histories captured the imagination of animal lovers across Europe and the growing American colonies.

But not until 1758 was there an accepted method of naming the world's bewildering array of insects. That was the year that the great Swedish taxonomist Carolus Linnaeus applied his system of *binomial nomenclature* to organizing the insect kingdom. (See the article on "Insect Classification," page 277.) Linnaeus' system, still used today, gave scientists throughout the world a consistent way to name insects and arrange them in related groups.

And so finally, in the early 1800s, the field of animal science acquired its newest branch:

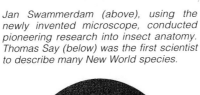

Jan Swammerdam (above), using the newly invented microscope, conducted pioneering research into insect anatomy. Thomas Say (below) was the first scientist to describe many New World species.

"entomology." The name, derived from the Greek *entomon*, meaning "cut-in," is descriptive of the insect's notched body. By tradition, entomology likewise includes the study of the insect's close relatives—the spiders, scorpions, centipedes, and other arthropods.

Early Entomologists

By the 1820s, entomological societies had sprung up throughout Europe and the Americas. The first entomologists kept busy just naming and describing the mind-boggling multitude of insects around them. Indeed, one of the enduring beauties of entomology is that its subjects are so numerous, and always close at hand. Even today, an estimated 1 million to 10 million insect species await discovery.

At the dawn of the 19th century, only a fraction of America's insects had been named or studied. The first to tackle the task was the Pennsylvania naturalist Thomas Say, the recognized "father" of American entomology. Not content to describe only the insects in his home state, Say traveled with many of the great Western explorers of his day. In 1820, he was among the first non–Native Americans to venture into the Rocky Mountains. He sketched and described several dozen new insect species.

Entomology continued to blossom throughout the 19th century. Say and other taxonomists amassed fantastic insect collections. Several such collections became exhibits in America's first natural-history museums.

Discovering Insect Pests

By the mid-1800s, America's entomologists were focusing less on describing nature's

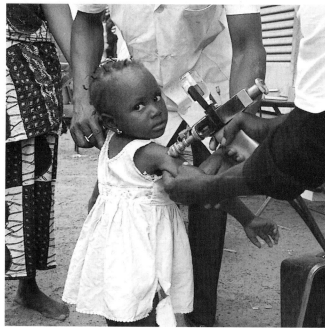

Agricultural entomologists inspect market-bound apples (left) and other fresh fruits and vegetables to determine if the produce has been damaged by insects.

nation's noted entomologists. Their work resulted in some of the first effective insecticides, from simple solutions of soap and tobacco juice to highly poisonous substances containing arsenic and kerosene.

Many states followed the federal government's lead. They established agricultural-research stations where entomologists could study the insect pests of their local areas. To this day, pest control remains a major part of the science of entomology—although only 5 to 10 percent of the world's insects actually cause problems for humans.

Medical Entomology

In 1879, the British physician Patrick Manson discovered that insects could cause human disease. Specifically, Manson found that the *Culex* mosquito could transmit the tiny parasite that causes filariasis, a painful inflammatory disease. A few years later, a British pathologist discovered that the bite of another mosquito, *Anopheles*, could transmit malaria. Then, in 1900, U.S. Army doctor Walter Reed

fantastic array of insects, and more on finding ways to exterminate them. Already in 1782, Thomas Jefferson observed that insects take a tremendous toll on crops and stored foods, and he called for further study. But it would be another 60 years before anyone would follow his advice.

In 1841, Massachusetts physician Thaddeus Harris published his monumental *Report on Insects Injurious to Vegetation*. This and other studies convinced American farmers that they could greatly increase their harvests by controlling insect pests.

Such books marked the beginning of what is now called *applied entomology*. Entomologists in this field apply their knowledge to either fighting problem insects such as crop pests or improving the productivity of useful insects such as honeybees.

To this end, in 1858, the federal government founded a new Bureau of Agriculture and hired some of the

Medical entomologists figured prominently in research that has led to the formulation of vaccines against some of the most serious insect-borne tropical diseases.

proved that still another mosquito, *Aedes aegypti*, could transmit yellow fever. This string of discoveries gave rise to the new field of *medical entomology*.

Since that time, medical entomologists have found an ever-increasing array of diseases that can be transmitted by insects, ticks, and other biting arthropods. Among the most devastating are bubonic plague, dengue, typhus fever, Rocky Mountain spotted fever, African sleeping sickness, Lyme disease, and West Nile virus. Livestock and pets also suffer a variety of insect-borne diseases, necessitating specialists in the field called *veterinary entomology*.

In many cases, the key to defeating or at least controlling such diseases lies in understanding the biology and life cycle of the insect carrier. Medical and veterinary entomologists must tease out the details of how and when insects become infected (for example, feeding on deer during a springtime juvenile stage) and how they transmit this infection (for example, feeding on humans or pets during a summertime adult stage).

Such entomology studies can lead to public-health recommendations. For example, an understanding of the life cycle of the deer tick has led to recommendations that all people who walk outdoors, particularly hikers, take extra precautions in summer and fall, when the ticks are most likely to transmit Lyme disease. Medical entomologists have likewise helped reduce the twin threats of malaria and yellow fever—not by mass exterminations, but by recommending that municipalities eliminate areas of standing water where mosquitoes tend to breed.

Fighting Insects with Insects

Entomologists have also been forced to become more sophisticated in their methods for controlling insect pests. By the end of the 19th century, many insects had grown resistant to common pesticides. At the same time, scientists were beginning to realize the terrible toll that toxic pesticides can take on surrounding wildlife and human health.

Wisely, entomologists turned to the insect world itself for allies in their battles against crop pests. In the 1880s, for example, pesticides had grown ineffective against the tiny scale insects that were destroying California's citrus crops. The answer came in the form of the predatory Australian ladybird beetle. Within a few years, this beneficial species had greatly reduced scale infestations, and the California citrus industry was on its way to recovery.

Entomologists have used ground beetles to eliminate destructive gypsy moths and ichneumon wasps to attack aphids. Today we know that more than half the world's insect species actual-

Entomologists use tent enclosures as part of a population-density study to determine if insect-pest species are present in excessive numbers.

ly prey on other insects. Still others can be used to eradicate plant pests. In the 1950s, U.S. entomologists employed flea beetles to clear southeastern waterways clogged with alligator weed.

HIGH-TECH ENTOMOLOGY

Entomologists today are pioneering a variety of new methods for controlling insect pests without harming the environment. The foundation of their work lies in their increasingly sophisticated understanding of insect biology.

Among the most interesting and productive areas of study is that of pheromones, "scent" chemicals that insects use to communicate with members of their own species. Some of the most

Careers in Entomology

Of all the animal sciences, only entomology offers the researcher a chance to discover hundreds, even thousands of new species in his or her lifetime. Many entomologists working for universities and natural-history museums spend at least part of the year "in the field," looking for new species to name and describe. Such work may take the entomologist no farther than a local lake, or to distant regions such as the Congo or Amazon. The world's tropical rain forests are an especially rich area of research, with countless species awaiting discovery. Entomologists also research insect biology, ecology, and behavior.

The greatest number of entomologists work in the field of applied entomology. They include medical entomologists, who study the relationships between diseases and the insects that can transmit them to humans. Medical entomologists often find work in the tropical-medicine departments of major medical centers and in government agencies such as the Centers for Disease Control and Prevention (CDC). A closely related field is that of veterinary entomology, the study of insect-borne diseases affecting livestock and pets.

Another broad area of applied entomology is agricultural research. Both the federal government and all 50 states employ entomologists to staff their agricultural extension services. Such entomologists identify insects that are causing crop damage, and they research methods to control these insects. The entomologists also enforce quarantines and regulations designed to keep problem insects from being accidentally imported from for-

Some of the most advanced research occurs in university labs, where devices like the insect-sound detector above can be tested in specially designed rooms.

eign countries or transferred from one state to another. Entomologists also work for private industries to develop new insecticides or new plant species that are resistant to insect damage. Those with advanced degrees may conduct research and teach about insects at colleges and universities around the world.

Young people interested in a career in entomology should prepare by taking classes in math and science during high school. Most careers in entomology require at least a bachelor's degree in science, usually with an emphasis on biology. Most entomologists pursue additional postgraduate study leading to a master's degree or doctorate.

---

powerful pheromones are released by female insects ready to mate. A female silkworm moth, for example, releases a pheromone that lures male silkworm moths from miles away. Entomologists use such insect "perfumes" to lure and trap specific insect pests without harming their beneficial cousins.

Entomologists have also found success with breeding sterile male insects, then releas-

ing them at the height of their natural mating season. In the wild, the sterile males mate with fertile females, which then produce sterile eggs or none at all. This tactic has helped control screwworms, a serious cattle pest in Texas.

Crime-fighting Bugs

The application of entomology to criminal investigations, called *forensic entomology*, has a history that goes back to 13th-century China. A murder committed with a sickle was solved by having local farmers lay their tools on the ground. Flies swarmed around the blade that bore invisible traces of blood, and the owner had no choice but to confess.

But it was not until the 1980s that forensic entomology became a recognized scientific field. Several American universities now teach courses in the subject. For the most part, forensic entomology involves the identification and study of insects and other arthropods recovered from a crime scene. The forensic entomologist identifies the species of insect, and then calculates its age and place of origin to pinpoint the time or location of a crime. An insect in a cache of illegal drugs, for example, can often be used to identify its country of origin. Fly larvae on a dead body can be invaluable. By determining the age of the larvae, investigators can tell when the eggs from which they hatched were laid, and thereby estimate the time of death.

ENTOMOLOGY FOR PLEASURE

Long before entomology became a profession, it was an enjoyable pastime. Today it remains so. As mentioned, one of the beauties of entomology is that insects can be found most anywhere, anytime. Some hobbyists enjoy capturing and mounting insects in a collection. Butterflies and moths are particularly popular among hobbyists. Others prefer sketching or taking pictures of the insects they observe. In any case, the amateur entomologist requires few tools, most of which are comparatively inexpensive.

Most valuable is a magnifying glass and perhaps a penlight to view the tiny details of insect anatomy. Especially useful are clear plastic "bug boxes" with a magnifying lens in the lid. Experienced entomologists recommend keeping a small piece of black and white cardboard on hand for use as a contrasting background against which to examine the insects you find.

Also helpful are field guides of the insects in your area. Still, no single field guide can list more than a fraction of the insect species in any region. At the least, they will help identify the most-common species. The best field guides organize species taxonomically, by order and family. To help identify unusual insects, identification keys are handy. They are a part of many

In Mexico, entomologists use pheromone-baited traps (like the one above, being attached to a tree) to capture Africanized "killer" bees and analyze their behavior.

good field guides, or can be purchased separately at nature stores or natural-history museums.

Since insects are masters of evasion, a few tools may be needed to safely capture a specimen for study. The classic entomology tool is the insect net, which is vital for fieldwork. Nets for capturing flying insects can be made of a nylon or silk webbing. "Sweep nets" of heavy white canvas can be used to scoop a sampling of insects from tall grass or weeds. Another method for gathering a variety of insects involves shaking a branch over a "beating tray." Budding entomologists can make such a tray by stretching a white cloth over a frame of two crossed sticks. Finally, a "light trap" helps attract nighttime insects. There are many types. The simplest is no more than a white sheet suspended over a line or branch with a flashlight illuminating the cloth from behind.

With such simple tools, anyone can join the ranks of entomology, the study of the most diverse group of living things on Earth.

What Is an Insect?

Insects are arthropods, alongside crustaceans, arachnids, and centipedes. Like other arthropods, insects have a hard outer covering called an *exoskeleton* and a segmented, or jointed, body. This relatively waterproof exoskeleton enabled the ancestor of modern insects to leave water for dry land some 350 million years ago. Soon after, insects became the first animals to fly. Most likely, the first winged insects did little more than flutter. Yet this fantastic adaptation enabled them to disperse far and wide to colonize new habitats.

Insect wings almost always come as a set of four (two pairs). In some species, such as flies, the second pair is reduced to mere stubs. Most insects also have many-faceted compound eyes; some have additional sets of simple eyes. Mouthparts come in an astounding variety of forms, variously modified for biting, chewing, sucking, stabbing, or lapping.

Needless to say, the above description barely touches on all there is to know about the bizarre and fascinating world of insects. Above all, insects represent the single most successful class of animals on Earth. To date, scientists have identified more than 900,000 species of insects—nearly four times as many as all other animal species combined. Scientists continue to discover another 5,000 species each year. Some experts believe there may be as many as 10 million in all. To look at it another way, for every person alive today, there are some 200 million to 300 million insects. For every pound of us, there are at least 4 pounds of them.

The largest insect known is a South American owlet moth with a 13-inch (33-centimeter) wingspan. Among the smallest are the near-microscopic lice.

FORMULA FOR SUCCESS

There is no doubt that the power of flight has enabled insects to spread far and wide. Still, because they are rather tiny, many insects live their entire lives within a small area, sometimes as little as a few square inches.

Insects can crowd even more closely together thanks to their varied eating habits. Some

A dragonfly (left) and a grasshopper (below) typify most insects in having a bilaterally symmetrical body that is divided into three parts: head, thorax, and abdomen.

consume plants; others parasitize animals; and still others consume dead organic matter. To add to the confusion, a single insect may eat different foods during different stages in its life. A nectar-sipping butterfly, for example, begins life as a leaf-eating caterpillar. As a result, two generations can live side by side without competing for food. This helps explain why so *many* insects can thrive in any area. But why are there so many kinds?

The secret to insect diversity may lie in their tremendous reproductive rate and low rate of survival. A typical female lays several thousand eggs during her brief life. A single housefly and her offspring can produce a mind-boggling 56 trillion eggs in one summer. Yet few of these offspring survive to adulthood. The result is a great winnowing-out process that can quickly give rise to new traits and even new species.

This process is called *natural selection*, or "survival of the fittest." It occurs with all organisms. Insects, however, have the added advantage of producing huge numbers of offspring. So within each new generation there are likely to be a few new traits, or variations, that just might prove beneficial to the species.

This variability enables insect species to adapt quickly to changes in their environment. Even if a change kills 99 percent of the individuals in a generation, the remaining 1 percent are sufficient to repopulate. If this new generation is different enough, it may eventually become its own separate species. Such adaptability also explains why insecticides rarely remain effective for very long. It takes only a few generations for insects to gain resistance to a given poison.

ANATOMY OF AN ADULT INSECT

Although insects are found in an almost infinite variety of forms, all adult insects have the same three major body parts—head, thorax, and abdomen—encased in an armorlike covering, or exoskeleton. Early scientists thus relied primarily on differences in body shape and appendages as criteria for grouping insects into different orders, families, and genera.

The Exoskeleton

The insect's outer covering, like that of all arthropods, is made of a stiff substance called *chitin*. It protects the insect from enemies and is divided into plates and segments that allow movement. Importantly, the covering is also pierced with many holes, called *spiracles*, that lead to internal breathing tubes, called *tracheae*.

The insect's exoskeleton also helps minimize water loss from the soft body within. Most species secrete a waxy substance that completes the waterproofing job. Evolution has likewise teased and shaped the insect's outermost layer into a variety of bristles, scales, and hairs. Depending on the species and its stage of development, the result may be fuzzy "fur," protective spines, or colorful wing patterns. Many insects also bear special cuticle hairs for touching, tasting, and smelling.

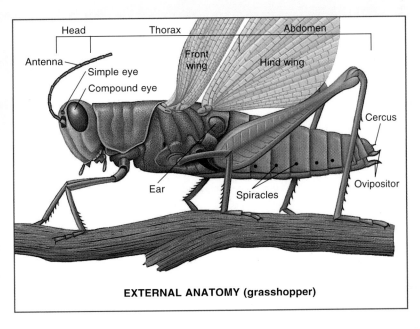

EXTERNAL ANATOMY (grasshopper)

The Head

The insect's head is encased in a capsule made of several fused plates. Near the top is a pair of compound eyes, often quite large and colorful. Each compound eye is made up of thousands of tiny lenses. Each lens projects its own image into the brain, giving the insect a mosaic view of life. In addition, most insects have one to three simple eyes, called *ocelli*, that provide sensitivity to light and motion.

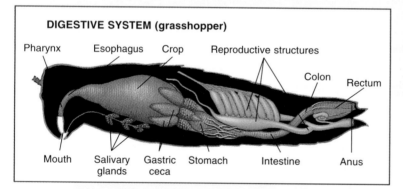

RESPIRATORY SYSTEM (grasshopper)

Brain · Aorta · Air sacs · Heart · Tracheae · Ganglia · Nerve cord · Spiracles

DIGESTIVE SYSTEM (grasshopper)

Pharynx · Esophagus · Crop · Reproductive structures · Colon · Rectum · Mouth · Salivary glands · Gastric ceca · Stomach · Intestine · Anus

Between or in front of the insect's compound eyes is a pair of segmented antennae. Depending on the species, they may be threadlike, stubby, feathery, comblike, clubbed, or beaded. All insects use their antennae for touch and smell; some use them for hearing.

Insect mouths are found in an even greater variety of forms. Species that chew their food have a pair of jawlike mandibles that open and close from side to side to cut, grind, and crush. Beneath the mandibles is a pair of mouthparts, called *maxillae*, for grasping. The maxillae of some species have *palps* for touching and tast-ing food. Insects that suck their food generally have some sort of beak or beaklike tongue.

The Thorax

The insect's *thorax*, or middle body part, has three segments, each bearing a pair of legs. The *tarsus*, or insect "foot," has several tiny segments and often bears a pad and a pair of claws at its tip. Leg size and shape vary tremendously from species to species. Forelegs may be modified for grasping, and back legs for jumping. Many bees have pollen brushes on their hind limbs. When present, wings grow from the top of the second and third thorax segments.

The Abdomen

The typical insect abdomen consists of 11 segments. The female's reproductive organs and ovipositor can be found between the seventh and eighth. Males have reproductive organs on the ninth segment, and sometimes a pair of claspers for grabbing their mates. The last segment sometimes has a pair of "tails," called *cerci*, for touching.

Internal Anatomy

The insect's internal anatomy is almost as simple as its outer form is complex. As mentioned, insects breathe through 10 pairs of spiracles in their outer shell. These holes extend into the body as tracheal tubes, which deliver oxygen directly to internal tissues. The insect's simple tubelike heart pumps its colorless blood through open spaces in the body. Insects also have a simple tubelike gut. Nutrients from the food pass through the sides of the gut, where they are picked up by the blood, or *hemolymph*.

The insect's tiny brain is little more than a cluster of fused nerves that allow the creature to react to stimuli (sights, scents, etc.) in the environment. The largest brains, found in social insects, may be able to store memories.

The tiny insect's legendary strength (ants can carry eight times their own weight) comes

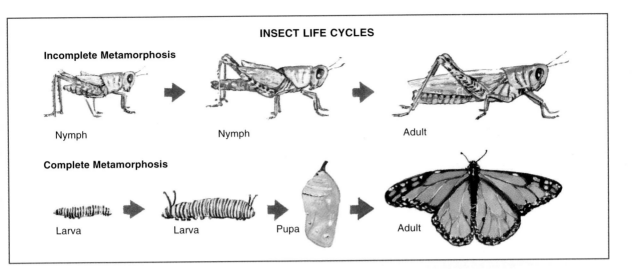

INSECT LIFE CYCLES

Incomplete Metamorphosis

Nymph → Nymph → Adult

Complete Metamorphosis

Larva → Larva → Pupa → Adult

from the special arrangement of its muscles: they are attached to the inner surface of the insect's exoskeleton. Some span adjacent segments, enabling the creature to flex and bend its body in many directions. Other muscles connect different parts of the same segment, enabling it to expand or contract.

LIFE CYCLE OF AN INSECT

Virtually all insects lay eggs—and lots of them. Such quantity makes up for the distinct lack of parental care that insects direct toward their eggs or hatchlings. A few species, including some flies, give birth to live young.

In shape and color, insect eggs are a varied lot. Some resemble tiny doughnuts. Others look like minuscule golf balls, milk bottles, barrels, or bullets. Contrary to popular belief, most are large enough to be seen with the naked eye—if one looks in the right places.

Some species of primitive insects look more or less like adults when they hatch. Their bodies undergo little change except to expand in size. By contrast, the vast majority of insects undergo several dramatic changes in body shape on the way to adulthood. This process is called *metamorphosis* and is divided into two general categories: "incomplete," or *hemimetabolous*, and "complete," or *holometabolous*.

Insects vary greatly in size, from the South American owlet moth (below), which has a 13-inch wingspan, to microscopic body lice, shown greatly magnified at right in a color-enhanced, electron-microscope image.

Insects that undergo incomplete metamorphosis include the cockroaches, termites, stone flies, crickets, grasshoppers, lice, cicadas, and "true" bugs. Most hatch as wingless *nymphs* that somewhat resemble adults. (A few, such as dragonflies and stone flies, begin life in the water as aquatic *naiads* that decidedly do *not* resemble adults.) Nymphs already have compound eyes and adult mouthparts, and so generally feed on the same food as do adults. Nymphs develop reproductive organs and wings gradually with each molt.

By contrast, "advanced" insects such as flies, beetles, butterflies, and social insects undergo complete metamorphosis. From their eggs hatch wormlike *larvae*. Some larvae, such as those of butterflies and moths, have many legs. Others, such as the fly's, have none. Typically, larvae have chewing or chewing-sucking mouthparts, stubby antennae, and several simple eyes. Larvae pass through several stages, or *instars*, that end in molts.

After its final molt, the larva *pupates*. During this crucial pupal stage, the larva stops feeding and rests within a hard outer covering or silken *cocoon*. Depending on the species, the pupal stage may last from four days to several months. During this time, larval tissues break down and are replaced by adult appendages, including new mouthparts, long antennae, compound eyes, segmented legs, wings, and reproductive organs.

When the adult pushes its way out of the pupal skin, its wings are crumpled and its body soft. Contact with air and internal fluid pressure unfurl the wings and harden their rigid framework of veins. Once its wings are dry, the adult insect launches into the air, ready to pursue its life's mission: to mate. The time allotted to do so ranges from just a few hours, in the case of some mayflies, to as long as several years, in the case of termite queens.

Mating itself may involve an elaborate courtship. Male crickets chirp. Fireflies flit about and blink. Moths release powerful scents. Other insects engage in elaborate mating flights or display dramatic and colorful wing patterns.

Be it brief or long, the aim of courtship is to demonstrate the male's fitness for mating. Once proven, the male transfers a packet of sperm into a special pouch on the female's abdomen. In a few species, the male remains with the female to guard her. But typically, the relationship ends with mating, and the male dies soon after. In the case of the praying mantis, the male usually ends up as a postcoital snack!

The female's final duty is to find a suitable place for her eggs, typically on or near a convenient source of food. She pushes her eggs through a tube, called an *ovipositor*, on her abdomen. Just inside the opening of the ovipositor, the eggs mix with the male's stored sperm, which fertilizes them.

While sexual reproduction is the rule among insects, a few exceptions occur. The unfertilized eggs of some social bees and wasps develop into males. Aphids, in turn, alternate between male-female generations that reproduce sexually and all-female generations that reproduce asexually.

DEFENSIVE BEHAVIOR AND MARKINGS

As mentioned, few hatchling insects survive to adulthood; those that do must avoid a wide variety of predators. Insects are certainly masters of camouflage, many of them blending with the foliage on which they feed. This type of camouflage is at its most remarkable among the leaf and stick insects, whose bodies and wings resemble a variety of plant parts.

Other insects avoid being eaten by becoming distasteful or downright inedible. Butterflies such as the monarch absorb toxic chemicals from their food to make their bodies poisonous. Any bird or mammal that snaps up such an insect is quick to avoid its kind in the future. This successful strategy gives rise to another type of insect defense—*mimicry*. The nonpoisonous viceroy butterfly, for example, closely resembles the poisonous monarch in appearance.

When attack cannot be avoided, speed becomes the insect's best defense. With six legs and four wings, most insects are well equipped to run, hop, or fly from danger. The speediest of all may be the hawkmoth, clocked at over 30 miles (48 kilometers) per hour.

Anyone who has ever been stung by a bee or wasp is certainly acquainted with the aggressive side of defensive behavior in insects. One of the more unusual forms of aggressive defense can be found among the cerambycid beetles. When threatened, this beetle slashes its attacker with long antennae tipped with sharp hooks!

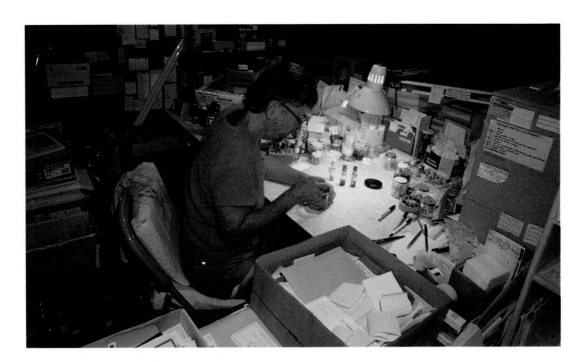

INSECT CLASSIFICATION

The task of naming and organizing the world's insects has intimidated scientists for centuries. And it's no wonder. There are nearly a million known species of insects, and more are being discovered every day. To confuse matters still further, many familiar insects have several popular, or common, names, and some of these overlap. Even the term "insect" is unclear to many people, who use it to describe any small creeping thing with more than four legs.

Fortunately, the great taxonomist Carolus Linnaeus eventually tackled the problem. In 1758, he assigned each known kind of insect a two-part scientific name using his binomial system of classification. He then grouped them all in the giant class Insecta, defined as segmented creatures with three distinct body parts (head, thorax, and abdomen) and six legs. Then, as today, this definition distinguishes the true insects from their cousins—the eight-legged spiders, the many-legged centipedes, and the even-more-legged millipedes. These three classes and the crustaceans belong alongside the insects in the larger grouping—phylum Arthropoda—the joint-legged animals, or arthropods.

Over the centuries, scientists have continued the task of grouping the world's insects into orders, families, and genera. Today there are 25 to 34 insect orders, depending on whom you ask. The classification of insects remains an active science, with some experts subdividing groups based on minute differences, and others lumping them together based on similarities.

Most recently, scientists have debated the classification of the three most-primitive insect orders, the minute proturans (order Protura), two-pronged bristletails (order Diplura), and springtails (Collembola). These wingless species differ from other insects in having their mouthparts enclosed in a cavity formed by the sides of the head. As a result, many experts have decided they are not proper insects at all. Instead, some scientists place these species alongside insects in a newly created "superclass" dubbed Hexapoda, meaning "six-legged animals." Yet, for simplicity's sake, many texts and field guides still consider class Insecta to include all arthropods with three main body parts and six legs—as we do here.

Of all members of the Animal Kingdom, insects present the most formidable challenge to the taxonomist, especially in view of the fact that there are more than a million known species—and many more to be described.

CLASS Insecta: *Arthropods with body segments grouped in three body parts—head, thorax, and abdomen—with one pair of antennae on the head, and three pairs of jointed legs on the thorax. Most have two pairs of membranous wings.*

SUBCLASS Entognatha: *Small, primitive, flightless insects with mouthparts enclosed within a cavity formed by the sides of the head. Muscles within the antennae.*

ORDER Protura: *Proturans. White, eyeless insects less than 0.06 inch (1.5 millimeters) long. Found in damp soil and organic matter. About 118 species. Example:* Protapteron.

ORDER Collembola: *Springtails. Slender, sometimes-colorful, tiny insects with forked "tail" that springs downward, causing insect to jump. Found in decaying organic matter and feeding on plants. About 2,000 species. Examples: snow flea, seashore springtail.*

ORDER Diplura: *Two-pronged bristletails. Blind, nocturnal insects with slender body and pincerlike "tail" used to catch prey. Some appear to have rudimentary abdominal legs. Found on ground under leaves, stones, and logs. About 400 species. Example:* Heterojapax.

SUBCLASS Apterygota: *Primitive wingless insects that do not undergo metamorphosis.*

Popular belief holds that the sighting of a single cockroach (above) means that many more of the creatures are lurking nearby. Perhaps even more difficult than roaches to exterminate is the silverfish (left), which often lives among paper products.

ORDER Archaeognatha: *Jumping bristletails. Brown insects about 0.5 inch (1.2 centimeters) long, with large compound eyes that meet on top of the head, and a long, three-pronged "tail" at end of the abdomen. Found under rubble and leaf litter and in cracks of seashore cliffs. About 350 species. Example: bristletail.*

ORDER Thysanura: *Common bristletails. Small, fast-running insects with slender, flattened bodies and long, bristly, three-pronged "tail." Found outdoors under light vegetation and indoors among paper products and food. About 250 species. Example: silverfish.*

SUBCLASS Pterygota: *Winged insects (as adults) whose immature forms undergo incomplete or complete metamorphosis. Contains 99 percent of all living insect species.*

ORDER Ephemeroptera: *Mayflies. Ancient brownish or yellowish insects that hold triangular forewings at right angles to the body. Adults do not feed, and live less than a day. Young found in water, adults nearby. Incomplete metamorphosis. About 2,100 species. Example: stream mayfly.*

ORDER Odonata: *Dragonflies and damselflies. Ancient predatory insects with large, slender bodies and movable heads with large compound eyes. Hold wings at right angles to body. Young found in water, adults nearby. Incomplete metamorphosis. About 5,000 species. Examples: green darner, golden-ringed dragonfly.*

ORDER Blattodea: *Cockroaches. Brownish, fast-running, nocturnal insects with flattened, oval bodies and long, swept-back antennae. Found in buildings and other warm places. Incomplete metamorphosis. About 3,500 species. Example: American cockroach, or "water bug."*

ORDER Isoptera: *Termites. Pale, soft-bodied social insects with biting mouthparts. Most species feed on wood. Found in dead timber, wooden buildings, or in nests in or atop soil. Incomplete metamorphosis. About 2,100 species. Example: subterranean termite.*

ORDER Mantodea: *Mantids. Slender, long-legged, predatory insects, 0.5 to 6 inches (1.2 to 15 centimeters) long, with movable, triangular head; large compound eyes; and threadlike antennae. Grasp prey with forelegs. Generally found in foliage. Incomplete metamorphosis. About 1,800 species. Example: praying mantis.*

ORDER Dermaptera: *Earwigs. Slender, flattened nocturnal insects with beaded antennae with pair of large pincers at tip of abdomen. Short, leathery forewings, when present, meet in a straight line down the back. Found on flowers, under bark, stones, and leaves. Incomplete metamorphosis. About 1,100 species. Example: common earwig.*

ORDER Plecoptera: *Stone flies. Drab-colored, flattened, weak-flying insects with hind wings that fold fanlike beneath the front pair. Young found in streams and lakes (where they feed on other insects), adults nearby. Incomplete metamorphosis. About 1,600 species. Example: common stone fly.*

ORDER Orthoptera: *Crickets and grasshoppers. Medium to large jumping insects with large, flat-sided heads; huge eyes; big chewing mouthparts; and large, powerful hind legs. Long, leathery forewings cover fanlike flying wings when at rest. Males known for musical mating sounds. Found among foliage on which they feed. Incomplete metamorphosis. About 23,000 species. Examples: lubber grasshopper, Mormon cricket, California katydid.*

ORDER Phasmida: *Stick and leaf insects. Large, slow-moving, sticklike insects, some wingless. Generally remain motionless during the day. Found in many types of foliage on which they feed. Incomplete metamorphosis. About 2,000 species. Examples: Mediterranean stick insect and leaf insect.*

ORDER Embioptera: *Web spinners. Small, slender brownish insects that live in colonies inside silken webs and tunnels. Found among ground mosses and in soil cavities. Incomplete metamorphosis. About 150 species. Example: web spinner.*

ORDER Psocoptera: *Book lice and bark lice. Tiny insects (not true lice) with relatively large heads and eyes and long, swept-back antennae. Found in houses among paper and outside on tree bark. Incomplete metamorphosis. About 1,100 species. Example: common book louse.*

ORDER Mallophaga: *Biting lice. Tiny, flattened, wingless insects with bristly bodies, relatively large heads, and chewing mouthparts. Found mainly on birds, which they parasitize. Incomplete metamorphosis. About 320 species. Example: elephant louse.*

The praying mantis (above) is considered a beneficial insect, since it feeds on destructive insect species.

ORDER Anoplura: *Sucking lice. Tiny, flattened insects with relatively small heads and sucking mouthparts. Found on mammals. Incomplete metamorphosis. About 250 species. Example: human body louse.*

ORDER Thysanoptera: *Thrips. Black, slender, specklike insects, some wingless. Found on foliage (often seen moving across flowers). Incomplete metamorphosis. About 4,700 species. Example: onion thrips.*

ORDER Zoroptera: *Zoropterans. Tiny, slender insects with chewing mouthparts and threadlike or beaded antennae and short legs. Found in colonies under bark of dead trees and in decaying wood. Incomplete metamorphosis. About 22 species. Example: Zorotypus.*

ORDER Hemiptera: *True bugs. Large group of diverse insects with beaklike, piercing-sucking mouthparts. Most have forewings that fold flat over the back. Most found on land, but some aquatic. Many suck plant juices. Incomplete metamorphosis. More than 40,000 species. Examples: water bug, bedbug, and stinkbug.*

ORDER Raphidioptera: *Snakeflies. Long-bodied, long-headed insects with transparent, veined wings, which are held rooflike over the body. Found in trees, feeding on smaller insects. Complete metamorphosis. About 50 species. Example: snakefly.*

ORDER Megaloptera: *Alderflies and dobsonflies. Large, broad-winged, nocturnal insects. Clumsy fliers. Young found in ponds and streams, where they feed on other insects. Adults found nearby. Complete metamorphosis. About 180 species. Example: common alderfly.*

ORDER Neuroptera: *Lacewings, mantis flies, and ant lions. Insects with large, lacelike, transparent wings held rooflike over the body; chewing mouthparts; big eyes; and long antennae that may be threadlike, comblike, or clubbed. Young of most species found on plants or in soil, where they feed on other insects. Those of family Sisyridae live in water and feed on sponges. Complete metamorphosis. About 4,500 species. Examples: mantis fly, lacewing, and ant lion.*

ORDER Coleoptera: *Beetles. Insects with armorlike forewings (elytra) that cover hind wings used for flying. Often brightly colored or patterned. All have chewing mouthparts; most have large eyes. Most found on plants, although some scavenge organic matter or prey on smaller insects. Complete metamorphosis. More than 300,000 species—the largest order of the Animal Kingdom. Examples: whirligig beetle, click beetle, firefly, weevil, and ladybug.*

ORDER Strepsiptera: *Twisted-winged parasites. Tiny, dark insects with club-shaped forewings that twist when the insect flies. Found under stones and debris, where they feed on bristletails. Complete metamorphosis. About 300 species. Example: stylopid.*

ORDER Mecoptera: *Scorpion flies. Soft, slender, long-legged insects with long, snoutlike heads that end in biting mouthparts. Males in family Panorpidae have large sex organ that curves over abdomen like a stinger. Young found on soil and moss, where they scavenge dead insects and other refuse. Adults found on ripe fruit and dead insects, on which they feed. Complete metamorphosis. About 400 species. Example: common scorpion fly.*

ORDER Siphonaptera: *Fleas. Tiny, wingless insects with flattened abdomens covered with bristles. Legs with large, springy "foot" for leaping. Found on mammals and birds, which they parasitize. Complete metamorphosis. About 16,000 species. Example: human flea.*

ORDER Diptera: *True flies. Insects with one pair of functional wings and one pair of small, stubby wings. A few species wingless. Most have large eyes, and piercing, lapping, or sucking mouthparts. Larvae of most species legless and headless (maggots). Found on the many types of plants, organic matter, and animals on which they feed. Complete metamorphosis. About 86,000 species. Examples: mosquito, midge, and housefly.*

ORDER Trichoptera: *Caddis flies. Mothlike insects with chewing mouthparts and long, slender antennae. Fine hairs cover body and wings. Wings held rooflike over body. Young found in freshwater, adults nearby. Complete metamorphosis. About 4,500 species. Example: northern caddis fly.*

ORDER Lepidoptera: *Butterflies and moths. Insects with four large, often dramatically patterned wings covered with powdery scales. Most have long, coiled, tubelike mouthparts. Butterflies fly by day on brightly colored wings, held flat over body when at rest. Most moths fly at night on drab-colored wings, although some brighter-colored species fly by day. Moths hold wings rooflike over body, curled around body, or flat against perching surface. Young found among plants on which they feed. Adults feed on flowers and sap. Complete metamorphosis. About 125,000 species. Examples: codling moth and monarch butterfly.*

ORDER Hymenoptera: *Bees, ants, wasps, and sawflies. Hard-bodied, active insects with chewing mouthparts. Bees, ants, and wasps have a narrow "waist" between the thorax and abdomen. Wasps and some bees and ants have a stinger at end of abdomen. Ants and some bees and wasps are social, building nests with worker castes and breeding castes. Sawflies found among plants on which they feed; bees and some wasps around blossoms; ants mainly on ground. Complete metamorphosis. About 108,000 species. Examples: common sawfly, ichneumon fly, digger wasp, army ant, leaf-cutter ant, Australian bulldog ant, yellow jacket, bumblebee, and honeybee.*

SOCIAL INSECTS

There is no counterpart among other animals to the military, food-gathering, cattle-keeping, and slave-making activities of the ants, or to the perfectly ordered system of the beehive. Ants and some bees and wasps form elaborate social organizations, and hence are known, appropriately enough, as *social insects*. In all the Animal Kingdom, such cooperative enterprises are rivaled only by those of humans.

Social insects belong to the order Hymenoptera, which constitutes perhaps the most highly developed group of insects. Not all hymenopterans live in communities, however; the order also includes such solitary insects as gall wasps, sawflies, horntails, and ichneumons (parasitic wasps that lay their eggs within the bodies of other insects' larvae). More than 100,000 species are known, and probably as many more still remain to be named.

All species of social insects have mouthparts specialized for biting, chewing, scraping, lapping, or sucking. Hymenopterans usually have two pairs of stiff and quite narrow wings; most ant species lack wings altogether.

ANTS

In the case of solitary insects, each individual must perform all the tasks necessary for its survival—collecting food, seeking shelter, fighting off enemies, and so on. Ants, by contrast, specialize. Most live in large nests, sometimes called *ant cities*, and divide their labor; each has its own individual duties.

Caste System

The inhabitants of a given ant nest are divided into three distinct classes, or *castes,* on the basis of the work they perform. There are various subdivisions—more than two dozen in all—among these three castes.

The largest caste comprises the wingless, normally infertile, females, which function as *workers* or *soldiers*. These insects are usually

Beekeepers removing a honeycomb from a bee box would be well-advised to wear special clothing to protect themselves from the stings of the angry insects.

the smallest members of the community. They enlarge, maintain, and defend the nest, gather food, and feed and nurse the queen and young. Occasionally a worker, if carefully fed and attended, may lay fertile eggs. The soldiers are workers with large heads and strong jaws for defending the nest.

The second caste is composed of the large, winged *queen* ants. They are the mainstay of the nest, producing eggs almost constantly, except during cold weather.

The winged males, which have small heads and small jaws, constitute the third caste. Some species have both winged and wingless queens or males.

Colony Formation

Ants live almost everywhere—in deserts and fields, in forests and mountains, on beaches, and in the cities, towns, and dwellings of humans. Their homes vary from galleries and chambers excavated in soil to nests built in hollow stumps. Some nests, constructed of paperlike material, are suspended from trees.

An ant colony may be formed either by a solitary queen or by several queens together. Each queen, having stored immense energy reserves within her body, departs on a so-called *nuptial flight*, during which the winged males and the queens swarm together. Mating occurs during or at the end of the flight. When she alights, the queen will be ready to begin her

egg-laying duties. The male, meanwhile, seeks shelter under stones, sticks, or fallen leaves, and dies in a matter of days.

Often the young queen must establish her own colony. She begins this task by casting off her wings and seeking an appropriate shelter— the underside of a stone or simply a hole in the ground. Then she digs, hollowing out a burrow with a chamber at one end. The queen blocks the entrance to the burrow and rests quietly, shut off from the outside. During this time, her wing muscles are gradually broken down and converted into fat bodies, for energy.

Finally the queen begins to lay eggs, and, in a short time, the first *larvae* hatch. The queen is a devoted mother to the first generation of offspring. She forces saliva, containing fat bodies, into the mouths of the young larvae, and they grow rapidly. Should her food supply fail, the queen may even eat some eggs and larvae so as to maintain herself and the nest. If mating occurred in late summer, cold weather comes while the brood is young. The queen and her larvae then hibernate until spring.

When the larvae of some species are still small, they spin cocoons and, enveloped in these wrappings, become *pupae*. As each pupa matures, its mother frees it from the cocoon. It is now a small but perfectly formed worker.

The workers of the first generation almost immediately dig their way to the surface and head off in search of food; whatever they find

The diagram below of a worker ant shows the inner structures of its body, including glands that secrete chemicals. Dufour's gland produces a substance that other ants can detect and follow as a trail; Pavan's gland contains poison; and anal and mandibular glands secrete chemicals used as alarm signals.

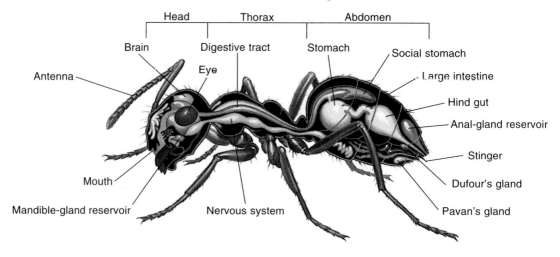

A herder ant (left) "milks" aphids by stroking the insects with its antennae. Below, slave ants perform such tasks as grooming the queen of the slaveholding community.

they bring back to the queen, who by now is in a rather sad state from feeding her brood with her own bodily substance. She soon recovers her strength and continues her egg-laying activities. Gradually, the workers take over care of the young, enabling the queen to become a sort of egg-laying machine. Workers feed her by cramming into her mouth food regurgitated from their stomachs.

As time goes on, the workers become larger and more numerous. Soldiers make their initial appearance sometime after the queen has established her colony. New queens appear upon the scene last of all.

All along, it is the workers that carry on the essential operation of the colony. They may even relocate the colony repeatedly, carrying the egg-laying queen, immature workers, larvae, and pupae to the new site. Although most workers are sterile, a few may lay eggs, which give rise to male or worker offspring.

Behavior

Much of the behavior of a young worker ant results from imitating its elders. The novice must learn the lay of the land around its nest to enable it to find its way home after a foraging expedition. Certain individuals seem to learn better than others. These key workers initiate the activities in the colony and set an example to the other ants. If these choice workers are removed from the nest, the activity of the colony is adversely affected, compromising the health of the queen and of the surviving workers.

Pheromones. Biologists believe that the seemingly intelligent activities of ants derive in part from inherited instinctual patterns. Ants also respond to stimuli released by other ants, "stimuli" mainly in the form of chemical secretions called *pheromones.*

By means of tiny sensory pits in their antennae, ants can sense the pheromone secretions emitted by other ants. They can thus recognize members of their own colony and detect the presence of hostile ants. In some cases, secretions are laid down as scent trails for other ants to follow, as when a food supply has been discovered by a foraging worker.

Pheromones can initiate alarm reactions, fighting, reproduction activities, nest construction, and other types of behavior in ants. Certain poisonous secretions are used to repel invaders or to subdue prey. At most stages of colony development, the queen ants secrete chemicals that prevent ordinary workers—infertile females—from developing into reproductive females or rival queens.

Food exchange and herding. Much of the apparently friendly behavior of ants and other social insects stems from the mutual exchange of pleasing food secretions. The larvae of ants, for example, exude substances that are greatly appreciated by the workers, who feed the young and receive the substances as a "reward." The adults of social insects also engage in this practice. The material may consist of regurgitated food or glandular secretions, exchanged in a process called *trophallaxis*, from the Greek words meaning "food exchange." "Foreign" insects that live in an ant nest may be tolerated because they "pay rent" in the form of food matter desired by their hosts. Certain ants "herd" other insects for the secretions the latter provide.

A worker ant called a replete (top) distends itself with honey, which it stores in its abdomen for later communal use when food becomes scarce. Leaf-cutter ants (above) gather vegetation on which to grow fungi.

One of the most amazing practices of some ant species is the keeping and milking of "cows." The "cow" in question is really an insect—the aphid, or plant louse, that deposits a secretion called honeydew on the foliage and stems of vegetation. The ants milk the aphids by stroking them with their antennae, thus coaxing the aphids to give droplets of honeydew.

The ants carry their insect livestock to different parts of the plant or to different plants in the area for "grazing." Some ants dig tunnels in the soil for the convenience of root-sucking plant lice. Certain ants even take the plant lice into their own nests for the winter.

Aphids are not the only animals that find hospitality in the nests of ants. A great number of beetles, cockroaches, flies, and arachnids take up their abode there, where they feed on the excretions of their hosts.

Parasitic ants. Parasitism plays an extremely important part in the life of ants. Different species or groups may live off others temporar-

ily or even permanently. For example, in temperate areas, various colonies of the genus *Formica* may establish themselves in the nests of other *Formica* communities. A single queen induces the workers of a foreign colony (of a similar species) to care for her and for the offspring from the eggs she lays in their nest. The original queen of the colony may remain, be killed, or be driven off—sometimes by her own workers! As the invading queen's larvae mature, they eventually replace all the original workers, who have been gradually dying off. At this point, there is little evidence that the thriving colony had begun by parasitism.

Occasional Pests

When ants make their way into human dwellings, they become unmitigated pests. One notable example is the pharaoh ant, *Monomorium pharaonis.* This tiny yellowish or reddish ant senses the presence of food and rushes to consume it—overrunning a house from the cellar to the attic in the process.

Carpenter ants, members of the genus *Camponotus,* live in ceiling beams, porch columns, and windowsills, where they do considerable damage by excavating galleries and chambers. Carpenter ants do not eat wood, however; rather, they feed on plant juices, animal remains, and the honeydew of aphids.

Representative Varieties

There are many interesting varieties of ants, including gardeners, living receptacles, and slaveholders.

Parasol (or leaf-cutter) ants. Members of the genus *Atta* cultivate various species of club fungi, which they use as food. To begin a fungus farm, a large ant expedition must first set out to obtain sections of leaves. The insects climb up nearby trees and cut off circular pieces of leaves. As the ants return to the colony with their booty, each one carries its piece of leaf overhead like an umbrella (hence the name parasol ants).

When the leaf sections have been brought to the nest, they are thoroughly chewed and then deposited on the floor of a large chamber. As the leaf layers accumulate, they acquire a sponge-

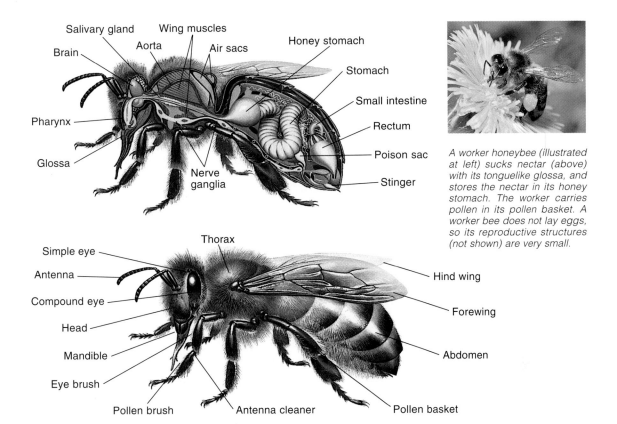

A worker honeybee (illustrated at left) sucks nectar (above) with its tonguelike glossa, and stores the nectar in its honey stomach. The worker carries pollen in its pollen basket. A worker bee does not lay eggs, so its reproductive structures (not shown) are very small.

like structure. Soon they are covered with the desired fungus growths.

The body of the fungus, called the mycelium, consists of many slender branched threads known as *hyphae.* Small spherical swellings develop on the hyphae, and these swellings provide food for the ants. The smaller workers in the colony rarely leave the nest, but spend most of their time "weeding" the fungus garden—removing unwanted growths.

Black honey ants. Black honey ants have a curious way of storing honey. Certain workers, known as *repletes,* gorge themselves with honey until their abdomens are greatly distended. They then serve as animated honey jars, ready to serve the needs of the other ants. When food is scarce, the members of the colony stroke the abdomens of the repletes and devour the droplets of honey that are regurgitated.

African driver, or army, ants. These carnivorous ants prey on insects and other small invertebrates, although they will attack any living thing in their path. Generally, animals such as mammals, including humans, and birds can easily avoid the driver ants. Animals fall victim to the little carnivores only if they are injured and cannot keep out of their way.

The two genera—*Eciton* and *Dorylus*—that make up the driver ants are found in widely separated areas. Ants of the genus *Eciton* dwell in the American tropics; those of *Dorylus*, in the African tropics. Although completely blind, these ants nonetheless advance in long columns with remarkable, almost military precision; their foragers fan out on all sides of the main columns. The ants form temporary bivouacs, consisting of clusters of insects hanging from the branches of shrubs and bushes.

BEES

The bees make up the superfamily Apoidea, comprising some 20,000 species. Not all bees can sting—and very few are social—but it is these characteristics that are most associated with this group of insects.

Female bees have an organ called an *ovipositor* at the end of the abdomen. This serves as an egg layer and also as a weapon: it can inflict a painful sting. In the case of honeybee workers, the ovipositor, or *stinger*, has barbs that turn inward. If the worker stings a foe, the stinger is generally left in the body of the victim, and the bee dies. The ovipositor of the hon-

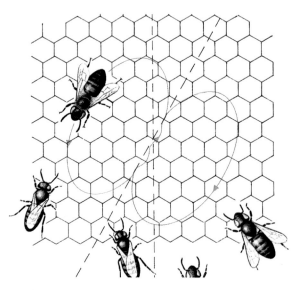

A scout honeybee traces out a figure eight as part of an elaborate dance to indicate to the other bees the location of—and distance to—a nearby source of nectar.

eybee queen is smooth, enabling her to sting a victim repeatedly without harming herself.

Bees store pollen and honey in their nests to provide food for their young. Pollen is collected by the hairs on a bee's legs and body, and also by specialized structures called *pollen brushes,* which are found on the hind legs and sometimes on the abdomens of female bees.

After pollen is collected, it is brushed off by the insect's head and feet, dampened with dew or some other form of moisture, mixed with honey from the bee's mouth, and formed into tiny pellets. The pellets are then pushed into the so-called *pollen baskets.* These baskets, consisting of long and stiff hairs on the hind legs, hold a great number of pollen pellets.

Honey is a product of nectar, a sweet liquid secreted by the glands found in certain flower petals. The bee sips nectar and swallows it. The substance is transformed into honey in the insect's crop, or *honey sac,* and is later disgorged. Honey is made up chiefly of the sugars levulose and dextrose and of water. It also contains dextrins, gums, vitamins, enzymes, pollen grains, and various minerals.

Bees also collect a sticky substance called *propolis,* derived from the resinous secretions of various trees. Propolis is used as a cement in the building of nests.

Solitary Bees

Contrary to popular belief, most bee species do not form communities but are solitary in habit. The female of the solitary bee builds her nest cell by cell. She stocks each cell with pollen mixed with nectar and then lays an egg on this food supply. She seals each nest before she goes on to the next one. After the entire nest has been completed, she closes it up and flies away, never to return. The larvae that are hatched from the eggs go through a series of molts, become pupae, and finally emerge from the nest as adult bees.

Honeybee Colonies

The social bees—bees that form communities—have developed distinct castes, which correspond more or less to those found among ants. In each hive, there are a mature queen bee; a number of males, known as *drones;* and a great many workers, or undeveloped females.

Perhaps the best known of the social bees is the honeybee, *Apis mellifera.* These familiar creatures build elaborate hives with wax secreted from eight wax pockets on the underside of the abdomen of each individual worker. The honeycombs in this hive are set vertically, side by side. Each comb consists of thousands of hexagonal cells. Some of the cells contain eggs, larvae, or pupae. Others are used for the storage of honey and pollen.

At the beginning of the spring season, the honeybee hive contains a queen and a comparatively small number of workers. The queen begins to lay eggs. Some of these will develop into workers, others into drones, and a few into queens. The latter are reared in special enlarged cells called *royal cells.* After about three days, the eggs hatch. The larvae, or *grubs,* are all fed for the first two or three days with *royal jelly,* a secretion from certain glands of the workers. After this period is over, the prospective workers and drones are gorged with honey and pollen. The larvae that are to be reared as queens—or rather, *princesses*—continue to be fed with royal jelly.

The larvae grow rapidly. After about six days, the cell is sealed by the attendant workers, and the larva becomes a pupa. The larvae that are to become workers or drones spin a complete cocoon about themselves before entering the pupal stage. The cocoons spun by the larvae

Beekeeping

Of the 25,000 known species of bees, only about six make honey. Honeybees—especially *Apis mellifera*, the most common species—collect nectar from flower blossoms and convert it into a concentrated, high-energy source of food that can be stored in their hives. Humans, of course, love the taste of honey.

It was not until the 17th century that people learned how to control bees with smoke and protect themselves from stings with veils. Gradually, over the next two centuries, a number of key discoveries made it possible to keep bees and harvest their honey and beeswax commercially. Those discoveries included the construction of movable frame hives, the deciphering of the mating behavior of the queen bee, and the fact that a colony of bees produces a new queen when the old one leaves or is taken away.

With such knowledge in hand, beekeepers learned to divide a colony themselves, instead of waiting for it to swarm naturally. Large-scale commercial beekeeping was made possible with the invention of centrifugal honey extractors, wax-comb foundations on which bees would build combs. In 2005, the beekeeping industry earned more than $200 million from the sale of honey and related products, such as beeswax.

Many beekeepers rent their hives to farmers and orchardists to aid in the pollination of their crops. The value of pollination to U.S. agriculture is estimated at $15 billion.

In recent years, pollination with rented bees has become increasingly important to agriculture, because infestations by mites have wiped out many wild-bee colonies. By and large, beekeepers have successfully fought the infestations with chemicals.

The recent widespread disappearance of honeybees has alarmed both beekeepers and farmers. Referred to as "colony collapse disorder" (CCD), the phenomenon was first reported in 2006 in Florida, where hives were found empty of all but a few sickly juvenile bees. By spring 2007, CCD had spread to 27 states, with beekeepers reporting losses of 30 to 90 percent of their hives. Early research implied that environmental and nutritional factors may have suppressed the bees' immune systems, leaving them susceptible to either new or known diseases. In 2007, the U.S. Department of Agriculture (USDA) announced a federal action plan to identify the causes of CCD and develop solutions.

that are to develop into queens enclose only the head, thorax, and part of the abdomen.

After 12 days or so, the workers cast off their pupal skins and chew their way out of the cell. It takes the drones about two days longer to pass through the pupal stage. Princesses develop from pupae to adults in about seven days. They do not emerge from their cells; attendant bees make a small hole in each royal cell and continue to feed the occupant.

In time, the honeybee colony becomes overpopulated, and a form of emigration, called *swarming*, takes place. The old queen, accompanied by many of the workers, leaves the hive and seeks a new nest. This may be the hollow of a tree or a human-made hive. One of the young princesses now emerges from her cell in the old hive. She makes her way to all the other royal cells and kills their occupants. If two or more princesses emerge at the same time, they fight until only one remains alive. The new queen then flies from the nest, mates with a drone, returns to the nest again, and begins to lay eggs. The drone dies immediately after mating.

The rest of the drones are tolerated in the hive for a time, although they perform no communal tasks. If the food supply dwindles, however, they are driven out of the nest and are not permitted to return. Since they are dependent on the food brought in by the workers, the drones are doomed to die from starvation once they are excluded from the nest.

The individual workers perform specific tasks. Some of them collect pollen and nectar. Others care for the young. Still others attend to the queen. A certain number fan the hive by means of rapid wing movements. This is a most important task; if the premises become too hot, the wax cells melt.

Dance Communication

As a result of research in the 1920s by Austrian zoologist Karl von Frisch, we now know that a worker bee conveys information about a promising food source to the other bees by means of a series of dances. When the food supply is near at hand, the returning bee performs a round dance on one of the vertical combs of the hive. It circles to the right and then to the left, over and over again, as its hivemates watch.

If the supply of food is 300 feet (90 meters) or more distant, the returning bee performs a tail-wagging dance. First it makes a short, straight run up or down the comb, wagging its abdomen from side to side. It then circles to the left. Again it makes a straight run with a tail-wagging motion, and this time circles to the right. The bee tells how far away the food is by the speed of the dance; the slower the dance, the farther away the food. It indicates the direction of the food by the direction of its straight run. If the dancer heads directly upward during the straight part of the dance, it means that the feeding place is in the same direction as the Sun. If the insect heads directly downward in its straight run, it means that the workers must fly away from the Sun to reach the food. If the bee goes 45 degrees to the right of vertical in the straight part of its run, it indicates that the feeding place is located at 45 degrees to the right of the Sun.

Other Social Bees

Bumblebees. These insects, which comprise the family Bombini, range in length from 0.04 to about 1 inch (1 to 2.5 centimeters).

Bumblebee colonies, like those of wasps, must be started anew each year. Each colony is established in the spring by a young fertilized queen, who has spent the winter under brush or debris or in a hole in a log. The queen seeks a site in or on the ground; this is often the vacated nest of a field mouse, chipmunk, or other small mammal. She may have to fight other bumblebee queens for the site.

Once established in her new home, the queen prepares balls of honey and pollen on which she lays her eggs. With the coming of cold weather, the old queen, her retinue of workers, and the drone hangers-on all perish. Only the young queens survive to begin the process again the following spring.

Stingless bees. The Meliponini are a third important group of social bees. They are much smaller than honeybees; some species are only 0.08 inch (2 millimeters) long.

The Meliponini build combs in horizontal sections. Some make their nests on the ground, others in the hollows of trees, and still others in the nests of termites or ants. In constructing their abodes, the bees use soil, leaf particles, dung, and other substances in addition to the wax that they secrete. They store honey in fairly large receptacles. Human beings occasionally use the honey as food—a dangerous practice, as it may be highly poisonous.

WASPS

The social wasps all belong to the family Vespidae. The most familiar representatives are the common wasps and hornets of the genus

Wasps destroy many insects that would otherwise harm crops. Unfortunately, wasps (including the bald-faced hornet above) also deliver a formidable sting to humans.

Vespa. The young *Vespa* queens mate in the autumn. They alone of all the members of wasp colonies survive the winter season, hibernating until the coming of spring.

Roused by the first warm days, each young queen seeks a place for a nest— perhaps under an eave, in a hollow tree, or on a bush. There she rapidly constructs a series of cells of paperlike structure, formed from woody fibers and other vegetable matter. She deposits an egg in each cell.

When the wasp larvae hatch, the queen feeds them with chewed caterpillars, flies, or fruit juices. When the time finally comes for the larvae to assume the pupa form, they close their cells, undergo metamorphosis, and emerge as undeveloped females, or workers. The workers assist the queen in making more cells and in feeding the larvae. Tier after tier is built, until the nest becomes a truly imposing structure.

The early generations of wasps have all been undeveloped females, or workers, some of which are capable of laying eggs that may develop into males. Toward late summer or early autumn, young queens and, after that, males appear. The young queens and males eventually leave the nest, never to return. The workers that remain behind destroy the larvae that are left in the nest. Then they themselves die.

Some wasps construct nests out of paperlike materials that they produce themselves. Most paper-wasp nests are built in trees or under the eaves of houses.

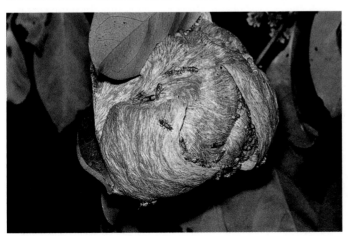

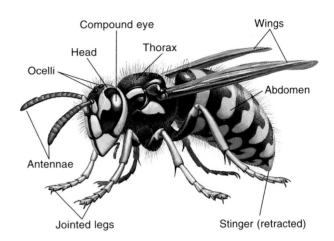

The yellow jacket illustrated above is a paper wasp with a striking, almost tigerlike pattern on its abdomen. Its external anatomy is typical of most wasps; the female has a stinger—a modified ovipositor—in the tip of the abdomen with which it delivers its infamous sting.

The social wasp whose life cycle was just described eats insects that are harmful to people. At the same time, it destroys much fruit and sometimes attacks human beings, particularly when it is molested (or thinks that it has been molested). The hornet is a large wasp whose sting is particularly formidable to people.

Solitary Wasps

Like bees, most species of wasps are solitary insects. Since a solitary wasp does not require the large communal dwellings of its social cousins, it frequently makes a simpler but still-efficient dwelling in sand, clay, or mud. Since solitary wasps lack a worker caste, the mother wasp must provide food to which the larvae, upon hatching, may help themselves. She undertakes this task by capturing various insects, particularly caterpillars and spiders. First the mother wasp stings the prey, paralyzing it; then she drags it off to her nest. The victims remain alive—albeit helpless—to await the attack of the newly hatched larvae. Thus, the young of the solitary wasps are assured of a bountiful and long-lasting food supply upon hatching.

Other especially remarkable species of wasps include those belonging to the genus *Pompilus,* which do not hesitate to attack even wolf spiders and other arachnids, and the gall wasp, or gallfly, which lays its eggs in plants and causes galls (areas of swelling) to form.

Ichneumons

The family Ichneumonidae includes some 40,000 known species of parasitic wasps. In general, ichneumon flies resemble wasps, but their antennae are usually longer and more seg-

A queen termite (inset below, being attended by workers) may reach gigantic proportions, as may the nests of certain species. In Africa, some termite mounds (below) are true achievements of animal architecture.

mented than those of wasps. Ichneumonidae flies are found all over the world.

The ichneumon fly deposits its eggs on or beneath the skin of various insect larvae. When these eggs hatch, the young feed on the tissues or vital fluids of the victims. Ichneumons kill great numbers of larvae of insects that are harmful to people, thus ranking them among our most valuable allies in the insect world.

TERMITES

The termites, or white ants, are not ants at all, but they deserve mention since they are ranked as social insects. They form the order Isoptera, a name that refers to the equal size and shape of the wings of those forms having wings. Unlike ants, termites are not slender-waisted, and their antennae are not elbowed.

Termite society is based on a caste system. A queen and king form the royal couple. The queen has an enormously enlarged, cylinder-shaped abdomen. During a year, she lays at least 3 million eggs. The small king is devoted to his queen throughout her life, fertilizing her eggs at intervals. Aside from this royal pair, individuals capable of reproduction are kept in readiness in the event of the queen's decline.

Workers are soft-bodied, pale creatures that labor continuously at constructing the nest, collecting food, caring for the eggs, and feeding the queen, soldiers, and young. In some species, nymphs instead of workers do these tasks.

The soldiers defend the nest against invading ants. Some soldiers have enlarged, armored heads with formidable jaws. Others, with small jaws, have a snoutlike projection that ejects a sticky, acrid fluid onto an enemy. Each caste includes termites of all ages and of both sexes.

Termites nest either below ground or above the surface in mounds, trees, and stumps. They build enclosed mud runways to their sources of food, which consists of dead tree stumps and limbs as well as the wood used for building houses or other structures. This wood is broken down in the digestive tract by protozoa. Termites also eat fungi and grasses.

BEETLES

by John C. Pallister

To many people, a beetle is a dark, scurrying little creature that evokes disgust and even apprehension. The very name of the insect reflects this attitude: the word "beetle" is derived from the Anglo-Saxon *bitol*, meaning "creature that bites."

Not all beetles are loathsome, however. Some species are very useful because they prey on other insects, ones that are generally considered to be pests. Other beetles are scavengers, burying small dead animals, cleaning up debris, and making the environment more attractive.

Unfortunately, there are thousands of species that destroy trees, crops, processed foods, clothing, and furniture. A few are parasitic on human beings. Some transmit a tapeworm to rats, other animals, and humans.

GENERAL CHARACTERISTICS

A beetle may be no larger than a pinhead, or it may be as big as an adult human's fist; dull in color or shiny like a precious jewel; and slender and graceful or antlike and ungainly.

Like all insects, a beetle has no bones. Its vital organs and muscles are protected by a jointed, segmented case of hard material called *chitin*. Its body is divided into three parts: the head, thorax, and abdomen. The head carries the eyes, antennae, and mouthparts, which are very complicated. The thorax, or middle section, bears the six legs and two pairs of wings, and, within it, some of the digestive organs. The abdomen—its 9 or 10 ringlike segments of chitin connected by a softer tissue—contains the organs for breathing, digestion, and reproduction. Stridulating organs, which produce sound, also occur on the abdomen of some beetles.

All beetles have one pair of jointed antennae, usually projecting in front of the eyes. These may be so short as to be almost invisible, as in carpet beetles and lady beetles. Or they may be two or three times as long as the insect's body, as in the long-horned wood-boring beetles. Under a low-powered microscope, the antennae show an astonishing variety of shapes—shapes that suggest a brush, a feather, a string of beads, a comb, or a club.

The most remarkable distinguishing structure of beetles is the outer, or first, pair of wings,

Beetles differ from other insects in having elytra—shield-like wing cases that cover their abdomens and hind wings. The familiar coloration of ladybugs (top) and the metallic look of a tiger beetle (inset) derive from their elytra.

called *elytra*. The elytra do not look at all like wings; rather, they are hard, shell-like structures that serve as a covering for the second, or inner, pair of wings and for the abdomen. The under-wings are thin and membranous, and, when not in use, are folded and refolded under the elytra. The elytra are of little help in flying.

All beetles have elytra or traces of elytra. Even the name of the beetles' order— Coleoptera, which means "sheathed wings"—is derived from this wing arrangement. Only a few other insects have wing sheaths, among them earwigs, some grasshoppers, and some aphids. Even so, their sheaths are not nearly as firm and shell-like as are those of the beetles.

A beetle's thorax is composed of three segments, each of which bears a pair of legs. The elytra are fastened to the top of the middle segment, covering it, the back segment, and part— or, more often, all—of the abdomen. The top of the front thoracic segment—the prothorax—is as hard and shell-like as the elytra. In some species, the prothorax fits so neatly against the elytra that when the beetle is resting, its back appears to be in one piece.

Life Cycle

During its life, a beetle passes through four distinct stages. First it is an egg. This hatches into a wormlike larva, commonly called a *grub*. The grub eats voraciously; this is the only stage of the beetle's life during which it increases in size. (Little beetles are never the young of large beetles; they are always of a different species.)

When the grub grows too big for its skin, it molts, or sheds the skin. Molting usually occurs five or six times before the creature is full-grown. Once the grub has eaten all it needs, it seeks a secure resting place, often in the plant or tree where it has been feeding. Sometimes the grub burrows into the ground, where it builds itself a little cell.

Once the grub is secure in its shelter, it becomes a *pupa*, eating nothing and remaining motionless while great changes occur in its body. This period may last only three to four days in the case of lady beetles, especially if the humidity and temperature are just right. In other species, the pupa stage can last all autumn and winter. Finally, the adult beetle emerges from the pupal case and lives for perhaps two to six months. Certain wood-boring beetles have a life cycle of several years.

DISTRIBUTION AND CLASSIFICATION

Land beetles are found all over the world, except in the extreme northern or southern areas. A few species dwell in freshwater ponds and streams, but none inhabit salt water.

The term "beetle" is applied to all the members of the order Coleoptera. With some 300,000 species, the beetles are the most numerous of all the orders of insects. These species are divided into about 150 families. The following discussion focuses on some of the more notable families.

Tiger Beetles

The term "tiger beetle" aptly describes the fierce and swift members of the family Cicindelidae. These creatures feed on other insects, which they stalk on sandy banks and beaches, at roadsides, and along woodland paths. These

The tiger beetle (Cicindela hybrida) *has outer structures common to all beetles. Mandibles, maxillary palps, and labial palps are jaws used for biting. The compound eyes contain thousands of lenses, or ommatidia.*

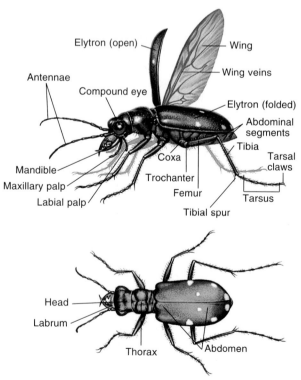

rather small, slender insects are just about the color of the sand or dirt upon which they run. One of the most common species in the eastern United States, however, is a brilliant metallic green, and several related species are greenish or bronze-colored. The elytra are often spotted or banded in lighter tints.

Tiger-beetle larvae are whitish creatures with big, metallic heads and very large mandibles (jaws). To their insect prey, these grubs are even more dangerous than the adults: they simply lurk in the small burrows they have dug, with their heads just protruding and their mandibles wide open, ready to seize any insect that walks over them. Hooks on the back of its abdomen serve to anchor the grub to the sides of the burrow, preventing the intended prey from launching a counterattack by jerking the larva out of its lair.

Diving beetles take unique advantage of their elytra by storing air underneath them. In doing so, they have an oxygen supply upon which to draw while hunting underwater or resting at the bottom of a pond.

Water Beetles

Although most beetles are strictly land insects, a few families spend much or all of their lives in ponds and streams. The diving beetles make up the Dytiscidae, the largest family of water beetles. These oval-shaped, medium- to large-sized beetles are brownish or greenish black. They have long, sturdy hind legs, which they use as oars. Under their wing covers, they carry a supply of air for breathing while they hunt or rest on the bottom. Both adults and larvae feed voraciously on all kinds of aquatic insects, tadpoles, and even small fish. Adult diving beetles sometimes migrate at night in great numbers from one pond to another, stopping on the way to whirl around a streetlight.

A silent approach to a pond or pool may reveal a group of whirligig beetles circling the surface of the water; disturb them, and they will quickly dive to the bottom. These small, dark insects comprise the family Gyrinidae. Their long, slender front legs are equipped to seize prey, while the middle and hind legs are broad and flat for swimming. Their habits and food are much like those of the Dytiscidae.

The third important water-beetle family, the Hydrophilidae, are sometimes nicknamed water scavengers after their habit of feeding on decaying vegetable and animal matter—although they will eat virtually any living creature they can catch. They somewhat resemble the diving beetles, but they use their legs differently and are not as good divers. Enough air clings to the hairy underside of the water scavenger to give the beetle a certain degree of buoyancy. The creature also carries air under its wings for breathing.

The insect called the black water beetle, which is found around kitchen sinks, drains, and other damp places, is not a beetle at all, but rather a type of cockroach.

Ground Beetles

Evening strollers frequently encounter small, dark beetles scurrying in front of them. The great majority of these creatures are ground beetles that belong to a large family called Carabidae. Carabids are most numerous in areas where there is plentiful rainfall.

Most ground beetles hunt at night, hiding by day under rocks, logs, or debris. If you raise an old board from the ground, you may catch a glimpse of some carabids. These black or brownish, oblong, medium-sized creatures will try to run away rather than fly.

Most ground beetles feed on the larvae and adults of other insects, and also upon slugs, snails, and every other creature they are able to capture. A few are seed eaters, and the grubs of a small number feed on sprouting corn.

To defend itself, the bombardier beetle (left) sprays enemies with an irritating gas from the tail end of its body.

eled in different shades of red with black spots. Usually these are the aphid eaters. Other species are black with red spots; many of these attack scale insects. The herbivorous lady beetles are likely to be yellow with black spots.

Carpet Beetles

Everybody hates the carpet beetles, or Dermestidae (skin eaters), and with good reason. These beetles feed on every animal product that people have processed for their own use. Fur and feathers, woolen cloth, ham, cheese, flour and meal, dried insects, stuffed birds and animals in museums—each of these products is a food for one or more dermestid species.

Dermestid larvae are small and brownish, covered with many black hairs and bristles. They can move very quickly: a closely observed one has a curious ritual—it runs a short distance, stops, vibrates its hair rapidly, and then starts running again. The larvae are more destructive than the adults, eating voraciously when food is available—although they can survive a long time without any food.

Click Beetles

A large variety of extraordinary beetles belong to the family Elateridae—click beetles, or elaters. The most amazing characteristic of the click beetles is their ability to hurl themselves up in the air. When disturbed, the creature drops on its back to the ground, feigning death. When it seems safe to move again, the beetle bends its head and thorax back, pushing a special spine on its prothorax almost out of the groove in which it lies. Suddenly the tension is released. The spine snaps back along its groove with a clicking noise, driving the base of the elytra against the ground with such surprising force that the little insect may be shot 4 to 5 inches (10 to 12.7 centimeters) into the air.

Click beetles are also known as skipjacks and snapping beetles. A conspicuous temperate species is the eyed elater, *Alaus oculatus*, a sturdy beetle

Carrion, or Burying, Beetles

Certain members of the family Silphidae help keep the surface of Earth clean by burying small dead animals. When a pair of these beetles find a dead mouse or small snake, the female deposits her eggs in it. Then the beetles quickly bury the body 3 to 4 inches (7.6 to 10 centimeters) under the ground. When the larvae are hatched, they feed on the decaying flesh.

There are many species of burying beetles. One of the largest and most conspicuous species, *Necrophorus americanus*, has a 1- to 1.6-inch (2.5- to 4-centimeter)-long heavy, oblong, shiny black body with two large reddish spots on each wing cover. The prothorax is hemispherical and red; the head is almost as large as the prothorax.

Ladybird Beetles, or Ladybugs

Unlike most beetles, the ladybirds, or coccinellids, have always enjoyed wide popularity. With approximately 4,500 species, these members of the family Coccinellidae were long considered omens of good luck; children throughout Europe and North America even sing affectionate little verses to them. Nowadays most people know that ladybirds eat the aphids or plant lice that attack house and garden plants. There are coccinellids, however, such as the squash beetle and the Mexican bean beetle, that eat food plants instead of other insects, and do considerable damage in gardens.

Both the helpful and harmful varieties of coccinellids are attractive in appearance. These rather small creatures are broadly oval or hemispherical. Many species of ladybirds are enam-

with a shining black back flecked with silvery scales. On top of its large prothorax, two big black spots, outlined by a ring of white scales, resemble two glaring eyes. Eyed elaters are found all summer long around old stumps and logs, where their larvae live, feeding on the rotting wood.

Elater larvae are long, slender, smooth, yellowish grubs, so hard and stiff that they are called wireworms. Many feed on decaying wood. Others live in the ground, annoying farmers by burrowing into bulbous roots, tubers, and sprouting corn seed.

Metallic Wood Borers

Nearly all the metallic wood borers, or Buprestidae, have striking colors. Their copper, gold, green, blue, or red backs shine with a metallic luster and often are decorated with intricate patterns in contrasting colors. Since their bodies are hard and the colors do not fade, buprestids are often used as decorations, not only by natives in tropical forests but by artists everywhere. Two of the loveliest species are called jewel beetles; Australians set them in mountings to wear as jewelry.

Buprestid species may be short and flat, or oblong and cylindrical. They are large in the tropics—a Brazilian giant is over 2 inches (5 centimeters) long—and small- to medium-sized in temperate regions. Most are tropical, and nearly all live in forests. The adults like to sun themselves, often in a small patch of sunlight amid an otherwise dark forest.

The larva is blind and legless, with a small head and a large, flat thorax. The thorax is often mistaken for the head, and gives the grub the name of flat-headed wood borer, or hammerhead.

Fireflies

Fireflies, or "lightning bugs," beetles of the family Lampyridae, add a certain mysterious charm to summer evenings. Even city

Most people know a firefly by its flashing glow rather than by its typical beetle characteristics.

dwellers may see a few sparklers on a park or lawn and around hedges.

In the daytime, with its bioluminescence machinery turned off, the firefly is decidedly unremarkable: medium- to small-sized, elongated or oblong, black or brownish, and edged with red or yellow. The elytra and the thoracic covering are not so hard as in most beetles.

The females of many species are wingless, wormlike creatures, sometimes four times as long as the male. They glow at night from spots along the sides of the abdomen and thorax. The European glowworm belongs to this group.

Each species of firefly appears to have its own code of signals. It has been assumed that the lights are signals between the sexes. But many larvae also are luminous, and so are a few pupae. In some tropical species, the larvae bioluminesce, but the adults do not. Not all lampyrids are bioluminescent; a great many species are diurnal and have no need of light.

Adults and larvae of nearly all species are carnivorous, feeding on small worms, snails, and the larvae of other insects.

Deathwatch Beetles and Their Kin

Members of the family Anobiidae are small insects, 0.25 inch (6 millimeters) or less in length. They are dull-colored scavengers, living on old, dry vegetable or animal material.

The most notorious member of this family is the deathwatch beetle, a tiny brown insect that feeds on decaying wood, as in old houses. As it eats, the creature makes a ticking noise that, in the still of night, sounds portentous.

You may find in your bathtub what looks like a little red spider, with a globular body, either smooth and shining or partly fuzzy, and long, slender legs. This is actually a beetle, one or another of a few species of the Anobiidae. It has likely fallen into the bathtub, in which it is trapped because this beetle cannot climb the slick sides of the tub and it has no wings for flying. Only against a white background is the little red beetle visible. Elsewhere it would blend completely with its surroundings and would therefore almost certainly escape detection.

Darkling Beetles

Darkling beetles, or tenebrionids, form the family Tenebrionidae. They prefer arid regions, where they are usually nocturnal scavengers, feeding on dead or decaying vegetable matter. Some species devour living plants, and sometimes become so numerous that they denude the sparse natural vegetation and damage cultivated crops.

The goddesses above pray to the Sun god Ra, symbolized by a scarab, a beetle sacred in ancient Egypt.

In general, darkling beetles are small to medium, black, and stoutly built. Many species are wingless, and their elytra have been fused together. Their legs are long, but they move rather slowly with an awkward, loose-jointed gait.

The long and slender larvae live in decaying wood and dried vegetable products. Some species of European and Asian origin feed only on grain and grain products. Now distributed around the world, they cause considerable damage. The mealworm, *Tenebrio molitor*, which attacks cereal products, has become a commercial product itself; it is raised in large quantities to feed pet birds.

Stag Beetles

Members of the family Lucanidae are relatively large beetles. The male's huge mandibles have led to a common name: "pinching bug." The other common name, "stag beetle," comes from the resemblance that the creature's mandibles bear to the antlers of deer.

It is not known what use the males make of their mandibles. They have been observed fighting each other—not by pinching, but by pushing or butting. If you push a small stick in front of the pinching bug, this beetle will grasp the stick with its mandibles and hold on tight while you lift the stick into the air. Do not offer a finger, however: this beetle can draw blood.

The giant male stag beetle, which lives in rotting logs and stumps of oak, maple, and apple trees, is a formidable-looking creature that ranges in length from 1.5 to 2.25 inches (3.8 to 5.7 centimeters). From the head of its highly polished chestnut-brown body protrude two mandibles that are almost as long as the entire body. The antennae are black, elbowed, and end in small combs. The strong black legs are edged with short spines. The female is smaller than the male; her mandibles are short and stout. These beetles require two or more years to mature.

Scarabs and Their Kin

The Scarabaeoidea are a numerous and well-noted family. They are so varied in form, size, and habits that about the only characteristics they have in common are antennae that end in a leafy club, large eyes, a large and prominent prothorax, and strong legs.

This group includes the largest beetles in the world and also some of the smallest, ranging in color from dull black to brilliant hues on metallic or enameled surfaces. Because of these variations, the Scarabaeoidea have been divided into a number of subfamilies. Some entomologists have even raised the family to the status of a superfamily, called Scarabaeidae—and the subfamilies to families. Either way, the relationship between the ranks is the same.

The scarab, the ancient Egyptian sacred beetle after which the entire family was later named, is one of the dung beetles. These useful scav-

Some beetles are pests. Every year, Japanese beetles (above) do untold damage to gardens and orchards.

engers clean up excrement by rolling it into little balls. The females deposit their eggs in the balls and then bury them. The Egyptians held one or two scarab species sacred, as a symbol of resurrection, and placed them in the tombs with their dead. They painted pictures of the scarab on their stone coffins, and made models of it in jewelry.

Another well-known group are the May beetles (perhaps more commonly called June bugs), big-bodied creatures that bumble about in the early evening. Tropical species are brilliantly colored; temperate varieties are brownish. These beetles are vegetarians—the adults eat leaves, and the larvae live underground on roots. The beautiful—albeit extraordinarily destructive—Japanese beetle, *Popillia japonica*, is closely related to the June bug.

Through photographs and museum specimens, many people are acquainted with the giant tropical scarabs and their grotesque horns. The horn projecting from the prothorax of the male Hercules beetle, *Dynastes hercules*, of the West Indies may be more than 2.5 inches (6 centimeters) long; the entire insect is often more than 6 inches (15 centimeters) long. The massive elephant beetle, which dwells in the tropical Americas, is the thickest and heaviest of all the beetles. It grows to be 4 inches (10 centimeters) long; its wingspread of 8 inches (20 centimeters) enables it to fly quite well. The males of the gigantic Goliath beetles of Africa and eastern Asia are 5 inches (12.7 centimeters) long. They have no large horns, but the prothorax is enormously swollen and beautifully marked.

Long-horned Wood-boring Beetles

The double-jointed name of the Cerambycidae aptly describes the majority of the species in this large family. The term "horned" refers to the insect's antennae and not to the protuberances on the head or prothorax found on some other beetles.

The cerambycids range in size from the pygmy beetle of central North America, which is about 0.1 inch (2.5 millimeters) long, with antennae of the same length, to the startling *Batocera* of New Guinea, whose 3-inch (7.6-centimeter) body carries antennae almost 7 inches (18 centimeters) long.

Cerambycids have large eyes and mouthparts; the mandibles of some males are very large and, in some tropical species, antlershaped. The legs are long and slender; sometimes the front pair are nearly twice as long as the others. The insects display all colors and color patterns. Usually they have large, powerful wings, although a few species are wingless. Many have stridulating organs that produce a peculiar squeaking noise.

Some species have a pleasant odor. The European musk beetle, for example, a beautiful copper and green insect, smells like attar of roses. Many longhorns are good mimics: some

The harmless Goliath beetle (below), one of the world's largest flying insects, lives high in the rain forest.

With its metallic colors glistening in the sunlight, the tiny leaf beetle above looks more like a gem than an insect.

drying themselves on the top of leaves on a summer morning after a heavy dew.

Each species has its preferred plant food. Many of the larvae feed on the outside of the leaf in company with the adults; they are active, bright-colored, chunky little grubs, in contrast to the pale, sluggish larvae that live in the ground or inside a plant stem.

Females of the beautiful genus *Donacia* drop down into the water to deposit their eggs on the roots and stems of aquatic plants. There the larvae will live until they pupate. *Donacia* beetles are gregarious. Large numbers of them can often be seen flying over or resting on the lush vegetation around ponds and swamps.

The chrysomelids include several destructive pests. The famous yellow and black Colorado potato beetle, *Leptinotarsa decemlineata*, has devastated crops in Mexico, eaten its way across the United States, and invaded Europe. Three or four species of brightly marked cucumber beetles do their share of damage to vines. Other species attack sweet potatoes, spinach, and other agricultural crops.

Weevils

The weevils, or snout beetles, comprise several families, most of which have beak-shaped heads. In some species, the beak is very long, slender, and rigid. Other species have spoon- or shovel-shaped beaks. In one family, the bark beetles, the beak is so short as to be hardly noticeable or is missing altogether.

The target tortoise beetle below derives its name from the resemblance that its back bears to a bull's-eye target.

look like bumblebees; others, like wasps. One African species is camouflaged to resemble a piece of velvety moss as it rests on a tree trunk; its antennae appear to be dried twigs.

All cerambycids are vegetarians. The adults feed on fungi, pollen, or green leaves. The larvae live inside a plant or tree, where they may spend from one to three or four years. In Mexico, the larva that lives in the agave, or century plant, is a shrimplike creature that is considered an appetizing addition to salads.

Cerambycids reach their greatest development in the tropics, where they are avidly sought by collectors; every natural-history museum has specimens of the larger and more striking species. Many of the North American species are quite attractive. The common milkweed longhorn, only a little more than 0.4 inch (1 centimeter long), is bright red with black spots. *Prionus imbricornis*, about 2 inches (5 centimeters) long, is a dark reddish brown with magnificent heavy plumed antennae.

Leaf Beetles

Wherever green leaves occur, so do leaf beetles, attractive little insects that are quite destructive from the human point of view. The Chrysomelidae, the third-largest beetle family, are small- to medium-sized and hemispherical, oval, or oblong in shape. Their mandibles, antennae, and legs are usually short. Some are enameled in brilliant colors. Many are striped and spotted. Others are dull black or brown.

Most leaf beetles live in the tropics, although there are 1,000 species in North America alone. It is not unusual to find these creatures

All weevils are vegetarians, attacking trees and cultivated crops. They have been a major pest for so long that some farmers refer to just about any damaging insect as a weevil, and the term "weevily" is used to describe damaged grains and grain products. Still, only a few of this enormous group actually cause economic destruction. The great majority feed on plants with which human beings are not at present concerned, or on weeds.

Brenthidae. The weevils of the family Brenthidae are odd-looking; their heads are often as long as their slender bodies—or even longer. This is especially true of the female, who uses her head to bore a deep hole in which to deposit her eggs. Sometimes she gets stuck and cannot withdraw her head. The male then tries to pry her loose by pushing down on the end of her upturned abdomen. Only a few Brenthidae are found outside of the tropics.

Curculionidae. The curculios are the largest family of beetles, with more than 40,000 described species. The curculios include many formidable crop pests: the cotton-boll weevil, the apple-blossom weevil, the plum curculio, the rose weevil, the grain weevil, and the rice weevil, among others.

Curculios range in size from minute to 3 inches (7.6 centimeters); all have prominent snouts, and a great many are colored dull gray or brown. When alarmed, curculios fold their legs close to their bodies and remain motionless, looking for all the world like seeds or bits of dirt. Some are quite beautiful. One of these, the diamond beetle of Brazil, is covered with scales reflecting brilliant blues and greens from minute grooves. At one time, this creature was in such demand for jewelry that it was almost completely exterminated.

Scolytidae. Bark beetles and ambrosia beetles belong to the weevil family of the Scolytidae; they are minute in size and dull in color. These creatures are serious forest pests. The female of

All of the many snout beetles, including the vividly striped specimen above, have a long, down-curving beak.

the bark, or engraver, beetle excavates a passageway along the grain of living trees, just under the bark, and deposits eggs on either side at regular intervals. The larvae work at right angles to the lengthwise passage through the cambium layer, so that the route of one never intercepts that of any other. This makes a pretty pattern, but it kills the tree.

Ambrosia beetles penetrate deep into the wood of dead trees. There the female lines tunnels with a yellow fungus, called ambrosia, probably as food for the larvae. The tunnels spoil the value of the trees as lumber. The beetles spend their whole existence in the tunnels, often remaining after the wood has been cut into lumber.

The people of Enterprise, Alabama, erected a statue in honor of the boll weevil to commemorate the beetle's role in forcing the local farmers to diversify their crops.

Other Beetles

The family Meloidae includes the blister beetle, which is well known to pharmacists. A variety of blister beetle—the Spanish fly, *Lytta vesicatoria*—is dried and reduced to powdered form to produce the pharmaceutical preparation known as cantharides, which is used in medicine as a counterirritant.

The smallest of the beetles are those of the Ptilidae family. All are less than 0.6 inch (15 millimeters) in length. They are particularly common under loose bark, where, to the naked eye, they appear to be mites. But the microscope reveals that they are true beetles, with elytra and wings.

Butterflies and Moths

by John C. Pallister

Butterflies and moths are among the most beautiful creatures in the Animal Kingdom. With their spectacular coloration and the elegant manner in which they delicately flit from flower to flower, butterflies are the favorites of amateur entomologists of all ages. Boys and girls often start their insect collections with butterflies. Many adults delight in collecting these lovely creatures, sometimes exploring isolated areas in search of new, unknown species.

Closely related to the butterflies are the moths. Both groups belong to the order Lepidoptera, which is second only to the beetles in number of species. More than 100,000 Lepidoptera species have been described.

Moths and butterflies are found throughout the world. A few species inhabit the subpolar regions and ascend to the snow line on mountains. Far more species live in temperate regions. In the tropics, the butterflies and moths attain the greatest variety, largest size, and most brilliant coloring.

GENERAL CHARACTERISTICS

The term "Lepidoptera" is derived from two Greek words: *lepis*, meaning "scale," and *ptera*, meaning "wings." The reference is to the minute scales that generally cover the rather broad, usually opaque and membranous wings of these insects. The scales are usually triangular or elongated modified hairs, each fastened by a stemlike base to the wing. They are laid on the wing in regular rows, each overlapping the row below, like shingles on a roof.

Since the scales are held only by the tiny stemlike base, they can be very easily dislodged. Such dislodged scales constitute the dustlike particles that coat your fingers when you try to hold a butterfly.

Luna moths (above) provide vivid testimony to the loveliness so often associated with butterflies and their kin.

The coloring of butterflies and moths is due in most cases to pigments embedded in the scales. In some Lepidoptera, different colors are produced as light is diffracted from tiny, closely spaced parallel lines, called *striae*, on the scales of the wings. This so-called *structural coloration* results in a variety of iridescent hues—violet, blue-green, copper, silver, and gold. The color changes as the surface is tilted.

Most lepidopterous scales are striated (that is, possess striae), but in only a few cases are the striae fine enough and close enough together to produce iridescent structural color. In such cases, the striae may be astonishingly fine. Some tropical species have thousands of striae per square inch.

There is sometimes considerable variation in the coloring of butterflies of the same species. Where there are two or more broods per season, the spring forms may differ radically in the shade of coloring from those in the summer brood; the latter are usually much lighter. If there is a fall brood, it may differ from both the spring and summer forms. Variation of this kind is called *seasonal dimorphism*. The two sexes of a given species are often differently colored. The male, which is usually somewhat smaller than the female, is quite apt to show more-brilliant coloring. This differentiation is known as *sexual dimorphism*.

Butterflies and moths have keen senses of sight, smell, and taste. Some moths can even hear! Butterfly eyes are especially sensitive to colors, most particularly red. Moths tend to be drawn to light colors. Many butterfly and moth species also use scents to attract potential mates and to drive away enemies.

Butterflies and moths are comparatively recent additions to the Animal Kingdom. In North America, butterflies occurred in the Eocene and Oligocene periods of the Cenozoic era, while in Europe, small moths were trapped in amber in the Baltic regions during the Oligocene period. Some European finds may go back more than 135 million years, to the Jurassic period in the Mesozoic era.

LIFE CYCLE

Butterflies and moths rank among the more highly developed insects—those having a complete metamorphosis. This means that they pass through four stages of development: egg, larva, pupa, and adult.

Eggs. The eggs are small; round, oval, or somewhat elongated; variously colored; and delicately sculptured with ridges or pits, according to the species. The female usually lays her eggs on or close to a plant whose vegetation will provide the young insects with food. With some exceptions, each species feeds only on one particular plant species or on a closely related group of species.

Larval stage. The creatures that hatch from moth or butterfly eggs are the *caterpillars*, scientifically known as larvae (singular: larva). The young of most butterflies and moths are herbivorous. A few species are carnivorous, feeding on aphids and scale insects. Of the four stages of development, this is the only one in which the insect can grow.

The caterpillar feeds as voraciously as its food supply will permit. As the skin, or covering, of the animal grows tight, it is shed, or

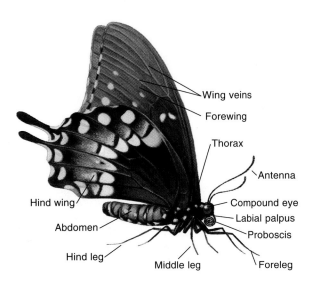

Spicebush Swallowtail Butterfly

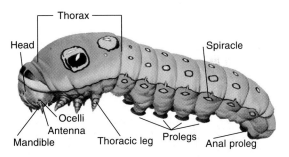

The typical butterfly (top) is slender, has knobbed antennae, and folds its colorful, often iridescent wings vertically when at rest. The moth (bottom), by contrast, is stout and hairy, has unknobbed, often feathered antennae, and spreads its usually dull-colored wings when resting. Anatomical features common to both butterflies and moths include mouthparts for sucking nectar and two pairs of wings that operate as one pair. The spicebush swallowtail caterpillar (center) has a striking pattern on the back of its head that resembles eyes, presumably to startle predators.

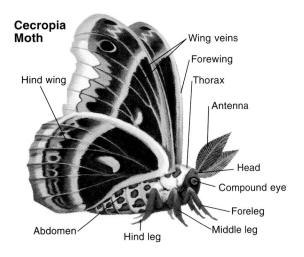

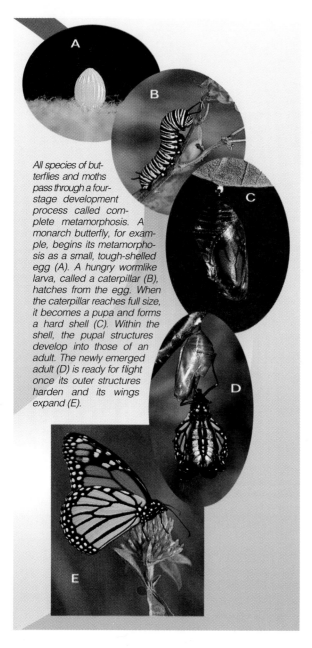

All species of butterflies and moths pass through a four-stage development process called complete metamorphosis. A monarch butterfly, for example, begins its metamorphosis as a small, tough-shelled egg (A). A hungry wormlike larva, called a caterpillar (B), hatches from the egg. When the caterpillar reaches full size, it becomes a pupa and forms a hard shell (C). Within the shell, the pupal structures develop into those of an adult. The newly emerged adult (D) is ready for flight once its outer structures harden and its wings expand (E).

pairs of prolegs, one pair each on the third, fourth, fifth, sixth, and last, or terminal, abdominal segment. Caterpillars travel by stretching out the front part of the body, taking hold with the true legs, and then drawing forward the rear part of the abdomen. The eyes are simple and arranged in pairs; there are from two to six on each side of the head.

Pupal stage. After a caterpillar has gone through the required number of molts, it becomes a pupa (plural: pupae). In butterflies and moths, the pupa is frequently called a *chrysalis*. It does not in the least resemble a caterpillar. In most cases, the appendages are "glued down" to the body (although frequently visible through the pupal skin), giving the creature a compact appearance.

The pupal stage is a quiescent period that may last from a few days to several months or more, depending on the species. Most butterfly pupae are found fastened to some stable object a short distance from the ground. Some hang head downward from a pad of silk, which the caterpillar spun on a sheltered object before molting. The swallowtail butterflies (family Papilionidae) and the white, sulfur, and orange-tip butterflies (family Pieridae) pupate in a more or less upright position, with the tip of the abdomen in a pad of silk; a silken strand, looped around the middle of the body, is fastened at each end to the support.

Moth pupae are sheltered in various ways. Most of them pupate on or near the ground under leaves, old logs, or loose bark, or in hollow trees. Many moth caterpillars burrow into the ground, where they form a smooth cell in which to pupate. Some line this cell with silk. Others, such as the tiger moths (family Arctiidae), also called woolly bears, use the spiny hairs from their bodies with a few strands of silk to form a rough cocoon in a sheltered place near the ground.

The most conspicuous cocoons are the beautiful silk ones spun by the larvae of a number of the giant silkworms (family Saturniidae).

Adult stage. After a certain period of inactivity as a pupa—a period that varies in length according to the species—life begins to stir

molted. The covering that has formed beneath the old one is soft and expands to accommodate the increased growth. There are five or six molts on the average—although some species may molt as many as 20 times.

Caterpillars have three pairs of true legs, one pair to each segment of the thorax—the part of the body between the head and the abdomen. On the abdomen, there are from one to five pairs of *prolegs*—fleshy protuberances armed with hooks for grasping twigs or leaves of the food plant. Most caterpillars have five

once again. With the final molt, the pupal case splits down the back, and out crawls a butterfly or moth. It is a poor, bedraggled creature at this time—its wings are limp and its body swollen. But soon the body fluids begin to flow into the veins of the wings, which start to expand and spread out. The spreading of the wings must proceed rapidly. If the air is too dry, the wings may dry out before they are properly spread, and the insect will be imperfectly formed. The last transformation of the butterfly or moth usually takes place in the dark of night. All the appendages now function properly, and the body has attained its normal size. Soon the lovely creature will be ready to fly off, seek food, and mate.

BUTTERFLY OR MOTH?

Over the years, many different systems of classification have been proposed for the Lepidoptera, although entomologists have still not universally agreed on a standard taxonomy for these creatures. Even the division of the Lepidoptera into the butterflies, Rhopalocera, and the moths, Heterocera, is considered by some to be artificial.

The antennae furnish the main point of difference between butterflies and moths. In butterflies, the tips of the antennae are distinctly knobbed or enlarged. In moths, the antennae assume a variety of forms: they may be slender, tapering to very fine points; feathery, or fernlike; or pectinate (having toothlike projections or divisions).

As with everything in zoology, there are exceptions. The skippers (family Hesperiidae) and the giant skippers (family Megathymidae)—which share characteristics of both butterflies and moths—have knobbed antennae. In most butterflies, however, the knob has a very fine, tapering, pointed tip, which is set at a very sharp angle. The antennae of the Sphingidae, which are moths, are tapering and very finely

pectinate (a moth characteristic), but the tip is curved, much as in the skippers.

Another distinguishing characteristic is that practically all butterflies fly only during the day (unless they are disturbed), while most

Once nearly extinct, the Schaus swallowtail butterfly (above) has made a strong comeback, thanks largely to an intensive captive-breeding program.

moths fly only at night (also unless they are disturbed). However, a few moth species, largely of the family Uraniidae, are diurnal. In this family, the creatures greatly resemble butterflies in their coloring, their broad wings, and, in some species, their "tails," or wing extensions.

SOME BUTTERFLY FAMILIES

The Lepidoptera number about 200 families. The following discussion focuses on some of the larger and more conspicuous ones.

Family Papilionidae. The members of this large group are known as swallowtails. Many of the species have "tails," or extensions, on their hind wings. A few even have two "tails"—a feature that accounts for the name "swallowtails."

The "tails" of the Papilionidae are not a positive identifying characteristic; indeed, certain members of the family have no "tails" at all. Conversely, certain butterflies and moths belonging to various other families have extensions on the hind wings.

In general, swallowtail species are medium to large in size, vividly colored or showing contrasting hues of black, yellow, red, and white. There are nearly 1,000 described species of papilionids. Most are found in the tropics, but many have invaded subtropical and temperate regions.

Dimorphism, both seasonal and sexual, is common among the swallowtails. Many of the caterpillars have eyespots on the thoracic region and a Y-shaped scent organ that can be extended from a slit on the dorsal (back) part.

Among the most magnificent members of this family are the bird-wing butterflies of the genus *Ornithoptera*. Some entomologists consider them a separate family. Most of these butterflies are gorgeously colored, with the males, which are generally smaller than the females, having the brighter colors. The front wings are very large and elongated; the hind wings are much smaller. These strong fliers usually prefer living in the protection of treetops in the forest canopy, which makes them difficult to collect. They are found particularly in New Guinea, Java, Sumatra, and Malaysia.

Countless reflective scales cover the wings of the male blue morpho butterfly (above), creating an extraordinary glimmering effect when the Sun shines on them.

Family Pieridae. These small- to medium-sized butterflies are worldwide in distribution, ranging from the tropics to the temperate regions. The cabbage butterfly hovering over garden cabbages and the common sulfur butterfly that children pursue over clover fields are familiar representatives of this family. The sulfurs of the tropics are medium-sized creatures that sometimes migrate in vast flocks to some unknown spot many miles away.

Family Morphidae. In the tropics of the Americas, from central Mexico south to southern Brazil, occur the gorgeous butterflies known as morphos. Tropical species show iridescent blues, greens, and purples, and the more than 100 species perhaps provide the best example of structural coloration.

Morpho butterflies are much sought after by collectors. Thousands are used for decorative purposes in the manufacture of trays, jewelry, and other items. So great has the trade in these colorful insects become that some countries have

The Palos Verdes blue butterfly (left), thought to have been extinct since 1983, was "rediscovered" in 1994. Zoologists now think that hundreds of them might exist.

The Uncompahgre fritillary butterfly (above), a recently discovered butterfly species, lives only in a few alpine meadows of the Rockies.

enacted strict regulations to prevent the morpho from being exterminated.

It is exciting to see a blue morpho flitting along a jungle pathway. With its slow, easy flight, it looks as if it would fly directly into an outheld butterfly net. Appearances are deceptive, however, for the morpho is an excellent dodger. It will dash under the net, or sweep upward and over a treetop, or backtrack down the path and lose itself in the foliage.

Family Nymphalidae. The brush-footed butterflies constitute a very large family. The front legs, greatly reduced in size, are often hairy and brushlike. This characteristic cannot be entirely depended upon to identify the Nymphalidae, however, because several other families, including the Satyridae, Danaidae, and Heliconiidae, have similar brushlike legs.

Nymphalidae are generally medium to large butterflies, garbed in varied patterns and colors. They occupy a wide belt around the world extending well into the temperate zones, making them readily available to butterfly lovers in the Americas and Europe. Descriptive common names have been given to several large groups, including the fritillaries, peacocks, tortoiseshells, and angelwings. Specific species of nymphalids have also received even-more-exact common names, such as mourning cloak and red admiral. These two species are noted for their ability to smell things through special structures on their feet!

Family Danaidae. The well-known monarch butterfly belongs to the Danaidae. Despite having relatively few species, this family accounts for an enormous number of individuals, which

Larvae As Pests

The larvae, or caterpillars, of the order Lepidoptera, particularly some of the moths, are often serious pests because, in order to satisfy their voracious appetites, they feed on plants and products that are useful to humans.

The larva of the gypsy moth, *Porthetria dispar* (see photo at right), is one of the worst pests. It devours the leaves of apple, oak, gray birch, alder, willow, and various other deciduous trees. When cankerworms—the caterpillars of the family Geometridae—are very numerous, they can strip the leaves of practically all the trees in extensive wooded areas. The caterpillar of the codling moth, *Laspeyresia pomonella*, feeds on apples and other pome crops. Wild cherry and other valuable fruit trees are attacked by the larvae of several species belonging to the family Lasiocampidae.

The cutworms—the larvae of various genera of noctuid moths—have been so named because they cut the tender stems and leaves of various young plants as they feed. The armyworm, *Pseudaletia unipuncta*, destroys grass, grain, and other crops. The tobacco worm, genus *Protoparce*, attacks tobacco plants; the cabbage webworm, *Hellula undalis*, cabbages and other vegetables. The larvae of several moth species belonging to the family Tineidae feed on woolens, furs, and feathers.

are found all over the world. Monarchs are noted for their very long migrations.

Family Heliconiidae. Butterflies in this family dwell in the tropics, where they flit gracefully from flower to flower along jungle trails on their long, narrow, brightly colored wings.

Family Brassolidae. Members of this family live in South America, the West Indies, and tropical North America. They are large and brightly colored on the upper side, which is usually brown, with lines and spots of various colors. A large eyespot adorns the center of each hind wing. When the wings are spread out, the underside, with its brown markings and two eyelike spots, suggests the head of an owl—hence the name owl butterflies.

Brassolidae are very difficult to collect. When disturbed, they hide in a thicket with their wings folded over their backs, thus covering the bright topside colors; the brown underside markings blend with the leaves and tendrils. If disturbed, they will dash from their retreat, circle a few times, and then make for cover in another thicket.

Family Hesperiidae. These swiftly flying butterflies are commonly known as skippers. The many species, small to medium in size, have color patterns in combinations of brown, yellow, and blue.

Contrary to folklore, scientists insist that absolutely no relationship exists between the coloration of the woolly-bear caterpillar and the severity of the upcoming winter.

These insects form a connecting link between butterflies and moths, although they are classified with the butterflies. The bodies are heavier and the scales more hairlike than those of most butterflies, giving them a mothlike appearance. Like most butterflies, however, skippers are diurnal creatures, flying at night only when disturbed—and then merely to find another hiding place. The antennae are knobbed as in the butterflies, but on the end is a tiny tapering extension as in the moths.

SOME IMPORTANT MOTHS

Family Sphingidae. These are the sphinx moths, so-named for the position many of the larvae assume when disturbed. Adults, often called hawkmoths, flit from flower to flower. A few hover in front of flowers, probing into the depths of the corolla with the long, coiled, springlike proboscis; these are called hummingbird moths. Various species of the Sphingidae pollinate flowers with long corollas.

Family Saturniidae. The giant silk-spinning moths are generally large and attractively colored, making them a popular group with collectors. The world's largest known moths occur in this family. The Atlas moth, *Attacus atlas,* of southern Asia and Malaysia has a wingspread of nearly 11 inches (28 centimeters). Two other species of this family—*Attacus edwardsii* of northern India and *Coscinocera hercules* of Australia and Papua—are just as large but are more rarely found in collections. The cecropia moth *(Samia cecropia),* spicebush silkworm *(Callosamia promethea),* luna moth

Tiny drops of dew make the European skipper at left look as if it is covered with hundreds of glass beads. Skippers, although classified as butterflies, might form a connecting link between moths and butterflies.

Unlike butterflies, moths tend to be active at night. The elephant hawkmoth (above) flits from flower to flower in search of nectar. The cecropia moth (right) is a large, colorful silkworm moth that lives in North America.

(Actias luna), and ailanthus moth *(Philosamia cynthia,* introduced from China) are noted family representatives that live in the United States.

Family Arctiidae. The tiger moths, whose more than 4,000 species occur worldwide, are generally small to medium in size, black or white, and decorated with contrasting black, red, brown, or white spots, lines, or blotches. Tiger moths are also called woolly bears because the larvae of most of the species are covered with a long and hairlike or thick and woolly covering. They weave together this hairy covering with a few strands of silk to create a cocoon when the time comes to pupate.

Family Noctuidae. Known as owlet moths, well over 10,000 species have been described, and new ones are constantly being added to the list. Many destructive lepidopterous pests, including the armyworms and cutworms, belong to this family.

The noctuids are medium in' size, and many of them are monotonously similar in their brown and gray markings. The hind wings of some species, especially those belonging to the genus *Catocala,* are most strikingly colored; they are jet black or alternately banded with red, black, orange, or yellow. Owlets are readily attracted to lights or sugar bait.

Family Geometridae. This family, whose name means "Earth measurers," is another very large family. The larvae are known as measuring worms, inchworms, spanworms, and loopers. Like the Noctuidae, Geometridae includes many destructive larva pests; the spring and fall cankerworms are familiar examples. Geometer moths rest with their wings spread out flat.

Family Psychidae. The bagworms are interesting because the larvae construct cases, or bags, of silk interwoven with leaves, bark, and other debris. The entire life of both the caterpillar and the pupa is spent in the bag. The female adult, usually wingless, also remains in her bag and lays her eggs in it. The adult male, however, has wings to seek out the female.

Family Limacodidae. The sluglike caterpillars of this family have no distinct legs. Some of the larvae, such as the saddleback, are covered with spines that cause severe irritation to the skin.

Family Cossidae. These moths are quite large. The small larvae bore into the wood or stems of trees or large plants. The adult females are sluggish and may frequently be found even in daylight, resting near the light that had attracted them during the night.

Family Aegeriidae. These small clearwing moths have wings that are largely transparent; scales occur chiefly along the margins. The larvae are borers in certain plants and shrubs.

Other moths. The Pyralididae are a very large family of very small moths. Many of these are destructive to hay, grain, and other crops. Tortricidae larvae roll the leaves on which they are feeding into a small case, in which they can hide and be protected.

The Tineidae include the three species of clothes moths. Most species feed on rotten fungi and other waste products.

THE PRIMITIVE CHORDATES

by Yvonne Bonnafous

Animals are usually divided into two general groups: the vertebrates, which have backbones; and the invertebrates, which have none. The vertebrates include mammals, birds, reptiles, amphibians, and fish. Animals such as insects, spiders, clams, worms, and corals have no backbone, and are therefore considered invertebrates.

Of course, as any zoologist will attest, nothing in the Animal Kingdom can be so clear-cut. When the question arises as to whether a certain creature is a vertebrate or an invertebrate, there are bound to be some species that do not fall clearly into either general group. Among them are the approximately 2,000 species of tunicates, lancelets, and acorn worms. These strange-looking creatures do not have true backbones, but at some point in their life cycle, they do at least develop a structure that is somewhat akin to a backbone.

How should these apparently intermediate animals be classified? Some zoologists have placed them in the same phylum as the vertebrates. The animals in this phylum—Chordata—are called *chordates*. The tunicates and lancelets have been ranked as primitive members of the chordates, and are called *protochordates*. Many zoologists, however, no longer consider the acorn worm to be a chordate, and therefore have placed this creature in a separate phylum, Hemichordata.

CHORDATE CHARACTERISTICS

All the chordates—vertebrates and protochordates alike—have certain features in common. They all possess—at some time in their lives—an internal, rodlike, cartilaginous structure called a *notochord*, the term from which the word "chordate" is derived. The notochord extends through the long axis of the body and gives it a certain degree of rigidity. In the higher chordates—the vertebrates—the notochord is enclosed and replaced early in the life of the embryo by the vertebral column, or backbone, a jointed, bony structure.

Second, all chordates at some time or another have *gill slits*, which open into the pharynx, the space in the back of the mouth that leads to the esophagus. In reptiles, birds, mammals, and other higher chordates, the gill slits disappear long before birth. Fish, however, retain them all through life.

Finally, all chordates have a *spinal cord*—essentially a hollow central nervous system that runs directly above the notochord. In animals with backbones, the vertebrae enclose the spinal cord from below.

The primitive chordates are commonly divided into two distinct classes based on the nature of the notochord. The urochordates ("tail-notochord animals"), or tunicates, have a notochord in the tail in the larval stage. The cephalochordates ("head-notochord animals"), or lancelets, are so called because the notochord extends into the head. It also runs the length of the body to the tail.

In the closely related phylum of hemichordates, a blind (dead-end) pouch made of stiff, cartilaginous tissue extends from the wall of the pharynx up into the proboscis. Many zoologists do not believe that this stiffened pouch of the acorn worms corresponds to the notochord that characterizes other chordates.

PROTOCHORDATES

Tunicates

Shallow seawater often contains orange, red, or purple baglike objects attached to rocks, piles, and seaweed. These colorful "bags" are tunicates, and the best-known tunicates are the so-called ascidians, or sea squirts. The term "sea squirt" is quite appropriate: when one of these animals is disturbed, it squirts small jets of

water from two openings, called siphons, in the unattached end of the sac, or bag. One of the siphons, the *oral pore*, is the animal's mouth. The other siphon is called the *atrial pore*—an all-purpose opening through which pass wastes, water, and sex cells.

The tunicate's body varies in diameter from 1 to 12 inches (2.5 to 30 centimeters), depending on the species. A material called *tunicin* is secreted on the outside of the body and forms a thick coat, or tunic, from which this group of primitive chordates derives its name.

In the adult animal, water passes through the mouth and is filtered through gill slits. Food particles suspended in the water are trapped by the gill slits and enter the intestine. The water then flows into a surrounding sac—the *atrium*—and out through the atrial pore. Undigested waste materials also pass out of the body via the atrial pore.

Tunicates can reproduce asexually by budding. An adult buds again and again, producing new individuals and—in time—a large colony on a rocky surface. Sexual reproduction also occurs. Tunicates are hermaphrodites—each

In sea squirts and other tunicates (facing page), a backbonelike structure exists only during the larval stage. A type of sea squirt called a sea vase (right) has a translucent body that is papery to the touch.

Unlike a tunicate, a lancelet (above) retains its backbonelike notochord throughout its life. Despite its resemblance to a fish, a lancelet is much more primitive, with only a simple nervous system, no brain, and no eyes.

animal produces both sperm and eggs. Fertilization may take place within the body, or the eggs and sperm may pass out of the body and unite elsewhere.

The link between the tunicates and the vertebrates is clearly seen in the larval stage. Free-swimming larvae develop from fertilized eggs. The young tunicates, which resemble tadpoles, have a tail within which the notochord is contained. As the animal matures, both the tail and the notochord disappear.

Not all tunicates are permanently attached to submerged surfaces or objects. Transparent forms called *salps* are free-swimming. They form colonies, which float about on the surface of the water like rafts. Other species of tiny tunicates also remain unattached, and spend their lives swimming about in the open sea.

Lancelets

The lancelet, also known as *branchiostoma* (formerly known as *amphioxus*), is closer to the vertebrates than are the tunicates. This tiny creature—rarely exceeding 2 inches (5 centimeters) in length—has a slender, translucent body, tapered at both ends, that looks very much like that of a fish. There is, however, nothing very fishlike about the creature's long

vertical fin. This structure starts at the back of the head and passes along the dorsal (top) part of the body. It widens as it goes around the tail. On the underside, it divides into two branches, which pass along the sides of the body to the head region.

Lancelets are the most widely distributed of all the protochordates, with species found in tropical and temperate waters around the world. Generally the animal spends its days almost entirely buried in sand, only its "snout" (that is, the structure that would correspond to a snout in a vertebrate) protruding. The little creature leaves its refuge from time to time—usually only at night or during the breeding season—and darts through the water. Soon it burrows into the sand again, tail first. Lancelets feed on microscopic organisms.

The snout of the animal consists of a cuplike depression surrounded by *cirri*, or bristles, which extend in front of the head. The cirri direct the flow of water into the lancelet's mouth. In a manner akin to that of tunicates, the water, carrying bits of food, passes into the pharynx, which is lined with gill slits. The pharynx is surrounded by a sac called the *atrium*. As water flows through the gills, the food particles are filtered out. The water then proceeds into the atrium and out of the body by way of an opening called the *atrial pore*. Food passes into the intestine from the pharynx. Undigested wastes leave the body via the anus.

Blood circulates in a closed system like that of the higher vertebrates. It first passes through the gill region. From there, it proceeds to the intestine and to the "liver" before it reaches the "heart," which is essentially a slightly enlarged blood vessel. From the heart, it is returned to the gill region. Oxygenation of the blood also takes place through the skin.

The muscles lie in a succession of V-shaped blocks along the body wall, with the point of the V facing the creature's head. This arrangement is also found in vertebrates.

The notochord of the lancelet extends lengthwise from head to tail. Unlike the tunicate, the lancelet retains its notochord throughout its life. Dorsal to the notochord—that is, above it—lies the hollow nerve cord. The nervous system is very simple; there is no brain, nor are there eyes. Instead, light-sensitive spots are present on the body and tail. A skin depression at the front end of the lancelet can detect chemicals in the water.

The acorn worm lives in the sand beneath warm, shallow waters. Some specimens reach a length of 80 inches, although most are substantially shorter.

Reproductive organs occur in 26 pairs along either side of the body cavity. They connect with the exterior by the atrial pore. The animals reproduce sexually. Sexes are separate; eggs or sperm are shed into the water in the early summer.

The lancelets are the only members of the protochordates that serve as food for human beings. Many tons of these tiny animals—the equivalent of hundreds of millions of lancelets—are consumed each year in China.

HEMICHORDATES

The phylum Hemichordata is best known for the acorn worm (class Enteropneusta), a creature that resembles an elongated worm with an acornlike head. The "acorn" is made up of a *proboscis,* or tubular structure, and a *collar,* into which the proboscis fits. The collar is attached to a long, flat, ruffled *trunk,* tapering toward the end. The animals range in length from 1 to 80 inches (2.5 to 200 centimeters); the average length is 6 to 10 inches (15 to 25 centimeters).

These relatively rare creatures are found buried in the mud and sand of low-tide zones. They are most common in warm waters. Like earthworms, acorn worms pass mud or sand through their bodies, extracting food particles and ejecting the wastes. The spiral castings are deposited outside of the animals' burrows. These castings resemble those of earthworms.

The proboscis of the acorn worm is long and muscular. The animal inflates and stiffens this structure by drawing in water, which it uses to burrow in sand and mud. The mouth, located between the collar and the neck, widens to form a pharynx.

The acorn worm's pharynx leads into the intestine, which is perforated with gill slits. The gills lead into a pouch, which opens to the exterior by gill pores. The intestine runs the length of the body, terminating in an anus at the tapered end of the trunk.

The reproductive organs occur at the front end of the trunk. The sexes are separate: males produce sperm, and females, eggs. Fertilization takes place outside of the body after the sperm and eggs have been ejected.

The larvae of acorn worms resemble those of the echinoderms (sea stars, sea urchins, and their kin) in both structure and development. For this reason, many biologists believe that the hemichordates are descended from the same stock as the echinoderms.

The phylum Hemichordata includes only one other class—Pterobranchia—rare, deep-sea-bottom dwellers that range in length from 0.02 to 0.2 inch (0.5 to 5 millimeters). These creatures, which reproduce asexually by budding, often form large colonies.

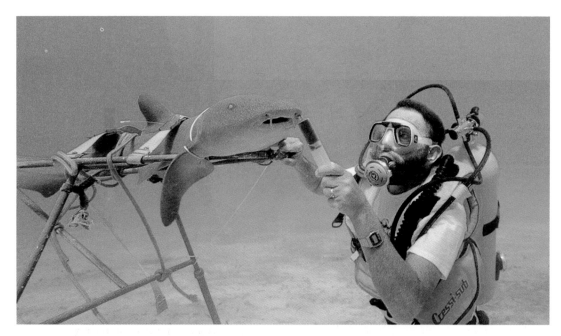

FISH BIOLOGISTS AND THEIR SCIENCE

A few miles off the Florida coast, five fish biologists dive into the turquoise water and scuba dive down to the 43-foot (13-meter) *Aquarius* research station. There they will spend 10 days studying the fish of the Florida coral reefs—an ecosystem as complex as any rain forest, and just as mysterious.

ICHTHYOLOGY

The scientific study of fish, or fish biology, is traditionally known by the rather intimidating name *ichthyology*. It is a very broad science that includes many specialized fields. The one thing that all fish biologists share in common is their fascination with the estimated 25,000 to 30,000 species of fish found in the world's oceans, lakes, ponds, rivers, and streams. Counted together, the three classes of fish—jawless, cartilaginous, and bony—make up the largest group of vertebrate, or backboned, animals on Earth.

Some ichthyologists study classification, the relationship of different fish species. Others research the anatomy, behavior, or physiology of one or more fish families, or even one particular species. Still others study fish breeding, or the care of fish kept in aquariums.

Of critical importance are the modern fields of fish conservation and fishery management. Scientists in these fields try to understand the needs of wild populations of fish and how they are affected by human activities. Their work has become critical in the fight to save the world's fisheries, those areas of the ocean that are harvested for human food. Indeed, fish supply nearly one-fifth of the protein that the people of the world consume each year—more protein than is derived from all red meats combined. Yet many of the world's fisheries are in serious decline or have already collapsed. In recent years, ichthyologists and fishery biologists have begun developing plans to better manage natural fish populations and maintain them for future generations.

History of Ichthyology

Ichthyology, like many of the life sciences, dates back to the work of the Greek naturalist Aristotle in the 4th century B.C. He was the first to record scientific observations about fish and to

As a matter of necessity, much of the original research conducted by fish biologists—known more formally as ichthyologists—must be carried out underwater.

In recognition of his pioneering observations on fish behavior and classification, Aristotle (right), the ancient Greek philosopher and naturalist, is generally considered the father of ichthyology.

classify them as a special group within a larger scheme of living things. During the European Renaissance, in the early 14th century, scientists began dissecting fish to better understand their unique biology. During the 17th and 18th centuries, European biologists stayed busy naming and classifying the many species being discovered by seafaring explorers.

A very important figure in the history of ichthyology is the Swiss-born U.S. naturalist Louis Agassiz. In the 1820s, Agassiz studied and classified an enormous number of Brazilian fish, mainly from the Amazon River. He also researched and published books on the natural history of Central Europe's freshwater fish.

Agassiz's greatest contributions were recognized after he moved from Switzerland to the United States in 1846. There he completed extensive research on the fish of both North and South America. He also popularized the study of ichthyology with his public lectures in many cities. Most important of all, perhaps, was Agassiz's legacy as a teacher. He taught his students to learn about fish by observing them in nature—not simply from books, as was the tradition in that day. Agassiz and his students pioneered the scientific methods of field research.

Many of the 19th century's greatest scientists began their careers as students of Agassiz. Among the most prominent of them was the American ichthyologist George Brown Goode, who wrote many important scientific books about North American fish. He also discovered and classified more than 150 new species of fish from the Atlantic Ocean.

Ichthyologists play a prominent role in the ecological aspects of fish biology by continuously monitoring the condition of water from important fishing grounds.

Another of Agassiz's students was David Starr Jordan. In the 60 years between 1870 and 1930, Jordan discovered, named, and classified more than 2,500 species of North American fish. For good reason, Jordan is considered the greatest American ichthyologist of his time.

In the past century, researchers developed better methods for keeping fish in tanks. As a result, fish became important laboratory subjects in the study of animal physiology, anatomy, toxicology (the study of poisons), and parasitology. Recent advances, such as underwater robots, allow scientists to better study fish in their natural environment.

A NEW ERA OF RESEARCH

In the 1940s and 1950s, the study of fish reached new heights—or, more precisely, depths—with the invention of equipment for underwater diving. The most important device by far was the *s*elf-*c*ontained *u*nderwater *b*reathing *a*pparatus, or scuba. Such equipment allowed ichthyologists to remain underwater for long periods, enabling them to observe their subjects under natural conditions. This gave rise to many discoveries about fish behavior and ecology.

The development of research submarines and deep-sea submersibles brought further dis-

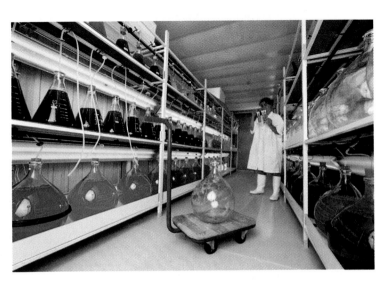

Careers in ichthyology and fishery science are open to people with a minimum of a bachelor's degree in biology, zoology, ecology, or marine science. There are scores of colleges, universities, and institutes that sponsor advanced research in ichthyology and its closely related fields. Among the most famous are the Scripps Institution of Oceanography, in La Jolla, California, and the Woods Hole Oceanographic Institution, in Woods Hole, Massachusetts. Traditionally, fish biologists known as "ichthyologists" focus primarily on academic research that advances the world's understanding of fish, as well as on teaching at the university level. Fishery biologists, in turn, apply this scientific understanding in ways that help protect and manage commercially valuable fish and their habitats. As might be imagined, these two fields are deeply intertwined.

By tagging fish, the student above can better monitor their movement and population.

Many federal and state agencies employ both ichthyologists and fishery scientists to help them manage coastal and wetland areas and their rich populations of fish life. Ichthyologists working for such agencies often research commercially important fish species. They may then publish guides that help identify these species and their larvae, or immature forms. The fishery scientists at these agencies often develop extensive regulations that control recreational and commercial fishing in a way that protects local fish populations.

Fishery scientists are also needed in the aquaculture industry, to advise fish farmers on how best to grow their "crop." Power companies and other industries often consult fishery scientists to better understand how their activities affect fish life in their areas.

Fishery biologists and ichthyologists with advanced college degrees (master's or doctorate) can also find work teaching and researching at major colleges, universities, and oceanography institutions. Such academic jobs typically involve a combination of teaching and original research.

Natural-history museums, zoos, and public aquariums need ichthyologists to manage their live or preserved fish specimens. Such jobs, called curatorships, often include the opportunity to conduct research on a particular group of fish.

Ichthyologists and fishery biologists with an interest in people as well as fish can sometimes find work as naturalists at state and national parks, nature centers, and public aquariums. Their job is to educate the public about the world of fish and their importance to humans and the environment.

coveries. Among the most famous of ocean research vessels is *Alvin*, a small, maneuverable research submarine operated by the Woods Hole Oceanographic Institution, in southeastern Massachusetts. Built in 1961, *Alvin* is still used today, ferrying ichthyologists and other marine scientists to the great ocean depths.

AQUARIUMS

Public interest in ichthyology has mushroomed in the past several decades. Today public aquariums rival zoos in popularity with both schoolchildren and tourists. One of the world's largest is the Miami Seaquarium, with more than 10,000 specimens from 400 different fish species. Marineland of the Pacific near Los Angeles features one of the world's largest fish tanks, with 1 million gallons (3.7 million liters) of seawater and more than 2,000 fish. The world's largest freshwater aquarium can be found in Chattanooga, Tennessee. Its three-story-tall tanks contain authentically re-created natural habitats featuring rivers and lakes across North America as well as the South American Amazon. Such exhibits have encouraged the growth of amateur ichthyology and the great popularity of home aquariums.

What Is a Fish?

A sockeye salmon leaps over a rocky waterfall. A stingray ripples through the ocean on enormous wings. A hagfish burrows in the sand, waiting to feed on dying fish that sink from the water above. These three creatures belong to very different classes of animals. But most people think of them all as simply "fish."

In fact, the three classes of fish—bony fish (Osteichthyes), sharks and rays (Chondrichthyes), and hagfish and lampreys (Agnatha)—are as different from each other as are the four classes of land animals we know as amphibians, reptiles, birds, and mammals. Taken together, these seven classes of animals make up the vast group that scientists refer to as vertebrate, or backboned, animals.

Bony fish such as salmon and trout are what most people have in mind when they think of "fish." As their name suggests, bony fish have skeletons made of true bone. Their bodies are covered with scales and thin, fanlike fins. Their gills, or breathing organs, are covered with a bony flap called an *operculum*. Of the 24,000 known species of living fish, more than 95 percent belong to this class. They can be found in oceans and freshwater around the world.

Sharks and rays, or *cartilaginous* fish, have skeletons that are made of cartilage, a softer, more flexible material than bone. Their gills are uncovered and open to the outside through several slits. Instead of scales, their skin is covered with toothlike *denticles*. Their fins are generally thick and fleshy. All sharks and rays live in the ocean, most of them in tropical waters.

The third class of living fish, Agnatha, is quite strange. It includes the snakelike hagfish and lampreys, the most ancient of all living vertebrates. So primitive is their form that they have no proper skull or jaws. They eat with a large sucker mouth that contains rings of sharp, horny teeth. Their slimy skin lacks scales of any kind. Their gills open to the outside through small, uncovered holes. Most lampreys live in

In a classic display of schooling, blue-striped snappers swim in unison as they slide by a coral reef. Perhaps one-quarter of all fish species exhibit schooling behavior.

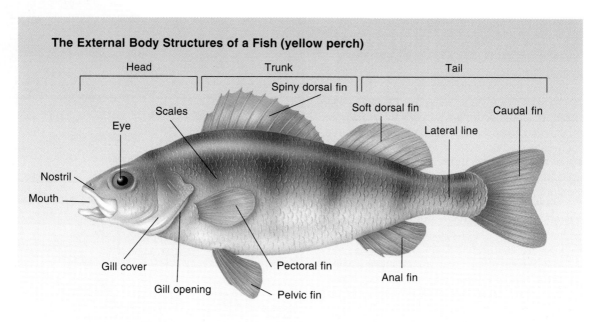

The External Body Structures of a Fish (yellow perch)

Head | Trunk | Tail

Spiny dorsal fin
Scales
Soft dorsal fin
Caudal fin
Eye
Lateral line
Nostril
Mouth
Gill cover
Pectoral fin
Gill opening
Anal fin
Pelvic fin

Although there is great variety in the sizes, shapes, and colors of fish, most species share some basic features. All have bodies designed for moving and breathing in water, most have fins, and many have scales. The external structures of the yellow perch above are common to most fish.

freshwater, although some move to the sea as adults. Hagfish (also called slime eels) live in salt water, primarily on the ocean floor.

FISHY ANCESTORS

All fish are thought to be descended from a group of small creatures called ostracoderms. The earliest ostracoderm fossil was found in rock some 500 million years old. About 6 inches (15 centimeters) long, this heavily armored creature had a tail but no fins. Its fully formed backbone made this the earliest known vertebrate, but it lacked jaws. The ostracoderm's immediate ancestor may have been a soft-bodied chordate similar to the modern lancelet, or *amphioxus*. Its direct descendants were the "jawless fish," or agnathans.

Despite their simple form, the agnathans dominated the seas for approximately 130 million years. Their descendants included two classes of now-extinct fish that appeared between 430 million and 400 million years ago: first came the sharklike acanthodians, or "spiny sharks," followed by the "plate-skinned" placoderms, a class of bizarre-looking, heavily ar-

mored fish. Both groups had biting jaws filled with sharp teeth.

The last of the acanthodians and placoderms disappeared about 280 million years ago. Before they did, they may have given rise to the modern-day sharks and rays and the bony fish. But the fossil record is not clear enough to say just who descended from whom.

FISH CHARACTERISTICS

Some 500 million years of evolution have shaped fish life into a stunning variety of forms—something to fit nearly every type of aquatic habitat in the world. The only permanent bodies of water that lack fish life are super-hot thermal pools and extremely salty lakes such as the Dead Sea.

In form, fish can be long, thin, broad, or flattened. Their fins can be spiky, frilly, winglike, or stumpy. The position of eyes, mouth, and nostrils can be twisted into a number of bizarre arrangements. Fish coloration ranges from cryptic camouflage to brilliant neon. Some fish can change color at will. A few can even produce their own bioluminescent light.

The Internal Body Structures of a Fish (yellow perch)

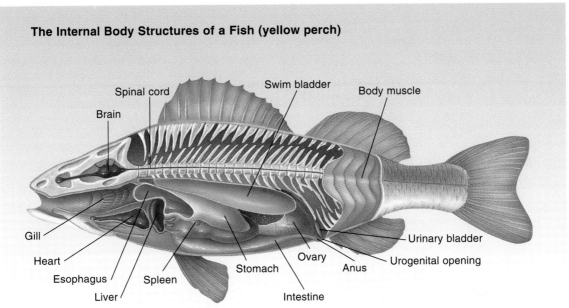

The internal organs of a fish comprise the systems that help the fish live and function. Each system performs a specific task, such as supporting the body, providing movement, pumping blood, or sensing the environment. The internal structures of the yellow perch above are common to most fish.

Despite these differences, all fish are designed to move and breathe in water. So it is not surprising that they share a basic body plan.

A Streamlined Shape

Most fish have streamlined bodies that slip easily through water. Despite the importance of this shape, there are a great many exceptions to the rule. Among the strangest of fish forms is that of the puffer fish. With its prickly, inflatable body, the puffer can make itself all but impossible for a predator to swallow. Still more difficult to explain is the bizarre shape of the hammerhead shark. Its enormous and awkwardly shaped head may contain special organs for detecting prey through their electrical charge.

The Importance of Fins

Whatever their shape, all fish have fins. The first fins probably developed from spines that early fish used to balance themselves. Among modern fish, the simplest fins are found on the most-primitive species. The hagfish has nothing more than a crude caudal, or tail, fin.

Sharks and rays have fleshy fins strengthened on the inside by rods of cartilage. The shark cannot flap or move its fins back and forth. Instead, it uses them for balance and to steer its body upward or downward through the water. The pectoral, or side, fins of the rays and skates form great "wings" that can be flapped or rippled for underwater "flying."

The fins of bony fish are fanlike in form, supported with rays of bonelike material. An unusual group of bony fish called the lobe-fins have fins supported by fleshy knobs that, in turn, are supported by muscle and bone. This type of fin may have been the model for the limbs of the first amphibians.

Fish Movement

Thanks to their streamlined bodies and variety of fins, fish have the capacity to propel themselves through their watery home. They do so in two basic ways. First, they bend their bodies from side to side. This motion pushes water aside like a wedge and so drives the fish forward. Hagfish, lampreys, and eels rely solely on this type of movement.

The second type of movement is a variation on the first. As it sways through the water, a typical fish gives the last third of its body a

How Fish Breathe

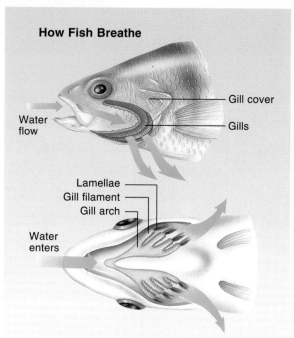

When water flows past a fish's gills, an important exchange takes place: oxygen from the water passes into the blood and is then distributed throughout the body; carbon dioxide and a variety of other waste products from the blood are released into the water and flow out through the gill openings.

muscular sweep to produce a powerful stroke of its tail. The fastest fish—the swordfish, mackerel, and tuna—derive their speed largely through this propeller-like motion of the tail.

Other bony fish, such as triggerfish and puffer fish, can flutter, or *scull*, their fins to brake and maneuver in different directions, including backward. This is an especially important adaptation for fish that live among rocks or coral, where they must make sharp turns to chase prey or escape their enemies. Among the most unusual of fish movements is that of the sea horse. With its head up, this creature fans its single dorsal fin to propel itself gently along. Not to be forgotten are the "flying" fish, which can leap out of the water and glide through the air on their winglike pectoral fins.

The drawings at right illustrate scale types on the basis of shape. Most often, scales overlap like shingles on a roof. A salmon's cycloid scale (enlarged) shows the ridges that reflect the fish's growth patterns.

Like swordfish and tuna, sharks rely on their tails for propulsion. As mentioned, the skates and rays have evolved oversized pectoral fins that work much like underwater wings. Some rays actually flap their pectoral fins. Others produce a wavelike movement that ripples through the fins from front to back.

Because a fish is heavier than water, it also needs to resist sinking. Sharks and rays do so by staying in constant motion. Most bony fish do so with a special organ called the *swim bladder*, located above the stomach. In essence, the swim bladder is a body cavity that holds a bubble of air or gas. Some fish fill the air bladder by swallowing air at the surface. (Their air bladders are connected to their stomachs.) More-advanced types of bony fish have a closed air bladder that they fill with gases produced by the body. By controlling the amount of air or body gas in the bladder, a fish can rise, sink, or hang at a particular depth with very little effort.

Breathing Water

Like all aquatic animals, fish take the oxygen they need from the water. A few species such as the lungfish can also breathe air through a special type of air bladder, or primitive lung. But the primary breathing organs are the *gills*.

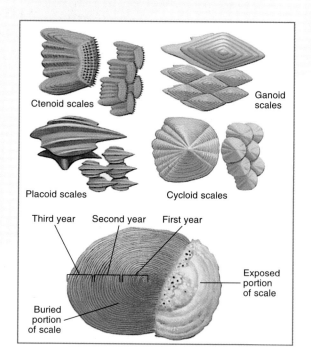

Classification of Fish

During the great Age of Fish (the Devonian period), from 450 million to 350 million years ago, there were five classes of fish, two of which are now extinct. The following classification chart helps show the place of fish in the greater kingdom of life.

PHYLUM CHORDATA

SUBPHYLUM Vertebrata: *Animals with backbones.*

CLASS Agnatha: *Jawless fish—the first vertebrates, lacking distinct skull, jaws, or scales. Cartilaginous skeleton and round, suckerlike mouth with rings of horny teeth. Mainly parasites or scavengers. About 80 living species in one order: Cyclostomata (lampreys and hagfish).*

CLASS Acanthodii: *Spiny sharks—extinct class whose earliest members were the first vertebrates with jaws. Most under 30 inches (75 centimeters), with many spines or spiny fins, large eyes, and powerful, sharklike tail. Lived in ocean and freshwater from 430 million to 280 million years ago. Example: Climatius, a 3-inch (7.6-centimeter)-long fish with 15 spiny fins.*

CLASS Placodermi: *Plate-skinned fish—an extinct class of heavily armored fish with strong jaws and biting teeth. Bony, interlocking plates shielded its head and front of body. Lived in open sea from 400 million to 360 million years ago. Example: Dunkleosteus, an 11-foot (3.3-meter)-long predator with a long, eel-like tail.*

CLASS Chondrichthyes: *Cartilaginous, or soft-boned, fish—jawed fish with skeletons made of cartilage. Fins paired and stiffened by rays of cartilage. Pelvic fins in males modified as simple sex organ. Skin protected by tiny, toothlike dermal denticles. About 750 species.*

SUBCLASS Holocephali: *Chimaera—tapered, sharklike fish with large eyes, large pectoral and pelvic fins, sharp spine in front of two dorsal fins, and whiplike tail. Weak swimmers, 24 to 80 inches (60 to 200 centimeters) in length. Found in rivers, estuaries, and open ocean. About 30 living species in one order: Chimaerae (ratfish, rabbit fish, and elephant fish).*

SUBCLASS Elasmobranchii: *Sharks and rays—mainly carnivorous fish with torpedo-shaped or flattened bodies, keen sense of smell, and five to seven gill slits. Found in all oceans. About 700 species in two major orders: Selachii (sharks and dogfish) and Batoidea (rays, skates, and stingrays).*

CLASS Osteichthyes: *Bony, or hard-boned, fish—jawed fish with bony skeleton, true scales, paired fins, and swim bladder. About 19,400 species.*

SUBCLASS Sarcopterygii: *Lobe-finned fish—primitive bony fish, mainly extinct, with fins borne on long, fleshy, muscular lobes supported by bone. Seven living species in two major orders: Crossopterygii (with one living species, the coelacanth) and Dipnoi (the lungfish).*

SUBCLASS Actinopterygii: *Ray-finned fish—bony fish with fins supported by parallel rays of bony material. Some 20,000 living species in three major infraclasses: Chondrostei (sturgeons, paddlefish, and bichirs); Holostei (bowfin and gars); and Teleostei (the modern bony fish, with 24 orders).*

Gills consist of thin flaps of fleshy filaments filled with small blood vessels that lend the structures a bright red color. The gills hang on bony supports called *gill arches* in two spaces called the *gill chambers*, one on each side of the head, directly behind the mouth.

When a typical fish opens its mouth, it sucks in water, which washes back and over the gills. A chemical exchange then takes place. Oxygen from the water passes through the surface of the gills and into the blood. At the same time, the blood releases carbon dioxide, a waste product of respiration, into the water. The fish then expels the water through the gill slits that open on either side of its head.

Life in water does not require as powerful a heart as is needed to survive in open air, under the full force of gravity. The fish heart has just two chambers, as compared to three in amphibians and most reptiles, and four in birds and mammals. One chamber of the fish heart collects oxygen-poor, carbon-dioxide-rich blood flowing from the rear of the body. The other chamber pumps this blood forward to the head and gills. As it flows through the gills, the blood exchanges carbon dioxide for oxygen and flows back through the rest of the body.

Like amphibians and reptiles, most fish are *ectothermic*, or cold-blooded, a term that has little to do with the blood. It simply means that a fish's body does not regulate its own temperature, as do the bodies of birds and mammals. Rather, a fish's temperature closely matches that of surrounding water. As a result, fish can die if the temperature around them suddenly drops or rises. A few fish, such as tuna, can generate internal heat, and therefore are technically *endothermic* (warm-blooded) creatures.

Fish Senses

As a group, fish have all the five senses found in land animals, plus a few more. Like humans, fish use their eyes for seeing (some in color), ears for hearing, nostrils for smelling, and tongues for tasting. Their skin contains nerve endings that provide the sense of touch.

In addition, a fish can sense distant sounds and movements with a sense organ called the *lateral line*—a network of small pores and internal canals that lie in a line from the head down either side of the fish's body. Filled with mucus, the canals contain small hairs that connect with sensitive nerves.

The vibrations produced by sound and movement can travel long distances through water. When they reach a fish, the vibrations move through the lateral-line pores and canals to move the small sensitive hairs and trigger a nerve signal to the brain. Depending on the size of the signal, it may alert the fish to prey or warn it of an approaching predator. A fish also uses its lateral-line system to navigate—by sensing the reverberations of its own vibrations as they bounce off objects around it.

The fish's seventh sense concerns electricity passing through the water around it. All species may have this sensitivity to one degree or another. Sharks use it to detect the faint electrical pulses produced by their prey. (All vertebrate animals produce electrical charges when their nerves signal their muscles to contract.)

Some fish can also generate weak electrical fields for locating prey. The electric catfish of Africa, the knife fish of Latin America, and the stargazers have bioelectric organs that produce such an electrical field and can sense the disturbance created by prey that enter it. Stronger bioelectric organs can be found in the electric eel, which stuns its prey with a powerful shock.

Fish Reproduction

Every species of fish mates and produces young in a slightly different way. In general, females lay large numbers of small, soft eggs. The male fertilizes them in the water by shedding his *milt*, or sperm, over their surface. Some fish have sticky eggs that they attach to underwater plants and other objects. Other fish simply scatter their eggs to the currents. Many species produce enormous numbers of eggs—often hundreds to thousands—because most are consumed by predators. Fish that protect their eggs tend to produce fewer of them. Many sharks, some rays, and even a few bony fish keep their eggs inside their bodies as they develop. The male of these species has a special organ to fertilize the female internally.

A variety of other fish are *hermaphroditic*. That is, one individual can produce both eggs and sperm through a combined ovary and testis, usually at different stages of its life.

All fish tend to grow most rapidly in their first year. Although they continue to grow throughout life, the rate slows dramatically after sexual maturity is attained. Among the smallest fish in the world is the 0.5-inch (1.27-centimeter) dwarf pygmy goby (*Pandaka pygmaea*); by far, the largest is the whale shark, with a length of up to 50 feet (15 meters).

IMPORTANCE TO HUMANS

The most obvious importance of fish to people is as a source of high-quality food. Worldwide, fish supply up to one-fifth of the protein humans consume. Once taken for granted, this important food resource has become threatened by overfishing, water pollution, and the destruction of habitat, especially that of the wetlands where fish breed.

Fish are also important for disease control. They eat a vast number of disease-carrying insects such as mosquitoes. People likewise treasure fish for their beauty and intriguing behavior—qualities that can be enjoyed both in the wild and in public and home aquariums.

THE JAWLESS FISH

"Disgusting!" It's a common and understandable reaction to the sight of a lamprey or hagfish. Slimy, jawless, virtually headless, they cling to the bodies of other fish, sucking blood and liquefied muscle. Yet these "living fossils" are as fascinating as they are bizarre. For starters, they are the most ancient of all living vertebrates.

EVOLUTION

Hagfish and lampreys belong to the superclass Agnatha, the "jawless fish." The first agnathan was also the world's first fish and the first animal to possess a backbone. Fossils of the early agnathans can be found in rock nearly 520 million years old. They had no actual skull, nor any true bone inside their bodies. Their skeletons were made entirely of cartilage, a softer material. They did, however, sport bone on the outside. A bony shield encased the head, and bony scales covered the body.

Then, as today, agnathans had a simple tail fin and dorsal (back) fin, but lacked paired fins on the sides, making them awkward swimmers. Rather than chase after prey, the first agnathans probably filtered bits of organic matter out of the water. Not surprisingly, they were all small, rarely longer than 1 foot (30 centimeters).

The agnathans thrived for 130 million years, filling lakes, rivers, marshes, and seas throughout the Northern Hemisphere. Then, 390 million years ago, they all but vanished. Most

Most jawless fish are parasites that feed on the vital fluids and tissues of larger fish. An exception is the brook lamprey (above), which does not feed after reaching adulthood. Instead, it quickly mates and dies.

likely, they could not compete with their own descendants—sharks and other fast-swimming fish with jaws and teeth.

How did the lamprey and hagfish survive? By inventing a new way of life. Some 400 million years ago, they became parasites, attaching themselves to the bodies of larger fish and feeding on their blood and tissues. More-advanced fish therefore did not compete with the lampreys and hagfish; they became their food!

CYCLOSTOMES

Scientists place lampreys and hagfish in the agnathan class Cyclostomata, meaning animal "with round mouth." Cyclostomes have a round sucking mouth armed with horny teeth. Like the

Jawless Fish (lamprey)

The jawless fish include some 70 species of lampreys and hagfish—slender-bodied fish that lack true jaws and have skeletons made of cartilage.

first agnathans, they have neither jaws nor proper skulls, and they swim weakly without paired fins. Otherwise, the cyclostomes look quite unlike their ancestors.

When they first appeared 400 million years ago, cyclostomes had already lost the bony armor worn by other agnathans. Their soft, scaleless bodies had become wormlike, perfect for burrowing in mud. Even more interesting, they had lost the agnathan's well-developed backbone. In essence, they became vertebrates without vertebrae. Their body was supported by a stiff internal rod called the notochord.

Although it may look bizarre to us, the cyclostome's form proved very successful. From fossils, we know that they have remained virtually unchanged to modern times. Today they are represented by 40 species of lampreys and 40 species of hagfish.

Lampreys

Lampreys begin life at the bottom of a freshwater stream, where they hatch as blind and toothless wormlike larvae. At three to seven years of age, the larva undergoes a dramatic change. Eyes develop. Its mouth becomes a suckerlike disk with rings of horny teeth and a rasping tongue. The adult lamprey has a long dorsal fin down its back and a series of small holes, or *gill spiracles*, along each side. Hidden beneath the skin between its large eyes is a primitive organ used to detect light.

Hagfish have a slithery, snakelike body that culminates in an eyeless stump of a head. The creatures defend themselves by secreting astounding amounts of slime from dozens of special pores.

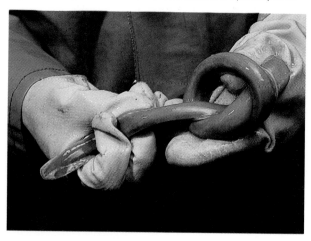

The adult lamprey begins to feed by attaching its sucker to a passing fish. It uses its teeth and rough tongue to file away the skin of its host. As the lamprey sucks blood, chemicals in its saliva partially dissolve the host's muscle and other tissues, enabling these structures to be sucked into the lamprey's mouth.

Most sea lampreys "ride" their hosts downstream to the ocean. Some landlocked species move downstream to large lakes. There they continue to parasitize fish. In many parts of the world, they cause considerable damage. In the early 1950s, for example, sea lampreys migrated into the upper Great Lakes and destroyed the region's trout population. Only after an aggressive program to trap and poison the lamprey could trout be reintroduced.

Lampreys grow to 6 to 40 inches (15 to 100 centimeters) in length, depending on the species. After several years in open water, adult lampreys stop eating and return to the streams where they were born. Back upstream, they dig nests, lay thousands of tiny eggs, and die.

Hagfish

Similar to the lamprey in shape and size is the even-more-bizarre-looking hagfish. Instead of a round sucker, its mouth is circled by long, fleshy barbels. Early sailors imagined these barbels to be the hair of a sea witch, or hag. Hagfish are also called slime eels, for they produce a thick coat of foul-tasting mucus to discourage predators. Hagfish are all but blind, with small eyes buried beneath the skin. They find prey with a keen sense of smell and touch, then bite with a slitlike mouth.

Hagfish live on the sea bottom in cold water. They seldom bother healthy fish, but feed on the dead and dying. They also attack crippled fish caught on lines and in traps. When the hagfish bores into its prey, it will sometimes tie its long body in a loop. It may do so to remove some of its copious body slime and give itself extra leverage.

Little is known about hagfish reproduction. Each individual has both male and female sex parts. But only one or the other functions. The female produces up to 30 tough-skinned, yolk-filled eggs, which the male fertilizes. They hatch into miniature adults.

THE CARTILAGINOUS FISH

Say the word "shark," and most people think, "*Jaws!*" Interestingly enough, they wouldn't be so far off the mark. Nearly 400 million years ago, sharks and their kin, the rays and chimaeras, were among the first vertebrates to develop jaws. And it was a great evolutionary invention indeed.

Jaws equipped with bony teeth enabled sharks, rays, and chimaeras to quickly become the top predators of the sea—a role they have dominated for all these millennia. Their success was ensured by yet another great adaptation—paired fins. These served as rudders for fast and efficient swimming.

EVOLUTION

The ancient history of cartilaginous fish remains unclear, essentially because their soft skeletons make poor fossils. Most likely, these creatures evolved from a class of now-extinct jawed fish called placoderms that had bony skeletons and body armor. What the first cartilaginous fish lost in armor and hard bone they made up for in aggressiveness. Swift attack became their means of survival. The earliest species were

sharklike in form, and may have lived in freshwater. These freshwater sharks vanished more than 200 million years ago. A separate group of marine sharks found greater success.

Some 150 million years ago, the marine sharks experienced a great flowering in number and variety. Most likely, they were taking advantage of an even greater increase in the abundance of bony fish, their prey. Each species of shark developed traits that enabled it to feed on certain types of prey.

One very large group of early sharks developed broad, flattened bodies suitable for life on the ocean floor. These became the rays. By the end of the Cretaceous period, 65 million years ago, there existed most of the families and many of the species of modern sharks and rays we know today.

Evolution also produced a second major group of cartilaginous fish, separate from the sharks and rays. These were the chimaeras. They appeared about 350 million years ago,

The cartilaginous fish include sharks—the most notorious creatures in the sea. The great white shark (above) may be the most dangerous of all fish to humans.

THE CARTILAGINOUS FISH 323

looking much as they do today—with delicate, tapering bodies, large eyes, and long, thin tails. Like the rays, chimaeras primarily ate shellfish on the ocean floor. So their teeth developed into plates specialized for crushing shells. Although abundant in ancient times, the chimaeras are rare today.

Unique Adaptations

Sharks, rays, and chimaeras have skeletons made of the gristly material *cartilage*, considerably softer than bone. But make no mistake—there is nothing soft about the bite of a cartilaginous fish. Predatory sharks, in particular, have the most powerful and deservedly feared bites in the world.

The mouth of a typical cartilaginous fish opens on the underside of its snout, rather than the tip as in most bony fish. Inside are thousands of triangular teeth arranged in rows. But the teeth are not actually attached to the jaws, as in most animals. Rather, they grow out of folds of skin. New rows continually rise up and move forward to replace worn and broken teeth in the front.

It can be said that cartilaginous fish have teeth outside their mouths as well. Their bodies bristle with a covering of toothlike scales called *dermal denticles*. Each denticle is a hollow cone of dentin covered with hard enamel, the same materials found in human teeth. As you might imagine, this produces an extremely rough surface. In fact, 18th-century carpenters used sharkskin as sandpaper!

Cartilaginous fish were among the first creatures to fertilize their eggs internally. Instead of shedding his sperm over eggs in the water, the male uses a pair of modified pelvic fins, called *claspers*, to insert his sperm into the female's body. Female sharks, rays, and chimaeras produce large, yolk-rich eggs covered in a leathery case. Inside, the embryo can grow quite large, hatching ready for life as a predator. In many species, the female keeps her eggs inside her body until they hatch, giving birth to live young. The embryos of some sharks remain inside the mother's body even after hatching—just long enough to consume the embryos of their unborn brothers and sisters!

Unlike most fish, cartilaginous species do not have swim bladders to buoy their weight. Instead, they must continually swim forward, or else they sink. Their senses of smell, hearing, and touch are especially keen. Sharks, in particular, can detect incredibly small amounts of blood dissolved in water—to less than one part per million, or one drop in 30 gallons (113.5 liters). Many cartilaginous fish hunt using special sensory organs that detect the small vibrations and electrical charges produced by prey fish.

CLASSIFICATION

Sharks, rays, and chimaeras are placed together in the animal class Chondrichthyes, which means "soft-boned," or cartilaginous, fish. Scientists generally divide the modern car-

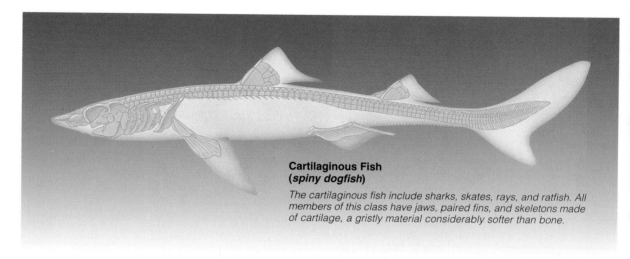

**Cartilaginous Fish
(*spiny dogfish*)**

The cartilaginous fish include sharks, skates, rays, and ratfish. All members of this class have jaws, paired fins, and skeletons made of cartilage, a gristly material considerably softer than bone.

tilaginous fish into two distinct groups, or subclasses. They isolate the unusual chimaeras into the subclass Holocephali, meaning "fused-head." The name refers to this group's unusual skull, in which the upper jaw is fused completely with the braincase. Sharks and rays comprise the second subclass, Elasmobranchii, a name that refers to their primitive, exposed gill slits. Elasmobranchii, in turn, is divided into two orders. The order Selachii contains all sharks, including several families of small sharks, called dogfish. The order Batoidea contains the rays.

The rarely encountered chimaeras (above) are slow-swimming and sluggish primitive cartilaginous fish that dwell deep in the oceans.

Chimaeras

The name "chimaera" refers to the sea monsters of Greek mythology. These pale-gray to pitch-black "monsters" of the deep are also called ratfish, a reference to their long, narrow tail. They can reach 5 feet (1.5 meters) in length, depending on the particular species.

Although chimaeras split off from the sharks and rays early in their evolutionary history, they clearly share a common ancestor. Like sharks, chimaeras swim by flexing the body and tail from side to side using their stiff, outstretched pectoral fins as rudders. The chimaeras, however, remained far weaker swimmers than their more aggressive cousins.

Although chimaeras have largely lost their scales, one thick line of toothlike denticles runs down the middle of the back. A sharp spine, often quite long, grows directly in front of the two dorsal fins.

Male chimaeras, like male sharks, have claspers for fertilizing their mates. But the chimaera has three additional clasping organs, called *tentaculums*. Two grow in front of the pelvic fins, and a third, shaped like a club, grows from the forehead. These strange appendages are unique to the cartilaginous fish.

Unlike the sharks and rays, chimaeras have a single gill opening on each side of the head. This structure is covered by a flap of skin called an *operculum*, similar to that of the bony fish. In breathing, chimaeras inhale water mainly through the nostrils rather than the mouth. Although chimaeras sometimes venture into rivers and freshwater estuaries, most live in very deep water, and are therefore seldom seen and little studied. When caught, they quickly die if removed from the water.

Scientists group the living chimaeras into three families with 34 species. The chimaeras known as rabbit fish belong to the family Chimaeridae and have distinctive, rounded snouts. The elephant fish belong to Callorhynchidae, and are recognized by a strange, flexible snout shaped like a hoe. The long-nosed chimaeras (Rhinochimaeridae) have lengthy, pointed snouts.

Sharks

Most people can quickly recognize the typical shark body: steel gray and torpedo-shaped with a pointed or flattened snout. Beneath this snout is a crescent-shaped mouth filled with many rows of intimidatingly sharp, triangular teeth. Sharks have five to seven pairs of uncovered gill slits, or *clefts*, above or in front of the pectoral fins.

A typical shark has large pectoral fins strengthened by cartilage rods. They extend straight out from the sides like airplane wings, providing the creature with lift, superb balance, and maneuverability at high speed. On its back, the typical shark has two triangular dorsal fins, which act as stabilizers. For propulsion, the shark uses the stiff caudal fin at the end of its muscular tail. As it swims, the shark holds the front of its body still, while whipping its tail from side to side like a propeller.

The hammerhead shark, readily identifiable by its bizarre head, can be dangerously aggressive.

A number of shark species differ from this typical form. In shape, they range from flattened to almost snakelike. Their coloration, though always drab, can include a variety of spots and stripes. Lengths vary from 6 inches (15 centimeters) to about 40 feet (12 meters).

Most sharks are carnivorous, and feed on comparatively large prey. Although primarily fish and squid eaters, they will swallow almost anything except the proverbial kitchen sink! Items found in shark stomachs include paint cans, raincoats, tires, license plates, sides of boats, even a small keg of nails. The shark's digestive system is very short compared with that of other vertebrates. A special organ called the *spiral valve* increases the surface area of the intestines to enhance digestion.

Sharks have keen eyesight, but they lack color vision. They are also sensitive to sound, although they have no eardrums; instead, sharks "hear" by sensing vibrations in the water around them.

A fair number of shark species are large or aggressive enough to attack swimmers, sometimes with deadly force. But humans pose a far greater danger to sharks. In recent decades, overfishing has seriously reduced many species of sharks. Smaller species such as dogfish, topes, and hound sharks are caught and eaten for their meat. A greater threat is the mass killing of sharks for their dorsal fins. Shark fins are valued as an ingredient in Asian folk remedies and gourmet soups. Because sharks occupy the important top rung on the food chain, experts warn that their continued slaughter will have serious consequences for all sea life.

Scientists divide the sharks into 13 to 22 families with about 300 species. Sharks are most abundant in tropical seas, but can be found in all the world's oceans at great depths. Some of the best-known families are discussed in the following pages.

Feeding Frenzy

Biologists are quick to point out that shark attacks, although serious, are rare. In 2006, there were 62 recorded shark attacks worldwide, resulting in four deaths. Far more people die from drowning each year.

Still, no one would belittle the fearsome quality of a full-fledged shark attack. The term "feeding frenzy" accurately describes the furious behavior that ensues when three or more sharks converge around a bleeding or thrashing victim.

For unknown reasons, most sharks circle their prey. When several sharks are present, their circling becomes quite rapid and progresses to zigzag passes. At this point, the sharks are primed for a *frenzy*. What triggers these wild attacks? It can be the scent of blood, or simply the ripples made by the thrashing movements of their frightened victims. Once a shark feeding frenzy has begun, indiscriminate attack on the prey and canni-

balism are common. Feeding sharks often turn on one another, regardless of size.

Sharks seldom come so close to a beach as to bother swimmers. But occasionally they are drawn by the kicking and splashing of people at play, or by some blood in the water—perhaps from a cut finger or even a hooked fish. In places such as Australia, where sharks are common, lifeguards keep watch from high towers and sound alarms when they see a shark approach.

Some species of rays have derived their common names from a particularly distinctive feature of their bodies. The shape of a guitarfish (left), for instance, bears a striking resemblance to that of the musical instrument. The snout of the sawfish (below) looks like a serrated blade.

• The dreaded *great white shark*, of the family Isuridae, may be the most dangerous shark to humans. Growing to nearly 30 feet (9 meters) in length, it is a powerful and voracious hunter of the tropical seas. Like many large tropical sharks, the great white occasionally strays into cooler waters. It appears periodically off both the Pacific and Atlantic coasts of North America, and may be responsible for most serious shark attacks on swimmers in U.S. waters.

• The *tiger shark*, another terror of the sea, is a member of the largest shark family, Carcharhinidae. Mature tiger sharks can rival the great white in size and are infamous for their unprovoked attacks on people. The family Carcharhinidae also includes several species that swim into coastal marshes and rivers. Some have even become landlocked in freshwater, including the *bull shark* of Lake Nicaragua in Central America.

• The strange *hammerhead shark*, another dangerous variety, belongs to the family Sphyrnidae. Even other sharks avoid this species! The weirdly enlarged lobes of its head may contain special organs for sensing the electrical impulses of prey. Its muscular body reaches a length of about 8 feet (2.4 meters). Although found in all seas, it is most common in the Indian Ocean.

• The *dogfish* include a number of small sharks in several families. The 3-foot (1-meter)-long spiny dogfish of the family Squalidae is equipped with poisonous spines, one in front of each dorsal fin. Dogfish often travel in rela-

tively large packs—much to the despair of deep-sea fishermen, whose nets they frequently rob. The dogfish also include the smallest known shark, the 5-inch (12.7-centimeter)-long tsuranagakobitozami, a Japanese word mercifully translated to "dwarf shark."

• The *whale shark*, the largest living shark by far, is the sole species in the family Rhincodontidae. Its whalelike body can grow to about 40 feet (12 meters) in length and weigh more than 10 tons. This behemoth of the deep feeds on plankton and other small organisms that it gulps into an enormous mouth filled with small, harmless teeth.

The usually harmless blue-spotted stingray (right) lashes out with the venomous spines of its tail only when threatened or attacked.

• The *basking shark* of the family Cetorhinidae is another gentle giant. As its name suggests, the basking shark drifts lazily near the surface, where it sifts plankton out of the water with its gills.

• The voracious *thresher shark* of the family Alopiidae feeds on a variety of large, fast, schooling fish such as mackerel and herring. Its name comes from the way it herds a school of prey fish into a frightened bunch. It circles them, all the while threshing, or beating, the water with its very long, slender tail. Common in all oceans, thresher sharks are harmless to humans.

• The *angel shark*, or *monkfish*, an unusually flattened shark with large pectoral fins, may represent an important evolutionary link with the rays. Like a ray, its eyes lie on the upper surface of its body; like a shark, its gill slits run along the side.

Rays

From the early torpedo-shaped sharks, there evolved a group with broad, flattened bodies adapted for life on the seabed. The first known "ray" was *Spathobathis*. From 150-million-year-old fossils, scientists have determined that its 20-inch (51-centimeter)-long body had eyes on the top of its head, with mouth and gill slits on the flat underside. Its pectoral fins had developed into great "wings" for "flying" through the water. Its teeth had become broad and flattened for crushing the shells of mollusks and crustaceans.

The rays quickly became a successful group that spawned many new species. Today their order—Batoidea—is the largest of the cartilaginous fish, with some 450 species. It includes five major groups, or suborders: the electric rays; sawfish; guitarfish; skates; and stingrays and devil rays. All have large, winglike pectoral fins that extend forward along the sides of the head above the gills. Most rays have long, slender tails, some equipped with sharp, poisonous spines. Except for the electric rays, all have rough denticle scales similar to those of the sharks. Most species are found in tropical seas, but some are temperate and a few are cold-water species.

Many rays breathe differently than do sharks. Instead of inhaling water through the mouth, they do so through large openings called *spiracles* atop the head. The water then passes over the gills and out the gill slits, as in other fishes. Except for the egg-laying skates, all rays give birth to live young. All species of rays are generally unaggressive toward humans, except when stepped upon.

The *electric rays* are famous for their shock tactics. Using highly developed electric organs on either side of the head, they can deliver a jolt of electricity—generally in self-defense, but occasionally to stun prey. This group is easily recognized by their discus shape, formed by their rounded wings and head. The largest electric rays are the torpedoes. A 40-pound (18-kilogram) Pacific torpedo can produce a discharge of 200 volts of electricity—strong enough to severely stun a human or to light several household lamps.

The *sawfish rays* are named for their unusual snout, modified into a long blade with a row of spikes on each side. To obtain food, a sawfish will swim into a school of smaller fish, then flail its saw from side to side. It then has an easy time catching the many injured fish around it. Sawfish have also been seen using their snouts to shovel crabs and mollusks out of the sand. The harmless *guitarfish* gets its distinctive shape from the broad base of its tail (the head of the guitar). Its pectoral fins are narrower and thicker than those of other rays.

By contrast, the *skates* are the broadest and most flattened of all the rays. Their extremely large pectoral wings extend all the way from the snout to the base of the tail. Some skates have peculiar "beaks," or long noses. Most skates are dangerous to step upon. They have a row of large, sharp spines down the middle of the back and tail. Some species can also deliver a mild shock with an electric organ in the tail. Skates lay eggs in square, leathery capsules known as "mermaid purses."

The *stingrays* comprise a large group of diamond-shaped rays with long, whiplike tails. Most have one or more barbed, venomous spines situated on the tail's upper surface. When frightened, the stingray lashes its tail to injure its enemy. The largest stingrays are the dramatic devil rays, or mantas, which can reach 25 feet (7.6 meters) in length. Their unique pair of hornlike head fins project forward on each side of the head. Most mantas are harmless unless attacked. Harpooned mantas have been known to demolish a boat in their efforts to escape.

Bony fish have evolved an almost infinite variety of methods of self-defense. The spiny puffer fish (above), for example, swells up its body and sticks out its spines to discourage would-be predators from swallowing it.

THE BONY FISH

In sheer number and variety, the bony fish—class Osteichthyes—are superstars. With more than 22,000 modern species, they outnumber not just all other types of fish, but all other vertebrates—nonbony fish, amphibians, reptiles, birds, and mammals—*combined*.

Bony fish are found in a seemingly endless variety of forms—with new, sometimes-bizarre-looking species still being discovered today. Those already known to science vary from the "typical" torpedo-shaped salmon to the weird anglerfish, porcupine fish, and sea horse. Bony fish also include such "living fossils" as the primitive coelacanth, as well as evolution's ultimate "swimming machine," the tuna.

Bony fish occur in virtually every aquatic environment, both freshwater and marine. They can fight their way up towering waterfalls, glide above the ocean surface, and dive to depths where no light shines.

BONES AND BLADDERS

Bony fish first appeared in freshwater lakes and streams some 400 million years ago. Like the cartilaginous fish (sharks and rays), which developed separately, bony fish evolved from one of two primitive groups of now-extinct fish—the sharklike acanthodians or the "plate-skinned" placoderms. Both groups had biting jaws filled with sharp teeth. Their skeletons were made of cartilage, covered in places by a thin film of true bone. The sharks and rays retained their ancestors' gristly cartilaginous skeleton. The bony fish developed something substantially stronger.

Bony fish were the first creatures to possess a skeleton in which cartilage was entirely replaced by hardened bone. Bone's great hardness and strength comes from a solid matrix of calcium phosphate. It is a truly remarkable adaptation that the bony fish passed on to all their land-living descendants.

The bony fish developed several additional important adaptations not found in other fish. They have a bony flap, called the *operculum*, covering the gill slits on each side of the head. When this flap closes, it creates within the head a suction that draws water over the gills. When the operculum opens, it causes the water to flush

The coelacanth (above, in its deepwater habitat off the coast of South Africa) may be the fish most closely related to the first land vertebrates.

out a rear opening. This adaptation greatly increases the efficiency of the bony fish's breathing over that of other fish.

The first bony fish also developed a special type of "float," called the *swim bladder*. A bony fish uses this air-filled pocket, located above the stomach, to maintain a chosen depth with little effort. The creature does so by inflating or deflating its swim bladder with air or body gases. By contrast, fish such as sharks, which lack a swim bladder, must constantly move, or else they will sink.

MAJOR GROUPS

Early in their evolution, the bony fish split into two main groups: the *ray-finned* fish (subclass Actinopterygii), and the *lobe-finned* fish (subclass Sarcopterygii). The fins of the ray-finned fish are thin structures with little or no muscle; their fanlike appearance derives from the membrane of skin that stretches over many stiff shafts, or "rays." By contrast, the lobe-finned fish developed fleshy, muscular fins supported by bone. Another difference: the nostrils of the lobe-finned fish connect to their mouths, a feature they share with air-breathing vertebrates. The nostrils of ray-finned fish do not.

Over the millennia, the number of lobe-finned fish

More than 22,000 living species make up the large and varied group known as the bony fish. Bony fish are distinguished by their jaws, paired fins, and skeletons made of bone.

remained small. Their primary importance to scientists lies in the fact that they may be the ancestors of all land vertebrates.

Lobe-finned Fish

In the deep waters of the Indian Ocean, a black hulk of a creature drifts over the seabed, its odd, fleshy fins turning slowly like propellers. It is a coelacanth, a primitive bony fish once thought to have disappeared 60 million years ago.

This one surviving species of coelacanth, together with six species of the equally ancient lungfish, make up the subclass Sarcopterygii—the lobe-finned fish.

Of special interest are the coelacanth's almost-leglike pelvic and pectoral fins. Unlike normal fins, each has a stumpy lobe of flesh that contains both bone and muscle. The bones of the pectoral fins connect with a sturdy shoulder girdle. Those of the pelvic fins connect with a hip girdle, or pelvis.

Scientists believe that the first land vertebrates—the amphibians—arose from a now-extinct freshwater relative of the coelacanth, the rhipidistian. Its stumpy pectoral and pelvic fins evolved into the first vertebrate legs. The rhipidistian's swim bladder may have become the first air-breathing lung. Like primitive fish surviving today, this creature had a tube connecting its swim bladder to its mouth through the stomach. This adaptation enabled the rhipidistian to fill its swim bladder by rising to the surface and gulping air.

Jawed Bony Fish (yellow perch)

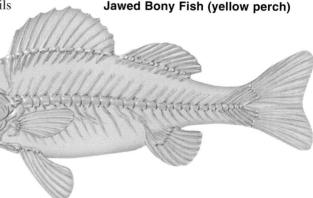

Until 1938, scientists believed that the coelacanths had died out with the dinosaurs. That year, fishermen in the Indian Ocean retrieved a coelacanth that scientists dubbed *Latimeria chalumnae*. It has since been studied and filmed in its deep-sea habitat. Females grow up to 6 feet (1.8 meters)—males are slightly smaller—and produce about 20 eggs the size of tennis balls. At least some females retain their eggs and give birth to live young. In 1998, a living coelacanth that appears to differ from *Latimeria chalumnae* was caught in the waters off the Indonesian island of Sulawesi. Zoologists are trying to determine if this specimen represents a separate species of coelacanth.

The coelacanth's closest living relatives are the lungfish of Australia, Africa, and South America. These unusual freshwater fish live in tropical rivers and lakes, where they grow to about 4 feet (1.2 meters) in length. Like the ancient rhipidistians, lungfish can use their swim bladder as a lung—rising to the surface to gulp air when oxygen levels in the water grow low.

Both the coelacanth and the lungfish have a *subterminal* mouth, located beneath the snout. By contrast, most ray-finned fish have a *terminal* mouth located at the snout's tip.

Ray-finned Fish

The ray-finned fish are the single most successful group of vertebrate animals ever, with more than 21,000 living species. The most successful division within this group is that of the advanced ray-fins (true bony fish), or *teleosts*. Today teleosts account for 95 percent of all ray-finned species, although they were not first. In fact, the ray-fins passed through three stages on their way to the teleosts.

The first ray-finned fish had long, spindle-shaped bodies; heavy, armorlike body scales; and stiff, barely movable fins. Their tails were asymmetrical, the top lobe being longer and larger than the bottom lobe. Their mouths, like those of the lobe-finned fish, were subterminal (beneath the snout). Today these primitive traits are retained in several species of "living fossils": sturgeons, paddlefish, and bichirs.

Sturgeons and paddlefish. Sturgeons are among the world's largest and longest-lived freshwater fish, growing up to 30 feet (9 meters) long and living more than 200 years. Sturgeons have a whiskery, shovel-shaped snout and five rows of bony body plates. Their flesh and eggs (caviar) have long been considered delicacies. Sturgeons live in rivers, lakes, and oceans of the Northern Hemisphere. Marine forms return to freshwater to breed.

The paddlefish's long, oar-shaped snout (its function remains a mystery) accounts for half its total length. Paddlefish feed on plankton. The 6-foot (1.8-meter)-long American paddlefish inhabits the Mississippi River in North America. Its only living relative swims in the Yangtze River of China.

The long, slender bichir and reed fish live in the streams of western and central Africa, where they forage in the mud for such small prey as worms and crustaceans.

Bowfin and gars. The middle stage of evolution for the ray-finned fish is represented by a group called the Holosteans. Only eight species survive today: one bowfin and seven kinds of gars. All are voracious predators, living in shallow, reedy lakes and rivers in North and Central

The red salmon is only truly red in the breeding season, when its back and sides become quite vividly colored. During this time, the male also develops a noticeably hooked upper jaw.

America. The scales of the bowfin and gars are not as chunky, nor their tails as lopsided, as those of the sturgeons, paddlefish, and bichirs. Their bodies are more compact, and their fins more flexible. Many have terminal mouths. All in all, their traits are intermediate between those of the primitive chondrosteins and those of the more modern teleosts.

The teleosts. Most teleosts have strong, compact bodies covered with thin, flat, overlapping scales; highly mobile fins; and symmetrical tails with upper and lower lobes of equal length, an arrangement that enables each flick to produce an even, efficient thrust. Their mouths are located at the tip of their snouts.

This giant group also includes some of the world's most unusual forms—fish that have developed strange and wonderful adaptations in the age-old quest to survive and reproduce. In size, teleosts range from tiny gobies a fraction of an inch long to marlins exceeding 11 feet (3.3 meters). They live everywhere from the subfreezing waters of the polar oceans to steaming desert hot springs. In all, there are more than 20,000 species of teleosts, grouped into 24 orders. Described below are the major groups and their most important and fascinating traits.

•*Tarpon* and *bonefish* are silvery, torpedo-shaped fish that still use their swim bladders as lungs. They can be seen gulping air at the surface of tropical swamps and lagoons. The air passes from the stomach to the swim bladder through a tube that no longer exists in more-advanced teleosts (whose swim bladders are filled with body gases).

Tarpon and bonefish migrate to the open ocean to spawn. Their eggs hatch into young called *leptocephalus larvae*, whose transparent, flattened bodies bear little resemblance to the adult forms. After they metamorphose into adults, these fish migrate back to their freshwater lagoons.

•*Eels* have distinctive long, slender, and scaleless bodies; their dorsal and anal fins form a continuous fringe around the tail. With some 500 species, eels can be found in all oceans. Morays, the largest and most dangerous eels, can grow to be 10 feet (3 meters) long; they use their long fangs for biting. Most eels are considerably smaller, with brushlike or flattened teeth.

Some eels spend a portion of their life in freshwater, migrating back to the ocean to spawn. Their young hatch as leptocephalus larvae similar to those of the tarpon.

•*Herring* and *anchovies* are small silvery fish, and among the most numerous in the sea. Most species travel in huge, shimmering schools. As a group, they provide more than one-third of the world's fish catch. The herring family includes the familiar sardines and shad. They and their close relatives, the anchovies, typically remain under 1 foot (30 centimeters) in length. They feed as they swim, sieving plankton from the water with their fleshy gills.

A notable exception in both size and behavior is the wolf herring, a voracious predator that grows to nearly 12 feet (3.6 meters); it uses large fangs to grip prey.

•*Bonytongues* and their close relatives—the elephant fish, featherbacks, and mooneyes—are a varied group that share one unusual trait: they have teeth on the tongue and the roof of the mouth in addition to the teeth in their strong jaws. These freshwater fish, with the exception of the mooneyes of North America, are

At the dark ocean depths where it lives, the deep-sea anglerfish (left) must rely upon its fleshy bioluminescent "lure" in order to attract curious prey.

Zoologists consider the leafy sea dragon at right to be among the oddest-looking of all ocean fish. Despite its daunting name, this "dragon of the deep" is quite harmless.

tropical species. The 10-foot (3-meter)-long bonytongues of the Amazon are renowned for their ability to leap high out of the water when cornered by fishermen—a habit shared by their tiny cousin, the African butterfly fish.

The African elephant fish are named for their strange, trunklike snouts, which they use to probe the mud for food. Elephant fish and featherbacks can create weak electric fields that help them distinguish prey, predators, and obstacles in dark or muddy water.

•*Salmoniformes*, or "salmonlike" fish, constitute nearly 1,000 species, including many important sport and commercial food fish—trout, whitefish, pike, char, grayling, and, of course, salmon—to name a few. Their common trait is a small, fleshy dorsal fin on the back. Salmoniformes inhabit just about every body of freshwater and salt water in the world.

Scientists consider salmoniformes to be the prototype, or ancestral model, for most other modern bony fish. Most of the species described below are thought to have evolved from salmonlike ancestors.

Many salmoniformes migrate long distances to spawn, typically traveling upriver from the sea or a lake. Each spring, the Pacific salmon swim hundreds of miles from the open ocean to the coast of British Columbia and Alaska, then swim hundreds of miles upriver. At one time, these fish traveled more than 1,000 miles (1,600 kilometers) inland; many of their paths have since been blocked by dams and other human-made barriers.

•*Carp, catfish*, and *minnows* make up the majority of the world's freshwater fish, with some 7,000 species. Among them are dozens of familiar aquarium fish: tetras, characins, loaches, danios, and the always-popular goldfish. Larger catfish and carp are important food fish. This large group also includes the piranhas, small South American predators that often attack in great numbers, tearing apart animals much larger than themselves.

Scientists credit the tremendous success of this large group to a number of remarkable adaptations. The most important is a special type of "hearing aid," called the *Weberian apparatus*, that virtually all catfish and carp have. This structure consists of tiny bony levers that connect the fish's ears to its swim bladder and convey sound waves traveling through the water, making this adaptation especially useful in habitats where muddy water and darkness limit sight. Many catfish and carp can use their swim bladders to produce sounds, including a variety of barks, chirps, and growls.

Among the most unusual features in this group are the "living batteries" found in electric catfish and the so-called electric eel (a catfish, not a true eel). The largest of these fish can produce a 600-volt shock, enough to stun any prey—or person. Another remarkable representative of this group is the hatchet fish of South America, which can literally fly—by flapping through the air on winglike pectoral fins! (By contrast, true "flying fish" only glide.)

•*Cod, toadfish*, and *anglerfish* share several unusual traits, most notably a large, gaping mouth with a distinctive muscular jaw. The pelvic fins on these fish are set far forward, closer to the head than to the tail.

With some 800 species, the cod include such popular food fish as haddock, whiting, pollack, and, of course, cod. Cod have been harvested from the North Atlantic for centuries. But overfishing has drastically reduced their numbers and size. Once 200-pound (90-kilogram) cod were common; today few survive long enough to reach 40 pounds (18 kilograms).

THE BONY FISH 333

The bizarre-looking anglerfish and toadfish are patient predators. They rely on camouflage and deception to lure small fish close enough to gulp. Anglerfish use a long, wormlike "fishing lure" that grows from the dorsal fin and dangles in front of the mouth. Those species living in coral reefs can be quite colorful, blending in with bright sea sponges and anemones. Anglerfish that live in deep-sea darkness are among the most-freakish-looking creatures in nature, with huge, gaping mouths filled with needlelike teeth. In some deep-sea species, the male is but a tiny parasite that attaches itself to the body of the larger female.

The toadfish derives its name both from its toadlike appearance and from its ability to croak—a sound amplified by its large swim bladder. The noise can be deafening, akin to an underwater foghorn.

•*Flying fish* and *silversides* live primarily in tropical seas, where they feed on plankton and small fish near the surface. All species can leap out of the water and skip along the surface to escape their enemies. Silversides simply skim over the surface for several feet. Flying fish go further, unfurling their winglike pectoral fins, lifting entirely out of the water and gliding through the air. This group of fish also includes the needlefish and the familiar grunions, which spawn at nearly full moon in large numbers along the coast of California.

•*Sticklebacks*, *sea horses*, and *pipefish* make up an order of unusual fish with narrow, armor-plated bodies and tubelike snouts. The males of several species are remarkably attentive fathers.

Sticklebacks are small silvery fish that live in streams and coastal waters. During breeding season, the male develops a red breast and becomes highly aggressive. Staking out a territory and defending it, he builds a nest of water weeds, where he invites females to lay their eggs. He guards the eggs and the newly hatched young until they are large enough to fend for themselves.

The stiffened bodies of sea horses and pipefish are encased in armored rings and plates; their tails have evolved into hooks for anchoring onto sea grass. These fish swim backward and forward through the water by whirring their tiny dorsal and pectoral fins. Most male sea horses and pipefish have a brood pouch on the

The pop-eyed mudskipper becomes a fish out of water whenever it hunts for food. When the creature feels hungry, it flip-flops ashore in search of some tasty insects.

belly, into which the female deposits her eggs. The swollen male then carries the eggs until they hatch, some four to six weeks later.

•*Scorpion fish* combine a masterly disguise with poisonous spines. Among the most dangerous are the stonefish, whose mottled, knobby bodies resemble rocks encrusted with barnacles and seaweed. This disguise enables them to lie in wait for small prey. But pity the poor person who steps on such a "rock." The fish's sharp body spines contain a dangerous, alarmingly painful, and sometimes-deadly poison. This group of fish also includes the sea robin. This unusual creature walks across the seabed on the stiltlike rays of its pectoral fins, which it also uses to overturn rocks in search of food to eat.

•*Perciformes*, or "perch-like fish," are the world's largest order of fish, with more than 6,000 species in 150 families. They are abundant in both freshwater and marine waters, from shallow ponds to the deep seabed. This order gives us many of the world's most important food fish, including tuna, mackerel, bass, and perch. It also includes popular aquarium fish such as gobies, angelfish, butterfly fish, stargazers, and blennies.

Perciformes vary in size from the 0.5-inch (1.27-centimeter) freshwater goby to the 11-foot (3.3-meter) bluefin tuna and black marlin; most measure between 1 and 8 feet (0.3 and 2.4 meters). They include both predatory and prey species, a difference based mainly on size. Many perciformes have torpedo-shaped bodies—streamlined forms that, together with powerful tail muscles, have produced the world's speediest fish. Indeed, tuna, marlins, and swordfish can cruise for long distances at speeds of 30 miles (48 kilometers) per hour.

Many perciformes lack the typical torpedo shape. The elegantly flattened butterfly fish are a favorite of aquarium enthusiasts. The comical-looking mudskipper has bulging, froglike eyes that sit high atop its head. Among the most feared of perciformes is the 6-foot (1.8-meter)-long barracuda. This voracious predator seldom

bothers human swimmers, but appears to follow them out of curiosity.

•*Flatfish*, which include the soles and flounder, have a truly unusual way of growing: they become asymmetrical as they mature! They are born resembling typical fish. Then one eye moves across the head to join the other. The mouth twists sideways, and the body flattens. Finally, the flatfish settles to the sea bottom, where it lies "eye-side" up. Adults can change their coloring to match their backgrounds. All eat small fish and invertebrates; some actively pursue their prey; others lie in wait.

•*Trunkfish* (or *box fish*), *puffer fish*, and *ocean sunfish* make up one of the strangest-looking groups of fish in the world. Puffer fish

Although barracuda (above) rarely make direct attacks on swimmers, those that do inflict savage bites with their large, dangerous-looking teeth.

are renowned for their ability to inflate their bodies with air or water—a tactic that makes them impossible for predators to swallow. The puffer fish (as well as the related porcupine fish) have spines that spring erect when they inflate. The closely related triggerfish have long, sharp spines in the dorsal fin that can be raised and locked in place.

The bizarre-looking ocean sunfish is often called the head fish, because it appears to be all head and no body or tail. In reality, its tail is reduced to a fringe at the rear of its rounded body. Ocean sunfish can reach great size, up to 10 feet (3 meters) long and more than 1 ton in weight. They hold the record for fish-egg production, laying up to 300 million eggs at one time!

HERPETOLOGISTS AND THEIR SCIENCE

by Kathy Svitil

Herpetologist Stephen Deban makes a habit of peeking under rocks. As a salamander specialist, he knows where to find his subjects. Among his favorite hunting grounds are the steep, rocky hillsides of California's Sierra Nevada. There, on a recent fall day, Deban lifted a stone and found his quarry. He quickly recognized the 4-inch (10-centimeter) creature as the web-footed Mount Lyell salamander, *Hydromantes platycephalus*. The discovery itself was no surprise. But what the salamander did next certainly was. Frightened by Deban's intrusion, the salamander tucked in its legs, wrapped its tail around its body, and rolled down the steep hill like a tiny log. Deban was impressed. Salamanders, being small-legged, slow-moving creatures, generally have a hard time escaping their enemies. Had this species found a clever new way to do just that?

Back at his lab at the University of California-Berkeley, Deban tested his hypothesis with the salamanders in his live collection. Indeed,

out of 16 salamanders tested, only *Hydromantes platycephalus* used the unique "rolling log" escape technique. And it did so whenever it had the chance.

In writing about the new behavior, Deban proposed that the web-footed salamander's steep habitat favored the evolution of this odd but useful escape technique. Such discoveries are part of the fascinating work of herpetology, the study of reptiles and amphibians.

THE FIELD OF HERPETOLOGY

Like ichthyology (the study of fish) and ornithology (the study of birds), herpetology is a branch of biology (the study of life). Although there is no logical reason for reptile experts and amphibian experts to both share the same label,

By spending time in the field, herpetologists can gain a clear understanding of how reptiles and amphibians survive and flourish in their natural habitats.

the fact that they do harks back to early European scientists, who lumped together reptiles and amphibians—two distinct classes of animals—as "creatures that creep."

As you might imagine, there are a great many things one can study about these fascinating creatures. A herpetologist may choose to investigate the anatomy, physiology, development, or genetics of either amphibians or reptiles, or both. Some herpetologists study reptilian or amphibian evolution, behavior, or habitat. Other herpetologists blend their science with that of paleontology to learn about extinct species—such as dinosaurs—through their fossils. Still others specialize in toxicology by studying snake venom or the poisonous skin secretions of salamanders and frogs.

THE FIRST HERPETOLOGISTS

Reptiles and amphibians figured prominently in many of the world's early civilizations. Pythons and cobras can be seen in the art of the Egyptian pyramids as well as that of the ancient Aztec temples of South America. No doubt, the respect shown these animals stemmed from fear of their deadly venom.

The scientific study of reptiles and amphibians began in the 4th century B.C. with Aristotle, the noted Greek philosopher and naturalist. When Aristotle created his great classification of living things, he placed reptiles and amphibians alongside mammals, birds, and fish in a group he called "animals with blood," and separated them from "bloodless animals" such as insects and crustaceans (which have colorless blood).

After Aristotle, herpetology fell into decline until the European Renaissance began in the early 14th century. At that time, naturalists began to dissect and compare the anatomy of many animals, including reptiles and amphibians. Such studies dispelled some of the superstitions people held about them. Snakes, in particular, were long thought to have magical powers. Salamanders were said to have the ability to walk through fire without being burned.

By the early 1700s, biology had developed into a full-fledged science. The study of reptiles and amphibians played an important role in its development. Early descriptions of embryonic growth, for example, came from the study of amphibian eggs. Their uniquely large cells make them especially easy to study.

Herpetology emerged as its own science in the late 18th century, with the founding of Europe's first herpetological societies. Most early herpetologists were amateur scientists. They included the German anatomist Johannes Muller, who, in 1835, discovered that caecilians had gills and were, in fact, amphibians, not snakes.

Throughout the 18th and 19th centuries, herpetologists kept busy collecting and naming the many new species brought back to Europe by early explorers. During this time, London and Paris were the leading centers for herpetological research. Many of the world's first textbooks on reptiles and amphibians came out of these two cities. But the leading herpetologist of

Snakes housed on the grounds of Brazil's Butantan Institute (below) are used by medical herpetologists for research into snake venom.

Years ago, a person with a keen interest in reptiles or amphibians could work in the field of herpetology without a college education. But today this is rare. A bachelor's degree in biology is typically a minimum requirement.

Most research and teaching careers in herpetology require advanced college study and a master's or doctorate degree in biology, zoology, or animal physiology. With such a degree, a herpetologist can often find a position as a college professor or postdoctorate "fellow." Herpetologists in these positions generally divide their time between teaching and conducting original research.

Some of the nation's most experienced herpetologists work as curators at zoos or natural-history museums, where they frequently have the opportunity to pursue separate independent research. A zoo curator's duties invariably include caring for live animals. A museum curator may need to develop exhibits and other educational material.

Wildlife management is another avenue for herpetologists. Federal and state governments, as well as private conservation organizations, offer such opportunities. In these positions, herpetologists plan and develop programs to monitor amphibians and reptiles in the wild. There are also herpetologists who breed the animals, or who focus specialized writing, photography, and film careers on the creatures.

the time was an American, Edward Cope of the Academy of Natural Sciences in Philadelphia. He described hundreds of new amphibians and classified them into closely related groups. He was among the first to classify animals based on their internal anatomy, especially the skeleton.

By the early 20th century, herpetology had blossomed into an international science. Major centers of study could be found at universities and natural-history museums around the world. Several of the most important were founded in the United States. In New York City in 1906, herpetologist Mary Dickerson helped establish an active amphibian-research program at the American Museum of Natural History, one that continues to this day. About the same time, the Museum of Zoology at the University of Michigan in Ann Arbor established one of the world's most important amphibian-breeding programs. Chicago's Field Museum of Natural History and the Smithsonian Institution both maintain extensive herpetological collections.

APPROACHES TO RESEARCH

The study of reptiles and amphibians has played a prominent role in advancing the scientific understanding of all animals, including humans. Amphibians, in particular, are ideal laboratory animals—easy to keep and able to survive procedures (such as partial dissection) that would kill other animals.

Many lizards and salamanders can regrow body parts such as the tail. Larval amphibians, or tadpoles, can regrow entire legs. As a result, some biologists study reptiles and amphibians to gain a better understanding of the basic processes of body growth and development. Perhaps their research will someday lead to new insights into nerve regeneration in humans.

The salamander known as the axolotl is an especially popular subject for such studies. A herpetologist can remove part of the amphibian's tail or leg, and then record how it grows back, all the while studying the cellular and molecular changes that occur during such regeneration. It is possible that such research may someday lead to methods that aid the recovery of patients with severely damaged tissues.

Many amphibians have unusually large chromosomes, the structures that contain genes, the molecular instructions for creating life. As a result, these creatures are very useful in studying gene structure, inheritance, and mutations.

At the first sign of spring, herpetologists in Massachusetts (above) and other temperate regions start looking for tadpoles in local ponds and marshes. In the subtropical Everglades (inset), herpetologists waste no time outfitting newly hatched crocodiles with radio transmitters.

Medical Herpetology

Medical herpetologists are interested primarily in the venom produced by snakes and some other reptiles, and in the poisonous skin secretions produced by many frogs and salamanders. Herpetologists with an interest in molecular biology or toxicology can study the proteins that make up these toxins. Together with physiologists and physicians, they can also study the effects that such poisons have on laboratory animals and human patients. Herpetologists also work with researchers to develop appropriate antivenins and other antidotes.

Other herpetologists study the disease organisms carried by reptiles and amphibians. Among the most common is salmonella, bacteria that grow on the skin and scales of many reptiles and can produce severe stomach distress in humans. It is now recognized that many people become ill after handling turtles, lizards, or other reptile pets infected with salmonella.

Field Studies

Many herpetologists enjoy studying their subjects in the wild. Such studies often involve tagging animals and releasing them to follow their movements and determine the size of their range. Field studies also enable herpetologists to estimate the size of a population, and thereby determine whether the population of a species is expanding or decreasing. How reptiles and amphibians respond to changes such as pollution in their environment can also be determined by herpetologists in the field.

Such studies have shown, for example, that amphibians are sensitive to a variety of human-made chemicals. This vulnerability is most likely due to their thin, absorbent skin. As a result, herpetologists studying amphibians are often the first to recognize potentially dangerous changes in the environment—problems that have not yet affected other animals.

Zoos and Museums

Many herpetologists work in zoos and animal parks, using their understanding of reptile and amphibian biology to tend to the animals in their care. Some of these herpetologists also work with the public, sharing their knowledge and interest in "scaly and slimy critters." National and state parks also employ herpetologists to educate visitors about native species. Still other herpetologists work with preserved specimens in natural-history museums.

AMPHIBIANS

Frogs and salamanders, together with the seldom-seen caecilians, make up the class Amphibia, a part of the subphylum Vertebrata, meaning animals "with a backbone." The direct ancestor of amphibians was the first vertebrate to venture out of water and onto land some 365 million years ago.

AMPHIBIAN EVOLUTION

Unlike other land animals, the amphibians never quite broke free of their wet ancestral home. Their name comes from the Greek *amphibios*, meaning "living a double life," referring to the creatures' dual existence on land and in water. Today, as in ancient times, most amphibians live on dry land, but must return to water to breed and lay their eggs.

Paleontologists (scientists who study fossils) believe that amphibians evolved from an ancient variety of freshwater, lobe-finned fish, perhaps a creature similar to the modern-day coelacanth. Such fish have a primitive type of lung in addition to their gills, enabling them to come to the surface to breathe air when the water grows muddy or low in oxygen. They also have muscular and bony fins that might prove useful for stumping about on land.

Still, scientists wonder just why the amphibians' ancestors first left their aquatic home. Perhaps they lived in ponds that dried up in times of drought. Or perhaps predators or competitors drove them out of the water. Whatever the reason, the first vertebrate on land would have discovered a new habitat teeming with food (the early insects), but completely free of enemies! The landscape was also friendly, covered with damp moss and shaded by giant ferns, club mosses, and horsetails some 50 feet (15 meters) high.

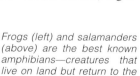

Frogs (left) and salamanders (above) are the best known amphibians—creatures that live on land but return to the water to breed and lay eggs.

In this idyllic world, there arose the earliest known amphibian, *Ichythyostega*. Found in fossils some 370 million years old, *Ichythyostega* was more than 3 feet (1 meter) long, with four fully formed legs, each ending in five toes. Another amazing first: *Ichythyostega* had a proper neck. It was the first vertebrate to be able to turn its head from side to side without moving the rest of its body.

Amphibians such as *Ichythyostega* ruled dry land for nearly 100 million years. In the end, they were pushed aside by their own descendants, the reptiles. Today only three orders of amphibians survive. Each of these orders may be distinguished by certain characteristics. The order Caudata, meaning animals "with tails," includes about 380 species of newts and salamanders. Order Anura, meaning "without tails," includes some 3,500 species of frogs. (The term "frog" also includes toads, which are considered to be dry-skinned terrestrial species.) And order Gymnophiona (formerly Apoda, "without limbs") includes 150 species of caecilians, unusual burrowing creatures that resemble large earthworms and live in the tropical regions of the world (see the box below).

Caecilians

The least familiar order of amphibians, Gymnophiona (formerly Apoda, "without limbs") is represented by a family of more than 150 species known as the caecilians. These little-studied animals—legless, nearly blind, hidden underground in remote forests—are like no other vertebrates. Their lives are spent burrowing in the moist soil beneath tropical forests everywhere except in Australia and Madagascar. A few South American species live in streams and ponds.

Caecilians vary in length from about 7 to as much as 54 inches (18 to 137 centimeters). With their narrow diameters—the largest is only about 1 inch (2.5 centimeters) thick—and the segmented grooves that ring their bodies, they can be easily mistaken at first glance for snakes or earthworms. Closer examination reveals that they have the firm bodies of vertebrates and well-developed teeth in a mouth designed for capturing and devouring prey. A groove on each side of the head contains a tentacle that can be extended or retracted—an appendage that serves as a sense organ, allowing the creatures to find their way in dark burrows. Most caecilians have poorly developed eyes; some species have none at all.

Some caecilian species have scales buried in their skin. Although no fossil caecilians have been found, the scales and other primitive characteristics suggest that the creatures are probably much older geologically than frogs and salamanders, and more than likely evolved independently from other types of amphibians.

Although much mystery surrounds the breeding habits and other behavior of caecilians, it is known that some species give birth to live young and that others lay eggs. In some species, the young pass through an aquatic larval stage, losing their tails—and their ability to live in water—when they transform into adults.

Caecilians in both their larval and adult stages are carnivorous creatures, burrowing through the ground to feed on worms, lizards, and insects. They are, in turn, preyed upon by certain species of snakes.

Jerry Dennis

FORM AND FUNCTION

Although many Paleozoic amphibians were as large as crocodiles, all of the modern-day forms are relatively small. Frogs range in size from the 0.25-inch (6-millimeter)-long Brazilian brachycephalid to the 1-foot (30-centimeter)-long West African goliath. Salamanders vary from a 1-inch (2.5-centimeter)-long Mexican species to the 5-foot (1.5-meter)-long giant aquatic salamanders of China. The worm-like caecilians range from 4 inches to 5 feet (10 to 150 centimeters) in length.

In form, adult amphibians remain intermediate between fish, their immediate ancestors, and reptiles, their immediate descendants. Like fish, most immature amphibians live in water and breathe through gills. Like reptiles, most adult amphibians live on land and breathe air through their lungs. The amphibian's heart is more powerful than that of a fish. It has three pumping chambers, like that of most reptiles.

Like fish and reptiles, amphibians are *ectothermic,* or cold-blooded, which means that their bodies do not control their own temperature. As a result, an amphibian's temperature more or less matches that of its surroundings.

Amphibians were the first vertebrate animal to develop legs—four of them, each ending in a foot with four or five toes. Yet another first: amphibians have eyelids, an important adaptation that keeps the eyes from drying out in open air. Amphibians are unique in having especially broad color vision, thanks to green rods in the retina of the eye. The exception is the unusual caecilian, which is all but blind.

Most remarkable of all, perhaps, is the amphibian's skin. In most species, it is exceptionally soft and smooth, although it may be dry and rough in some toads and salamanders. This thin skin is especially rich in blood vessels that come close to the surface to exchange oxygen and carbon dioxide. Quite literally, therefore, many amphibians can breathe through their skin. Special mucous glands help keep the amphibian's skin moist. In many species, the skin has specialized poison glands to discourage predators. Except for these glands, the amphibian's skin lacks special adaptations such as scales, bristles, feathers, hair, or claws. Like reptiles, amphibians periodically outgrow and shed their skin, which does not expand with them.

AMPHIBIAN LIFESTYLES

The term "amphibian" can be interpreted two ways: as an animal that begins life in water and then changes to an air-breathing, land-living adult, or as an animal that is able to move in and out of the water throughout its entire life. Many amphibians fit both definitions. But a few spend their entire lives in water, while others never enter it at all.

Most amphibians enter freshwater to breed and lay eggs. Typically, the female lays a string or mass of eggs coated with a protective jelly-like material. Hatching time varies from 20 days to nine months, depending on the species and the temperature of the water. (Development slows as temperatures drop.) The eggs hatch into larval forms called tadpoles.

Metamorphosis

As mentioned, the hatchling larvae resemble fish, with gills and fishlike skin and internal organs. This larval stage typically lasts a couple of months, although it varies from two weeks to well over a year, depending on the species, water temperature, and the availability of food. A few species of salamanders, such as the axolotl, never quite "grow up."

During development, the aquatic larva of a typical amphibian gradually loses its fishlike features and develops legs and amphibian skin. Its gills are absorbed and give way to lungs, and many other internal organs undergo dramatic change. In a number of ways, this metamorphosis follows the evolutionary changes that produced the first amphibian.

So transformed, the young amphibian emerges from the water as a small adult. If it is a frog, it is equipped with powerful jumping legs. Salamanders emerge with a slender body and a long tail. The seldom-seen caecilian looks remarkably like a giant earthworm.

Some adult amphibians travel far from water. They generally seek shelter from the drying effects of sunlight in underground burrows and other damp places, such as the leaf litter on a forest floor. Despite their delicate, easily parched skin, amphibians have moved into every habitat from low-lying deserts to frozen mountain peaks. Indeed, they can be found on every continent except Antarctica, and in every climate but permanent ice cap.

The sound begins gradually, like musicians in an orchestra warming up their instruments. A trill, then more trills. Then comes a chorus, swelling as the darkness deepens. "Quackety, quackety, quackety. Preep, preep, preep. Waaaaaah!"

Such pond-side concerts are a sure sign that spring has arrived. The crazy music will build through the summer as a new generation of frogs joins in the nightly song. Then, with the first chill of autumn, the voices fade away. The singers sleep till spring.

Most of us half-consciously know the life cycle of the frog by the ebb and flow of its evening song. And thanks to biology class, many of us have glimpsed its anatomy—both inside and out. But there is much more to frogs than this. Their story begins some 225 million years ago, in early Triassic times.

The first amphibians had already conquered land at the end of the Devonian period, about 350 million years ago. A million years later, some of these early amphibians were on their way to becoming true frogs. The earliest froglike creature was *Triadobatrachus*. From fossils, scientists know that it had a squat body about 4 inches (10 centimeters) wide, with a flat skull and nubby tail. Its powerful hind legs were designed for kicking through the water with a motion like that of the breaststroke. This frog also had a distinct, broad eardrum, clearly designed to pick up sounds in open air.

Whatever followed *Triadobatrachus* is a mystery. No other froglike creature appears in the fossil record for another 50 million years. Then, in the early Jurassic, we find *Vieraella*, a fully formed frog with a very short body, no tail, narrow hips, and long jumping legs.

Today frogs are among the most unusual as well as the most successful of vertebrate ani-

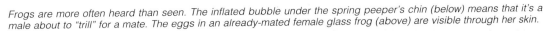

Frogs are more often heard than seen. The inflated bubble under the spring peeper's chin (below) means that it's a male about to "trill" for a mate. The eggs in an already-mated female glass frog (above) are visible through her skin.

A typical frog starts life in the water as a fertilized egg covered by a protective jellylike substance (A). A tiny fish-like larva, called a tadpole, emerges from the egg (B). As its growth continues, the tadpole becomes increasingly froglike—legs and lungs form, and internal systems develop to accommodate the habits of an adult, such as eating live animals (C). When the tadpole has finally transformed into an adult frog, its metamorphosis is complete.

changed little since they first appeared on Earth more than 150 million years ago. Other groups have developed new forms and behaviors to help them survive in different habitats. In fact, over the past 50 million years, frogs have invaded every known habitat outside of Antarctica and the Arctic ice cap. The familiar wood frog of North America can survive sub-zero winters above the Arctic Circle. The squat spadefoot toad can withstand the withering heat and dryness of the desert. As might be expected, the wood frog and the spadefoot toad have very different adaptations and lifestyles. Indeed, any description of a "typical" frog life cycle will include many exceptions to the rule.

LIFE CYCLE OF A FROG

Like a rolling wheel, a life cycle has no real beginning or end. For frogs, it is perhaps most convenient to begin this discussion with the quiet time of hibernation or estivation. Like other cold-blooded, or ectothermic, animals, frogs cannot warm or cool their bodies from the inside. To survive, they must therefore avoid extreme heat and cold.

In areas where winters are cold, frogs hibernate in a burrow in the soil or in some other protected shelter. There the frog's body functions slow. Its heart pumps just enough to keep blood circulating through the body. Under these conditions, frogs expend little energy. They can survive for months on stored fat (from summer feeding) and oxygen absorbed through the skin.

The length of hibernation varies between species and according to the conditions outside. The common European toad can hibernate up to three years when conditions are harsh. In general, frogs awaken from hibernation in the spring, when the days lengthen and the temperatures rise. The hardy wood frog emerges from its blanket of leaves before the ice has completely melted from its breeding ponds.

Estivation is the equivalent of hibernation in hot, dry regions. The spadefoot toads of the North American prairie avoid drought and heat by digging into the soil. Inside their deep burrows, the temperature and humidity level remain

mals. They have the shortest backbones of any vertebrates, with only five to nine vertebrac. Their powerful jumping legs are enormous compared to their body size. And with more than 3,000 species, frogs account for nearly 90 percent of all modern-day amphibians.

FROG BIOLOGY

Frogs display a great variety of body shapes and lifestyles. Some, such as the primitive bell frogs (family Leiopelmatidae), have

Toads are not always what they seem. The cane toad (left), imported to Australia to eat insect pests, instead prefers to feed on beneficial species. And despite its name, the Texas horned toad (right) is actually a lizard!

surprisingly comfortable. Some species, such as the giant burrowing frog from Australia and the African bullfrog, spend many months underground. Their skin produces a thick coating of waterproof slime to doubly protect their bodies from drying. Most estivating frogs burst out of their burrows with the first downpour of the rainy season.

Although it has not eaten in months, an emerging frog's most urgent desire is not food: it is the desire to mate. So driven, most frogs find their way to water, be it a lake, pond, stream, or puddle. Then, as dusk falls, they begin their familiar chorus.

Virtually all of the world's frogs produce some type of song, which is, to put it plainly and simply, the male's mating call. With each bird-like trill or cowlike bellow, he advertises his fitness as a potential father. The female also produces a song, but it is only a quiet croak.

Frog or Toad?

What's the difference between a frog and a toad? The answer to this frequently asked question is not a scientific one. The two words come from early England, where slippery varieties were dubbed "frogs," and, dry, warty varieties were called "toads." As it turns out, many "slippery" species are more closely related to "dry-rough" species than to other slippery species, and vice versa. Scientists have also discovered frog species that fall into neither category.

To avoid confusion, scientists refer to all "tailless" amphibians as "anurans" (Order Anura), or simply "frogs." This distinguishes them from the "tailed" amphibians, the salamanders, and the wormlike caecilians.

The word "toad" can be considered a nickname for members of the frog family Bufonidae. (Yes, most are dry and warty.) So all toads are frogs. But not all frogs are toads.

The spadefoot frog spends most of the year buried deep in the soil of the Arizona desert, emerging only during brief muddy spells (left) to lay its eggs. The female pygmy marsupial frog (below) tucks her eggs into special pouches on her back until they grow into tadpoles.

The simplest frog mating call may be that of the clawed African toad: he produces a loud clicking noise underwater. By contrast, most frogs produce calls designed to carry across open air. Many species have vocal sacs to amplify their calls. The male forces air in and out of the sac through two small holes in the floor of his mouth. Some species have a single sac under the chin. Others have a pair of sacs on either side of the mouth. Still other species have all three.

The females, in turn, wait to hear the special patterns and tones of their species. In the dark of night, they follow this special sound until they reach their mates. Once a female comes within reach, the male grabs her around the waist or clings to her back. Typically the female is larger than her mate. So she may carry him for some distance before she is ready to lay her eggs. Once she does so, he sheds his sperm to fertilize them.

From Egg to Adult

Most frogs lay long strings or large clumps of eggs that number several hundred to a thousand. Each is coated with a slippery jelly that swells on contact with water. This slimy substance is usually quite distasteful to predators.

Over the next few days, each egg grows longer. It then begins to move about in the water. Inside is a quickly growing and already active tadpole embryo that lives on the food substances stored in the yolk. By the end of the week, it hatches. First, it simply clings to the protective jelly that was its egg; it may also eat the jelly for nourishment. Within a day, the tadpole begins swimming and feeding. At first, it eats algae, tiny water plants, and decaying matter. But within a few weeks, it develops a voracious appetite for insects and other small invertebrates.

In form, a larval frog looks like a plump little fish. Its body functions are also fishlike—a tadpole even breathes through three pairs of feathery gills on either side of its head. But a few weeks after hatching, back legs appear.

Soon after, the tadpole's body absorbs its tail, front legs appear, and gills give way to functioning lungs. The tadpole now comes to the surface to breathe air. Within a few days, it will hop onto land.

The larval stage between hatching and adulthood typically lasts a few months. Eggs laid in spring or early summer generally produce small frogs between midsummer and early fall. But the length of metamorphosis can vary depending on the species, outside temperature, and the availability of food. Spadefoot toads have the most-rapid metamorphosis. They lay their eggs in small puddles. The spadefoot tadpoles must mature quickly—in as little as two weeks—before their nursery evaporates around them. At the other extreme is the slow-maturing bullfrog. In the cold northern reaches of its range, the bullfrog's tadpole form can take two years to mature into an adult frog.

Unusual Development

Not all frogs develop in a typical manner. The greenhouse frog of Florida lays its eggs on damp leaves. Inside the egg, the embryos undergo complete metamorphosis, hatching as miniature adults two to three weeks later. The female Suriname toad, or "marsupial frog," lays just a few eggs, which the male then packs into a sunken chamber on her back. There the eggs complete their development. They hatch as fully formed froglets that literally spring from their mother's back.

ADULT ANATOMY

Adult frogs are among the world's most easily recognized animals. With their flat-topped heads; short, tailless bodies; and long jumping legs, they resemble no other creature alive today. Evolution compacted the frog's body by reducing the number of vertebrae in its rigid spine to nine or fewer, depending on the species. The vertebrae of the neck and tail are likewise reduced to a minimum. Most frogs therefore have neither a visible neck nor tail. By contrast, evolution has lengthened the frog's pelvis, or hip girdle, as well as its hind legs. Adding to the length of its back limbs are an extra pair of long foot bones and five exaggerated toes. Most species have webbed feet to help them swim. The toes of tree frogs have tiny suction disks that help them to cling to small

Frogs That Sweat Poison

Danger can put certain frogs into a deadly sweat. When threatened by predators, many species of tiny, brilliantly colored frogs of Central and South America emit creamy or foamy secretions from glands in their skin. The secretions are distasteful, and predators almost always spit the frogs out immediately. The experience is so unpleasant that most predators never make the same mistake twice.

Sometimes they don't get a second chance. The poison emitted by at least three species of Colombian frogs is so potent that a mere taste of it is enough to kill. One species of tiny 1-inch (2.5-centimeter) frogs produces enough lethal poison to kill 100 people!

Almost all brightly colored frogs produce toxins. The brilliant coloration is a defensive tactic that helps keep predators away. Several of the most-toxic species are known as poison-dart frogs, because human hunters in the region use their secretions to make lethal weapons. After tormenting the frogs to stimulate their poison glands, the hunters rub the tips of their darts and arrows over the backs of the frogs. Once treated in this way, an arrow can remain deadly for months. The poison is so potent that even grazing the skin of a monkey with it paralyzes the animal within minutes.

Scientists have studied poisonous frogs for years, but only recently have they discovered how frog poisons are made. The species that produce the most-potent poison feed primarily on ants and mites, both of which contain small amounts of toxins. It is theorized that the frogs use a "toxin uptake system" to concentrate the poisons in their skin glands. Some species, however, seem to have an internal production system much like that of rattlesnakes. Poison-dart frogs, for instance, produce a chemical called batrachotoxin, which is found in no other animal except the hooded pitohui bird of New Guinea. The substance, one of the deadliest poisons ever discovered, causes instant muscle paralysis.

Scientists believe that such toxins might have medical value. In laboratory studies, some frog toxins have been tested as painkillers and appetite suppressants. Others have shown potential for treatment of Alzheimer's disease and as alternatives to morphine and other drugs.

Jerry Dennis

branches. Other species have spadelike bumps on their legs, which they use for digging. A frog's smaller forelegs have four toes each.

The frog's lightweight skull is quite flattened on top. The frog's sizable eyes and ears are important for seeing and hearing small prey in the dimness of night. A frog's eyes sit atop its head, enabling the creature to sit half-submerged in water and still see insects flying over the surface.

A frog's mouth is truly enormous in proportion to the rest of its body. Most species have a few small teeth in the upper jaw. But these teeth are used to hang onto prey, not chew it. All frogs swallow their food whole.

A few primitive frogs simply pounce on their prey and use their front legs to push the food inside their mouths. More typical is the frog that uses its long tongue to capture its prey. The frog tongue is unique among vertebrates. Attached to a spot at the bottom front of the mouth, the tongue curls backward into a ball when the creature's mouth is closed. A special gland near the tip of the tongue produces a sticky slime. So equipped, the frog snaps out its tongue at its prey like a marksman. So lightning fast is the motion (about 0.15 second) that it is invisible to the human eye.

Skin

Frogs have two types of skin glands. One produces mucus to prevent the skin from drying. This mucus also helps the frog literally breathe through its skin.

The second type of skin gland secretes a poisonous or distasteful fluid. As a result, most predators will quickly spit out a frog and avoid their kind in the future. The most-poisonous species of frogs tend to be brightly colored as a warning to would-be predators.

Not all enemies are so easily repelled, however. Herons, cranes, and other marsh birds delight in "frog legs" for lunch. To avoid such predators, frogs rely on camouflage and their ability to remain motionless. This tactic accounts for the large number of species that have developed green or mottled-brown skin to match their surroundings. When all else fails, many frogs evade capture by emptying their bladders. The foul-smelling liquid is sometimes enough to cause a predator (or person) to drop the frog in surprise or disgust.

FROG CLASSIFICATION

The amphibian order Anura contains 16 families. Among the most familiar are the true frogs (family Ranidae), tree frogs (Hylidae), and the so-called toads (Bufonidae).

True frogs can be recognized by their large size, slim hips, and spectacular jumping ability. They include the American bullfrog, which grows to 8 inches (20 centimeters) and produces a deep-pitched "jug-or-rum" call that can be heard a quarter mile away.

As their name implies, tree frogs are expert climbers, aided by sticky pads on their toes. They are among the most successful of frog families, with more than 600 species, most of them in tropical and subtropical areas.

The toads of the family Bufonidae spend most of their life on dry land, returning to water briefly to breed. Their tough skin resists drying, enabling this family to thrive in arid habitats such as prairie and brushland. The largest and most familiar group of toads are the 200 species in the genus *Bufo*. They include the American toad of the Northeast, the western toad of the West, and the Great Plains toad of the Midwest.

IMPORTANCE TO HUMANS

In addition to being loved (or at least tolerated) for their song, frogs benefit humans by eating an enormous number of insect pests. In some parts of the world, frogs are also eaten as food. The skin secretions produced by frogs may someday prove equally important. Scientists have found that the skin secretions of some species contain natural antibiotics and other substances of possible value pharmaceutically.

It is important that humans do not take the existence of frogs for granted. Indeed, because of their thin, absorbent skin, frogs have always been vulnerable to the effects of pollution. Concern for their welfare has grown in recent years, as scientists see a decline in frog populations around the world, with some species more affected than others. But the exact reasons for their decline remain a mystery. Possible culprits include acid rain, water pollution, global warming, ozone depletion, or infectious microbes. The latest suspect is chytrid, a virulent, parasitic fungus that some scientists believe may be responsible for the decline of frogs in Australia, New Zealand, and the United States.

The steady but gentle rainfall on an unusually warm late-winter evening can mean only one thing in the Animal Kingdom: it's a perfect night for salamanders! Drab or vividly colorful, speckled or boldly striped, half a dozen species emerge from the leaf litter and head for water. Silently and slowly they creep, their slender bodies twisting from side to side with each tiny step. Some follow familiar scents to the same pond from which they emerged several years before. Others may navigate by the magnetic field of Earth itself!

Few people know these shy and secretive creatures, although millions live throughout North America, Europe, and Asia, and a few can be found in Africa. Unlike their noisy cousins the frogs, salamanders are all but voiceless. Much of their lives are spent hidden beneath logs, rocks, and leaves.

The name "salamander" is derived from the Greek term for "living in flames." This mythical reputation arose in ancient times when people saw the slender amphibians escape from damp logs placed in the fire. On a more scientific note, all salamanders belong to the order Caudata, meaning "animals with tails." Alongside the frogs (order Anura) and caecilians (order Gymnophiona), salamanders make up the class Amphibia, or amphibians.

Like other amphibians, salamanders are cold-blooded, or ectothermic, vertebrates (animals with backbones) recognized by their soft, moist skin. This remarkable skin is extremely thin and enriched with blood vessels that absorb oxygen directly from the surrounding air or water. In other words, salamanders—like other amphibians—can breathe directly through their skin, although some also use lungs or gills. To keep their skin moist, salamanders exude a slick liquid and live in damp places away from the drying effects of the Sun.

The bright coloration of many salamanders is often accented by spots or stripes. Special glands secrete substances that protect the salamander's delicate skin.

LIFE CYCLE

Most salamanders breed and lay eggs in water. Typically, their young hatch as fishlike, water-breathing larvae that feed on smaller aquatic animals. Voracious predators, they even bite the legs and tails off other larval salamanders. Remarkably, the damaged larva simply grows its lost limb anew.

The salamander's immature stage can last from a few days to several years, depending on the species and outside conditions. During a brief period of rapid change, most larval salamanders lose their gills and fins and develop lungs and fully formed legs. Unlike frog tadpoles, larval salamanders do not lose their tails. They emerge from the water as miniature adults that breathe air and walk on land.

The adult salamander is unique among amphibians in having a distinct, bendable neck, slender body, and long tail. It creeps slowly on four small legs. The salamander holds its legs to the sides of its body rather than beneath it. This arrangement produces a side-to-side movement of the body with each step. The salamander's back feet end in five toes (as do a frog's), but its

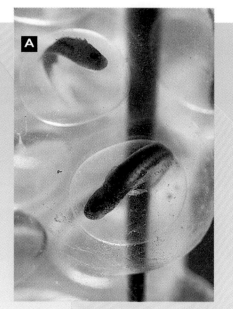

front feet have just four toes each. At first glance, some people mistake salamanders for lizards. But the salamander's soft, moist body lacks both scales and claws.

The salamander's movements, like its metabolism (body functions), are generally slow. Except during breeding season, these creatures generally sit in one place, waiting the approach of prey—mainly insects, snails, and worms. Such a drowsy lifestyle may account for the salamander's remarkably long life. A few species live 30 years or more, barring an accident or other violent end.

The salamanders' predators include raccoons, shrews, owls, snakes, fish, and large frogs. Some species discourage these enemies with poisonous and foul-tasting skin secretions and bright warning colors. Some salamanders can shed their tails when attacked. The dismembered tail continues to wriggle, distracting the predator while the salamander escapes to grow another.

In a typical sequence of salamander metamorphosis, eggs (A, with developing embryos visible) are laid singly or in clumps in or near the water. The water-dwelling larva (B) has a well-developed head; gills; and a voracious appetite. This stage may last for weeks or even years. Finally, following a rapid burst of development, the salamander emerges from the water as an air-breathing adult; some species, including the hellbender (C), retain an aquatic lifestyle as adults.

EVOLUTION

As a group, the salamanders evolved in the Jurassic period, some 200 million years ago. Salamander-like amphibians appear in the fossil record even earlier. But it remains a mystery which, if any, of these early amphibians (all since extinct) gave rise to the salamanders we see today.

Salamanders evolved a stunning variety of forms and behaviors over the past 100 million years. Most grow to a length of 4 to 6 inches (10 to 15 centimeters). Species range in size from the 1-inch (2.5-centimeter) Cherokee salamander of Georgia to the 60-inch (152-centimeter) giant salamander of China.

As mentioned, many salamanders live a typical amphibian existence, hatching fishlike in water before transforming into air-breathing adults. Some skip the water stage and live entirely on land. Still others remain in the water, never losing their fishlike gills and fins.

SALAMANDER FAMILIES

Scientists generally divide salamanders into 6 to 10 families, based on common physical traits and behaviors. Presumably, those in each family share common ancestors. Of 350 known species, the vast majority live north of the equator. A full one-third of salamander species can be found in North America.

By far, the largest family is that of the lungless salamanders (Plethodontidae), with about 215 species worldwide. Among the most familiar of this group is the dusky salamander of eastern North America. Like all of the lungless salamanders, the dusky variety breathes neither through gills nor lungs, but absorbs the oxygen it needs through its skin. The lungless salamanders are famous for their elaborate courtship rituals. The male rubs and prods the female, who then climbs atop his tail for a ride. In the process, the male deposits a cone-shaped packet of sperm on the ground. The female lowers herself over the packet, pressing

Unlike other salamanders, newts have rather rough, dry skin as adults. When agitated, many species (including the crested newt above) produce patches of vivid warning coloration.

it into an opening on the underside of her body. When she lays her eggs, they will pass through the sperm to be fertilized. Most lungless salamanders lay their eggs in damp places on land. At hatching, their young look like miniature adults. A few species in this family live in underground caverns and streams.

The salamanders called newts belong to the family Salamandridae. They are unique among salamanders in having rather rough, dry skin as adults. Their development is also unusual. Most begin life in the water as tadpolelike larva. After losing their gills and developing legs, they emerge as brightly colored forms called *efts* that creep about the forest floor for one to three years. When ready to mate, the efts return to the water and undergo a second body change. Their skin grows thin as the tail becomes flattened like a long fin. Some males also grow large body crests. So transformed, the adults breed, and their cycle begins again.

Other interesting families include the mud puppies (Proteidae) common to eastern North America. They live entirely in water, where they feed on fish, insects, and crayfish. Although most mud puppies develop legs, they never entirely lose their gills. The olm is a blind, colorless mud puppy found in underground caves in Eastern Europe. This species can alternately lay eggs or give birth to live young; scientists do not yet understand what determines the choice.

The sirens and congo eels (families Sirenidae and Amphiumidae) are aquatic, eel-like salamanders found in ditches, swamps, and other waterways in eastern North America. Adult congo eels have four puny, almost useless legs. The sirens have no hind legs at all.

A particularly unusual salamander is the axolotl of Lake Xochimilco, near Mexico City. This salamander lives a kind of Peter Pan existence. It spends its entire life in an immature larval form, except to develop sexual organs for mating. Nineteenth-century scientists were astounded to learn that the axolotl is actually a form of the tiger salamander, a normal-looking species common to North America. Axolotls mature into tiger salamanders in water that contains trace amounts of iodine, a chemical that stimulates their metabolism. The axolotl's strange prolonged "youth" is called *neoteny*. A few other species of salamanders can similarly prolong their larval stage under certain conditions.

REPTILES

What has a backbone, breathes air, and wears scales instead of feathers or fur? O.K., so we gave away the answer in the title. Still, this puzzler is a good definition of what it means to be a reptile.

Reptiles make up a class of animals that includes snakes, lizards, crocodiles, alligators, turtles, and the ancient tuatara. Not to be forgotten are the extinct pterosaurs and dinosaurs—reptiles that ruled land and air for nearly 140 million years. About 60 million years ago, the reptiles yielded their kingdom to their direct descendants, the birds and mammals. Today about 6,500 species of reptiles remain, none of them close in size to the largest dinosaurs. Most of these living species belong to the order Squamata, the lizards and snakes.

In form and behavior, reptiles lie midway between their ancestors, the amphibians, and warm-blooded animals. Like amphibians, reptiles cannot raise or lower their body temperature with internal processes such as shivering or sweating. But unlike the amphibians, reptiles do exert a kind of active control over their temperature. To warm themselves, they seek sunny places where they can bask, or "sunbathe." When temperatures rise too high, reptiles seek shade.

AN EVOLUTIONARY LEAP

The first amphibian may have crawled out of the water 370 million years ago. But it remained for the reptiles to break all ties to a water-bound life, some 70 million years later. This liberation required two great evolutionary changes. First, the reptiles evolved scales that prevented their skin from losing water. Second, they developed the eggshell, a protective case that enabled the reptiles to lay their eggs away from moisture.

From their beginnings in the Carboniferous period, 300 million years ago, the first reptiles diversified into many forms, including the "Ruling Reptiles," the dinosaurs. No one knows what caused the dinosaurs' ultimate demise, some 65 million years ago. Most likely something caused a general cooling of Earth, and this favored the success of warm-blooded animals such as birds and mammals.

MODERN-DAY REPTILES

Today four orders of reptiles survive out of the 17 orders that thrived in Precambrian times. The order Squamata includes the lizards and snakes. Chelonia includes the turtles and tortoises. Crocodylia contains all crocodiles, a group that includes the alligators, gavials, and caimans. The ancient, lizardlike order Rhynchocephalia has one surviving member—the lizardlike tuatara of New Zealand. Like its extinct relatives, the tuatara has in the middle of its head a unique eyelike organ whose function remains a mystery to scientists.

Most modern reptiles live in tropical and subtropical areas, although a substantial number inhabit temperate regions. The lacertid lizard and a snake, the common viper, live the farthest north, reaching the Arctic Circle in parts of Europe. These cold-climate reptiles survive by hibernating through winter.

The largest modern reptiles include the reticulated python and the saltwater crocodile. The python reaches a length of more than 30 feet (9 meters), while the crocodile can grow to as long as 23 feet (7 meters). The largest lizard is the Komodo dragon, which can reach almost 15 feet (4.5 meters) in length. The largest turtle is the 9-foot (2.7-meter), 1,500-pound (680-kilogram) marine leatherback.

The smallest living reptiles are the geckos, some of which grow to just over 1 inch (2.5 centimeters). A few burrowing snakes are less than 4 inches (10 centimeters) long; the smallest turtles weigh less than 1 pound (0.45 kilogram).

REPTILE CHARACTERISTICS

Say the word "reptile," and people think "scales." And they are right: a reptile's body is covered in tiny plates made of a tough, horny substance similar to fingernail material. The exact shape, texture, and arrangement of scales differ between species. In general, snake scales feel smooth.

Those of lizards can be rough or spiky. The scales of crocodiles and the shells of turtles are hardened with actual bone.

The reptiles' scaly covering came at a cost, however. Their ancestors, the amphibians, could actually absorb oxygen and eliminate carbon dioxide and waste fluid through their soft, thin skin. Scales prevent this exchange. Reptiles were therefore forced to evolve more-sophisticated lungs for breathing and more-efficient kidneys for the excretion of urine.

Most reptiles have sharp, cutting teeth. The exception is the turtle, which snaps up its food with a sharp beak. A typical reptile tooth is a long cone with a sharp point. The exception is the pair of long, slender fangs found in venomous snakes. Most snake fangs have grooves that carry poison.

Without flat molars, reptiles cannot effectively chew their food. Most simply swallow it whole, a process made possible by the unique design of the reptilian jaw, which can literally become unhinged. Snakes and lizards also have jointed skull bones that enable them to open their mouths even wider. As a result, some can engulf prey many times larger than their own heads. Snakes are especially dramatic eaters. Some can swallow a pig or young gazelle.

Less impressive is the size of the reptilian brain. An 8-foot (2.4-meter) crocodile has a brain about the size of a large walnut. The reactions of reptiles are fairly automatic. Many can react with lightning speed to the sight or sound of prey. In general, they have keen eyesight, hearing, smell, and sense of touch.

The tuatara (right), a large lizardlike reptile that lives only in New Zealand, is a relic of an ancient reptilian order. The gecko (facing page) attests to the decidedly primitive appearance of many reptiles.

Lizards and snakes have in the roof of the mouth an additional sense organ, called Jacobson's organ, a unique kind of chemical receptor that functions somewhere between tasting and smelling.

Reptile Movement

Although reptiles can react quickly, they cannot remain active for long periods of time, a limitation likely due to their primitive circulation systems. Most reptiles, like amphibians, have a three-chambered heart. (Birds and mammals have four.) Crocodiles are the exception, with a four-chambered heart. But even the crocodilian heart is not nearly as efficient as that of a warm-blooded animal. As a result, reptiles must take prolonged rests between periods of activity.

When reptiles do move, the motions are fascinating and complex. The legs of a typical lizard splay out to the side of the body. As a result, the reptile twists slightly from side to side with each step. A few unusual lizards can rear up and run on their back legs, although only for short distances. These include the speedy basilisk, also called the "Jesus Christ lizard," of Central America. Its nickname derives from its unique ability to literally run across water for short distances.

Crocodiles can bring their legs beneath their bodies to charge a short distance. But most prefer to swim, aided by their powerful tails. Snakes, of course, have no legs at all. Snakes thrust themselves forward by pushing against rocks, sticks, or any fixed point, be it only a small bump in the ground. Most snakes move in a curving motion because each joint of the body must push against the same rock, stick, or bump. A few snakes such as boas and certain rattlesnakes can move in a straight line by stretching and contracting their bodies lengthwise.

Snakes, including the twin-spotted rattlesnake above, are perhaps the reptiles most feared by humans.

Reptilian Life Cycle

Courtship is an important prelude to reptile mating. In some species of freshwater turtles, the male swims in front of the female and uses his front feet to give her a vibrating head massage. If she likes his touch, the female allows mating to occur. Many male snakes administer their own type of courtship massage.

Perhaps the simplest courtship is performed by the male crocodile: he simply bellows for his mate! Lizards, by contrast, conduct quite elaborate courtship rituals. The males of many species are decorated with colorful patches, flaps, and inflatable pouches on their throats and sides. So equipped, they strut, bob, and puff their stuff to impress potential mates.

When the first reptiles developed their hard-shelled eggs, they also had to develop a special way to fertilize them. The male cannot simply shed his sperm over the eggs as they are

The granddaddy of reptiles—and perhaps the longest-lived of all animals—is the giant tortoise. The oldest on record was still healthy at the ripe old age of 150.

laid, as can fish and amphibians, because the hard shell forms a barrier to fertilization. As a result, the male reptile must fertilize his mate's eggs inside her body before they harden. The exception to this rule is the male tuatara. He deposits his sperm in a packet, and the female presses it into herself.

The fertilized reptile egg is considered an evolutionary wonder. Not only does it have a hard shell for protection, it is also filled with food in the form of a yolk. Together, the shell and yolk transform the reptile egg into a self-contained life-support unit. Within the egg, the embryo develops through larval stages, including fishlike forms seen in amphibians. Young reptiles hatch looking like miniature versions of the adults.

Like all reptiles, crocodiles require long periods of rest between brief spurts of activity. All reptiles are cold-blooded, and therefore spend much time basking in the sunlight.

Most reptiles deposit their eggs in a nest, crevice, or hole, and then abandon them. But a few keep their eggs inside their bodies and give birth to live young. Reptiles that lay eggs can produce as many as 200, depending on the species. Reptiles that give birth to live young typically have small numbers of offspring. An exception is the anaconda, a snake that gives birth to as many as 75 young.

A few reptiles guard their eggs. Female crocodiles remain nearby to chase away intruders. Male and female cobras take turns wrapping their long bodies around the rim of their nest. Female pythons curl up around their eggs, never leaving except to drink. Reptile eggs typically hatch after two months, although the time varies with each species.

Most reptiles grow rapidly during the first few years of life. As they reach sexual maturity, growth slows, although it never entirely stops. The reptile's stiff skin does not grow, and so must be shed and regrown every few weeks, months, or years. Depending on the species, reptiles take anywhere from four months to nine years to reach adulthood. They mature more quickly when warm and well nourished.

With a few exceptions, reptiles are meat eaters. In general, the larger the reptile, the larger its prey. Small- to medium-sized lizards tend to eat insects. Crocodiles and large snakes can eat large mammals. Reptile vegetarians include the land tortoise and the green iguana.

All but the largest reptiles themselves become food for other predators. Young turtles, small snakes, and lizards are especially popular among hawks, owls, herons, and other birds of prey. Those reptiles that survive to adulthood can live very long lives. Turtles may be the longest lived—several species live 150 years or more. Crocodiles in zoos have lived more than 56 years. The upper limit for snakes and lizards seems to be about 40 years.

REPTILES AND HUMANS

With the exception of turtles, reptiles have never been an important food item for people. But this has not stopped overhunting. Reptile skin has long been a popular leather, fashioned into shoes, handbags, belts, and luggage. As a result, several species of crocodiles are on the brink of extinction, and many large lizards and snakes are close behind.

Although greatly feared, poisonous snakes pose little danger to people except in isolated areas. Even the most dangerous species prefer to flee rather than attack a human. The same cannot be said of crocodiles. The largest species have been a danger to humans since prehistoric times.

LIZARDS

Glistening like a holiday ornament in the morning sunlight, a blue-tailed skink basks on a garden wall. With almost cheeky indifference, it ignores the approach of a human. But then, as if an invisible line had been crossed, the little creature flicks its azure tail and darts from view. Thus concludes another close encounter with a lizard, one of the Animal Kingdom's most fascinating vertebrates.

THE SCALY ONES

Delightful to watch, nearly impossible to catch, lizards seldom inspire the dread that people reserve for other reptiles. Perhaps this is because, with rare exception, they are neither aggressive nor venomous. Lizards can also be undeniably beautiful. Their skin and scales are found in a rainbow of colors, and their movements are nimble and graceful.

Lizards—together with the snakes and the mysterious *amphisbaenans*, or worm lizards—make up the reptile order Squamata, meaning "scaly creatures." In truth, all reptiles are scaly to some degree. A better distinction for the *squamids* might be their flexible and powerful jaws. This trait stems from large jaw muscles and a unique hinged joint within the skull. Also, unlike other living reptiles, male lizards and male snakes possess paired copulatory organs that enable them to fertilize their mates internally. Such adaptations have helped make the squamids the most successful and diversified order of reptiles, with more than 6,000 species. Half of these are lizards.

LIZARD EVOLUTION

It is tempting to think of lizards as tiny left-over dinosaurs. But reptile evolution is not that simple. In truth, the first lizards appeared before the dinosaurs, more than 250 million years ago, and the two groups evolved along separate lines. Most likely, the lizard's direct ancestors were among an ancient group of primitive reptiles known as *eosuchians*.

Although fossils of the earliest lizards are rare, they do reveal that about 150 million years ago, lizards underwent a great burst of evolution. During this time, there appeared all four groups of lizards we know today: geckos, skinks, iguanas, and varanids (or monitors).

About 90 million years ago, the lizards gave rise to a more distinct group—the snakes.

When crossing water, the American basilisk (above) appears not to break the surface—an illusion created by the way the creature rapidly paddles with its hind limbs.

The common iguana is the largest lizard in the New World. The crest of long spines that runs down its back gives the creature a distinctly prehistoric appearance.

Some scientists believe that snakes are the descendants of a burrowing lizard that, over time, lost the use of its limbs. Others believe that the ancestor of modern snakes was an aquatic lizard that developed a long, undulating body to enable it to move through the water. About 65 million years ago, yet another split occurred. The amphisbaenans appeared, clearly the descendants of some extinct type of burrowing lizard. These three groups of squamids have continued to develop along separate lines to modern times.

Today, lizards can be found on every continent except Antarctica. They are most common in warm habitats. But their range extends from the Arctic Circle in parts of northern Scandinavia to nearly the Antarctic Circle, on the cool, southernmost tip of South America. In North America, lizards barely range into southern Canada. Some species of lizards are even found at high altitudes in the Himalayas, in the Andes, and among some volcanic peaks.

FEATURES AND ADAPTATIONS

Lizards exist in a great variety of forms. Yet, as a group, they share many common and remarkable traits. In size, most lizards are small, averaging 6 to 8 inches (15 to 20 centimeters) in length. The world's tiniest lizard, *Sphaerodactylus ariasae*, a forest-dwelling Caribbean gecko discovered in 2001, averages only 0.6 inch (1.5 centimeters) long. At the other extreme are the monitors. The largest include the 10-foot (3-meter) Komodo dragon of Indonesia and the equally long but less bulky Salvadori monitor of New Guinea.

The majority of lizards have four strong legs on either side. Typically, they move by stepping one front leg and the opposite hind leg at the same time. The result is a distinctively awkward wriggle. Yet lizards are among the speediest and most agile animals for their size. The fastest known lizards are the race runners, or whiptail lizards, of North, South, and Central America. Some can reach speeds of up to 15 miles (24 kilometers) per hour.

The lizard's skeleton includes a skull with two openings separated by no more than one bony arch. The sternum and pectoral girdle are present in all lizards; many species also have special break points in the tail vertebrae.

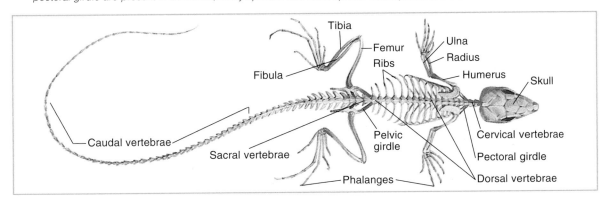

In most species of lizards, the hind legs are longer and stronger than those in front. Extreme examples of this can be seen in species that rear up and sprint on their hind legs. The most famous example is the basilisk lizard of South America, which can actually run across the water for short distances. At the other end of the spectrum are the burrowing lizards, whose legs have grown small and useless; a few species have even lost their limbs altogether. But these creatures still have the remnants of leg bones and hipbones inside their bodies.

A number of tree-dwelling geckos have remarkable toes equipped with special gripping pads called *lamellae*. These geckos can climb up smooth surfaces such as tree trunks and walls, and even cling upside down on branches and ceilings. Many anole lizards have similar toe pads, although not nearly so impressive in function. A very different type of foot structure is seen on lizards that live in sandy deserts. The fringe-toed lizards of the American West have rows of long scales along each toe. These toe fringes act like "snowshoes" to keep the lizard's feet from sinking in loose sand.

Old World chameleons have yet another type of specialized foot. The two inner and two outer toes of each foot are separated by a web of skin. The result is an *opposable* foot, in which the inner toes can be brought together against the outer toes. This enables the chameleon to firmly grasp each stem as it climbs through bushes and trees.

A most unusual adaptation is seen among the flying dragons of Southeast Asia. These lizards have winglike flaps of skin between the front and hind legs. Their wings are supported by long ribs that literally stick out from the sides of the body. Flying lizards do not take to the air like birds; instead, they use their "wings" to glide and parachute between trees high above the rain-forest floor.

Still other lizards are strong swimmers. The dragonlike marine iguana of the Galápagos Islands remains mainly in shallow water, where it feeds on algae. Occasionally the iguana ventures far out to sea, propelling itself through the water with its muscular tail.

The Tail

The lizard tail serves many purposes. Climbing lizards use it to balance, as do lizards that stand up to run on their back legs. Old World chameleons and a few other kinds of lizards have *prehensile*, or grasping, tails—used much like an extra "hand" for climbing. Lizards have fat reserves in their tails from which they can draw when food is scarce.

The tails of many lizards are brightly colored to help distract predators from more-vulnerable body parts. In fact, many species have a special *fracture point*, where the tail breaks off quite easily. The detachable tails often continue to twitch after they break. Such movements frequently distract a predator long enough for the rest of the lizard to escape. Most lizards can regrow the lost tail again and again.

Scales and Skin

The skin of most lizards is completely covered in scales of various shapes, sizes, and arrangements. Depending on the species and the part of the body, the scales may lie smooth and flush against the skin, or be raised to form rough bristles, crests, and spines. The North American alligator lizards represent

The skin of a gecko's toes (top) is arranged in rows, or lamellae, that are covered with microscopic suction disks. This adaptation allows the lizard to climb vertical surfaces (above) and walk upside down across ceilings.

one extreme with their heavy armor of large, overlapping plates. By contrast, the geckos have virtually naked and easily torn skin.

A lizard's scales grow from thickened patches of skin. The outer portion of each scale is made of a horny material similar to fingernails. The lizard sheds this dead outer layer as it grows. Unlike snakes, which periodically shed their entire skin, most lizards continually shed small bits and pieces.

A well-known trait of chameleons and anoles is their ability to rapidly change the color of their skin. A frightened or angry chameleon will change from plain green or brown to a pattern of bars, stripes, or spots. Anoles tend to change from bright green to chocolate brown in response to temperature. Typically, they darken when cold, enabling them to better absorb heat from the Sun.

The Worm Lizards

Children playing in a Florida field accidentally dig up a long, pink ... well, they are not sure *what* it is. A giant pink earthworm? Before the children can recover from their surprise, the 10-inch (25-centimeter)-long "worm" wriggles backward into a small hole in the earth and disappears.

These children are not alone in their confusion. For a long time, scientists did not know what to make of the strange "worm lizards," or *amphisbaenans*. At first, they classified them as snakes, then as lizards. Today these reptiles have their own suborder, Amphisbaenia, alongside the snakes (suborder Ophidia or Serpentes) and the lizards (suborder Sauria) in the order Squamata.

Like snakes, amphisbaenans have a long, typically legless body and just one lung. But it is the left lung that evolution left behind in the amphisbaenans, instead of the right lung, as in snakes. Also, some amphisbaenans are equipped with front legs and feet like those of lizards. These weak limbs appear immediately behind the head, almost like ears. Adding to the amphisbaenans' strange appearance are their tiny, skin-covered eyes and ears, and the ringlike arrangement of their smooth scales. The result is a very strong resemblance to an earthworm.

Fossil records suggest that amphisbaenans appeared some 65 million years ago, presumably the descendants of a true lizard. Today there are about 130 species. Seldom seen above ground, they live in underground burrows in Africa, Asia, and the Americas. In North America, worm lizards are found only in Florida and Mexico.

The name *amphisbaenan* means "animal that moves in both directions"—an apt reference to the creature's ability to inch backward through its tunnels just as easily as it moves forward. All in all, the amphisbaenan's movements are unique and quite strange. It moves by expanding and contracting the rings of skin that cover its body. These rings are loosely attached to underlying flesh and bone with muscle, allowing the amphisbaenan to slide its skin forward over the rest of its body, then press its skin outward against its tunnel walls. Finally, the creature contracts the muscles that connect body and skin to pull itself forward.

Some amphisbaenans lay eggs. Others give birth to live young. All feed on a variety of worms, insects, and small vertebrates. Despite their weak, wormlike appearance, amphisbaenans have surprisingly powerful jaws filled with sharp teeth. Thanks to their extreme sensitivity to the vibrations of passing prey, an amphisbaenan can burst out of its burrow to grab a frog or mouse. Crushing its prey in an instant, the amphisbaenan then quickly disappears back underground.

A more gradual type of color change is seen during the breeding season. Many male lizards become quite brightly hued to attract mates, then lose their showy colors when the breeding season is over.

A lizard's coloring may also change with age. This is particularly true of many species of skinks. Typically, they begin life with a bright blue tail, which serves to distract predators. As the skink grows larger and less vulnerable to predators such as birds, its bright blue tail fades to brown.

The slow process by which a lizard is able to change the color of its skin is controlled by special skin cells called melanophores, which contain colored grains of pigment. Body temperature, hormones, and nerve activity are all known to change the shape and arrangement of these cells. This alters the color of the lizard's skin in a kaleidoscopic fashion.

The Gila monster (left) likes nothing better than to happen upon a clutch of quail eggs. Geckos (center), unlike most lizards, lay hard-shelled eggs. At bottom, a showy collar makes the frilled lizard look more imposing than it really is.

Teeth

Most lizards have sharp, small teeth designed for grabbing and holding onto insects and other small prey. A few vegetarian lizards such as the iguanas have broad molars with roughened edges for chewing fibrous food. Some aquatic species such as the freshwater caiman lizard have molars strong enough to crush the shells of mussels and crustaceans.

The world's two species of poisonous lizards—the Gila monster of the Southwest and its cousin, the Mexican beaded lizard—are equipped with special grooved teeth for injecting their deadly venom.

Senses

Most lizards have especially keen vision and rely on it to locate their prey. As a result, the typical lizard has large, prominent eyes, equipped with movable eyelids to protect them. In general, nocturnal lizards have the largest eyes. By contrast, some burrowing lizards are entirely blind, with skin covering the remnants of their eyeballs. Geckos, in turn, have a unique type of eye covering—a large transparent scale that permanently encloses the eyeball without reducing its vision.

The majority of lizards have visible ear openings, although chameleons and some monitors do not. Hearing seems to be most keen in nocturnal lizards that might otherwise have difficulty finding prey and mates.

Like most vertebrates, lizards have scent organs in their nostrils. They also possess a special smelling organ—called the *Jacobson's organ*—in the roof of the mouth. Like a snake, a lizard will flick its tongue to transfer scent particles in the air to small pits in the Jacobson's organ.

Metabolism

Like all modern reptiles, lizards are *ectothermic* (cold-blooded)—they must warm their bodies with external heat. Many do so by basking in the sunshine. Others absorb heat from Sun-warmed surfaces such as rocks and bare ground.

Although not a dragon in the classic sense—no wings, no fire shooting from its mouth—the Komodo dragon is the world's largest lizard and certainly deserves to be respected, if not feared. Found on Komodo and several other remote islands among the Lesser Sunda Islands of Indonesia, these members of the monitor-lizard family can reach 10 feet (3 meters) in length and 300 pounds (135 kilograms) in weight—large enough to prey on goats, pigs, deer, water buffalo, and even, on occasion, people. Although they feed primarily on carrion, the giant lizards are not slouches when it comes to hunting. Armed with long claws, sharp teeth, and powerful jaws, they lie in ambush along game trails; when pursuing prey, they can climb trees, swim, dig, and run faster than any human. Although equipped with poor hearing and eyesight, their sense of smell is very acute.

When sexually mature, Komodo monitors dig burrows as deep as 25 feet (7.6 meters) to lay their eggs. But they are not devoted parents. Adults tend to be cannibalistic, so young hatchlings escape their burrows and scramble quickly up the nearest trees, where for several years they feed on insects, geckos, and other tree-dwelling prey. They descend to the surface only when large enough to be relatively safe from marauding adults. Healthy individuals can live 25 years or more; some are thought to have reached 100 years of age.

Young and adults alike are solitary animals, staking out protected territories and marking them with their scents. Groups of the lizards gather only at kill sites, where all their social activity takes place at once. A dozen of the monitors might gorge on the carcass of a water buffalo while simultaneously establishing rank, performing courtship rituals, and mating. When the meal and the social activities are finished, the animals disperse until the next communal meal.

Only about 5,000 Komodo monitors (350 of which are female) remain alive in the wild, and only a few others survive in zoos. Their future is threatened by illegal hunting and by habitat destruction. The Lesser Sunda Islands have proven to be rich in oil and mineral deposits. As development of those industries expands, the natural range of the world's largest lizard is certain to shrink.

Jerry Dennis

In general, heat enables a lizard to become more active. But like all ectothermic animals, the lizard must avoid extreme heat. It typically does so by moving into shade, especially during the heat of midday. In very warm regions, lizards such as geckos rest during the day in shaded retreats, becoming active at night.

LIZARD LIFE CYCLES

Most lizards lay eggs, typically depositing them in a damp hole or other hideaway. In general, the number of eggs increases with the size of the lizard. Anoles lay just one egg at a time. Most geckos lay one or two. Large iguanas, by contrast, can lay 50 or more eggs at one time. Most lizard eggs are leathery and expand with the growing embryo. A few species lay hard-shelled eggs. A typical lizard begins life by breaking open its own egg with a special egg tooth, which it then loses.

In recent years, herpetologists have discovered that the temperature at which a lizard egg is incubated can determine the sex of the young. Such is the case with the leopard gecko. An increase in incubation temperature of just 4° F (7.2° C) will produce a clutch with significantly more females than males. Conversely, lowering the incubation temperature will result in more males than females. The benefit of this unique adaptation eludes scientists.

At least five families of lizards contain viviparous species—that is, species that give birth to living young. The females retain their eggs inside the body until they hatch. In a few species of skinks, the females even develop a placenta that supplies nourishment to the embryos.

Whether it hatches from a shell or is born alive, a newborn lizard must quickly fend for itself. Few species show any type of parental care. Not surprisingly, a great many young lizards do not survive to adulthood. Adult lizards, being substantially larger, have far fewer predators than do juveniles.

Small- and medium-sized lizards tend to mature very quickly. A good example is the side-blotched lizards of the western United States. Those that hatch in July are fully mature

Snakes vs. Lizards

Distinguishing lizards from snakes and worm lizards is generally easy. Typical lizards have four well-developed legs, visible ear openings, and eyelids. Snakes and worm lizards have none of the above (although a few have vestigial, or "remnant," limbs).

Just to confuse matters a bit, a few species of lizards also lack visible limbs and ears. So scientists distinguish lizards from snakes by their internal attributes. In lizards, the lower jawbone is fused into one piece, the braincase is incompletely closed, and pelvic bones are always present—even when outer legs are not.

and ready to mate by October. By contrast, large lizards such as the marine iguana take several years to mature. Lizards seldom reach 10 years of age, although one lizard is known to have lived 54 years.

Courtship

Lizard courtship can be quite colorful and dramatic. As with many types of animals, it is the male who tends to be the showier. The courtship display of the anole lizards is familiar to many North Americans. Typically, the male bobs up and down as if doing push-ups, all the while inflating and deflating his brightly colored throat pouch. Such bobbing movements are a common lizard courtship display, as is tail waving. Other lizards display a variety of colorful skin patches or dramatic skin crests.

Nocturnal lizards, on the other hand, tend to have more vocal than visual displays. Certain male geckos, for example, will croak in a decidedly froglike manner.

All such courtship displays serve to advertise a male lizard's fitness. In this way, he attracts females of his species while warning away competing males.

Once a female approaches, the male climbs on her back. To transfer his sperm into her body, he must twist his tail beneath her so that their sexual organs meet. At the same time, he may bite her behind the head and hold her tightly in his jaws until mating is finished. Typically, lizards mate several times during their breeding season, which may last several days or weeks. The female can store the sperm for months before using it to fertilize her eggs.

Defense Mechanisms

In general, a lizard's life is a speedy game of eat or be eaten. Lizards typically avoid their enemies by remaining hidden from view. They tend to stay motionless until danger is very near—and then flee with amazing rapidity.

Exceptions to this rule include the mastigure of Africa and Asia, which does not hesitate to attack in self-defense. It can inflict a nasty wound with a flick of its spiky tail. Even more dangerous are the poisonous Gila monsters and beaded lizards. Still other lizards bluff their way out of danger with hissing and various showy flaps of skin. The frilled lizard of Australia, for example, can rapidly erect a large ruff around its neck.

The prevailing notion of snakes should come as no surprise: most people think snakes are slimy, ugly, dangerous creatures. But snakes are not slimy. Few are dangerous. Most are not ugly. In fact, many are strikingly handsome, with stripes, bands, and blotches of brilliant colors. And many have gracefully tapering bodies.

There are about 2,300 known species of snakes. Somewhat less than one-third of snake species have poison glands, although only a small number of these are dangerous to humans. Even those few dangerous species tend to shy away from humans, striking and biting only when threatened or attacked.

Snakes may, in fact, rank among our most valuable allies. Some prey on pesky rodents that destroy valuable grain crops and other vegetation. Others feed on insect pests. Still others eat slugs and snails.

SNAKE EVOLUTION

The oldest known fragmentary snake fossils are some 200 million years old; well-preserved fossils exist from almost 100 million years ago. Spanning these dates is a substantial period in which little is known of snake evolution.

Some zoologists believe that the snakes' ancestors began to inhabit areas where high grasses flourished. There legs would be almost useless for quick and easy passage through the dense vegetation. Once the legs were lost, snakes became something akin to the so-called glass snakes of today—elongated lizards that have no limbs.

Another theory holds that the ancestors of snakes were underground burrowers whose legs gradually degenerated because of their mode of life. According to this theory, the eyes of these burrowing creatures also degenerated. In time, when the snakes again began to live above ground, their powers of vision reevolved. In support of this theory, scientists note that the eyes of snakes are quite different from those of lizards and other animals.

SNAKE CHARACTERISTICS

However snakes evolved, there is no question about one thing: the most obvious feature of snakes is their lack of limbs. Some primitive snakes still possess internal traces of hind limbs and pelvic bones, or hipbones. All other snakes entirely lack such vestiges. No snake has a breastbone for the attachment of forelimbs.

The skull has a rather loose construction that allows the upper and lower jaws substantial

The black-tailed rattlesnake (below), like all snakes, uses its forked tongue as an instrument of smell and touch. Snakes lack senses of hearing and taste.

freedom of movement. The two halves of the lower jaw do not fuse in front, but are jointed by an elastic ligament. Needle-sharp, backwardly curved, replaceable teeth stud the jaws.

As the body became longer in the course of evolution, the internal organs were considerably affected. The heart, for example, became an elongated organ. The gallbladder, instead of being embedded in the liver as is usual, came to lie far behind it. One lung degenerated to leave room for the other, functional one.

Snakes are covered with thousands of horny scales. The top of the head may have large scales, called *head shields*, or smaller scales. Large scales, known as *chin shields*, also occur on the underside of the head. Big, straplike scales, or *scutes*, run across the underside. Scales may be either smooth or *keeled*—that is, with a ridge over the center of each. The color of the scales is derived from numerous tiny bodies called chromatophores. Some chromatophores contain pigments that are responsible for blacks and browns. Other scales lack pigment altogether, but break up light into its various colors, much as tiny prisms would.

Well-developed Senses

Snakes have evolved several keen senses. Vision is very acute in all but the burrowing types. The lens of the eye focuses accurately on objects at various distances within a comparatively limited range. This adaptation is a great asset to the hunter as it stalks its prey. The eyes have no lids, but instead are capped with a transparent scale. Snakes that hunt by day have rounded pupils. Night roamers have vertically oval pupils, much like those of a cat.

A highly developed sense of smell allows a snake to trail prey and to recognize others of its own species. The forked tongue helps the animal to smell. As the tongue flicks out, it picks up tiny particles on its tips. The tongue carries these particles to two small pits lying at the front part of the roof of the mouth. Branches of the olfactory nerve lead to these pits, which are lined with sensitive cells and form part of the smelling part of the nose. The tongue serves also as a delicate instrument of touch, although it seems to lack taste buds.

The absence of structures for receiving airborne vibrations suggests that snakes lack a sense of hearing. There are neither external ears nor eardrums. Snakes can, however, perceive (and therefore react to) vibrations transmitted through the ground.

Locomotion

A snake's ability to move from place to place is not hampered by its lack of limbs. Snakes can negotiate fairly smooth or rough terrain, swim well, and climb trees.

A snake moves in several ways. It may throw its long form into *horizontal waves*, since its backbone is very flexible. Each curve pushes against obstacles—clumps of grass, shrubs, ridges on the ground, small stones, and so on—to force the body forward. Swimming is accomplished in this manner, too, except that the body curves push against the water.

Another type of motion is the *caterpillar method*: the snake crawls by pushing the free edges of its belly scutes, which are powered by strong muscles, against irregularities on the ground. Scutes are also useful in climbing, as are the keeled scales found along the lower sides of the body of certain tree snakes.

A third type of motion is a *hitching gait*. The snake thrusts its front end forward, holds it steady, and then pulls the rear end along.

Desert-living species—including several African horned vipers and the horned rattlesnake of North America—move by a method called *sidewinding*. The snake passes with ease over flat, sandy ground in a sidewise direction. As it moves, the animal's body contacts the ground only at several places at any one moment, each part of the body flowing through an S-shaped curve above the ground as the body is transferred from one contact point to the next. The horned rattlesnake gained its other name—sidewinder—from this form of locomotion.

The apparent speed of a snake is deceiving. The fastest snakes probably do not exceed 3 miles (4.8 kilometers) per hour, and this speed cannot be maintained for any length of time.

Attack and Defense

Snakes capture and subdue prey in various ways. Sometimes the animal simply grasps the prey in its jaws and swallows the victim. Such prey as insects and their larvae, worms, snails, fish, salamanders, frogs, and toads are easily handled in this way. Other prey is held to the ground by a loop of the snake's body.

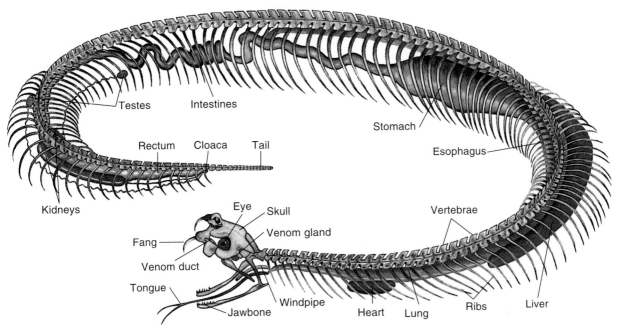

A snake's skeleton consists of a skull, with loosely attached jawbones, ribs, and numerous vertebrae—more than 400 in some species. The long, thin internal organs are adapted to the snake's slender body. The digestive system includes a thin esophagus and a flexible stomach with an extremely large capacity. All snakes lack limbs.

Some snakes subdue prey by constriction—throwing several coils around the victim's body and squeezing. When the prey exhales, the coils tighten so that fresh air cannot be inhaled. The victim dies quickly. The constrictor does not break bones or crush its victim to a pulp.

The most notorious way in which a snake kills is by poison. Venom is introduced into a wound by poison-conducting teeth, or *fangs*.

The size of a snake roughly determines the size of its prey, although animals several times as large as the snake's girth are readily swallowed. Typically, the snake's teeth firmly seize the victim. Since these teeth are curved backward, the only path the prey can take is inward—that is, down the snake's gullet. The lower jaw of the snake is loosely attached to the skull so that the mouth can open wide. The throat is very elastic, and each side of the upper and lower jaws can move independently. The snake literally draws its mouth over the prey. Each side of the upper and lower jaws in turn releases its hold, moves forward a little, and then holds fast again. The snake is able to breathe while struggling with such a mouthful by thrusting out the end of its windpipe between the separated halves of the lower jaw.

A snake can go without a meal for considerable stretches of time. Since it is less active than an energetic mammal, it does not burn up its food so quickly. But it cannot do without water for long. It drinks by thrusting the lower part of its head into the water and sucking up the water by contractions of the throat, in much the same way as a horse does.

If threatened with danger, a snake displays the defensive behavior peculiar to its species. The great majority of snakes will not attack people; cobras are a notable exception.

Hibernation

Unlike a bird or mammal, a snake cannot keep its body at a constant temperature. Usually its body temperature is just slightly above or below that of its surroundings. Consequently, a snake does not live long when exposed to direct sunlight or when the temperature drops below freezing.

In temperate regions, snakes avoid extreme cold by hibernating. During early autumn, they seek out a den on the side of a mountain, reached by fissures in the rocks, or a secure place under a pile of rocks or in the base of a hollow tree. There they pass the winter in a state of dormancy. Often several species hibernate together, as is the case with the copperheads, timber rattlesnakes, and pilot blacksnakes of the northeastern United States.

Mating and Reproduction

During the first warm days of spring, snakes begin to emerge from their winter quarters. At first, the chilly spring nights keep the snakes from roaming very far from their retreats. During this period, the males seek out the females for the purpose of mating.

The sex of a snake is difficult to determine by its external appearance. Generally, females are longer and plumper, while males have a longer tail, and the tail has a stouter base.

Apparently the males find females by using their sense of smell. The female gives off an odorous substance from her skin as she crawls along. The male picks up the trail and follows it until he finds the female.

Courtship behavior varies with different species. The male water snake, for example, rubs his chin along the back of his mate; so does the male garter snake. The male whip snake gives chase to the female, which dashes over rocks, through ponds, and over bushes. When the male finally overtakes his mate, each crawls through the coils of the other. Then each animal raises the front part of its body, holding its head close to that of its mate, but keeping the portion below the head well away. The pattern thus formed by the animals is strikingly like the shape of a lyre. The snakes maintain this figure as they move in an elegant courtship dance that may last for more than an hour before mating occurs.

Female snakes either bring forth their young alive or lay eggs. Those that produce live young do so during late summer or early fall. Some species retain eggs until they hatch inside the body. Others seem to nourish their embryos, or developing young, in more or less the same manner as mammals do. The gestation period—the interval between fertilization and the birth of young—is not known.

Each young of live-bearing species emerges from the mother's body enclosed in a thin, membranous sac. This sac is ruptured by the newborn snake, which is now completely capable of taking care of itself. The mother shows no interest whatsoever in her offspring.

Egg-laying snakes lay their eggs during the summer in places where moist heat is available, such as manure

Once hatched, the green mamba (above, emerging from its egg) will grow to resemble its parents. As a snake grows, it periodically molts—sheds its outer skin, or cuticle—by crawling out of it (left). The old cuticle peels off inside out.

Every year an estimated 40,000 to 50,000 people worldwide die from snakebites. Nearly a quarter of them are killed in India, where each year about 200,000 people are bitten by venomous snakes. Burma's 15 human deaths for every 100,000 in the population is perhaps the highest rate in the world.

In the United States, where about 8,000 people are bitten each year, only 9 to 15 die. Although there is some disagreement about the best ways to treat snakebites, all doctors agree that quick medical attention is essential in keeping the number of fatalities low.

Modern treatment of snakebite no longer includes the "cut and suck" method—incising the area around the wound and attempting to withdraw the venom—nor applications of ice and tight tourniquets. In fact, such efforts can cause more damage than the bite itself. The Red Cross recommends a three-step program for first aid: (1) Wash the area of the bite with soap and water. (2) Immobilize the bitten area and keep it lower than the heart. (3) Seek medical assistance. If it is not possible to reach medical care within 30 minutes, a bandage a few inches above the bite, wrapped loosely enough for a finger to be slipped beneath it, can slow the spread of the venom.

Treatment of snakebites is an inexact science. Snakes produce many kinds of venom, depending on a number of factors, including species, age, genetic differences, region, and time of year. In most cases, the only effective treatment for serious bites is antivenin, a serum produced by introducing small amounts of snake venom into horses and withdrawing the natural antibodies produced. When promptly administered to humans, either by injection or intravenously, antivenins neutralize most kinds of snake venom.

Not everyone can receive antivenins. People who are allergic to horses and their products must be carefully screened to protect them from dangerous allergic reactions. Before antivenins are administered, snakebite victims must undergo a special skin test designed to identify such sensitivity.

The safest defense against snakebites is simple common sense. Most bites occur when people handle or torment the creatures. When walking in areas known to be inhabited by snakes, wear thick leather boots and remain on well-traveled hiking paths whenever possible. Never place your hands and feet on ledges or other places you cannot see, and be especially alert while climbing among rocks. If snakes are encountered, give them a wide berth. These fascinating—and potentially deadly—creatures are best appreciated from a distance.

Jerry Dennis

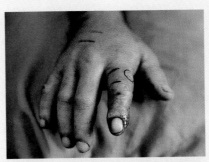

A snakebite (top) requires immediate medical attention. Snake venom (obtained by "milking" snakes, above) is used in the production of antivenins—often the only treatment for a serious snakebite.

The rain forest is home to many tree-dwelling boa species, most of them handsomely marked (left). A snake is able to swallow prey several times its girth; it may take several days for the bloated anaconda (below) to digest its latest meal: a caiman!

piles, rotting vegetation, and holes in embankments. Most snakes abandon the eggs after laying them. Female pythons, however, coil about their eggs to incubate them. The python's body temperature is several degrees higher at this time than is normal under other conditions.

The white or cream-colored shells of snake eggs are composed of several layers of tough, threadlike fibers. Each little snake cuts its way through the shell by means of a special *egg tooth* at the front of the upper jaw. The number of young produced by snakes varies greatly from species to species.

Growth and Molting

Snakes continue growing as long as they live. Young snakes generally double their length during their first year, but the growth rate diminishes as the animal matures. Food consumption and ambient temperature have much to do with growth. Snakes that hibernate grow little, if at all, during the dormant period. Zoologists have only data from captive species with which to estimate typical life spans.

As a snake grows, it periodically sheds, or *molts*, its skin by actually crawling right out of it. This skin, which peels off inside out, represents an old layer of *cuticle*, or outer skin, that has been replaced prior to shedding by a new cuticle layer.

About 10 days before molting, several physical changes take place. The snake's eyes take on a milky or smoky appearance. The body colors become dull. Then the eyes clear again. The cuticle begins to peel back from the edges of the lips. The snake rubs its head against

stones, bark, or other rough surfaces to help push the skin back over the head. By muscular contractions and more rubbing, the snake quite quickly frees the rest of its body from the skin. Then, its molting process complete, the snake emerges with fresh and brilliant colors—thanks to the transparency of the new cuticle.

SNAKE DISTRIBUTION

Snakes are found throughout the tropical and temperate regions of the world. Only the extreme northern and southern parts of the globe, the Hawaiian Islands, Ireland, and New Zealand are free of native varieties. Snakes are hardy animals and will live wherever they are able to hibernate underground below frost level during winter. The tropics contain the greatest number of snakes, although temperate regions also contain many species.

Some snakes are burrowers, spending the greater part of their lives underground. Their heads are wedge-shaped or conical for penetrating the soil. Ground-dwelling snakes may be either heavy-bodied or slender in shape. They often go underground via crevices in rocks or burrows made by other animals. Most can climb bushes and trees and swim in case of necessity.

REPRESENTATIVE SPECIES

Snakes are reptiles belonging to the order Squamata. They are closely related to lizards and more distantly akin to crocodiles, alligators, turtles, and the curious tuatara of New Zealand, and are descended from early reptiles.

Nonvenomous Snakes

Blind snakes. These wormlike snakes— often less than 12 inches (30 centimeters) long—make up two families. Members of the family Typhlopidae are small burrowing snakes, widely distributed in the tropics and on many islands. Their blunt, rounded heads and short, stumpy tails give them a wormlike appearance. They possess rudimentary hipbones and rear limbs, which are hidden beneath the skin. The upper jaw has very tiny teeth. The small eyes are concealed beneath scales. The body scales are smooth and shiny.

Typhlopids live underground, eating worms and insect larvae. Sometimes they invade termite and ant nests and feed on the larvae and pupae inside. They typically lay eggs in underground burrows.

The other family of blind snakes—Leptotyphlopidae—is quite similar in appearance and habits to the typhlopids. Leptotyphlopids, however, have teeth only in the lower jaw. They live underground in semiarid areas where some moisture occurs and rocks and boulders are plentiful. These snakes are head-burrowers, coming to the surface in the early evening to crawl about, all the time flicking out their tongues and aiding their motion by pushing with the spine at the end of the tail. They are entirely harmless, never attempting to bite even when picked up. Most members of this family live in tropical parts of Africa, Southwest Asia, and in North and South America.

Boas. Members of the family Boidae are strikingly handsome creatures, varying in size from very large species to small ones not exceeding 24 inches (61 centimeters) in length. They are, for the most part, tree-dwelling creatures with prehensile tails. A few are ground dwellers and burrowers.

Boas are primitive snakes with two well-developed lungs and vestiges of pelvic bones. Also present are hind-limb bones, which end in

The common garter snake (below), abundant throughout North America, is harmless to humans. The brown tree snake (above), accidentally introduced to Guam, is blamed for the extinction of nine bird species there.

spurlike appendages that emerge from the side of the body at the base of the tail. The male uses these spurs to strike the female during courting. Boas have large curved teeth in both jaws. These muscular animals kill their prey—birds and mammals—by constriction, coiling around the prey animal so tightly that it dies of suffocation. The young are born alive.

have an average length of 8.2 feet (2.5 meters).

Africa is home to a small burrowing python *(Calabaria)* and the ball python, which attains a length of about 5 feet (1.5 meters). The ball python derives its name from its habit of curling itself up into a sphere if frightened.

Most members of the family Pythoninae roam at night, generally in the vicinity of water. They are excellent climbers. Females lay eggs, which they brood. The larger pythons are capable of swallowing small goats, antelope, and medium-sized pigs.

Burrowing snakes. The false coral snakes (family Aniliidae) of South America and much of southeastern Asia constitute a small group of harmless burrowing species with cylindrical bodies. They have vestigial pelvic and hind-limb bones and clawlike spurs at the base of the tail; some may reach 3 feet (1 meter) in length.

The shield-tailed snakes of southern India and Sri Lanka, another small family (Uropeltidae) of burrowers, are related to the false coral snakes, but lack hipbones and hind-leg bones. These small snakes have moderately stout bodies; small eyes; smooth, glossy scales; and a flat shield at the tip of the tail.

"Common" snakes. The largest family of snakes—the Colubridae—includes the typical harmless Old and New World snakes, which occur in all types of habitats. The burrowers are cylindrically shaped, have blunt or cone-shaped heads and, usually, smooth scales. The snakes that roam about over the ground are generally long and moderately slender, with a distinct neck and a long, tapering tail. Semiaquatic species are usually stout-bodied with keeled scales. Arboreal forms are exceedingly slender with elongated heads and prominent eyes.

The burrowers of the Colubridae family include the rainbow snake *(Farancia erythro-*

The largest boa is the South American anaconda, *Eunectes murinus*, which may grow to an intimidating length of 24.5 feet (7.5 meters). Semiaquatic in habit, this snake preys upon waterfowl, young tapir, and large rodents such as agoutis and capybaras.

The boa constrictor, *Boa constrictor*, of South America is a tree dweller measuring only 11.5 feet (3.5 meters) at most. Its close relatives inhabit Central America and Madagascar. If annoyed, the Central American species will strike repeatedly and hiss loudly.

The sand boas *(Eryx)* of North Africa, southeast Europe, and Central Asia, and the rubber boa *(Charina bottae)* of the western United States are burrowing, drab-colored snakes with small heads, tiny eyes, and stubby tails. The harmless rosy, or California, boa, *Lichanura roseofusca*, coils into a ball if disturbed.

Pythons. Snakes of the subfamily Pythoninae resemble boas, but have an extra bone in the skull above the eye. This family includes the longest snake in the world—the reticulated python, *Python reticulatus*, of Southeast Asia and the Malay Peninsula. A length of 32 feet (9.7 meters) has been recorded for the species, but that is far above average. Close relatives are the Indian and African rock pythons, which are substantially shorter creatures. The diamond and carpet pythons of Australia and New Guinea

grammus), mud snake *(Farancia abacura)*, western ground snake *(Sonora)*, hook-nosed snake *(Ficimia)*, hog-nosed snake *(Heterodon)*, worm snake *(Carphophis)*, and banded sand snake *(Chilomeniscus)*. Usually they are secretive animals that feed primarily on salamanders, toads, frogs, earthworms, insects, and spiders. The small ring-necked snake, *Diadophis punctatus,* lives beneath stones and debris.

Among the more active members of the Colubridae are the green snakes *(Opheodrys)*; the graceful blacksnakes, racers, and whip snakes *(Colubrid)*; indigo snakes *(Drymarchon)*; patch-nosed snakes *(Salvadora)*; leaf-nosed snakes *(Phyllorhynchus)*; rat snakes *(Elaphe)*; bull, pine, and gopher snakes *(Pituophis)*; and king snakes *(Lampropeltis)*. These terrestrial snakes sometimes climb into bushes and trees; many are nocturnal. All whose breeding habits are known lay eggs. The smaller species eat insects, frogs, salamanders, and lizards; the larger ones prey on rodents. The rat snakes, bull snakes, and king snakes constrict their prey. Bull snakes destroy great numbers of rodent pests; king snakes devour other snakes, both harmless and venomous varieties. The indigo snake, pilot blacksnake (one of the rat snakes), and bull snake are the largest nonvenomous snakes in the United States, growing to a length of 6.5 to 8 feet (2 to 2.4 meters).

The whip, or tree, snakes *(Leptophis)* of tropical America are completely arboreal—in fact, they look almost like vines when they loop their coils around a branch. Lizards and tree frogs make up their diet.

The widely distributed Colubridae known as water snakes make up the genus *Natrix*. They live near freshwater streams and lakes, where they prey on aquatic animals. The females bring forth their young alive. Closely akin are the common garter snakes *(Thamnophis)* of North America, perhaps the most abundant of all snakes. They are found in a variety of localities, and prey on earthworms and frogs.

The De Kay's and red-bellied snakes *(Storeria)* are small relatives of the water and garter snakes. The little De Kay's snake, which feeds on slugs, snails, worms, and insect larvae, occurs in areas that other snakes have abandoned, such as vacant lots and backyards.

The Colubridae just described demonstrate a variety of behaviors when annoyed. The rainbow and mud snakes push the sharply pointed scale at the end of the tail against an attacker. The hog-nosed snake flattens its body, widens its head, hisses, and strikes repeatedly. If these actions do not discourage the enemy, the little snake writhes in apparent agony, rolls on its back, and goes limp—even letting its tongue hang out of its partially open mouth!

The cobras above are responding to the movements of the snake charmer's instrument, not to the music. The coral snake (below), a New World relative of the cobra, is a shy, inoffensive creature, but will bite if provoked.

Whip, rat, king, and bull snakes vibrate their tails; some hiss fiercely. The leaf-nosed snake hisses and strikes from a coiled position. Water and garter snakes flatten themselves and smear the ground with a foul-smelling secretion from their anal glands. The typical tree snake holds its mouth agape and weaves its head from side to side. A number of these species bite, but the wounds tend to be harmless to people unless infection sets in.

The egg-eating snake. *Dasypeltis scaber,* the only species in the subfamily Dasypeltinae, feeds exclusively on eggs. An accordion-like pleated mouth lining and a stretchable throat allow this little snake to swallow eggs of diameters three or four times that of its body. The

The eastern copperhead (above) inflicts most of the venomous snakebites that occur in the eastern United States outside of Florida.

snake compresses its throat muscles so that the egg contents flow into the stomach while the eggshell is ejected from its mouth. This African snake eats eggs voraciously during the bird-nesting season; the rest of the year, the snake lives on stored fat.

Venomous Snakes

The venomous snakes have developed a most effective method for paralyzing prey or causing its death: they inject poison by means of enlarged grooved or tubular fangs. Modified salivary glands, which produce the poison, are located in the tissues of the head below and to the rear of the eye. Ducts lead from the glands to the poison-conducting fangs. Depending on the species, the fangs are either at the back of the mouth or at the front.

The venom injected through the fangs either destroys red blood cells and breaks down blood capillaries, producing hemorrhage, or works on the nervous system, affecting in particular the centers that control breathing and heartbeat. Rear-fanged snakes possess blood-destroying venoms, as do vipers and pit vipers. Coral snakes, sea snakes, and cobras and their kin produce nerve-affecting venoms. The venom of rattlesnakes affects the prey's blood and nervous system.

Of the 114 species of snakes in North America, only 20 are venomous. About 8,000 venomous snakebites are reported in the United States each year; 9 to 15 victims die, and many survivors are left with permanent aftereffects.

Rear-fanged families. The widely distributed rear-fanged snakes are generally only mildly venomous. Since their grooved fangs, which lie at the rear of the upper jaw, are not easily brought into play, these snakes are not considered dangerous to humans. Frogs, lizards, small birds, and mice are their principal fare. Prey is seized and held firmly well back in the mouth until the venom has had its effect.

The majority of rear-fanged snakes belong to the family Colubridae. They closely resemble, in habit and appearance, the nonvenomous colubrines (common snakes): racers, whip snakes, king snakes, and slug-eating snakes. The African boomslang, *Dispholidus typus,* has a very toxic venom. It threatens by inflating its windpipe, thus compressing its neck so that it spreads vertically. A boomslang bite killed the noted U.S. herpetologist Karl Patterson Schmidt. The "flying" snake, *Chrysopelea ornata,* of Southeast Asia can expand its ribs and draw in the belly. In this way, the snake produces a surface that allows it to glide downward from considerable heights. The tropical American mussurana, of the genus *Clelia,* kills prey by constriction, often attacking and subduing even the large pit vipers of the region.

The stout-bodied, rear-fanged water snakes (family Homalopsinae) of southeastern Asia and nearby islands have nostrils on the top surface of the snout. They are similar in habit to the nonvenomous river and water snakes.

The rear-fanged, egg-eating snakes (family Elachistodontidae) of India, like the colubrid *Dasypeltis*, have projecting spines in the throat for cutting eggshells.

Cobras and their relatives. Among the deadliest of the front-fanged snakes are the highly venomous cobras, kraits, mambas, and coral snakes (family Elapidae). Outwardly, most resemble racers and whip snakes. Their fangs are teeth whose grooved edges meet so as to form a tube. Usually these snakes seize their prey and inject the venom into the wound as they chew.

The king cobra, *Ophiophagus hannah*, of southeastern Asia is considered the world's most dangerous snake, not only because its venom is so potent, but also because of its aggressiveness and size—some attain a length of 18 feet (5.5 meters). It feeds almost exclusively on other snakes. The female lays from 21 to 40 eggs into a nest she makes by pushing leaves or other debris into a pile. She remains close by the nest to guard the eggs.

The Asian, or Indian, cobra, *Naja naja*, is a jungle or open-field dweller that preys upon rodents, frogs, birds, and other snakes. When annoyed, the cobra erects the forward one-third of its body and expands its larger ribs below the neck upward and outward. The skin stretches over this framework to form the so-called *hood*. The snake hisses and occasionally ejects two streams of venom, apparently aiming for a foe's eyes. The creature can "spit" venom thanks to the arrangement of its fangs, which are adapted for directing the venom forward and out of the mouth.

The African ringhals, *Hemachatus haemachatus*, and the spitting cobra, *Naja nigricollis*, are even more notorious as spitters. The African water cobras *(Boulengerina)* are stoutly built creatures that lead a semiaquatic existence, feeding on fish.

Kraits, which make up the genus *Bungarus*, dwell in Southeast Asia. These nonaggressive snakes never attempt to bite unless stepped on or handled. They have a small head, blunted nose, and smooth, lustrous scales. A ridge runs from neck to tail along the top of the body. These night hunters feed on frogs, toads, small mammals, and other snakes.

The mambas *(Dendroaspis)* are very active, swiftly gliding snakes of Africa with elongated and extremely slender dark olive or green bodies. The head is narrow but distinct from the

The water moccasin rarely leaves water except to hibernate (above). Its other name—cottonmouth—refers to the snake's whitish mouth lining.

neck. The slender fangs are advanced farther than those of other Elapidae, and the venom is highly potent. Infrequently, perhaps at mating time, mambas attack people. In habit, they are semiarboreal, climbing through bushes and small trees in search of birds or moving along the ground, hunting small mammals.

The coral snakes are shy burrowers, living in the American tropics and subtropics; similar snakes are found in the Old World. Coral snakes are generally inoffensive creatures, but occasionally will bite. The head is small and blunt, and the scales are smooth and glossy. The majority are ringed with black, yellow, and red. Lizards and small snakes constitute the diet of these creatures.

The venomous snakes of Australia all belong to the family Elapidae. The smaller forms are inoffensive or secretive; by contrast, three of the larger species—the blacksnake, tiger snake, and death adder—can be exceedingly dangerous. The blacksnake *(Pseudechis)*, a 5-foot (1.5-meter)-long racerlike snake, spreads its neck horizontally when threatened. The highly venomous tiger snake *(Notechis)* is quick to take offense and strikes savagely. The death adder *(Acanthophis)* resembles a viper, having a wide head and thickset body. These three snakes prey on lizards, frogs, and mammals, and bring forth living young.

Sea snakes. Snakes of the family Hydrophiidae are aquatic species related to coral snakes and cobras. Although highly venomous, they are docile, inoffensive creatures that use their venom to benumb fish and other prey.

The head is indistinct from the neck. The nostrils, which can be closed by a flap or valve so as to exclude water, are on the top of the snout. The tail is flattened vertically and resembles an oar.

One species—the yellow-bellied sea snake, *Pelamis platurus*—lives in tropical waters of the Western Hemisphere, occurring as far north as the Gulf of California. All other members inhabit Indian Ocean and western tropical Pacific coastal waters. Most Australia-area sea snakes lay eggs; all others bear live young.

Vipers. Vipers, Old World snakes of the family Viperidae, are, as a rule, comparatively stout-bodied, with wide heads and venom-conducting tubular fangs that are attached to very short, hinged upper jawbones. When the mouth is closed, the enlarged fangs lie in a horizontal position against the roof of the mouth. As the mouth opens to strike, the jawbones rotate forward, bringing the fangs into full play. Muscles contract to squeeze venom into the fangs as they sink into the prey—usually small mammals, lizards, and frogs. Most vipers shy away from humans, hissing only when threatened.

Of the European vipers, the common viper, or adder, *Vipera berus*, is the only venomous snake in the British Isles. It ranges farther north than any other known venomous species, living in Norway, Sweden, Finland, and Siberia.

Of the Asian vipers, the 5-foot (1.5-meter)-long Russell's viper, *Vipera russelli*, is considered one of the more dangerous.

Africa, however, is the true headquarters of the vipers. The vividly patterned puff adder, gaboon viper, and river jack, or rhinoceros, viper, all of the genus *Bitis*, are outstanding representatives. These chunky creatures have very broad heads and short, abruptly tapering tails. Other African vipers include the bush vipers *(Atheris)*, which have prehensile tails; the secretive burrowing vipers, or mole vipers *(Atractaspis)*, and the desert-living sand and horned vipers.

Pit vipers. Snakes of the family Crotalidae have a special organ that opens by means of a pit, or chamber, on the side of the head below and in front of the eye. This organ, lined with sensory tissue, serves to detect the body heat given off by the snake's prey. Thus, it aids the snake in locating the direction and distance of the prey, and directs the snake's strike.

Pit vipers usually strike the prey with a lightning thrust and then draw back to let the venom do its work. If the prey moves away before dying, the snake tracks it down through its sense of smell. Many pit vipers threaten a foe by coiling the body and arching the front end in an S-shaped loop. The water moccasin threatens by exposing its white mouth lining.

The majority of pit vipers inhabit the Americas, but a few species occur in southeastern Asia and nearby islands. The bushmaster, *Lachesis mutus*, which differs from other American pit vipers by laying eggs, is an agile, up to 10-foot (3-meter)-long snake of the tropical American forests. The fer-de-lance, *Bothrops atrox*, another tropical American species, is a common, highly venomous snake that may attain a length of over 8 feet (2.5 meters). Relatives of the fer-de-lance include the arboreal palm vipers, the chunky jumping vipers, and the slender hog-nosed vipers.

Copperheads, water moccasins, and rattlesnakes are pit vipers that have gained wide notoriety in the United States. The richly colored copperhead and the semiaquatic moccasin of the genus *Agkistrodon* are heavy-bodied snakes of the eastern states. The rattlesnakes *(Crotalus)* and pygmy rattlers *(Sistrurus)* are unique among snakes in possessing a rattle at the end of the tail. This curious device consists of a series of dry, horny segments built up, segment by segment, when the snake sheds its skin. When the rattler vibrates its tail, the segments strike against each other, giving the characteristic buzzing sound, or rattle. This is not intended to give warning, but is a display of annoyance.

Each species of turtle has a distinctive shell. The Indo-Pacific ridley (above), noted for its olive-colored shell, is just one of the many species of turtles whose numbers have been seriously depleted by overexploitation.

Turtle, tortoise, terrapin—is there a difference? Traditionally, those species that live on land have been called tortoises, those species that live in water have been called turtles, and those species used for food have been called terrapins. But as far as zoologists are concerned, such distinctions are unnecessary. To them, all are turtles, plain and simple.

A SHELL OF BONY PLATES

Turtles belong to the reptilian order Chelonia. Most of the approximately 250 species are characterized by a hard shell of bony plates covered by a layer of tough scales. Underneath this plating lie the ribs. Since the ribs serve only to stiffen the shell, they are fused to the top shell, called the *carapace*; the bottom shell is called the *plastron*. The ribs do not encircle the body as they do in most vertebrates.

The spine of the turtle also differs greatly from the spines of other vertebrates. In the region of the shell, many vertebrae have been lost over time; others have been fused into a single tube that runs the entire length of the carapace. As the shell evolved, the spine lost its supporting function and now serves solely to encase the nerve cord.

The presence of the shell has resulted in still further peculiarities. In all other backboned animals, the pectoral and pelvic girdles lie outside the main, or axial, skeleton. In turtles, the growth of the shell is so rapid—and its influence on the ribs so great—that the normal arrangement is reversed. The bones that support the limbs—both front and rear—are entirely enclosed within the central skeleton.

The presence of a rigid shell has also caused turtles to evolve an unusual way of breathing. Most reptiles, like other land vertebrates, normally breathe by expanding and contracting the rib cage—a process not possible in the turtles. Instead, the function of expanding the lungs is taken over by the flank (side) muscles. In many species of aquatic turtles, sensitive patches of skin in the lining of the throat are specialized to absorb oxygen from the water. Although these patches do not supply the entire oxygen needs of the turtle, they do enable the creature to stay submerged for hours.

COLD-BLOODED AND SLUGGISH

Turtles vary greatly in size. In length, turtles range from less than 4.5 inches (11 centimeters) to more than 8 feet (2.4 meters); an ex-

The term "tortoises" refers to turtles that live on land. The formidable-looking spur-thigh tortoise (above) inhabits certain arid regions of Central America.

tinct species is known to have been 11.5 feet (3.5 meters) long. The weight of a full-grown turtle can range anywhere from less than 1 pound (0.5 kilogram) for the smaller species to upwards of 1,500 pounds (680 kilograms) for the giant sea turtles, such as the leatherback. In many species, the female weighs several times as much as the male.

The heaviest species tend to be aquatic. Despite their huge, unwieldy bodies, the aquatic turtle species are surprisingly agile when their weight is supported by water.

On land, a turtle is dull and sluggish when compared to other land vertebrates; it engages in only a fraction of the activity of a mammal of comparable size. Its food and oxygen consumption are correspondingly reduced. For example, a 9-pound (4-kilogram) South American land turtle can reportedly satisfy its entire food requirement for four weeks with less than 6.5 ounces (184 grams) of banana—an amazingly tiny amount, especially when compared with the amount of food consumed by a warm-blooded animal of similar weight, such as a small dog.

Turtles feed on the softer parts of plants, on carrion, and on small, slow-moving animal life. Because they lack teeth, turtles cannot eat tough, fibrous plants. Their slowness generally prevents them from actively pursuing fast-moving creatures.

As might be expected of such a sluggish animal, the turtle takes passive measures to pro-

tect itself from enemies. In some species, the turtle withdraws its body into its shell and clamps the upper and lower parts together. The fact that its normal respiratory rate is so low enables the creature to survive in this suffocating position for hours. Eventually the potential predator gives up and goes away.

Like other cold-blooded animals, turtles cannot survive in truly cold climates. Since the body temperature of a turtle usually approximates that of the outside air or water, a very cold environment will cause the life processes to slow down to a point where the animal is incapable of motion. In temperate regions, turtles hibernate during the winter.

The mating habits of the turtle follow the usual reptilian pattern. As a rule, turtles do not

All turtles are egg layers, all deposit their eggs on land, and all the eggs are white. The hatchlings of most species look like miniature versions of adults.

conduct complex mating rituals, although the males of some freshwater species woo potential mates by swimming around them and stroking their cheeks with their front claws.

Shortly after mating, the female lays eggs; she quickly buries the eggs and then promptly abandons them. When the baby turtles hatch, they must fend for themselves.

TURTLE CLASSIFICATION

The order Chelonia includes approximately 250 species of turtles, which are divided into two suborders: Cryptodira and Pleurodira. Most species are classified as Cryptodira. The snake-necked and side-necked turtles comprise the suborder Pleurodira.

Sea Turtles

Most sea turtles belong to the family Cheloniidae. The most commercially valuable species is the green turtle, *Chelonia mydas*, the main ingredient in turtle soup. Like many other sea turtles, green turtles are quite large, sometimes reaching weights of 500 pounds (225 kilograms). They are often found sunning themselves on beaches and rocky ledges.

Because both their eggs and meat are taken as food, green turtles are in danger of extinction. Efforts to protect them and to increase their numbers have not been very successful, largely because researchers do not yet know enough about their nesting grounds, migratory habits, and breeding behavior.

The largest of the sea turtles is the leatherback, *Dermochelys coriacea*, which makes up the family Dermochelyidae. The

The leatherback, the largest living species of turtle, may reach a length of 8 feet and weigh 1,500 pounds or more. Leatherbacks only go ashore to lay eggs (above).

leatherback is named for its tough, leathery hide. The hide, in which pieces of bone are embedded, is considered by evolutionists to be closely related to the original bony shell of the ancestral turtles. Scientists consider the leatherback to be the most primitive of the turtles.

Although basically tropical creatures, leatherbacks are found in all parts of the world except the polar regions. They are at home in the water, but exceedingly clumsy on land.

As with most aquatic turtles, the female leatherback is particularly vulnerable when she emerges from the water to lay and bury her

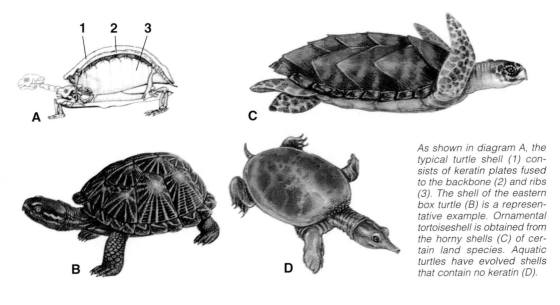

As shown in diagram A, the typical turtle shell (1) consists of keratin plates fused to the backbone (2) and ribs (3). The shell of the eastern box turtle (B) is a representative example. Ornamental tortoiseshell is obtained from the horny shells (C) of certain land species. Aquatic turtles have evolved shells that contain no keratin (D).

The distinctive shell designs of the odd-looking mata mata (below) and the strikingly marked delta map turtle (bottom) readily blend in with the background. The more typical-looking box turtle (right) is in great demand as a pet both here and abroad.

eggs. First she camouflages herself by heaping sand upon her back as she starts to crawl out of the water and onto the beach. Then, when the nesting spot is reached, a large hole is dug and the eggs deposited in it. After the eggs are buried, the female paws over the surrounding area so that they cannot be found readily. She leaves behind a heavy, musklike odor in the vicinity to mask the slight odor of the eggs. Once all this is done, the female heads back to the sea, leaving the young entirely on their own.

Soft-shelled Turtles

These odd creatures belong to the family Trionychidae. After undergoing millions of years of evolution to develop a hard shell and the anatomical peculiarities that go with it, the Trionychidae proceeded to lose the shell while still retaining most of the characteristic turtle features. Why or how this happened is not completely understood. What is perfectly clear, however, is that—disencumbered of a hard shell—the soft-shelled varieties are more active and mobile than any other types of turtles. It is said that they strike with the speed of a snake and move with the agility of a mammal.

Perhaps, at some point in the distant past, the competition for food made speed and activity more important for survival than pure defensive ability, and so the protective (albeit weighty) shell was lost. Further evidence supporting this view is the fact that soft-shelled turtles are predominantly carnivorous.

The various species of soft-shelled turtles inhabit freshwater in North America, Asia, and Africa, spending much time burrowing in soft, muddy stream bottoms. Their flattened shape has led some people to call these creatures "pancake turtles."

Freshwater and Land Turtles

Species of the families Chelydridae, Kinosternidae, Emydidae, and Testudinae are characterized by hard shells, relatively unspecialized limbs, and a straight withdrawal of the head into the shell.

A well-known North American member of this group is the snapping turtle, *Chelydra serpentina*, which is generally considered more aggressive than other turtles. Legend holds that once this snapper has seized a victim in its jaws, it will not let go until sunset—or until the sound of thunder is heard. Oddly enough, this creature, which is so pugnacious on land, loses all its aggressiveness in water, and simply swims away from potential danger.

A close relative of the snapping turtle is the alligator snapper, *Macroclemys temminckii*, a

The world's largest species of tortoise lives on the Galápagos Islands off the Pacific coast of South America. Scientists are unsure of how (or if) the almost-constant presence of tourists affects these 500-pound reptiles.

large creature that may attain a weight of 200 pounds (90 kilograms). This turtle's large, blunt head, rough shell, and prominently peaked plates produce a particularly fierce appearance. Surprisingly, the alligator snapper is less active and less combative than its smaller relative.

Perhaps the best known of all turtles, and the species most commonly kept as a pet, is the box turtle. Two types native to North America are the eastern box turtle (*Terrapene carolina*) and the ornate box turtle (*Terrapene ornata*). Unlike many turtles, these species are active primarily in the daytime. Box turtles are predominantly land-dwelling, but seek out water in very hot, dry weather. They eat almost anything their jaws and throat can manage, including vegetables, meat, and insects. In recent years, box turtles have become immensely popular among European gardeners, creating a demand that may soon exceed the supply.

When European naturalists first came upon the Galápagos turtles, *Geochelone elephantopus*, on the Galápagos Islands, they were truly astounded. Nothing approaching the size of these giant tortoises had ever been seen before

by Europeans. These creatures are closely related to the genus *Testudo*, which includes some 50 separate species. Many members of this widely distributed genus are found on a comparatively small number of oceanic islands. Apparently, isolation from the mainstream of evolution helped them to survive.

Many *Testudo* species have been wiped out by humans. Their large size made them a prime source of food, and their sluggishness made them easy to catch and slaughter. When whalers and traders realized that a *Testudo* laid on its back could survive for weeks without any attention, they began to transport large numbers of them to markets thousands of miles from their native islands.

Side- and Snake-necked Turtles

These turtles, of the suborder Pleurodira, all live in the Southern Hemisphere: Africa, Australia, South America, and New Guinea. When one of these creatures withdraws into its shell, the neck is pulled in, doubled over to one side. The snake-necks are distinguished from the side-necked turtles chiefly by the length of their necks.

THE CROCODILIANS

Crocodiles, alligators, caimans, and gavials have walked the planet virtually unchanged in form and habit since the great Age of Reptiles, more than 160 million years ago. These creatures stand as reminders of that far-distant past, when there were great numbers of fierce-looking armored animals that have long since become extinct.

In that remote, almost unimaginable era, the most remarkable land animals were the "ruling lizards," or *archosaurs*. Among these were the dinosaurs, the crocodiles, and the reptilian ancestors of our birds. Although these animals had four legs, the hind legs were long and quite powerful, while the front legs were short and comparatively weak. This arrangement led them to develop what is called *bipedal habits*—when these animals needed to get somewhere in a hurry, they would rear up and lumber along on their hind legs, their bodies heavily protected by thick, horny armor, not unlike that of their crocodilian descendants that inhabit tropical swamps and rivers today.

CROCODILIAN CHARACTERISTICS

Modern crocodilians use all four legs to heave their cumbersome bodies along the ground. But their front legs are short, like those of their ancestors that flourished during the Age of Reptiles. When they swim, crocodilians fold their legs close to their bodies and move through the water by means of powerful strokes produced by their tails. The hind feet are webbed in most species of crocodilians; sometimes the forefeet are also webbed.

Crocodiles and other living members of the subclass Archosauria form the order Crocodylia. These animals occur only in temperate and tropical regions. The crocodile itself lives in parts of five continents: Africa; Asia; tropical parts of North and South America; northern Australia; and the long chain of islands extending southeastward from the Malay Peninsula. Alligators live in China and the southeastern United States. The caiman lives in Central and South America. The gavial, or gharial, is found primarily in India and parts of Southeast Asia.

To the anatomist, the vital organs of the Crocodylia are of particular interest, for, like those of the birds, they are a reminder of the crocodilians that flourished with the great di-

If it survives, the tiny American crocodile hatchling (inset above, emerging from its egg) could ultimately mature into an adult of truly gigantic proportions (top).

nosaurs. This is especially true of the arrangement and structure of the heart and lungs, which are highly specialized in these animals.

Laying Eggs on Land

A characteristic that crocodilians share with birds is that their young are hatched from eggs. Each egg contains its own watery medium, the *amniotic fluid,* which provides for the needs of the embryo. The porous shell allows for the exchange of oxygen and carbon dioxide, all the while keeping the amniotic fluid from leaking out. A crocodile may lay from 20 to 90 eggs in a single clutch. The eggs have a thick, tough shell; when the time comes, the young crocodile uses a special egg tooth at the end of its snout to chip its way out of the shell. This egg tooth drops off almost immediately after the baby is hatched. The youngster, essentially a miniature version of its parents, is at once completely able to cope with the world about it without any help from its mother or father.

Life in the Water

Crocodilians are found in tropical rivers, lakes, marshes, saltwater lagoons, and the deltas of large rivers. In these habitats, they do most of their feeding, comparatively safe from humans and other predators. They also spend a great deal of time sunning themselves on riverbanks or along the shores of seas or lakes.

On land, these reptiles usually move slowly and rather clumsily. But when charging prey or an enemy, or when escaping danger, they travel at a good pace, their bodies well off the ground on extended legs. Only the tip of the tail drags along the ground.

Crocodilians sport an armor of horny scales. This covering is reinforced on the back and, in some species, on the belly as well by small bony *scutes,* or plates. Such a coat is all but impenetrable to the attacks of other animals and to primitive human weapons such as arrows. (Unfortunately, high-powered rifles and other modern weapons have proved more than a match for the crocodilian's tough hide.)

In addition to its use in swimming, the powerful crocodilian tail is employed as a weapon of defense. A well-placed blow of this appendage will snap a small tree or knock a large animal off its feet. The jaws and teeth also constitute weapons formidable enough to crush the leg bones of an ox.

In keeping with their aquatic habits, crocodilians have a streamlined shape, with more or less elongated and tapering jaws. The eyes are placed well up on top of the head, enabling the reptiles to scan the water's surface and edge while being almost completely submerged. The nostrils are elevated high on the tip of the snout. Inhaled air follows a channel, above the bones of the roof of the mouth, to the windpipe. Croc-

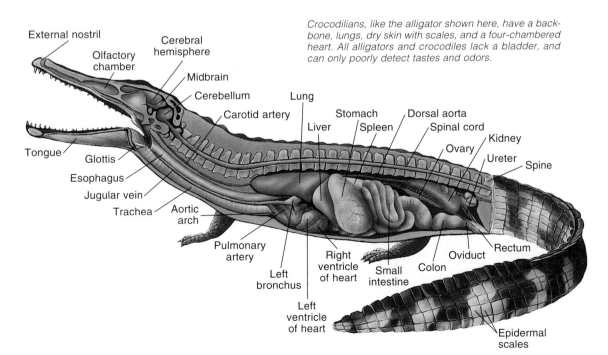

Crocodilians, like the alligator shown here, have a back-bone, lungs, dry skin with scales, and a four-chambered heart. All alligators and crocodiles lack a bladder, and can only poorly detect tastes and odors.

External nostril
Olfactory chamber
Cerebral hemisphere
Midbrain
Cerebellum
Carotid artery
Lung
Stomach
Liver
Spleen
Dorsal aorta
Spinal cord
Kidney
Ovary
Ureter
Spine
Tongue
Glottis
Esophagus
Jugular vein
Trachea
Aortic arch
Pulmonary artery
Right ventricle of heart
Small intestine
Colon
Oviduct
Rectum
Left bronchus
Left ventricle of heart
Epidermal scales

odilians have a flap of skin that closes off the mouth from the windpipe, an adaptation that allows these creatures to remain openmouthed underwater (to forage for and attack prey) without flooding their vital air passages. The American alligator can remain submerged for quite some time—three or four hours—without drowning.

Diet

All kinds of animal food, depending on the environment, may make up a crocodilian's diet. Insects, spiders, crayfish, shrimp, crabs, snails and other mollusks, frogs, snakes, and turtles are preyed upon. The gavial's exceedingly long jaws and sharp, slender teeth are well adapted for seizing fish. Mammals—such as rodents, deer, and hogs—are grabbed by the snout when they come to the water's edge to drink. Ducks, other swimming and diving birds, and unwary wading birds are also fair game. The decayed remains of animals may also form a substantial part of the diet.

Once captured, the smaller animals are downed in one gulp. Large animals have to be torn apart in a unique way, since the crocodilian's flat jaws and spikelike teeth allow for no grinding or shearing action. The reptile firmly grasps its victim and then rolls over and over until the prey is twisted apart. (The prey's bulk prevents it from rolling over together with the reptile.) Sometimes a large animal is killed, hidden, and then consumed later—after aging has

A crocodile (right) can be distinguished from the similar-looking alligator (left) by its narrower snout and by the manner in which the fourth lower tooth protrudes when its mouth is closed.

softened the carcass so that it can be easily broken apart for swallowing.

Breeding Behavior

Both male and female crocodilians possess two pairs of scent glands: one pair is located in the lips of the cloaca (discharge chamber), the other pair on the right and left sides of the lower jaw. During the breeding season, these glands produce a musklike secretion that, trailed on the ground or discharged in the water, presumably enables crocodilians to find one another.

Mating occurs in the water. The eggs are deposited by the female in burrows that are then covered over, or in moundlike nests made of vegetation and sand or mud. Females are often found in the vicinity of their nests, presumably guarding them against marauders.

TYPES OF CROCODILIANS

Scientists categorize the 23 species of crocodilians into three families.

Alligators and Caimans

The family Alligatoridae includes the alligators and caimans. Alligators dig burrows, or dens, which may extend back 40 feet (12 meters) from the water's edge. The reptiles retreat from danger to these "gator holes" and retire to them during the winter. From October to late March, alligators eat little or nothing.

Many crocodilian species are seriously endangered. A notable exception is the enormous Nile crocodile (left), which thrives in rivers and lakes throughout Africa.

Alligators are generally not dangerous to people. Yet a cornered individual or a female guarding its nest can be readily provoked into attacking. Legend holds that when a big alligator angrily crashes his jaws together, the sound suggests a stroke on a bass drum. Certain alligators in zoos have become fairly tame, but their keepers are always careful to stay a reasonable distance from the animals' jaws.

Once found across much of the southern and coastal portions of the United States, the American alligator has seen its range shrink substantially. Professional hunters—seeking the alligator's leatherlike hide—and habitat destruc-

The gavial (above), also known as the gharial, is readily identifiable by the curious enlargement at the tip of its snout. Gavials rarely—if ever—attack humans.

Caimans

All species of caimans (sometimes spelled caymans) are native to Central and South America, from southern Mexico to northern Argentina. These close relatives of alligators have broad snouts, like alligators, but are smaller and less notorious than other crocodilians. Like alligators and crocodiles, they are amphibious carnivores that inhabit the edges of rivers and lakes, are armored with horny plates, and lay hard-shelled eggs in nests constructed and guarded by breeding-age females. Also like alligators, caimans are noteworthy for their vocal abilities. They snort, growl, croak, and, when injured or mating, roar like lions.

Most of the several species of caimans range in length from 3 to 7 feet (1 to 2.1 meters) at maturity and feed on fish, birds, crabs, snails, small mammals, and even insects. Because they are smaller than alligators and crocodiles, they have not captured the public imagination as have those larger carnivores. However, one species, the black caiman, can reach a length of 15 feet (4.5 meters) and is considered dangerous. The most familiar and widely distributed species is the spectacled caiman, named for an arching ridge of bone between its eyes that resembles eyeglasses. The spectacled caiman can reach a length of 9 feet (2.7 meters).

The smooth-fronted caiman is named for the lack of bony ridges around its eyes. This smallest of caiman species—rarely exceeding 6 feet (1.8 meters)—usually inhabits fast, rocky streams and rivers in the Amazon River Basin. What it lacks in size it makes up for in defenses: the smooth-fronted caiman is fast, strong, and is protected by the thickest horny plates of any of the crocodilians.

Like many animals of the tropical Americas, most species of caimans have been reduced in number recently due to human encroachment and habitat destruction. They have been exterminated altogether from large portions of the Amazon Basin.

Although no caimans are native to the United States, thousands of spectacled caimans were imported and sold as pets soon after the alligator was declared endangered and placed under legal protection. Enough of these imported caimans escaped or were deliberately released to establish small, isolated populations in Dade County and Palm Beach County, Florida.

Jerry Dennis

tion have combined to nearly eradicate the alligator from many areas. Conservation efforts in recent years have been very successful, however, and the alligator is again abundant in many parts of its original range.

The Chinese alligator is restricted to the basin of the Yangtze River. Comparatively little is known about this animal's habits.

The female American alligator lays her eggs in nests made of vegetation or in sandbanks, and remains with the eggs until the heat of the Sun causes them to hatch about two months later. It is believed that she digs up the young when they begin to call, and either carries them in her mouth or leads them to the water. At this early period of their existence, the young alligators are exposed to many dangers and are a favorite prey of fish and turtles.

Alligators prey upon fish and waterfowl, and on small mammals that go into the water or too near its edge, where the reptiles lie in wait. Land animals are dragged underwater by alligators, to be drowned and eaten. If the prey is too large to be gulped down at once, it is torn to pieces before swallowing.

Many myths persist about alligators. One legend insists that alligators grow very slowly. That may be so, although certain specimens are known to have grown in just five years to a length of 5.2 feet (1.6 meters) and a weight of 55 pounds (25 kilograms). The typical life expectancy of an alligator is not precisely known, but the big reptiles are probably not as long-lived as scientists once believed.

Caimans live in Central and South America. Like the alligators, caimans have stub-nosed snouts. These creatures are discussed in greater detail in the box on page 383.

Crocodiles

Members of the family Crocodilidae are much more widely distributed than alligators. In North America, the only species, the American crocodile *(Crocodylus acutus)*, is listed as endangered, with only 200 to 400 living along the coast of southern Florida.

These largest of reptiles—saltwater crocs can reach nearly 30 feet (9 meters) in length—move quickly on land and strike powerful blows with their tails. Young crocodiles feed chiefly on fish. Adults prey on waterfowl and on land animals that come to the water to drink. In water where the temperature drops below 44° F (7° C), crocodiles become inactive and—for all intents and purposes—helpless.

As with the alligators, an entire body of folklore has developed around the crocodile. Certain crocodiles, for example, are still noted as being notorious man-eaters. In 1926, C. F. M. Swynnerton, a game warden in Tanganyika (now Tanzania), exhibited to a London gathering of scientists the contents of the stomach of a crocodile that he had killed. Among other things, the contents featured 11 heavy-brass arm rings worn at the time by the members of local tribes; three coiled-wire armlets; a glass-bead necklace; 14 human arm and leg bones; three spinal columns; and cord that had probably bound some bundle borne on the head of a Tanganyikan who had become a meal for the crocodile.

The 19th-century Scottish explorer David Livingstone had many unpleasant experiences with crocodiles in the course of his African travels. He wrote how one of his bearers was suddenly seized by a crocodile while swimming in a river. When the reptile pulled him down to the bottom of the river, the man whipped out a knife and stabbed the creature behind the ear. Writhing with pain, the reptile released the man and swam off at a great rate. The man carried the marks of this encounter on his thigh for the rest of his life.

In ancient times, the Egyptians worshiped the crocodiles that infested the waters of the Nile River. They tamed the animals and kept them in tanks at the temples. When these sacred crocodiles died, they were preserved in mummy form as holy relics. Crocodiles are still considered objects of veneration in parts of India.

The Gavial

The family Gavialidae contains only one living species, *Gavialis gangeticus*. This animal has a long, thin snout that is very useful in catching the fish that constitute its diet.

The gavial inhabits rivers in India and can also be found in Myanmar, Borneo, and Sumatra. It spends most of its life in the water, although the female will climb onto land to lay eggs—40 or more at a time—on the sandy riverbanks. Despite so many eggs, gavials have become quite scarce in the wild. Recently instituted preservation programs may help the species make a comeback.

ORNITHOLOGISTS
AND THEIR SCIENCE

Ornithologist Donna Dewhurst steps out-side her summer cabin on Mother Goose Lake in the Alaskan Peninsula Refuge. Across the water, sandhill cranes dance, while the songs of warblers mingle with the rustle of cottonwood leaves. Dewhurst is here, in one of North America's most productive and remote songbird breeding grounds, to decipher why songbird populations are plummeting. Assisting her each summer are small teams of volunteers from Earthwatch, a group that organizes research "holidays" for laypeople. Between June and September, Dewhurst and her volunteers will band more than 3,000 songbirds belonging to some 30 different species. They will locate nests, identify predators, and describe much of the bird's breeding habitat.

WHAT IS ORNITHOLOGY?

Such work is one small part of ornithology, the study of birds—a broad science with many subdisciplines. It is also one of the few scientific fields that still rely heavily on the contributions of amateurs. Some amateurs directly work with professionals such as Dewhurst. Many

more amateurs participate in population studies by observing and counting the birds in their own backyards and neighborhoods (see the box on pages 388 and 389).

Professional Specialties

Many ornithologists—or bird biologists—work in the field, charting changes in bird populations across entire continents. Others follow a particular species, a task that may take them thousands of miles, from summer breeding grounds in the Arctic to winter feeding grounds in the Amazon. Other field ornithologists focus on a single aspect of bird behavior or ecology, such as how birds find food—or even how one particular species finds its food. Still others look at how well (or poorly) birds adapt to changes in their environment.

Like other animal sciences, ornithology is by no means restricted to fieldwork. Some ornithologists study birds from the inside out, examining how the parts work together to make a bird what it is. Others study bird physiology, examining the unique processes of bird digestion, respiration, circulation, or excretion. Still other ornithologists focus on avian biochemistry—for example, what metabolic changes occur in birds during the breeding season or prior to migration.

Bird taxonomists classify new bird species or populations, or identify the fossils of extinct forms. Their work often involves the analysis of body fluids and the genetic fingerprinting of different bird populations and species.

Other ornithologists study the behavior, or *ethology*, of birds. Mysteries still under investigation include how birds navigate when they migrate great distances, and what prompts them to commence their great journeys in the first place. Such work takes place both in the laboratory and in the field.

Finally, some ornithologists pursue studies in veterinary medicine with a specialty in avian diseases. These are just a smattering of examples of the diverse work done by bird biologists.

Some ornithologists focus on the care and preservation of owls (above) and other wild species of birds. Domestic fowl (below) are of special concern to those ornithologists who have a degree in veterinary medicine.

THE HISTORY OF ORNITHOLOGY

Like all the life sciences, ornithology has evolved through the ages, with interest shifting from one area to another. Aristotle, the father of all science, described 140 species of birds and speculated about where and how they "disappeared" at migration time. (He thought swallows hibernated in the mud beneath ponds!) The first great ornithologist may have been the Holy Roman Emperor Frederick II, who studied the behavior and anatomy of his beloved hunting falcons as well as their processes of molting, flight, and migration. In all, he published seven ornithology books before his death in 1250. Most other ornithology books of the Middle Ages were also of a practical rather than academic nature, focusing on hunting birds, such as falcons, or game birds, such as quail.

In the mid-18th to late 19th centuries, ornithology enjoyed a great flowering. European explorers were returning from their travels with an awesome variety of new animal species, including a dazzling array of parrots, toucans, hummingbirds, and other tropical birds. Ornithologists of the day were kept busy simply describing these new species and classifying them into families and orders.

The Age of Illustrators

This period also saw the beginning of a rich tradition of ornithologist-artists, whose works led to the first bird guides—illustrated books for identifying species in a local area.

During the late 1800s, many wealthy European ornithologists made scientific expeditions to the Americas, from the Amazon to the Northwest Territories of Canada. The "father of American ornithology," however, arrived under less auspicious circumstances. Alexander Wilson left Scotland an impoverished weaver, newly released from prison for writing satirical political verse. He found work as a teacher in Philadelphia, where he met the great American naturalist William Bartram. Encouraged by Bartram and the engraver Alexander Lawson, Wilson studied art and ornithology and began the illustrations that would become the great classic work *American Ornithology*, published between 1808 and 1814. This nine-volume set was the first of its kind and helped establish the science of ornithology in North America.

Following in Wilson's footsteps was the great artist-ornithologist John James Audubon, whose bird illustrations many people still consider the finest in history. In 1827, the first volume of Audubon's four-volume *The Birds of America* quickly became world-famous for its beauty. The legacy of Audubon's love of birds and nature is the modern-day Audubon Society, one of the largest and most active conservation groups in the world.

Still, except for a few well-published illustrators such as Audubon, the ornithologists of the 1800s were amateurs who pursued their science in their spare time. Many, including Bartram, Wilson, and Audubon, were members of Philadelphia's Academy of Natural Sciences.

In 1899, Frank Chapman of the American Museum of Natural History began publishing *Bird-Lore*, America's first popular "birders'" magazine. It later evolved into *Audubon* magazine, still an American favorite.

A program sponsored by Cornell University helps budding ornithologists learn about bird behavior and gain experience on how to collect scientific data.

Careers in Ornithology

In its narrowest sense, a career in ornithology involves the scientific study of birds. Such work is usually connected with an academic institution such as a university, a government wildlife agency, or a private organization concerned with conservation.

A career pursuing such research requires a minimum of a bachelor's degree in a life science, preferably biology or physiology, with some coursework in bird-related subjects. Such a degree opens the door to a limited number of research positions in a broad array of fields. Advanced degrees, offered at universities across the United States, are required for many jobs. Ornithologists work both in the field—observing birds, their behavior, and their habitat—and in the laboratory, studying birds' anatomy, physiology, biochemistry, and genetics. Some ornithologists find work as curators at natural-history museums and as keepers at zoos, animal parks, or nature reserves.

With the recent decline of many of the world's bird populations, there is a great need for both field observation and laboratory research. Ornithologists at universities such as Cornell (Ithaca, New York) and the University of Michigan (Ann Arbor) have long traditions in these areas.

Although opportunities for full-time work in ornithology are limited, a large number of ornithologists and ornithology students find seasonal work as field researchers, as guides for nature-club expeditions, and as naturalists at national or state parks.

In a broader sense, a career in ornithology involves anything that furthers the understanding and enjoyment of bird life. A great many careers fit this wider definition. In fact, the popularity of "birding" has created entirely new industries in recent years. A growing number of bird lovers have opened up "wild bird" stores, selling a variety of birdhouses, bird feeders, birdbaths, and various bird-themed items. Importantly, such shopkeepers share their expertise on attracting local birds and meeting their needs for food, shelter, and nesting materials.

Aviculture is a separate field, concerned with the breeding of birds as pets or produce. The breeding of exotic birds has grown considerably in recent years, especially now that laws forbid the importation of rare birds collected in the wild. The popularity of pet birds also creates a need for veterinarians who specialize in their care.

An estimated 40 million people worldwide (and 25 million in the United States alone) observe wild birds as a hobby. Much of today's interest in observing birds can be credited to a single man: the late artist and ornithologist Roger Tory Peterson. When Peterson published *A Field Guide to the Birds* in 1934, he made it possible for untrained enthusiasts to readily identify birds from a distance, based on "field marks." Before that, most ornithologists collected specimens with a shotgun and studied the birds in their hands.

Peterson's simple system of identification—noting prominent features and patterns that could be seen even while birds winged past overhead—initiated a revolution in backyard bird study. Instead of examining dead specimens, ornithologists began studying the day-to-day behavior of living birds. Armed with their "Peterson," amateur birders could now identify the birds they saw and could understand their behavior. Little wonder that Roger Tory Peterson's landmark field guide has sold more than 7.5 million copies and remains the bible of modern birding.

To many enthusiasts, birding is more than just a hobby. Perhaps only in ornithology are amateurs so important to the advancement of a discipline's scientific knowledge. Each year, tens of thousands of amateur ornithologists regularly contribute to the field by assisting scientists involved in programs to study avian population shifts, breeding success, mortality, migration routes, and other crucial information.

One of the oldest of these "cooperative research" programs is the Christmas Bird Count, sponsored by the National Audubon Society. Since 1900, as many as 45,000 people per year record the total number of birds of each species they see during a specified period in late December. This information is used to monitor the changes of wintering populations throughout North America and to help keep track of population trends.

Another Audubon Society program, the Breeding Bird Census, was begun in 1937 to keep track of the number of breeding pairs of various species on study sites varying from 10 to 400 acres (4 to 162 hectares) in size. About 2,000 "advanced" birders, each of whom can identify local species by sight and song, make at least eight visits to each site during the breeding season. Their observations help ornithologists understand regional population trends and habitat requirements.

Each spring, during the peak nesting season, about 2,500 advanced birders throughout North America participate in one of the longest-running bird-population studies in the world: the North American Breeding Bird Survey administered by the U.S. Fish

In the 1930s, the popularity of bird observation was greatly stimulated by another great American ornithologist. An artist in the tradition of Audubon, Roger Tory Peterson began publishing his popular *A Field Guide to the Birds* in 1934. His books, together with a pair of binoculars, became the basic tools of amateur ornithology in North America.

THE MODERN SCIENCE

In the academic arena, ornithology gained new status in 1915, when Cornell University in Ithaca, New York, granted its first ornithology degree. About this time, ornithology itself underwent a great change as well. Although the majority of the world's birds had been identified and classified (primarily by external features or behavior), very little was known about the actual biology of birds. Ornithologists at Cornell and the American Museum of Natural History in New York City began studying the internal anatomy of different species. This work, in turn, transformed bird taxonomy. Based on internal similarities, ornithologists recognized the evolutionary relationships of many birds that looked quite different from the outside.

By the mid-20th century, the focus of ornithology had shifted yet again as scientists began exploring the uncharted areas of bird behavior and ecology. Less-violent ways were used to study avian subjects: instead of shooting

and Wildlife Service. The volunteers each drive a 24.5-mile (39.4-kilometer) length of country road, stopping every 0.5 mile (0.8 kilometer) to record every bird they see and hear within a 0.25-mile (0.4-kilometer) radius. Since the 1960s, the Breeding Bird Survey information has provided ornithologists throughout the Western Hemisphere with important data about bird-population trends. Such information has aided scientists in recognizing declines of many bird species that nest in North America but migrate to Central and South America for the winter.

Other volunteer programs include several organized by the Cornell Laboratory of Ornithology at Cornell University in Ithaca, New York. For Cornell's Project FeederWatch, volunteers keep records of the numbers and species of birds that visit their feeders throughout the winter.

Like many other pursuits, bird-watching has embraced the Internet. In 1997, the National Audubon Society and the Cornell Laboratory of Ornithology launched BirdSource (www.birdsource.org), a Web site that provides the results of the annual Christmas Bird Count, the Breeding Bird Survey, and Project FeederWatch. The site also gives amateur birdwatchers the opportunity to report sightings during other times of the year. For instance, since 1998, BirdSource has sponsored the Great Backyard Bird Count, an annual survey in which participants count birds they see in their backyard or other areas and send in their findings.

In all, more than 50,000 volunteer birders throughout the Americas take part in these and other annual ornithological events. Millions of others simply take pleasure in watching chickadees, finches, and cardinals flitting through trees and landing on feeders stocked with sunflower seeds and suet. Armed with binoculars and field guides, they discover that nature is alive and well in trees, shrubs, ponds, and meadows—even in their own backyards.

Jerry Dennis

and mounting birds, ornithologists "captured" them on film and recorded their songs on portable audiotaping equipment.

Banding became another important means of studying birds in the wild. Ornithologists learned to carefully net their subjects and mark them with small leg bands. Engraved on these metal rings were special identity numbers as well as details such as when and where the bird was captured. Banding systems enabled ornithologists to track bird movements around the world, and to estimate the maximum life spans of different species.

In recent years, ornithologists have been greatly aided by advanced electronic technology. In addition to banding, a number of other techniques are at the ornithologist's disposal. An ornithologist may, for example, attach a tiny radio transmitter on or even inside a bird's body. Radar tracking systems can be used to follow the movements of large flocks of migrating or foraging birds.

Modern bird taxonomists now have a host of biochemical tools to study the genetic material of a bird. Using this information, ornithologists can accurately gauge how close or distant two species are in their evolutionary relationship. Similarly, ornithologists can use such techniques to track the relationships between populations within a single bird species. This supplies information about how interbred or isolated two populations of birds may be.

What Is a Bird?

Borne aloft on feathered wings, birds have invaded every known habitat on Earth. Their soaring silhouettes are a familiar sight in the woodlands, on the prairies, in the desert, in suburban backyards, along the beaches—even in cities where little other wildlife can be seen.

What is a bird? In a sentence, it is a warm-blooded, egg-laying vertebrate that has feathers. As a distinct class of animals, birds are also the undisputed "masters of the air," with some 200 families and more than 8,500 species. Their success lies in that unique marvel of animal engineering—the feather. The story of its development—and that of the class Aves—begins more than 150 million years ago.

THE FIRST BIRD

The earliest known bird was *Archaeopteryx*, a pigeon-size species that lived in what is now Europe about 150 million years ago. *Archaeopteryx* had a body similar to that of a small, two-legged dinosaur, covered in feath-

ers except for the head. Its long, bony tail bore a feathery fringe on each side. Each wing bore three clawed fingers. Small, sharp teeth filled its beaklike jaws.

Paleontologists suggest that *Archaeopteryx* descended from a lightly built, running dinosaur that used its clawed forelimbs to climb into trees in search of insects and other small prey. A likely ancestor of *Archaeopteryx* is the coelurosaur *Compsognathus*. In 2000, the 130-million-year-old fossil of another feathered dinosaur, the dromaeosaur, was discovered in China. This small, fast-moving relative of the velociraptor appeared to have traces of downy fibers covering most of its body. This find gave paleontologists even more evidence to support the theory that a link exists between dinosaurs and birds.

The greatest mystery, no doubt, is why this ancestral dinosaur developed feathers in the first

Colorful plumage and melodious songs are just two of the traits that make cardinals (above) and other species of birds beloved and familiar creatures to humans.

place. Some experts believe that the first feathers were a downy covering on the bodies of baby dinosaurs. This fits with the currently held theory that the ancestors of birds were warm-blooded, or endothermic, dinosaurs. A covering such as feathers would have helped these avian ancestors retain their body heat.

The leap from feathers to flight may have come when these "dinobirds" began jumping, then gliding from tree to tree. Another theory is that these creatures first used their feathered wings to increase running speed, eventually lifting up off the ground. What all scientists seem to agree on is that this evolutionary process took a very long time.

By the time *Archaeopteryx* arrived on the scene, it already possessed fully developed feathers and wings, similar to those seen in birds today. It appears to have been a weak flier, as its breastbone was small, and so provided little leverage for wing muscles.

Other ancient birds followed *Archaeopteryx*, including an unusual group of toothed marine birds. They lacked *Archaeopteryx*'s bony tail, but retained the tail feathers. They had also developed the large breastbones needed to anchor powerful flight muscles. Ironically, some of these birds had already lost the ability to fly, becoming the first flightless birds.

By the end of the Cretaceous period, 65 million years ago, birds had evolved most of the features we see today. The tail was short. The breastbone was broad and strong. The remnants of fingers and teeth had all but disappeared.

About this time, many new types of birds appeared. Some were large, flightless predators such as the 10-foot (3-meter)-tall "elephant birds." Among the first vultures was the enormous *Argentavis magnificens*, which rode updrafts of air on wings spanning an amazing 24 feet (7.3 meters)!

Most of these large, ancient birds disappeared with the coming of the Ice Ages, about 2 million years ago. When Earth warmed again 12,000 years ago, the small songbirds far outnumbered their larger relatives.

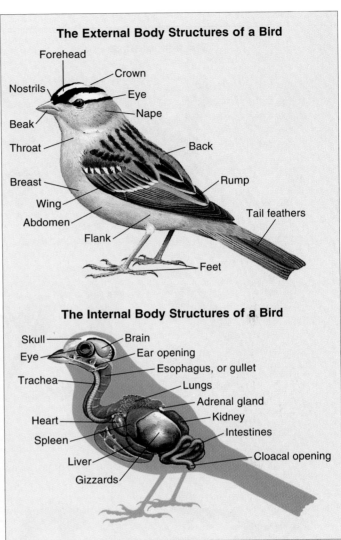

The External Body Structures of a Bird

Forehead
Crown
Nostrils
Eye
Nape
Beak
Throat
Back
Breast
Rump
Wing
Abdomen
Tail feathers
Flank
Feet

The Internal Body Structures of a Bird

Skull
Brain
Eye
Ear opening
Esophagus, or gullet
Trachea
Lungs
Adrenal gland
Heart
Kidney
Spleen
Intestines
Liver
Cloacal opening
Gizzards

FEATHERS

The feather is the characteristic that distinguishes birds from all other creatures. Lightweight, strong, and flexible, feathers display a remarkably simple structure that has remained largely unchanged for 150 million years.

Like reptile scales, feathers grow from follicles in the skin and are made of a horny protein called *keratin*. Each feather follicle produces a cone-shaped sheath that unfurls as it emerges. Once fully grown, the feather loses its blood supply, but remains embedded in the skin. When old feathers fall out, new ones grow in to take their place.

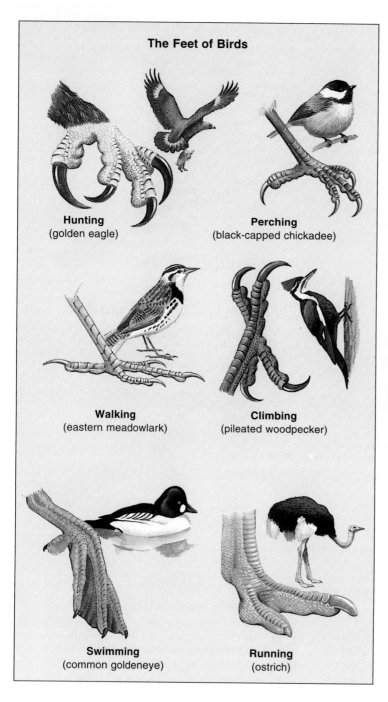

The Feet of Birds

Hunting
(golden eagle)

Perching
(black-capped chickadee)

Walking
(eastern meadowlark)

Climbing
(pileated woodpecker)

Swimming
(common goldeneye)

Running
(ostrich)

stiff, air-filled center shaft called a *rachis*. Each side of the rachis has a row of tiny barbs. The edges of each barb have tiny teeth and hooks, called *barbules* and *hooklets*. These zip together to form a flattened, tightly woven surface called the *vane*. Beneath the contour feathers lie the small, fluffy *down* feathers. Down feathers have a short, thin shaft that gives rise to barbs that lack hooks. Instead of forming vanes, they remain fluffy. Down traps air to insulate the bird's body. The young of many birds begin life covered with down.

Waterfowl and some other birds have another type of feather, the *semiplume*, on the belly. Semiplumes have a long center rachis, but the barbs remain fluffy. They repel water and help a bird float. *Filoplumes* are feathers with very few barbs. These feathers commonly appear as "whiskers" around the beaks of insect-eating birds such as flycatchers. Presumably, they are used for touch.

The colors of feathers play an important role as well. Drably colored feathers enable birds to blend with their surroundings and avoid predators. Many male birds sacrifice their camouflage during breeding season for brightly colored plumage. Some tropical birds remain brightly colored year-round.

Birds keep their feathers in good working order by *preening*. Using feet and beak, they comb their feathers to repair separated vanes and remove dirt and parasites. Most birds also waterproof their feathers with an oil produced by a gland near the tail.

All birds shed old and damaged feathers and regrow new ones. Some birds lose many of their feathers during a period called *molting*, and it can leave a bird unable to fly for several weeks. Ducks molt nearly every year, as do male birds that lose their bright plumage after breeding season.

Birds have several types of feathers. The largest and most visible are the *contour* feathers that cover a bird's outer surface and produce its streamlined shape. The flight feathers of the wing and tail are contour feathers. Each has a

ANATOMY OF A FLYING MACHINE

As the mythical Greek Icarus quickly discovered, it takes more than feathers to fly. Birds must be light and compact, and yet powerful enough to launch themselves into the air. Flight also requires tremendous amounts of energy and high levels of endurance.

The bones of most birds are slim, thin-walled, and filled with tiny sacs of air. Even the skull is amazingly light. As an example, the skeleton of a frigate bird, with an enormous wingspan of 7 feet (2 meters), weighs just 4 ounces (0.1 kilogram).

The most massive bone in a bird's body is its broad, keeled sternum, the anchoring point for large, powerful wing muscles. The bird's backbone is rigid, its vertebrae fused together to keep its trunk stiff in flight. The bones inside the wing are highly adapted arm bones. The outermost flight feathers, or *primaries*, arise from lengthened hand bones. The secondary flight feathers are borne on the *ulna*, or forearm.

Another adaptation of great importance for flight is the bird's streamlined shape. A typical bird wing is an airfoil, with a rounded leading edge tapering to a thin trailing edge. The upper surface curves outward, while the lower one is flattened or curved inward. This shape deflects air in a way that increases pressure below the wing and decreases it above the wing, pushing the wings upward.

The tail feathers come into play as a steering mechanism that can be angled up, down, or sideways. When fanned out, tail feathers produce additional lift or braking, depending on their position.

Most birds glide whenever possible, and some birds glide almost exclusively. They do so by holding the wings fully extended to the sides. A gliding bird slowly loses altitude, but maintains its speed thanks to the force of gravity. The most-artful gliders—vultures, albatrosses, and eagles—can even glide upward on rising currents of warm air.

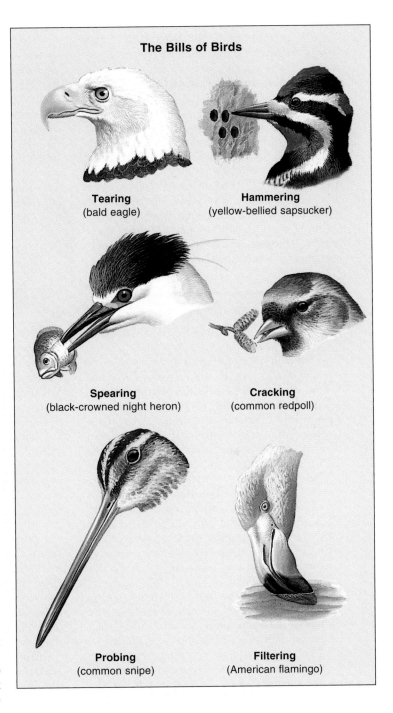

The Bills of Birds

Tearing
(bald eagle)

Hammering
(yellow-bellied sapsucker)

Spearing
(black-crowned night heron)

Cracking
(common redpoll)

Probing
(common snipe)

Filtering
(American flamingo)

In general, birds fly by flapping their wings. Typically, a bird does so by beating its wings downward and forward, and then, more rapidly, lifting them upward and back.

Energy for Flight

Clearly, it takes an enormous amount of energy for a bird to operate its powerful flight muscles for any substantial period of time. The effort requires a relatively high body temperature (104° to 113° F—40° to 45° C), excellent blood circulation, and very efficient respiration. Birds have a four-chambered heart that beats extraordinarily rapidly—some 500 times per minute in a sparrow, and up to 1,000 times per minute in a hummingbird.

A bird's lungs have a highly developed system of branching air tubes that increases the exchange of oxygen from the air and carbon dioxide from the blood. In addition, a bird's lungs connect with air-filled spaces in its bones and between its organs and muscles, enabling oxygen to diffuse throughout the body.

To maintain their high body temperature, birds must eat constantly and digest their food quickly and efficiently. Birds have no teeth. Instead, their digestive system breaks up their food. Once swallowed, food passes into the bird's *crop*, where fluid softens it. From there, food passes into the stomach,

Migration

Most animals move from place to place in their search for food and nesting sites. With their gift of powerful flight, many birds take this journey to the extreme. Every fall, the majority of birds in the Northern Hemisphere fly thousands of miles south for the winter. A similar migration takes place among the marine birds of the cold southern seas. The following spring, the birds make the long journey back to their summer nesting grounds.

Anyone who has endured a cold, snowy winter can understand the desire to head to warmer places. But why do so many birds make the long journey back to high latitudes each spring? Certainly, the trip requires tremendous effort, and many birds do not survive its dangers.

Experts believe that birds return to high latitudes each year for several reasons. The higher latitudes tend to offer wide-open spaces with ample food and fewer predators. Summer in high latitudes also promises long hours of daylight—so important for the time-consuming task of raising young. In the northern reaches of its range, the American robin, for example, feeds its young an astonishing 21 hours a day.

Even more intriguing is the question of *how* birds migrate. How do they know when to start their journey, and how do they find their way? Length of day plays a role in triggering the desire to migrate. But even in a windowless laboratory, a migrating bird will begin to flutter and hop in the appropriate direction at a specific time of year. No doubt, migrating birds possess some type of internal, or biological, clock and compass. Its exact nature remains a mystery to science.

Migrating birds navigate by a variety of means, depending in part on the species. Most songbirds migrate only at night. Experiments show that they navigate in part by the position of stars. Other birds such as crows, hawks, and hummingbirds migrate by day and use the Sun as a compass. Still other migrating birds such as geese fly day and night until they reach their destination. In addition, most, if not all, birds somehow sense Earth's magnetic fields and use them to stay on course.

Some of the shortest migrations occur among birds that summer in the mountains and then move into valleys for the winter. The premier long-distance travelers are the oceanic birds. The arctic tern travels from summer breeding grounds in the North Atlantic to winter feeding grounds in the Antarctic Ocean, for a round-trip journey of more than 22,000 miles (35,400 kilometers).

where it mixes with acid; beyond that, it passes into the muscular *gizzard*, which grinds the food into particles. The gizzard of most birds contains small stones, sand, or grit to help in this grinding process.

Food then passes through the intestines, where water and nutrition are absorbed. Finally, undigested waste passes into a chamber called the *cloaca* and is eliminated as feces.

Diet varies tremendously from species to species. Most birds eat insects, which they supplement with seeds. Hummingbirds both eat insects and sip nectar. Birds of prey seek out primarily small animals for food. Scavengers eat

primarily seeds have short, conical beaks for crushing them. "Pickax" beaks such as that of the woodpecker are designed for boring holes in wood—to find insects, store food, or excavate a nest hole. The hummingbird's needlelike bill and long tongue are designed for extracting nectar from flowers. The long, slender, and curved bill of a shorebird is perfect for probing water and mud for crustaceans and other food. The broad, flat bills of ducks have strainer plates for sifting

the flesh of dead animals. Marsh and oceangoing birds mainly catch fish, as do kingfishers.

Bird Feet

When not in flight, birds depend on their feet for locomotion. What we think of as a bird's "foot" is actually toes—typically four of them. The rest of the foot is raised above the ground. The form of the foot depends on the way of life of the particular species. The feet of perching birds are designed to grasp twigs. Woodpeckers and other birds with *zygodactyl* feet have two toes pointing forward and two to the rear. This enables them to climb steep, flat surfaces such as tree trunks. The powerful feet of predatory birds are equipped with sharp, curved claws for killing and grasping prey. Ground birds such as quail have long, clawed toes suited for scratching for food. In the winter, many grouse develop fleshy fringes on their toes that act like snowshoes. Swimming and diving birds typically have webbed feet, while marsh birds that walk on mud tend to have very long toes.

Bird Beaks

Bird beaks, or bills, also come in a variety of forms. Birds use their beaks for feeding as well as for nest building and fighting. Predatory birds tend to have stout, curved beaks with sharp edges for ripping apart prey. Birds that eat

food from water and mud. Fish-eating birds such as the merganser tend to have beaks with saw-toothed edges for gripping their slippery prey. Wading birds, such as the heron, have long, sharp, daggerlike bills that they use to spear fish and frogs.

Bird Senses

Many experts believe that birds have the most highly developed vision in the animal world. Typically, the eyes are quite large compared to the bird's size, with the bulk of each eyeball lying inside the skull. In most birds, the eyes lie on either side of the head, providing two independent fields of vision. The fields overlap in the front, for binocular view. Although binocular vision is quite limited in most birds, it is of particular importance for birds that chase moving prey. The owl's forward-facing eyes maximize its binocular view.

Many special adaptations work together to heighten bird vision. Among them is a unique eye shape and special eye muscles that allow for quick refocusing from far to near objects and from light to dark conditions.

Ears lie hidden beneath feathers on either side of a bird's head. Typically, hearing is keen. Nocturnal birds such as owls rely on hearing to find prey. So do robins, which can hear earthworms moving in the soil. Most birds lack highly developed senses of touch and taste.

BIRD BEHAVIOR

The complexities of bird behavior are enough to fill many volumes. A striking difference between birds and simpler forms of life (reptiles, amphibians, and fish, for example) is the bird's ability to learn. Birds can learn from past experiences and adapt their knowledge to new situations. This adaptability helps explain why birds have been able to thrive in altered environments such as cities and suburbs. The advent of automobiles, for example, has given rise to new bird behaviors such as mockingbirds scraping insects off the radiators of parked cars.

Breeding

More instinctual are the fascinating and complex behaviors seen during breeding season. Breeding males establish territories, which they defend with loud songs and colorful plumage displays. These same behaviors help attract females. Depending on the species, courtship rituals can include song and dance, elaborate feather fluffing, and the giving of gifts such as berries and twigs. Typically, courtship is a two-sided affair. The male's display elicits a special response from the female. Her reaction then elicits a response from the male, and so on.

Mating is an unsteady affair with most birds. The male climbs on the female's back, then twists and lowers his tail while the female raises and twists hers so that their cloacae meet. Millions of sperm enter the female's oviduct to fertilize her eggs.

After mating, most birds build nests. Some species simply use cavities that they line with nesting materials. Many others, including most perching birds, build elaborate, cup-shaped affairs. A few birds make no nest at all. The white tern simply lays an egg on a forked branch. Brood parasites such as cowbirds leave their eggs in the nests of other birds.

Typically, the job of nest building falls primarily on the female, although her mate may fetch materials such as twigs. Exceptions include house wrens, woodpeckers, and swallows, which share equally in nest building. In most weaverbirds, the male builds the nest.

Care of Eggs and Young

Within several weeks of mating, the fertilized eggs inside the female have developed a tough, mineralized shell. She lays them one at a time, typically a day apart. The total number varies from 1 to 35, depending on the species, although clutches of more than 10 are rare. Egg size, color, and shape also vary with species. Typically, eggs are oval with splotchy coloring for camouflage. The smallest is the pea-sized egg of the hummingbird. The largest is the football-sized egg of the ostrich.

All birds except the megapode fowl incubate, or warm, their eggs. One or both parents develop an almost-featherless *brooding patch* on the belly. Typically, the female takes charge of incubation, although the male may remain nearby to guard her and occasionally relieve her for a short while. Roles are reversed among emperor penguins and tinamous, with males taking charge of incubation. The megapode fowl of Australia leaves its eggs in mounds of dead plants or sand, allowing sunshine and the heat of decay to incubate them.

Incubation time varies from 10 to 12 days among some woodpeckers to 81 days for the royal albatross. Two to three weeks is typical.

The hatchling pecks its way out of its shell with a temporary *egg tooth* at the tip of its bill. The newborn of some birds, such as pheasant and ducks, emerge covered with down and can leave the nest within a few hours. They are called *precocial* young. Most perching birds hatch naked and helpless, or *altricial*.

With the exception of megapodes, all birds begin life dependent on their parents. Altricial young must be fed in the nest. Precocial young follow their parents, who teach them how to find food. Most altricial young develop the ability to fly between one and five weeks. The bond between parent and chicks then weakens, and eventually the chick becomes independent.

Most young birds have dull-colored plumage that provides camouflage from enemies. Adult plumage develops by the first breeding season. Weather, predation, and injury kill many birds before they reach adulthood, and prevent most from reaching their maximum life span. In general, longevity increases with size. Very small species such as hummingbirds and wrens seldom live longer than five years. Gulls live into their 30s; hawks and owls, into their 50s and 60s. The record for longevity goes to the cockatoos, which occasionally live more than 100 years in captivity.

BIRD CLASSIFICATION

What was the first bird? Which is the most advanced? What are the relationships among the thousands of species in existence today? Taxonomy, the science of classifying species of living things, helps answer these questions by grouping birds with similar traits.

The 18th-century taxonomist Carolus Linnaeus devised the classification system used today, and he established the class Aves, into which all birds are placed. Over the centuries, ornithologists have added innumerable species and modified Linnaeus' work. Today they recognize 27 living orders and one extinct order of birds divided into about 200 families containing more than 8,500 species. Closely related species within a family group share a common genus name—such as *Laurus* in the case of *Laurus argentatus*, the herring gull, and *Laurus delawarensis*, the ring-billed gull.

The largest order of birds, by far, is the order Passeriformes, the "perching birds," with some 60 families. Ornithologists consider the perching birds to be the most recently evolved and specialized, or advanced, species. Among the most ancient, or primitive, are the six families of flightless birds, such as ostriches and penguins. The following classification begins with the most ancient order and progresses to the diverse and successful Passeriformes.

In an ongoing effort to clarify avian taxonomy, ornithologists conducting a field study analyze a bird's outward appearance, internal anatomy, habits, and behavior.

Avian Classification

PHYLUM: Chordata

SUBPHYLUM: Vertebrata: *Animals with backbones.*

CLASS Aves: *Birds*

ORDER Archaeopterygiformes: *The extinct "dawn birds," with one known family and one known species. Identified from pigeon-sized fossil about 140 million years old. In essence, a feathered, flying reptile. Example:* Archaeopteryx.

ORDER Struthioniformes: *Ostriches, with one family and one species. The world's largest living bird, flightless, found in arid regions of Africa. Example: ostrich.*

ORDER Rheiformes: *Rheas, with one family and two species. Large, flightless birds, found in scrublands of South America. Example: common rhea.*

ORDER Casuariiformes: *Cassowaries and emus, with two families and four species (one emu and three cassowaries). Large, flightless birds, found in wooded and grassy areas of Australia, New Guinea, and Indonesia. Example: double-wattled cassowary.*

ORDER Apterygiformes: *Kiwis, with one family and three species. Small- to medium-sized, flightless birds, found in brushy habitats of New Zealand. Example: brown kiwi.*

ORDER Tinamiformes: *Tinamous, with one family and 46 species. Chickenlike ground birds, found in forests, bushlands, and grasslands of Central and South America. Examples: great tinamou and crested tinamou.*

ORDER Sphenisciformes: *Penguins, with one family and 18 species. Flightless marine birds with paddlelike wings, found in cold, southern oceans. Example: emperor penguin.*

ORDER Podicipediformes: *Grebes, with one family and 19 species. Fast-swimming freshwater birds of Eurasia, Africa, Indonesia, and Australia. Example: little grebe.*

ORDER Gaviiformes: *Loons, with one family and five species. Freshwater and marine diving birds of the high Northern Hemisphere. Example: red-throated loon.*

ORDER Procellariiformes: *Albatrosses, shearwaters, and petrels, with four families and 80 to 100 species. Birds of the open sea, with unique external, tubular nostrils. Found in all oceans. Example: wandering albatross.*

ORDER Pelecaniformes: *Pelicans, gannets, boobies, tropic birds, cormorants, darters, and frigate birds, with six families and 60 species. Medium to large web-footed waterbirds, most of which eat fish. Found worldwide in freshwater and oceans. Examples: brown booby, rough-billed pelican, and anhinga.*

ORDER Ciconiiformes: *Herons, storks, ibises, and flamingos, with six families and about 125 species. Storklike wading birds with long legs and unwebbed feet, many of which have long necks and pointed or down-curved beaks. Found worldwide near water. Examples: cattle egret and Japanese crested ibis.*

ORDER Anseriformes: *Screamers, swans, geese, and ducks, with two families and about 143 species. Web-footed waterbirds. (Screamers have partially webbed feet.) Found worldwide. Example: Canada goose.*

ORDER Falconiformes: *Birds of prey, with five families and about 300 species. Daytime hunters such as hawks, New World vultures, ospreys, falcons, and secretary birds. Found worldwide. Examples: bald eagle, red-tailed hawk, California condor, turkey vulture, and great horned owl.*

ORDER Galliformes: *Wildfowl (also called upland game birds), with seven families and about 250 species. Includes the curassows, hoatzins, and pheasants. Adapted for living on the ground and eating seeds, with the exception of curassows and hoatzins. Found worldwide. Examples: peafowl, quail, and turkey.*

ORDER Gruiformes: *Cranes, rails, bustards, and their relatives, with 12 families and some 200 species. Diverse and ancient group of wading and ground birds, some quite rare. Found worldwide. Example: whooping crane.*

ORDER Charadriiformes: *Plovers, sandpipers, gulls, terns, auks, and their kin, with 15 families and some 300 species. Diverse group of water- and shorebirds, grouped together for their common skeletal traits. Found worldwide. Example: herring gull.*

ORDER Columbiformes: *Sandgrouse and pigeons, includes two living families with 310 species, and the extinct dodo family with three species. Typically stout, strong birds of plains and open woods, found worldwide. Example: mourning dove.*

ORDER Psittaciformes: *Parrots, lories, and cockatoos, with three families and about 310 species. Typically brightly colored, noisy birds, with hooked beaks and zygodactyl feet (two toes pointing forward, two backward). Found in forests of Southern Hemisphere and tropics. Examples: cockatiel, lovebird, macaw.*

ORDER Cuculiformes: *Cuckoos and turacos, with two families and 146 species. Typically slender, strong-billed insect eaters with long tails and unusual arrangement of toes. Found in woodland and scrub. Examples: cuckoo and roadrunner.*

ORDER Strigiformes: *Owls, with two families and 146 species. Nocturnal predators with large eyes, taloned feet, and powerful wings. Found worldwide. Example: barn owl.*

ORDER Caprimulgiformes: *Goatsuckers, frogmouths, potoos, nightjars, and their kin, with five families and 94 species. Typically nocturnal insect eaters, with mottled brown plumage. Most found in tropics. Example: whippoorwill.*

ORDER Apodiformes: *Swifts and hummingbirds, with three families and about 390 species. Fast-flying, acrobatic birds with small feet. Hummingbirds include the smallest of birds, many of them brilliantly colored. Examples: palm swift and ruby-throated hummingbird.*

ORDER Trogoniformes: *Trogons, with one family and 36 species. Brilliantly colorful birds with short, stout beaks. Typically eat fruits. Nest in tree cavities. Found in Africa, India, Southeast Asia, and the Americas. Example: collared trogon.*

ORDER Coliiformes: *Mouse birds, with one family and six species. Small, crested birds with short, strong bills, soft plumage loosely attached to the skin, and long tail feathers, found on African savanna. Example: speckled mouse bird.*

ORDER Coraciiformes: *Kingfishers, todies, motmots, bee-eaters, rollers, hoopoes, and hornbills, with 10 families and about 194 species. Typically colorful birds with large, strong beaks. Third and fourth toe jointed at the base. Found in forests and along shores worldwide. Examples: Eurasian kingfisher and red-billed hornbill.*

ORDER Piciformes: *Jacamars, puff-birds, honeyguides, woodpeckers, toucans, and barbets, with six families and about 390 species. Strong-billed birds with zygodactyl feet. Found in woodlands worldwide. Example: toco toucan.*

ORDER Passeriformes: *Perching birds, with two suborders, 60 families, and about 5,000 species. Typically small birds, with unwebbed feet adapted for perching on twigs. All have 9 or 10 primary flight feathers and about 12 tail feathers. Young born naked and helpless. All sing, although vocal ability varies. Found on dry land in all habitats. This large order is generally subdivided into one large and three small suborders. The three small orders are grouped together as the suboscine, or primitive, perching birds. Their vocal organs and songs are simpler than that of the fourth and largest suborder— the oscines, or songbirds.*

NONPERCHING BIRDS

When scientists discuss birds, they talk about them according to their taxonomy—using terms such as Struthioniformes to describe ostriches, or Strigiformes to describe owls. When the rest of us talk about birds, we tend to group them according to their habits.

In its most general sense, "nonperching birds"—an unscientific term, to be sure—refers to all birds whose feet are not specialized for perching. Several types of nonperching birds have evolved traits unusual enough to warrant individual articles in this volume. These include flightless birds (page 409), birds of prey (page 414), wildfowl (page 422), the pigeons (page 428), and waterbirds and shorebirds (page 432).

Of course, many types of nonperching birds fall into categories not mentioned above. Some are casually grouped together for their behavior, others for their unique songs, still others for the food they eat. These, and several other unrelated groups of nonperching birds, are the subject of this article.

The African parrots called lovebirds (above) are named for the strong attachment exhibited by mates. Even in the wild, pairs tend to roost directly next to one another.

CLASSIFICATION

The nonperching birds discussed in this article are a truly diverse group. Scientists have assigned them into eight orders:

• Order Psittaciformes, which contains such tropical birds as macaws, parrots, parakeets, and cockatoos;

• Order Cuculiformes, which contains the cuckoos, roadrunners, and some tropical birds;

• Order Caprimulgiformes, which contains whippoorwills, nighthawks, frogmouths, and other birds with very wide mouths, small beaks, and tiny feet;

• Order Apodiformes, which contains the swifts and hummingbirds;

• Order Coliiformes, which contains the colies, or mousebirds;

• Order Trogoniformes, which contains the trogons;

• Order Coraciiformes, which contains hornbills, kingfishers, and bee-eaters, among others; and

• Order Piciformes, which contains woodpeckers, puffbirds, toucans, and other birds adapted for climbing and digging into wood.

PARROTS AND THEIR KIN

Members of the order Psittaciformes use their short, hooked bills to crack nuts and hard fruits. Each of their feet has four toes, two forward and two backward—an adaptation for climbing and grasping. They are brightly plumaged birds, and most are strong fliers, traveling long distances in search of the plant matter or insects that make up their diets. These gregarious birds have harsh, shrieking voices. In captivity, many can be taught to speak, making them popular pets and zoo animals. One species, the kakapo (*Strigops habroptilus*) of New Zealand, is flightless.

This order occurs primarily in tropical and subtropical areas, particularly in Australia and nearby islands. Unfortunately, advancing human settlements have decreased the parrots' numbers and threaten the existence of some of the approximately 320 species that make up the order.

Representative Species

One of the most-familiar parrots is the cockatoo, a medium- to large-sized bird distinguished from its cousins by the erectile crest atop its head. Its tail tends to be relatively short and square-ended. The plumage is largely white, gray, or black. Cockatoos inhabit Australia, New Guinea, and the islands of Indonesia.

Lories are distinguished by the brushlike tip of the tongue. This, together with the narrow bill, is useful in obtaining the nectar and pollen that form most of the bird's diet. These brilliantly colored members of the parrot family live in Australia, New Guinea, and nearby islands. Smaller species are called lorikeets.

Lovebirds, small African parrots of the genus *Agapornis*, are renowned for the preening and affection they shower on one another.

Macaws are large, brightly colored parrots that inhabit tropical forests from Mexico into South America. The largest, the scarlet macaw (*Ara macao*), may grow to be more than 36 inches (90 centimeters) long.

CUCKOOS AND THEIR KIN

Most birds of the order Cuculiformes render a valuable service by feeding on insects. These birds have long bodies and tails; slender, down-curving bills; and 8 to 10 stabilizing feathers. The four toes on each foot are arranged in pairs: two point forward, two backward.

Cuckoos

The cuckoo family, Cuculidae, contains more than 200 species and subspecies. These

The vividly plumed cockatoo (above, center) has reversed toes: two point forward, two point back. In the South American jungles, many colorful parrots (left inset) and macaws (lower inset) are captured and sold as pets.

birds, ranging from sparrow size to pheasant size, live everywhere that insects do. Cuckoos are shy, furtive birds, more likely to be heard than seen. In general, they have dull brown, gray, or black plumage, although some tropical varieties are brilliantly colored and plumed. All species have long tails and short wings.

New World varieties of cuckoos build their own, rather haphazard nests and care for their young. The Old World species, on the other hand, are parasitic. They lay their eggs in the nests of smaller birds and depend on the foster parents to raise the young. Typically, only one cuckoo egg is laid in each parasitized nest. That egg has a shorter period of incubation than the eggs of the host. When the cuckoo egg is hatched, the young chick grows more rapidly than its nestmates and frequently pushes the rightful occupants out of the nest. The parasitized birds never seem to realize what has happened. In fact, they seem to take a certain parental pride in filling with food the cavernous mouth of the strange young bird.

Young cuckoos do not have juvenile plumage. Instead, their growing feathers remain in the sheaths until fully developed. When the feathers are mature, the sheaths burst open at about the same time so that the change to adult plumage takes place in only a few hours.

Eurasian cuckoos, *Cuculus canorus*, whose song inspired the notes of the cuckoo clock, are associated with the coming of spring. They are migratory birds, wintering in Africa and returning to Europe with the first of the spring birds.

The scarlet macaw (top), the largest macaw, is relatively abundant. Spix's macaw (above), by contrast, is nearly extinct in the wild, although a few survive in captivity.

Other Representative Species

Anis are fascinating jay-sized cuckoos of Central America, South America, the West Indies, and Mexico. They follow cattle, pecking ticks off their backs and catching insects that the livestock stir up. Their plumage is black with a metallic sheen; they have large, convex bills. Anis are weak fliers, perhaps because their long tails have only eight feathers, the smallest number of any bird. Anis lead a communal way of life. When the breeding season arrives, the entire flock builds a common nest, into which all the females lay their eggs. If there is not enough room for all the eggs, green leaves are placed over the first layer, and the rest of the eggs are laid on top. The lower layer does not usually hatch. The females incubate and feed the young together.

Another curious member of the cuckoo family is the roadrunner (*Geococcyx californianus*), which lives in arid regions of Mexico and the southwestern United States. This bird has brownish-streaked feathers tipped with white; bright, alert eyes accented by blue and orange skin; a very long, bronze-green tail; and strong legs. The bird can erect the feathers on its crown to form a ragged crest.

The roadrunner has been clocked at speeds of 15 miles (25 kilometers) per hour; although it can fly, it prefers to travel by running and by fast, gliding jumps.

THE GOATSUCKERS, OR NIGHTJARS

The order name for these birds, Caprimulgiformes, is derived from the Latin *capri mulgus*, meaning "milker of goats." As is so often the case, this name is traced to a very old legend. Even the ancient Greek philosopher Aristotle thought that the birds used their unusually large mouths to suck milk from goats! Actually, goatsuckers feed on small flying insects, which they catch on the wing, using their gaping beaks as scoops. Since goats ordinarily attract myriad insects, the goatsuckers often hover around goats, taking advantage of the free insect feast.

These birds are also called *nightjars*, because their booming calls "jar" the night. The order contains five families, which are distributed over wide areas of the world.

The roadrunner (above), a fast-running member of the cuckoo family, lives in the arid scrublands of the southwestern United States and Mexico. The roadrunner rarely flies, preferring to rely on its swiftness afoot to make an escape.

True Goatsuckers

To confuse matters even further, taxonomists consider the approximately 70 species that comprise the family Caprimulgidae to be "true" goatsuckers; they include the nighthawk, whippoorwill, poorwill, and chuck will's widow, the last three named for the sound of their calls. The poorwill (*Phalaenoptilus nuttalli*) displays a phenomenon absolutely unknown in any other bird: hibernation. In western North America, it is often found in protected niches, hibernating through the winter.

The long feathers and pointed wings of the true goatsuckers make the birds appear much larger than they actually are. For example, the nighthawk, whose body is smaller than that of the robin, appears, on the wing, to be about the size of a sparrow hawk.

Goatsuckers do not build nests. Instead, they lay their eggs on bare ground—not even in a depression to keep them from rolling! The eggs are whitish or cream-colored, marked with gray and purple. The young, hatched blind and helpless, soon develop long grayish or brownish down, not so different from that which covers young owls. Both parents incubate the eggs and care for the young.

Nighthawks prefer pasture or prairie country, spending the day perched on a rock or post. At dusk, they begin seeking out their insect prey. These birds consume great quantities of gnats, mosquitoes, and other flying insects. At dusk, they can sometimes be seen along the shoulders of country roads, busily pursuing grasshoppers. In ever-increasing numbers, nighthawks visit urban areas, where they have little competition for the host of flying insects that are attracted by streetlights, neon signs, and other illuminated objects.

The whippoorwill is a bird of the woodlands, spending the day on the ground under the trees and emerging into clearings or along the forest borders at night to feed. Whippoorwills prey on larger insects than do nighthawks. These birds are particularly fond of the large, night-flying moths, whose larvae are very destructive to tree foliage.

The true goatsuckers are extraordinarily beneficial to humanity, since they feed almost exclusively on insects, especially destructive night-flying insects that for the most part have few other predators.

Other Representative Species

The potoos (family Nyctibiidae) are large, owl-like night birds of Central and South America. Their huge mouths are large enough to close over a tennis ball!

The family Steatornithidae contains only one species: the oilbird, or guacharo (*Steatornis caripensis*). It lives colonially in caves in isolated parts of the Caribbean and South America.

Local people trap the oilbird and melt down its body fat to make lamp oil and a variety of butter substitutes.

Another interesting species, the owlet nightjar or frogmouth, belongs to a small family (Aegothelidae) of birds found in Australia and New Guinea. This rather odd nightjar has a wide—and, as might be expected, froglike—mouth, and very sluggish habits.

HUMMINGBIRDS AND SWIFTS

Even close inspection fails to reveal much similarity among adult hummingbirds and swifts—except in the shape of the long, narrow wings and the tiny feet. Nevertheless, kinship exists. A relationship can most clearly be discerned by comparing the bills and mouths of swifts and of newly hatched hummingbirds.

Hummingbirds

By far, the smallest bird in the world is the bee hummingbird of Cuba, measuring barely 2.25 inches (5.7 centimeters) in length. Not all hummingbirds are tiny, however. The giant hummingbird of the Andes is more than 8 inches (20 centimeters) long. Still, the majority of the 580-odd species and subspecies measure less than 4 inches (10 centimeters)—and half of that length consists of bill and tail.

Hummingbirds are renowned for their brilliant colors. John James Audubon, the noted 19th-century American ornithologist, called them "glittering fragments of the rainbow." Sometimes extremes of color, in wonderful combinations, are found on the back or breast of individual birds. Interestingly enough, the colors are not derived from pigments, but occur through light diffraction, a result of the peculiar structure of the feathers. The plumage may actually appear quite somber if viewed in shadowy light. Hummingbirds are most brilliant when flitting about from flower to flower in ever-changing bright light. Many species of hummingbirds are further ornamented with tufts of feathers in various places on their bodies.

Hummingbirds live only in the New World, with the majority of species found in the Colombian and Ecuadorean Andes. The birds have spread all the way south to Patagonia and as far north as Alaska, although most species have quite localized ranges, some limited to just a single valley.

These birds live on the nectar of flowers and the insects within them. They always dwell in areas with multitudes of flowers. The bills of many hummingbird species have become adapted to particular flowers. In all species, the bill is probelike and the tongue tubular for sucking flower nectar.

Bill lengths vary from 5 inches (12.5 centimeters) to scarcely 0.25 inch (6 millimeters). Curiously enough, regardless of bill length, the birds feed from the same long, tubular flowers. The long-billed variety sips the nectar in the conventional way. The other drills a hole through the base of the flower into the nectar, and then inserts its bill. Many flowers depend on hummingbirds for cross-fertilization. The pollen is usually carried on the head or bill as the bird moves from flower to flower.

The hummingbird derives its name from the distinctive sound made by its rapidly beating wings. During the mating season, the male of most species expresses his feelings with excited chirpings as he flies, with flashing wings, back and forth past the female. A few species are capable of producing melodious songs of surprising volume.

Hummingbird nests are skillfully constructed of plant down or catkins, and fastened in place by spiderwebs. The outside of the nest is usually ornamented with lichen and bits of moss. Usually the nest is set upon a branch, and often looks like a knot in the tree. Some species fasten the nest to the underside of a large leaf or even to a projecting cliff or overhanging rock.

Hummingbirds are noted for their colors. People wishing to draw these birds to their gardens should plant brightly colored tubular or trumpet-shaped flowers.

Swifts

The nearly 100 species of swifts (family Apodidae) are, with few exceptions, sooty-black birds, sometimes with white on the rump or underparts, but often with no marks whatsoever. The chimney swift, for example, entirely sooty-colored above, is only slightly lighter below. In the East Indian tree swifts, by contrast, the plumage has a metallic gloss, and the feathers are quite silky. Overall, though, most swifts have short, drab plumage.

Swifts make nests from sticks, straw, feathers, or other material, and shape it all into a shallow saucer. The materials are cemented together and fastened to the wall of a cave, hollow tree, or chimney by means of the bird's gluelike saliva. In one group of swifts off the east coast of Asia, the nests are made entirely of this saliva. These are the same nests from which the Chinese make their famous bird's-nest soup.

The feet of swifts are small and too weak to support the weight of the body. Therefore, all feeding, nest-material gathering, and contacts between the birds must take place while in flight. When forced to rest or to climb the walls of its home, the swift remains vertical, grasping the wall with the aid of its sharp, curved claws and the spiny protuberances of its tail feathers. It rarely perches or stands on the ground.

As their name implies, swifts are fast fliers. Even the smaller ones reach speeds of almost 62 miles (100 kilometers) per hour—a fair speed for a small bird, but not uncommon. The larger swifts of Asia and the Middle East have been clocked at 170 to 200 miles (275 to 320 kilometers) per hour, making swifts, together with certain falcons, the fastest living birds.

MOUSEBIRDS

The mousebirds, or colies, are small, long-tailed birds of sub-Saharan Africa that resemble mice both in appearance and behavior. Their short legs terminate in feet that are equipped with sharp, hooked claws and an outer toe that pivots, and therefore can point either backward or forward. This adaptation enables the mouse-

Alone among the trogons, only the elegant, or coppery-tailed, trogon (above) ranges into the United States. This bird, less than 1 foot long, feeds primarily on insects, other small prey, and fruit.

bird to run along tree branches—in a mouselike fashion. Its plumage consists of grayish, hairlike feathers and a head crest.

Mousebirds feed mainly on fruits. They are graceful fliers, although they generally fly no farther than from one tree to another. At night, they gather in small groups in a bush or tree and fall asleep, cuddled against one another.

TROGONS

The 35 species of trogons, which comprise the order Trogoniformes, are beautiful, brightly colored birds. The male plumage often includes vivid shades of red, pink, orange, or yellow on the breast and belly; some are a bold green. These hues contrast sharply with the glossy colors of the throat and neck. The square tail has a black-and-white design. The female's plumage is generally more subdued.

These tree-dwelling birds inhabit tropical areas around the world. Their stout, heavy bodies range from 9 to 14 inches (22.5 to 35 centimeters) in length. They have a long tail; short, rounded wings; and a short, broad, and curved beak. The two inner toes on the trogon's feet are turned backward. Most species feed on fruits and large insects.

Most trogons excavate nests in soft, decaying wood, although some nest in termite mounds or wasp nests. The female usually lays two or three eggs, which take 17 to 19 days to hatch. The parents share the tasks of incubation and caring for the young.

By far, the most-spectacular-looking trogon is the resplendent quetzal, *Pharomachrus mocinno*, which inhabits the mountain forests of Central America. It is colored in brilliant shades of green, blue, and crimson, and has extravagant tail feathers. The quetzal is the national bird of Guatemala and was long considered sacred by the Aztecs and other ancient civilizations of Central America.

KINGFISHERS AND THEIR KIN

Members of the order Coraciiformes are noted for their long tails, strong beaks, and plume crests. The three front toes on each foot are partially joined. The order includes kingfishers, hornbills, bee-eaters, todies, motmots, rollers, and hoopoes.

The magnificent trailing feathers of the male quetzal (above) may extend well beyond the bird's body; the female has only a short train.

Kingfishers

The kingfisher family, Alcedinidae, contains 250 species and subspecies. Only 11 of these brilliantly colored bird species are found in the Americas; most occur in the Malay Archipelago and New Guinea.

The kingfisher is readily identified by its characteristic top-heavy appearance. It has a large, crested head; heavy body; short tail; long, straight bill; and feeble feet, with the second and third toes united. The most-common colors are metallic greens and blues, satiny whites, russets, and reds. The males and females are very similar in appearance; sometimes the females may even have brighter plumage than the males.

The Alcedinidae are divided into three natural groups: kingfishers, water kingfishers, and tree kingfishers. The kingfishers and tree kingfishers live in woodlands, open country, and gardens, where they feed on insects, snails, frogs, lizards, and occasionally young birds and mammals. The water kingfishers are found near streams and lakeshores, where they subsist almost entirely on fish and other water creatures.

All the New World kingfishers are fish-catching birds that prefer freshwater. They live on the seacoast only where there are estuaries.

The water kingfisher stakes out a fishing territory along the edge of a stream or lake and boldly defends it against other avian trespassers. The bird's call, a harsh, penetrating rattle, is often heard as it fishes. Sometimes the kingfisher sits patiently on an overhanging branch and waits for fish to swim past. Other times, it flies over the water until it sees a fish near the surface. Once the prey is sighted, the kingfisher makes a rapid, head-foremost plunge with closed wings, and the fish is grasped or speared with the bird's sharp bill. When the kingfisher returns to its perch, it beats the fish against a branch to kill it. Then, juggling its prey about, the bird swallows it headfirst. The kingfisher can swallow surprisingly large fish, spitting up any indigestible bones and scales in the form of pellets.

The water kingfisher nests in a hole that it digs, using its bill as a shovel and its feet as rakes. It begins by building a long tunnel into a sandy bank. At the end of the tunnel, the bird digs out a rounded chamber in which it lays from five to eight white eggs.

The belted kingfisher (*Ceryle alcyon*), the most-common North American species, is about 13 inches (33 centimeters) long, with grayish-blue upperparts and a band across its chest. Its wings are tipped with white, and its tail is banded in the same color. The white of its underparts extends around its neck in a broad collar. This species is found from the Arctic to the Gulf of Mexico, where it winters.

The common kingfisher of Europe and Asia (*Alcedo atthis*) displays habits much like those of the American species, although it is a substantially smaller bird—approximately 7 inches (17.5 centimeters) long, and has more brilliantly colored plumage—bright blue on top and a rusty orange-red underneath. Many charming legends tell of this kingfisher, or halcyon, as the ancient Greeks called it. It was believed that the bird built a floating nest of fish bones upon the sea, and that during its two-week brooding period, or "halcyon days," the god of winds kept the waters calm and peaceful.

The largest and most unusual kingfisher is the kookaburra (*Dacelo gigas*), known also by the less elegant moniker "Australian laughing jackass." This brown and grayish-white, 20-inch (50-centimeter)-long bird is noted for its discordant, abrupt cry, or laugh. The kookaburra feeds on crabs, reptiles, rats, and young birds.

Other Representative Species

Motmots. Motmots are solitary forest dwellers that occur in the Western Hemisphere from Mexico to Argentina, although primarily in the northern part of this range. They feed on fruits and insects. The plumage is boldly colored, especially around the head. The motmot has a serrated bill; short, rounded wings; and a tail with long central feathers.

Motmots use their bills to dig a nesting tunnel in a bank of soft earth. Most species lay three or four eggs, which take up to a month to hatch. The parents share incubation duties.

Hornbills. These Old World birds inhabit dry wooded savannas and tropical forests in Africa and Asia. They eat mainly fruits, although some also feed on insects, lizards, and small mammals.

A hornbill is distinguished by its huge bill, which is usually topped by an equally large—and sometimes larger—boldly colored casque, a helmetlike, usually hollow structure.

Hornbills nest in tree holes. After the female settles into the nest, the male closes up the opening to the outside with mud and other materials until only a hole large enough for the female's beak to emerge remains. During the entire period of incubation—some 30 to 50 days—the female is fed through this hole by her mate. After the eggs hatch, the female remains with the chicks in the "predator proof" nest—perhaps another 30 to 50 days. Only when the young are able to fly on their own is the wall finally broken down.

WOODPECKERS AND THEIR KIN

The woodpeckers, toucans, honeyguides, jacamars, barbets, and puffbirds make up the order Piciformes. All members of this order have feet with two toes pointing forward and two pointing backward—creating an effective pincer for grasping the bark of trees. The wings are usually rounded. The feathers are stiff and brightly colored; males and females have different-colored plumage.

These tree dwellers inhabit tropical and temperate woodlands and forests throughout the world, with the exception of Australia, New Zealand, and the island of Madagascar.

The largest species of toucans have black plumage offset by brightly colored throats. The most notable feature of any toucan is, of course, the enormous bill.

Woodpeckers

Woodpeckers (family Picidae) dwell not only in forests and woodlands, but also in city parks and rural areas. The North American woodpeckers known as flickers are often seen on lawns and in gardens, diligently searching for ants and grasshoppers.

As a rule, woodpeckers are solitary birds. Family groups break up and go their separate ways after the young are able to care for themselves. The Picidae do not migrate great distances as do many other species of birds.

Woodpeckers are highly specialized for tree-climbing and grub-hunting activities. Their strong feet are equipped with sharp, curved claws. The stiff tail feathers end in spines that, when pressed against the ridges in a tree's bark, help to prop the bird as it digs for grubs or excavates a nesting site.

The woodpecker has a large head and a short, powerful neck, adaptations that enable the bird to deliver rapid and forceful blows with its stout beak. This beak, with its chisel-shaped tip, is an effective woodcutting tool. With it, the bird penetrates the bark and wood of trees, where wood-boring grubs, hibernating insects, and insect eggs are to be found. Once a small hole is made, the woodpecker's long and slender tongue dislodges the insect prey. The tip of the tongue is usually pointed, barbed, and covered with an adhesive secretion.

These birds produce harsh and rather unmusical notes. During the mating season, the males display acrobatic courting dances in flight and replace the mating call with the characteristic woodpecker "tattoo."

All woodpeckers obtain food by drilling holes in the bark of trees and extracting insects. Some species, like the red-cockaded woodpecker (left), are endangered.

Woodpeckers have remarkably uniform nesting habits. They drill a small hole in a tree and then lay their eggs on the chips in the bottom of the cavity. The hole is drilled into the trunk for a short distance and then dips down, sometimes for 1.5 feet (0.4 meter). It is enlarged at the bottom and covered with chips to prevent the eggs from rolling about. The various species lay from 2 to 12 glossy, white, and unspotted eggs that hatch in about two weeks. Most woodpeckers excavate new nesting cavities each year, with both male and female participating.

Sapsuckers

The North American woodpeckers known as sapsuckers, genus *Sphyrapicus*, derive their name from the way they eat one of their favorite foods: tree sap. Typically, one bird taps several trees in various places and then makes the rounds each day. The sapsucker's tongue is brushlike at the end instead of covered with barbs, a modification for collecting sap.

Surprisingly, sap is not the main part of the sapsucker's diet. The bird is primarily an insect eater. The sap holes serve, among other things, to attract insects, on which sapsuckers feast when making their sap-collecting rounds.

Piculets

Piculets—the smallest woodpeckers—range in length from 3 to 4 inches (7.5 to 10 centimeters), and usually lack the pointed, stiff tail feathers found on other woodpeckers. These species live in South America, Africa, and Asia.

Toucans

The outstanding body structure of a toucan is its bill—highly specialized, very colorful, and several times as large as the bird's head! The bill—filled with air chambers—is surprisingly light; it is nonetheless very strong.

These birds range in length from 12 to 24 inches (30 to 60 centimeters); in some species, more than half of this length is taken up by the bill. The plumage, mainly black or green, has patches of vivid colors on the head and neck.

The 37 species of these noisy, gregarious birds live in tropical forests from Mexico south to Argentina, sometimes as much as 1 mile (1.6 kilometers) above sea level. Toucans feed mainly on fruits, although they will also eat insects—and even the eggs and young of other birds.

FLIGHTLESS BIRDS

To many people, the defining characteristic of a bird is its ability to fly. And yet there exist, scattered in varying numbers in the far-flung corners of the world, several dozen species of birds that have lost this ability. These so-called flightless birds constitute less than 1 percent of the avian world, but, tragically, represent approximately one-third of the 75 or so bird species that have met extinction during the past 400 years.

Most flightless birds gradually lost their power of flight as they adapted to life on land in a habitat free of predators. Often this worked well for the birds until humans arrived. Then, for an ungainly flightless bird such as the dodo, whose habitat was limited to a few Indian Ocean islands, extinction came quickly. A particularly swift extinction befell the only known flightless songbird, the Stephen Island wren. These tiny creatures, discovered in 1894 by a lighthouse keeper, were, within a matter of months, wiped out by the lighthouse keeper's pet cat.

Some flightless birds barely hold on at the brink of extinction. The kakapo (*Strigops habroptilus*), or owl parrot, is a flightless species whose 50 or so survivors are native to Stewart Island, New Zealand. These nocturnal creatures—the largest parrots on Earth—subsist on ferns and fungi. About 100 or so members of another species, the brilliantly colored takahes, survive in the remote alpine meadows of New Zealand.

The foregoing discussion is not meant to imply that all flightless birds are defenseless. Ostriches, rheas, and emus are all famous for their superb running ability and the ruthlessness with which they kick and claw their enemies. Others, such as the penguins, can outswim most predators. The plumage of most forest-dwelling flightless species helps these creatures blend in with their natural surroundings.

A number of bird orders have representatives that do not fly. The extinct dodo, for instance, is a form of pigeon. The flightless cormorant is the largest member of an aquatic family of birds whose other representatives can—and do— fly. Generally, however, the

To characterize a bird as flightless seems contradictory. Nevertheless, about 75 species of birds lack the ability to fly, including the flightless cormorant (above), which has only stunted wings. The kakapo (left) is a flightless species of parrot.

A small population of ground-dwelling takahes—flightless but brightly colored members of the rail family—survives in the remote alpine meadows of New Zealand.

term "flightless birds" refers to members of six orders: Struthioniformes, the ostriches; Rheae, the rheas; Casuarii, the cassowaries and emus; Apteryges, the kiwis; Tinamiformes, the tinamous; and Sphenisciformes, the penguins.

THE OSTRICH

Several million years ago, about half a dozen species of ostriches were distributed through the continents of Africa, Asia, and Europe. Today the only surviving species, *Struthio camelus*, lives in Africa, south of the Sahara, typically in dry savanna or brushland. The birds usually feed in groups of 6 to 10, although they occasionally gather in bands of 50 or more. Ostriches often associate with antelope, zebras, and other grazing mammals. The two groups have a mutually beneficial relationship: the grazing animals disturb small rodents, lizards, and insects, which are then eaten by the ostriches; the tall, sharp-eyed ostriches can spot an enemy a long way off, and warn the mammals of danger.

Ostriches are indeed tall and are, in fact, the largest living birds. A male may stand 10 feet (3 meters) high and weigh more than 330 pounds (150 kilograms). The ostrich has a number of adaptations that compensate for its inability to fly. For example, each of its feet is equipped with two clawed toes of very unequal size. This configuration gives the foot greater strength and thrust, which is useful to an animal adapted to a walking and running way of life. And speaking of running, an ostrich can sustain 30 miles (50 kilometers) per hour for 15 minutes or more, and can achieve 43 miles (70 kilometers) per hour for short bursts.

The male has black body plumage with white tail feathers and wing quills. The smaller females are dusky gray in color. In both sexes, the heads and long necks are sparsely covered with down. Alone among birds, ostriches eliminate liquid and solid waste separately.

A flock of ostriches, the largest living birds, gallops across the sandy plains of Africa. Although their wings are useless for flight, ostriches can maintain a steady pace for an extended period, thanks to their powerful legs.

Single-wattled cassowaries (left) come together only for breeding. Below, a well-camouflaged emu tends to his nest, which holds eggs from several hens. An interesting characteristic of both of these flightless species is that the males alone incubate the eggs.

Ostriches are nomadic animals, wandering to wherever food is available. They are indiscriminate eaters. In addition to invertebrates and small vertebrates, they consume all sorts of plant material—and will even gulp down such shiny objects as bottle tops. Ostriches can go long periods without water.

Ostriches are polygamous. Typically, a male has a harem of three to five mates. The females in the harem generally lay their eggs—usually six to eight apiece—in a common, shallow, sandy depression in the ground scraped out by the male. Although an ostrich egg is comparatively small in relationship to the bird's size, the eggs are nevertheless the largest produced by any bird. A single ostrich egg may weigh more than 3.5 pounds (1.6 kilograms)—as much as 20 or 24 chicken eggs! The females in a harem incubate the eggs during the day; the male sits on them at night. The eggs take about six weeks to hatch.

Such a large clutch of eggs would make a grand meal for predators such as vultures and jackals. But any ostrich-nest raider must first deal with the muscular ostrich legs, which can deliver a maiming kick, and the toenails, which can disembowel a jackal.

RHEAS

These birds—represented by two species in South America—are similar to, but much smaller than, the ostrich. The greater rhea, *Rhea americana*, may stand 5.6 feet (1.7 meters) and weigh 55 pounds (25 kilograms). This dull-gray bird lives on the grassy plains of Brazil and Argentina—an ever-shrinking habitat. A second, smaller species—Darwin's rhea, *Pterocnemia pennata*—has brownish, white-spotted plumage, and lives in the foothills of the Andes.

Rheas—with their long, powerful legs and three-toed feet—are swift runners and surprisingly good swimmers. Like ostriches, rheas roam in groups for most of the year. When the breeding season begins, the males fight each other for control of a harem. After the victorious male acquires his harem, he constructs a nest—essentially a shallow lined pit in the ground. After mating, the male leads the female to the nest, where she lays her egg. Once all the eggs of the harem members are together in the common nest, the male assumes full incubation duties. The eggs hatch after about 40 days. As soon as they are able, the young rheas follow the male parent in search of food. The father tends to the young brood for about six weeks.

The brown-spotted kiwi (below), a nocturnal flightless bird native to New Zealand, relies on its probing bill and sense of smell to find food on the forest floor.

CASSOWARIES AND EMUS

Like their flightless cousins, cassowaries and emus are swift runners, an ability they use to avoid most enemies. When a direct confrontation does occur, these birds are by no means helpless. They can be very aggressive creatures, delivering vicious kicks and inflicting wounds with their long, sharp claws.

These birds are distinguished by their hair-like feathers. Each feather has two shafts, and does not interlock with other feathers, as is the case in most birds.

Cassowaries inhabit dense rain forests in northern Australia, New Guinea, and nearby islands. There are three species, all members of the genus *Casuarius*.

These birds live in pairs or small family groups. The male incubates the three to six large eggs and also takes care of the young.

The largest and most common species, the double-wattled cassowary, *Casuarius casuarius*, may stand more than 5 feet (1.5 meters). Its black, glossy plumage has a hairlike appearance; its blue neck and head lack feathers altogether. Two red wattles, or folds of loose skin, hang from the neck. Atop the head is a flat, horny structure that looks like a tall crown; this structure, called a casque, may be 6 inches (15 centimeters) high. When the bird dashes through the forest, the casque helps to deflect obstacles that might otherwise cause injury.

The emu, *Dromaius novaehollandiae*, is native only to Australia, where it holds the distinction of being that continent's largest bird. Emus, typically a drab, brownish-gray color, grow to a height of 5 to 6 feet (1.5 to 1.8 meters) and weigh up to 120 pounds (55 kilograms). Female emus are larger than the males.

Emus live in a variety of environments, from scrubland to rain forest. This adaptability has led to their exportation to the United States and other

Penguins gather in large colonies to breed and to raise their young. These flightless birds use their wings to propel them through the water.

countries, where they are raised on ranches for their meat. Emus feed mainly on plant matter, although they eat insects as well.

Emus breed in the winter. The female lays 8 to 10 dark green eggs in a nest on the open ground, usually beneath a tree. The male incubates the eggs and cares for the young.

KIWIS

Kiwis live in the damp forests of New Zealand. The three species of kiwis, all in the genus *Apteryx*, each have grayish or reddish-brown plumage and a long, slender bill well adapted for probing the soil in search of insects and their larvae, worms, snails, and other small animals that comprise their diet. The nostrils of the kiwi are located at the tip of the bill, and the sense of smell seems to be highly developed. The eyes are small and weak, which perhaps explains the bird's nocturnal habits. The kiwi has long, muscular legs, making it a swift runner. Its wings are very tiny—only 2 inches (5 centimeters) long—and the bird lacks a tail.

Kiwis range from 14 to 22 inches (35 to 55 centimeters) in length. They have heavy claws, which they use to excavate a nest on the forest floor. Female kiwis lay the heaviest eggs, relative to their size, of any bird: a single egg can be as much as one-quarter the weight of the entire bird! Most kiwis lay only one egg, which the male incubates for 75 to 80 days.

TINAMOUS

The 50 or so species of tinamous live in a variety of habitats from southern Mexico to the tip of South America. The tinamou can fly, but only clumsily, and then—thanks to its short, rounded wings—for just very short distances.

Tinamous have compact bodies ranging from 8 to 20 inches (20 to 50 centimeters) long; all species have long necks, short tails, and strong legs. The patterned brown and gray plumage blends in well with the background.

These are solitary birds, except during the breeding season, when they are polygamous. The males alone incubate the 1 to 10 eggs and care for the young.

PENGUINS

The 18 species of penguins all belong to the order Sphenisciformes, a term derived from the Greek word *spheniskos*, which means "small wedge"—a reference to these birds' highly specialized flippers. These flippers are used by the penguin to propel itself underwater at speeds of 25 miles (40 kilometers) per hour or more. Penguins have a number of other adaptations to marine life: their bodies are streamlined; their feet are webbed; and their feathers form a dense, waterproof insulation.

Penguins live in the Antarctic and on islands as far north as the Peruvian coast. The largest species, *Aptenodytes forsteri*, the emperor penguin, is more than 3 feet (1 meter) tall and weighs 77 pounds (35 kilograms). It lives and breeds on the Antarctic ice, never setting foot on dry land. The smallest penguin, *Eudyptula minor*, the little blue penguin of Australia, is about 16 inches (40 centimeters) tall.

Most penguins are monogamous, remaining with their mates throughout their long lives. They breed in colonies that may contain many thousands of birds. Most species lay two or three eggs. The parents share the tasks of building the nest, incubating the eggs, and caring for the young. During the nesting period, most species undergo a long period of starvation, living off fat reserves in their bodies. During other times of the year, the birds feed primarily on fish, squid, and shrimp.

BIRDS OF PREY

Few sights in nature can match the grandeur of a bird of prey on the hunt. First, from high in the sky, the bird flies in wide circles. Then its extraordinary vision and hearing discern an almost imperceptible movement on the ground far below. In seconds, the bird silently swoops down on its victim and makes the kill.

Eagles, vultures, and owls are birds of prey—a group of animals that includes some of the most powerful fliers and fiercest hunters, for their size, in the entire Animal Kingdom. They are graceful on the wing and utterly ruthless when unwary prey reveals itself.

Unlike most animals, the birds of prey are grouped together based on their similarity in habits, rather than on their physical similarities. Zoologists recognize two orders of birds of prey: Falconiformes, those that hunt by day, and Strigiformes, those that hunt by night. The diurnal (daytime) hunters include vultures, hawks, eagles, kites, falcons, and ospreys. The nocturnal (nighttime) hunters include most species of owls.

A small rodent has little chance of escape once a snowy owl (above) or other bird of prey spots it. Within seconds, the bird will seize its victim with its razor-sharp talons and kill it.

GENERAL CHARACTERISTICS

All birds of prey—or *raptors*, as they are often called—have stout, hooked, wavy-edged beaks with a soft area, called the *cere*, at the base. Most have three toes set forward and one directed backward. The owls and ospreys have a reversible outer toe—that is, it can be turned either to the front or to the rear.

Birds of prey range in size from the condor, which measures over 10 feet (3 meters) from wing tip to wing tip, to the pygmy falcon of India, scarcely larger than a sparrow. Female birds of prey tend to be larger than males.

Long, well-curved, sharp *talons* characterize all birds of prey except the vultures. With such truly formidable weapons, these birds seize and dispatch their victims before ripping the prey to pieces with their hooked beaks. Vultures live on carrion (remains of dead animals) and therefore do not need talons.

The eyes of the diurnal raptors are placed at the sides of the head so that the two eyes never look in the same direction. In owls, the eyes, which are larger than those of the other birds of prey, are set in front of the rather flat face, so that both look together in the same direction. The owl, therefore, has binocular vision, while the other birds must survey an object first with one eye, then with the other.

The eyesight of birds of prey is remarkably keen. From more than 300 feet (90 meters) overhead, these creatures scan the ground, their extraordinary vision capable of spotting the tiniest mouse or lizard. In the instant required for the birds to drop from that height and pounce on their victims, their eyes are able to change focus quickly enough to maintain constant sight of the prey.

Soft shades of brown and gray characterize the plumage of most raptors, although striking patterns of blue and reddish brown occur in some species. A few species of eagles and vultures have ornamental crests. Young hawks are marked on the underparts with perpendicular stripes, which become horizontal (adult markings) after the first molt. It is easier to distinguish between species by size or shape than by color. Eye color varies according to the family, genus, or species. It may be yellow, ruby red, gray, or brown. The eye color may also vary according to the bird's sex or age.

Perhaps the most outstanding raptor characteristic is their fearlessness and truculence. The goshawk will courageously attack any person coming near its nest. The European sparrow hawk, although hardly 1 foot (30 centimeters) in length, will fall upon any other creature in the air, no matter how large. Many hawks will attack animals as large as themselves, or even larger.

The voices of the diurnal preying birds are harsh, discordant screams. The short-winged species that lie in wait for their prey are usually silent. Vultures merely hiss. The other raptors call frequently. The owl's voice is perhaps best described as bloodcurdling—at least to small animals!

All birds of prey are exclusively carnivorous. Most kill their food; a few, the scavenger species, feed on decaying animal matter. The larger birds eat other birds and small mammals. Small ones feast on insects, mice, frogs, lizards, and snakes. Only the short-winged hawks and occasionally the marsh hawks are destructive to game birds and domestic birds.

Certain birds of prey, especially ospreys and eagles, repair and use the same nest year after year. A number of hawks and eagles mate for life, but are quick to find another mate if the old one dies. The other raptors, however, find a new mate and build a new nest each year. Many construct nests of sticks and branches high up in trees. Some nest on cliffs and high ledges, or on the ground in prairie or marshland. All birds of prey lay strong, heavy-shelled eggs with granular surfaces.

DIURNAL BIRDS OF PREY

The order Falconiformes is made up of five families. The family Cathartidae contains the New World vultures. The family Accipitridae includes the Old World vultures, hawks, eagles, and kites. The falcons are placed in the family Falconidae. The osprey by itself makes up the

Because it feeds almost exclusively on carrion (the remains of dead animals), the vulture's feet are adapted for standing rather than for seizing.

A California condor chick, hatched in captivity, is fed and "raised" by a condor puppet (right). Scientists contend that rearing the chick this way reduces its dependence on humans. Many such birds have been raised to adulthood and released into the wild (below).

family Pandionidnae. The secretary bird of Africa is the lone species in its family, the Sagittariidae; it is primarily a predator of snakes.

Vultures

The vulture is a heavy bird—weighing 22 pounds (10 kilograms) or more—with weak legs, feet adapted for standing or walking, and a long middle toe that helps balance its ungainly body. It feeds almost exclusively on dead animals—a diet made possible by the bird's immunity to the poisons produced in decaying flesh.

Vultures seek food just about everywhere. In the United States, they have even learned to patrol highways in search of roadkill! With their remarkable eyesight, they can detect the smallest dead animal from dizzying heights. When a vulture swoops down on a find, its descent is seen by others for miles around; within minutes, a flock has gathered. After eating, the birds are often too full to fly, making them particularly vulnerable to capture.

Vultures lay several spotted eggs on the ground, under a log, in a hollow tree, or in a cave. The young—noisy little creatures covered with whitish down—are dependent on their parents for quite some time.

There are six species of New World vultures and 14 species of the Old World variety.

The turkey vulture, *Cathartes aura,* is the most widely distributed of the New World species, with a range extending from Canada to the southern part of South America. This creature has a distinctive reddish head, neck, and wings. The Andean condor, *Vultur gryphus,* one of the largest living birds, has a wingspan stretching 10 feet (3 meters); it lives in South America. The gravely endangered Californian condor (*Gymnogyps californianus*) is just slightly smaller than its Andean cousin. A well-publicized captive-breeding program has greatly increased the species' population, but it has met with mixed results in returning these birds safely to the wild.

True Hawks and Eagles

Broad-winged hawks. The broad-winged, fan-tailed hawks include the red-shouldered, red-tailed, broad-winged, Harris', Swainson's, and rough-legged hawks, as well as the bald and golden eagles. With wings extended and tails spread, these birds circle high overhead.

In general, broad-winged hawks live in wooded areas but hunt in open fields. Most feed mainly on small rodents and larger insects, and thus are considered beneficial to humans.

These hawks are readily distinguished by the dark marking on their underparts. The undersurface of the broad-winged hawk's wings is pure white with the exception of a dark tip formed by the dark first primary feathers. The undersurface of the red-shouldered hawk's wings is barred but lacks distinct black patches. The red-tailed hawk has a crescentlike black patch at the second joint of the wing.

Eagles are usually recognized by their large size. From ancient times, the eagle has been regarded as a symbol of bold strength and courageous character. The American bald eagle, *Haliaeetus leucocephalus*, was chosen as the national bird of the United States because of its majestic appearance rather than for its habits. This raptor feeds mainly on fish cast up by the waves or on those that it steals from an osprey. In the adult, the head and tail are white; they are brown in the nestlings. The young require four years to develop adult plumage.

Young bald eagles are very similar to the dark brown golden eagles except in the feathering of the legs. The lower leg of the bald eagle is bare. That of the golden eagle is feathered all the way to the toes.

The golden eagle, *Aquila chrysaetos*, lives in mountainous areas throughout the Northern Hemisphere. Compared to its bald cousin, the golden eagle is a much more active predator. Overhunting by humans has greatly diminished the number of both golden eagles and bald eagles.

Goshawks or short-winged hawks. These birds, genus *Accipiter*, include three common North American species: the sharp-shinned hawk, Cooper's hawk, and the goshawk. Short-winged hawks typically lie in wait and then suddenly burst forth with great speed from a stationary position and seize their prey. These three species are responsible for most of the killing of poultry and game birds for which the hawk family as a whole is blamed. The sharp-shinned hawk itself has sometimes been hunted for food by people, but this bird is now protected by law.

A short-winged hawk seldom wheels aloft in search of food. Instead, it flies swiftly from place to place, flapping its wings rapidly for a few seconds and then gliding noiselessly, ready to drop like an arrow among a flock of poultry. It seizes the victim in its talons and leaves quickly. After the hawk reaches some favored branch or log, it settles down to the mundane task of plucking its prey before eating it.

Kites and Marsh Hawks

The kites are the lightest and most graceful of the hawks, characteristics perhaps best exemplified by the New World's swallow-tailed kite, *Elanoides forficatus*. This 18-inch (45-centimeter)-long, strikingly marked white and black bird has a deeply forked tail that lends the creature a decidedly swallowlike appearance. Many a bird-watcher has been moved by the beauty of a troop of these birds as they skim the water like a band of swallows, darting after one another in playful sport, rising abruptly high into the air, then diving, then sailing.

Another species, the Everglade kite, *Rostrhamus sociabilis*, which ranges from Florida south to Argentina, depends entirely on a certain large freshwater snail for its food supply. Its bill, adapted to draw the snail from its shell, is very long and slender.

The hen harrier or marsh hawk, *Circus cyaneus*, lives in Eurasia and North America. In spite of its light body and long wings, it does not resemble its fellow kites. Except during migration, this bird is usually found near marshes or feeding in open fields where mice are abundant.

The bald eagle has staged a stunning comeback from the brink of extinction, thanks largely to intensive conservation programs. In 2007, the bird was removed from the endangered-species list.

The marsh hawk nests on the ground, usually in the marshes but sometimes by stumps in pastures, and lays from five to seven pure-white eggs. During the mating season, the male conducts curious courtship rituals in the air, sometimes plunging somersault-style from high altitudes or performing dramatic "loop-the-loops" on an angular course across the marsh.

Ospreys

The osprey, *Pandion haliaetus*, is abundant along seacoasts, but also is found inland near most large bodies of water from the tropics to the Arctic Circle. With slight variations, it occurs all over the world. This bird of prey is often confused with the bald eagle, owing to their similar wingspans and the large white areas on their heads. Unlike the eagle, however, the osprey has white underparts and a dark tail.

The osprey sometimes nests in small colonies where food is abundant and protection is afforded. It builds an enormous nest of sticks, usually atop a broken tree, although occasionally on the ground.

A favorite alternate name for the osprey is "fish hawk," an appropriate moniker in view of the bird's fish-only diet. Typically, an osprey hovers over the surface of a body of water until it locates its next meal. Then, with a plunge—often from a substantial height—the osprey

snatches up the fish with its talons. The fish might weigh up to 4.5 pounds (2 kilograms)!

Falcons

The approximately 50 known species of falcons (family Falconidae) have pointed wings adapted to give them great speed rather than soaring ability. Found on all continents except Antarctica, falcons pursue and strike their prey in full flight. Some species of these powerful birds have been tamed and trained to assist humans on the hunt (see the box on page 419).

A common group of falcons are the kestrels (genus *Falco*), which are worldwide in distribution. The American kestrel *(F. sparverius)* is sometimes called the sparrow hawk because it eats small birds—although it prefers rodents and insects.

Also classified in Falconidae are the nine species of caracaras, carrion-eating birds that inhabit semiarid regions of the southwestern United States, Mexico, and Central and South America. Caracaras sometimes scavenge in the company of vultures, which they dominate.

NOCTURNAL BIRDS OF PREY

Unlike the other birds of prey, the owl usually hunts at night. This hardy bird can adapt to desert, mountainous, or swampy terrain. In most cases, it migrates only short distances. At least one of the roughly 300 species of owls can be found in each and every country in the world.

Owls range from small, rather mild-mannered 6-inch (15-centimeter)-long insect eaters to fierce raptors more than 2 feet (60 centimeters) long. The latter are even capable of taking over an eagle's nest!

Throughout recorded history, the owl has been the object of superstition, thanks perhaps to the aura of mystery that surrounds a bird that hides during the day and emerges only at night. Not until relatively modern times did people realize that when an

Volunteers across the United States have erected special nesting boxes to accommodate kestrels (left), North America's smallest and most common falcon.

The Fine Art of Falconry

Birds of prey are the very emblem of airborne freedom, so it may seem surprising that they can be domesticated and taught to hunt for the pleasure and benefit of humans. Yet the sport of hunting hare, pheasant, herons, partridge, and other small animals with falcons and other birds of prey dates back to at least the 8th century B.C., in Assyria. Falconry, also known as hawking, was practiced for centuries in China, Persia, and Egypt before it made its way to Europe in the Middle Ages, where the sport enjoyed great popularity for many centuries.

Only a dozen or so species of falcons and hawks are suitable for falconry. The most desirable is the peregrine falcon, a fast and powerful hunter that can be readily trained. The saker falcon is popular among Middle Eastern falconers, as is the arctic gyrfalcon, which is so prized that royal families in the Middle East are reported to have spent up to $100,000 for a healthy specimen. Among the short-winged hawks, the goshawk and the European sparrow hawk are frequently used.

Most birds used by falconers are taken from their nests when they are fledged but are too young to fly. Migrating birds are also captured. Birds are *hacked*, or prepared for training, by regular hand-feeding with fresh meat. Once a falcon or hawk begins responding to training, it is taught to capture meat attached to a bird's wing and swung on a cord. Eventually the bird is trained to accept a hood over its head, to stand motionless on a falconer's wrist, and to fly at prey. Once the prey is killed, the bird stands over it but does not eat it.

Traditionally, falconry was a sport of royalty and the nobility. The expense and time involved in training the birds ensured that it would be enjoyed primarily by the wealthy. Although it declined in popularity in the 17th century, a few falconers continue to practice this ancient sport in the United States, Europe, and Asia.

Jerry Dennis

Few can afford the time and expense required to excel at the ancient sport of falconry. Only after much training will a falcon accept a hood over its eyes (above).

owl came nearby, it was to rid the barn or garden of mice and rats.

General Characteristics

Coloration. Owls that live in woodlands have predominantly brown and gray plumage, frequently streaked, mottled, and barred in shades that imitate the colors of dead wood and bark. Such hues effectively hide the birds during the day, when they conceal themselves in hollow trees or perch on branches close to the trunk. On their heads, many species bear tufts of feathers, called horns or ears, which break up the outline and make the protective coloration even more effective.

No owl has brilliantly colored plumage, although some tend away from the brown and gray. The short-eared owl, a dweller of open marshes, is pale buff in color and finely streaked with brown, which makes it inconspicuous in the dead and tangled low vegetation. The burrowing owl has dull, sandy-colored feathers. The plumage of the snowy owl of the Arctic is almost entirely white.

Eyes. An owl's eyes are set immovably in their sockets and directed toward the front. In order to look at a particular object, therefore, an owl must move its entire head, and not simply turn its eyes toward the object.

The eyes of owls are very large. The size of the retina is further increased by an appendage, called the *pecten*, situated in the middle of the eyeball. Thus equipped, the eye is able to register the faintest light rays, a necessity for birds that hunt primarily during the night.

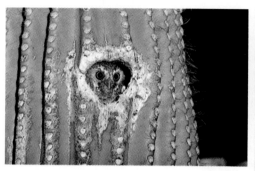

Owls have adapted to a variety of habitats. The tiny elf owl (above) peeks out from within a saguaro cactus, where it makes its home. Saw-whet owls (right) find food and shelter among groves of aspen trees.

Owls can also see very well during the day. Certain species hunt regularly by day, and some owls emerge occasionally, particularly if they have young to feed. The snowy owl lives most of the year in the Arctic, where the days are exceedingly long during the summer. This species is well adapted to daylight hunting.

Unlike most birds, owls have well-developed eyelashes. When the owl closes its eye, the upper eyelid moves downward. In other birds, the lower eyelid moves upward.

Ears. The acuity of owl vision is matched by a very keen sense of hearing. The owl is the only bird with an external ear like that of a mammal. The ear is concealed and partly protected behind the radiating feathers of the bird's facial disk. In some species, a funnel-like arrangement of feathers serves as a sort of ear trumpet. An owl can hear even the slightest rustle in the leaves or grass, then can swoop down on its prey noiselessly. Even in total darkness, the owl can locate its prey by sound.

Feet. Owls differ from all the birds of prey (except the osprey) in the arrangement of the toes. The outer toe may be turned forward, backward, or outward. When it is turned back in perching, the owl achieves a much stronger grip. This outer toe is also turned back when the bird is about to strike its prey, thus making its foot a most efficient weapon.

Feathers. The feathers—especially the wing feathers—are soft and fringed with down, making these birds very silent fliers. North American Indians dubbed the owl "hush wings" for its quiet flight.

Diet. Small nocturnal animals—especially small rodents—form the bulk of the owl's diet. Some species also feed on insects, snails, frogs, or larger animals. The great horned owl is the only species that preys on poultry to any extent. A fierce, bold hunter, it will also attack skunks, turkeys, and domestic cats.

The rest of the owls are very beneficial to humans through their role of keeping in check the population of small rodents. The meadow mouse, for example, which feasts on stored grain and attacks the bark of young fruit trees, has from five to eight young in a litter and from three to six litters per year. If their numbers increased unchecked, meadow mice could do untold harm. It is fortunate indeed that the mice are sought so greedily by owls.

The roving habits of some owls make them particularly efficient protectors of grain crops. When, for example, meadow or field mice become abundant in a locality, a group of short-eared owls often follows. The owls remain in the area, nesting if need be, until the rodents once again become scarce.

Reproductive Activities

Unlike many birds of prey, most owls do not build a nest; instead, they lay their eggs in cavities of trees and other convenient places, or they use the old nests of crows, hawks, and even squirrels. A few species, notably the screech owl and the short-eared owl, hastily build crude nests on the ground.

Owls breed very early. There are generally three to five white or whitish spherical eggs per single clutch, or brood. Incubation begins when the first egg is laid. Sometimes both parents sit on eggs side by side. The first eggs may hatch long before the last.

Newly hatched owlets are thickly covered with down. Almost immediately they display certain instinctive defense reactions. For example, if molested, they fluff out their feathers and either hiss or make clicking sounds with their bills. It takes a comparatively long time for the young bird's flight feathers to develop.

Representative Species

Most owls belong to the family Strigidae. The barn owls are placed in a separate family, the Tytonidae. The distinguishing feature in barn owls is the furcula, or "wishbone," which differs from that of other owls.

There are 10 species of barn owls. An especially widespread species is aptly known as the common barn owl, *Tyto alba*. This 18-inch (45-centimeter)-long bird has a mottled buff and grayish back and speckled underparts. The feathers of the face radiate outward, forming a heart-shaped disk.

A hollow tree, a barn, a silo, a steeple, or even a hole in a riverbank may provide this odd-looking owl with a satisfactory egg-laying site.

The great gray owl, *Strix nebulosa*, an especially handsome although rarely observed member of the family Strigidae, haunts the forests of Canada and Alaska; in winter, it migrates south into the northern part of the United States. It is a large bird—measuring 30 inches (76 centimeters) in length—with grayish-brown plumage.

The great horned owl, *Bubo virginianus*, is a magnificent North American bird some 24 inches (60 centimeters) long with prominent ear tufts about 2 inches (5 centimeters) long. This owl's sooty-brown or dusky-colored feathers are streaked or mottled with grayish white.

The barred owl, *Strix varia*, ranges from southern Canada to Mexico, where it hunts in the deep solitudes of dense forests and forbidding swamps. It is a 20-inch (50-centimeter)-long bird with brown plumage decorated with whitish bars. This species has no ear tufts.

The snowy owl, *Nyctea scandiaca*, is a predominantly white bird (although lightly barred with brown) about 22 to 26 inches (55 to 66 centimeters) in length. It spends the summer on the Arctic tundra, and winters from the Arctic shores southward.

The long-eared owl, *Asio otus*, lives in coniferous forests throughout Europe, Asia, and North America. Although its ear tufts resemble those of the great horned owl, this bird is much smaller and more slender, and lacks the white throat patch of the larger bird.

The short-eared owl, *Asio flammeus*, is found near grassy marshes, pastures, or coastal dunes throughout the Northern Hemisphere and in South America. Groups of these birds spend the day together, usually on the ground (where they nest) or in areas of tangled vegetation.

The most common owl in all of North America is the little screech owl, *Otus asio*, not much larger than a robin, although it is substantially heavier. This bird even survives in large cities—living in the hollows of trees or in crevices around buildings—and feeds on the mice that are virtually everywhere. Individual specimens vary in color from tan to gray to brown regardless of age or sex. The call of the screech owl is really not a screech, but is better described as a low, tremulous whistle.

Perhaps the most widely known owl subspecies in the United States today is the northern spotted owl, *Strix occidentalis caurina*. In the early 1990s, this bird of prey found itself in the center of a controversy between environmentalists, who wished to preserve the owl's old-growth-forest home, and loggers, who make their living harvesting the forests' wood. A 1993 compromise reduced the maximum logging harvest in these forests by nearly 80 percent. In the late 1990s, a new danger threatened the northern spotted owl: interbreeding with the eastern barred owl. Currently, the birds face several other threats to their habitat, including urban and suburban development, water works, and agriculture and mining activities. Debate over conservation efforts remains contentious.

The northern spotted owl has gained a certain degree of celebrity as the focus of a heated controversy between environmentalists and loggers.

WILDFOWL

Quail, grouse, turkeys, and pheasant comprise what are perhaps the four most-familiar types of wildfowl. Populations of these splendid birds and of many of their less-familiar cousins have fluctuated greatly in the past century as habitat destruction and uncontrolled hunting took their toll. Fortunately, conservation efforts in recent years have helped return many (but not all) populations of wildfowl back to sustainable levels, and special programs continue to safeguard a number of species.

The other name for wildfowl—*upland game birds*—has a twofold derivation. These birds are usually found in grasslands and forests (rather than in low-lying marshy areas or at the edge of water); they also rank among the favorite game birds for hunters.

GENERAL CHARACTERISTICS

Wildfowl are mainly ground dwellers. They tend to be rather large birds, with heavy bodies, small heads, and stout, short bills. All are equipped with short, rounded wings that are strong, although the birds do not fly long distances. Their stout legs are moderately long, and the three front toes are often slightly webbed.

Most wildfowl have inconspicuous plumage that blends in with the surroundings. Exceptions include turkeys and pheasant, which have some areas of rich color, and the most

Mating displays reach a dazzling extreme among the peafowl. The peacock's plumage, besides impressing females, tells them that he's a healthy specimen.

spectacularly plumed of all birds: the male peafowl—the famous peacock.

Wildfowl flock together at mating season. Then they go their separate ways, making nests in various natural hiding places on the ground, and laying from 6 to 18 eggs. The young are hatched already covered with down and prepared to care for themselves. Wildfowl have a varied diet depending upon the season. Primary foods include weed seeds, buds, berries, insects, and snails.

Classification

All wildfowl are members of the order Galliformes. The order contains more than 250 species, classified into seven families:

• Family Phasianidae, which includes pheasant, partridge, peafowl, quail, and the domestic chicken;

• Family Tetraonidae, which includes the grouse, ptarmigan, and prairie chickens;

• Family Meleagrididae, which contains the turkeys;

• Family Megapodiidae, which includes mallee fowl, brush turkeys, and other fowl found only in Australia and on nearby islands;

• Family Numididae, which contains the guinea fowl of Africa;

• Family Cracidae, which contains curassows, chachalacas, and guans—forest-dwelling birds found primarily in Central and South America; and

The California quail (above) rarely flies unless alarmed. Unlike other quail, this West Coast species tends to roost in dense trees or shrubs rather than on the ground.

• Family Opisthocomidae (sometimes considered a superfamily by certain ornithologists), which contains only one species, the tropical hoatzin, *Opisthocomus hoazin*.

THE PHEASANT FAMILY

Quail

Scientists have identified approximately 100 species of plump, small to medium-sized, nearly tailless wildfowl as quail. New World species have large, heavy bodies and small heads. Old World quail, belonging to the genus

Fowl Foul-Ups

Much confusion revolves around the correct usage of such common names as "grouse," "partridge," and "quail." These terms are applied to quite different birds in some parts of North America and interchangeably in others. For example, the harlequin quail is also known as the Montezuma quail, massena quail, fool quail, fool hen, and black quail. Similarly, the mountain quail is often called the plumed partridge.

This confusion of names can probably be traced back to the early European settlers in the United States and Canada, the first English-speaking people to name the birds. These men and women often mistook the American birds for similar species native to their homelands. For example, an immigrant who might have been familiar with a certain species of European partridge might well be inclined to call any similar birds he or she saw in the New World by the name of that partridge. In many cases, the bird to which he or she was referring was not a partridge at all, but a turkey, quail, or grouse.

Coturnix, are much smaller than their American cousins—some no larger than sparrows.

All quail bills are invariably stout, short, and convex. The outer edge of the lower mandible is distinctly serrated, or notched, in the New World quail. The Old World quail differs in that the edges of both the upper and lower mandibles are smooth.

The legs and toes of quail are usually scaly and featherless. Occasionally the three front toes are webbed, and the hind toe is elevated. Most American quail lack the tiny nostril feathers that characterize the English quail. Quail wings are normally short, arched, rounded, and quite strong.

In habit and habitat, most quail are strictly ground dwellers. Some favor open and cultivated fields, while others prefer the protection of wooded areas and mountains.

The mating season for quail usually occurs sometime during February. The birds tend to become promiscuous, with the males engaging in very elaborate courtship rituals and even collecting harems. The females lay 10 to 15 eggs in May or June. Both make devoted parents: the female constantly cares for the eggs while the male guards the nest. In some species, when danger approaches, the male has been known to purposely attract attention to himself so as to spare the nest any harm. As with most wildfowl, the quail hatchlings are well developed and, within a matter of hours, are able to forage for their food themselves. Some fly when only a week old.

The best-known North American quail is the northern bobwhite, *Colinus virginianus*, which occurs from southern Canada to Mexico. Other bobwhite species, also of the genus *Colinus*, are common in Mexico and Central America. All bobwhite species have a call that sounds distinctively like their name: "bob-white."

The northern bobwhite enjoys great popularity for several reasons. It has always been a favorite game bird for hunters, and its call is considered by some to be quite musical. This bird is now protected in some parts of the United States because it feeds upon the destructive cotton-boll weevil.

Unlike other quail, the bobwhite is not polygamous. The typical male is a devoted mate and a conscientious father, helping to incubate the eggs and care for the young. It selects a protected area under a fallen branch or in high grass that can be bent to form a roof. The male then scratches out a depression where the female lays eggs and incubates them until they hatch. Bobwhite eggs are the whitest and most pointed of any of the gallinaceous birds.

At the close of the breeding season, the bobwhites gather in large flocks, or *coveys*, which may constitute all the members of one or perhaps two families. The coveys generally tarry in open fields or gardens where food is plentiful, remaining together (unless scattered by hunters) until winter, when they retire to more-wooded areas. At night, the coveys form circles, reminiscent of the wagon-train arrangement of early European settlers in North America. Each bird in the circle stands with its tail pointing toward the center, and its head pointing outward. When the birds are disturbed and take to the air, the circle seems to explode.

The California quail, *Lophortyx californica*, ranges from southwest Oregon to Southern California. This slate-blue bird has a crest of club-shaped feathers that remain erect and curved forward, giving the appearance of a helmet. From this plumed headgear, the California quail derives its other name: the helmet quail. The feathers are bare at the base and swollen at the tips. The male's plumage includes areas of

The conspicuous plumage of the male ring-necked pheasant (above) helps hunters spot the bird on open land. The female has more subdued coloration.

soft grays and warm browns; the female's coloring is considerably more subdued.

The scaled quail, *Callipepia squamata*, lives in semidesert regions of the southwestern United States and Mexico. This bird is predominantly gray in color, although the feathers of the neck and breast are edged with black, giving the appearance of scales—hence its name. The inconspicuous tuft of white feathers on its crown accounts for another of this quail's names: "cottontop."

The common European quail, *Coturnix coturnix*, is a solitary animal except during migration. It lives in pasture and croplands, and is a difficult bird for hunters to flush.

The True Pheasant

The true pheasant are native to continental Asia and the nearby islands. Most of the males are brilliantly colored; the female's plumage is rather dull by comparison. For example, the head and neck of the male ring-necked pheasant (*Phasianus colchicus*) are peacock blue and glossed with green, purple, and bronze metallic reflections; the sides of the head are scarlet. The feathers of its back are orange-brown, with streaks of green, buff, and black; the tail is olive-brown with black bars; and the breast is a glossy copper-brown edged with purplish hues. The female, on the other hand, is a plain brown.

The common pheasant was successfully introduced into England many years ago—according to some accounts, by the Romans. It is still raised there for hunting purposes. The Chinese ring-necked pheasant was introduced into the United States in 1880. However, the well-known ring-necked pheasant now found in the United States is not the same species that was brought over in 1880. Rather, it is a hybrid—a cross between the original Chinese ring-necked variety and the English common pheasant. This hybrid has flourished in the New World.

Pheasant have strong legs with which they can flee to cover quite rapidly. They can fly for short distances, but only with considerable effort, owing to the relative stubbiness of their wings. The tail is certainly the outstanding feature of these birds. One notable species, the great argus pheasant, *Argusianus argus*, of Southeast Asia is about 8.2 feet (2.5 meters) long, of which 6 feet (1.8 meters) is tail!

THE GROUSE FAMILY

The family Tetraonidae may be divided into three distinct groups: the ptarmigan; the grouse proper; and the prairie chickens.

The birds of this family are generally larger than quail, measuring approximately 14 to 20 inches (35 to 50 centimeters) in length, as compared with the approximately 12-inch (30-centimeter) length for quail. Another distinguishing feature is the presence of full leg feathering in most species of grouse, an adaptation for living in areas subject to snowfall. In species of the far north, even the toes are feathered, enabling the birds to walk readily atop the snowpack.

Ptarmigan

The ptarmigan inhabit Arctic and subarctic regions and rocky areas on the peaks of lofty mountain ranges. They are the only birds in the entire gallinaceous order whose plumage changes from one season to another. As is common with animals that spend a large part of their lives in snow-covered areas, the ptarmigan has a pure-white winter coat; this blends admirably with the snowy background, helping to conceal the bird from predators. The summer coat of mottled gray and brown also provides excellent

Alone among the wildfowl, the ptarmigan (above) develops special winter plumage—a pure white coat of feathers that allows the bird to blend with its snowy habitat.

camouflage, blending beautifully with the lichen-covered rocks amid which the ptarmigan makes its home.

All ptarmigan belong to the genus *Lagopus*. There are many species, each native to specific areas. *L. mutus rupestris* is found in North America; *L. hemileaurus*, on the polar island of Spitsbergen; *L. leucurus*, in the Canadian Rockies and the Sierra of the United States. Another species, the red grouse of Great Britain, is actually a ptarmigan, *L. scoticus*. It is the only member of the genus whose population is confined to the British Isles.

Grouse Proper

These birds are inhabitants of wooded areas in the temperate zone. Perhaps the most familiar species is the ruffed grouse, *Bonasa umbellus*, of North America, an upland game bird of average size whose generally red to brown plumage is occasionally mixed with patchy areas of gray and yellow. The "ruffed" in its name refers to the tufts of black feathers on the sides of its neck. These feathers can be raised and spread so as to form a ruff.

The ruff plays a role in this bird's curious courtship ritual. During the breeding season, the male mounts a hollow log, struts back and forth with its tail spread and ruff erect, and rapidly beats its wings, producing a hollow rumbling sound known as "drumming."

The black grouse, *Tetrao tetrix*, of Europe and Asia displays a similar mating ritual, during which the male dances about and sings. Although it nests on the ground, the black grouse may be found in trees. Generally, though, it inhabits moors and rocky, heather-covered areas.

Wild turkeys (above) have become abundant in recent years. Conservation efforts have helped many species of wildfowl make dramatic population recoveries.

Prairie Chickens

The prairie chickens of the genus *Tympanuchus* inhabit the open plains and semiarid regions of North America. Normally about 18 inches (45 centimeters) long, a prairie chicken can weigh nearly 0.5 pound (1 kilogram); it has reddish-brown plumage with small markings of red and black. On the sides of its neck are air sacs that can be inflated at will. During its elaborate courtship ritual, the male inflates these sacs and then rapidly expels the air, producing a loud booming sound calculated to attract interested females. A characteristic dance completes the courtship routine.

The heath hen, *Tympanuchus cupido cupido*, also called the eastern prairie chicken, was once found in large numbers throughout the coastal plain of New England and the Middle Atlantic states. Over the years, relentless hunting of the birds caused their numbers to diminish sharply. Finally, only one flock of these birds survived— and only on the island of Martha's Vineyard, where they were protected by rigidly enforced laws. Unfortunately, this protection did not avail. The last heath hen disappeared on March 11, 1932, and the bird is now considered extinct.

THE TURKEY FAMILY

Turkeys belong to the family Meleagrididae. The name "turkey" is the result of mistaken identity. An Old World relative of the turkey, the African guinea fowl, was imported into Europe via Turkey. The guinea fowl then became known as the turkey cock in Europe. When Europeans settled in the New World, they confused the American bird with the turkey cock. Thus they called the American bird "turkey."

The original North American common turkey (*Meleagris gallopavo*) has five subspecies found in eastern Canada, the United

States, and Mexico. One other species of North American common turkey, the ocellated turkey (*Agriocharis ocellata*), is restricted to Mexico's Yucatán Peninsula. This bird owes its name to *ocelli*—eyelike spots on its tail feathers.

The turkey that the Pilgrims ate at the first Thanksgiving was a northern subspecies of *Meleagris gallopavo*. At that time, common turkeys were plentiful throughout the wooded areas of the region. They were overhunted until, by the 1960s, they were quite rare. Now, thanks to stringent restoration programs, common turkeys are abundant again. The male stands almost 3 feet (1 meter) tall and weighs about 20 pounds (9 kilograms). The plumage shines with a metallic luster, reflecting browns, reds, greens, blues, and blacks.

The North American common turkey may be distinguished from the ocellated turkey by having a peculiar tuft of hairlike feathers hanging down from the breast—the so-called "breast beard." The common turkey has powerful legs and wings. Although it prefers to remain on the ground and run from danger, it is quite capable of flying for short distances.

Male turkeys of both the common and domestic species are polygamous and constantly seek to add more females to their harems. Consequently, during the breeding season, most males strut about trying to attract prospective mates. Often their promenading is interrupted as they fight among themselves.

The original domestic turkey is a Mexican subspecies domesticated by the Aztec Indians in Mexico long before Europeans ever voyaged to the Americas. This Mexican bird was brought back to Spain in 1519 and then distributed throughout Europe. It was introduced into England sometime between 1524 and 1541.

Hoatzins (above) are exotic-looking South American birds that nest in groups near water. Better swimmers than fliers, hoatzins dive into the water when threatened.

The Mexican subspecies was crossbred with other varieties after it was brought to Europe. Some modern domestic-turkey types resulted from this crossbreeding. Eventually a number of these domestic breeds were reintroduced into North America.

OTHER WILDFOWL

A number of other families of wildfowl are generally restricted to the tropics or to remote areas of the Southern Hemisphere.

The best-known member of the family Megapodiidae is the brush turkey. The males of these Australian species build huge mounds of debris into which several females lay their eggs. When the young hatch, they must burrow their way out of the mound.

Six species of guinea fowl make up the family Numididae. The birds of this family, closely related to pheasant, inhabit the brushlands of Madagascar and of Africa south of the Sahara.

Perhaps the most widely distributed members of the family Cracidae are the curassows. Thirteen species of these large, turkeylike birds inhabit the lower levels of dense tropical and subtropical forests from Mexico to Argentina. Many are noted for their bushy crests. Their large size makes them favorite targets of hunters, and some species are now quite rare. The only cracidan whose range extends into the United States is the plain chachalaca (*Ortalis vertula*), a popular game bird in Texas.

With claws on its wings, a cowlike digestive system, and a host of unusual behaviors, the hoatzin may well be the world's strangest bird. It has traditionally been considered the sole species in the family (or superfamily) Opisthocomidae. Recent studies suggest that the hoatzin may require its own special order, or that it could even be an exceedingly unusual member of the cuckoo family.

The ubiquitous street pigeon (above left) is so common as to go practically unnoticed. In London (above) and in almost every other large city in the world, the streets, parks, and squares teem with huge flocks of the birds.

The
Pigeons

When the Romans coined the word *ubique* to mean "everywhere," they must have had pigeons and doves in mind. Classical cities teemed with huge flocks of these birds, much as modern cities do today. Homing pigeons were used to carry messages as far back as the time of Christ. And more than 2,600 years before that, the ancient Egyptians raised pigeons for food.

The Latin *ubique* has given rise to the English "ubiquitous," and that word is equally descriptive of the current distribution of pigeons and doves. Today these birds flourish almost everywhere except for the extreme Arctic and Antarctic regions. Almost every large city in the world has hordes of domestic pigeons firmly entrenched in parks, public squares, window ledges, and rooftops—just about anyplace where the birds can do what they do best: walk about and coo.

CLASSIFICATION

Pigeon is an inclusive name for birds of the family Columbidae. Scientists do not recognize any technical differences between pigeons and doves; as a general practice, the larger species are called pigeons, and the smaller species are called doves. The family Columbidae includes about 300 species altogether.

Several species related to pigeons figure prominently in the annals of avian extinctions. Perhaps most tragic was the extinction of the passenger pigeon *(Ectopistes migratorius),* which had once darkened the skies of eastern North America in flocks of millions (see the box on page 431). A terrible fate also befell the family of flightless birds known as dodos, the three species of which each inhabited an island in the Indian Ocean. Dodos were about the size of a turkey and weighed approximately 50 pounds (23 kilograms); the plumage color and beak shape varied according to the species. When Europeans and their domestic animals arrived on the dodos' islands, the species rapidly became extinct. No surviving species of pigeon approaches the dodo in size.

GENERAL CHARACTERISTICS

Pigeons and doves are decidedly plump and full-breasted birds with rather small heads. Their feet are adapted such that they can live with equal facility on the ground or in the trees. Their bills, horny at the tip, have a swelling, called the *cere*, at the base. The powerful wings are pointed. Most wild pigeons and doves produce soft, cooing sounds.

These birds feed chiefly on fruits, grains, and weed seeds, although insects also form a part of their diet. Most birds drink in small gulps, hold up their heads, and swallow with the aid of gravity. When a pigeon or dove drinks, however, it immerses its bill to the nostrils and sucks in continuously.

Some pigeons and doves live in large flocks; others are solitary creatures. The male and female mate for life; a "widowed" pigeon often waits for some time before accepting a new mate. Typically, though, both share the duties of building the nest, sitting on the eggs, and feeding the young. Into the nest—a very flimsy structure composed of twigs—are laid one or two snow-white or buff-colored eggs. The young are fed on pigeon milk, a substance secreted from the lining of the parent's crop. The adult bird pumps the substance into the mouth of the young.

Pigeons and doves dwell in the temperate and tropical zones throughout the world. The greatest number of species occur on the island chains off southeastern Asia. The plumage of these Asian birds is particularly handsome, with brilliant shades of red, green, and purple.

One of the first birds to become extinct in historical times was the dodo (above), a large, flightless relative of the pigeon that weighed as much as 50 pounds.

REPRESENTATIVE SPECIES

Wild Pigeons

As mentioned earlier, the most colorful species of pigeons inhabit areas of the Eastern Hemisphere. The topknot pigeon, *Lopholaimus antarcticus*, of Australia has gray feathers offset by a bright rust-red topknot on its head. The crowned pigeons of the genus *Goura* derive their name from the rigid feathers on their heads. Their slate-blue feathers are highlighted with areas of brick-red plumage. These birds are the largest of all living pigeons, equivalent to a large chicken in size.

The band-tailed pigeon, *Columba fasciata*, is an American species with a range from southern Canada to Nicaragua. About the size of the domestic pigeon, this bird has brownish and grayish upperparts, a purplish-pink head and underparts, a white collar on the back of the neck, and its namesake pale gray broad band on the end of the tail, which is black above. This pigeon feeds largely on acorns, young sycamore balls, and wild berries.

Domestic Pigeons

The parent species of the domestic pigeon is the rock dove, *Columba livia*. In Europe, this bird inhabits the rocky seacoasts, but in Asia and North Africa, it lives inland. There are about 15 subspecies, all of which have the grayish-blue coloration characteristic of pigeons on city streets. It is interesting to note that ornamental domestic pigeons will revert, in a few generations, to this type of "street coloration" if they are not carefully selected for mating.

In the domestic state, the pigeon has been carried to all parts of the world. More than 150 different kinds that breed true are now recognized by fanciers. Among the most interesting of the domestic strains is the homing pigeon. This amazing creature has been clocked at speeds of up to 90 miles (145 kilometers) per hour, and can find its way back to its home loft when released up to 1,250 miles (2,000 kilome-

The homing pigeon's reliability as a message carrier made these birds especially valuable during times of war.

ters) away. It must be said, however, that this is not an unusual avian performance: many wild birds have an even stronger homing instinct, and will find their way to their home loft from substantially greater distances.

Other strains developed from the wild stock include the fantail pigeon, whose tail may have an amazing 42 quills instead of the normal 12, and the pouter, which is able to inflate its gullet to great size. The pompous swagger of the pouter pigeon seems almost a parody of the ordinary male pigeon's inflated posture when cooing and strutting.

North America's mourning dove (right) and Europe's turtledove (below) are very similar in appearance and habit. Both species help farmers by eating harmful insects.

Doves

In its role as a symbol of gentleness, love, and purity, the dove figures prominently in poetry and legend, both ancient and modern.

Perhaps the most familiar dove in the United States is the mourning dove, *Zenaida macroura*, which averages about 12 inches (30 centimeters) in length. In flight, a distinctive white band is visible on the tips of the outer tail feathers, making this bird easily identifiable. Another distinguishing characteristic is a black spot on the side of the head behind and below the eye. The breeding range of the mourning dove extends through southern Canada and the United States southward into Mexico. Three or four broods may be raised each season.

Mourning doves are among the first migrants to return north each year. Their mournful calls on a spring morning are in sharp contrast to the bubbling lay of the song sparrow. When the dove flies, the whistling sound produced by the wings can be distinctly heard. The mourning dove feeds principally on weed seeds and grasshoppers, making it an ally of farmers and gardeners alike.

The turtledove, *Streptopelia turtur*, of Europe is very similar to the North American

Passenger Pigeons

Passenger pigeons once flew over much of the United States in numbers that defied belief. Written accounts from the 18th and 19th centuries described flocks so enormous that they darkened the sky for hours. When the birds roosted in forests at night, their combined weight sometimes stripped limbs from trees.

During August 1813, the wildlife illustrator John James Audubon saw a flock of passenger pigeons in Kentucky that he estimated numbered more than 1 billion birds. The flock was 1 mile (1.6 kilometers) wide and passed overhead continuously from noon until sunset, obscuring daylight "as by an eclipse."

It was calculated that at their peak, there were more than 3 billion passenger pigeons—a number equal to 25 to 40 percent of the total bird population in the United States, making it perhaps the most abundant bird in the world. Even as late as 1870, when their numbers had already been reduced by excessive hunting, a flock estimated to be 1 mile wide and 320 miles (515 kilometers) long was seen near Cincinnati.

Ironically, the abundance of passenger pigeons may have been their undoing. Where the birds were most abundant, people assumed there was an inexhaustible supply and slaughtered them by the thousands. Wherever the pigeons congregated to roost and nest, they were netted, clubbed, and shot.

They were shipped to large cities and sold in restaurants, or, when the market was glutted, fed to hogs. Commercial hunters baited small clearings with grain, waited until pigeons had settled to feed, then launched large nets over them, taking hundreds at a time. While roosting in trees, the birds were so tightly massed that a single blast from a shotgun could kill dozens.

By the closing decades of the 19th century, the hardwood forests where passenger pigeons nested had been decimated by logging, scattering the flocks and forcing the birds to migrate farther north, where cold temperatures and spring storms contributed to their decline. Soon the great flocks were gone, never to be seen again.

In 1897, the Michigan legislature passed a law prohibiting the killing of passenger pigeons, but by then, no sizable flocks had been seen in the state for 10 years. The last confirmed wild pigeon in the United States was shot by a boy in Pike County, Ohio, in 1900.

For a time, a few birds survived in captivity. The last of them, known affectionately as Martha, died at the Cincinnati Zoological Garden on September 1, 1914.

Jerry Dennis

---

mourning dove. It is a fawn-colored bird with a larger black mark on the sides of the head. The attention that the turtledove pays its mate is legendary: paired birds sit and coo to each other for hours at a time.

The Inca dove, *Scardafella inca*, is distributed from the southwestern United States through Mexico and southward into Central America. About 8 inches (20 centimeters) long, it has grayish brown plumage above, and grayish red and buff on its underside. This bird nests in bushes, often quite close to human dwellings. In agricultural areas, Inca doves often share a grain dinner with chickens.

Birds of the Water

Hearing the cry of a loon for the first time is an experience not soon forgotten. The sound begins on a low note. Then, gradually, it rises in pitch and increases in volume. Finally the cry culminates in a terrible spasmodic gasp. The loon's voice has been variously described as sinister, wolflike, defiant—even compared to hysterical laughter. Perhaps unexpectedly, the owner of this distinctive voice is a large, handsome diving bird.

Other waterbirds and shorebirds also have distinctive calls. The magnificent trumpeter swan produces a decidedly unmagnificent honk. The sooty tern's cry can perhaps be best described as "kerwacky-wack." The hoglike grunt of Australia's Cape Bareen goose has led to its particularly apt nickname: pig goose.

The birds just noted represent only a few of the many avian species that live on or near the water. For classification purposes, ornithologists have organized the various species into the following eight orders:

• Order Podicipediformes, which contains the grebes;

• Order Gaviiformes, which contains the loons;

• Order Charadriiformes, which contains the so-called shorebirds—gulls, plovers, skimmers, sandpipers, terns, puffins, and so on, as

Dozens of species of birds live on or near bodies of water. Many of these birds are most vocal early in the morning, just as the Sun begins its slow ascent over the horizon, or late in the evening, just before sunset.

well as such related species as the woodcocks, snipes, lapwings, and many others;

- Order Gruiformes, which contains the marsh birds—cranes, rails, and coots;
- Order Anseriformes, which contains waterfowl—ducks, geese, and swans;
- Order Ciconiiformes, which contains the stilt-legged birds—herons, storks, ibises, spoonbills, flamingos, and other species;
- Order Procellariiformes, which contains the seabirds—albatrosses, petrels, and shearwaters; and
- Order Pelecaniformes, which contains the cormorants, anhingas, gannets, boobies, frigate birds, tropic birds, and, as the order's name suggests, the pelicans.

In the following pages, we will look at representative members of these orders.

LOONS AND GREBES

The loons (family Gaviidae) and the grebes (family Podicipedidae) spend almost all their time in the water. The two families share a number of characteristics. Both are diving birds. Both also have elongated bodies and necks and are able to submerge their bodies so that, as they swim, only their necks and heads remain above water. And both have short wings and short tails, dense plumage, and an extensive layer of underlying fat.

An important characteristic that distinguishes the two families is the toe structure: in loons, the toes are webbed; in grebes, the toes are broadly lobed.

Loons

The loon, an accomplished diver and swimmer, can overtake even the swiftest fish, using its powerful wings to—for all intents and purposes—"fly" under the water. Unlike most other birds, however, the loon is almost helpless on land. When danger threatens, the bird must awkwardly flop to the water's edge, since it cannot become airborne from the ground. Once in the water, the loon escapes by either diving or rising in flight.

The loon is a solitary bird, usually found alone or in pairs. Occasionally several pairs may nest fairly close together, but only if the marsh or lake is unspoiled and the fish supply is plentiful enough to feed all.

The nest—never very far from the water's edge—is essentially a depression in the ground, sometimes crudely lined with bits of weed stalks or marsh vegetation, into which two mottled, olive-colored eggs are laid. The newly hatched young are covered with down and are immediately capable of swimming. Usually, though, the female carries the babies on her back for several days.

The common loon, *Gavia immer*, also known as the great northern diver, is widely distributed in North America. During the nesting season, it ranges from Alaska across Arctic Canada to Greenland and, southward, from northern California across the United States to New England and Labrador. During the winter, the loon migrates to Southern California and Mexico on the West Coast and to Florida and nearby on the Atlantic seaboard. The common loon is sometimes found inland along the largest rivers.

Boobies are closely related to pelicans. The blue-footed boobies below, natives of the Galápagos Islands, are conducting a curious courtship ritual called skypointing.

In summer, the plumage of the great northern diver is glossy black above, spotted with white; its underparts are white. The head and neck are velvety black except for patches of white streaks on the lower throat and sides of the neck. The feathers are thick and compact, making an effective cloak for shedding water. The loon's winter plumage is a dull black or gray above, without white spots.

The loon's three front toes are completely webbed. Its wings are short, narrow, pointed, and placed well back on the body; and the tail is short and stiff. The heavy beak resembles a sharp-edged spear, making it an excellent weapon for capturing and holding the fish that make up the main part of the loon's diet.

Grebes

The grebes measure under 24 inches (61 centimeters) in length. Like the loons, they excel as divers and swimmers, but are helpless on land because their feet are too far back on the body to be very efficient in walking.

The grebe's plumage occurs in softly patterned tones of white, gray, black, or brown; its very short tail is little more than a tuft of feathers. The bill is pointed, while the toes are individually webbed, or lobed. The grebe's stomach invariably contains a ball of its own feathers, which the bird instinctively has swallowed to prevent sharp fish bones from continuing into the intestine.

The grebe is able to stay underwater for lengthy periods of time. When it does come up, usually after having been frightened, it rises to the surface very quietly, and then only until the bill shows above the water. The grebe can dive either headfirst with a flip of its feet, or it can settle backward so carefully as to leave scarcely a ripple on the surface. No matter how it dives, it can do so with amazing speed. The grebe, in fact, seems to prefer diving over flying as a means of escaping enemies; indeed, it takes much effort for the bird to fly. Ordinarily, the grebe must patter along the surface of the water for some distance before it is able to gain enough speed to lift itself.

The most-common species is the pied-billed grebe, *Podilymbus podiceps*, which ranges from Canada southward to Chile and Argentina. It is an inconspicuous, brownish little bird with unremarkable breeding plumage. Its most readily identifiable feature is its chicken-like bill, which is encircled by a black band. This bird is usually found on reed-bordered ponds and marshy lakes, where it builds a floating nest (really just a pile of debris) and anchors it securely to the reeds. The grebe's eggs, white when laid, are soon discolored by the decaying vegetation.

Young pied-billed grebes are covered with black-and-white striped down. The first hatchlings almost immediately slip into the water and follow their father, while the mother incubates the remaining eggs. When cold, the young snuggle beneath the wings of one of the parents. When the babies get tired of swimming, they simply climb aboard a parent's back for a ride.

SHOREBIRDS

As their name suggests, these birds are most commonly seen in marshy areas and along shores. They are strong fliers, and many migrate long distances in the spring and fall. Most species have long, slender beaks that are well adapted for seizing the insects, shellfish, and worms that are their primary foods.

Gulls

Along the seacoast, there is perhaps no bird more familiar—or more ubiquitous—than the

Carelessly discarded rubbish can end up causing great harm to shorebirds. The gull below caught its neck in a plastic six-pack ring that had been left lying on a beach.

graceful, long-winged seagull. This creature is an absolute master of the air, and flourishes even in the most severe climates. Several of the approximately 50 species live far from the shore, on and around inland bodies of water.

The gull's skill at airborne wheeling and dipping combines with its strong, curving bill to prepare it admirably for a career as scavenger of port and harbor. Wherever it is found, the gull follows ships, ready to pounce on anything thrown overboard. Gulls also congregate in large flocks in harbors. Even far inland, gulls are regular visitors to landfills and outdoor dumps. Both at sea and on land, gulls render a valuable service by consuming enormous amounts of refuse.

The typical seagull is about 24 inches (61 centimeters) long. Most are white, with the back and upper surfaces of the wings (called the mantle) washed with gray, black, or brown. The head is often black during the nesting season; black markings sometimes occur on the flight feathers. The tail is square. The gull's webbed feet resemble those of a duck.

Seagulls can often be seen sleeping on the ocean waves, but they never plunge beneath them in search of food. The seagull is a surface feeder—and not a very picky one! In coastal areas, this clever bird is often seen carrying bivalve mollusks into the air and dropping them onto rocks in order to break the shells. It occasionally preys on the eggs and young of other waterbirds.

In its large nesting colonies, the female lays three heavily marked eggs in a crude nest of seaweed. The birds are sociable but quarrelsome, and often behave quite harshly toward one another's young. Baby gulls have the distinctive habit of announcing their hunger by tapping on the bill of one of their parents.

Terns

The tern, another graceful flier of the seacoast, is typical of this tribe of water-loving birds: its plumage is white below and gray above, and the bird has a black or gray cap. From a distance, the tern can be distinguished from the seagull by its more-slender body and by its forked tail—the feature from which it derives its nickname "sea swallow." Worldwide,

The Atlantic puffin above is carrying a mouthful of fish to its hungry chick. The puffin holds the fish between its tongue and the sharp spines on the roof of its mouth.

there are 39 species of terns, several of which are endangered.

Thanks to its long, straight, slender bill, the tern is well equipped to fish for a living. The bird spends much of its time diving for small fish and catching insects with its bill agape while on the wing.

The migrations that certain species of terns undertake are truly astonishing. Most notable is the migration of the arctic tern, which makes an annual round-trip migratory flight of approximately 22,000 miles (35,400 kilometers)—the longest known of any creature. Some species of terns do not take these extended migratory flights, instead simply flying to coastal regions in warm latitudes.

Terns nest in colonies. Into their nests—really just slight hollows scraped in the sand—they lay one to three white eggs mottled with dark brown. Some species build nests of seaweed in bushes. Instead of a nest, the fairy tern balances its single egg on the gnarled bark of a horizontal limb!

Skimmers

The skimmer differs from all other birds in having a vertically flattened, knifelike bill, in which the lower part of the bill is much longer than the upper part. This feature has led the skimmer to be nicknamed "scissorbill." The skimmer also differs from other birds in eye structure—it has a vertical, slitlike pupil. Thanks to these two unusual adaptations, the bird is able to fly low over the water with its bill cleaving the surface, seeing and seizing small marine organisms and fish.

Three species of these long-winged birds make up the family Rynchopidae. The black skimmer, *Rhynchops niger*, nests along the U.S. East Coast and southward to Argentina. Its plumage is black, with the forehead, sides of the face, and underparts white; it has red legs. The skimmer lays black-blotched, buff-colored eggs in a hole scraped in the sand. The female alone incubates the eggs, but the male assists in feeding the young, which rely on their sand coloring for protection. Of the remaining two species, one (*R. flavirostris*) lives in Africa; the other (*R. albicollis*) lives in India.

Both sexes of crested auklets compete for mates, perhaps explaining why, during breeding season, feathers adorn the foreheads of both the female (above) and the male.

Sandpipers

The term "sandpiper"—the common name for members of the family Scolopacidae—has a twofold derivation: the birds live mostly on sandy beaches, and they produce a distinctive piping cry.

Sandpipers have long, flexible bills with which they probe the sand for food. Their sizes vary considerably, from the least sandpiper—no longer than a sparrow—to the curlews and godwits, standing 12 inches (30 centimeters) tall. Aside from size, though, all sandpipers look very much alike, plumaged with similar patterns of gray, brown, chestnut, and white.

There are about 100 species of sandpipers living in various parts of the world. During their nesting seasons, they occur mainly in the temperate and northern portions of the Northern Hemisphere, many of them nesting within the Arctic Circle. Sandpipers mainly inhabit sea-coasts, although some are found inland on the shores of bodies of freshwater.

Sandpipers are great travelers. Some traverse the entire length of both the Americas in their extended migrations. The majority of species summer in the far north, heading south to the Caribbean, then to northern South America during the winter. Some species migrate no farther than the North American Gulf Coast, while others fly south thousands of miles to Chile and Patagonia.

When a sandpiper begins its migration, it has stored up thick layers of fat. By the time it reaches its winter quarters, however, the bird has become decidedly thin. This is particularly true of those that have undertaken the long flight from Nova Scotia to Venezuela or from Alaska to the islands of Hawaii without a single stop. A nonstop flight of 2,500 miles (4,000 kilometers) seems almost incredible, but such a feat is not at all unusual for these birds. Some sandpipers have even been observed at Cape Horn—about 9,000 miles (14,500 kilometers) from their nesting grounds.

During the nesting season, sandpipers tend to live alone; at migration and during the winter, they gather in large flocks. With the exception of the solitary sandpiper, all the members of this group nest on the ground. The solitary sandpiper, however, utilizes the old nests of other birds such as robins and grackles. A sandpiper typically lays three or four eggs of a size out of proportion to the bird. The eggs are sharply tapered at one end so that they fit together like the pieces of a pie, which allows the parent bird to cover them all during incubation. The eggs vary greatly in color, although most are spotted with black, brown, or lavender.

Upon hatching, the young sandpipers are covered with down, sometimes with a striped pattern. The babies are able to run about and follow their parents—and even swim across streams. The first plumage is similar to that of the adults in the fall; the following spring, all molt into the breeding plumage.

Sandpipers subsist primarily on insects—mosquito and fly larvae, grasshoppers, and other destructive insects. Their long legs enable them to wade through shallow water and mud in search of their food.

The most-common species of sandpiper in North America is the spotted sandpiper, *Actitis macularia*. In summer, it is found along almost every stream and lake from northwestern Alaska to Louisiana, and in winter from Louisiana to southern Brazil. This species—about 7.5 inches (19 centimeters) long—has light brown upper parts and white underparts spotted with black. In the fall, it loses its spots, but it is still easily identifiable because of its jerky walk. Several other species jerk their heads when they walk, but the spotted sandpiper teeters its tail or its whole body as though it had difficulty balancing on its slender legs.

Plovers

The members of the plover family, Charadriidae, somewhat resemble sandpipers. They are about 10 inches (25 centimeters) long and have plump bodies; long, pointed wings; and short necks and tails. Their bills are short and shaped much like a pigeon's, with an enlargement at the tip.

All of the plovers' movements are quick and energetic. They run rapidly over the ground—much like mechanical toys. There are about 75 species in this family, which also includes the lapwings, turnstones, and surfbirds.

The plovers are most remarkable for their migrations. The American golden plover, *Pluvialis dominica*, for example, covers 8,000 miles (13,000 kilometers) in its round-trip migratory flight, flying south from Nova Scotia to the northeast coast of South America—a distance of 4,000 miles (6,500 kilometers). This flight over long stretches of open ocean is often made without a stop. In the spring, the bird returns to its northern nesting grounds by a different route, via the northwest coast of South America and the Mississippi Valley.

Like all birds, waterbirds and shorebirds must constantly maintain their plumage. The egret (above) spends several hours a day preening and fussing over its feathers.

The golden plover has upper parts spotted with golden yellow and with black; its underparts are uniformly black in summer and grayish white in winter. A white stripe from the forehead down the side of the neck and breast is a conspicuous feature of the summer plumage.

The grey plover, *Pluvialis squatarola*, is very similar to the golden plover. It also has a change of plumage with the seasons, but lacks the golden-yellow spots on the upper parts. This bird is found over nearly the entire world. It, too, is a great traveler.

The golden and the grey plovers have quite similar habits. They rarely enter the water. Instead, these birds feed on sandbars and mudflats exposed by the falling tide. The plovers run along the beach in search of stranded aquatic insects and crustaceans, which they pick up with a vigorous tilt of the body. These birds are also seen in plowed fields or pastures.

An interesting member of the plover family from the Eastern Hemisphere is the Nile plover, noted for its symbiotic (mutually beneficial) relationship with the Nile crocodile. The bird picks leeches and other parasitic creatures from the mouth of the reptile and feasts on them. The crocodile, in turn, benefits both from being rid of these pests and from having an

In just the past few decades, the whooping crane has made a dramatic comeback from the brink of extinction, thanks largely to intensive conservation efforts.

avian sentinel warning the reptile of approaching danger.

Plovers nest in small depressions on the ground. Occasionally the depression is lined with moss or grass. Like sandpipers' eggs, the plover's eggs are much larger at one end than at the other. Egg color is neutral, with specklings of dark brown, black, or lilac.

Other Shorebirds

Phalaropes, family Phalaropodinae, are the most aquatic of all shorebirds. Wilson's phalarope, *Phalaropus tricolor*, spends many months at sea during the winter. It is well adapted for this type of life, with its weblike toe lobes and dense, gull-like plumage. It often nests in the interior marshes of North America. The female phalarope, in a role reversal of sorts, assumes the bright plumage and does the courting at breeding time; the male phalarope incubates the eggs and cares for the young.

Avocets and stilts, family Recurvirostridae, are long-legged wading birds with long, upcurved bills. They build their nests on sandy banks, in muddy flats, or in marshes. The black-winged, or common, stilt, *Himantopus himantopus*, of southern Europe is easily recognized by its exceptionally long pink legs, which project some 7 inches (18 centimeters) beyond its tail when the bird is in flight.

The jacanas are tropical birds whose long legs and long toes are adapted for walking on floating water plants—a habit that has earned them the nickname "lily-trotters."

Auks and puffins, family Alcidae, often live together in huge groups that also include murres and gulls. They inhabit cliffs and islands in the northern seas. Most migrate south in winter, returning north in the spring to breed. Auks and puffins do not build nests, but lay their eggs on ledges or niches in the rocks. Each female lays only one egg. She and her mate take turns guarding it.

The shy woodcock, species *Scolopax*, ventures into the open only after dark, spending its days hidden in thickets. The woodcock has a protective coloring of grayish brown, reddish brown, and black. Its long, thin bill takes up a third of its length. The large eyes, set far back in the head, give the bird a very distinctive appearance. It likes to feed in the lowlands, where it can bore into the soft mud for worms and other small invertebrates.

MARSH BIRDS

Although not well adapted for flight, the members of the order Gruiformes are very well adapted for life on land and in the water. The order's three major families are the Gruidae, or cranes; the Rallidae, which includes rails, gallinules, coots, soras, and wekas; and the Otididae, or bustards.

Cranes

These birds are found on every continent except South America. The American whooping crane, *Grus americana*, is well known because of the tremendous efforts that have been made to try to save this beautiful creature from extinction. The whooping crane summers in western Canada and winters on islands off the coast of Texas. It flies from one site to another—a total distance of more than 2,300 miles (3,700 kilometers)—at an average rate of 100 miles (160 kilometers) per day.

The common crane, *Grus grus*, also migrates great distances. It summers in north-central Europe and Asia and winters in northern

Africa. Migrating cranes typically fly in a familiar V or line formation, with their necks and legs extended.

Rails, Gallinules, and Coots

Nature has given the members of the family Rallidae slender, compressed bodies that enable them to slip easily through bunches of marsh grasses. These secretive birds are mostly freshwater marsh dwellers.

There are about 225 different species of Rallidae. Family characteristics include short, rounded wings; long necks; and muscular legs with long, slender toes that help the birds to scamper easily across the marshes. The coot has lobes on each side of its toes to assist in swimming. Coots are much more aquatic than the other species, and often gather in large flocks on the water like ducks.

Many species have a somewhat chickenlike appearance, thanks especially to their short, erect tails and short wings. Even the clucking voice resembles that of a chicken. The gallinules, coots, soras, and yellow and black rails have short, thick, pointed bills. The Virginia clapper and king rails have rather long, slender, and somewhat down-curving bills.

In the water, both coots and gallinules are very ducklike except for their small heads, which they continually pump as they swim. Strutting and running along the border of the marsh, they look more like little hens as they peck at seeds and insects on the ground. Some of the most startling sounds that come from the marshes can be traced to these birds. Their ordinary calls sound somewhat henlike: "cut-cut" or "tuka-tuka." But occasionally they give vent to loud, angry screeches that shatter the air. Unlike the rails, coots and gallinules rarely call at night, instead being most vocal in the early morning or in the evening toward dusk.

Coots and gallinules build their nests of dried rushes, hidden in clumps of marsh vegetation, and sometimes lodged in tall stalks growing 1.5 to 4.5 feet (0.5 to 1.4 meters) above the water. Some are floating platforms that can rise and fall with the floods. The eggs are buff-colored, the coot's being evenly spotted with black and brown, the gallinule's more sparsely spotted with brown and lavender.

Few birds can match the elegance of the mute swans (below). Still, since their introduction from Europe less than a century ago, these majestic birds have multiplied at a rate high enough to threaten the habitats of native American waterfowl.

Canada geese often migrate in sizable flocks, their characteristic honking sounds audible long before the birds come into view. Those geese that are fed by humans in their summer habitat tend not to migrate south for the winter.

The young of most species of coots, gallinules, and rails are covered with glossy black down when hatched, the coots being ornamented with an orange, beardlike fringe around the throat. The coots and gallinules lay their eggs at the rate of one a day, and begin to incubate each one as soon as it is laid. The young are able to swim and run almost as soon as they hatch, which helps to explain why they leave the nest very shortly after hatching.

Rails in general are the most secretive members of this elusive family, and seem to take wing only when an escape by dashing through the weeds is impossible. Their nests are built on the ground, hidden in the grassy marshes. The sparrow-sized black rail, the smallest and rarest representative of the family, conceals its nest very effectively in a small depression in the ground.

WATERFOWL

Waterfowl include swans, geese, mergansers, and ducks—all members of the order Anseriformes and the family Anatidae. More than 200 species of waterfowl have been recognized.

These birds are well adapted for life on the surface of the water. They have broad, flat bodies that are lightened by air sacs and hollow bones. They keep their feathers well oiled to prevent water from reaching the skin. Their swimming ability is aided by webbed feet and strong leg muscles.

Waterfowl have long necks with which they reach to the bottom of streams and ponds for food. Their center of gravity lies forward, making it unnecessary for them to tip up as the bill searches for food on the bottom. In most species, the bill is broad and flat and has grooves at the side, forming a strainer when the bird dabbles after small water organisms.

One interesting characteristic of waterfowl is that they lose all the wing quills at the same time that they molt their mating plumage after the breeding season. As a result, they are unable to fly until new quills have grown in. For awhile, therefore, they must depend on swimming to escape their enemies.

Swans

These elegant birds have much longer necks than the other waterfowl—even longer than their bodies. Their beauty and grace has given them a position in the poetry and legends of many nations. Of the eight species of swans, two are found in North America—the trumpeter and whistling swans. Both species are pure white except for their black bill and feet. The adults are more than 3 feet (1 meter) long. These two species closely resemble the common domesticated swan, which has been derived from the European mute swan and which can always be identified by the tubercle, or knob, on its bill.

A particularly unusual species is the black swan, *Cygnus atratus*, of Australia. A Dutch explorer who saw these beautiful birds in 1697—at the mouth of what is now called the Swan River—captured some of them and carried them back to Europe, where they had never before been seen.

Geese

There are about 30 species of wild geese. The Canada goose, *Branta canadensis*, is the most abundant and the best known of the species in North America. It has been introduced to Europe, where it may often be seen in parks and on golf courses. This 3-foot (1-meter)-long bird is gray-brown above, grayish beneath, and has a black head and neck. A white patch runs under its chin and up both cheeks like an incomplete chin strap.

The Canada goose nests from the northern United States northward to the limit of trees. It winters from the Great Lakes southward into Mexico. The travelings of the Canada geese are among the most conspicuous of bird migrations. One hears their loud honking long before they become visible high overhead in a great wedge or Y. These birds migrate both by day and by night. On their journeys, they are great vegetarians, with a particular fondness for grazing on young wheat, both in the spring and fall. In the south, in their wintering grounds, they seem to prefer to feed in the shallow water of bays and lagoons, tipping like dabbling ducks for aquatic plants and organisms.

The snow geese, *Anser caerulescens*, have easily recognized white feathers offset by black flight feathers; sometimes the head is stained or-

In many duck species, the female alone cares for the eggs and tends to the young. The mother duck reacts aggressively when an intruder nears her nest.

ange. Found in both North America and Europe, these are colonial birds that generally breed on lake islands and tundra.

The greylag, *Anser anser*, is the best known—and most domesticated—of the European wild geese. This ashy-brown bird is the species from which the domestic goose has been derived. The greylag has the same nasal, reedy voice as its domestic cousin.

Mergansers

The fish-eating mergansers are easily distinguished from other members of the family Anatidae by their crested heads and narrow, saw-toothed bills, which end in a strong hook to aid them in grasping slippery fish. These birds seldom venture far from the water's edge and must patter along the water's surface before flying.

Of all duck species, the mallards are the most widespread. The two sexes look remarkably different: the male has an iridescent green head, white neck band, and rust-colored breast; the female has mottled brown plumage.

Mergansers can pursue their finny prey underwater, thanks to the drive of their powerful feet, which are set far back on their bodies. They first locate their prey by lowering their heads until their eyes are beneath the surface film—a position in which they often swim about. Their predominantly fishy diet gives the bird a coarse, rank taste that makes merganser unappealing to the human palate.

Three of the nine merganser species are found in North America. All of them nest either on the ground or in hollow trees. Six to 18 eggs are laid, and the young enter the water immediately upon hatching. Mergansers breed in the far north and migrate as far south as Mexico as the colder season approaches. The females of all three species are grayish birds with conspicuously crested reddish-brown heads. The males have bold black-and-white markings.

Ducks

Ducks (subfamily Anatinae) are divided into two tribes: the surface-feeding ducks (tribe Anatini) and the diving ducks (tribe Aythyini). Despite this seemingly straightforward classification, surface feeders sometimes dive for food, and diving ducks sometimes feed on the surface. Most diving species lack a conspicuous feature seen on most surface feeders: the so-called "beauty spot," an area of iridescent color formed by the secondary feathers of the wing.

For the most part, surface feeders live in marshes and on lakeshores. These ducks feed in shallow water by tipping their bodies, and they frequently feed on land. They seek food mostly at night or on overcast days, and are also frequently seen feeding on land.

The diving ducks, on the other hand, feed far offshore, where they readily dive for mollusks and the roots and buds of aquatic plants in water up to 145 feet (45 meters) deep. They seldom feed on land, since they do not walk as well as their surface-feeding cousins.

Diving ducks commonly gather in large flocks—often by the thousands on larger bodies of water. The diving ability of these ducks can hardly be exaggerated. Some members of the family are repeatedly captured in gill nets set for fish at great depths.

Diving ducks also feed more during the day than at night, since their offshore foraging is not apt to expose them to enemies. The feeding grounds of diving ducks do not freeze over as readily as do the marshes and shallow waters where the surface feeders live, and so the divers tend to migrate at a later time.

As their name suggests, diving ducks are especially well adapted for plunging deep beneath the surface. Compared to surface feeders, diving ducks have larger feet, stockier bodies, shorter necks, and shorter wings. Their hind toes have distinctive lobes that make them resemble paddles. These lobes are not present in the surface feeders.

When swimming, diving ducks float lower in the water than do the surface feeders, and they do not hold their tails up from the surface. To become airborne, the surface feeders spring directly up without a preliminary run. Diving ducks must run over the surface of the water to work up enough speed for flight.

Around midsummer, the males, or drakes, shed their bright plumage for two months or longer. Those feathers are replaced by duller plumage that resembles that of the females. This so-called eclipse feathering appears at the same time that the bird sheds its flight feathers. Scientists are baffled by this periodic change of dress, especially since it occurs only among ducks native to—or transplanted to—the Northern Hemisphere.

Most ducks pair and nest the spring following hatching. Wild ducks are monogamous, but the domesticated male is polygamous. Most surface feeders build crude nests of grasses and weeds on the ground, usually near water. Diving ducks prefer to nest in marshes, where they can

Only recently did zoologists learn that the spectacled eider, after passing the summer in relative comfort (above), winters in small holes in the Bering Sea pack ice.

slip directly into the water without having to walk on dry land.

As incubation proceeds, the female plucks down from her breast, which she uses to cover the eggs, thus keeping them warm when she goes off to feed. The drakes do not make devoted fathers, usually abandoning the female as soon as incubation is well under way.

The mallard, *Anas platyrhynchos*, is a common and very widely distributed species of surface-feeding duck. It breeds readily in captivity as well as in the wild. The males have bright green heads and white rings around their necks. The females are uniformly streaked yellowish or grayish brown.

Another surface feeder, the pintail, *Anas acuta*, is also widely distributed throughout the Northern Hemisphere. The male has a chocolate-brown head and neck, with a conspicuous white streak up each side of the neck. Its tail is long and pointed. The female looks much like the mallard female.

Perhaps the most familiar diving duck is the canvasback, *Aythya valisineria*, named for the white back of the male. This duck is easily recognized because of its long, flat, gradually sloping profile. The male has a reddish head and neck. The female's back is gray; her head and neck are cinnamon brown.

Eider ducks, *Somateria mollissima*, are divers that inhabit northern regions around the world; these hardy birds are the world's largest ducks. The male is the only duck that has a black belly and a white back. The female is brown. Like various other ducks, the female eider covers her eggs with down plucked from her breast. This down, taken from the nest by humans, is the eiderdown of commerce.

Many superstitions surround the habits of the European white stork. According to legend, the arrival of a stork signals good luck; its departure is an omen of calamity.

Pink plumage enhances the beauty of both the roseate spoonbill (above) and the greater, or scarlet, flamingo (left). Both species live in tropical or subtropical environments, and both tend to congregate in large, noisy groups.

STILT-LEGGED BIRDS

Members of the order Ciconiiformes are well suited for their life as waders. In addition to their long legs, they have long necks and long bills, adaptations that help them catch fish, snakes, frogs, and so on. The approximately 120 species are widely distributed. These birds are strong fliers, and many of the temperate-zone species migrate long distances.

Herons, Bitterns, and Egrets

The members of this family of birds vary in size from the least bittern, whose body is not much larger than that of a robin, to the great white heron, which is more than 3 feet (1 meter) long. Colors range from the streaked brown plumage of the bitterns through various shades of blue, gray, and chestnut, to the snowy white of the egrets. Herons are ornamented with elongated feathers on the crown, foreneck, breast, or middle of the back, particularly during the mating season.

The long-legged herons are wading birds that live in marshes of saltwater lagoons, freshwater lakes, and rivers. The birds have a voracious appetite, consuming fish, frogs, tadpoles, crayfish, small snakes, meadow mice, and shrews—all with great relish. Still, no matter how much they eat, herons always look emaciated, thanks to their long necks and legs and light, bony bodies.

Herons are patient creatures; they are frequently observed standing quite still in the water, seemingly waiting for prey to come near. Some herons wander about in search of food, staring at the water and lifting each foot and putting it down so carefully that no ripples are created to warn potential prey. The heron's stiletto-shaped bill makes a most formidable weapon. The voices of the heron family resemble hoarse croaks and squawks.

Herons are gregarious birds, roosting and nesting in colonies. The nests—bulky platforms of twigs and sticks lined with grass—are usually built in trees or large bushes in swamps. Nest construction is usually begun by the male but completed by the female after the pair has mated. Three to six pale greenish-blue eggs are laid. Some older birds double up their long legs underneath themselves when brooding.

Newly hatched young are covered with down. When frightened, the young herons stretch up their long, slender necks and remain perfectly quiet—so still, in fact, that they look more like sticks than birds. Should the nest be disturbed, the young may welcome the intruder with their thrown-up stomach contents: partially digested food from the parent's crop.

Bitterns are smaller than herons. Like the other members of this family, they live and nest in reedy marshes. Bitterns are difficult to observe, however, as they are shy and skulk about among the reeds. When approached closely, a bittern seems to freeze into position with head, neck, and bill pointing to the sky, the streaks along its throat blending with the surrounding reeds. The bittern has a booming call in the springtime and is a skilled ventriloquist.

Egret is the name usually applied to the white members of the family that grow long mating plumes, or aigrettes, on their back during the breeding season. These plumes, which look as if they are made of spun glass, nearly led to the egret's extinction: back when plumed hats for women were the style, egret aigrettes were in great demand. They could be obtained only by killing the adult birds; the fledglings would thus be left to starve. As a result, the egrets all but disappeared. Thanks to the efforts of legislators and environmentalists—not to mention a change in fashion—most species of egrets are no longer endangered.

Flamingos

Rosy pink or bright, vivid scarlet plumage make the flamingos unquestionably one of the world's most beautiful birds. These lovely creatures have very long necks and legs. Their distinctive bills have a lower, boxlike bottom section and an upper part that fits the bottom like a box lid. The sides of the bill have gill-like structures that serve as sieves. When the bill is thrust into mud, the sieve strains out shellfish, frogs, plant matter, and other food from the inedible particles.

The most widely distributed species is the greater, or scarlet, flamingo, *Phoenicopterus ruber*. In the New World, this bird ranges from the Bahamas through the Caribbean and into parts of Central and South America. In the Old World, it is found around the Mediterranean

Hungry pelicans wait for a handout from fishermen working the waters of Lake Edward, a large, deep lake in central Africa. Pelicans will travel many miles to find food.

The albatross (below) drinks seawater exclusively and without any ill effects, thanks to special glands in its head that remove the extra salt via hypersaline teardrops.

Sea, Caspian Sea, and Persian Gulf. Everywhere it favors shallow coastal waters.

The female lays one or two eggs in a conical nest made of mud. The young birds have dull grayish-brown plumage. Several years pass before they attain the vivid adult colors.

Spoonbills and Ibises

These birds, members of the family Threskiornithidae, are, for the most part considered tropical or subtropical species, although some summer as far north as Scandinavia and Southern California.

The spoonbill has, as its name suggests, a spoon-shaped bill that is well adapted to catching the frogs, shellfish, insects, and fish on which the bird feeds. The ibis has a long, slender, more or less cylindrical down-curving bill. Its diet is similar to that of the spoonbill.

Spoonbills are gregarious birds, often forming large colonies during the breeding season. Some ibises are colonial and often live with spoonbills and herons; other species are generally solitary. Spoonbills and ibises build their nests in a variety of sites: on trees, bushes, in holes, in rock ledges, or on the ground.

Plumage ranges from white to shades of pink and rose. The white ibis, *Eudocimus albus*, has pure white plumage, with a few large feathers tipped in black. The glossy ibis, *Plegadis falcinellus*, has green, purple, and bronze tints on its plumage. The roseate spoonbill, *Ajaia ajaia*, has pink plumage, pink legs, and a yellow bill.

SEABIRDS

Four families of seabirds make up the order Procellariiformes: albatrosses; storm petrels; diving petrels; and shearwaters and fulmars. These birds spend nearly their entire lives in the air or on the water's surface, coming ashore only to breed. Seabirds are sometimes called tubenoses, because their nostrils open through tubes that extend along the top or sides of the bill. The tip of the bill is hooked and enlarged. The upper half of the bill is longer than the lower half, and is curved downward.

Every part of the world is visited by Procellariiformes. Individual species may be very wide ranging. The sooty shearwater, *Puffinus griseus*, for example, makes its home in the oceans of the Southern Hemisphere, but in summer it flies as far north as California and northern Europe. It returns every year to the same nesting site.

The albatrosses are the largest members of the order. The wandering albatross, *Diomedea exulans*, may attain a length of more than 4.5 feet (1.4 meters) and a wingspan of over 10 feet (3 meters). Storm petrels—the smallest seabirds—look much like swallows.

Seabirds lack the brilliant plumage typical of their avian cousins. Most have gray, black, or white feathers, with little or no variations between the sexes or from season to season.

PELICANS AND THEIR KIN

All members of the order of Pelecaniformes have long bills and an expandable membrane, or throat pouch. In pelicans, this pouch—sometimes more than 6 inches (15 centimeters) deep—is very noticeable, and is used by the bird to scoop up and store fish. In frigate birds, the pouch plays a role in courtship display. The male attracts a female by inflating his normally invisible pouch, which gradually turns scarlet, and by rattling his bill.

The order consists of six families of birds: pelicans; cormorants; anhingas; gannets and boobies; frigate birds; and tropic birds. All feed exclusively on fish.

Pelicans

Pelicans are large birds, with a length ranging anywhere from 4 to 6 feet (1.25 to 1.8 meters). Some Eastern white pelicans, *Pelecanus onocrotalus*, have a wingspan measuring 10 feet (3 meters). White pelicans are found in temperate areas in both the New and Old worlds, along coastal lagoons and marshes, and near large inland bodies of water.

The brown pelican, *Pelecanus occidentalis*, is a New World species most commonly found from the Gulf of Mexico to South America. Occasionally it will wander as far north as Canada. It is a spectacular sight to see this bird as it dives headlong from high in the sky into the water, emerging soon thereafter with a fish in its distinctive pouched bill.

Pelicans are gregarious birds, breeding in large colonies and building their huge nests out of sticks, reeds, and mud on the ground or in trees. The two to five eggs are a bluish white. Pelicans catch fish in their pouches, swallowing some and feeding the remainder to their young. They undertake long journeys in search of food or during their seasonal migrations.

Related Species

Cormorants have long necks; thin, hooked bills; and metallic black plumage. They dive after their prey. One species, the Galápagos cormorant, cannot fly. The nests, of sticks and seaweed, are built on the ground or in trees. Usually there are two to four eggs. Cormorants occur throughout the world.

Anhingas—also called snakebirds or darters because of their very long necks—are found on every continent except Europe. They live in colonies, where they build tree nests in which they lay three to six eggs.

Gannets prefer cooler waters, while boobies like warm waters. Both are colonial nesters, and both are excellent divers.

Perching Birds

The melodious songs that waft through the window on a sunny spring morning are produced by the flying vertebrates known as perching birds—the bird group that has most successfully adapted to human environments. Most species of perching birds can be further narrowed into another category: songbirds. In fact, there's little question that these merry creatures are the birds that are most familiar to humans.

Of the 9,000 or so species of birds officially known to us, well over half—some 5,500—are classified as perching birds. Perching birds comprise the order Passeriformes. The great majority of passeriformes are members of the suborder Oscines—the songbirds.

GENERAL CHARACTERISTICS

On each foot, perching birds have four toes, one of which points backward. This arrangement enables the bird to easily perch on everything from leaf stems to thick branches. Tendons in the feet help the bird to flex its toes and grasp its perch tightly. Any movement that threatens the bird's equilibrium will cause the feet to tighten their grip. This explains why perching birds do not fall off thin telephone wires—even when the creatures are asleep on a windy night.

Perching birds vary greatly in appearance. In size, they range from tiny wrens only 3 inches (7.6 centimeters) long to the lyrebirds, which may be more than 40 inches (100 centimeters) long—counting their 30-inch (75-centimeter)-long tail. Colorwise, some species—such as the Baltimore, or northern, oriole and the cock-of-the-rock—have brilliant plumage. Others, such as the wood warblers and the house sparrows, are dressed in dull-colored feathers.

The beaks vary, depending on the food eaten by the bird. For example, wrens have long, slender, slightly downcurved bills—ideal for picking insects off leaves. Cardinals have large, heavy bills adapted to crushing seeds. The strong bills of the drongos hook at the tip and

Although named for their ability to perch nearly anywhere, perching birds such as the robin above are also well-known for the care they lavish on their young.

The hooded pitohui (above), a colorful songbird on the island of New Guinea, holds the dubious distinction of being the only known bird with poisonous plumage.

are slightly notched—the better to hold insects captured while in flight.

Most songbird species can be recognized by their distinctive song or songs. A few, such as crows and jays, imitate the calls of other birds.

A number of different taxonomic systems are used by scientists to classify the Passeriformes. In general, the group is divided into more than 50 families; more than 40 of these families comprise the suborder Oscines—the songbirds. Members of the other families are sometimes called Suboscines.

SUBOSCINES

Many of these perching birds can sing. However, their vocal organs are not as well developed as those of the Oscines.

Woodcreepers

About 50 species of woodcreepers make up the family Dendrocolaptidae. These solitary tree dwellers live from Mexico and the Caribbean islands south to Argentina.

The woodcreeper ranges in length from 5 to 16 inches (12.7 to 40 centimeters); most species have olive plumage with reddish wings

and tail. Its legs are short and strong; its bill is stout, long, and adapted for probing bark to find insects and spiders—its main foods.

Ovenbirds

The family Furnariidae consists of approximately 220 species of ovenbirds. These small- to medium-sized drab brown South American birds live in a variety of habitats, from the coast to the Andes, from swamps and jungles to grasslands and rocky mountain slopes.

The ovenbird family derives its common name from members of the genus *Furnarius*, which build large, elaborate mud-and-cow-dung nests that look like old-fashioned ovens.

American Flycatchers

The tyrant flycatchers make up the family Tyrannidae. There are more than 350 species, found throughout the Americas but most numerous in the tropics. They are not to be confused with Old World flycatchers, birds that belong to the thrush family (Muscicapidae).

In temperate areas, the American flycatcher prefers open country, thin woods, orchards, or gardens. It spends much time perched on branches and poles, from which it darts after insects, its chief food. Other species live in deserts and tropical rain forests.

The American flycatcher has small, weak feet, a short neck, and a large head. Its bill, broad and flat at the base, tapers down to a hooked tip. The mouth, which has bristles at its corners, can open wide.

The male vermilion flycatcher (below) is the only brightly plumaged American flycatcher that ranges into the United States. The female's feathers are rather drab.

The "tyrant" nickname derives from this bird's aggressive behavior—perhaps most obvious when it drives off larger birds, such as hawks and crows, that encroach on its territory.

Among the most fearless Tyrannidae are the kingbirds, genus *Tyrannus*. The Eastern kingbird, *Tyrannus tyrannus*, is a bit smaller than a robin; its plumage is white, black, and gray, with an orange crown. This bird nests in rural areas in eastern North America, and winters in Central America and parts of northern South America.

A particularly striking member of the family is the many-colored rush tyrant, *Tachuris rubrigastra*, of South America. Its plumage includes vibrant shades of greens, oranges, and reds, as well as black and white.

The family also includes the small phoebe, of the genus *Sayornis*, and the Eastern wood pewee, *Contopus virens*. These sparrow-sized creatures have gray-brown or olive feathers above and whitish ones below. Pewees prefer woodlands; phoebes, human habitations.

Cotingas

The 90 species of the family Cotingidae all live in the New World, from Central America south into South America. These forest dwellers have short, sturdy legs and large, hooked beaks. Cotingas usually eat insects and fruits.

The birds in this family differ greatly in appearance from one species to another. Most have dull-colored plumage, but some are brightly colored. The male cock-of-the-rock of the genus *Rupicola* has bright red or orange feathers; atop its head is a flattened, disklike crest. The female, by contrast, while also having a crest, is substantially smaller and has unremarkable brown plumage.

Lyrebirds

The beautiful lyrebirds (family Menuridae) are perhaps best known

Extravagant tail feathers, a trait of lyrebirds, are also a feature of the male whydah (above), a perching bird of the weaver family.

for the adult male's magnificent tail—a true extravaganza in which two large outer feathers fringe 12 filamentary feathers; all the tail feathers have silvery undersides. On some males, the feathers reach 2.5 feet (76 centimeters) in length! During the courtship ritual, the male spreads the tail feathers and brings them forward over his back, all the time dancing and singing to the female, often mimicking the songs of other forest birds.

Without its remarkable tail, the lyrebird looks somewhat like an ordinary hen. It has a large head; long neck; and short, rounded, and rather weak wings. Its long legs terminate in feet equipped with heavy claws.

OSCINES

Larks

Only one of the 75 species in the family Alaudidae is native to the Americas; the remainder inhabit Europe, Asia, and, especially, Africa. In general, larks are sparrowlike birds with small, rounded bills, rounded shanks, and greatly elongated hind toenails. Many species are noted for their very lovely songs.

The horned lark, *Eremophila alpestris*, is widely distributed throughout North and South America. It averages 7 inches (17.7 centimeters) in length and has curious black markings about the face and little tufts of erectile black feathers on the head.

These beneficial birds frequent open farm country and prairie land, where they run along roads or soar aloft, whistling cheerfully. They feed largely on the seeds of weeds, except during the nesting season, when they consume a great many harmful insects.

The horned larks begin nesting very early in the spring. Prior to mating, the males perform daring aerial courtship rituals. Olive or grayish speckled eggs are laid in the nest—essentially a depression in the grass.

The barred antshrike is a relatively common species in Central and South America. The female barred antshrike (above) has reddish-brown plumage, while the body of the male (below) has bold black and white bars.

Not so long ago, horned larks were captured in huge numbers and sold as game birds. Today they are protected by law.

Swallows

The swallows (family Hirundinidae) have long appeared in literature as symbols of spring. The nesting swallows greet the early sun of a summer morning with pleasant warbling. They are day birds, and birds of the air. Their bodies express this adaptation beautifully; they have a thin, streamlined shape; long, tapered wings; and graceful forked or notched tails. The swallow's smooth glide over the surface of a pond, as it quenches its thirst in flight, is an inspiring sight. The bird rarely walks on the ground, as its feet are small and weak—fit only for perching.

The swallow family is worldwide in distribution. Its 75 species are insectivorous, which,

as with all insect-eating birds, means that they have short, flat bills.

The migration of swallows is linked to the abundance of insects in the air. As insects begin to disappear with the approach of cold weather, thousands of swallows assemble in flocks, preparing for their journey to warmer lands. In the spring, the swallows dependably return with the first warm weather and the accompanying reappearance of insects.

Cuckoo-shrikes

The members of this group (family Campephagidae) are related neither to cuckoos nor shrikes. The 70 species, distributed from Africa through Asia to the Philippines and Australia, are tree dwellers, living in forests and woodlands and feeding on insects and small fruits. They range in length from 5 to 13 inches (12.7 to 33 centimeters).

The black-faced cuckoo-shrike, *Coracina novaehollandiae*, spends the summer in southern Australia and Tasmania, where it usually nests on a thick, horizontal branch of a eucalyptus tree. Like most cuckoo-shrikes, the black-faced species builds a shallow, frail nest. Both parents share the tasks of nest building, incubating, and caring for the young. The birds fly to warmer locales for the winter.

The minivets, also members of the Campephagidae family, are a group of slender, brightly colored birds found mainly in tropical forests of Asia. The sharply hooked bill is well adapted to picking insects from leaves or catching them in midair.

Shrikes

The shrikes (family Laniidae) comprise an Old World family of 70 or so species. Only two of these, the loggerhead and the northern, are found in North America.

The shrike, a frequent predator of other birds, well deserves its nickname "butcherbird." Unlike a bird of prey, the shrike has ordinary songbird feet, and is therefore unable to attack birds with its talons the way an eagle might. Instead, it uses its powerful, sharp, and hooked bill to impale its prey on a thorn or on a barb of a wire fence, or even to wedge the hapless victim into a forked tree branch. Then the shrike perches on one side of its trapped prey, braces itself, and begins feeding.

The shrike does not limit its diet to small birds such as sparrows and chickadees; it also preys on insects, mice, and snakes. In time of plenty, a shrike may kill more than it needs and leave the surplus impaled on thorns.

Shrikes usually select a prominent fence post or the top of a tree from which to survey the countryside and locate their prey. They can adjust their eyes for different distances, enabling them to keep their victim in focus at all times. Some ornithologists claim that a shrike can fly directly to a spot several hundred yards away and catch a grasshopper.

The shrike builds a large open nest into which four or five mottled grayish eggs are laid. The bird is known to boldly defend its family.

The shrike's song can be described as a subdued "shek-shek," sometimes prolonged into a magpielike rattle—a curious mixture of harsh sounds and musical notes. The bird's anxiety cry is a grating "jaaeg."

Waxwings

The waxwing is noted for its dignified carriage and its quiet coloring and conduct. The family name of this feathered aristocrat—Bombycillidae—is derived from the word *bombyx* ("silkworm" in Latin), a reference to the silky texture of its brownish plumage. A reddish-chestnut crest, yellow-tipped tail feathers, and red, waxlike appendages on the inner wing feathers further distinguish this creature. Adults have a black eye stripe and throat patch.

Waxwings are widely distributed throughout the Northern Hemisphere, despite their being one of the smallest families of birds, with only three species. Eastern Asia is home to the Japanese waxwing, *Bombycilla japonica*, which

Songbird Populations: Something to Sing About?

For decades, ornithologists and amateur bird-watchers in North America have observed an apparent decline in the numbers of songbirds, especially the Neotropical varieties which nest in North America and migrate to the tropics in winter. Deforestation in tropical regions and increasing hazards to migrating birds seemed the likely culprits in what appeared to be an alarming collapse of many cherished bird species.

But the population of many Neotropical migrants is now stable, and, in some cases, steadily increasing. In addition, the Neotropical Migratory Bird Conservation Act was signed into law in 2000, and has addressed the need for protecting the habitats of many migratory songbirds. Although some species—especially grassland birds—are declining in numbers, the majority of woodland bird species are benefiting from the gradual reforestation of regions of the United States and Canada that were clear-cut in the 1800s. While observers have noticed a decline in local bird populations, the total number of birds, when averaged over large areas, appears to be holding steady.

According to Scott K. Robinson, Ph.D., of the University of Illinois in Urbana, large areas of deep forest, especially in the Midwest and Northeast, serve as "reservoirs" that overflow with surplus birds. These birds repopulate smaller woods, farms, and suburban areas. But small and lightly wooded habitats are perilous places for songbirds. Predation by house cats, raccoons, and other creatures takes a heavy toll, giving the impression that bird numbers are declining.

Grassland species such as the bobolink, meadowlark, and grasshopper sparrow are indeed in trouble, largely because of changing farming techniques. Pastures and hay fields are being converted to cropland, where few birds can nest. And with new species of fast-growing grasses being used, hay fields are being harvested earlier in the season, often while ground-nesting birds are still on their nests. One recent study has also suggested that pesticides have played a role in the birds' decline.

Overall, however, the trend is encouraging. Large, dense woods are relatively safe places for songbirds to nest, and with the number of natural bird sanctuaries increasing, woodland birds should have plenty to sing about for years to come.

Jerry Dennis

has a rosy-red tail band instead of a yellow one. The Bohemian waxwing, *B. garrulus*, is found in North America, Europe, and Asia. The cedar waxwing, *B. cedrorum*, ranges throughout the United States and Canada.

The waxwing's call note is a weak and high-trilled "zhreee"—more like the whistle belonging to a street vendor's peanut roaster than a melodious tune. Legend holds that the waxwing gave up music because it hindered the bird's success in eating cherries. Interestingly, the waxwing prefers wild fruits. Still, it will likely become a pest around commercially grown sweet cherry trees, especially when native fruits or mulberries are scarce. Therefore, the best way to protect a cherry-growing business against the waxwing is to plant plenty of native fruits throughout the orchard to sate the bird's appetite. The waxwings more than pay for the fruits they eat by devouring insect pests found in orchards and trees.

Waxwings love company. They travel in compact flocks, and they even eat together. Sometimes members of a small flock arrange themselves on a branch where only the one at the end can reach the fruit. It plucks the fruit and very politely passes the food to its neighbor and so on down the line until the last bird is reached. The last bird then swallows the morsel. This avian conveyor belt may continue for some time before the birds scatter and commence feeding by themselves.

Rather late in the breeding season, the waxwing finally builds a bulky nest 7 to 10 feet (2 to 3 meters) above the ground, into which it deposits three to five spotted bluish-gray eggs.

Wrens

The energetic, small brown wrens (family Troglodytidae) occur in both hemispheres, although the majority of the 350 species dwell in the tropics of South and Central America.

Despite their numbers, wrens are remarkably uniform in their plumage, sporting browns and grays in very inconspicuous patterns. The birds are from 4 to 6 inches (10 to 15 centimeters) long, with rounded wings and short tails, which they characteristically hold erect or tilt forward over the back. Their small, plump brown bodies and their habit of haunting brush piles or walking on the ground give them a strikingly mouselike appearance. They constantly flutter about as though on springs, scolding trespassers in a loud voice.

Individual species can be identified by their distinctly different songs. The male sings a song of surprising volume and sweetness; the female seldom sings except in some tropical species, when the mates sing "duets."

The house wren (*Troglodytes aëdon*), one of the most common of all wren species, is found throughout North and South America from Quebec to Argentina. It is uniformly dark brown above, faintly barred with black, and brownish gray below.

The house wren somewhat resembles another quite common species, Bewick's wren, *Thryomanes bewickii*. The latter, however, has a light line over its eye and light spots on the corners of its tail.

Both species are fond of the habitations of people, and both are quick to avail themselves of nesting boxes put up for them.

The long-billed marsh wren (*Cistothorus palustris*) of North America frequents the cattails and sedges of marshes bordering lakes, creeks, or sloughs. There its incessant song will always be heard. Even after dark, when most birds are quiet, the marshes will resound with their chorus. Often the wrens seem to be carried away by the exuberance of their own songs and, springing from the cattails, seem actually to explode upward. With their feathers shaken out, their short wings vibrating, and their cocky tails tilted far forward, their plump little bodies look like cotton balls.

The long-billed marsh wren is noted for its amazing nest-building habits. Each season, it typically builds several elaborate nests—for no known reason.

In the arid regions of the western United States dwells the largest and most unwrenlike of the family—the cactus wren, *Campylorhynchus brunneicapillus*—a gray bird with a white-spotted breast. Its large, retort-shaped nests are among the most characteristic sights in cactus country. The cactus wren's song is less musical than that of any other wren, although it is delivered in pure wren fashion—with the tail drooping and the head thrown back.

Although at present the cactus wren is found primarily in arid, uncultivated desert land, its dietary preferences may, at some future date, be put to very valuable use by humans.

These birds feed on insects injurious to valuable crops; fostering this species in agricultural areas would bring a powerful ally to the side of farmers in their never-ending battle against harmful insect pests.

A Family of Mimics

Members of the family Mimidae imitate other birds. In fact, one mockingbird holds a record for imitating 32 different species in 10 minutes of continuous singing! Not all members of the family are such good mimics, or mockers. Many confine themselves to their own brilliant notes.

There are 34 species in the family Mimidae, all limited to the New World. Included in the family are mockingbirds, catbirds, and thrashers.

When perched, the hermit thrush has a habit of slowly cocking its reddish tail and then dropping it slowly. This spotted brown bird is especially fond of the berries that grow on dogwood trees (above).

Mockingbirds. On the average, the typical mockingbird is about the size of a thrush. The best-known species is the northern mockingbird, *Mimus polyglottos*. This bird is quite abundant along the Gulf of Mexico, where its rich songs are frequently heard—even at night.

The northern mockingbird is a slender ashy-gray robin-sized bird with white marks in the darker wings and tail. It thrives wherever there is a thicket for hiding and an exposed perch for singing.

Catbirds. The catbird (*Dumetella carolinensis*), a common species of Canada and the United States, resembles the mockingbird in its long, slender silhouette, but it is darker and lacks white bars on the wings and tail. Its only marks are a black cap, black tail, and reddish-brown feathers at the base of the tail. The catbird's name derives from the harsh, catlike notes with which it scolds every intruder and with which it ruins an otherwise-melodious song. Many catbirds learn to imitate with great skill the notes of other birds.

Catbirds are either very sympathetic to the troubles of the avian world or they are very inquisitive. Indeed, whenever a bird is in distress and gives an alarm cry, all the catbirds of the neighborhood assemble to stare at and to scold the disturber. In the defense of their own nests, catbirds are seldom excelled for bravery.

The catbird is largely insectivorous and therefore beneficial. However, together with

many other birds, it shows a partiality for cherries and other small fruits in season. Where mulberries and wild fruits are available, cultivated varieties seldom suffer.

Thrashers. Thrashers are the most numerous of the Mimidae family. Their center of distribution is the southwestern United States, from which they extend southward through Mexico and westward through Southern California and Baja California.

Only one species, the brown thrasher (*Toxostoma rufum*), occurs east of the Rocky Mountain region, ranging throughout eastern North America as far north as Quebec and occasionally even somewhat farther away. The brown thrasher is often confused with the wood thrush, although the thrasher differs in its much longer, slightly curved bill; its long tail; and its streaked, rather than spotted, underparts. It is a shy bird, much more often heard than seen. Indeed, this thrasher keeps to the undergrowth, where it scratches the leaves on the ground or digs holes with its bill in search of food.

The brown thrasher produces a snortlike sound when it apparently blows soil from its nostrils. When singing, the male flies to the topmost branches of a tree and bellows forth loud, ringing notes that can be heard for long distances. The song is a rich, ringing medley. Although limited in its range and confined to one tune, the thrasher's song rivals the mockingbird's in its exuberance.

Occasionally the thrasher lives near gardens, especially if some effort is made to develop a tangle of shrubbery in which it can find seclusion and safety from enemies. Like the mockingbirds and catbirds, the thrasher will fly to a food shelf for suet and crumbs and may even become quite friendly. When the bird is angry or in active defense of its nest, it vigorously flies about in a thrashing motion, the characteristic from which it derives its name.

The Thrush Family

Members of the family Muscicapidae are found in most parts of the world, although the greatest numbers live in the Eastern Hemisphere. The family includes many well-known birds: the robin, bluebird, and wood thrush of North America; the garden warbler and blackbird of Europe; the fantail and tomtit of New Zealand; and so on.

The birds of this family are generally insectivores that capture their prey in the air. Others hunt for insects in foliage, on branches, or on the ground.

Thrushes. The widely distributed subfamily Turdinae encompasses more than 300 species, including the robins, wood thrushes, bluebirds, wheatears, bluethroats, rock thrushes, and nightingales. These familiar birds inhabit parks, gardens, fields, and woodlands.

Thrushes are medium-sized songbirds—averaging less than 12 inches (30 centimeters) in length—with strong wings and legs; long, slender bills that are slightly curved at the tip;

and uniformly colored (rather than streaked) plumage. Most thrushes are dull brownish to grayish, although some species have more brightly hued feathers. The underparts are white, with spots. Most thrushes produce beautifully melodious songs.

Except during the nesting season, thrushes travel in scattered flocks, hunting food. They usually eat insects during spring and early summer, and wild fruits or berries in late summer and fall. Some thrushes winter in cool areas, while others prefer to spend the cold months in tropical regions.

The American robin, *Turdus migratorius*, with its black head and reddish breast, is one of the most familiar thrushes in the United States. It is famed as a herald of spring, although some robins remain in one area during the entire winter. The robin builds its mud nest wherever it finds a sheltered ledge near a house or garden.

To shape the nest, the female robin uses her breast, turning around and around. The eggs are the familiar "robin's-egg blue." The robin's merry phrase, "cheerily, cheerily," and the brisk, businesslike manner with which it dispatches earthworms and insects makes it one of the most beloved wild birds in North America.

The "robin redbreast" of children's rhymes is the European robin, *Erithacus rubecula*, a smaller bird than its American cousin. The upperparts are olive brown, while the forehead, throat, and breast are bright orange-red. The European robin uses its lovely song to define its territory and warn other birds to stay away.

Several small North American thrushes of the genus *Sialia* are commonly known as bluebirds. Of the two sexes, the males have more blue in their plumage, and even then, the bird must be in bright light for the blue to stand out strongly enough to make a clear species identification. This beautiful bird is very devoted to its family, as befits a symbol of happiness. It nests in an abandoned woodpecker hole, a cavity in a tree or fence post, or in a birdhouse. The bluebird destroys an enormous

Even considering the male's faint red breast streaks, no other warbler has such extensively yellow plumage as does the yellow warbler (left), a common songbird in the United States.

The cheerful, inquisitive black-capped chickadee (above) is a familiar visitor to bird feeders throughout the United States. In the northern parts of its range, the great tit (right) is reputed to store food for the winter in crevices in tree bark.

number of insects, making it a most welcome visitor to gardens.

Few birds have sweeter songs than that of the hermit thrush, or American nightingale, *Catharus guttatus*. One seldom hears this very shy bird, as it frequents woodlands rather than gardens. It is easily identifiable by its tail, which is a much brighter brown than the rest of its back, and its dark-spotted white breast, a typical thrush characteristic. The hermit thrush nests in Canada and in the hills and mountains of the northern United States, always above a height of about 45 feet (14 meters).

The name "blackbird" is commonly given to several species of thrushes. The "4 and 20 blackbirds" of nursery-rhyme fame refers to the European blackbird, *Turdus merula*, which has also been introduced into Australia and New Zealand. Some 10 inches (25 centimeters) in length, the male is entirely black, except for a yellow bill. The female is dark brown, with a paler throat and a brown bill. Blackbirds live in many different types of environments. They are ground feeders, favoring insects and fruits.

Flycatchers. Flycatchers range from Europe and Asia through the islands of the Pacific to Australia and New Zealand. Some 50 species are found in New Guinea alone.

These birds vary greatly in appearance: some have brightly colored plumage, while others are dull in color; some have wattles on the face; a few have crests. Most are comparatively small-sized, with long, pointed wings and relatively short tails. A typical species is the spotted flycatcher, *Muscicapa striata*. This European bird is brownish gray with a creamy breast. Its song is a monotonous chirp.

Warblers. Warblers are small, insectivorous birds with thin, pointed bills. The common name comes from the trilling, or warbling, song that these creatures produce. Many have very melodious songs, while other species sing monotonous or even unpleasant tunes. The 275 species live throughout the Old World.

Two species, known as kinglets, are found in North America, Eurasia, and Taiwan. The kinglets sometimes follow the winter flocks of chickadees and nuthatches southward. More often, however, these small grayish-olive-green birds keep very much to themselves among the evergreens, searching for scale insects and aphids. Their movements are quick, their wings constantly flitting. Their bright gold or red crowns are partially concealed except when they raise their head feathers.

True Tits and Chickadees

The family Paridae contains some 60 bird species that are common in the woodlands of the Northern Hemisphere and Africa.

As a group, these birds have the common characteristics of small size; short, cone-shaped

The brown, or tree, creeper (above) is a wide-ranging, stiff-tailed bird that lives in cool, wooded areas of North America and Eurasia. The Hawaiian honeycreeper (below) is a nectar-feeding perching bird.

bills; blunt-ended tongues; rounded and well-developed wings; and rounded tail feathers. Their plumage is never spotted, streaked, or barred. Grays, browns, and olives predominate on the upperparts, dull white and gray on the lower ones. Some of these birds may have black, gray, or yellow around the head, or—as in the case of the tufted titmouse—they may sport protruding tufts.

Although a titmouse will eat almost anything, it prefers a diet of insects. When these are not available, it will eat various seeds and the larvae and eggs of insects.

Only a few species migrate south for the winter. After the nesting season, members of most species of these sociably inclined little birds join forces in loosely organized groups and spend the cold winter months foraging for food together. Seeming to enjoy their society, other winter birds, such as the downy and hairy woodpeckers and the golden kinglets, often fol-

low titmouse flocks. Not only do these birds get along well together, but they seem to have little fear of people and gather about suburban dwellings wherever food is offered to them.

In North America, by far the most beloved titmice are the chickadees—dull grayish birds with lighter plumage below and conspicuous black crowns and throat patches. Although they differ slightly, all 10 species can be easily identified as chickadees.

The songs and call notes of the different species vary considerably, but all have a family similarity. The call of the common species gives the name to the family, for it is a clearly enunciated "chick-a-dee" or "chick-a-dee-dee-dee." In other species, the call is less clear, more highly pitched, or more nasal. The common chickadee has a song of two or three whistled notes resembling the syllables "phe-be" or "phe-be-be" so exactly that amateur bird-watchers are often led to believe that it is a phoebe calling. When flying through the woods, the chickadees have a variety of conversational notes that are rather difficult to describe. They also utter a hissing sound when protecting their eggs or their young against intruders.

Chickadees are friendly, inquisitive birds, especially at winter feeding stations. They are always ready to answer an imitation of their "phe-be" call, and even will greet the person uttering the call. These cheerful little creatures will perch on the branches above the person's head, sometimes even dropping to the person's shoulder or hovering in front of his or her face in a vain effort to discover the whereabouts of the other "chickadee."

Nuthatches

The 70 species of nuthatches (family Sittidae) are confined largely to the Northern Hemisphere. This creature is an acrobatic little inspector of the trunks and larger branches of trees. It climbs with equal facility whether its head is upward or downward, devouring vast numbers of insects along the way. In clinging to trees, it does not use its tail as a balancing prop, but relies on its large, strong feet. Its feet are of the ordinary perching type, but the toes and claws are much better developed than in most other perching birds. In fact, the nuthatch has been known to sleep hanging head downward, clinging to the bark beneath a jutting limb.

The nuthatch is a lively little creature, seemingly always on the move. The "hatch" in its name comes from the Middle English *hake,* meaning "hack," an apt reference to the manner in which the bird wedges nuts or seeds into crevices in a tree's bark, and then hacks away at them in order to get at the tasty contents.

Tree Creepers

Members of the family Certhiidae are weak fliers; instead, they "creep" up and down tree trunks in search of insects. They can accomplish this feat thanks to their large feet and strong tail feathers, which, when pressed against a tree, lend the bird support. The beak is slender, rather long, and curved—well adapted for probing into crevices in search of insects.

The tree creeper, *Certhia familiaris,* is a slender bird about 5.5 inches (14 centimeters) long. Its streaked brown back provides camouflage in that it makes the bird resemble a bit of animated bark as it climbs about the trunks of trees, using its stiffly spined tail feathers as a prop. The brown creeper has a slender, curved bill, and dines on such insects and larvae as it can find in the crevices of the bark. This bird's song consists of a few weak notes.

The largest creeper, the wall creeper, *Tichadroma muraria,* is about 7 inches (17.7 centimeters) long and lives in mountainous parts of Europe and Asia. Its plumage is dull gray, with black on the chest and throat; patches of red on its wings are visible during flight.

The seven species of Australian tree creepers, which are similar to other tree creepers except that they lack the strong, rigid tail feathers, belong to the subfamily Climacterinae.

Sunbirds

Sunbirds are very small, brilliantly colored birds comprising the family Nectariniidae, a word derived from the eating habits and favorite food of these creatures. Sunbirds have long, slender bills (curved downward in many species) and a partly tubular tongue—two adaptations that help the bird reach into flowers to gather nectar and insects.

Sunbirds are Old World birds, distributed from Africa and the Middle East across Asia to New Guinea and Australia. The greatest variety is found in Africa. These birds live in many different habitats, from mountains to coastal lands, from tropical forests and swamps to grasslands and semidesert areas. Some are common near human settlements.

The males of most species have metallic-colored plumage—bright greens, purples, and bronzes—on the back and breast, and nonmetallic belly plumage. The female plumage is usually a dull olive or brown.

Buntings

The buntings (family Emberizidae), closely related to the finches, have a worldwide distribution. They are essentially ground birds, more common in grasslands than in forests. The bill is short and cone-shaped—an adaptation to a diet largely composed of seeds.

In North America, many buntings are commonly called sparrows or finches. "True" spar-

The painted bunting (above) is considered the most garishly colored songbird of North America. The plumage of the pine grosbeak (below), although conspicuously red, is substantially more subdued than that of the bunting.

rows and finches, however, are members of other families (Passerinae and Fringillidae). Among the best-known and most-beloved buntings of the Americas are the grosbeaks and the cardinals.

The northern cardinal, *Cardinalis cardinalis*, makes its home from southeastern Canada to Mexico. It may be more than 9 inches (22.8 centimeters) long, with a tail of up to 5 inches (12.7 centimeters) in length. The male is a brilliant scarlet, except for black around the stout red bill. The female is brownish, with some red in the plumage and a red bill. Both sexes have conspicuous crests.

Tanagers

The brightly colored tanagers are New World birds. Most of the more than 200 species of the subfamily (Thraupinae) are confined to Central and South America. The greatest number live in tropical areas.

These stout little woodland birds have a tail that is shorter than the wings; the heavy bill has a large, naked nostril. Males have the brilliant feathers, with much red, green, yellow, blue, and black in their plumage; the females tend to be a yellowish-green color, which blends with the leaves of the treetops where they nest and feed. Males may assume a more subdued garb in the late summer. These birds live on insects and fruits. Most of them are about 7 inches (17.7 centimeters) long.

Tanagers generally have wheezy or squeaky voices. The scarlet tanager *(Piranga olivacea)*, the most familiar North American member of the Thraupinae, also has perhaps the most pleasant song of the family, sounding much like a hoarse robin giving a hurried performance. During the summer, the male has bright scarlet plumage and a black tail and wings. In winter, these colors change to olive green. The female is olive green throughout the year. The scarlet tanager summers in the eastern United States and Canada; it winters in South America.

Wood Warblers

The New World wood warblers usually have an unwarbler-like song and probably were named for their Old World counterparts because of their similar body shape, quick movements, and insectivorous habits. In addition to their songs, a prime difference between the New World wood warblers and the Old World warblers is that the former have nine primary feathers, whereas the latter have 10.

The wood warblers form the family Parulidae, the second-largest family of American birds (after the finches). Wood warblers have thin bills and attractive plumage with pleasing color patterns. Yellow is the dominant color, combined with markings of white, black, chestnut, olive green, or gray-blue. The female's feathers are generally drabber than the male's.

The male western tanager (above) has a red face and head. The male bowerbird (below left) has the unusual habit of decorating his nest with trinkets. The red-eyed vireo (below right) is a common songbird of the forests.

Many wood warblers dwell in the trees of parks, gardens, and forests, where they hunt insects. Others inhabit low trees and bushes. Still others live on the ground, especially along the shores of streams or ponds.

Except for the myrtle warbler, most northern species head south for the winter. Many fly from the northern United States and southern Canada to the southern United States. Other warblers winter in Mexico, Central America, the West Indies, or South America.

The wood warblers travel mainly at night in their southern migrations, although they continue their journey slowly during the day, feeding as they go. They make long flights across bodies of water, occasionally by day but much more often by night.

The wide variety of plumage and of feeding and nesting habits among the wood warblers is likely the result of a relatively recent evolution. The woodlands and forests contain so many species of warblers that competition would be extremely severe if each warbler species had not adapted itself to a slightly different manner of existence.

Although almost all the wood warblers are insectivores, they differ in the manner of catching their food. Some snap insects up in flight, others glean them from the bark of trees, and still others snatch up the insects as they flit along the ground. Some wood warblers simply search them out of the debris on the forest floor. This diet is often supplemented with aquatic organisms and the juice of various fruits.

As mentioned, the name warbler is a misnomer for most of these birds. Their ordinary calls are shrill, unmusical, wheezy sounds—such as the myrtle's *tchep-tchep*, the blackpoll's rising *east-east-east-east*, and the sewing-machine trill of the worm-eating warbler. Nevertheless, a few have songs of subtle beauty—such as the Swainson's clear, rich whistle; the Nashville's eight full-voiced notes and rolling twitter; and the myrtle's "sleigh bell" trill.

The trees in the forest where wood warblers live are in constant danger from leaf-eating insects and caterpillars. It is indeed fortunate that such pests fall prey to insect-eating birds.

Vireos

Vireo is a Latin word meaning "I am green," and green is indeed the basic color of

The spotted-breasted oriole (above, with young) is a vibrantly colored and vocally gifted bird of Mexico and Central America. More familiar to North Americans is the distinctive orange breast of the Baltimore oriole (below).

the birds we call vireos (family Vireonidae). Usually the green is combined with gray and yellow in attractive combinations. Vireos often travel in the company of warblers, from which they can be distinguished by their softer color combinations, slightly larger size, proportionately larger heads, and heavier bills. Vireo movements are more deliberate than those of the nervous little wood warblers. Even their song has an unhurried quality. The vireo sings from dawn to dusk: it even sings after the exhausting molting season has caused most other birds to fall silent.

The vireos form an exclusively North and South American family of about 40 species.

The finch family includes species from every corner of the world. An Old World goldfinch (above) attends to its young in a typical cup-shaped finch nest. The sparrow-like house finch (below) lives throughout North America.

With only a very few exceptions, they are arboreal birds frequenting shade trees of city streets, brush, and woodlands. Vireos feed greedily on insects and insect larvae; in the fall, berries are added to the diet.

These birds are found from sea level to about 9,800 feet (3,000 meters). Most vireo species breed in the cold parts of the Northern Hemisphere and then migrate to the tropics for the winter months.

One of North America's most common forest birds is the red-eyed vireo, *Vireo olivaceus*. Its intermittent song is heard wherever trees occur in any substantial number. It is olive green above and white below, with a slate-gray cap bordered on either side by black. There is a white line over the eye, which is red in the adult and brown in the young.

American Blackbirds

The varied family Icteridae, found only in the Americas, includes blackbirds, bobolinks, cowbirds, grackles, meadowlarks, and orioles—about 95 species in all. All have stout bills with exposed nostrils, strong perching feet, pointed wings, and tails of 12 feathers, the tips of which are square or rounded—never forked. Black is usually prominent.

The Icteridae eat seeds, insects, and fruits. During the summer, when their diet is composed principally of insects, they are very valuable birds. In the fall, however, many species assemble in large flocks and often do considerable damage to grainfields. This family has the dubious distinction of containing the only American parasitic bird species: the cowbird, which lays its eggs in the nests of other species.

The red-winged blackbird, *Agelaius phoeniceus*, is about 10 inches (25 centimeters) long. The female is streaked gray and black like a large sparrow; the male, by contrast, is glistening black with red epaulets. This bird summers in the cattail marshes of eastern North America, and flies south for the winter.

Grackles may attain lengths of 16 inches (40 centimeters) or more, making them particularly large members of the blackbird family. Most have a metallic bronze and dark purple sheen to the plumage; the tail is shaped like the keel of a boat. The grackle walks jerkily over lawns, "conversing" in its harsh, squeaky voice.

The bobolink, *Dolichonyx oryzivorus*, is a valuable field bird with ground-nesting habits. The male bobolink is black with buff or yellowish-white markings, while the female is streaked brown. Its joyous song is most delightful—except to rice growers in the southern regions of the United States, where the bobolink feasts on the growing plants.

There are about 40 species of orioles, distributed throughout temperate and tropical America. (The Old World orioles belong to another family—the Oriolidae.) Although not great singers, orioles produce sweet whistling calls. The males are quite grand in their orange, chestnut, yellow, and black plumage. Orioles devour great numbers of destructive insects.

A well-known oriole is the Baltimore, or northern, oriole, *Icterus galbula*, so named because the orange and black colors of the male resemble the colors on the coat of arms of Britain's Baltimore family. The bird summers throughout eastern North America, and winters from Mexico south to Colombia. Adults measure about 8 inches (20 centimeters) long.

The Finch Family

The large finch family, Fringillidae, has representatives all over the world, except for some Pacific islands and Antarctica. Finches are most abundant in the Northern Hemisphere, where they range in length from 4 to 10 inches (10 to 25 centimeters). Among their distinguishing characteristics are a thick-based, conical bill and the presence of only nine primary flight feathers. These birds feed mainly on seeds, but they also eat other plant matter and some insects. They build open, cup-shaped nests.

Many members of the Fringillidae are commonly called sparrows. (Other birds that are called sparrows belong to the weaver family, Ploceidae.) The typical sparrows are rather dull-colored, brown and gray birds, usually heavily streaked to blend in with the pattern of the grasses where most of them live. Others, such as the goldfinches, have striking colors.

Many species produce beautiful songs and are well-known cage birds—the canary and European bullfinch being prime examples.

Sparrows adapt themselves readily to their environment. They are hardy birds, with many species never migrating. An excess of light and aridity tends to make them pale in color. They turn darker in extreme humidity or shade.

Weavers

The 300 species in the family Ploceidae resemble the Fringillidae, but have 10 primary

Some Old World weaverbirds create breeding colonies in which numerous nests dangle from a single tree (above). The house sparrow (below) is a species of weaverbird known more for its noisy behavior than for its skillful nest building.

flight feathers and build dome-shaped nests. These are Old World birds, although some species have been introduced into the Americas. The Old World sparrows belong to this family.

The English, or house, sparrow, *Passer domesticus*, is well known around the world. In some countries, this pugnacious, hardy, noisy little bird has become *too* well naturalized, since it has at least partially displaced several native species. At a Shakespeare festival, for instance, a few house sparrows were introduced to the East Coast of the United States. In less than 30 years, the species had spread across the continent to the Pacific Ocean.

The house sparrow is about 5.5 inches (14 centimeters) long. The male adult has a dark gray crown, chestnut neck, black throat, whitish cheeks, brown back, and a grayish-white belly. The females and young have duller plumage (brown above and whitish below).

Starlings

Until 1890, there were no starlings in North America. At that time, 60 common starlings, *Sturnus vulgaris*, were released in New York City; 40 more were released in 1891. From these 100 birds have descended all those that now swarm over most of the North American continent.

There are about 60 species of starlings—family Sturnidae—native to Southeast Asia and Africa. As with the house, or English, sparrow, America was warned against the starling by European ornithologists. Unfortunately, the warning came too late.

Studies of the starlings' food consumption throughout the year show that, economically, they do much good. Unfortunately, this domineering bird displaces many more-valuable birds—such as swallows and flickers—by driving them away from their nesting sites and feeding grounds. Since starlings withstand northern winters, they appropriate the best nesting and feeding sites before migratory birds return in the spring.

After the nesting season, starlings gather in enormous flocks. Before retiring and upon arising, the entire flock performs a series of aerial maneuvers with all the precision of trained soldiers. In the air, starlings can be recognized by their strong, direct flight, their pointed wings, and their square tails. On the ground, they walk like blackbirds, but have longer bills, which are yellow during the nesting season. Their much shorter tails are quite distinctive. During the fall and winter, their iridescent black feathers are spotted with buff, but this coloring wears off as spring approaches.

Birds of Paradise

These birds, which make up the family Paradisaeidae, are famous for the beautiful colors of their plumage and for the elegant translucent feathers displayed by the males during courtship. In some but not all species, males and females have similar coloration.

Birds of paradise live in the forests of New Guinea and nearby islands; a few species are found in the Moluccas and Australia. These birds are primarily fruit eaters, but also feed on insects, lizards, and other small animals.

Birds of paradise may reach lengths of 18 inches (45 centimeters). The largest species is the greater bird of paradise, *Paradisaea apoda*. The male has a yellow head, green throat, and spectacular metallic yellow plumes projecting from the sides of his body.

The Crow Family

The crows, jays, ravens, magpies, jackdaws, rooks, and choughs make up a single family: Corvidae. The more than 400 species and subspecies of Corvidae are found everywhere except New Zealand. All make interesting but mischievous pets, and some can be taught to articulate a few words. In their natural state, they are greatly disliked by farmers and feared by other birds.

All members of the family have stout, heavy bills with thick tufts of bristles concealing the nostrils. They have strong legs and toes, which are adapted for walking and perch-

The starling (top) has proved itself a nuisance since its introduction to the United States in 1890. All but unknown to Americans is the red bird of paradise from Oceania. The male develops extravagant plumage (left), which he displays to females as part of an elaborate courtship ritual.

ing, and strong, rounded wings. The American crows and ravens are uniformly black with metallic reflections. The jays and magpies are brilliantly colored; blues, greens, blacks, and whites predominate. The crows and ravens have short, square tails. Jays and magpies have long, tapered tails.

Corvidae eat nearly everything—insects, fruits, grains, nuts, crustaceans, fish, and the eggs and young of other birds—whatever is most easily procured. Consequently, they are often of considerable value during insect outbreaks, because they then feed on insect pests to the exclusion of nearly everything else. However, when grain or eggs are more readily available than other foods, these birds can do considerable damage. Many spend the winter in northern climes.

Jays. These noisy woodland birds bully smaller birds and rob their nests. They are mischievous creatures that delight in mobbing a sleepy owl; following and tormenting a dog, cat, or fox; or mimicking a hawk—to the consternation of smaller birds. Jays store up grains and seeds for winter use, and so are important factors in the natural dispersal of nut, oak, and fruit trees.

Jays nest early in the spring, building bulky affairs of twigs lined with fine grass and feathers. They lay four or five eggs, mottled with gray and brown. Both male and female take part in building the nest and feeding the young. The birds are pugnacious when their nest is disturbed.

The plumage of many jays features blue. Some species are exceptionally colored. The green jay, *Cyanocorax yncas*, which ranges from Mexico to Peru, has a green back, yellow belly and outer tail feathers, and a blue crest.

Crows. Crows are much more destructive than jays. In addition to their egg-destroying habits, they are larger and bolder than jays. They often fly into the poultry yard looking for young chickens and eggs; they regularly feed on corn and other grains. At the same time, crows also destroy large numbers of harmful insects.

Steller's jay (above) is common in the coniferous forests west of the Rocky Mountains. In the eastern United States, the blue jay (below, incubating its eggs) is well-known for its bold, noisy behavior.

Ravens. Several large, dark crows of the genus *Corvus* are known as ravens. These birds, found throughout the Northern Hemisphere, have been immortalized by many writers.

The common raven, *Corvus corax*, is about 25 inches (63 centimeters) long. Its plumage is sable brown. It feeds on the ground of forests and other wild areas, eating a variety of foods: fruits, small birds and mammals, and carrion. With the spread of human habitation, ravens have been displaced by crows in many areas.

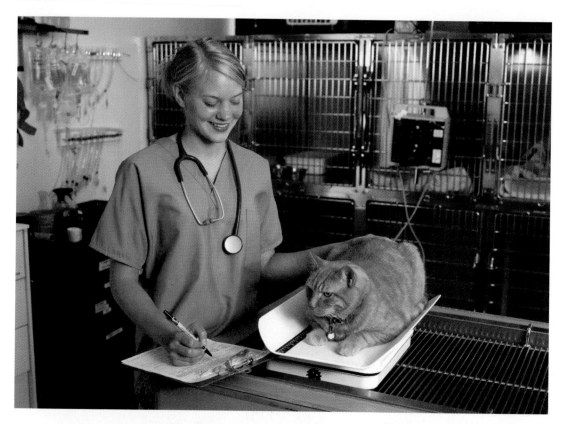

VETERINARIANS
AND THEIR SCIENCE

by Jenny Tesar

Charlie had stopped eating and was losing weight: a painful abscess had developed under one of his teeth. Instead of pulling the tooth, the dentist performed root-canal therapy and put a crown on the tooth. Meanwhile, Sarah Anne is recovering from cataract surgery, and Willie is getting accustomed to his hip implant. Pablo is back to his old self after having had open-heart surgery, Billy has a new pacemaker to regulate his heartbeat, and Millie is feeling better since the surgeon removed a tumor.

None of this sounds unusual until you realize the patients under discussion are not human beings. They're animals: dogs, cats, birds, cows, horses, dolphins, seals, and other species. And their doctors are veterinarians.

WHAT IS VETERINARY SCIENCE?

Veterinary science is the branch of medicine that is concerned with the health and welfare of animals. Veterinarians diagnose, prevent, and control animal diseases; treat sick and injured animals; and advise owners on the proper care of their animals. They care for wildlife, too, particularly animals in zoos, but also creatures in the wild that are threatened by extinction; their responsibilities include not only maintaining the health of these animals but also ensuring successful reproduction. They help enforce laws dealing with the import and export of animals, including laws designed to prevent illegal trade in endangered species.

Veterinarians protect human health and welfare, too. More than 100 animal diseases, called zoonoses, can be transmitted to humans, and veterinarians participate in control programs designed to check the spread of these dis-

For the healthy cat or dog, the first order of business during a routine visit to the veterinarian's office is to have the animal's medical records brought up to date.

Some veterinarians work to ensure the survival of endangered species. A zoo-born rhinoceros (right) will likely be doted upon by staff veterinarians.

eases. Veterinarians also maintain economically important animals on farms and aquaculture operations, and they often oversee the production of meat, milk, and processed foods.

Once lagging far behind human medicine in its sophistication and capability, veterinary medicine has now all but caught up—and in some cases has advanced further. For instance, veterinarians administer a vaccine that protects cats against feline leukemia; no vaccine is yet available to combat any form of human cancer. Virtually anything the medical community can do for human patients, the veterinary community can do for animals.

A veterinarian's medicine cabinet contains many of the same drugs prescribed by physicians. Captopril or hydralazine may be prescribed to dilate the blood vessels of a dog suffering from high blood pressure, thus making it easier for the heart to pump blood through the vessels. Analgesics such as aspirin may be given to relieve the pain experienced by a bird suffering from gout. Daily injections of insulin are the treatment for a cat that has diabetes. Antidepressants and antianxiety drugs are prescribed for treating obsessive-compulsive disorders, such as a cat's incessant chewing of its tail.

Preventive health measures, such as removing plaque and tartar that accumulate on teeth, play an important role in veterinary medicine. Alternative therapies have a place, too, particularly in combination with conventional therapies. These therapies include homeopathy, chiropractic, shiatsu massage, Chinese herbal remedies, and acupuncture. For instance, veterinarians have had some success in using acupuncture to treat a skin condition called lick granuloma, a disorder in which a dog or cat obsessively licks its fur.

Psychological therapies also are part of a veterinarian's arsenal of treatments. Aggression, excessive vocalization, and other antisocial behavior often can be reduced through a combination of behavior-modification techniques and drug therapy. As with humans, physical examinations are needed to rule out disease, metabolic disorders, and other medical causes for the undesirable behavior.

VETERINARY SPECIALTIES

Many veterinarians are generalists, much like the family physicians who treat human patients, but with an important difference: a physician needs to understand only one species, *Homo sapiens*, whereas a veterinarian may treat everything from household pets to barnyard creatures.

Before embarking on an expensive breeding program for Galápagos tortoises, veterinarians must first screen individual specimens (left) by conducting extensive tests.

No two species of animals are identical. Each has its own anatomy, biochemistry, nutritional needs, behavioral patterns, and, hence, responses to medical treatment. Each species also has unique medical problems. For this reason, some veterinarians may treat only cats, while others concentrate on birds, horses, or zoo animals. Still others specialize in a particular branch of medicine, such as veterinary cardiology, dermatology, oncology, parasitology, pharmacology, radiology, or surgery.

Companion-Animal Veterinarians

About half of the veterinarians in the United States focus on companion animals: cats, dogs, birds, guinea pigs, and other animals that are family pets. An animal's visit to such a veterinarian typically begins much like a person's visit to a family physician. The veterinarian will ask about the animal's medical history, including its age, vaccinations, previous injuries, and any problems observed by the owner. Then the veterinarian will perform a physical examination, looking at the animal's general appearance, taking its temperature and pulse, listening to its heart, checking its ears, and so on. Samples of the animal's blood, urine, and feces may be examined, and diagnostic tools such as X rays, ultrasound, CAT scans, or an electrocardiogram may be needed. A biopsy is sometimes taken for

Careers in Veterinary Science

To become a veterinarian, a person must complete two to four years of undergraduate study before attending a veterinary college, where the educational training is comparable to that completed by medical doctors. Typically, the first two years of the curriculum at a veterinary college focus on classroom and laboratory studies in subjects such as anatomy, physiology, pathology, pharmacology, and microbiology. The second two years focus on clinical work, giving students the opportunity to treat animals under the supervision of faculty members.

Gaining admission to veterinary school is considered at least as difficult as getting into medical school. Graduates must pass state examinations and acquire a license before going into practice.

Upon graduation, veterinarians who wish to work in private practice must pass an examination and acquire a license from the state in which they wish to conduct their work. But they never leave behind their days of study and learning. They must keep up to date by reading scientific journals and attending professional meetings and seminars.

Veterinarians work in a variety of settings. The majority are in private practice, most working exclusively with companion animals. Other veterinarians teach and conduct research at veterinary schools; work for government agencies such as departments of agriculture, the military, environmental agencies, and city health departments; work for pharmaceutical, agricultural-chemical, and pet-food companies; and practice at zoos, aquariums, wildlife preserves, racetracks, and so on.

Assisting veterinarians are veterinary technicians and assistants, who handle such chores as preparing animals for surgery, collecting specimens, dressing wounds, and performing certain laboratory procedures. A career as a veterinary technician requires completion of a two-year college-level program. Veterinary assistants typically receive training on the job, in secondary schools, or at less than the two-year college level. In addition to working in veterinary practices, technicians and assistants are employed by pharmaceutical companies, food-inspection agencies, public-health organizations, research institutions, and other facilities.

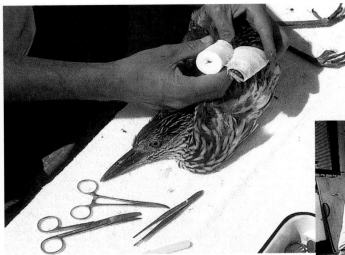

Aquariums (below) almost always employ their own veterinarians to care for their animals. Most city veterinarians specialize in household pets, although injured birds and other wild animals are sometimes brought in for emergency treatment (left).

examination under the microscope. Based on the veterinarian's findings, a course of treatment is determined. This may include a special diet, medication, or hospitalization and surgery.

At one time, infections such as feline respiratory disease and canine distemper killed many pets. Today these diseases can be prevented by vaccinations. Boosters against the diseases usually are necessary to maintain immunity. Vaccinations against rabies also are critical protection not only for the animals but also for humans with whom they come into contact. Another important part of a companion-animal practice is surgery to sterilize, or neuter, animals so that they cannot reproduce. Animal sterilization can often be arranged at minimal expense through local humane societies.

Medical advances have helped to extend the life span of companion animals; it is not unusual, for instance, to hear of cats living into their 20s. But with old age come significant physiological changes, including decreased immunity to disease, difficulty in regulating body temperature, impaired kidney function, and declining ability to absorb food nutrients. If the animal becomes incurably ill and has a great deal of pain, the veterinarian may need to administer a lethal injection.

The care of horses can be part of a companion-animal or large-animal practice, but it also is sometimes considered a separate specialty. The latter is particularly common in regions where horses are bred and raised, as well as in places where horse racing takes place.

Large-Animal Veterinarians

Large-animal veterinarians typically specialize in the care and treatment of livestock. In North America, the category comprises mainly cattle, sheep, goats, pigs, and, in some cases, horses and bison. Elsewhere, it includes animals such as reindeer or llamas. Farmers and ranchers depend on regular, frequent visits by veterinarians to keep their herds disease-free and to help them make decisions about their livestock that will maximize profits.

When treating livestock, veterinarians must be careful in their use of antibiotics, hormones, and other medications. If residues of these chemicals contaminate meat or milk, the products may not be suitable for sale. Veterinarians also perform blood-chemistry tests and review farmers' feed programs, making nutritional recommendations that will improve milk production or weight gain. Veterinarians often are present for the birth of babies, particularly if complications are expected.

As advances have been made in genetics and reproductive science, livestock-breeding programs have become extremely sophisticated. A process called artificial insemination, for example, now accounts for the majority of dairy-cattle births, and is also used to aid reproduction in other livestock. In another procedure, a hormone may be injected into a cow that is a heavy milk producer, causing her to produce a dozen or more eggs during ovulation, rather than the usual one or two. The eggs are fertilized by artificial insemination and removed from the cow. The veterinarian then implants each fertilized egg, or embryo, into the uterus of a surrogate-mother cow, where it will develop into a normal calf with the characteristics of its genetic parents. If not needed immediately, the fertilized eggs can be frozen for later use.

Veterinary Research

Veterinarians involved in research increase our understanding not only of animals and disease-causing organisms but also of humans. For instance, much of our understanding of heart disease, drug addiction, and pain mechanisms was derived from animal research.

The development of antibiotics, vaccines, and other drugs, both for animals and for humans, is an important area of research. Vaccines for protection against parvovirus in dogs and Lyme disease in humans, drugs to treat cholera in pigs and manic depression in humans, anesthetics for surgical procedures—all were made possible by animal research.

Surgical techniques and the development of prosthetics are other areas of research. For instance, researchers have developed intraocular lenses that can be implanted in the eyes of animals following cataract surgery. Therapeutic soft contact lenses—for species from birds to elephants—bathe the eye with medication and can be used to treat corneal abrasions, corneal ulcers, and other eye problems.

The newest techniques in biotechnology and genetic engineering are aimed at producing hardier, more-productive livestock, poultry, and fish. Among the most exciting yet controversial genetic procedures is cloning, or producing offspring that are exact genetic replicas of a single adult animal. In 1996, the first clone of an adult farm animal (a sheep) was reported. Since then, scientists have successfully cloned a bull, horses, a mule, a gaur, a dog, and several pigs. Pigs have also been genetically altered to make them better suited to donate organs to humans.

Veterinarians oversee animal facilities at universities, pharmaceutical companies, and other research centers. They monitor the care and use of animals, perform standard diagnostic and other medical procedures, maintain breeding programs, and ensure that the institutions' animal facilities and programs meet government-mandated standards.

VETERINARY SCIENCE IN THE FUTURE

The challenges facing veterinarians are expected to increase in the coming years due to various factors, including:

• The need to understand how diseases are transmitted from animals to humans. Each year brings news of yet another disease that has "jumped" from animal to human. AIDS (acquired immune deficiency syndrome), for example, is caused by a virus that may have evolved from related viruses in African monkeys.

• Concern about the quality and safety of food. Consumers want beef that contains limited amounts of fat and is free of pesticides, hormones, and other chemicals. They want pork that is germ-free, but they shy away from irradiated food. Veterinary care and research can play a role in resolving issues such as these.

• The multitude of threats to wildlife, ranging from oil pollution to diminishing habitats. Veterinarians will search for improved ways to treat animals harmed by environmental pollutants, and will increasingly use techniques such as artificial insemination and embryo transfer to maintain endangered species.

• Rising prominence of animal-welfare issues. Nearly all biomedical research relies on testing in animals and humans, and government regulations require tests in animals before a treatment can be tested in humans. Increasingly, however, objections to the use of live animals are forcing veterinarians and other scientists to search for humane yet valid alternatives. For instance, new drug compounds are now first tested in cell cultures; if they are found to be toxic, they are not tested on animals.

• The growing number of companion animals, coupled with people's willingness to seek and pay for the very best care for these animals. People recognize that today there are numerous alternatives to putting an animal to sleep. Even if a beloved pet develops heart disease or cancer, all is not hopeless. The prognosis for recovery and a return to good health may be excellent, thanks to modern veterinary science.

ZOOS AQUARIUMS & WILDLIFE PARKS

by Jessica Snyder Sachs

The colorful creatures inside the glass-walled enclosure chatter, squeal, and press against the windows of their pen at the Central Park Zoo in New York City. On the rocky shore outside, three polar bears ignore the antics and continue their morning sunbath. After a few minutes, the still-chattering crowd moves on to a new enclosure, this one on the edge of a penguin colony.

Welcome to the modern zoo—a place designed to give captive animals as much freedom as possible, while minimizing the intrusion of their human visitors. The result is a win-win situation that lets zoo-goers glimpse wild animals living near-normal lives.

At its most expansive, the world's "new zoos" take the form of wildlife parks, where animals wander freely over hundreds of acres that visitors view from trams or protected walkways. In recent decades, many of the world's most-

visited public aquariums have likewise taken this all-surrounding approach to animal exhibition—with visitors literally walking under water inside glass-walled tunnels and canyons.

WHY ZOOS AND AQUARIUMS?

For thousands of years, people have been caging animals for personal and public entertainment. Today, "going to the zoo" still ranks among the most popular of family pastimes. In North America, zoo attendance surpasses that of all professional sports combined, and virtually everyone (98 percent) has visited a zoo or aquarium at least once by adulthood.

Today's zoos try to re-create the natural living conditions of their residents. At New York City's Central Park Zoo, polar bears (above) dwell in roomy "habitats," while human visitors observe unobtrusively from afar.

Over the past 50 years, the mission of the world's major zoos and aquariums has expanded beyond public recreation. As the last refuge for many endangered species, a significant number of these institutions sponsor captive-breeding programs, zoological research, and conservation-education projects.

ZOOS THROUGH HISTORY

Some 3,100 years ago, China's Emperor Wen-Wang created the first known zoo, a walled animal park called the "Garden of Intelligence." But only royalty and monks enjoyed its pleasures. Macedonia's Ptolemy I built the first public zoo around 300 B.C. in Alexandria, Egypt. Around 1240, England's King Henry III opened his royal menagerie to the public, in effect creating the first London Zoo. Long before 1517, when the Spanish conquistadores arrived in Mexico, the Aztecs kept colorful birds in large and elaborate aviaries. During the late 1600s and early 1700s, the Renaissance spread the popularity of public menageries throughout Europe. The first public aquarium opened at Regent's Park, England, in 1853.

In 1862, the first U.S. zoo opened in New York City's Central Park, followed by Chicago's Lincoln Park Zoo in 1868, and Washington, D.C.'s National Aquarium in 1873. In addition, countless carnivals and circuses displayed trained and caged animals as part of their traveling exhibits. Soon every major American city wanted its own zoological garden.

Early zoos depended largely on hunters to capture wild animals for their collections. Zoo hunters typically shot older animals in order to take their young. Adding to the carnage, fewer than half of captured animals survived their long-distance journey to the zoo. Moreover, many of the new arrivals died within days to months. A large part of the problem was diet. A gorilla in a typical 19th-century zoo, for example, might be fed boiled potatoes and mutton, instead of its natural diet of fresh leaves and fruit. Zoo visitors routinely fed animals candy, peanuts, and whatever else they might have in their pockets.

To gain some reaction from the listless animals, visitors commonly banged on bars,

Until recently, most zoos confined their animals in cages. Many patrons inadvertently caused harm by feeding the animals (above). Often, the creatures seemed frightened or even bored (center). Once encaged, a large cat, like the snow leopard (top), might spend the rest of its life in enforced inactivity.

yelled, or pelted the creatures with food and other objects. Not surprisingly, few zoo animals mated or gave birth in those days.

At the dawn of the 20th century, zoos remained mere collections of caged animals, the aim being to have a single specimen of as many species as possible. Zoos typically grouped types of animals together in side-by-side cages within ape houses, bear houses, and the like.

A New Vision

Carl Hagenbeck, a German animal dealer, had a vision of a zoo without bars. In 1900, he used moats, hedges, and rocks to create a naturalistic zoo with no visible barriers between visitors and animals, and with the illusion of predators and prey living side by side. In doing so, he became the first to bring animals and zoo visitors out of cramped, dank buildings and into a beautiful landscape.

Visitors of all ages can meander among the wildlife on special walkways and bridges at Disney's Animal Kingdom Park (right). SeaWorld (below) and other large marine aquariums have gained fine reputations for the work they do with marine animals. At nearly all modern zoos, animal nutritionists look after the appetites of their charges (above).

Hagenbeck also established the convention of grouping animals according to geography instead of taxonomy. For example, he grouped lions with zebras, gazelles, and hyenas to evoke the African savanna (instead of with cougars and tigers in a "cat house").

Hagenbeck's approach proved popular with visitors. But the world's zoos were slow to adopt his ideas. Not until the 1960s did major zoos begin to use moats instead of steel bars, and to place animals on dirt and grass instead of concrete or tile.

The second half of the 20th century brought huge improvements in zoo animal care. The American Association of Zoo Veterinarians (AAZV), established in 1960, developed training programs for the new specialties of exotic-animal medicine and nutrition. For the first time, zoo animals began living longer, on average, than those in the wild.

At the same time, zoo directors realized that happy creatures made baby creatures. Building enclosures roomy and comfortable enough to encourage

The safe and rapid transport of an animal from one zoo to another requires an enormous amount of planning on the part of zoo curators.

ed by the association, a zoo or aquarium must meet high standards in areas such as animal care, ethics, science, and conservation.

By the beginning of the 21st century, more than 99 percent of the large mammals in accredited U.S. zoos came from captive-breeding programs. Collecting from the wild has become largely unnecessary, except when wild animal species need rescuing from poaching and habitat destruction.

Sadly, not all zoos and aquariums have shared in the progress of the past century. In contrast to the 200-odd AZA-accredited parks, more than 1,000 small North American zoos and game ranches still display animals in cramped cages, concrete pits, and other inadequate conditions.

breeding became more affordable than hunting down increasingly rare animals. In the 1970s, the birthrates of animals in zoos began surpassing the death rates.

The 1970s saw the first wildlife parks, with visitors riding trains and trucks through giant preserves of roaming animals. Notable among these early preserves was the San Diego Wild Animal Park—an 1,800-acre (700-hectare) simulated African plain that visitors toured on a quiet monorail.

Public aquariums such as Marine World in Vallejo, California, followed this immersion-in-nature trend with clear tunnels that allowed visitors to enter underwater worlds teeming with life. Even more popular with the public were the live whale and dolphin shows featured at marine-aquarium theme parks such as SeaWorld.

Around the same time, zoos began enriching the lives of their animals with naturalistic activities. Rather than simply feeding animals in troughs, zookeepers began dangling treats from branches or hiding them in hollow logs drilled with holes. They also found ways to use traditional animal shows to meet a creature's need for mental and physical activity. This proved especially important for intelligent and athletic animals such as whales, dolphins, and seals.

In 1972, the American Zoo and Aquarium Association (AZA) incorporated to oversee conditions at North American zoos. To be accredit-

ACQUIRING WILD ANIMALS

Today, international, national, state, and local laws strictly control how and when animals can be taken from the wild. The AZA likewise requires its member organizations to acquire animals only from reputable dealers who use humane methods for capture and transport.

Special red lighting encourages nocturnal animals to be active—and visible to zoo patrons—during the day.

State-of-the-art aquariums and marine parks have vastly broadened the scope of their presentations. At the Oregon Coast Aquarium, in Newport, Oregon, starfish, sea urchins, and other inhabitants of the intertidal zone are displayed in a visitor-friendly, albeit closely supervised, exhibit (below). At the Audubon Aquarium of the Americas' Caribbean Reef, in New Orleans, patrons can walk through special glass tubes (right) to gain the sensation of entering the marine habitat.

As previously noted, the world's major zoos now rely almost entirely on captive-breeding programs rather than wild capture. To maximize the success of these programs, the AZA coordinates the trade and loan of animal mates between member institutions.

Zoos also serve as safe havens for many illegally or inhumanely kept exotic pets and circus animals. Zoo rescue work involves saving rare wild animals threatened by the destruction of their natural habitat. New York City's Wildlife Conservation Society (WCS), for example, recently rescued 500 specimens of a newly discovered Tanzanian frog when the construction of a hydroelectric dam threatened to wipe out the entire population of the species.

TRANSPORTING WILD ANIMALS

The safe transport of animals—either from the wild or between zoos and aquariums—presents a great logistical challenge. Minimizing

transit time is key, says WCS curator Nilda Ferrer. So, weeks to months before, curators begin to carefully plan every step of the move, with backup plans for emergencies (such as airline delays).

Typically, the most challenging step in the shipment process is prevailing upon an animal to enter its shipment crate. Zoo veterinarians sometimes use a mild, temporary tranquilizer. Today, many curators help animals grow accustomed to entering and exiting crates as part of their behavior-enrichment exercises.

For health and safety reasons, zoo animals never travel while under sedation. To calm an easily excited animal such as a bird, keepers may block the animal's view by placing burlap or some other breathable covering over crate openings. One or more familiar keepers may accompany a traveling animal. But many animals destined for the zoo, from birds to gorillas, fly unaccompanied—sometimes in a cargo hold, other times in first class.

Typically, an animal arriving at a zoo or aquarium from the wild is placed in isolation, where it can be monitored for possible disease before it is released to live among other animals. Often zookeepers will use a see-through barrier such as a fence to separate new animals from established residents until they have had a chance to get acquainted.

The designers of aviaries face parallel challenges: the exhibits must be bright, natural-looking, and appealing to visitors, but they must also be heavily screened and otherwise secure enough so that the birds cannot simply fly away.

DISPLAYING WILD ANIMALS

Over the years, zoos and aquariums have developed many ways to display creatures. The least desirable (some would say criminal) of these methods is the barren cage or tank. Animals kept in such conditions often suffer from lack of physical activity and mental stimulation. Some species tend to develop compulsive behaviors such as relentless pacing; others sink into a listless state.

The Enriched Cage

Many small mammals can thrive in a relatively limited space if given a stimulating environment. Nesting material, climbing structures, and other naturalistic features can help make a cage a "home," and stimulate natural behaviors such as burrowing, swimming, or running. Caged animals also need space or time away from the intrusion of visitors. In the Nocturnal House of Seattle's Woodland Park Zoo, for example, zookeepers use red lights to encourage nocturnal animals to remain active during the day, then switch on white lights in the evening, so the animals can sleep peacefully after their visitors have gone.

Aquariums

Maintaining proper water chemistry remains a major challenge for all public aquariums. Before the first fish arrives, aquatic biologists must balance a tank's mineral content, pH (acidity), and aeration (oxygen content). A typi-

Thick safety glass encloses the exhibits of venomous snakes and other animals that could potentially cause harm to patrons or zookeepers.

Zoo and aquarium employment is not always glamorous, the American Zoo and Aquarium Association tells would-be keepers, curators, and wild-animal veterinarians. "It takes a special kind of dedication to provide care to captive animals that require attention 24 hours a day, seven days a week, come snow, rain, or shine."

Of course, animal care is just one type of position found in a typical zoo or aquarium. Zoos cannot operate without competent administrators, groundskeepers, and membership directors, many of whom enjoy the opportunity to work around animals. Zoos and aquariums likewise employ educators to work with school groups and run informative programs for animal lovers of all ages. Most also employ horticulturists, or plant experts, to develop and maintain botanical collections. These may range from ordinary landscaping to entire mini–rain forests, deserts, and other habitats inside and around wildlife enclosures. The exhibit curators use their artistic talents and strong communications skills to convey information in graphic and eye-catching ways.

Those wishing to pursue a career working directly with zoo animals would do well to attain a college degree in animal science, zoology, marine biology, conservation biology, wildlife management, or animal behavior. Today, even entry-level zookeeper and aquarist positions often require a four-year college degree. Animal curators—scientists who oversee part or all of an institution's animal collection—generally hold advanced academic degrees in some aspect of animal science.

Wildlife veterinarians provide health care for zoo and aquarium animals, and may assist in captive-breeding programs. Preparation for a career as a zoo vet requires four years of undergraduate college study with a strong emphasis in biology and chemistry, followed by four years at a veterinary college and several years of specialized training in exotic-animal or wildlife medicine.

Assisting the wildlife veterinarian is the veterinary technician. Some veterinarians still train their own technicians. But increasingly, this position is filled by graduates of two-year veterinary technical programs.

During high school, would-be keepers, curators, veterinarians, and veterinary technicians should complete college-preparatory courses in science, mathematics, and English; volunteer opportunities at local zoos and aquariums should also be explored. Many zoos and aquariums offer summer and after-school programs for highschoolers and internships for college students.

A favorite task at any zoo is feeding and otherwise doting over the baby animals (left). The personnel who work with wild animals (below) require extensive specialized training.

Insects won't inherit the earth—
they own it now

Thomas Eisner, Entomologist

Insects are very difficult to contain and exhibit. Some zoos have discovered an especially useful approach: present displays of live insects and preserved specimens side-by-side.

est aviary at Riverbanks Zoo and Garden in Columbia, South Carolina, can even enjoy thunderstorms at scheduled intervals throughout the day.

Herpetariums and Insectariums

Many amphibians, insects, and reptiles thrive only within a narrow range of temperatures, humidity, and other environmental conditions. It follows, then, that their enclosures may be grouped inside climate-controlled reptile, amphibian, or insect houses. The museum-like Insect World at the Cincinnati Zoo, for example, features exotic insects such as Hercules beetles and venomous bullet ants alongside hands-on educational activities and displays. The San Diego Zoo's Reptile House has separate environmental controls for side-by-side displays of rattlesnakes, pythons, cobras, tropical frogs, and Komodo dragons.

Open-Air Enclosures

Open-air enclosures have become the norm in most major zoos. The best of these exhibits re-create minihabitats for their resident animals.

cal oceanarium tank, for example, may contain 150,000 pounds (68,000 kilograms) of salt and 100,000 pounds (45,000 kilograms) of other minerals and chemicals evenly dissolved in 750,000 gallons (2.8 million liters) of freshwater. Once fish and other sea life take up residence, room-sized filters must continually clean the water of animal waste.

Some of the world's best public aquariums create diverse habitats filled with a variety of species. In the 138,000-gallon (522,000-liter) Nickajack Lake exhibit of the Tennessee Aquarium, for example, flathead catfish perch on rocks surrounded by branches, sunfish hang motionless beneath sunken tree trunks, and striped bass position themselves in the fast-flowing current that delivers water into the 25-foot (7.6-meter)-deep tank.

In many wildlife parks, visitors travel among the animals in trams or other open-air vehicles intended to resemble those on safaris.

Aviaries

A typical zoo aviary consists of a large, mesh-covered bird enclosure placed out-of-doors, with nesting boxes or other shelters provided for cold weather. Houses and indoor rooms can likewise be transformed into aviaries, with the addition of plants and other perches where birds can take refuge. A well-designed aviary allows visitors to witness natural bird behaviors such as courting, nesting, and the fledging of young. The largest aviaries enclose mini-forests and other habitats that zoo-goers can enter. Visitors to the rain-for-

Zoo-managed captive-breeding programs have helped bring a number of species back from the brink of extinction. The Arabian oryx (above) has been successfully reintroduced to its Middle East habitat using zoo-bred herds.

The Asian tigers of the San Diego Zoo, for example, inhabit a grassy hillside complete with waterfalls and pools for bathing and rocks and logs for climbing.

Wildlife Parks

Many consider the wildlife park to be the best way to watch zoo animals live as freely as possible. Of course, in actual wilderness situations, animals fight and eat each other. So wildlife-park curators must artfully separate natural enemies with the use of moats and other hidden barriers. Typically, visitors tour wildlife parks in enclosed vehicles. The San Diego Wild Animal Park and Disney's Animal Kingdom in Florida, for example, offer safari-type adventures in trams, trains, and flatbed trucks. The wildlife park of the Arizona-Sonora Desert Museum features miles of paths through natural areas alive with native animals from the surrounding deserts and mountains.

ZOOS AND CONSERVATION

Over the past 50 years, the world's major zoos and public aquariums have committed themselves to the role of "protectors, not just collectors." As wild populations and their natural habitats continue to shrink, these institutions have become the new breeding ground for many rare and endangered species.

Central to this mission is the Species Survival Plan adopted by the American Zoo and Aquarium Association in 1981. As part of the plan, the AZA's 200-odd member organizations lend and borrow rare animals in order to ensure breeding success. On a global level, the International Species Information System maintains a worldwide computer database of more than 700,000 animals suitable for breeding, at more than 450 zoos and aquariums in 54 countries.

The goals of such programs include reintroducing threatened and endangered animals back into the wild. Some have been remarkably successful. The Arabian oryx, for example, was extinct in its native home for more than 20 years before the first zoo-bred herds were returned to the Middle East in 1982.

Zoos also help ensure the survival of rare animals through research and field projects. The Wildlife Conservation Society, for example, has helped protect hundreds of millions of acres of wild habitat around the world, and funds the work of more than 150 conservation scientists (this in addition to running New York City's public aquarium and five zoos).

Notable Zoos in the United States

Name of Zoo	Location	Area Acres (Hectares)	Number of Species
Arizona-Sonora Desert Museum	Tucson, Arizona	75 (30)	300+
Bronx Zoo	Bronx, New York	265 (107)	578
Brookfield Zoo	Brookfield, Illinois	216 (87)	375
Cincinnati Zoo & Botanical Garden	Cincinnati, Ohio	75 (30)	510
Cleveland Metroparks Zoo	Cleveland, Ohio	165 (67)	600+
Columbus Zoo and Aquarium	Powell, Ohio	588 (238)	10,362
Dallas Zoo	Dallas, Texas	97 (39)	524
Denver Zoo	Denver, Colorado	80 (32)	700+
Detroit Zoo	Royal Oak, Michigan	125 (51)	270
Houston Zoo	Houston, Texas	55 (22)	500+
Indianapolis Zoo	Indianapolis, Indiana	64 (26)	190
Los Angeles Zoo & Botanical Gardens	Los Angeles, California	100 (40)	250
Louisville Zoo	Louisville, Kentucky	135 (55)	366
The Maryland Zoo in Baltimore	Baltimore, Maryland	160 (65)	200
Memphis Zoo	Memphis, Tennessee	70 (28)	500
Miami MetroZoo	Miami, Florida	300 (120)	390
Milwaukee County Zoo	Milwaukee, Wisconsin	200 (81)	350+
Minnesota Zoo	Apple Valley, Minnesota	500 (203)	388
North Carolina Zoo	Asheboro, North Carolina	500 (203)	250
Oklahoma City Zoo	Oklahoma City, Oklahoma	203 (82)	1,500
Omaha's Henry Doorly Zoo	Omaha, Nebraska	130 (53)	1,000
Philadelphia Zoo	Philadelphia, Pennsylvania	42 (17)	300+
Phoenix Zoo	Phoenix, Arizona	125 (51)	200+
Riverbanks Zoo and Garden	Columbia, South Carolina	170 (69)	350
San Diego Wild Animal Park	San Diego, California	1,800 (730)	400+
San Diego Zoo	San Diego, California	100 (40)	800+
Smithsonian National Zoological Park	Washington, D.C.	90 (36)	800
Woodland Park Zoo	Seattle, Washington	92 (37)	300
Zoo Atlanta	Atlanta, Georgia	39 (16)	220

Zoo curators offer the following tips for making the most out of a day at a zoo, aquarium, or wildlife park.

• *Time your visit.* Cooler months can be a great time to see lots of animal activity with a minimum of crowds. During hot summer months, animals in outdoor exhibits tend to be most active in the early morning. Call ahead or check the park's Internet site to find out the schedule and locations of animal shows and feedings.

• *Brush up before you go.* Reading a book or two about zoos, aquariums, or a particular group of animals can enliven an upcoming visit by piquing curiosity and deepening understanding.

• *Come equipped.* Remember to wear comfortable shoes, clothing to suit the weather, and Sun protection such as a hat and sunscreen. Binoculars bring distant animals up close, and cameras are a must.

• *More to explore.* Call or check the Internet to find out about special opportunities such as behind-the-scenes tours, overnight zoo camps, photo safaris, and talks by animal curators.

A day at the zoo is a treat for the whole family. A little research prior to the visit can provide ideas on what exhibits not to miss. Much of this information can be found on the zoo's Internet site, which will also provide hours of operation, descriptions of special activities, and downloadable maps showing how to best get around the facility. The guided tour (right) is often the highlight of a trip to the zoo.

ZOOS AND EDUCATION

More than 100 million people visit North American zoos and aquariums each year. Globally, the number exceeds 600 million, or nearly 10 percent of the population. For many visitors, the zoo will be the only place where they will come into close contact with wildlife. For children, their first-ever visit to a zoo can make an indelible impression.

Consequently, zoos and aquariums share an unprecedented opportunity to educate entire communities about the importance of preserving wildlife and wild habitats. This increasing emphasis on education has led to many new, innovative exhibits and visitor activities, including hands-on laboratories, computer simulations, behind-the-scene tours, and safari camps (where groups can spend the night within earshot of roaring lions and other wild animals).

"One thing is certain," says Terry Maple, director of Zoo Atlanta, "if we're to be successful in our conservation, science, and education missions, we must not abandon our commitment to recreation." Thankfully, zoos can always bank on a certain universal appeal: the opportunity to gaze into the eyes of a tiger, touch an elephant's trunk, or turn over a living starfish. Such close encounters touch something deep inside almost everyone.

pets

Pet ownership may be the world's ultimate animal science. Every year, hundreds of millions of pet owners learn volumes about animal psychology, physiology, aging, and medicine. But it's not research into animal behavior that has made pet keeping one of the world's favorite leisure activities; rather, it is the fact that pets, by definition, are companions. Their status as cherished friends and confidants distinguishes them from all other categories of domesticated animals, including those used for food, labor, and medical studies.

In many circumstances, pets double as working animals—whether herding or hunting alongside their owners or bearing their masters on their backs. Other pets, such as fish, serve an essentially decorative function, enlivening a room with color and movement.

A responsible owner, in turn, supplies a pet's physical and emotional needs, from health-ful food and fresh water to veterinary care and opportunities for enjoyable physical activity. Making the choice of an appropriate pet hinges on a clear understanding of a particular animal's requirements, and how that animal's needs fit into the lifestyle of the potential owner. Unfortunately, millions of pets end up abandoned each year by owners who failed to appreciate what caring for an animal entails.

PET CAPITAL OF THE WORLD

Pets enjoy popularity from the Arctic to the Amazon—and especially in the United States, where they rank highest in sheer numbers. Pet

Everyone knows that the perfect pet—be it dog, cat, bird, or fish—can make an enormous difference in its owner's life. Less clear is what type of animal will make that perfect fit into its owner's lifestyle.

cats now reign supreme, with around 73 million in this country, although dogs take a close second—around 68 million. Add to this: 165 million aquarium fish (but many fewer fish tanks), 19 million pet birds, 19 million rodent pets (guinea pigs, gerbils, mice, etc.), 9 million pet reptiles, and nearly 6 million pet livestock (horses, pigs, llamas, etc.).

In all, nearly two-thirds of households in the United States own at least one pet and, taken together, spend an estimated $29 billion per year on pet food, veterinary care, and related supplies and services.

While randomly bred, or "mixed-breed," dogs and cats have always been common, pet-keeping also has its fads. Handsome but difficult breeds such as Dalmatians and Rottweilers, for example, enjoy a certain vogue, only to be eclipsed a few years later by other breeds. Some pets, once considered "exotic," have continued to grow in popularity in recent decades. They include ferrets, iguanas, snakes, and tarantulas.

For thousands of years, pets have played an important role in the lives of humans. A painting of a dog on its master's coffin (above) testifies to the status of pets in ancient Egypt. Many tombs from those days also included feline-shaped vessels (right) containing the mummified remains of the deceased's cat.

HISTORY

Stone Age cave drawings suggest that the dog became humankind's first established pet more than 12,000 years ago. The first domesticated canines may have been either wolf pups hand-raised by humans, or adult wolves that started lingering near human campfires and following human hunters for cast-off bones and other leftovers.

However the transition occurred, over the course of thousands of years, domesticated wolves gradually evolved into a new breed—the domestic dog, with an appearance similar to that of the Australian dingo. Even today, feral, or free-running, dogs left to interbreed gradually return to this "generic" body type: medium-sized and short-haired, with a pointed snout and upturned tail.

By 5000 B.C., the people of Persia and Egypt had begun producing the first "designer" breeds by selectively mating dogs with certain characteristics. The earliest of all may have been the elegant, long-legged saluki, a pampered pet of royalty also used to chase down antelope. Cleopatra and Muhammad both cherished their salukis. The wealthy women of ancient Rome kept Maltese terriers and Italian greyhounds as lapdogs. The fluffy Pekingese held a privileged position in China's imperial palaces.

Humans first welcomed cats into their households more than 5,000 years ago. Presumably, the first "house cats" were semiwild creatures that preyed on mice and other rodent pests around granaries and farms. Their ancestors may have included a variety of small, wild cats in different parts of the world.

The first records of fully domesticated felines come out of Egypt, where they were worshiped as sacred animals as far back as 1500 B.C. When an Egyptian cat died, its human household went into mourning and mummified the pet's remains. Today, some of the most elaborate cat mummies can be seen in the Egyptology exhibits of many world-class museums.

The ancient Romans, Phoenicians, and Chinese likewise cherished cats. During Europe's Dark Ages, superstitions associated cats with witchcraft, notions which ultimately led to the tragically misguided torture—and even deaths—of many helpless felines.

Customers should only patronize pet stores in which the animals are clean, well-nourished, and disease-free.

Throughout history, royal and wealthy households have kept rare and expensive pets such as cheetahs and monkeys as showpieces. The fashion of keeping parrots emerged in Greece more than 2,000 years ago. Around the same time, the sport of falconry, or hunting with hawks, emerged in Central Asia. By the 16th century, caged songbirds were popular throughout China and Europe.

THE PET–OWNING EXPERIENCE

By nature, the relationship between a pet and its owner is one of symbiosis, or mutual benefit. The pet receives shelter, protection, and food from its owner. Depending on the pet, the benefits of ownership can include companionship, entertainment, affection, and obedience. Working pets help earn their keep by guarding, hunting, herding, and performing other duties. Guide dogs and canine assistants serve as trained aides to people with disabilities.

Research has shown that the companionship of a pet can even enhance a person's emotional and physical well-being. Just as friends and family help one deal with life's stresses and strains, so, too, can a pet. After all, people, like many kinds of pets, are social animals.

In many cities, professional walkers exercise the dogs of pet owners who lack the time or ability to do so themselves.

Choosing a Pet

Undeniably, a great many people become pet owners without understanding the needs of their newly chosen companions. The result: an epidemic of unwanted pets, abandoned to roam the streets and fill animal shelters. More than half of discarded dogs and cats are euthanized, or "put to sleep" (killed). Other pets end up pining for company in an empty house, pen, or backyard after their master's initial interest wears off. Not surprisingly, many of these neglected pets often cause problems for themselves and their owners by digging, scratching, chewing, barking, or otherwise venting their frustration, boredom, and loneliness.

For the most part, researching and answering a few key questions before adopting any pet can avoid such problems.

Why do you want a pet? If it's because you cannot resist a cute and cuddly puppy or kitten, stop and think about what the animal will be like as an adult. Some people pick a certain breed or type of animal because of its trendiness or rarity. Unfortunately, the "coolness" of owning a popular or exotic animal usually wears off quickly.

The title of "man's best friend" recognizes the loyalty and companionship that a dog bestows upon its master. In return, a good master invests time every day training, feeding, grooming, and exercising his or her dog.

Fish do not demand high levels of human attention. The fish tank may well be the only "pet habitat" that needs to be worked into a room's decorating scheme.

The desire for a pet's companionship is usually the best reason to adopt, as long as you remember that pets have their own personalities and emotional needs. If you want an especially affectionate and cuddly pet, remember that such animals can become extremely distressed when left alone for long periods of time. If you want an active pet for outdoor play, remember that such animals need ample daily exercise—even when the owner is not in the mood.

In addition to companionship, you may want a pet that has a special quality such as protectiveness or the ability to learn tricks. Researching the "personality" of different pets and breeds can help you make a good choice. This is not to say that purebred dogs and cats are necessarily more predictable than mixed breeds. A shepherd-collie mix, for example, is likely to have a blend of characteristics from both breeds.

In addition, a pet's early experiences powerfully affect its behavior as an adult. A puppy or kitten that receives ample affection and attention usually turns out to be a calmer and friendlier adult than does one that is mistreated or ignored.

Mice, gerbils, and other small rodents require little care beyond feeding and cage-cleaning. A pet hamster will readily avail itself of any convenient exercise apparatus (above) and, like most rodents, see to nearly all of its own needs.

How much time do you have for a pet? No pet can be ignored simply because its master is too busy. At one end of the spectrum, goldfish in a self-cleaning aquarium require little more than a sprinkle of food twice a day. A dog, on the other hand, requires daily feeding, fresh water, exercise, and lots of affection. Canine pets cannot be left indoors all day without a chance to relieve themselves, and someone must

A parrot (below) can form an extremely strong bond with its owner. Unlike birds and cats, dogs need to be brought outside at regular intervals to attend to their natural functions.

care for them when the owners are away. Some kinds of dogs and cats also need regular grooming, not just for appearance but for good health. Bulldogs, for example, need painstaking skin care. Many cats develop hair balls in their stomachs if they are not frequently brushed.

What kind of pet can you afford? Typically, a pet's purchase price or adoption fee represents a tiny fraction of the animal's lifetime expense. For starters, immunization and spaying or neutering can quickly add up to hundreds of dollars for a kitten or puppy. In addition, there is no way to predict what emergency care a pet may need.

In general, dogs, cats, and exotic birds such as parrots tend to be much more expensive to maintain than are small pets such as gerbils, mice, and guinea pigs. Fish vary in expense from easy-care guppies and goldfish to pricey and difficult-to-maintain saltwater species.

Do you have patience? Puppies chew things and have accidents. Some cats scratch furniture and yowl at night. Even good pets make messes at times, whether this means fur on the furniture or a litter box to be cleaned. Many pets misbe-

A certain amount of training helps a dog learn its role in the household. Obedience classes have the further benefit of teaching dogs to tolerate their fellow canines.

periences greatly influence whether an individual cat will grow up to be cuddly or aloof. Siamese cats have a perhaps undeserved reputation for being standoffish and temperamental. Kittens of any breed will tend to become semi-wild if they do not receive gentle and frequent handling when young.

A cat is less likely than a dog to come when it's called—unless it's in the mood to do so! On the other hand, cats have the wonderfully convenient instinct to use a litter box. So, with adequate food and water, they can be left alone indoors for the day. Most cats should also be spayed or neutered, for their own health as well as to avoid worsening the cat overpopulation problem. Unaltered males have a tendency to mark their "territory" by spraying urine.

Where people once thought nothing of letting pet cats run free outdoors, it is now clear that outdoor cats take a toll on wildlife, especially birds. Free-running cats also pick up parasites and other ailments and frequently fall victim to dogs, other cats, and cars. For these reasons, the Humane Society of the United States urges people to keep their cats indoors.

have when bored, and any pet can take ill at inconvenient times. Like children, pets require care and patience on bad days and good.

What kind of pet suits your home? Does your apartment building have restrictions on pets? Do you have a backyard or nearby park where you can exercise a dog? Size is not the only factor in matching pet to home. Some highly active small dogs need more running room than do certain large and mellow breeds.

How long of a commitment are you prepared to make? Depending on the breed, dogs live an average of 8 to 15 years. Cats can live to be 20. Some birds, such as parrots and macaws, commonly outlive their masters. By contrast, the life span of a healthy hamster or gerbil ranges from two to four years. Before obtaining a pet, consider whether you are willing to commit to care for it *for its lifetime*.

POPULAR PETS

Cats are often described as independent, unpredictable, and mysterious; they can also be wonderfully affectionate and playful. Cats vary widely in personality, but breeding and early ex-

Cats demonstrate the affection and loyalty of dogs, but require much less direct care. Today, cats are the number-one pets in the United States.

A horse can make a wonderful pet, although the time required for exercising, cleaning, and grooming is considerable. In financial terms, the cost of maintaining a horse is beyond the means of most families.

Dogs are highly social animals that need as much loving attention as they lavish on their owners. Many breeds, both large and small, also need vigorous physical activity and prove destructive when cooped up for too long. Some breeds are prone to physical ailments, such as hip problems or blindness. As with cats, dogs benefit from spaying or neutering.

In general, dogs have a strong instinct to please their masters. Given this characteristic, they can be readily trained using praise and play as their reward. Physical punishment is rarely, if ever, appropriate.

Some dog breeds are better with children than are others. Herding dogs such as collies tend to be protective around children, and retrievers such as Labradors are known for their gentleness. On the other hand, certain breeds, such as traditional fighting dogs can be unpredictably dangerous around toddlers, perhaps because a child's small size and quick movements can trigger their attack instincts.

Fish vary dramatically in their hardiness, expense, and ease of care. Goldfish and guppies tend to be the easiest and least expensive to keep. At the other end of the spectrum are saltwater fish, whose expensive marine aquariums demand careful and time-consuming attention.

Birds kept as pets include small songbirds such as parakeets (budgies), canaries, finches, doves, pigeons, and parrots. Certain birds, such as lovebirds and finches, mate for life, and should therefore always be purchased in pairs. Parakeets, or budgies, are also happiest in the company of their own. Doves and pigeons do best in small flocks inside large coops.

A solitary parrot or mynah will bond with its master for companionship, and so requires lots of attention. Like parakeets, parrots and mynahs can be patiently taught to repeat simple phrases and sounds. Parrots and mynahs, in particular, can be very affectionate. But they can also bite when irritated. Importantly, getting a parrot or mynah is a long-term commitment. They can live 40 to 50 years.

Each kind of bird has specific dietary requirements. All need clean cages, fresh water, and a cuttlebone for calcium and other minerals. Birds also need a certain amount of exercise. A caged bird needs room for limited flight, and a pole, ladder, or other "gym" equipment for climbing.

Potentially dangerous "pets" should only be handled by trained individuals. Many people find the idea of keeping a boa constrictor (below) objectionable.

Most people have seen or read about guide dogs, which assist their blind or near-ly blind masters. Through special training, dogs can also serve as the hands and ears of the disabled—picking up dropped objects, opening doors, even "calling" for help when it is needed. Some dogs even learn how to recognize an approaching epileptic seizure, presumably by detecting subtle changes in a person's behavior or odor. Such dogs are trained to alert their master to lie down or otherwise seek a safe spot until the seizure has passed.

Other animals serve as "pet therapists." Spe-cially trained handlers bring gentle dogs, cats, rabbits, and other mild-mannered animals into nursing homes and hos-pitals, where residents

and patients enjoy the soothing experience of holding, petting, and talking to them.

Medical studies also show that animal com-panionship can help re-lieve depression, lower high blood pressure, improve cholesterol levels, and even increase survival rates from heart attack. In other words, pets are more than just fun. They can be good medicine as well.

A service dog (top) fetches items and performs other tasks for its owner; guide dogs (center) help their masters navigate a sidewalk. Therapy pets visit hospitals and other facilities; at left, a golden retriev-er gives an ailing man a few moments of distraction.

Rodent pets include hamsters, gerbils, guinea pigs, and domesticated mice and rats. All like to gnaw and burrow. Their cages should in-clude concealed sleeping quarters and appropri-ate chewing toys. Pet stores sell specially for-mulated food pellets for each type of rodent pet. All need fresh water and enjoy many types of fruits and vegetables.

Horses can be as rewarding as they are de-manding of care. Unless you have your own sta-ble and pasture, the cost of boarding can be con-siderable. A horse must be ridden regularly (at least twice a week) if it is to remain a good "mount." As herd animals, horses need to share pasture with others of their kind, although sometimes a related animal such as a donkey will fulfill this need for companionship.

Reptiles and amphibians (snakes, lizards, turtles, and salamanders) can be interesting pets. They vary widely in life span, hardiness, and

Mrs. Warren Harding and "Laddie Boy"

George W. Bush's dog "Spotty"

U.S. Presidents and Their Pets

The White House has been home to more than 400 pets since 1800, when President John Adams and his wife, Abigail, moved in. Here is a sampling of more-recent presidential families and their beloved pets.

Herbert Hoover and "King Tut"

Franklin Delano Roosevelt and "Fala"

John F. Kennedy and "Macaroni"

President	Term	Pets
Rutherford B. Hayes	1877–81	Siamese cat (first in America), mixed-breed dogs, canaries, mockingbird
Theodore Roosevelt	1901–09	Horses, pony, bull Chesapeake Bay retriever, mixed breed, spaniel, snakes, macaw, cat, badger, guinea pigs, lion, hyena, wildcat, coyote, five bears, two parrots, zebra, barn owl, snakes, lizards, rats, roosters, raccoon
Warren Harding	1921–23	Airedale ("Laddie Boy"), English bulldog ("Old Boy"), canaries
Calvin Coolidge	1923–29	White collies, terrier, Airedale, Shetland sheepdog, chow chows, brown collie, bulldog, police dog, yellow collie, bird dog, canaries, thrush, goose, mockingbird, cats, raccoons, donkey, bobcat, lion cubs, wallaby, pigmy hippo, bear
Herbert Hoover	1929–33	Police dogs ("King Tut" and "Pat"), fox terriers ("Big Ben" and "Sonnie"), collie ("Glen"), Eskimo dog ("Yukon"), wolfhound ("Patrick"), setter ("Eaglehurst Gillette"), elkhound ("Weejie")
Franklin Delano Roosevelt	1933–45	German shepherd ("Major"), Scottish terriers ("Meggie" and "Fala"), Llewellyn setter ("Winks"), English sheepdog ("Tiny"), Great Dane ("President"), mastiff ("Blaze")

Barbara Bush with "Millie" and pups

Bill Clinton's cat "Socks"

Lyndon B. Johnson and "Him"

Gerald R. Ford and "Liberty"

Amy Carter and "Grits"

Ronald Reagan and "Lucky"

President	Term	Pets
Dwight D. Eisenhower	1953–1961	Weimaraner ("Heidi")
John F. Kennedy	1961–63	A number of dogs, including Welsh terrier ("Charlie") and German shepherd ("Clipper"); cat; a canary ("Robin"); parakeets; ponies ("Macaroni," "Tex," and "Leprechaun"); hamsters ("Debbie" and "Bill"); rabbit ("Zsa Zsa"); and horse ("Sardar")
Lyndon B. Johnson	1963–69	Beagles ("Him and Her"), white collie ("Blanco"), mixed-breed dog ("Yuki"), hamsters, lovebirds
Richard Nixon	1969–74	Poodle ("Vicky"), terrier ("Pasha"), Irish setter ("King Timahoe")
Gerald Ford	1974–77	Golden retriever ("Liberty"), Siamese cat ("Shan")
Jimmy Carter	1977–81	Siamese cat ("Misty Malarky Ying Yang") and spaniel mixed-breed ("Grits"), which had to be given up due to "poor manners"
Ronald Reagan	1981–89	Two dogs: Bouvier des Flandres ("Lucky") and Cavalier King Charles spaniel ("Rex")
George H.W. Bush	1989–93	Springer spaniels ("Millie" and "Ranger")
Bill Clinton	1993-2001	Cat ("Socks") and Labrador retriever ("Buddy")
George W. Bush	2001-	Springer spaniel ("Spotty," a puppy of "Millie," the elder Bush's pet), Scottish terrier ("Barney"), cat ("India"), long-horn cow ("Ofelia")

Millions of abandoned and neglected pets die each year in this country—some put to death humanely in animal shelters, others killed by injury, disease, starvation, or exposure to extreme heat or cold. To reduce the problem, animal advocates encourage people to adopt pets from animal shelters rather than to buy them from stores and breeders. Animal advocates urge that dogs and cats should be spayed and neutered to stop them from breeding.

The following national statistics, compiled by the Humane Society of the United States, illustrate the current situation.

- 6 million to 8 million: Number of cats and dogs entering shelters each year
- 4,000 to 6,000: Number of animal shelters in the United States
- 600,000 to 750,000: Number of lost cats and dogs reclaimed by owners from shelters each year (30 percent of dogs and 2 to 5 percent of cats)
- 3 million to 4 million: Number of cats and dogs euthanized in shelters each year
- 3 million to 4 million: Number of cats and dogs adopted from shelters each year
- 3: Average number of litters a fertile cat can produce in one year
- 4 to 6: Average number of kittens in a feline litter
- 6 to 10: Average number of puppies in a canine litter

special needs. Since these pets are exothermic, or "cold-blooded," their homes must be constructed and maintained in specific ways to accommodate their sensitivity to changes in temperature and humidity.

Land turtles and iguanas can subsist on fresh greens and various fruits. Snakes, salamanders, insectivorous lizards, toads, and frogs generally need live food such as mice, earthworms, or insects.

The skin of reptiles and amphibians often harbors *salmonella*, a bacterium that can cause life-threatening blood infections in people. For this reason, it is important to thoroughly wash your hands with soap and warm water after handling these creatures. Because of salmonella, experts recommend against keeping reptiles and amphibians in homes with small children or people with weakened immune systems.

Wild animals as pets are seldom, if ever, a good idea. They do not become truly tame or content in captivity; indeed, nature has bred them for independence and survival, not human companionship. Exceptions to this rule include certain insects such as ants and caterpillars, which lend themselves to temporary captivity if properly housed and fed. It can be fascinating to watch their transformation from juvenile to adult form.

IF YOU CANNOT KEEP YOUR PET

Sometimes it happens. Even the most responsible and caring pet owners may have to give up their pets for reasons such as a personal illness, a move, or financial hardship. Clearly, the best solution is to find a good replacement home, which can take time and effort. If these endeavors fail, find an animal-rescue group in your area. Some work very hard to avoid the destruction of any animal. If worse comes to worst, you can take a pet to an animal shelter. Most animal shelters euthanize animals not adopted within a relatively short period of time, such as two to three weeks.

Under no circumstance should anyone simply abandon a pet. Beyond such an act being extremely cruel to the animal, pet abandonment can also endanger other animals and people who encounter the frightened orphan.

SELECTED READINGS

PLANT LIFE

Attenborough, David. *The Private Life of Plants: A Natural History of Plant Behavior.* Princeton, N.J.: Princeton University Press, 1995; repr. 1996; 320 pp., illus.—A fascinating look at the sometimes strange world of plant reproduction; based on the television series.

Bown, Deni. *Encyclopedia of Herbs & Their Uses.* New York: DK Publishing, 1995; 424 pp., illus.—A beautifully illustrated encyclopedia listing 1,000 herbs, from aloe to *Zea.*

Brenner, Barbara. *One Small Place on a Tree.* New York: HarperCollins, 2004; 32 pp., illus.—Explores the relationships between a single tree and the various organisms that make it their home; for younger readers.

Brickell, Christopher, ed. *The American Horticultural Society Encyclopedia of Plants and Flowers, rev. ed..* New York: DK Publishing, 2002; 720 pp., illus.—A definitive guide to the horticulture of North America, featuring more than 8,000 plants and 4,000 photographs.

Brodo, Irwin M., et al. *Lichens of North America.* New Haven, Conn.: Yale University Press, 2001; 628 pp., illus.—A comprehensive and beautifully illustrated guide to more than 1,500 species in this primitive and relatively unknown plant group.

Burdick, Alan. *Out of Eden: An Odyssey of Ecological Invasion.* New York: Farrar, Straus & Giroux, 2005; 336 pp., illus.—An in-depth look at the environmental problems caused by invasive plant and animal species, and the human causes of their migrations.

Burleigh, Richard. *Chocolate: Riches from the Rainforest.* New York: Harry N. Abrams, 2002; 40 pp., illus.—The evolution of cacao seeds into one of the world's most popular foods; for younger readers.

Camenson, Blythe. *Careers for Plant Lovers and Other Green Thumb Types.* Lincolnwood, Ill.: VGM Career Books, 1995; 160 pp.—A basic guide to careers in the world of plants.

Campbell-Culver, Maggie. *Origin of Plants: The People and Plants That Have Shaped Britain's Garden History since the Year 1000.* North Pomfret, Vt.: Headline/Trafalgar Square, 2002; 256 pp., illus.—The fascinating, fact- and legend-filled story of how many of the world's most popular garden plants came to live in domesticity.

Gately, Iain. *Tobacco: The Story of How Tobacco Seduced the World.* New York: Grove Press, 2002; 403 pp., illus.—A lighthearted history of the lethal leaf.

Greenaway, Theresa. *The Plant Kingdom: A Guide to Plant Classification and Biodiversity.* Austin, Tex.: Raintree/Steck-Vaughn, 1999; unpaged, illus.—The science of plant classification; for younger readers.

Hudler, George W. *Magical Mushrooms, Mischievous Molds.* Princeton, N.J.: Princeton University Press, 1998; repr. 2000; 272 pp., illus.—A delightful and lucid look at the kingdom of the fungi, both beneficial and destructive.

Hughes, Meredith Sayles, and E. Thomas Hughes. *Buried Treasure: Roots and Tubers.* Minneapolis: Lerner Publications, 1998; 80 pp., illus.—Historical facts and current uses of potatoes, carrots, cassavas, turnips, beets, and radishes; for younger readers.

Johnson, Sylvia A. *Roses Red, Violets Blue: Why Flowers Have Colors.* Minneapolis: Lerner Publications, 1991; 64 pp., illus.—An examination of why colors are important to plants; for younger readers; includes several experiments.

Knapp, Sandra. *Plant Discoveries: A Botanist's Voyage through Plant Exploration.* Westport, Conn.: Firefly Books, 2003; 336 pp., illus.—The fascinating stories of adventurer-botanists who risked their lives to obtain plant specimens.

Meinesz, Alexandre, trans. by Daniel Simberloff. *Killer Algae.* Chicago: University of Chicago Press, 1999; 360 pp.—How a giant seaweed originally cultivated for use in aquariums is taking over the bottom of the Mediterranean Sea.

Munger, Susan H., et al. *Common to This Country: Botanical Discoveries of Lewis and Clark.* New York: Artisan, 2003; 112 pp., illus.—A wonderful combination of history and science, with beautiful botanical illustrations and horticulture notes that may inspire personal collecting and journal keeping.

Pavord, Anna. *The Naming of Names: The Search for Order in the World of Plants.* New York: Bloomsbury USA, 2005; 384 pp., illus.—A history of the science of naming plants.

Pollan, Michael. *The Botany of Desire: A Plant's-Eye View of the World.* New York: Random House, 2001; 271 pp.—How flowering plants have prospered by exploiting human desires.

Preston, Richard. *The Wild Trees: A Story of Passion and Daring.* New York: Random House, 2007; 294 pp., illus.—A look at some of the world's oldest and tallest trees, found in the redwood forests of northern California—and at the often unusual people who are obsessed with exploring them.

Rocco, Fiammetta. *The Miraculous Fever-Tree.* New York: HarperCollins, 2003; 348 pp., illus.—The scientific inquiry involved in the discovery of quinine, which cured malaria.

Ryden, Hope. *Wildflowers around the Year.* New York: Clarion Books, 2001; 96 pp., illus.—Wonderful photographs and information about habitat and uses for 38 different wildflowers.

Sacks, Oliver. *Oaxaca Journal.* Washington, D.C.: National Geographic Society, 2002; 159 pp., illus.—The ever-curious amateur pteridologist describes a field trip to a state in southern Mexico where nearly 700 different species of fern—one of the oldest forms of life—have been identified.

Steinberg, Ted. *American Green: The Obsessive Quest for the Perfect Lawn.* New York: Norton, 2006; 224 pp., illus.—A lively look at America's preoccupation with keeping lawns green and weed-free.

Tudge, Colin. *The Tree: A Natural History of What Trees Are, How They Live, and Why They Matter.* New York: Crown, 2006; 459 pp., illus.—A descriptive catalog of all the trees in the world, and their essentialness on the world stage.

Turner, Nancy J., and Adam F. Sczawinski. *Common Poisonous Plants and Mushrooms of North America.* Portland, Oreg.: Timber Press, 2d ed., 1995; 324 pp., illus.—A comprehensive and easy-to-understand reference work.

Whittle, Tyler. *The Plant Hunters: Tales of the Botanist-Explorers Who Enriched Our Gardens.* New York: Lyons Press, rev. ed., 1997; 288 pp.—An introduction to the adventures of the intrepid explorers who brought back the plants that now fill our gardens.

ANIMAL LIFE

GENERAL WORKS

Arnold, Caroline. *Did You Hear That? Animals with Super Hearing.* Watertown, Mass.: Charlesbridge Publishing, 2001; 32 pp., illus.—One means of animal communication; for younger readers.

Brooks, Bruce. *Nature by Design.* New York: Farrar, Straus & Giroux, 1991; repr. 1994; 80 pp., illus.—Explores the intricate world of natural design, from the chambers of the nautilus to the spiderweb; for younger readers.

Conniff, Richard. *Every Creeping Thing: True Tales of Faintly Repulsive Wildlife.* New York: Henry Holt, 1998; 255 pp., illus.—Well-told tales of interactions between various creatures and humans.

Downer, John. *Weird Nature.* Toronto, Ont.: Firefly Books, 2002; 168 pp., illus.—The companion book to the BBC/Discovery Channel series on the amusing, odd, and sometimes grotesque world of animal adaptation.

Earle, Sylvia A. *Sea Critters.* Washington, D.C.: National Geographic Society, 2000; 32 pp., illus.—A beautiful book on various marine-animal families; for younger readers.

Flannery, Tim, and Peter Schoutin. *Astonishing Animals: Extraordinary Creatures and the Fantastic Worlds They Inhabit.* New York: Atlantic Monthly Press, 2004; 208 pp., illus.—A fascinating look at some evolutionary marvels.

Fleisher, Paul. *Parasites: Latching On to a Free Lunch.* Minneapolis: Lerner Publications, 2006; 112 pp., illus.—A beautifully illustrated look at parasites of all kinds and why they exist.

Friend, Tim. *Animal Talk: Breaking the Codes of Animal Language.* New York: Free Press, 2004; repr. 2005; 288 pp., illus.—The grand story of communication from the rain forests to our own backyards.

Heinrich, Bernd. *The Snoring Bird: My Family's Journey Through a Century of Biology.* New York: Ecco/HarperCollins, 2007; 461 pp., illus.—The fascinating tale of a family of research biologists by one of its members, a noted nature writer whose works include *Winter World: The Ingenuity of Animal Survival* (2003; repr. 2004) and *Bumblebee Economics* (1979).

Hickman, Pamela, and Pat Stephens. *Animals in Motion: How Animals Swim, Jump, Slither, and Glide.* Buffalo, N.Y.: Kids Can Press, 2000; 40 pp., illus.—Focuses on six types of animal motion and includes experiments; for younger readers.

Hrdy, Sarah Blafer. *Mother Nature: A History of Mothers, Infants, and Natural Selection.* New York: Pantheon Books, 1999; repr. 2000; 723 pp.—A look at the biological basis of maternal instincts.

Johnson, Jinny, et al. *National Geographic Animal Encyclopedia.* Washington, D.C.: National Geographic Society, 2000; 264 pp., illus.—Strikingly illustrated overview of animal groups and facts.

Kaner, Etta. *Animal Defenses: How Animals Protect Themselves.* Buffalo, N.Y.: Kids Can Press, 1999; 40 pp., illus.—A well-illustrated look at unusual animal defense mechanisms; for younger readers.

Lang, Susan S., et al. *More Nature in Your Backyard: Simple Activities for Children.* Brookfield, Conn.: Millbrook Press, 1998; 48 pp., illus.—Easy science activities; for younger students.

McLain, Bill. *What Makes Flamingos Pink? A Colorful Collection of Q and A's for the Unquenchably Curious.* New York: HarperResource, 2001; 304 pp., illus.—A fabulous look at crazy and entertaining facts.

McLeod, Beatrice. *Hunters and Prey.* Woodbridge, Conn.: Blackbirch Press, 2000; 40 pp., illus.—A fascinating and easy-to-read look at how animals adapt to survive.

Montgomery, Sy. *Quest for the Tree Kangaroo: An Expedition to the Cloud Forest of New Guinea.* Boston: Houghton Mifflin, 2006; 80 pp., illus.—For budding young naturalists, a look at some of the incredible ways scientists study animals in their natural habitat.

Peieribone, Vincent, and David F. Gruber. *Aglow in the Dark: The Revolutionary Science of Biofluorescence.* Boston: Harvard University Press, 2006; 288 pp., illus.—The discovery and evidence of bioluminescence.

Quinlan, Susan E. *The Case of the Monkeys That Fell from the Trees: And Other Mysteries in Tropical Nature.* Honesdale, Pa.: Boyds Mills Press, 2003; 172 pp.—Introduces students to scientific inquiry by solving a series of ecological mysteries set in the tropical forests.

Settel, Joanne. *Exploding Ants: Amazing Facts about How Animals Adapt.* New York: Atheneum/Simon & Schuster, 1999; 40 pp., illus.—A fascinating look at animal habits that have developed to enable various species to survive.

Shedd, Warner. *Owls Aren't Wise & Bats Aren't Blind: A Naturalist Debunks Our Favorite Fallacies about Wildlife.* New York: Random House, 2000; 304 pp.—An entertaining look at myths and misconceptions about 27 North American animals.

Singer, Marilyn. *What Stinks?* Plain City, Ohio: Darby Creek Publishing, 2006; 64 pp., illus.—A fascinating and easy-to-read discussion of "stinky" organisms, where they come from, and the science behind the stink.

Thain, M., and M. Hickman. *The Penguin Dictionary of Biology.* New York: Prentice Hall, 10th ed., 2004; 704 pp., illus.—Covers issues in biology ranging from recent discoveries in paleoanthropology to gene mapping and manipulation.

Waldbauer, Gilbert. *The Birder's Bug Book.* Cambridge, Mass.: Harvard University Press, 1998; repr. 2000; 320 pp., illus.—A fascinating look at the complex relationships among birds, bugs, and plants.

Wolfe, Art, et al. *The Living Wild.* Seattle: Wildlands Press, 2001; 230 pp., illus.—A photographic record of more than 140 threatened species in their natural habitats in more than 40 countries, with a plea to end world habitat destruction.

INVERTEBRATES

Alcock, John. *In a Desert Garden: Love and Death among the Insects.* New York: Norton, 1997; repr. 1999; 192 pp., illus.—Required reading for those who think of insects as the enemy.

Berenbaum, May R. *Buzzwords: A Scientist Muses on Sex, Bugs, and Rock 'n' Roll.* Washington, D.C.: Joseph Henry Press/National Academies Press, 2000; 320 pp.—A collection of whimsical essays by an entomologist.

Bishop, Holley. *Robbing the Bees: A Biography of Honey—The Sweet Liquid Gold That Seduced the World.* New York:

Free Press, 2005; repr. 2006; 366 pp., illus.—Everything you might want to know about bees and beekeeping.

Brown, Andrew. *In the Beginning Was the Worm.* New York: Columbia University Press, 2004; 244 pp.—How three scientists won the Nobel Prize for their research on the genetic makeup of a nematode worm known as *C. elegans*, which led to the sequencing of the human genome.

Buckman, Robert. *Human Wildlife: The Life That Lives On Us.* Baltimore, Md.: Johns Hopkins University Press, 2003; 208 pp., illus.—A look at the various microbes, fungi, viruses, parasites, and bugs that live on human beings.

Camp, Roger. *Butterflies in Flight.* New York: Thames & Hudson, 2002; 104 pp., illus.—In this unique slipcased book, digitally enhanced photographs of 285 colorful butterfly species appear against a black background in an accordion-like folio; includes a removable identification guide to the species and their habitats.

Cranshaw, Whitney. *Garden Insects of North America: The Ultimate Guide to Backyard Bugs.* Princeton, N.J.: Princeton University Press, 2004; 672 pp., illus.—What's eating your garden besides you.

Dance, S. Peter. *Shells.* New York: DK Publishing, 1992; 256 pp., illus.—A comprehensive reference work as well as an easy-to-use guide for the amateur collector.

Eisner, Thomas. *For Love of Insects.* Cambridge, Mass.: Belknap Press of Harvard University Press, 2004; 448 pp., illus.—The fascinating and unusual memoirs of an entomologist who helped to found the discipline of chemical ecology.

Farrell, Jeannette. *Invisible Allies: Microbes That Shape Our Lives.* New York: Farrar, Straus & Giroux, 2005; 176 pp., illus.—Bacteria may cause illness, but they also help preserve and digest food, make medicines, and treat waste products.

Froman, Nan. *What's That Bug?* Toronto, Ont.: Madison Press Books/Little, Brown, 2001; 32 pp., illus.—A fascinating look at nine of the most familiar orders of insects; for younger readers.

Glausiusz, Josie. *Buzz: The Intimate Bond between Humans and Insects.* San Francisco: Chronicle Books, 2004; 144 pp., illus.—A grisly and gorgeous look at the bugs around us through an electron microscope.

Halpern, Sue. *Four Wings and a Prayer: Caught in the Mystery of the Monarch Butterfly.* New York: Vintage, 2001; repr. 2002; 224 pp.—The story of these amazing butterflies and the entomologists and amateur enthusiasts who migrate with them.

Kneidel, Sally. *Stinkbugs, Stick Insects, and Stag Beetles and 18 More of the Strangest Insects on Earth.* New York: John Wiley, 2000; 114 pp., illus.—Describes 21 curious members of the arthropod class of insects; by the author of *Slugs, Bugs, and Salamanders* (1997).

Lockwood, Jeffrey A. *Locust: The Devastating Rise and Mysterious Disappearance of the Insect That Shaped the American Frontier.* New York: Basic Books, 2005; 320 pp.—A fascinating history of the insect that was once the scourge of the Great Plains.

Markle, Sandra. *Inside and Outside Killer Bees.* New York: Walker, 2004; 40 pp., illus.—Describes the key differences between European honeybees and Africanized bees; for young readers.

Purser, Bruce. *Jungle Bugs.* New York: Firefly Books, 2003; 128 pp., illus.—Glorious photographs and text examine some of nature's freakiest camouflage artists.

Robertson, Matthew, ed. *The Big Book of Bugs.* Mount Vernon, Wash.: Welcome Enterprises, 1999; 448 pp., illus.—Loaded with facts, fiction, and lore; includes many experiments and activities and remarkable 3-D images.

Ross, Michael Elsohn. *Spiderology.* Minneapolis: Lerner Publications, 2000; 48 pp., illus.—Provides a wealth of information about spiders; for younger readers.

Schwerd, Richard. *The Cockroach Papers: A Compendium of History and Lore.* Portland, Oreg.: Four Walls Eight Windows, 1999; 266 pp.—A zesty survey of nature's evolutionary success story.

Snedden, Robert. *Yuck! A Big Book of Little Horrors.* Old Tappan, N.J.: Simon & Schuster, 1996; 32 pp., illus.—A fun look at the microscopic creatures found in the everyday world; for younger readers.

Spielman, Andrew, and Michael D'Antonio. *Mosquito: A Natural History of Our Most Persistent and Deadly Foe.* New York: Hyperion, 2001; 247 pp., illus.—Everything you ever wanted to know about this insect.

Stewart, Amy. *The Earth Moved: On the Remarkable Achievements of Earthworms.* New York: Algonquin Books of Chapel Hill, 2004; 223 pp., illus.—The important role of the earthworms in gradual geologic changes.

Sutton, Patricia Taylor, and Clay Sutton. *How to Spot Butterflies.* New York: Houghton Mifflin, 1999; 160 pp., illus.—A comprehensive guide to this delightful pastime.

Wade, Nicholas, ed. *The Science Times Book of Insects.* New York: Lyons Press, 1998; 256 pp., illus.—Essays about insects and the scientists who study them, from the weekly science section of the *New York Times*.

Waldbauer, Gilbert. *What Good Are Bugs? Insects in the Web of Life.* Cambridge, Mass.: Harvard University Press, 2003; 384 pp., illus.—Answers to just about everything you've ever wanted to know about bugs by the author of *Millions of Monarchs, Bunches of Beetles: How Bugs Find Strength in Numbers* (2000).

Wolfe, David W. *Tales from the Underground: A Natural History of Subterranean Life.* New York: Perseus Books, 2002; 240 pp.—Describes the fascinating diversity of underground life.

FISH, AMPHIBIANS, AND REPTILES

Berman, Ruth. *Sharks.* Minneapolis: Carolrhoda Books, 1995; 47 pp., illus.—A beautifully illustrated book for younger readers in the *Nature Watch* series.

Blum, Marc. *Amphibians and Reptiles in 3-D.* New York: Chronicle Books, 1999; 96 pp., illus.—Dazzling photographs and fascinating facts.

Casey, Susan. *The Devil's Teeth: A True Story of Obsession and Survival Among America's Great White Sharks.* New York: Henry Holt, 2005; 304 pp., illus.—A fascinating look at the mysterious and frequently misunderstood world of the great white shark.

Corson, Trevor. *The Secret Life of Lobsters: How Fishermen and Scientists are Unraveling the Mysteries of Our Favorite Crustacean.* New York: HarperCollins, 2004; 289 pp.—The ecology of *Homarus americanus* along the rocky coast of Maine.

Crump, Marty. *Amphibians, Reptiles, and Their Conservation.* North Haven, Conn.: Linnet Books, 2003; 149 pp., illus.—A wonderful introduction to the field of herpetology.

Dugatkin, Lee Alan. *The Imitation Factor: Evolution beyond the Gene.* New York: Free Press, 2001; 243 pp.—The biology and culture of the guppy.

Ellis, Richard. *The Search for the Giant Squid: An Authoritative Look at the Biology and Mythology of the World's Most Elusive Sea Creature.* New York: Viking Penguin, 1999; 336 pp., illus.—A zoologist and expert on life-forms of the deep seas of the world, whose other works include *Monsters of the Sea* (1994), investigates facts and lore about the giant squid.

Greenberg, Dan. *Lizards.* San Marino, Calif.: Benchmark/Marshall Cavendish, 2004; 112 pp., illus.—A lively look at lizard basics; for younger students interested in reptiles.

Greene, Harry W. *Snakes: The Evolution of Mystery in Nature.* Berkeley: University of California Press, 1997; repr. 2000; 351 pp., illus.—A beautifully illustrated look at diverse snakes, their habitats, and their history; for older readers.

Hofrichter, Robert, ed. *Amphibians: The World of Frogs, Toads, Salamanders, and Newts.* New York: Firefly Books, 2000; 264 pp., illus.—A magnificent book covering the biology, physiology, ecology, behavior, and evolution of these animals.

Kurlansky, Mark. *Cod: A Biography of the Fish That Changed the World.* New York: Walker, 1997; repr. 1998; 294 pp., illus.—Describes the way in which dried and salted cod, one of the world's first nonperishable foods, shaped human history.

Lasky, Kathryn. *Interrupted Journey: Saving Endangered Sea Turtles.* Cambridge, Mass.: Candlewick Press, 2001; 48 pp., illus.—The miraculous journey of a stranded and rescued sea turtle; for younger readers.

Mattison, Chris. *Snake.* New York: DK Publishing, 1999; 192 pp., illus.—Describes more than 60 types of snakes.

McPhee, John. *Founding Fish.* New York: Farrar, Straus & Giroux, 2002; 358 pp.—A tale of the ocean-dwelling shad, which must find its way to rivers to spawn, that is both a fishing book and a mini-encyclopedia.

Parker, Steve. *Frogs and Toads.* San Francisco: Sierra Club Books, 1994; 57 pp., illus.—An easy-to-read and well-illustrated overview of frogs and toads; a volume in the *Look into Nature* series.

Rotman, Jeffrey L. *Shark!* New York: Ipso Facto, 1999; 228 pp., illus.—An underwater photographer takes an intriguing and up-close look at sharks.

Sandford, Gina. *An Illustrated Encyclopedia of Aquarium Fish.* New York: Howell Book House, 1995; 256 pp., illus.—Stunning photographs and informative text showcase 700 freshwater and marine-aquarium fish.

Schweid, Richard. *Consider the Eel.* Chapel Hill: University of North Carolina Press, 2002; 181 pp.—Everything you ever wanted to know about the eel, which is still a popular food elsewhere but has largely vanished from the American table.

Snedden, Robert. *What Is a Reptile?* San Francisco: Sierra Club Books, 1995; repr. 1997; 32 pp., illus.—For younger readers; answers the question of what turtles, snakes, crocodiles, and tuataras have in common, and describes the characteristics and behavior of these creatures.

Wade, Nicholas, ed. *The Science Times Book of Fish.* New York: Lyons Press, 1997; 240 pp., illus.—A wide variety of fascinating articles collected from the weekly science section of the *New York Times.*

BIRDS

Arnold, Caroline. *Ostriches and Other Flightless Birds.* Minneapolis: Lerner Publications, 1990; 48 pp., illus.—A guide to the flightless birds; for younger readers.

Bateman, Robert. *Birds.* New York: Pantheon, 2002; 176 pp., illus.—Lush paintings of birds by a noted artist.

Cocker, Mark. *Birders: Tales of a Tribe.* New York: Atlantic Monthly Press, 2002; 230 pp.—An avid bird fanatic tries to explain the sometimes strange ways of his fellow bird-watchers.

Fiennes, William. *The Snow Geese: A Story of Home.* New York: Random House, 2002; 288 pp.—The author follows the snow geese on their 3,000-mile migration from southern Texas to the Arctic Ocean.

Gessner, David. *Return of the Osprey: A Season of Flight and Wonder.* New York: Algonquin Books of Chapel Hill, 2001; 286 pp.—The author's observations on the return of the osprey to the salt marshes of New England.

Green-Armytage, Stephen. *Extraordinary Chickens.* New York: Abrams, 2000; 112 pp., illus.—Fabulous photos and informative text on a wide variety of exotic chickens.

Grimes, William. *My Fine Feathered Friend.* New York: North Point, 2002; 85 pp.—A restaurant critic relates the amusing tale of the chicken that suddenly appeared in his New York City backyard, along with other chicken trivia.

Harris, Joan. *One Wing's Gift: Rescuing Alaska's Wild Birds.* Anchorage: Alaska Northwest Books, 2005; 64 pp., illus.—Details the response to the 1989 *Exxon Valdez* oil tanker spill.

Heinrich, Bernd. *The Geese of Beaver Bog.* New York: HarperCollins, 2004; repr. 2005; 240 pp., illus.—A beautifully illustrated look at the Canada goose by an award-winning nature writer.

Hoose, Phillip. *The Race to Save the Lord God Bird.* New York: Farrar, Straus & Giroux, 2004; 208 pp., illus.—Tales of the astonishing ivory-billed woodpecker, whose likely extinction may prompt questions about the loss of other species.

Johnson, Jinny. *Simon & Schuster Children's Guide to Birds.* New York: Simon & Schuster, 1996; 96 pp., illus.—A clear guide to more than 9,000 species of birds for the beginning bird lover; illustrated with photographs and drawings.

Laubach, Christyna M., et al. *Raptor! A Kid's Guide to Birds of Prey.* Williamstown, Mass.: Storey Kids, 2002; 128 pp., illus.—A wonderfully illustrated and informative look at a magnificent group of predators.

Mahnken, Jan. *The Backyard Bird-Lover's Guide: Attracting, Nesting, Feeding.* Williamstown, Mass.: Storey Communications, 1996; 312 pp., illus.—Advice for birders at all levels, with delightful illustrations.

Markle, Sandra. *Outside and Inside Birds.* Old Tappan, N.J.: Simon & Schuster, 1994; 40 pp., illus.—A vivid description of the various characteristics of birds, including how and why they fly.

Mattheissen, Peter. *The Birds of Heaven: Travels with Cranes.* New York: North Point Press, 2001; repr. 2003; 349 pp., illus.—A beautifully illustrated look at the world of cranes, most species of which are imperiled.

Nielsen, John. *Condor: To the Brink and Back—The Life and Times of One Giant Bird*. New York: HarperCollins, 2006; 272 pp., illus.—The ongoing effort to save this remarkable species, which became almost extinct in the 1970s.

Nixon, Rob. *Dreambirds: The Strange History of the Ostrich in Fashion, Food, and Fortune*. New York: Picador USA, 2000; 289 pp.—A flightless-bird history that is part science, part commerce, and part memoir.

Obmascik, Mark. *The Big Year: A Tale of Man, Nature, and Fowl Obsession*. New York: Free Press, 2004; 268 pp.—The quirky tale of three hypercompetitive birders.

Perrins, Christopher, ed. *The Firefly Encyclopedia of the Birds*. Westport, Conn.: Firefly Books, 2003; 640 pp., illus.—A profusely illustrated reference for students, naturalists, and birders.

Porter, Eliot. *Vanishing Songbirds: The Sixth Order: Wood Warblers and Other Passerine Birds*. Boston: Bulfinch Press, 1996; 159 pp., illus.—A posthumous collection of Porter's work on this subject; includes detailed color photographs.

Rhodes, Richard. *John James Audubon: The Making of an American*. New York: Knopf, 2004; 528 pp., illus.—The biography of the world's most famous bird artist.

Ross, Michael Elsohn. *Bird Watching with Margaret Morse Nice*. Minneapolis: Carolrhoda Books, 1997; 48 pp., illus.—A fascinating look at a famous ornithologist, with information for young readers about birds and how to become an effective bird-watcher.

Roth, Sally. *The Backyard Bird Lover's Field Guide: Secrets of Attracting, Identifying, and Enjoying Birds of Your Region*. Emmaus, Pa.: Rodale Books, 2007; 336 pp., illus.—Learn about the birds commonly found in your part of the United States, and how to identify and attract them.

Rothenberg, David. *Why Birds Sing: A Journey Through the Mystery of Bird Song*. New York: Basic Books, 2005; 258 pp., illus.—A unique look at birdsong that is as much about music as science.

Safina, Carl. *Eye of the Albatross: Visions of Hope and Survival*. New York: Henry Holt, 2002; repr. 2003; 377 pp., illus.—Follows the fortunes of one of the world's most beautiful birds, which has unusual wings built for gliding, not flapping.

Sattler, Helen Roney. *The Book of North American Owls*. New York: Clarion Books, 1995; 64 pp., illus.—A look at owl classification, history, hunting, habitat, courtship, and nesting, plus the complex relationship between owls and humans.

Sayre, April Pulley. *If You Should Hear a Honey Guide*. New York: Houghton Mifflin, 1995; 32 pp., illus.—A mesmerizing journey to the East African bush-country habitat of this small bird that feeds on wild honeycomb; for younger readers.

Schaefer, Lola M. *Arrowhawk*. New York: Henry Holt, 2004; 32 pp., illus.—The disturbing and heartwarming story of a red-tailed hawk that was shot with an arrow; for younger readers.

Sibley, David Allen. *Sibley's Birding Basics*. New York: Knopf, 2002; 154 pp., illus.—A beautifully illustrated guide to identifying and enjoying birds.

Sibley, David Allen, with the National Audubon Society. *Sibley Guide to Birds*. New York: Knopf, 2000; 544 pp., illus.—More than 6,000 watercolor illustrations by one of America's most famous birders provide a wealth of detail on 810 species and 350 regional populations of birds.

Skutch, Alexander F. *The Minds of Birds*. College Station: Texas A & M University Press, 1997; 200 pp., illus.—A distinguished ornithologist investigates and interprets the avian mental landscape.

Souder, William. *Under a Wild Sky: John James Audubon and the Making of "The Birds of America."* Berkeley, Calif.: North Point Press, 2004; 367 pp., illus.—The artist's long quest to publish his lifelike bird drawings.

Tennant, Alan. *On the Wing: To the Edge of the Earth with the Peregrine Falcon*. New York: Knopf, 2004; 304 pp., illus.—Studying how peregrine falcons—and, by implication, humans—have been affected by the chemicals of civilization.

Wade, Nicholas, ed. *The Science Times Book of Birds*. New York: Lyons Press, 1997; 288 pp., illus.—A collection of essays from the science section of the *New York Times*.

Webb, Sophie. *Looking for Seabirds: Journal from an Alaskan Voyage*. Boston: Houghton Mifflin, 2004; 48 pp., illus.—A view of scientists at work studying the relationships of Antarctic animals, by the author of *My Season with Penguins* (2000).

Wechsler, Doug. *Bizarre Birds*. Honesdale, Pa.: Boyds Mills Press, 1999; 48 pp., illus.—Discusses the physical characteristics, breeding habits, flight ability, and other strange traits of a number of bizarre species of birds.

Weidensaul, Scott. *Living on the Wind: Across the Hemisphere with Migratory Birds*. New York: North Point Press, 1999; 432 pp., illus.—The miracle of migration, coupled with a plea for the conservation of habitat; by the author of *National Audubon Society First Field Guide: Birds* (1998).

ZOOS, AQUARIUMS, AND WILDLIFE PARKS

Brazaitis, Peter. *You Belong in a Zoo: Tales from a Lifetime Spent with Cobras, Crocs, and Other Creatures*. New York: Villard Books, 2003; 345 pp.—Memoirs of a lifetime working in New York zoos, including involvement in wildlife forensic science to help prosecute smugglers of protected animals.

Hancock, David. *A Different Nature: The Paradoxical World of Zoos and Their Uncertain Future*. Berkeley: University of California Press, 2001; 392 pp., illus.—A history of zoos, and questions about their role in the modern world.

Segaloff, Nat, and Paul Erickson. *A Reef Comes to Life: Creating an Undersea Exhibit*. Danbury, Conn.: Franklin Watts, 1991; 48 pp., illus.—Describes the design and construction of an exact replica of a Caribbean reef at the New England Aquarium; for younger readers.

Sutherland, Amy. *Kicked, Bitten, and Scratched: Life and Lessons at the World's Premier School for Exotic Animal Trainers*. New York: Viking, 2006; 320 pp.—Life at California's Exotic Animal Training and Management Program, which produces animal trainers and zookeepers.

Zoehfeld, Kathleen Weidner. *Wild Lives: A History of the People and Animals of the Bronx Zoo*. New York: Knopf/Random House, 2006; 96 pp., illus.—For zoo lovers everywhere, the history of the Bronx Zoo, the animals who live there, and the people who care for them.

Illustration Credits

The following list credits or acknowledges, by page, the source of illustrations used in this volume. When two or more illustrations appear on one page, they are credited individually left to right, top to bottom; their credits are separated by semicolons. When both the photographer or artist and an agency or other source are given for an illustration, they are usually separated by a slash.

162 USDA-ARS
165 © Breck P. Kent/Animals Animals
166 © Steven J. Krasemann/DRK Photo
168 © Frank Balthis; © John Gerlach/Animals Animals
169 © Richard Shiell/Animals Animals
170 USDA-ARS
171 USDA-ARS
172 USDA-ARS
173 © Keith A. Szafranski
174 © Walter Chandoha
175 © Michelle Litvin
176 © Fred Bavendam
177 © U-AT/The Stock Market
178 © Tom Bean/DRK Photo
179 © Robert C. Burke; Keith Weller/USDA-ARS
180 © Jim Tuten/Animals Animals
181 © James Prince/Photo Researchers; © Jack Dykinga/USDA-ARS
183 © Frans Lanting/Minden Pictures
184 © Giles Martin/*Figaro* Magazine/Gamma Liaison
185 © Scott Neilsen/DRK Photo; © John Shaw/Tom Stack & Associates
186 © Gerard Lacz/Animals Animals; © Hans Reinhard/Okapia/Photo Researchers
188 Nina Leen/*Life* Magazine © Time Inc.
189 © John Mitchell/Photo Researchers
190 © Renee Lynn/Photo Researchers; © Fred Bavendam
191 © David Hosking/Photo Researchers; inset: © Johnny Johnson/Animals Animals
192 © Larry West/Photo Researchers
193 Both photos: © Kim Taylor/Bruce Coleman
194 © Jane Burton/Bruce Coleman; © Miriam Austerman/Animals Animals
195 © Michael Fogden/DRK Photo
196 © Toni Angermayer/Photo Researchers; © Jack Drafahl/Image Concepts
197 © Art Wolfe
198 The Granger Collection
200 Art Resource
201 The Granger Collection
202 The Granger Collection
203 Popperfoto/Archive Photos
204 Smithsonian Institution: Department of Anthropology
205 © Robert C. Burke
206 © Stanley Flegler/Visuals Unlimited
208 © M. Abbey/Photo Researchers; © Stephen Dalton/NAS/Photo Researchers
209 © James H. Robinson/Photo Researchers; © M. Abbey/Visuals Unlimited
210 Top photos: © M. Abbey/Photo Researchers; bottom left: © Frederica Georgia/Photo Researchers
212 © Stephen Dalton/Photo Researchers; © Sue Ford/Science Photo Library/Photo Researchers
213 Both photos: © A.M. Siegelman/Visuals Unlimited
214 © Robert Holland/DRK Photo
215 © Peter Parks/Mo Young Productions/Norbert Wu
216 © Dave B. Fleetham/Tom Stack & Associates
217 © R. & V. Taylor/Bruce Coleman
218 © Dr. Frieder Sauer/Bruce Coleman
219 © Doug Perrine/Innerspace Visions; © Stuart Westmorland/Tony Stone Images
220 © Rainiero Maltini and Piero Solaini/Scala, New York
221 © Oxford Scientific Films/Animals Animals; © Fred Bavendam; © J. Spurr/Bruce Coleman
222 © Carl Roessler/Animals Animals; © Brian Parker/Tom Stack & Associates
223 © E.R. Degginger/Animals Animals; © Zig Leszczynski/Animals Animals; © Steve Earley/Animals Animals
224 © Peter D. Capen/Terra Mar Productions
225 © David Scharf/Peter Arnold
226– Crossover photo: © Manfred Kage/Peter Arnold; right: © Drs. Kessel &
227 Shih/Peter Arnold
228 © Dr. Jeremy Burgess/Science Photo Library/Photo Researchers; © Sinclair Stammers/Science Photo Library/Photo Researchers
229 © Ed Reschke/Peter Arnold; © R. Calentine/Visuals Unlimited
231 © Fred Bavendam/Peter Arnold
232 © Peter David/Planet Earth Pictures; © Norbert Wu
233 © Kathleen Campbell/Liaison International
234 © Frederick Ayer/Photo Researchers
235 © Roudnitska/Gamma Liaison
236 © James Carmichael/Bruce Coleman
237 © Mike Okoniewski/Gamma Liaison
238 © Marty Snyderman
239 © Jane Burton/Bruce Coleman
240 © John Markham/Bruce Coleman
241 © Kjell B. Sandved/Photo Researchers; © Gilbert Grant/Photo Researchers
242 USDA-ARS
244 © Geoff Tompkinson/Aspect Picture Library Ltd.; © Peter Menzel
245 © Joe McNally
246 © R. Calentine/Visuals Unlimited
249 © Arthur Morris/Visuals Unlimited
250 © Jean-Paul Ferrero/Auscape/Peter Arnold
252 Photo: © Sinclair Stammers/Science Photo Library/Photo Researchers
253 © Roy Waller/Natural History Photo Agency; © Fred Bavendam
255 © Larry Ulrich/DRK Photo
256 © Peggy Starborn/Visuals Unlimited
258 © Patrick Landmann/Gamma Liaison; © Dr. Paul A. Zahl/Photo Researchers
259 Courtesy, M. Fergione, Pfyzer Central Research
260 © Larry Ulrich/DRK Photo; © Carol Hughes/Bruce Coleman
261 © Kim Taylor/Bruce Coleman
262 © Hans Pfletschinger/Peter Arnold
264 © Bill Beatty/Visuals Unlimited
265 © Patrick Landman/Gamma Liaison
266 National Museum of Natural History, Smithsonian Institution
267 Both illustrations: Corbis-Bettmann
268 USDA-ARS; © Alain Noques/Sygma
269 USDA-ARS
270 USDA-ARS
271 USDA-ARS
272 © Larry West/Bruce Coleman
275 Photos: © Leroy Simon/Visuals Unlimited; © Oliver Meckes/Photo Researchers
277 © John Cancalosi/DRK Photo
278 © Adrian Davies/Bruce Coleman; © Adrian Wenner/Visuals Unlimited
279 © Michael Lustbader/Photo Researchers
281 Photo: USDA-ARS
283 © Dwight Kuhn/DRK Photo; © Mark Moffett/Minden Pictures
284 © Mark Moffett/Minden Pictures; © Varin/Jacana/Photo Researchers
285 Photo: © Hans Pfletschinger/Peter Arnold
287 © Aaron Strong/Strong Images, Inc./Liaison International
288 © Stephen J. Krasemann/DRK Photo
289 Photo: © Stanley Breeden/DRK Photo
290 © B. Brander/Photo Researchers; © Kjell B. Sandved/Photo Researchers
291 © Glenn M. Oliver/Visuals Unlimited; inset: © Maria Zorn/Animals Animals
293 © Hans Pfletschinger/Peter Arnold
294 © Charles Mohr/Photo Researchers
295 © Ed Degginger/Bruce Coleman
296 © Erich Lessing/Art Resource
297 © Michael P. Gadomski/Photo Researchers; © Simon Trevor/Bruce Coleman
298 © Hans Pfletschinger/Peter Arnold; © George Dodge/Bruce Coleman
299 © Michael Fogden/Bruce Coleman; © Bruce Roberts/Photo Researchers
300 © Michael Lustbader/Photo Researchers
302 © Runk/Schoenberger/Grant Heilman Photography; © Ed Reschke/Peter Arnold; © Grant Heilman Photography; © Ken Cole/Animals Animals; © Ed Reschke/Peter Arnold
303 © Dr. Thomas C. Emmel
304 © E.R. Degginger/Animals Animals; © B. Moose Peterson
305 © Daniel Goodyear; © Michael P. Gadomski/Photo Researchers
306 © Charles Mann/Photo Researchers; © John Shaw
307 © Adrian Davies/Bruce Coleman; © D. Cavagnaro/DRK Photo
308 © Nancy Sefton/Photo Researchers
309 © Andrew J. Martinez
310 © Cleveland P. Hickman, Jr./Visuals Unlimited
311 © Cabisco/Visuals Unlimited
312 © Doug Perrine/DRK Photo
313 Erich Lessing/Art Resource; © Patrick Aventurier/Gamma Liaison
314 © W.A. Banaszewski/Visuals Unlimited
315 © Fred McConnaughey/Photo Researchers
321 Photo: © Hans Reinhard/Bruce Coleman
322 © Tom R. Stewart
323 © Jeffrey L. Rotman/Peter Arnold
325 © Visuals Unlimited
326 © Tui De Roy/Bruce Coleman; © James D. Watt/Animals Animals
327 © Louisa Preston/Photo Researchers; © Norbert Wu/Peter Arnold; © Robert Yin/Gamma Liaison
329 © W. Gregory Brown/Animals Animals
330 Photo: © Peter Scoones/Planet Earth Pictures
331 © Victoria McCormick/Animals Animals
332 © Peter David/Planet Earth Pictures
333 © Fred Bavendam
334 © W. Gregory Brown/Animals Animals; © Zig Leszczynski/Animals Animals
335 © Fred Bavendam
336 © Martin Wendler/Peter Arnold
337 © Loren McIntyre
338 © Rick Poley/Visuals Unlimited
339 © Budd Titlow/Visuals Unlimited; inset: © Jeffrey W. Lang/Photo Researchers
340 © Gary Meszaros/Visuals Unlimited; © Zig Leszczynski/Animals Animals
341 © David M. Dennis/Tom Stack & Associates
343 © Richard LaVal/Animals Animals; © Ron Austin/Photo Researchers
344 Top: © Barry L. Runk/Rannels/Grant Heilman Photography; middle photos: © Runk/Schoenberger/Grant Heilman Photography; bottom: © Breck P. Kent/Animals Animals
345 © Suzanne L. & Joseph T. Collins/Photo Researchers; © T.A. Wiewandt/DRK Photo; © Jane Burton/Bruce Coleman
346 T.A. Wiewandt/DRK Photo; © Michael Fogden/DRK Photo
347 © Michael Bacon/Tom Stack & Associates
349 © Suzanne L. Collins & Joseph T. Collins/Photo Researchers
350 © L. West/Photo Researchers; © Marty Cordano/DRK Photo; © R.J. Erwin/DRK Photo
351 © Jane Burton/Bruce Coleman
352 © David T. Roberts/Photo Researchers
353 © Tom J. Ulrich/Visuals Unlimited
354 © John Cancalosi; © Frans Lanting/Minden Pictures
355 © Clem Haagner/Bruce Coleman
356 © Stephen Dalton/Animals Animals
357 Photo: © Peter Jordan/Gamma Liaison
358 © Breck P. Kent/Animals Animals; © Zig Leszczynski/Animals Animals

359 © John Cancalosi/Tom Stack & Associates
360 © Tom Brakefield/Bruce Coleman; © Bruce Davidson/Animals Animals; © Klaus Uhlenhut/Animals Animals
361 © Wolfgang Kaehler
363 © Joe McDonald/Bruce Coleman
366 © Anthony Bannister/Oxford Scientific Films; © Mark Cardwell
367 © W. Rudhart/Argus Fotoarchiv/Peter Arnold; © John B. Dobbins/Photo Researchers
368 © Joe McDonald/Bruce Coleman; © Erwin and Peggy Bauer/Bruce Coleman
369 © Michael Fogden/Animals Animals; © Lynn M. Stone/Bruce Coleman
370 © Joe McDonald/Animals Animals
371 © Charles Preitner/Visuals Unlimited; © E.R. Degginger/Photo Researchers
372 © R. Andrew Odum/Peter Arnold
373 © John Cancalosi/Peter Arnold
375 © Luiz C. Marigo/Peter Arnold
376 © Joe McDonald/Visuals Unlimited; © Kelvin Aitken/Peter Arnold
377 Photo: © Jany Sauvanet/Photo Researchers
378 © A. Kerstitch/Visuals Unlimited; © Larry Miller/Photo Researchers; © Joseph T. Collins/Photo Researchers
379 © Inga Spence/DDB Stock Photo
380 © Adam Jones/Photo Researchers; inset: © Caulion Singletary
382 © Michael Cardwell; © Shaen Adey/Anthony Bannister Photo Library
383 © Michael Fogden/DRK Photo; © Schafer & Hill/Peter Arnold
385 © William H. Mullins/Photo Researchers
386 © Mark C. Burnett/Stock Boston; Ken Hammond/USDA-ARS
387 © Tim W. Gallagher
389 © Tim W. Gallagher
390 © Maslowski/Visuals Unlimited
397 © Dan Guravich/Photo Researchers; © Bob and Clara Calhoun/Bruce Coleman
398 © Roland Seitre/Peter Arnold
399 © M. Philip Kahl/Bruce Coleman
400 © George D. Dodge/Bruce Coleman
401 © Labat/Jacana/Photo Researchers; left inset: © Jean-Claude Carton/Bruce Coleman; right inset: © Tom McHugh/Photo Researchers
402 © Charles Munn/Bruce Coleman; © Claus C. Meyer/Agencia TYBA
403 © Joe McDonald/Visuals Unlimited
404 © Robert A. Tyrell
405 © J.H. Robinson/Animals Animals
406 © Michael Fogden/Animals Animals
407 © Renee Lynn/Photo Researchers
408 © Stephen G. Maka/Wildlife Photography
409 © Tui De Roy/Auscape International; © G.J.H. Moon/Bruce Coleman
410– Upper left: © John Cancalosi/DRK Photo; crossover: © Jan & Des
411 Bartlett/Bruce Coleman; upper right: © Tom McHugh/Photo Researchers; © Jean-Paul Ferrero/Auscape International
412 © Erwin & Peggy Bauer/Bruce Coleman
413 © Ben Osborne/Tony Stone Images
414 Photo: © Jack Barrie/Bruce Coleman
415 © James R. Fisher/Photo Researchers
416 © E. Sander/Gamma Liaison; © Zoological Society of San Diego
417 © Tom & Pat Leeson
418 © Art Gingert/Comstock
419 © Christophe Lepetit/Gamma Liaison
420 © Craig K. Lorenz/Photo Researchers; © Henry H. Holdsworth
421 © Michael Sewell/Peter Arnold
422 © F.J. Hiersche/Okapia/Photo Researchers
423 © Bob & Clara Calhoun/Bruce Coleman
424 © Stephen J. Krasemann/DRK Photo
425 © Bob & Clara Calhoun/Bruce Coleman
426 © Stephen J. Krasemann/DRK Photo
427 © Diana Rogers/Bruce Coleman
428 © Robert Maier/Animals Animals; © Mike Birkhead/Oxford Scientific Films/Animals Animals
429 The Granger Collection
430 Top: © Culver Pictures; bottom photos: © Roger Wilmshurst/Bruce Coleman; © Maslowski/Visuals Unlimited
431 © Glenn Wolff
432 © S. Nielsen
433 © Wolfgang Kaehler/Gamma Liaison
434 © Fred Bavendam
435 © John Gerlach/Animals Animals

436 © John Shaw/Tom Stack & Associates
437 © M.H. Sharp/Photo Researchers
438 © Lynn M. Stone/DRK Photo
439 © Frank Krahmer/Bruce Coleman
440 © David Madison/Bruce Coleman
441 © Scott Nielsen/DRK Photo
442 © Jack A. Barrie/Bruce Coleman; inset: © Gary W. Carter/Visuals Unlimited
443 © Michael Francis/The Wildlife Collection; © Fritz Polking/Peter Arnold
444 © M. Phillip Kahl, Jr./Bruce Coleman; © Charlie Heidecker/Visuals Unlimited
445 © George Holton/Photo Researchers; © Frans Lanting/Minden Pictures
447 © Barbara Gerlach/Visuals Unlimited
448 © W. Peckover/Vireo; © Summer Hays/Audubon/Photo Researchers
449 © Nigel J. Dennis/Photo Researchers
450 Both photos: © Paul Schwartz/Audubon/Photo Researchers
453 © Stephen Collins/Photo Researchers
454 © Alvin E. Staffan/Audubon/Photo Researchers
455 © Ken Brate/Audubon/Photo Researchers; © J.A. Hancock/Audubon/Photo Researchers
456 © Dan Sudia/Audubon/Photo Researchers; © Michael Ord/Audubon/Photo Researchers
457 © Dan Sudia/Audubon/Photo Researchers; © Stephen J. Krasemann/Photo Researchers
458 © L.F. Wanlass/Audubon/Photo Researchers; © Dick Halney/Audubon/Photo Researchers; © Dan Sudia/Audubon/Photo Researchers
459 © Ron Willocks/Audubon/Photo Researchers; © S.C. Fried/Photo Researchers
460 © Stephen Dalton/Audubon/Photo Researchers; © Walter E. Harvey/Audubon/Photo Researchers
461 © Mitsuyoshi Tatematsu/Nature Productions; © J.A. Hancock/Audubon/Photo Researchers
462 © S.R. Maglione/Photo Researchers; © Tom McHugh/Photo Researchers
463 © Bill Reasons/Audubon/Photo Researchers; © Ed Degginger/Bruce Coleman
464 © Royalty-Free/Corbis Images/Jupiter Images
465 © Zoological Society of San Diego; © Peter Menzel
466 © Robert Pearcy/Animals Animals
467 © Dan Guravich/Photo Researchers; © Sea World, Inc.
469 © Rudi Von Briel/PhotoEdit
470 © Don Riepe/Peter Arnold, Inc.; © M. Gunther/BIOS/Peter Arnold, Inc.; © Patricio Robles Gil/Bruce Coleman Inc.
471 © Steven Senne/AP/Wide World Photos; © Bill Bachmann/PhotoEdit; © Norman Owen Tomalin/Bruce Coleman Inc.
472 © Mark Baker/Reuters/Landov; © Jennifer Weinberg/Danita Delimont, Agent
473 © Tom Bean/DRK Photo; © Mark Stouffer/Animals Animals/Earth Scenes
474 © Jennifer Weinberg/Danita Delimont, Agent; © Bao Mai
475 © Dennis Demello/Wildlife Conservation Society; © Bao Mai
476 National Museum of Natural History/Smithsonian Institution; © Bao Mai
477 © Michael Gunther/BIOS/Peter Arnold, Inc.
479 Both photos: © Bao Mai
480 All images: © G.K & Vikki Hart/PhotoDisc/Getty Images
481 © Enric Marti/AP/Wide World Photos; © Dagli Orti/Egyptian Museum Cairo/The Art Archive
482 © Richard Hutchings/Photo Researchers; © Norbert von der Groeben/The Image Works
483 © Renee Stockdale/Animals Animals/Earth Scenes; © Gregory K. Scott/Photo Researchers
484 © Carolyn A. McKeone/Photo Researchers; © Susana Pashko/Envision Stock Photography, Inc.; © Ken Cavanagh/Photo Researchers
485 © Kent & Donna Dannen/Photo Researchers; © Myrleen Ferguson Cate/PhotoEdit
486 © Margaret Miller/Photo Researchers; © Joe McDonald/Animals Animals/Earth Scenes
487 © Carolyn A. McKeone/Photo Researchers; © John Pontier/Animals Animals/Earth Scenes; © William B. Plowman/Getty Images
488 Clockwise from bottom left: John F. Kennedy Library/Hulton/Archive/Getty Images; Brown Brothers; Library of Congress/Hulton/Archive/Getty Images; Brown Brothers; © Paul Morse/The White House/AP/Wide World Photos
489 Clockwise from top left: Time Life Pictures/Getty Images; © Marcy Nighswander/AP/Wide World Photos; Pictorial Parade/Getty Images; © James Pozarik/Getty Images; courtesy, Jimmy Carter Library; © Diana Walker/Time Life Pictures/Getty Images
490 © G.K & Vikki Hart/Photo Disc/Getty Image

Cover credits, front and back: © Keith Kent/Science Photo Library/Photo Researchers, NY; spine: © Lester Lefkowitz/Photographer's Choice/Getty Images

498   **ILLUSTRATION CREDITS**

INDEX

ALPHABETICAL INDEX

The index that follows is a complete set index: it covers all the articles found in each of the six volumes of *The New Book of Popular Science*. This index is repeated in its totality in the back of each volume.

Throughout this index, a subject heading that is covered by an entire article is printed in boldface capital letters and is followed by the volume and page numbers, indicating where the article appears in *The New Book of Popular Science*. For example, the entry:

ACCOUNTING 1:453–59

indicates that an article on accounting can be found in volume 1, pages 453 to 459 inclusive. A subject that is covered within an article is printed in boldface capital and lowercase letters, and the volume and specific pages are noted. For example, the entry:

Acetic acid 3:94, 99, 114

indicates that information on acetic acid can be found on pages 94, 99, and 114 of volume 3. In all text references throughout the index, volume numbers are printed in boldface type. Page numbers referring to the entire article about the subject heading are in boldface; other page numbers are in lightface type. Multiple volume and page references to one subject are filed in numerical order.

Illustrations are identified by the abbreviation *illus.* References to the illustrations, as well as to the charts, tables, and diagrams, are filed after all references to the text.

Subjects in this index may be subdivided to make information on specific aspects of the topic readily accessible. These subentries are indented and listed alphabetically below the main entry. The example below has two subentries.

Aerospace engineering 6:20
aeronautical engineering **3:**192
composite materials **6:**230–31

Some entries include a brief identification of the subject. The identification, enclosed in parentheses, may note the scientific field in which the term is commonly used, define the subject in a few words, or describe a person's nationality and profession.

Absorption (in physics)
Ada (computer language) **6:**376
Adams, John Couch (English astronomer) **1:**79, 152; **3:**182
American Woodhenge (archaeological site, Missouri) **1:**471

The index includes *see* and *see also* references. *See* references guide the reader from one term to another. They are used for abbreviations, for synonyms, for inverted headings, and for alternative spellings.

Accelerators, Particle *see* Particle accelerators
ALU *see* Arithmetic/logic unit
Amebas *see* Amoebas
Ascorbic acid *see* Vitamin C

See also references direct the reader to related subject entries.

Accidents *see also* Safety
Air *see also* Atmosphere
Astronauts *see also* Cosmonauts
Atomic theory 3:3–4, 304–5 *see also* Atoms

Subjects are filed alphabetically, letter by letter. When a subject heading is made up of more than one word, it is still arranged alphabetically, letter by letter.

Air *see also* Atmosphere
Air-conditioning systems 3:236
illus. **2:**479
Airglow 2:151–52
Air masses 2:186–88
Airplanes 6:153–60
air pollution **2:**468
engines **6:**162–64
Air-traffic-control radar 6:259

Cassiopeia A (supernova remnant)
illus. 1:58; 3:280
Cassowaries 4:412
illus. 4:411
Caste system
ants 4:281–82
bees 4:286
termites 4:290
Cast iron 6:29–30, 175, 178, 187–88
Cast-iron pipes 2:449
Castor (star) 1:32
Casuariiformes 4:398
Catalysts 3:55, 62; 6:206
Catalytic converters 2:468; 3:73; 6:140–41
chemistry 3:62
negative effects 6:134
Catalytic cracking 2:331
Catamounts *see* Cougars
Cataracts (in the eyes) 5:271, 508
Catbirds 4:453
Catenary curves 6:33
Caterpillars 4:301–2, 304, 305, 307
illus.
monarch butterfly 4:302
spicebush swallowtail 4:301
woolly-bear 4:306
CAT FAMILY 5:84–92 *see also* Cats, Domestic
endangered species 2:500
evolution 1:489
Catfish 4:333; 6:90
illus. 6:87
Cathedrals 6:7, 25, 33
illus. 6:36
Catheter ablation 5:440
Catheters
angiogram 5:439
angioplasty 5:439, 490, 491
post-surgery monitoring 5:480
Cathode-ray tubes (CRTs) 6:249–50
television 3:300; 6:295–96
illus. 6:249
Cathodes 3:102; 6:247, 248
illus. 6:247, 249, 250
Cations 3:31, 50, 63, 97, 102
Catopril 5:467
Cats, Domestic 4:190; 5:324
pets 4:480–81, 482, 484, 485–86, 490
illus. 5:85, 90
CAT scans 5:452–53, 458, 459
illus. 6:372
Catskill Mountains 2:80
illus. 2:68
Cattails
illus. 4:150
Cattle 5:134
beef tapeworm 4:226
dairy farming 6:64–66
evolution 5:127
feedlots 6:60

grasslands 4:140
methane production 2:146, 478
milking machines 3:186
selective breeding 6:71
illus. 2:76; 6:58
Caudata *see* Salamanders
Caustic soda *see* Sodium hydroxide
Cavendish, Henry (English scientist) 3:178
illus.
gravity experiment 3:177
Cave of the Winds (Niagara Falls, New York) 2:129
Cave painting
illus. 6:4, 333
Cave pearls 2:128
CAVES AND CAVERNS 2:125–31
carbon dioxide–water solution 3:84
coastal formation 2:291, 292
lake formation 2:110
water changes the land 2:418
illus. 2:1; 3:87
cutaway view 2:127
wind caves 2:431
Caviar 4:331
Cavies 5:45
Cayley, Sir George (British scientist) 6:152
Caymans *see* Caimans
CB (citizen-band) radio 6:242
CBT *see* Computer Based Training
CCDs *see* Charge-coupled devices
CD-4 cells (Helper T cells; T-helper lymphocytes) 5:236, 237, 442, 443
AIDS 5:239
CDMA (Code Division Multiple Access) (cellular standard) 6:245
CDPD (Cellular Digital Packet Data) (cellular standard) 6:245
CD-ROMs 6:299, 300
CDs (Compact discs) 6:285–87; 6:299, 370
Cecropia moths 4:306
illus. 4:301, 307
Cecum 5:8, 254
Cedars 4:85, 86, 87, 92
wood construction 6:28
Cedars of Lebanon 4:92
Cedar waxwings 4:452
Cedros Island mule deer 5:122
Ceilometers 2:164
Celera Genomics 3:420
Celestial equator 1:36
Celestial globes 1:66
Celestial navigation 6:165, 166
Celestial sphere 1:32, 36, 385
Cell biology (Cytology) 3:366; 4:181
Cell body 5:171

CELL DIVISION 3:440–45, 459–60, 467
CELL DYNAMICS 3:432–39
Cell membranes 3:428–29 *see also* Plasma membrane
Cell phones 6:242–45
Cell plate 3:442–43
Cells (in air pressure) 2:210
Cells (in biology) 5:161–63 *see also* Cell division; Cell dynamics; Cell structure
aging 3:467, 468
algae 4:47–48
animals 4:185
biology, history of 3:369
cancer 5:433–34
death 3:468, 470
early life 4:184
glossary 3:430
human growth 5:325
life, characteristics of 3:376, 378
life, origin of 1:319
malignant 5:434
membranes *see* Cell membranes
osmosis 3:80
plant cytology 4:4
plants 4:9, 14, 65
prokaryotes 4:26–27
types of 3:432–33
viral infection 3:391–93
illus. 5:162
human cheek cells 6:341
malignant 5:433
muscle cells 3:439
plants 4:10
potato 6:74
Cells (in telecommunications) 6:242–43
CELL STRUCTURE (in biology) 3:424–31
glossary 3:430
illus. 5:162
Cellular Digital Packet Data *see* CDPD
Cellular One (company) 6:243
Cellular respiration 3:436–38; 5:203
Cellular response 5:237
Cellular slime molds 4:51, 52
Cellular technology 6:242–45
digital photography 6:274
health and cell phones 3:277
Celluloid 6:215
Cellulose 3:118, 119
algae 4:48, 51
commercial plastics 6:214–15
plant cells 4:9, 14
portland cement mixture 6:26
ruminants' digestion 4:35
Cellulose acetate 6:215
Cell walls 3:426, 430, 431; 4:14, 28–29
microbiology 3:448, 451
Celsius, Anders (Swedish astronomer) 3:191

Clarinets **3:**216
Clark, Laurel (American astronaut) **1:**289
Clark, Ronald W. (author) **6:**16, 20
Classes (in biological classification) **3:**397
Classical conditioning 5:338, 359
Classical physics 3:144–45
CLASSIFICATION OF LIVING THINGS 3:394–99
 animal-like protists **4:**211
 arachnids **4:**262–63
 Aristotle **3:**367
 birds **4:**397–99, 400
 botany **4:**3–4, 54–57
 butterflies and moths **4:**303
 cartilaginous fish **4:**324–25
 crustaceans **4:**254
 early classifications **4:**183–84
 fish **4:**319
 fungi **4:**41
 insectivores **5:**24
 insects **4:**277–80
 mammals **5:**11–13
 monerans **4:**29
 plantlike protists **4:**52–53
 turtles **4:**377–79
 zoological **4:**179, 198–205
Clastic rocks *see* Fragmental rocks
Clavicle 5:178
 illus. **5:**165, 174
Clavius (lunar crater) **1:**113
Clavius, Christopher (Bavarian mathematician) **1:**477
Clawed African toads 4:346
Clay 2:35
 caves **2:**126–27, 129
 ceramics **6:**217
 climate analysis **2:**216
 groundwater **2:**113, 114, 119
 tablets for writing **1:**454
Clay, Jacob (Dutch scientist) **1:**226
Clean Air Acts (U.S.) **2:**471
 1963 **2:**471
 1970 **6:**134
 1990 **2:**172, 358, 474
Clean Water Act (U.S., 1970) **2:**458
Clear-cutting of timber 4:129; **4:**146, 149
Clear Skies Act (U.S., 2003) **2:**476
Clearwing moths 4:307
Cleavage (in biology) **3:**460; **5:**162
Cleavage (in minerals) **2:**137; **3:**64
C-Leg (prosthetic leg) **5:**503
Clementine spacecraft 1:114; **1:**298
Clermont (steamboat) **6:**110
 illus. **6:**111
Click beetles 4:294–95
Cliffs 2:418, 422

CLIMATE CHANGE 1:109; **2:**477–82
 Antarctic ice shelf melting **2:**91
 Arctic, effect on **2:**88–89
 climate changes **2:**219
 climates of the world **2:**214
 coral reef damage **2:**287
 endangered species **2:**500
 environmental pollution **2:**453
 geological studies **2:**8
 greenhouse effect **2:**154
 methane **2:**146
 savanna grasses **4:**143
CLIMATES OF THE PAST 2:215–20
 archaeology **1:**464
 geological studies **2:**8
 geologic record **2:**19, 21
 paleoecology **1:**482–83
CLIMATES OF THE WORLD 2:207–14
 air pollution **2:**8, 469–70, 477–82
 Arctic Ocean's effects on **2:**235
 biomes **3:**492–93, 498
 climatology **2:**146
 climax communities **4:**125
 convection currents **3:**235
 erosion, factor in **2:**121–22
 greenhouse effect **2:**154
 ocean currents **2:**242
 ocean's effects on **2:**222
 past ages **2:**215–20
 polar regions **2:**87–92
 precipitation **2:**170–72
 rain forests' role **4:**161
 seawater's salt content **2:**229
 volcanoes' effect **2:**62
 water diversions **2:**410
 wetlands' role **4:**155
 map(s) **2:**208
Climatology 2:142, 146, 209, 300
Climax communities 3:483; **4:**122, 125
Clinical genetics 3:404
Clinical psychology 5:345, 346
Clinker construction (of ships) **6:**109
Clipper Graham Single-Stage-to-Orbit rocket 1:262–63
Clipper ships 6:110
Clitoris
 illus. **5:**295
Cloaca 4:395; **5:**14
Clock genes 3:380
Clock paradox 3:352
Clocks and watches 3:91
Clock speed (of computers) **6:**361, 368
Clonidine 5:470
Cloning 6:14
 genetic technology **3:**422–23
 Lincoln's genes **5:**318
 mitosis **3:**443
 monoclonal antibodies **5:**471–72

 organ transplants **5:**479
 sheep **6:**75
 veterinary science **4:**468
Closed control systems (in automation) **6:**195
Cloth *see* Textile industry
Clothing, Protective
 coal miners **2:**355
 illus.
  nuclear-power plant workers **2:**371
Clothoid loops 3:159
Clotting *see* Blood clotting
Cloud chambers
 cosmic rays **1:**225, 227–28
 illus. **1:**226
Clouded leopards 5:88
Cloud Garden (book, Dyke) **4:**2
CLOUDS 2:159–65
 hurricanes **2:**197–98, 199
 precipitation **2:**166–67
 thunderclouds **2:**175–76
Cloud seeding 2:145
Cloud streets 2:163
Clown fish
 illus. **4:**219
Clozapine 5:356
Club fungi 3:455; **4:**41, 44–45
 parasol ants **4:**284–85
CLUB MOSSES 4:13, 56, 60, **74–75, 76–77**
Clumber spaniels
 illus. **5:**3
Clumped populations 3:479
Cluster (spacecraft) **2:**158
Cluster galaxies *see* Galactic clusters
Clutches 6:144
Clydesdale horses
 illus. **5:**108
CMOS *see* Complimentary metal oxide semiconductor
Cnidaria *see* Coelenterates
Coagulation (in physiology) *see* Blood clotting
Coagulation (water treatment) **2:**444–45
COAL 1:90; **2:**35–36, **346–60**
 acid rain **2:**473
 alternative energy **2:**395; **2:**396
 chemical reaction **3:**62
 combustion **3:**62
 composition **2:**133
 conservation **2:**415
 energy **2:**305, 398
 formation **3:**188
 fossils **1:**485; **4:**74
 gasification *see* Coal gasification
 heat energy **3:**219
 hydrogen production **2:**399
 liquefaction *see* Coal liquefaction
 minerals **2:**136
 organic chemistry **3:**108
 peat **4:**62
 pollution **2:**306–7

Dogs, Domestic (cont.)
life span 5:324
pets 4:481, 484, 485, 486, 490
tapeworms 4:226
illus. 5:3
Clumber spaniels 5:3
heart with heartworms 4:229
veterinary care 4:464
Dog Star *see* Sirius
Dogwood anthracnose
illus. 4:44
Dogwood trees
illus. 4:100
Doldrums (winds) 2:184, 196
Dollar as unit of measure 1:457
"Dolly" (cloned sheep) 3:422;
6:14, 75
Dolly Sods Wilderness (West
Virginia) 2:512
Dolomite 2:111
Dolomites (mountains, Italy)
illus. 2:124
DOLPHINS 5:55–60
killer whales 5:53
limits on taking 2:413
pilot whales 5:53
Domain names 6:307
Domes (in architecture) 6:26, 33,
41
illus. 6:35
Domesday Book 1:455
Domestication of animals 6:4
camels and llamas 5:117
cattle 5:134
cheetahs 5:89
dogs 5:78
falconry 4:419
pets 4:481
river otters 5:98
water buffalo 5:133–34
yaks 5:135
Dominance hierarchies 5:10,
147
Dominant genes 3:407, 408;
5:315, 316, 318, 420; 6:70
illus. 3:407
Dominican Republic 2:52
Donacia 4:298
Donkeys 3:396; 5:110
Donora (Pennsylvania) 2:468
Donor organs for transplants
5:497–98, 499
Doolittle, Jimmy (American pilot)
6:155
Doorbells 3:260
illus. 3:265
Dopamine 5:233; 5:334, 356
Doping (in electronics) 2:389;
6:232
Doppler color flow imaging
5:454, 459
Doppler effect 1:19
navigation 6:171
sound 3:207
Sun's spectrum 1:87
illus.
sound 3:207

Doppler radar 2:205, 206;
6:255–56
electromagnetic spectrum 3:279
tornadoes 2:194
weather forecasting 6:261
illus.
tornado tracking 2:191
Doppler ultrasound 5:303
Dormancy
bryophytes 4:59
desert animals' eggs 4:169
desert plants 4:168
fern spores 4:79, 82
fungi 4:38, 39, 40, 42
grasses 4:139
perennials 4:107
seeds 4:104, 105
Dormice 5:44
Dot-matrix printers 6:366
Double bonds (in chemistry)
3:109, 111, 112, 113
Double covalent bonds 3:52
Double-entry bookkeeping
1:456
Double helix (form of DNA
chains) 3:91, 123
illus. 3:116
Double-star theory 2:11–12
Double-wattled cassowaries
4:412
Douglas, David (Scottish bota-
nist) 4:92
Douglas DC-3 (airplane) 6:156
Douglas firs 4:86, 91–92
illus. 4:84
Doves 4:430–31
Downers *see* Depressant sub-
stances
Down feathers 4:392
Downloading (of data files)
6:307, 384
Down quarks 3:20, 318, 319
Down syndrome 3:416; 5:421
illus. 5:419
Downwelling, Oceanic 2:236,
237, 238
Downy mildew 3:451
Doxirubicin 5:474
Draco (constellation) 1:26
Drafting (in bicycling) 6:94
Drag (Resistance) 3:192–93
air 6:94
aviation 6:158
falling objects 3:154, 155
water 6:91–92
Dragonflies 4:154, 276, 278
fossils 1:488
illus. 4:184, 246, 272
Drainage basins (of rivers) 2:419
Drais de Sauerbrun, Baron Karl
von (German inventor)
6:92
Drake, Edwin L. (American oil
producer) 2:323
Drake, Frank (American scientist)
1:322
Drake Equation 1:322–23
Drakes 4:443

Drawing, Scientific 3:515; 6:336
see also Scientific illustration
Drawing pads (of computers)
6:364
Dreamcast (video-game system)
6:301
Dreams 5:342, 407
Dredging 2:290, 294
deep-sea exploration 2:273
fishing 6:87
Drela, Mark (American aircraft
designer) 6:95
Drexler, K. Eric (American scientist) 6:347
Drift-bottle method 2:236, 242
Drift mines 2:350, 354
illus. 2:350
Drift nets 6:87
Drilling
deep-sea exploration 2:275–76
geothermal energy 2:394
lasers in manufacturing 6:355
natural gas 2:340–41
oil wells 2:326–27
tunnels 6:47–48
water wells 2:439–40
illus.
natural gas 2:338
oil wells 2:324, 325, 327
water wells 2:116
Drills (animals) 5:143
Drills, Dental 5:491
Drinker-Collins respirator *see*
Iron lung
Dripstones 2:127
Driven wells 2:441
Driver ants 4:285
Drivetrains 6:135, 138
illus. 6:135
Drizzle 2:167
Drogues 1:241
illus. 1:257
Dromaeosaurs 4:390
Dromedaries 5:117
illus. 5:116
Drones (bees) 3:457; 4:286;
4:287–88
Drongos 4:447–48
Drosophila 4:181
Droughts 2:172
Dust Bowl 2:123
hydrometeorology 2:145
irrigation 2:409
water conservation 2:409
wells 2:117
Drug abuse *see* Substance
abuse
DRUG DELIVERY TECHNOL-
OGY 5:468–75
implantable pumps 1:254
illus.
implantable pumps 1:255
DRUGS (Medications) 5:460–67
AIDS research 5:445
allergic reactions 5:448
allergy treatment 5:241, 449

Heisenberg uncertainty prin-
ciple *see* Uncertainty prin-
ciple
Helical scan 6:281
Helicobacter pylori 5:256
Helicopters 6:160–61
Helictites 2:128
Heliocentric system *see* Coper-
nican system
Heliopause 1:293
Helios (solar-powered aircraft)
6:157
Helios (space probe) 1:301
Helioseismology 1:190
Heliosphere 1:234
Heliozoans 4:211
Helium 3:33, 38
airships 6:151
atomic structure 3:48, 63
balloons 3:188
discovery of 3:5
Jupiter 1:136
Mercury (planet) 1:98
Moon 1:260
stars 1:192, 193, 195, 197
Sun 1:86, 88, 89, 191
weight of 3:184
illus. 3:336
Hell Gate (New York City)
tidal current 2:248
Helmet quails *see* California
quails
Helmets
illus. 2:355
Helmont, Jan Baptista van
(Flemish biochemist) 3:369
Helper T cells *see* CD-4 cells
Hematocrit reading 5:213
Hematologic system 5:196
Hematomas 5:234
Hemichordates 4:204, 308, 309,
311
Hemipseudospheres 1:401, 402
Hemiptera *see* Bugs, True
Hemispheres (in geometry)
1:401, 402
Hemlocks 4:87, 93
Hemoglobin 5:203, 206, 211,
213
adaptation to high altitude 5:7
anemia 5:210
genetics 3:402
genetic technology 5:475
Hemolymph 4:274
Hemolytic anemia 5:211
Hemophilia 5:212, 319, 421
AIDS from transfusions 5:443
illus.
heredity 5:317
Hen harriers *see* Marsh hawks
Henry III (English king) 4:470
Henry of Portugal (Portuguese
prince) 6:167–68
Heparin 5:207–8, 467
Hepatitis 5:375
Hepatitis B (Serum hepatitis)
5:210, 430, 475
Heptane 3:75, 111

Herald of Free Enterprise (ferry-
boat) 6:112
Herbals (books) 4:3; 6:335
illus. 6:333
Herbicides 2:462, 502
Herbivores 3:485; 5:8
bison, buffalo, and oxen
5:132–35
camels and llamas 5:116–17
deer family 5:118–23
giraffes and okapis 5:124–25
marsupials 5:17–20
Hercules (constellation) 1:30
Hercules beetles 4:297
Hereditary diseases *see* Genetic
diseases
HEREDITY 3:395, 406–15 *see
also* Evolution; Genes;
Genetic technology; Heredity, Human
genetics 3:400–405
HEREDITY, Human 5:308–22,
323, 325
allergies 5:447
body weight 5:392
cancer 5:435
genetic diseases 5:418–22
Hermaphrodites 3:457; 4:187,
244, 320
Hermes (asteroid) 1:169
Hermit crabs 4:216
Hermit thrushes 4:455
illus. 4:453
HERO-2 *see* Einstein X-Ray
Observatory
Herodotus (Greek historian)
2:322
Heroin 5:373, 374, 376
Herons 4:444
illus.
beak 4:393
Hero of Alexandria (Greek math-
ematician and physicist)
6:96
Herpes viruses 3:388, 392;
3:393
illus. 3:385, 451
HERPETOLOGY 4:336–39 *see
also* Amphibians; Reptiles
Herrick, Richard (American kid-
ney transplant recipient)
5:496
Herring 4:332
Herschel, Sir William (German-
English astronomer)
infrared radiation 1:60; 3:274
Saturn 1:140
star survey 1:184
Uranus 1:147
Hertz (unit of measurement)
6:288
Hertz, Heinrich R. (German scientist) 3:276; 6:255
Herzsprung-Russell diagram
illus. 1:193
Hesperornis regalis 1:497
Hess, Harald (American physi-
cist) 3:450

Hess, Harry (American geologist)
2:41
Hess, Victor F. (Austrian physi-
cist) 1:225
HETE-2 *see* High Energy Tran-
sient Explorer
Heterocysts 4:35
illus. 3:448
Heterodyning 3:218
Heterografts 5:496
Heterotrophs 4:11, 30
Hewish, Antony (British astrono-
mer) 1:209
Hexactinellida 4:200, 216
Hexadecanol 2:439
Hexadecimal numeral system
6:362–63
Hexagonal crystals 3:90
Hexane 3:75
Heyerdahl, Thor (Norwegian
explorer) 2:235, 464
HHS *see* Health and Human Ser-
vices, U.S. Department of
Hibernacula 4:111–12
Hibernation 5:5
bats 5:30–31
bears 5:71, 74
dormice 5:44
frogs 4:344
poorwills 4:403
snakes 4:365–66
Hibiscus 4:158
Hidalgo (asteroid) 1:168–69
Hieroglyphic system 1:339
illus. 1:340
Higgs, boson 3:324
Higgs, Peter (Scottish physicist)
3:324
High blood pressure *see* Hyper-
tension
High-definition television
(HDTV) 6:293, 297
High-density lipoproteins
Nutrition 5:383
High Energy Astrophysical
Observatory-2 *see* Ein-
stein X-Ray Observatory
High-energy-density physics
(HEDP) *see* Inertial-con-
finement fusion
High Energy Transient Explorer
(HETE-2) 1:59
High-intensity discharge (HID)
lights 3:362; 6:141
Highland climates 2:214
High-latitude biomes 3:496–97,
498
High-level wastes 2:370
Highly active antiretroviral
therapy (HAART) 5:239;
5:445
High-quality proteins *see* Com-
plete proteins
High species richness and
diversity 4:132
High-speed trains 6:130–32
illus. 6:129
High-sulfur fuel oil 2:473

KAGUYA (space probe) **1:**124, 298
Kaifeng pagoda (China) *illus.* **6:**29
Kakapos 4:401, 409 *illus.* **2:**497
Kalahari Desert 2:83
Kamerlingh-Onnes, Heike (Dutch physicist) **6:**220
Kamptozoa 4:202
Kanellopoulos, Kanellos (Greek bicyclist) **6:**95; **6:**157
Kangaroos 4:140; **5:**8, 17–19 *illus.* **5:**7, 16
Kansas City, Missouri 2:201
Kant, Immanuel (German philosopher) **2:**9
Kaolin 6:217
Kaolinite 2:122
Kaons (K-mesons) 3:20, 315, 316
Kaplan reaction turbines 2:316 *illus.* **2:**378
Kaposi's sarcoma 5:239, 441, 443
Kapteyn, J. C. (Dutch astronomer) **1:**184
Karst region (Slovenia–Croatia) **2:**126, 172
Kasner, Edward (American mathematician) **1:**359
Katmai (volcano, Alaska) **2:**433
Katrina (hurricane, 2005) **2:**199, 200
Kauris 4:87
Kay, John (English inventor) **6:**189
Kayaks 6:92
Kearns-Sayre syndrome 5:321
Keck Observatory (Hawaii) **1:**13, 41, 179
galactic core **1:**187 *illus.* **1:**43
Keels 6:109
Keller, Horst Uwe (German astronomer) **1:**161
Keloids 5:239
Kelp 2:397–98; **3:**476; **4:**47, 50 *illus.* **4:**7, 46, 48
Kelvin, William Thomson, Baron (British physicist) **2:**27
Kelvin temperature scale 3:74, 135–36, 223
superconductors **3:**305 *table(s)* **6:**424
Kennedy, John F. (American president) **1:**240
Kentucky 2:131
Kenya
wilderness preservation **2:**514
Kepler, Johannes (German astronomer)
Copernican system **1:**473
planetary motion **1:**12, 78; **3:**141, 161
supernovas **1:**198
Keratin 4:391; **5:**112, 263, 507

Kermode's bears 5:74
Kerogen 2:395–96
Kerosene 2:323, 330, 332
Kestrels 4:418
Ketones 2:467; **3:**114; **5:**245, 381
Ketosis 5:394
Kettledrums 3:216
Kevlar fiber 6:229
Keyboards (of computers) **6:**364
Key deer 5:121–22
Keyhole surgery *see* Minimally invasive surgery
KH-11 (artificial satellite) **1:**313
Kiangs 5:110
Kidneys
babies **5:**327
cancer **5:**437
drug elimination **5:**461
excretory system **5:**258–60, 262
mammals **5:**4
pain **5:**290
primate kidneys transplanted **5:**496
scarlet fever **5:**238–39
transplants **5:**496, 498 *illus.* **5:**168
Kidney stones 5:262, 491–92
Kilauea (volcano, Hawaii) **2:**55, 58, 61
Kilby, Jack (American scientist) **6:**253
Kilimanjaro, Mount (Tanzania) **2:**67, 71
Killer T cells 5:237
Killer whales 3:476; **5:**53, 67 *illus.* **5:**3, 56
Kilns 6:26, 27, 29, 218
Kilocalories 3:58, 61, 225
Kilowatt-hours 2:319; **3:**257
Kilowatts 2:319
Kinesthesia 5:286
Kinetic energy 3:71, 75, 76, 78, 190
entropy **3:**241
work **3:**164
Kinetic theory 3:71–72, 141
heat energy **3:**221
King, Mary-Claire (American geneticist) **3:**400
Kingbirds 4:449
King cobras 4:373
King crabs *see* Horseshoe crabs
Kingdoms (in biological classification) **3:**396, 398, 399
Kingfishers 4:406–7
Kinglets 4:455
King rails 4:439
King snakes 4:371
Kinkajous
illus. **5:**75
Kirchhoff, Gustav (German physicist) **3:**5
Kiss II (holographic movie) *illus.* **6:**276
Kitasato, Shibasaburo (Japanese bacteriologist) **5:**424
Kites (birds) **4:**415; **4:**417

Kitti's hog-nosed bats 5:32
"Kitty Hawk" (Apollo command module) *illus.* **1:**244
Kiwis (birds) **4:**398, 413 *illus.* **4:**412
Klinefelter's syndrome 5:314
Klipspringers 5:131
Klystrons 6:249
K-mesons *see* Kaons
Kneecap *see* Patella
Knee jerk 5:227, 408
Knees (of cypress trees) **4:**153
Knees, Artificial *see* Artificial knees
Knife fish 4:320
Knight, Charles (American artist) *illus.* **1:**483
Knot (unit of speed) **2:**236; **6:**167
Knuckles 5:179
Koalas 5:20
Kobe (Japan) **2:**52, 54
Kobs 5:130
Koch, Robert (German physician) **3:**447; **4:**25; **5:**424
Kodiak bears 5:73
Köhler, Georges (German physiologist) **5:**472
Köhler, Wolfgang (German-American psychologist) **4:**193
Kokia kookei (plant) *illus.* **2:**496
Koko (gorilla) **5:**149
Kolhörster, Werner (German physicist) **1:**225, 226
Kolyma Range (Siberia) **2:**89
Komarov, Vladimir M. (Soviet cosmonaut) **1:**247
Komodo dragons 4:353, 357, 361 *illus.* **2:**495
Kookaburras 4:407
Koonwarra plants *illus.* **4:**99
Köppen, Vladimir (German meteorologist) **2:**211
Korea, Republic of *see* South Korea
Korn, Arthur (German inventor) **6:**244
Kovalevskaya, Sofia (Russian mathematician) **1:**330
Kraits 4:373
Krakatau (volcano, Indonesia) **2:**433
Krebs citric acid cycle 3:437 *illus.* **3:**435
Kremer Prizes 6:94–95
Krikalev, Sergei (Soviet cosmonaut) *illus.* **1:**268
Krill 5:49
Kristall (space module) **1:**283
Kruger National Park (South Africa) **2:**513
Krypton 2:364; **3:**33, 39, 68
Krypton 85 2:372

Miscarriage 5:302
Missile-carrying submarines (SSBNs) 6:121; 6:122
Missiles (weapons) 6:121
  radar control 6:258
  space-based defense 1:262–63
Missing mass see Dark matter
Mission Control Center (Houston, Texas)
  illus. 1:257, 294
Mission to Planet Earth see Earth Science Enterprise
Mississippian period 1:488
  table(s) 2:18–19
Mississippi River 2:419, 420, 421
  delta plain 2:76, 105
  flood control 2:105
  meanders and oxbows 2:103, 104
Mississippi Valley 2:77
Missouri 2:51, 463
Miss Waldron's red colobus 5:141
Mist 2:160, 167
Mistletoe 3:483; 4:104, 112, 119
Mistral 2:186
Mitch (hurricane, 2004) 2:200
Mites 4:248, 257, 258, 262, 263
Mitnick, Kevin (American hacker) 6:395
Mitochondria 3:430, 431; 4:14
  aging 3:467–68
  bacteria 3:428
  cell dynamics 3:437
  DNA 5:321
  genetics 3:400
  illus. 3:429; 5:162
Mitosis 3:441–43; 5:162–63, 310
  illus. 3:442
Mitral (Bicuspid) valve 5:198, 199
Mnemonic devices 5:362
Moa plants 4:82
Mobitex 6:245
Mockingbirds 4:192, 396, 453
Mode (type of average) 1:409–10, 411
Models 6:337
Model T Ford (automobile) 6:192
  illus. 6:136, 191
Modems 6:306, 364, 387–88
  faxes 6:244
Moderators (of nuclear reactors) 2:366
Modern physics 3:145
Modulation 6:289
Modulators 6:256
Moebius Strip
  illus. 1:334
Moeritherium 5:103
  illus. 5:104
Mohole Project see Project Mohole
Mohorovičić, Andrija (Croatian seismologist) 2:25
Mohorovičić discontinuity 2:25
Mohs' hardness scale 2:137

Mojave Desert 4:166
Molarity 3:80
Molar mass 3:56
Molars (teeth) 5:279, 280
Molasse 2:71, 72, 73
Molding (of plastics) 6:212–14
Molds (fungi) 3:375, 451; 4:38, 41
  antibiotics 5:463
  decomposition 3:470
  reproduction 3:455
  illus. 3:375; 4:38
Mole (unit of measurement) 3:56, 58, 80, 335
Molecular beam epitaxy 6:232
Molecular biology 3:373
Molecular compounds 3:65
Molecules 3:17, 53–54, 64–67
  aromatic compounds 3:112
  chemical bonding 3:47
  covalence 3:50–52
  liquids 3:75, 76, 77, 78
  smell 5:283, 284
  water 3:82–83; 3:85
  illus. 3:84
Mole rats 5:43
Moles (animals) 5:24–26
Moles (on skin) 5:267
Moles, Mechanical 6:48
Mole vipers 4:374
MOLLUSKS 4:202–3, 231–41
  carbon cycle 3:489–90
  fishing 6:87
  fossils 1:487
Molniya (communications satellite) 1:309
Molting 5:6
  arthropods 4:247
  beetles 4:292
  birds 4:392
  butterflies and moths 4:301–2, 303
  crustaceans 4:251
  reptiles 4:355
  snakes 4:368
  illus. 4:366
Molybdenum 3:40
Momentum 3:141, 156, 313–14
  Newton's third law 3:158
Monadnock, Mount (New Hampshire) 2:425
Monadnocks 2:425
Monarch B (human-powered aircraft) 6:95
Monarch butterflies 4:276, 305–6; 6:75
  illus. 4:190, 302
MONERANS 4:25–35, 54, 55, 184
  classification of living things 3:398, 399
  illus. 3:448; 4:55
Mongolian asses see Kulans
Mongolian wild horses see Przhevalski's wild horses
Mongooses 5:100, 101
  illus. 5:99

Monier, Joseph (French gardener) 6:31
Monitors (lizards) 4:356, 357
Monitors (of computers) 3:300; 6:365
Monkey-puzzle trees 4:85
  illus. 4:87
Monkeys 5:7–8, 10, 138, 139–43, 146–47, 148
Monkey's dinner-bell trees 4:119
Monk parakeets 4:197
Monoamine oxidase inhibitors 5:356, 466
Monoclimax theory 4:125
Monoclinic crystals
  illus. 3:90
Monoclonal antibodies 5:437, 471–73
Monocoque fuselages 6:153–54
Monocots 4:57, 106–7
Monoculture 2:412
Monocytes 5:208
Monoecious plants 4:101
Monomers 6:210
Mononucleosis 3:392
Mononychus
  illus. 1:498
Monophonic recording 6:279
Monoplanes 6:153
Monopoles 3:262
Monorails 6:128, 130
  illus. 6:128, 129
Monosaccharides 3:118; 5:380
Monosodium glutamate 6:84
Monosodium urate 5:429
MONOTREMES (Egg-laying mammals) 1:498; 5:5, 11, 14–15
Monounsaturated fats 3:120; 5:382, 383
Monsoon Drift (ocean current) 2:240
Monsoons 2:183, 230
  climates of the world 2:212
  ocean currents 2:234, 237
Monsters (science fiction) 1:504
Montana
  coal 2:360
  farmland 6:64
  Glacier National Park 2:108
  wilderness areas 2:511
  illus. 6:18
Montane squirrels 5:40
Monterey Canyon (submarine canyon, California) 2:269
Monterey cypresses 4:92
Monterey pines 3:507
Montezuma cypresses
  illus. 4:91
Montgolfier, Joseph-Michel and Jacques-Étienne (French inventors) 6:149
Month (time period) 1:474, 475, 478
Montreal Protocol (1987) 2:482
Mont St. Michel (France)
  illus. 2:246

NIBIN *see* National Integrated Ballistic Information Network

Nicaragua 2:52

Niches (in ecosystems) 2:454; 3:477

Nickajack Lake (exhibit, Tennessee Aquarium) 4:476

Nickel 3:41
  atomic number 3:20
  Earth's interior 2:28
  electroplating 3:103
  meteorites 1:172

Nickel-cadmium batteries 1:306; 3:253

Nicotinamide *see* Niacin

Nicotine 5:370–71, 376–77
  nasal sprays 5:474
  transdermal skin patches 5:470

Nicotinic acid *see* Niacin

Nielsbohrium *see* Bohrium

Night blindness 5:270; 5:383

Night-blooming cacti 4:115

Night crawlers 4:243

Nighthawks 4:403

Nightingale, Florence (English nurse) 5:482, 483

Nightjars *see* Goatsuckers

NIGHT SKY 1:24–36; 2:155–58

Night terrors 5:409

Night-vision goggles
  illus. 3:273

Nikolayev, Andrian G. (Soviet cosmonaut) 1:241

Nile crocodiles 4:437–38
  illus. 4:382

Nile plovers 4:437–38

Nile River
  flooding 2:105
  meanders 2:103
  sediment 2:419
  water supply 2:435–36

Nilgais 5:128

Nim (game) 1:451

Nimbostratus clouds 2:165

1984 (novel, Orwell) 1:502

99s, The (women's aviation organization) 1:288

Niño, El *see* El Niño

Nintendo (video game company) 6:298; 6:299, 300, 301

Niobium 3:41, 306

Nios, Lake (Cameroon) 2:61, 109

Nipples 5:294

Nipride *see* Sodium nitroprusside

Nitrates 2:411–12; 3:491

Nitric acid 2:473–74, 476; 3:96, 99

Nitric oxide 2:154

Nitrile 3:110

Nitrogen 3:31, 32, 41
  atmosphere 1:105; 2:149, 151, 152
  atomic structure 3:69
  auroras 2:157
  bacteria, nitrifying 4:31
  blood 5:221

ceramic superconductors 6:221
covalence 3:52
cryosurgery 5:479
fertilizers 6:205
fuel gases 2:359
geysers on Triton 1:155
life, origin of 3:380
lightning 2:179
microbiology 3:450
organic compounds 3:114–15
plants 4:68; 6:75
protein 5:378
  illus.
    liquid nitrogen 3:26

Nitrogen cycle 3:490–91

Nitrogen dioxide 3:69

Nitrogen engines 6:148

Nitrogen family of elements 3:31–32

Nitrogen fixation 3:491; 4:35, 122–23; 6:73

Nitrogen oxides 2:467; 2:471, 473–74, 475, 476; 3:73

Nitrogen trichloride *see* Agene

Nitroglycerin patches 5:470

Nitro group 3:110

Nitrous oxide (Laughing gas) 2:479; 5:465

Nix (moon of Pluto) 1:79, 157

Nixon, Richard (American president) 1:239, 248

NMR scans *see* Magnetic resonance imaging

NOAA (weather satellite) 1:314

Nobelium 3:41

Nobel Prize winners in science 6:407–18

Noble firs 4:91

Noble gases 3:28–29; 3:33, 48, 63, 69
  food packaging 6:85

Noble metals 3:27, 30

No Child Left Behind (NCLB) Act (U.S., 2001) 6:329

Nociceptors 5:288

Noctilucent (Night-shining) clouds 2:151, 162

Nocturnal animals and plants 3:380; 5:6
  owls 4:418–21
  zoo exhibits 4:474
  illus.
    animals 4:472

Nodes (in computer networking) 6:383

Nodes (in ocean basins) 2:246

Nodes (of the Moon's orbit) 1:118, 176

Nodes of Ranvier 5:224, 225

Noise
  careers in acoustics 3:202
  hearing 5:277
  tornadoes 2:191
  illus.
    damaging levels 3:201

Noise pollution 2:451

Noise-reduction headphones 3:208

Nomads 2:86
  illus. 2:212

Nomex fiber 6:229

No More War! (book, Pauling) 3:9

Noncarbonate hardness 2:447

Nonconsumptive demands on forests 4:127, 131

Nonelectrolytes 3:101–2

Nones (Roman dates) 1:476

NON-EUCLIDEAN GEOMETRY 1:329, 401–3

Non-ionizing radiation 5:436

Nonliving environment 2:453

Nonmetals 3:25, 26, 27–29
  halides 3:33

Nonnucleoside reverse transcriptase inhibitors (NNRTIs) 5:445

NONPERCHING BIRDS 4:400–408

Nonrenewable resources 2:413–15

Nonsense syllables experiment 5:359, 360

Nonspecific defense mechanisms 5:236

Nonsteroidal anti-inflammatory drugs (NSAIDS) 5:240, 291–92

Nonvascular plants *see* Bryophytes

Nonverbal learning disabilities 5:366

Non-zero-sum game 1:429–30

Noordung, Hermann von (Austrian rocket engineer) 1:265

Noradrenaline (Norepinephrine) 5:246, 356

Norfolk island pines 4:84

Nori 4:50

Normalizing (of steel) 6:182

Normal sulfate salt 3:97

Normandie (ship) 6:114

North, Marianne (British illustrator) 6:337

North America
  acid rain 2:474
  continental islands 2:281
  extinct birds 2:496
  extinct mammals 1:498, 499; 2:495, 496
  forest density 4:131; 4:146–47
  grasslands 4:140
  ice ages 2:218
  rain forests 4:159

North American water lily
  illus. 4:vi

North Atlantic Current 2:241, 242

North Atlantic right whales *see* Right whales

North Carolina 2:292, 512

North celestial pole 1:36

Northeasterlies 2:185

Northeast trade winds 2:184

Regeneration 3:456; 4:187
    crustaceans 4:248, 251
    earthworms 4:243–44
    lizards 4:338, 358
    Planaria 4:228
    salamanders 4:338, 349
    sea cucumbers 4:224
    starfish 4:223
    illus. 4:222
Regional anesthesia 5:477
Regional geography 2:297
Registered dietitians 5:390
Registered nurses 5:483, 486
Registers (of computers) 6:368
Regulator proteins 3:459
Regulator stations (natural gas industry) 2:344
Regulus (star) 1:29
Rehabilitation Act (U.S., 1973) 5:368
Rehabilitation medicine 5:486, 501
Reid, John B., Jr. (American geologist) 2:5–7
Reiki 5:514
Reindeer *see* Caribou
Reindeer moss 4:60, 163
Reinforced concrete 6:30–31
    building techniques 6:40
    road construction 6:44
    water pipes 2:449
Reinforced plastics 6:214
Reinforcement (in psychology) 5:338
Rejection of transplanted organs 5:497
Rejuvenated streams 2:425
RELATIVITY 3:142, 344, 346–56
    black holes 1:204, 208
    subatomic particles 3:311
    wormholes 1:214
Relaxation techniques 5:289, 357
Relay (communications satellite) 1:309
Relay systems, Microwave 6:239–40
Reliability (in statistics) 3:511, 513
Religion 1:3
Rem (radiation unit) 2:372
Remainder 1:347
Remotely operated vehicles 6:200–201
Remote manipulator system 1:252
REM sleep *see* Rapid eye movement sleep
Renaissance 4:470; 5:412; 6:8, 10
Renal anatomy *see* Kidneys
Renewable resources 2:406–13
Renin (hormone) 5:246
Rennin 5:250
Rensselaer Polytechnic Institute (RPI) (Troy, New York) 6:19

Repetitive stress syndrome 5:182–83
ReplayTV 6:287
Repletes (honey ants) 4:285
Report Program Generator *see* RPG
Reports, Laboratory *see* Laboratory reports
Reprocessing of nuclear fuel 2:370
Reproducibility (in experiments) 3:513
REPRODUCTION 3:452–57 *see also* Alternation of generations; Asexual reproduction; Sexual reproduction
    acorn worms 4:311
    alligators 4:384
    animals 4:185–86
    bacteria 4:31–32
    bats 5:31
    birds 4:396
    bryophytes 4:59–60, 61
    cartilaginous fish 4:324
    cell division 3:440–45
    cloning 3:422–23
    conifers 4:87–88
    crocodiles 4:381
    crustaceans 4:255
    dinosaurs 1:493
    dolphins 5:59
    egg-laying mammals 5:14–15
    elephants 5:106
    embryology 3:458–63
    ferns 4:80–81, 82–83
    fish 4:320
    flowering plants 4:102–4
    frogs and toads 4:345–47
    fungi 4:38–39
    ginkgo and cycads 4:95
    humans *see* Human reproduction and birth
    insects 4:273, 275, 276
    lancelets 4:311
    life, characteristics of 3:375
    life span 3:465–66
    light's effects on mammals 5:6
    lions 5:86
    livestock breeding 4:467–68
    lizards 4:361–62
    marsupials 5:16–17
    myriapods 4:265
    owls 4:420–21
    plants 4:9, 12, 13, 15
    primates 5:145–46
    rabbits and hares 5:37–38
    reptiles 4:354–55
    salamanders and newts 4:351
    sponges 4:215–16
    tigers 5:87
    tunicates 4:309–10
    whales 5:48
    zoos 4:471–72, 477
Reproductive potential (of populations) 3:477, 478
Reproductive system 4:185–86
    human 5:293–95

REPTILES 4:205, 352–55
    crocodilians 4:380–84
    dinosaurs 1:492–96
    extinct species 2:496–97
    fossils 1:488, 489
    genetic variation 3:505
    herpetology 4:336–39
    lizards 4:356–62
    mammals' ancestors 5:2–3
    monotremes resemble 5:14–15
    pets 4:481, 490
    prehistoric animals 1:492
    pterosaurs 1:496
    snakes 4:363–74
    turtles 4:375–79
    zoo exhibits 4:476
Reptiles, Age of *see* Mesozoic era
Research papers, Scientific 3:512; 6:315, 321
RESERVOIRS 2:110, 410, 437–39, 450; 6:51–56
    geological effect 2:48
    hydroelectric power 2:377, 378, 379, 380
    table(s)
        largest 2:438
Residency (in medicine) 5:414
Residual fuel oils 2:332
Resin 4:89
Resistance (in physics) *see* Drag
Resistance (of microbes to drugs) 5:464, 465
    bacteria 4:34
    evolutionary biology 3:506
Resistance (of the immune system to infection) 5:425, 426
Resistance, Electrical 2:320; 3:256, 258; 6:220
    superconductors 3:305
Resistance, Environmental *see* Environmental resistance
Resistance heating 2:320
Resnik, Judith (American astronaut) 1:289
Resolution (Resolving power) 1:43–44
    microscopes 3:450; 6:338
    radio telescopes 1:56
Resolution (research ship) 2:276
Resonance 3:200
Resource Conservation and Recovery Act (U.S.) 2:491
Resource partitioning (in ecology) 3:481
Resources, Conservation of *see* Conservation
Respiration
    amphibians 4:342
    animal 4:185–86
    arachnids 4:258
    arthropods 4:247
    atmosphere 2:149
    babies 5:326
    baby's first breath 5:304
    bacteria 4:30
    birds 4:394

Watson, John B. (American psychologist) 5:338
Watson, Thomas A. (American engineer) 6:237
Watson-Watt, Robert A. (British physicist) 6:255
Watt (unit of measurement) 3:167; 3:256
Watt, James (Scottish inventor and engineer) 3:256; 6:97, 190, 195
illus. 3:255
Watt-hour 3:257
Watt-hour meters (Wattmeters) 2:319; 3:257
Wave cycle 3:195
Wave farms 2:399
Wavelength 3:195, 272
  sound waves 3:198–99
  telescopes 1:43–44
  visible light 3:282, 293
  X-rays 1:58
  illus.
    measurement 3:334
Wave mechanics 3:278–79, 338–40
  electron behavior 3:19
  light 3:291–92
  plasma 3:361–62
Wave-particle duality *see* Wave mechanics
Waves *see* Electromagnetic spectrum; Mechanical waves
WAVES, Ocean 2:250–55
  cave formation 2:129
  coastal formation 2:291–92
  coasts 2:289
  earthquakes 2:50
  erosion 2:120, 124
  hurricanes 2:200
  lakes 2:106, 111
  physical oceanography 2:223
  solitons 2:221
  tsunamis 2:256–59
  illus. 2:123
    solitons 2:226
Wave speed 3:196
Wave tanks
  illus. 2:255
Wax
  beeswax 4:287
  earwax 5:277
  petroleum products 2:333
  rain-forest products 4:159
Waxwings 4:451–52
W-bosons (W particles) 3:21, 324
Weak force 3:21, 324
Weak interactions 3:312, 324
  symmetry violations 3:315, 316
Weakly Interacting Massive Particles *see* WIMPs
Weasels 5:6, 93–94
  illus. 5:95
Weather
  air pollution 2:469–70
  archaeology 1:464

atmosphere 2:149
climates of the world 2:207–14
coastal formation 2:290, 292
convection currents 3:235
hurricanes and typhoons 2:195–200
precipitation 2:166–73
Spitzer Space Telescope 1:62
tornadoes 2:189–94
water's specific heat 3:84
weather forecasting 2:201–6
wind 2:181–88
Weather balloons *see* Balloons
WEATHER FORECASTING 2:142–44, 146, **201–6**
  atmospheric study 2:153
  cloud patterns 2:164
  computer modeling 2:226
  hurricanes and typhoons 2:200
  radar 6:260–61
  tornadoes 2:193–94
  waves, ocean 2:255
Weathering 2:120–22
Weather modification 2:145–46
Weather satellites 1:312, 313, 314; 2:164
Weaverbirds 4:396
  illus.
    nests 4:461
Weavers (birds) 4:461–62
Webcam images
  illus. 6:389
Weberian apparatus 4:333
Web-footed tenrecs 5:28
Web pages 6:310, 376
Webs, Spider *see* Spider webs
Web sites 6:310
Web spinners 4:279
WebTV *see* MSN TV
Weddell Sea 2:91
Wedges 3:171–72
  illus. 3:173
Weeds 4:174
Week (time period) 1:476
Weevils 4:298–99
Wegener, Alfred (German scientist) 2:38–39
Weight (in physics) 1:104
  gravity 3:178–79, 180, 181
  mass, compared to 3:11, 21
  Moon 1:125
Weight, Body
  AIDS 5:443
  low birth weight 5:301
  weight control 5:391–94
  table(s)
    healthy weights 5:392
WEIGHT CONTROL 5:391–94
  calories 3:61
  exercise benefits 5:402
Weightless Environment Training Facility 1:277
  illus. 1:273
Weightlessness 1:250, 253
Weight lifting 5:404
  illus. 5:151, 397
Weight Watchers 5:394
Welding 3:363; 6:356

Welles, Orson (American actor) 1:506
Wells (water supply) 2:116, 117, 439–41
  contamination 2:119
  earthquake prediction 2:54
  geological effect 2:48
  hot water wells 2:391
Wells, H. G. (English author) 1:213, 500–501; 6:304
Welwitschia 4:96
Wertheimer, Max (Czech psychologist) 5:339
West African manatees 5:62
West Australia Current 2:239
Westerlies 2:184–85, 237
  illus. 3:494
Western blot test 5:213, 444
Western ground snakes 4:371
Western larches 4:92
Western tanagers
  illus. 4:458
Western toads 4:348
Western yellow pines *see* Ponderosa pines
West Indian manatees 5:62
West Indies 2:281, 283
Westinghouse, George (American inventor)
  illus. 2:317
West Nile virus 2:481
  illus. 3:393
West Virginia 2:512
West Wind Drift 2:239, 240
Wet cells *see* Storage batteries
WETLANDS 2:407–8; 4:136–37, **150–55** *see also* Bogs; Marshes; Swamps
  illus. 3:496
Whale (nuclear submarine)
  illus. 6:122
Whalebone *see* Baleen
Whaler sharks *see* Bull sharks
WHALES 5:8, 9, **46–54** *see also* Dolphins
  blue whales 5:2
  classification 5:12
  endangered species 2:500–501, 505
  fossils 1:482
  heart rate 5:197
  life span 5:324
Whale sharks 4:320, 327
Whale songs 5:47, 51, 56
Whaling 2:413; 5:54
Wheat 4:170, 172; 6:71
  illus. 4:19, 23
Wheat-barberry rust *see* Cereal rust
Wheel and axle 3:173
  automobiles 6:146
  Bronze Age 6:6
  illus. 3:174
Wheeler, John (American scientist) 1:204, 214
Wheeler, Sir Mortimer (British archaeologist) 1:468
Whelks 4:240

XV-15 (aircraft) *see* Tiltrotor XV-15
Xylem **4**:12, 65, 67, 88, 99
  aging **3**:468
  leaves **4**:70, 71
  stems **4**:69
Xylophones **3**:216
Yahoo! (Internet search engine) **6**:310
Yaks **5**:135
  illus. **5**:6, 132
Yale University (New Haven, Connecticut) **6**:328?
Yang, C. N. (American physicist) **3**:315
Yangtze River **2**:380, 410; **6**:22; **6**:56
Yawing
  illus. **6**:159, 160
Yazoo tributaries **2**:104
Y chromosomes **5**:313–14, 319, 420
  illus. **5**:322
Yeager, Charles (American aviator) **6**:157
Year (time period) **1**:110–12, 474–76, 476–77, 478
Yeasts **3**:455; **4**:37, 40–41
  illus. **4**:39
Yellow baboons **5**:142
Yellow-bellied sea snakes **4**:374
Yellow fever **4**:182, 269; **5**:431
Yellow jackets (insects) **5**:448
  illus. **4**:289
Yellow pines *see* Ponderosa pines
Yellow River **2**:105
Yellowstone National Park (Idaho–Montana–Wyoming) **2**:44, 63, 65, 509, 512
  bison **5**:133
  cyanobacteria in water **4**:33
  microorganisms in water **3**:2
  obsidian **2**:34
  telemedicine **5**:493
  illus. **2**:66, 80; **3**:8, 78
Yellowstone Plateau **2**:79
Yellowtail **6**:90
Yellow-throated martens **5**:95
Yellow warblers
  illus. **4**:454
Yerkes Observatory (Wisconsin) **1**:39
Yews **4**:86, 89, 93
Yoga **5**:404
  illus. **5**:399

Yohkoh satellite **1**:93, 301
Yolk **3**:462
Yolk sac **5**:297
Yorktown (ship) **6**:124
Yosemite National Park (California) **2**:98, 123, 509
Young, John W. (American astronaut)
  illus. **1**:281
Young, Leo C. (American physicist) **6**:255
Young, Thomas (English physician and physicist) **3**:338
Yo-yo dieting **5**:393, 394
Ytterbium **3**:46
Yttrium **3**:46; **5**:488
Yucca moths
  illus. **4**:169
Yucca Mountain (Nevada) **2**:307, 371; **2**:490
Yuccas
  illus. **4**:169
Yukawa, Hideki (Japanese physicist) **1**:229
Zahniser, Howard (American wilderness advocate) **2**:510
Zambezi sharks *see* Bull sharks
Zarontin *see* Ethosuximide
Zarya (space-station module) **1**:269
Z-bosons (Z particles) **3**:21, 324
Zebra mussels **4**:237, 239
Zebras **5**:109–10
  illus. **4**:141; **5**:vi, 5, 89
Zebus **5**:134
Zeiss planetariums **1**:67
  illus. **1**:67, 68
Zeolite **2**:447, 448
Zephyr (train)
  illus. **6**:127
Zeppelin, Count Ferdinand von (German aeronaut) **6**:150
Zeppelin, Wolfgang von (German aeronaut) **6**:151
Zeppelins **6**:150
Zero **1**:330
Zero-sum games **1**:425, 426
Zidovudine *see* AZT
ZIFT *see* Zygote intra-fallopian transfer
Zimbabwe **2**:513
Zinc **3**:46
  corrosion **3**:103
  metals and alloys **6**:182, 184

  soil pollution **3**:129
  storage batteries **3**:105
  trace mineral **5**:387
Zinc chloride **3**:105
Zinc oxide **3**:103
Zircon **2**:18
Zirconium **3**:46
  nuclear energy **2**:366, 370, 371, 374
Z number *see* Atomic number
Zodiac **1**:29, 30, 32
  Babylonian astronomy **1**:472
  China **1**:478
Zodiacal light **2**:153
Zollinger-Ellison syndrome **5**:246
Zoloft *see* Sertraline
Zombie computers **6**:392
Zona pellucida **5**:306
Zone of audibility
  illus. **3**:204
Zone of silence **3**:204
Zoogeography **2**:300; **3**:475
ZOOLOGICAL CLASSIFICATION **4**:198–205
ZOOLOGY **1**:7; **4**:178–82 *see also* Animals; names of animals and groups of animals
  biology **3**:366; **3**:372–73
  ecology **3**:475
Zoom lenses **6**:265
Zoom-lens microscopes **5**:494–95
Zoonoses **4**:464–65
ZOOS **4**:180, 338, 339, **469–79**
Zoospores **4**:48
Zooxanthellae **2**:285, 287
Zoropterans **4**:279
Z particles *see* Z-bosons
Zvezda (space-station module) **1**:269
Zweig, George (American physicist) **3**:317
Zyban *see* Bupropion hydrochloride
Zygomycetes **4**:39, 41
Zygosporangia **4**:39
Zygospores **4**:48
Zygote intra-fallopian transfer (ZIFT) **5**:307
Zygotes **3**:445; **5**:295
  algae **4**:48
  embryology **3**:459, 460